MW01630157

Ezra Stoller
Photographer

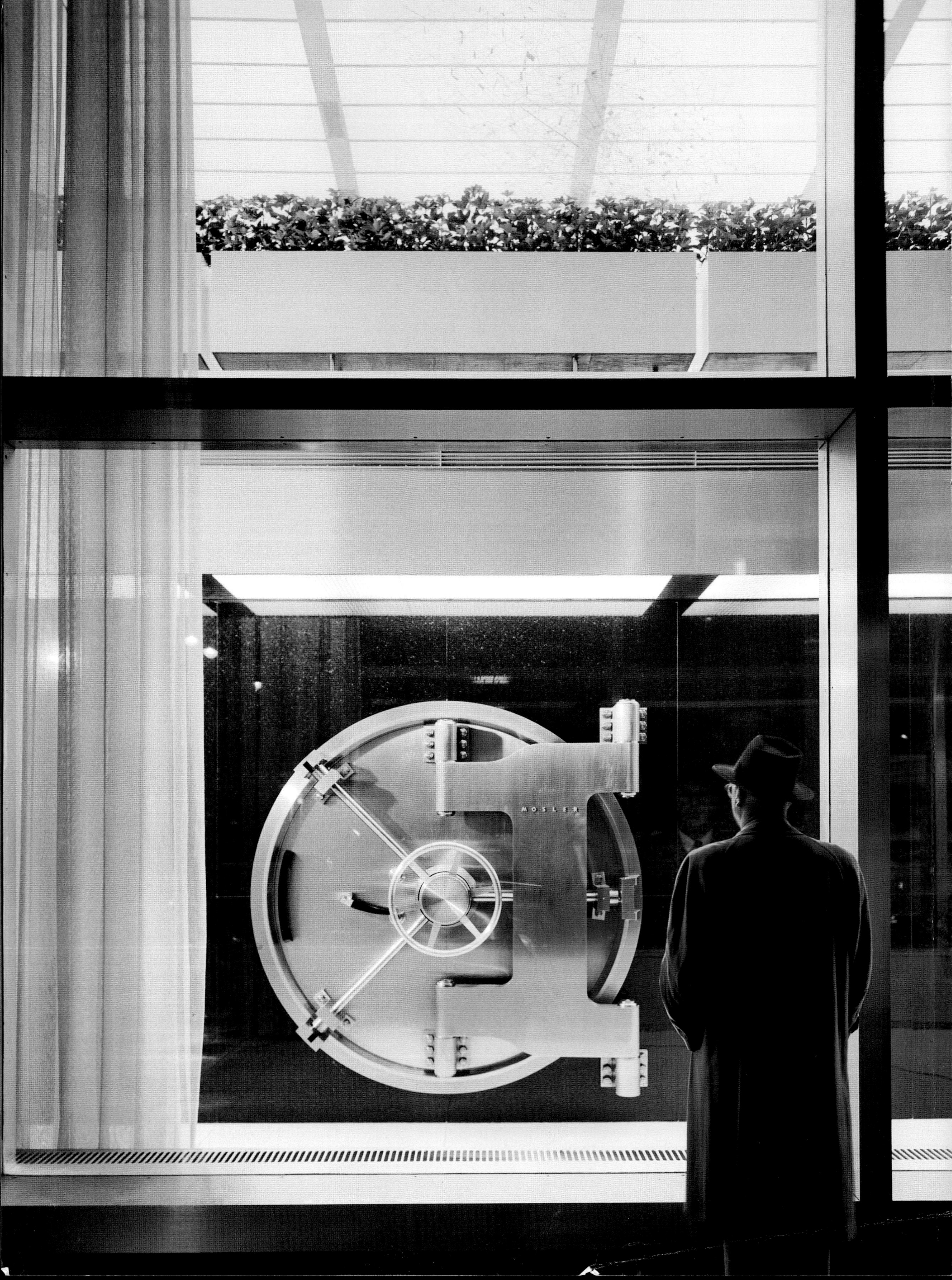
MOSLER

Nina Rappaport
and Erica Stoller

Introduction by
Andy Grundberg

With essays by
Akiko Busch and
John Morris Dixon

Ezra Stoller
Photographer

Yale University Press
New Haven and London

Published with assistance from the Graham Foundation for Advanced Studies in the Fine Arts.

yalebooks.com/art

Designed by Yve Ludwig, Pentagram
Set in type by Yve Ludwig
Printed in China through Asia Pacific Offset

Library of Congress Cataloging-in-Publication Data
Rappaport, Nina.
Ezra Stoller, photographer / Nina Rappaport and Erica Stoller ; introduction by Andy Grundberg ; with contributions by Akiko Busch and John Morris Dixon.
p. cm.
Includes bibliographical references and index.
ISBN 978-0-300-17237-9 (cloth : alk. paper) 1. Stoller, Ezra. 2. Photographers—United States—Biography. 3. Architectural photography. I. Stoller, Erica. II. Stoller, Ezra. III. Title.
TR140.S733R37 2012
770.92—dc23
[B] 2012021493

Page 2 and back of jacket: Manufacturers Trust, 510 Fifth Avenue, New York. Skidmore, Owings & Merrill, 1954. Vault designed by Henry Dreyfus, 1954.
Page 6: Connecticut General Life Insurance, Bloomfield, Connecticut. Skidmore, Owings & Merrill, 1957.
Front of jacket: TWA Terminal at Idlewild (JFK) Airport, New York. Eero Saarinen, 1962.

A catalogue record for this book is available from the British Library.

This paper meets the requirements of ANSI/NISO Z 39.48-1992 (Permanence of Paper).

10 9 8 7 6 5 4 3 2 1

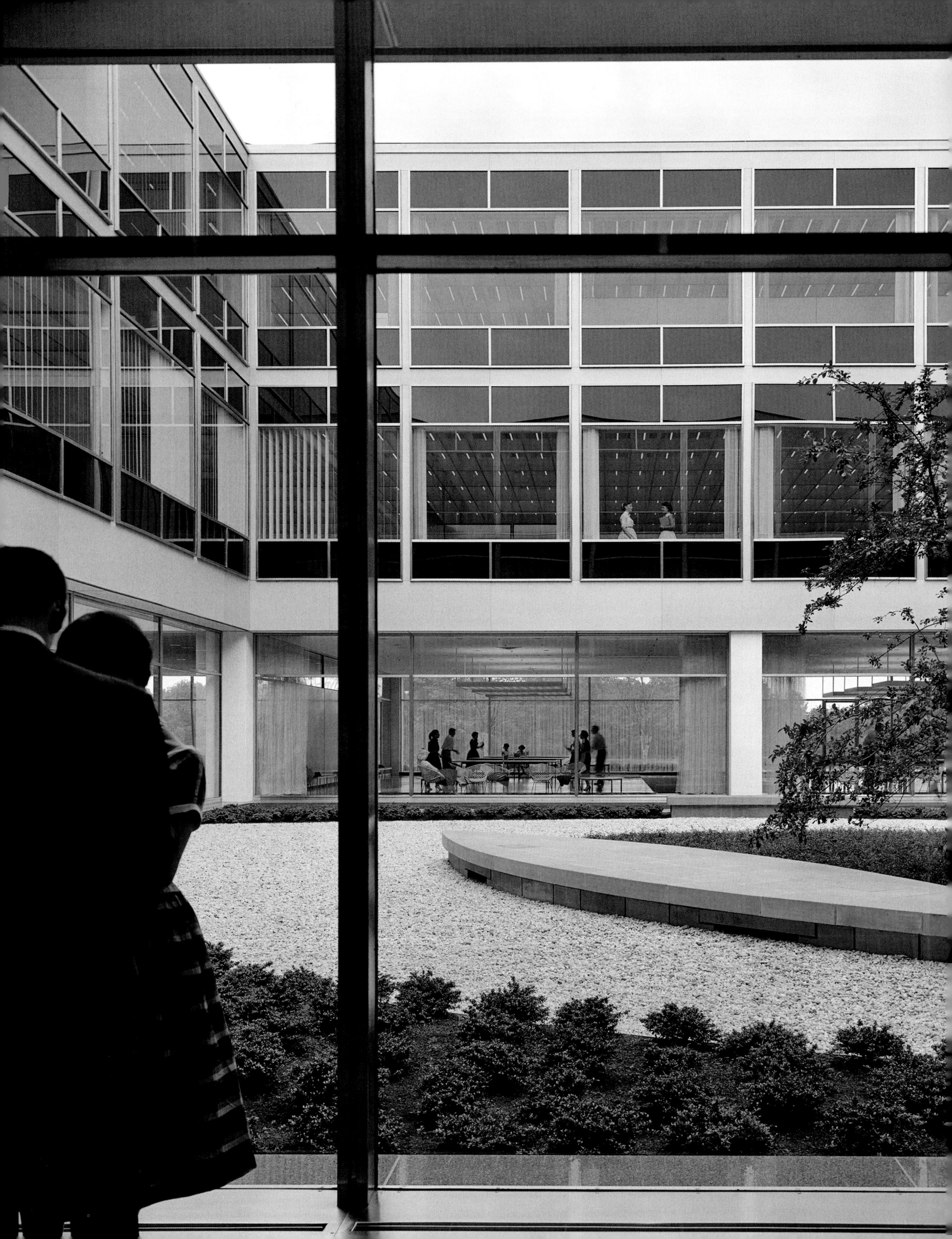

Erica Stoller

Preface

Ezra Stoller's approach to photography was formed by the functionalist tenets of Modern architecture. He believed in the honest ability of photography to reveal the structure, function, and material qualities of a building. His commitment to the visual transcended the need for words: if one could look at an image, then text was redundant. And if photographs were second to physically being in the space, verbal descriptions were further removed from the architectural experience.

My father (1915–2004) was a storyteller. To explain the flow of space through a building, he spent a long time getting to know the project, following the sun from dawn to dusk even before setting up a camera. His thorough approach to documentation involved a relationship between the part and whole: instead of relying on the power of an individual image, he considered photographs in sets and groups. Back at the studio, once the film was processed, he would spend hours studying the photographs, cropping and organizing them in sequence. His carefully arranged tours often included a corner or an edge of one image in the next, providing a framework for entering and moving through the spaces. Each image was composed to reveal a considerable amount of detail: the closer you look, the more there is to see. With that in mind, one of his favorite photographs was taken at the Salk Institute; it is a complicated weave of layers and angles that encloses in the foreground and opens to the courtyard in the distance. Looking at this view, one's eye travels through the space, left, right, up, and down, near to far. One's mind understands three dimensions, and my father would often mention a fourth: time, which included the moment of making the image, the man forever walking across the courtyard, and time for the viewer to explore the intricacies of space within the photograph. I recall hearing about a problem at the Salk and his fearing that the equipment had been damaged; even with the tilts and shifts of the view camera, he couldn't get the lines straight. Finally, he realized that the camera was okay—it was the building that was the problem. In construction, some of the concrete pours had bellied, creating vertical lines that were not exactly straight.

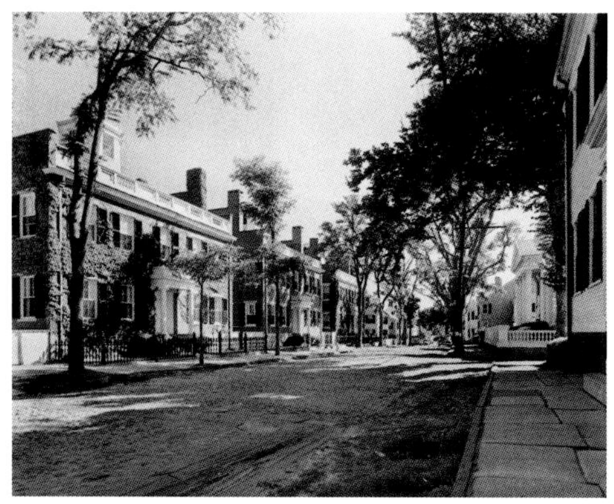

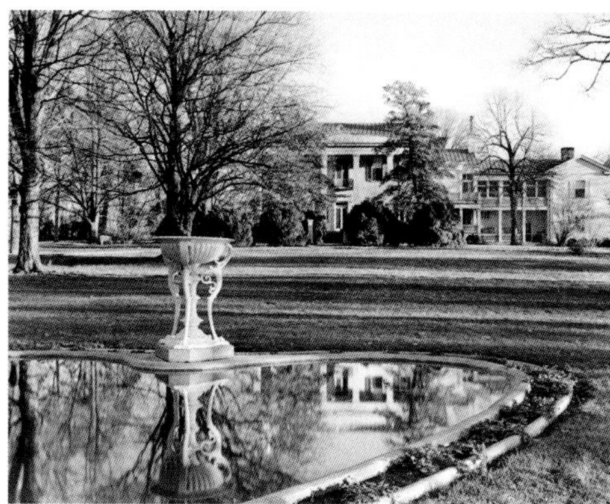

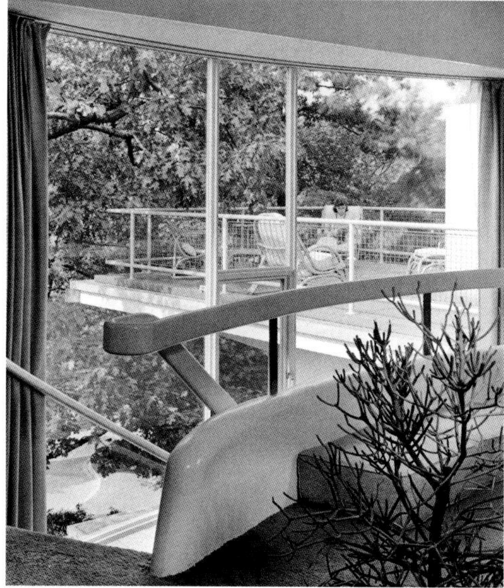

Fig. 1. Jethro Coffin House, Nantucket, Massachusetts, 1948.

Fig. 2. Belle Meade, Nashville, 1948.

Fig. 3. Frank House, Pittsburgh. Walter Gropius and Marcel Breuer, 1941.

Ezra Stoller did not grow up with the idea of a career related to architecture. Because he was mechanically inclined, in his early teens he attended a technical trade school in New York. A drafting class introduced him to depicting three-dimensional space, which then led him to pursue training in architecture. To complete academic credits, he went to one high school in the daytime and another at night before applying to New York University to study architecture. He and his contemporaries were interested in Modern design, working against the Beaux Arts program of the school; one of his instructors was Edward Durell Stone.

My father purchased his first camera while a student at NYU. The story is that he borrowed fifteen dollars from his uncle Harry to buy the box Linhoff to photograph models for other architecture students, and the work of painters and sculptors. My mother was then a student at Cooper Union, and the two collaborated on at least one design project—a Rome Prize submission that involved a team with several disciplines: architecture, sculpture, painting, and photography. However, he decided to concentrate on photography rather than architecture, and he never completed the full set of requirements for a B.Arch., instead receiving a degree in industrial design in 1938.

Ezra's first architectural photography assignment was a new suburban building completed by an architecture firm that employed one of his NYU classmates. "It had columns, but they were square, so it was Modern," he described, "and it included glass block." For a Pittsburgh Glass competition the architects needed to submit photographs, which my father made for the firm. The project won the award. On the strength of those pictures he got to know the editors of architecture magazines, and was on his way.

During the Depression he found that he could work independently, remain involved in Modern architecture, and make a more significant contribution as a photographer than as an architect. Among early notable assignments was a 1941 trip to Boston, commissioned by *Architectural Forum*. In Cambridge he met Walter Gropius and his colleagues, later partners at The Architects' Collaborative (TAC), who were working on their Six Moon Hill homes in nearby Lexington. It was after this introduction to Gropius and others that Ezra began to collaborate with architects, magazine editors, and corporations.

Early in his career my father worked with Richard and Dorothy Pratt of *Ladies' Home Journal* to document many Colonial-style homes around the country.

The images were published first in the magazine and later as *The Treasury of Early American Homes,* in 1949 (figs. 1, 2). On more than one occasion I heard him say that his work for *Ladies' Home Journal* paid for the house we lived in.

In 1945, Ezra Stoller took his first trip to Frank Lloyd Wright's Taliesin and Taliesin West. At about the same time he met Will Burtin, the art director at *Fortune,* a friendship that led to industrial editorial commissions and features in the magazine. Later, after Burtin left *Fortune,* they worked together on technical and scientific projects for Upjohn, IBM, and Kodak. My father found this work so satisfying that for a time he considered giving up architectural photography to concentrate on photographing scientific processes, machinery, and production.

Following these successes, in the mid-1940s, my father built a house for the family on a rocky piece of land in Westchester County, not far from New York City. This was a collective venture somewhat like TAC's Six Moon Hill houses in Lexington, and Frank Lloyd Wright's Usonian houses in Armonk, New York. The primary designer for our neighborhood was Henry Wright, son of the city planner of the same name and himself an architect who had been the editor of *Architectural Forum.* My father worked with his school friend, Abe Geller, to design our house with a butterfly roof, redwood, stucco, and lots of glass. As a child, I thought it was surprising that the early Breuer houses were so much like ours, not realizing that there was a strong Bauhaus influence.

In our family there are not many snapshots, and the ones that exist are hard to find. It's the cobbler's children syndrome. But my mother, brothers, and I all have recollections—sometimes mistaken—of our interactions with my father's work. My mother insisted she wasn't in Pittsburgh in 1941 for photography of the Frank House by Gropius and Breuer. Yet, when Esto made large prints using the 8 × 10 negatives for a recent exhibition, there she is in the background (fig. 3). There was an arrangement with GE to provide kitchen and laundry equipment in return for photographs, including a story that ran in *McCall's* magazine (fig. 4). I vaguely recall helping my father during his shoot at Alvar Aalto's Louis Carré House outside of Paris. There is no pictorial evidence in family albums of my having been there with the exception of a familiar-looking hand opening the door (fig. 5). And there is an image of my ten-year-old brother, Lincoln, at

Fig. 4. Stoller House, Rye, New York. Nemeny & Geller, 1949.

Fig. 5. Louis Carré House, door handle, Bazoches-sur-Guyonne, France. Alvar Aalto, 1965.

Fig. 6. Whitney Museum with two figures; Lincoln Stoller and Gary Szanto, New York. Marcel Breuer, 1966.

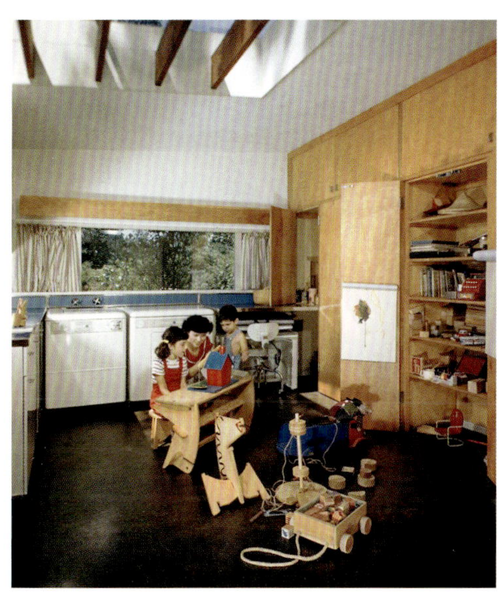

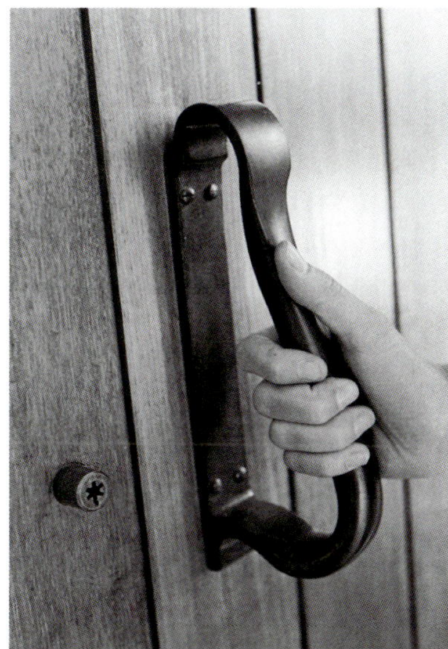

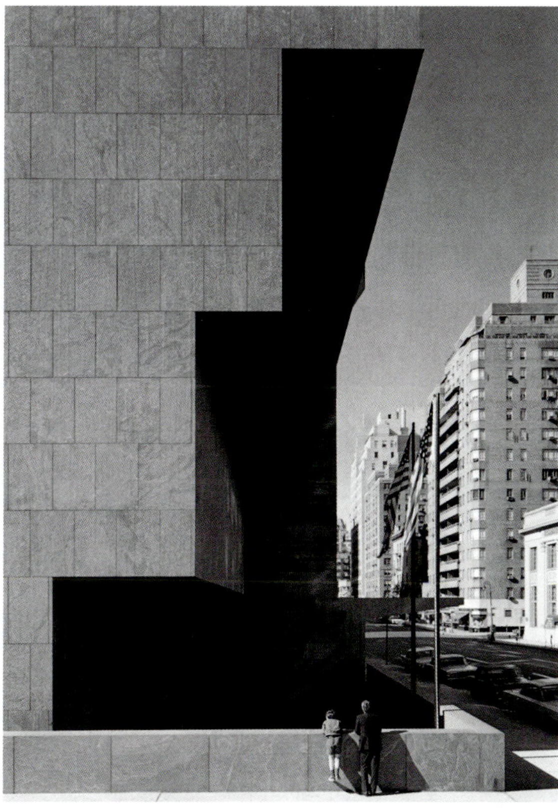

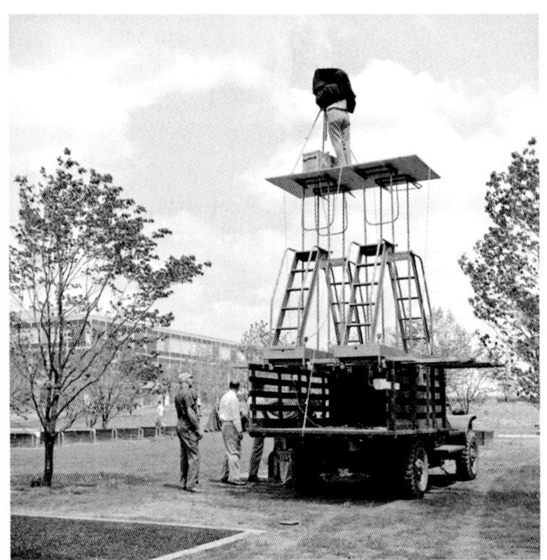

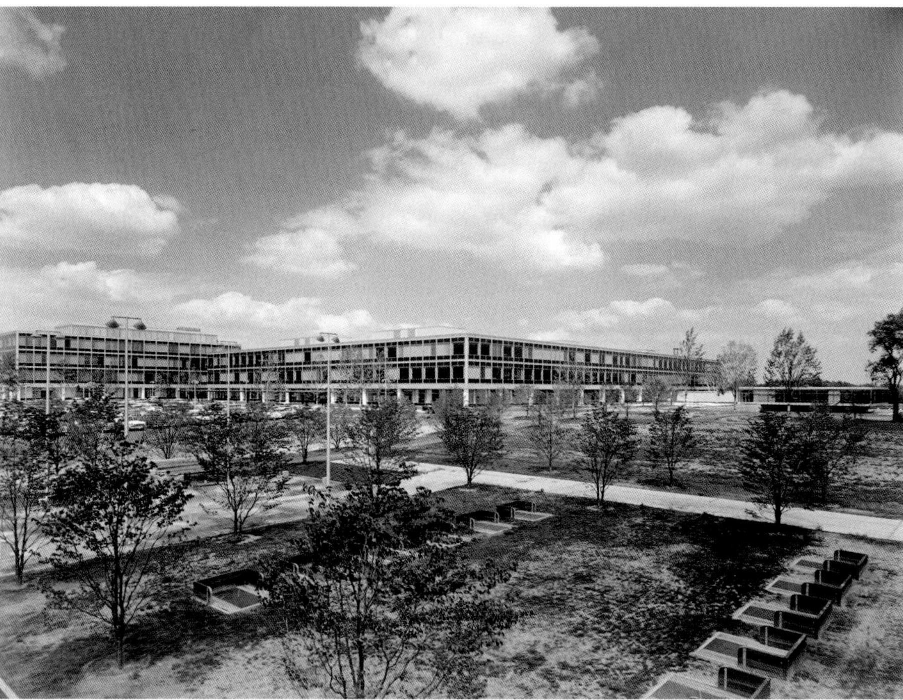

Fig. 7. Ezra Stoller photographing Connecticut General Life Insurance, Bloomfield, Connecticut. Skidmore, Owings & Merrill, 1957.

Fig. 8. View from shooting platform of Connecticut General Life Insurance, Bloomfield, Connecticut. Skidmore, Owings & Merrill, 1957.

the Whitney Museum. For years he recalled standing next to our father, but of course the photographer was behind the camera. My brother, with his feet off the ground, is beside an assistant (fig. 6).

My father was a ferocious and energetic worker. He handled every assignment with an exacting rigor that combined journalism, artistry, and a kind of zealotry. He attacked every project with total commitment, and his goal was perfection, even for the most pedestrian projects. Over and over again he proved what he could do with his camera and technique. His intensity and stamina seemed boundless to those who worked with him. He produced over 50,000 images during his long career, an amazing feat in both quantity and practice. Consider the heavy, cumbersome equipment, the early 8 × 10 film, which was costly and hard to load on location, the hot lights, and cases of flashbulbs. There were no strobe lights and no Polaroids. A recently discovered image of the Connecticut General building illustrates the frequently complicated, daredevil setups that he created to make his images (figs. 7, 8).

His best-known architectural assignments involved commercial buildings and residences, but he also frequently documented factories and hotels. The range of this work is evident in a consecutive series of assignments, all completed in a few months during 1963. After photographing Fallingwater he traveled to New Haven, Connecticut, to photograph Yale University's new Art & Architecture Building, then to a house by E. Fay Jones in Little Rock. Next he photographed hi-fi equipment in a New York apartment, two architectural models for Paul Rudolph, a model of the Kennedy Center for Edward Durell Stone, and bottles of cognac for a liquor catalogue, followed by a building in Kansas City for Skidmore, Owings & Merrill. With all of his traveling, my mother, Helen, brothers Evan and Lincoln, and I didn't see much of him in those days.

Ezra's parents had been strong supporters of labor unions, and while he was not overtly political, he was deeply concerned with artists' and photographers' rights. He was an active member of ASMP (originally the American Society of Magazine Photographers, now the American Society of Media Photographers) and served as the organization's president in the early sixties. He also set up his own business with the goal of furthering these efforts. His professional studio, started in the late thirties, became Esto in 1965. It had three components: assignment photography, a darkroom production facility, and a stock archive. As my father aged, and his energy and assignments slowed down, he began to work with younger photographers as a natural extension of the existing procedures. For more than thirty years Esto has included the work of a number of architectural photographers, a roster that has changed over the years.

After my father died in 2004, Esto digitized his images and stored the negatives, color transparencies, contact proofs, and prints in archival conditions. Only when the material was in digital form, key-worded and searchable online, could one see the full scope of the collection. This access was invaluable in preparing this book, which redefines Stoller's work in the broader context of twentieth-century photography. Now, with distance and time, we can also see Ezra Stoller's photographs as documents of social history. While he didn't strive to be an artist, in the end, the photographs are meaningful and beautiful works of art.

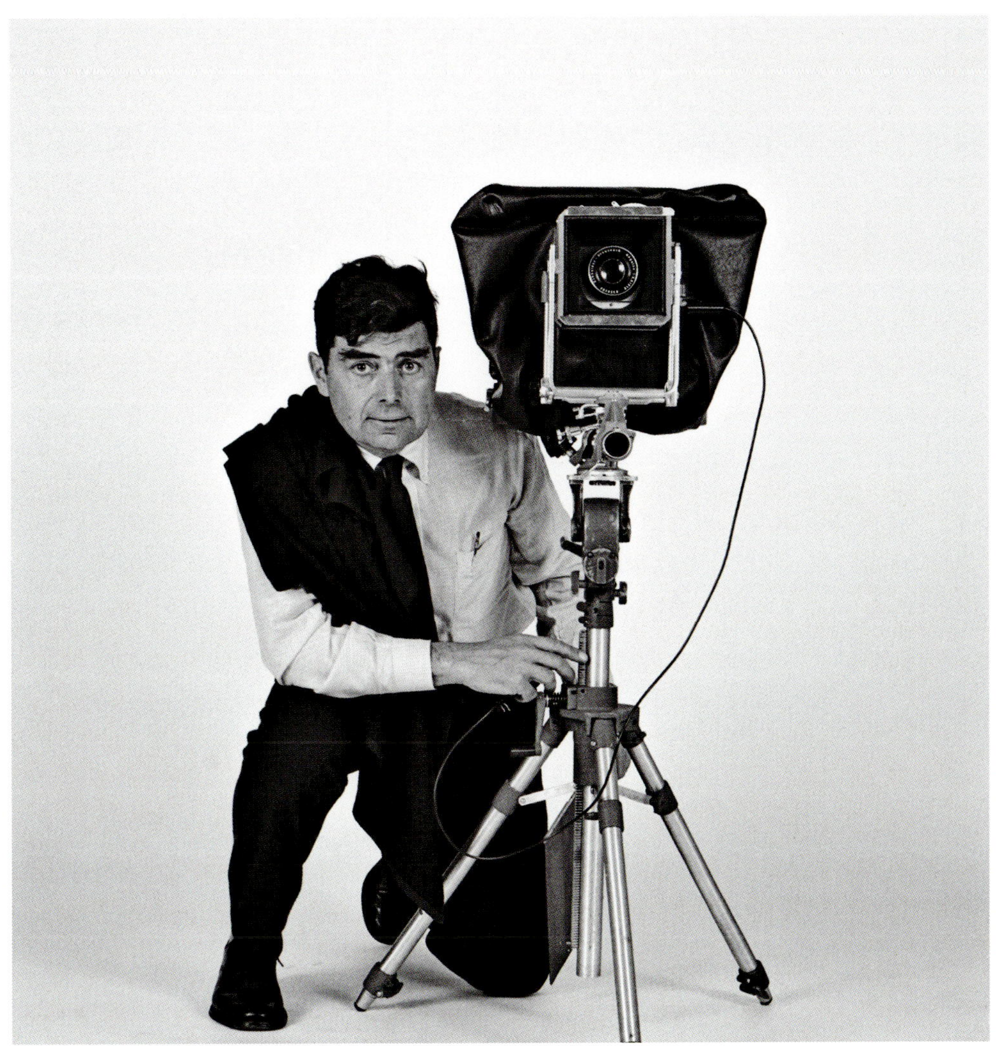

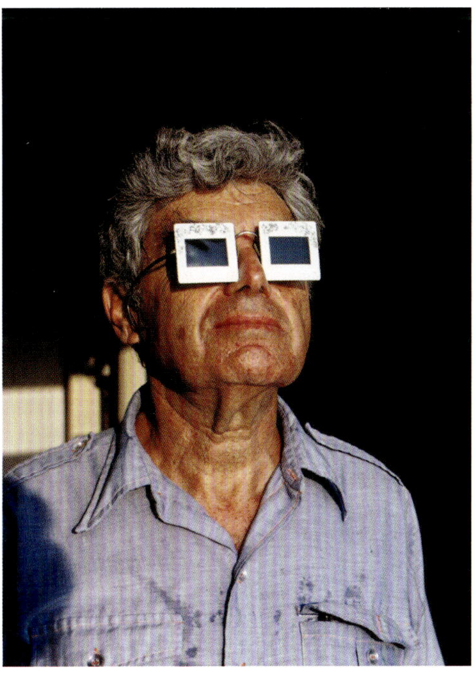

Fig. 9. Portrait of Ezra with view camera, circa 1955.

Fig. 10. Portrait of Ezra with "slide" glasses, circa 1975.

Andy Grundberg

Introduction
The Double Life of Ezra Stoller's Photographs

Photographers who earn their living by taking on assignments—referred to, sometimes disparagingly, as commercial photographers—have long been looked on as second-class citizens of the photography and art worlds. Even if we now agree that all art functions as a negotiation between its maker and its audience, we cling to the idea that the true artist exists in an autonomous, self-willed state of grace where the demands of the real world matter little or not at all.

This is a special problem for the art of photography, which most frequently takes the real world as its essential subject. In curator John Szarkowski's famous formulation, is the photograph a mirror or a window? If a mirror, then it reflects the intentions of its maker. If a window, then it provides a document of what the camera saw. Szarkowski resolved this dilemma by observing that the photograph is almost always inescapably both: it is a creation of a singular vision or approach *and* it is a report on something that exists in the world. This is the essential basis of photography's claim to fame and what distinguishes it as an art form.

Still, the prejudice persists that by aiming to please a client, photographers sacrifice their ability to remain true to the inner dictates of their own visions, thereby compromising any claim to making art themselves. This is particularly true when it comes to genres like architectural photography. The art in a picture of a building, as far as an architect may be concerned, is the building itself, which the image has distilled from a three-dimensional lived experience to a flat plane seen from a fixed, single perspective. What claim does the photographer have to being the artist? The same question could be asked of all photographers who, submerging their egos, devote their careers to recording the structures and environments constructed by their forebears or contemporaries.

Yet a great many photographers who have taken the constructed world as their subject matter have come to be admired, respected, and placed among the greatest photographers in the medium's history. There is Edouard Baldus, who took on the job of documenting the construction of the new Louvre in 1855; Eugène Atget, who produced what is considered the medium's greatest work of urban documentation by photographing the buildings, streets, and denizens of Paris at all hours and in all seasons; and more modern figures, such as Werner Mantz and Albert Renger-Patzsch in Germany and Berenice Abbott and Walker Evans in the United States, who worked on assignments or commissions in the 1930s, many of them industrial or architectural in nature. All have found a place in the history of photography.

There is, in short, an estimable tradition of documentation of great and not-great architecture, of architect-designed buildings and of vernacular, unheralded ones, that forms a broad backdrop against which we might consider the career and accomplishments of Ezra Stoller, the preeminent photographer of architect-designed buildings built in the United States in the decades after World War II. Stoller of course was more than this; he photographed workplaces, homes, factories, industrial machinery, and much else, as the images and essays in this book make clear. But what built his reputation, and what serves as the center of his archive of more than sixty thousand negatives and transparencies, are his iconic images of the great imaginative leaps made by American architects in the economic euphoria of the postwar years.

Stoller was not alone in wanting to freeze the monuments of new building technologies and the forms they inspired. Julius Shulman, working in Southern California in the same period, took memorable images of the now-fabled Case Study Houses and of homes constructed in the boomtown of Palm Springs—work focused on architects such as Charles and Ray Eames, Pierre Koenig, and Richard Neutra. In Chicago, the Hedrich Blessing firm specialized in the Second City's skyscrapers and much else, including Ludwig Mies van der Rohe's apartment towers and his low-rise Farnsworth House.

Stoller's advantage over these competitors was twofold. He was based in New York, home to most of the magazines giving out assignments and to many important architects. Secondly, he was particularly sympathetic to and understanding of the aims of the Modern architects whose work he photographed. As a student of architecture and design prior to devoting himself to photography, he brought an informed view to all his work, one that reflects not only a great technical sophistication in using his camera but also an intuitive feel for how to tell the story of a building in pictures.

William S. Saunders, a design editor and writer, has said that Stoller's pictures tell "one true story wholly: the real ideal of the building," adding that Stoller as a photographer was the "honorable architect's perfect servant." The idea of a real ideal is of course a curious one, but its complexity suggests what animates Stoller's photographs: they incorporate an obvious love for the purity of structures with an equal appreciation for the living, breathing aspects of the spaces they define. Stoller's best images reverberate between revealing the fundamental rationality of the Modernist built environment and instilling a sense of personality or place-ness that both distinguishes the buildings from one another and reveals them to be inflected by their human uses.

We might see Stoller's pictures of buildings as contemporaneous equivalents of Arnold Newman's so-called environmental portraits. Newman gained fame in the 1950s and 1960s for images that seemed to capture the personalities of politicians and celebrities by including visual metaphors of their public image; his portrait of Igor Stravinsky, for example, shows the piano at which the musician is seated as a kind of looming quarter note. Like Stoller, Newman defined his subject in formal terms, but the elements of composition and juxtaposition he employed intentionally serve to heighten the viewer's recognition of what the subject is. In Stoller's case, what comes across most often is the distinctive vocabulary of each architect's style.

The notion that Stoller is the architect's perfect servant thus seems obvious. Stoller shows the buildings he photographed in their best light. This is literally true, given the marvelous use of sunlight, shadows, and reflective surfaces to define the structures' exterior and interior forms and spaces, and metaphorically so, since there is never in any of his pictures a sense of architectural failure or moral ambiguity. The photographer also apparently took pains to leaven the geometric severities of much Modernist architecture by including automobiles, parked in carports and in front of office buildings, as well as other traces of human presence, including a half-peeled orange on a deck next to a pair of empty sandals and the remains of a traditional tea service in the middle of a then radically new sunken living room. Often he added human presence directly, letting people compete with, and occasionally upstage, the architectural view.

The vision that Stoller brought to the table of mid-twentieth-century architecture pleased practically the entire pantheon of major architects of his time, yet it was only incidentally and rarely their vision. If we believe that representations are a form of thought, then clearly Stoller did not think in the same way that architects do. Although, as others have pointed out, Stoller occasionally placed his camera to create an image that duplicates what architects refer to as a front elevation (the straight-ahead, perspectivally parallel frontal face of the building), for the most part he chose points of view from which no architectural drawing would have been made. Whereas Modernist architects might choose an axonometric view to show what a building would look like from a 45-degree approach, their drawings lacked the perspectival normalcy of a photograph, not to mention the flexibility to change the perspective by incrementally shifting the point of view side to side and up and down. By photographing the real thing in real space, Stoller gave architects a kind of visual final report on the success of their practice.

His pictures also helped give architects the kind of celebrity status that they enjoy today, and to introduce the idea that they are as much artists as are painters and sculptors. Through publication and other means of distribution his photographs spread the gospel of Modernist architecture across a culture that once knew only the names of buildings, not the names of their designers. Stoller's work helped to make the architects synonymous with their buildings.

Stoller's photographs are doubly Modernist. Their subject matter is first of all from a time when the "form follows function" decree of Louis Sullivan was being played out by a generation of young and ambitious architects and designers. This particular brand of Modernism favored clarity of form and transparency of structure, innovative use of materials like tempered glass and reinforced concrete, and a strict but playful planarity that defined three-dimensional space both internally and externally.

Stoller's pictures are also paragons of Modernist photography. They show the devotion to precise description and full tonal rendition that an earlier generation of photographers—among them Ansel Adams, Walker Evans, Paul Strand, and Edward Weston—pioneered as the hallmarks of photography intended to be seen as Art. At the beginning of the twentieth century this so-called straight style was a radical break from the norms of art photography, but by Stoller's era it had become the norm. (Witness, for example, Margaret Bourke-White's pictures for *Life* and *Fortune* in the 1930s and 1940s.)

The precision of Modernist photography is most easily achieved through the use of large-format cameras that produce a negative as large as eighty square inches, multiple-element glass lenses designed to be as sharp as possible, and a tripod, which eliminates any chance of camera shake and any doubt about where the edges of the final image will lie. Like Adams and Weston, who briefly associated themselves with a West Coast movement called Group f/64 (a term for an extremely small lens aperture), Stoller would stop down his lens to ensure that sharp focus prevailed from the foreground of the photograph all the way into the distance. This technique minimizes the sense, when we look at the picture, that the photographer has intervened in the scene by choosing what part is most important; instead, we see the world within the frame as if it had chosen to present itself.

But Stoller's choices of equipment and technique were as much a matter of practicality as of aesthetics. His clients—magazines and architects in equal measure—needed to show buildings in great detail to satisfy their customers, without special effects or obvious artificiality (which also explains why Stoller took pains to disguise the addition of any artificial lighting to a scene). The crisp edges, where glass meets steel, ask for crisp rendition, and the patterns on poured concrete left by the forms that defined them beg for a wealth of detail. Equally important, the camera Stoller used (generically known as a view camera) allows a photographer, looking at an upside-down image of the scene while hidden under a black cloth, to adjust the rectilinearity of the image. Building verticals that would seem to tilt backward when the camera is tilted up can be brought into perfect square by adjusting the camera's back; horizontals can be induced into squareness in much the same way.

Other evidence of Stoller's mastery lies in his choices of time and place. Usually he would arrive soon enough after a building's completion so that it still looked fresh and clean, but long enough after that evidence of construction had disappeared. He would wait out the weather, picking the moment of sunshine or clouds that complemented the building or revealed its voids and penetrations. For Frank Lloyd Wright's Johnson Wax Tower (1950), he photographed at dusk, when the lights revealed the building's solid internal columns, in effect producing an X-ray of its structural bones. He also surveyed sites in a progression, starting from far enough away to include most or all of the building and then moving progressively closer to show juxtapositions of solids and spaces that evoke rather than describe an architect's particular style.

His extended set of photographs of Louis Kahn's Salk Institute, taken in the twilight of the photographer's career, is an example of how thoroughly and cogently he would approach his job—although, in this case, he was not on assignment. He took vistas of the central plaza of the campus, looking out to sea; medium-range views of the layers and levels of the interlocking laboratories; and details, including close-ups of the raw concrete walls and of the maze of pipes and ducts running within a floor of their own. In total, the pictures show that what to a casual pedestrian comes across as austere and forbidding is in fact a cleverly disguised living organism.

Given the compelling evidence of Stoller's command of his medium and of the clarity of his vision throughout his career, should we call him an artist? This is a question that likely matters more to us than it would to him. Stoller was of a generation of photographers for whom the motive of making art was less compelling than that of making a living. That is to say, the chance of a photographer earning a living by pursuing his or her own inclinations and then marketing the results was, until the 1970s, virtually nil. Even Ansel Adams spent most of his career doing commercial assignments and commissions to help underwrite the landscape work for which he is now known. Adams did exhibit his photographs at Alfred Stieglitz's An American Place gallery in New York in the 1930s, it is true, but the market for selling photographs as works of art, despite Stieglitz's lifetime of efforts, was four decades away.

For most of Stoller's career the way to success in photography was through publication, not exhibition. In the public mind, at least, the apogee of great photography was to be found in the pages of *Life, Look, Collier's, The Saturday Evening Post,* and other heavily illustrated, general-interest magazines modeled largely on the newsy "picture magazines" developed in Germany and England before World War II. Other magazines devoted to more specific topics and audiences, like *Fortune, Harper's Bazaar, Holiday, Town and Country,* and *Vogue,* provided equally impressive venues for the display of ambitious and innovative photographs. Stoller found his niche at Time, Inc.'s, *Architectural Forum.*

Since so-called editorial rates could be meager (in the 1960s, as head of the photographers' organization ASMP, Stoller led a long fight to raise them), advertising, annual reports, and other categories of commercial assignments were important alternatives to magazine work. As Nina Rappaport's essay on Stoller's industrial photographs makes clear, he repeatedly crossed the line between work done for magazines and work done for corporations, architectural firms, and other clients. This not only kept him busy but it gave him access to photograph subjects he might not otherwise have encountered. In Columbus, Indiana, for example, he photographed the interiors of the Cummins Engine factory and the Eero Saarinen–designed house of Cummins' owners, J. Irwin and Xenia Miller, who were responsible for making the town a magnet for world-class architecture.

As a result, and as this collection of pictures demonstrates, Stoller was not merely nor exclusively the photographer of Modern architecture as we have come to know him. He was confident and fluent in photographing domestic settings, men and women at work, even portraits of architects. In this work, as in all his pictures of buildings, he uses the tools of his medium—lighting, point of view, lens angle, perspective, detail—to fashion images that command and captivate our attention. Still, in the same way that Picasso will always be remembered for his Cubist period despite his years of painting before and afterward, it seems safe to say that Stoller will always be remembered for taking the iconic images of the best buildings of the middle two quarters of the twentieth century.

The art world's belated attention to his photography reinforces this impression. Perhaps the first recognition of Stoller's work in the art world came with a one-person exhibition at the Max Protetch Gallery in New York in 1980. Protetch, an art dealer who started his career in Washington, D.C., moved his operations to West 57th Street in Manhattan in 1978; soon thereafter he expanded from showing mostly contemporary painting and sculpture to selling architectural drawings and design objects. He was among the first to recognize that architects' drawings and sketches had their own claims to esthetic value and to create a market for them. He focused on the new generation of Postmodernist architects, such as Michael Graves, John Hedjuk, and Peter Eisenman, but he also sold works by their predecessors, including Louis Kahn, Mies van der Rohe, and Frank Lloyd Wright.

Protetch's interest reflected a growing awareness (and a growing marketplace) for architecture as art. Photography, of course, had also recently broached the glass ceiling of the contemporary art world and, together with video, was being viewed as the art world's hot new enterprise. Stoller's work, spanning both these bases, found a new home in gallery shows and in museum exhibitions and collections, including the Whitney Museum of American Art, the Canadian Centre for Architecture, and the San Francisco Museum of Modern Art.

The work also began to be collected in books, and with a depth that individual magazine articles could rarely achieve. The 1990 publication *Modern Architecture: Photographs by Ezra Stoller* (Abrams) was the first attempt to comprehend Stoller's career, although it was limited to just his architectural work. *Modern Architecture* was reissued in 1999, the same year Princeton Architectural Press began a series called "Building Blocks," small volumes of Stoller's pictures, each examining a single site, including Wright's Fallingwater, Rudolph's Yale Art + Architecture building, and Kahn's Salk Institute, with essays by art and architecture critics.

The upshot is that Stoller's photographs, like those of Julius Shulman and the Hedrich Blessing firm, entered a second life no less useful than their original function. Whereas once they served as fodder for magazines and brochures advocating for Modern architecture at a time when modernity was controversial (and, in the case of Brutalism, widely disparaged), they now enshrine both its style and ambitions as artifacts of a golden bygone era. It seems no coincidence that Stoller decided to stop actively photographing at the moment Modernism was giving way to Postmodernism in architecture. Tellingly, Robert Venturi's Vanna Venturi House of 1962, an early landmark of the new style, was built while Stoller was still active, but he left it to his then partner, Bill Maris, to photograph it.

If the heyday of Modernist architecture ended at roughly the same time as Stoller's active career, the same might be said of Modernist photography. By the end of the 1970s the art world's interest in the medium had shifted the terms of its reception from formal concerns to conceptual ones. A new generation of artist/photographers was less interested in the documentary capabilities of precisely made black-and-white prints than in reflecting on photography's presence in the mass media and narrative. Instead of photographing the world, Postmodern artists often photographed reproductions of photographs. The visually based aesthetic values that underlie the work of Stoller, Ansel Adams, Arnold Newman, and many others came to be seen as artifacts of a more innocent, optimistic, and naïve time.

But as Modernist photography has come to be less current, it has also come to seem more interesting. This is especially true of work, like Stoller's, that abjured any claim to being aesthetically autonomous. The sense of obligation to its subject, to the near exclusion of any inflection that might suggest the "hand" or artistic sensibility of its maker, finds its counterpart in the twenty-first-century documents of photographers like Katy Grannan, Candida Hofer, and Thomas Struth, and more arguably in the more complicated cases of Gregory Crewdson, Thomas Demand, and Andreas Gursky. The current reconsideration of what used to be called commercial photography is, in a sense, a recapitulation of what happened half a century ago with the work of Timothy O'Sullivan, William Henry Jackson, Carleton Watkins, and other nineteenth-century photographers who lived on commissions or by selling their work in galleries. Instead of being seen as commercial photographs, their images became landscapes, and thus antecedents of twentieth-century art photography.

Considered in light of today's broad embrace of photography created for many different purposes and audiences, from photojournalism to snapshots, Ezra Stoller's photographs no longer carry the stigma of having been made to be useful. In fact, their utility is part of their charm and ultimately their beauty: they were made to beguile us, and these many years later they still do. They are, in short, first-class citizens.

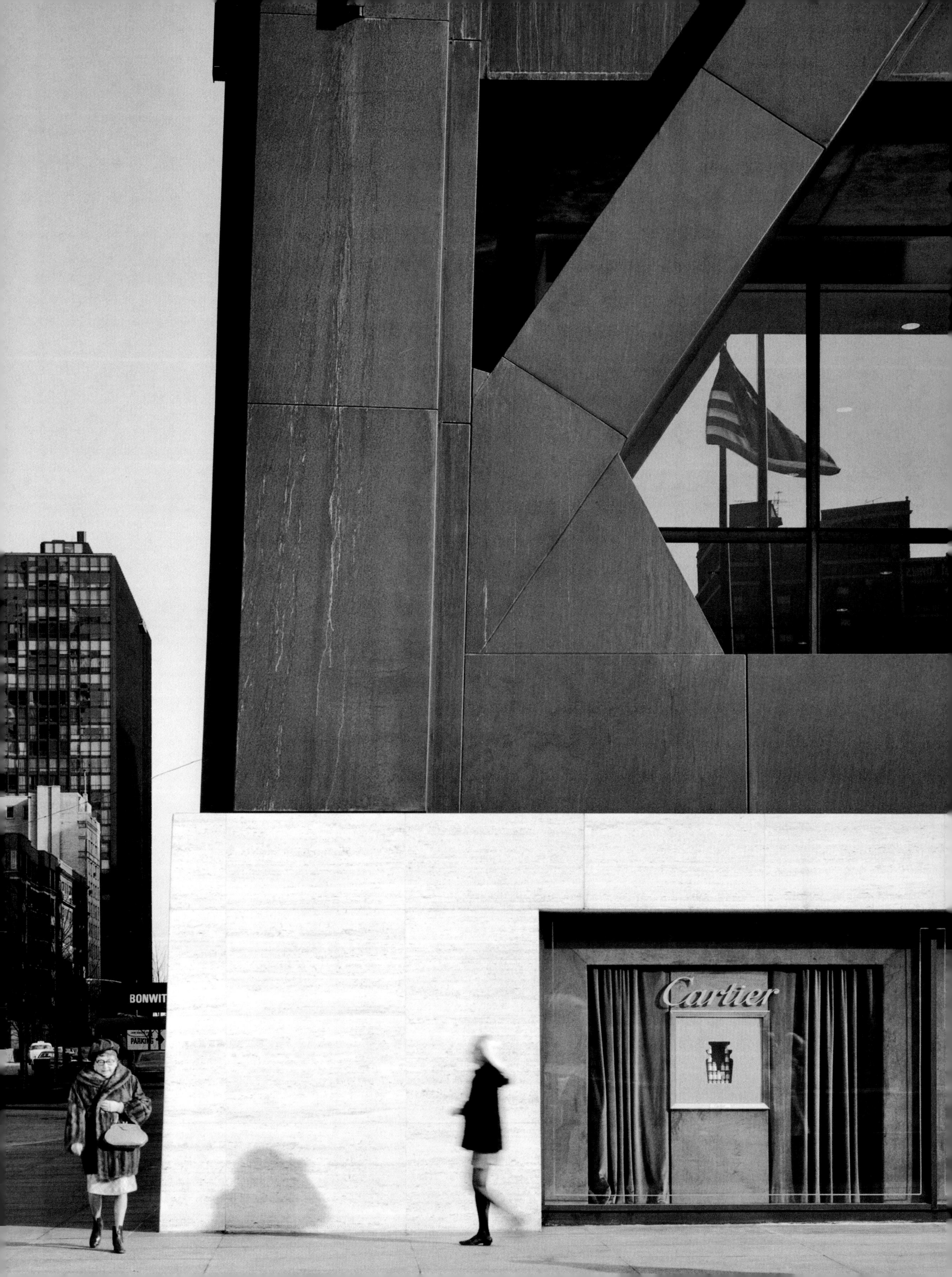
BONWIT
PARKING
Cartier

John Morris Dixon

Architectural Photography

Stoller and the Landmarks of Modernism

Like many of the architects whose buildings he photographed, Ezra Stoller practiced his art not as a means of self-expression but to fulfill the needs of clients. And just as certain architects become prominent for the brilliance of their designs, Stoller became the photographer of choice to record many of the outstanding design accomplishments of the twentieth century.

While other portions of this book examine assignments Stoller carried out for manufacturers and for the home-oriented "shelter" press, here I deal with Stoller's photography of what is considered capital-A Architecture, exemplary works interpreted through his camera. To a greater degree than other types of photographs, such portrayals of buildings have to capture three-dimensional reality in a two-dimensional format.

Why do Stoller's architectural photographs excel? First, there is his commitment, which he spoke of often, to portray space. He conveyed a sense of depth, often by the inclusion of foreground elements—a device that must be executed subtly to avoid cliché. Less obvious to the viewer is his manipulation of daylight to give shape to forms and spaces—and for Modern architecture daylight is often as crucial for interiors as for exteriors.

On an assignment, Stoller reports, he would typically spend the first day establishing camera locations with consideration of the optimum natural light. As he became more proficient, he was able to tour sites more quickly, anticipating the light conditions at specific locations and times without actually seeing them. Artificial light was used, sometimes even for outdoor daytime shots, to fill in shadowy areas, but always so that its effect was not obvious. Stoller maintained, as well, that the architectural photograph was meant to convey the architect's intentions, which he understood exceptionally well. And, finally, the photograph itself had to present a satisfying two-dimensional composition.

John Hancock Center, Chicago. Skidmore, Owings & Merrill, 1970.

His photographic assignments were commissioned variously by the architects, the owners of buildings, or the magazines that featured the latest design achievements. Sometimes a museum would commission him to take photos for an exhibition. On rare occasions Stoller would shoot works of special interest "on spec," taking photographs for which there might or might not be immediate demand.

As his career became established, Stoller couldn't be available for every potential assignment. But certain prominent architects could be assured of his documentation for most of their works. Among them were Philip Johnson, Eero Saarinen, Paul Rudolph, and Richard Meier. Skidmore, Owings & Merrill, the firm that accounted for more Stoller assignments than any other, called on him for most projects by their New York design partner, Gordon Bunshaft, and for works of their Chicago and West Coast offices that they considered especially important.

Among the publications that were major outlets for Stoller's work, the magazines *Fortune* and *Architectural Forum* gave him some of his early choice assignments. Both were published by the mid-century giant Time, Inc., which could fund more ambitious assignments (photography fees, travel and related expenses, film and processing costs) than could its rivals of the time. Stoller credited Howard Myers, editor of *Forum* in the 1940s and 1950s, with helping to launch his career. Even during *Forum*'s final decade, 1965–74, when it no longer had the backing of Time, Inc., the loyalty between Stoller and the magazine was reflected in the frequent appearance of his images on its pages.

In my own experience on the staffs of architecture magazines, extending from 1960 through 1995, Stoller's work always set the standard by which other architectural photography was judged. It is important to recognize that these magazines' art directors had at least as much input as the editors did on the choice of photographers and of photographs for publication. And it was primarily art directors' decisions on such matters as page layout and cover design that revealed a photographer's skill. Owing to the quality of his work, Stoller maintained a relationship of mutual respect with the best art directors in the field.

Whatever buildings Stoller was assigned to photograph, he typically did a thorough documentation. His goal was a virtual tour of the building—from surroundings to exterior to a series of interiors, often including some of a building's less glamorous, functional spaces. Architects and owners often wanted the full range of such photos to illustrate the breadth of their accomplishment. But only a few pictures, those that most vividly illustrated the design intent, would be chosen for publication.

Launching an Exceptional Career

Stoller's career as a photographer grew out of his courses in architecture and industrial design at New York University and the contacts he made there among faculty and fellow students. As soon as his photos appeared in print he became the photographer of choice for several architects in the Northeast. His network of admirers among architects was reinforced by contacts made through his younger brother Claude Stoller, who studied architecture at Black Mountain College, and, after World War II, at Harvard. Claude later launched his architecture practice in San Francisco.

Stoller's education and early experience nurtured his commitment to Modernism. For him, Modern architecture represented progress and high social purpose. Almost everyone he knew and dealt with—at least up to the mid-1960s—saw Modern design as a force for the improvement of the human condition. He and his family lived in a rigorously Modern house in an enclave of homeowners with similar design convictions. Aesthetically, Modernism's bold, unadorned forms lent themselves to the strong compositions Stoller strove for in his photos.

One of Stoller's earliest assignments didn't quite fit his convictions. He documented parts of the New York World's Fair of 1939, most of which displayed a streamlined Art Deco style reviled by committed Modernists. But Stoller was able

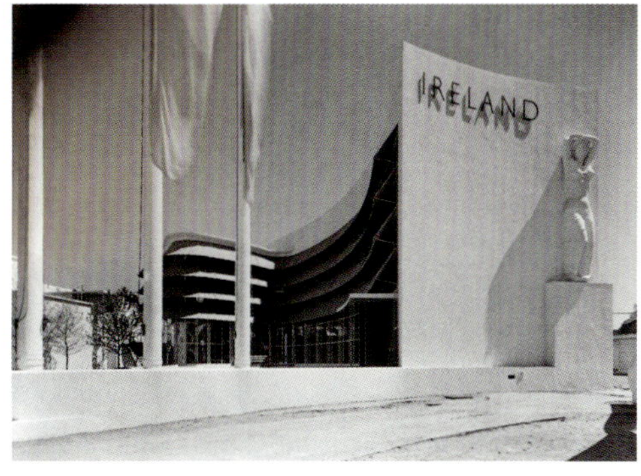

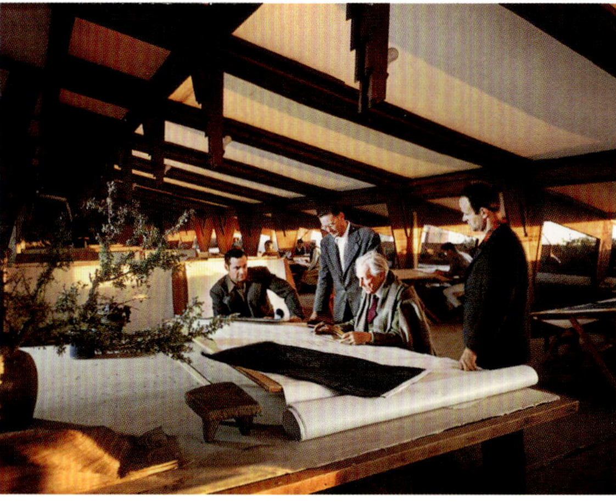

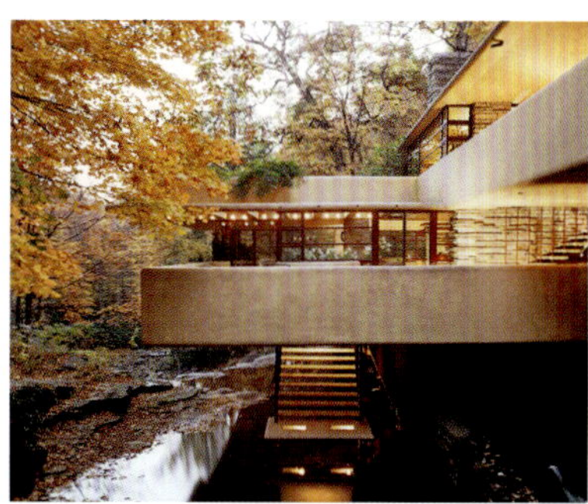

Fig. 1. World's Fair 1939, Irish Pavilion, Queens, New York. Michael Scott, 1940.

Fig. 2. Frank Lloyd Wright at Taliesin West, Scottsdale, Arizona, 1951.

Fig. 3. Fallingwater, Bear Run, Pennsylania. Frank Lloyd Wright, 1963.

to reveal the Modernist potential embodied in the fair's structures, such as the Irish Pavilion (fig. 1). And he took what became the iconic photo of the Finnish Pavilion, a Modern masterpiece by Alvar Aalto, though it was only an interior created inside a multi-tenant pavilion.

In the early years of his career Stoller was able to enhance his portfolio—and advance the art of architectural photography—with photographs of the greatest works by the senior American architect Frank Lloyd Wright. In 1946 he was assigned by *Architectural Forum* to document Wright's Taliesin West in Arizona, the winter headquarters of the master's design and teaching enterprise. On one of his two visits there he took a revealing photo of Wright with some of his reverent apprentices (fig. 2). His photos of Wright's Fallingwater in rural Pennsylvania, first visited in 1963 on assignment for the Museum of Modern Art, include some that have long represented this structure to most of the world (fig. 3). Some of his shots are from relatively unfamiliar viewpoints and depend on subtly adjusted artificial lighting. The scale of Stoller's subjects expanded with the prominence of architectural commissions available to the Modern architects who emerged in the 1940s. Most of them started practicing with modest commissions—for houses, elementary schools, even motels. Stoller's photos celebrated the austerity of these works: the simple geometries, minimally expressed structural support, and inconspicuous details.

In Untrammeled Nature

The early Modern houses Stoller photographed were mostly in rural or nearly rural settings, where houses with architectural aspiration often have been located. So the relationship of house to landscape was a key consideration in his photos during those years—the constructed and the natural portrayed with equal elegance. And the land around Modernist houses of those times was usually intended to look undisturbed (see Busch essay, fig. 11). The house in the pristine landscape continued to be a choice subject for architectural photography, and it remains so today. But Stoller often concentrated on the sculptural qualities of a house itself—revealed through light, shadow, and textures.

It wasn't long before forward-looking (and tax-averse) corporations began to follow their middle-class work forces to the suburbs, and Stoller began to document their then-novel additions to the landscape. Although the scale and complexity of these developments called for considerable alteration of the immediate landscape, the aesthetic intent again was the contrast between new structure and largely untouched surrounding property. As suburban office buildings became more sophisticated, the demand for parking was met with more advanced provisions than just acres of asphalt, and Stoller documented such facilities with artistry, sometimes even going airborne to get the most telling view in compositions and perspectives (fig. 4).

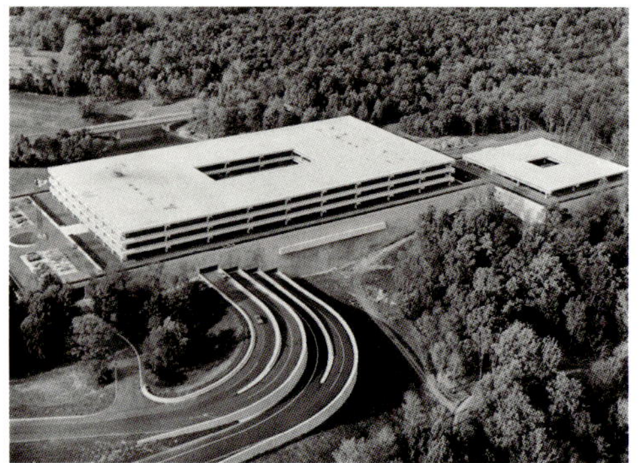

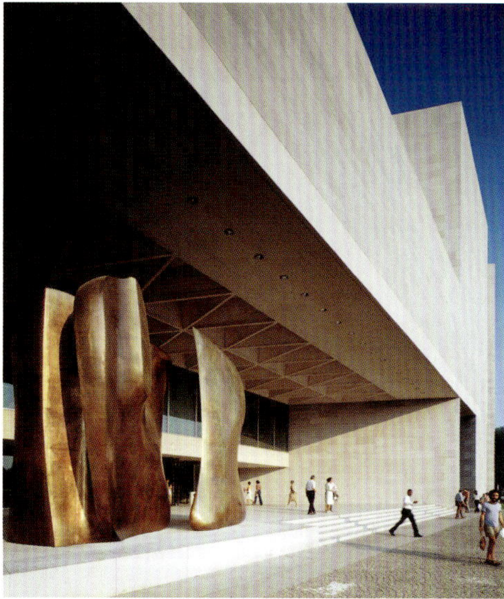

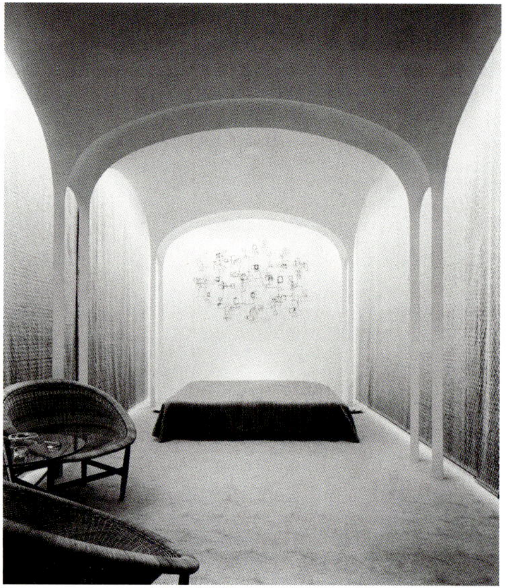

Fig. 4. American Can Company, Greenwich, Connecticut. Skidmore, Owings & Merrill, 1970.

Fig. 5. East Wing, National Gallery of Art, Washington, D.C. I. M. Pei, 1978.

Fig. 6. Interior of Guest House, New Canaan, Connecticut. Philip Johnson, 1954.

Corporate and Civic Visions

Back in the central cities Stoller was the photographer of choice for architects of curtain-walled corporate landmarks. In these photographs he included just enough surroundings to show how they related to their urban settings. They often included passersby, bringing them into the composition. For the jewel-box Manufacturers Trust bank on Manhattan's Fifth Avenue, designed by Skidmore, Owings & Merrill, he juxtaposed the building to Fifth Avenue's pedestrian stream, then zoomed in on the bank vault just inside its glazed envelope. For the John Hancock tower in Chicago, Stoller's many images include fine portrayals of the structure as a whole, as well as its presence at sidewalk level on Michigan Avenue. The street-level photo, in its subtle colors, served elegantly as a cover for the July–August 1970 *Architectural Forum*.

As office buildings demonstrated the virtues of Modernism in both the cities and suburbs, the design of the interiors was undergoing something of a revolution. The typical pre–World War II office environment had been made up of walled-off rooms and open clerical areas, generally furnished with standard products chosen by purchasing agents. The office that Philip Johnson designed for himself as director of the architecture department at the Museum of Modern Art (1946–54) represented aspirations for future workplaces—informal, with movable, industrially produced furniture. From the 1950s on, corporate offices became consciously integrated environments, and office interiors became a major segment of design practice. All the requisite elements—from air-supply grilles to floor coverings, with the demountable partitions and furnishings in between—were coordinated by architects and interior designers, the two disciplines frequently collaborating within the same firm. Stoller's task was often to document these revolutionary working environments.

The years of Stoller's rise to prominence coincided with some of the country's most ambitious government-sponsored building and rebuilding projects. Early in Stoller's career a committee of international all-stars designed the ultimate world-government institution, the United Nations complex in Manhattan. Stoller documented it from its role in the cityscape to its imposing interiors, using careful framing to enhance the new Modern forms.

Concurrent opportunities for Modern architects to rebuild the urban fabric at monumental scale are represented in his sweeping view of the Albany Mall government complex in New York State's capital city, oddly unscalable without a figure. Another grand government-related commission was I. M. Pei's East Wing of the National Gallery in Washington, D.C., illustrating Stoller's reconstruction in images of a procession from the building's approach to its innermost spaces (fig. 5).

Recording a Parade of Isms

An early movement against the strictures of the International Style was the 1950s effort to marry Modernism with the staid geometries and symmetries of historical classicism. By the 1950s the modernist pioneer Ludwig Mies van der Rohe had adopted classical massing for otherwise Modern structures such as the Seagram Building in New York. And the next-generation architect Philip Johnson, initially a Mies disciple, moved toward a more literal classicism. Stoller, as Johnson's preferred photographer, documented his adaptation of classical forms in works such as the Sheldon Museum of Art in Nebraska and the guest house at Johnson's own Glass House compound in Connecticut (fig. 6).

In another 1950s challenge to the reigning International Style, the impulse toward sculptural, expressionist architectural forms made a striking comeback. The revival was launched by Le Corbusier, the leading light of the International Style, who shocked his more rule-bound contemporaries and acolytes with his 1954 pilgrimage chapel at Ronchamp in France. The chapel's willfully expressionist forms and coarse textures shook up the functionalist establishment. Stoller made a visit to the chapel in 1955, and his photos capture the building's complex curvatures and the modulation of light on its stucco and concrete surfaces. A monk in the distance contrasts with the building's form, humanizing the sacred space.

In New York, Frank Lloyd Wright's Guggenheim Museum, completed in 1959, inserted some vigorous expressionist forms into the heart of Manhattan. Stoller captured this contrast with the dramatic strength of black-and-white film. Soon after, an intrepid innovator of the next generation, Eero Saarinen, completed his TWA Terminal at New York's Idlewild (now John F. Kennedy) Airport, where ambitious architectural statements were greeting the jet age. Stoller's photograph of this terminal from the apron beautifully relates the forms of aircraft to a structure shaped to express the wonder of flight. Interior views of this terminal capture the exhilarating, futuristic experience of passing through it. His images with individuals using the terminal show vividly that its concrete shell structure, while presenting a delicate, billowing image from a distance, is actually quite massive. Stoller depicted a similar linkage of lyrical curves and monumental structure at Saarinen's Dulles Airport outside Washington, D.C.

Other American Modernists were also adopting the sometimes theatrical forms of expressionism and offering Stoller opportunities for some dramatic photographs. Some choice examples include Wallace Harrison's First Presbyterian Church in Stamford, Connecticut, and Paul Rudolph's Tuskegee Chapel in Alabama. The Shrine of the Book in Jerusalem, by New York architects Frederick Kiesler and Armand Bartos, gave Stoller a chance to juxtapose smooth, curvilinear Modern forms with a rugged, ancient setting.

By the early 1960s, American Modernists had become seduced by the muscular forms made possible by the use of cast-in-place concrete—often more massive than necessary and cast with a heavily textured surface—in an aesthetic generally referred to as Brutalism. Like the more fluid, expressionist designs, these owed a strong debt to Le Corbusier—in this case to his pioneering use of *béton brut,* or rough-formed concrete. Stoller captured the brooding, almost menacing sculptural qualities of two prime American examples of American Brutalism: the Yale Art + Architecture Building by Paul Rudolph (fig. 7) and Boston City Hall, a competition-winning design by Kallmann, McKinnell & Knowles.

Brutalism didn't have to be executed entirely in rough concrete. Marcel Breuer, whose buildings often displayed massive exposed concrete elements, chose to clad most of his Whitney Museum in New York with granite, the slabs somewhat roughened up by flame treatment. Stoller captured the building's massive yet strangely levitating forms in day and night photos (fig. 8).

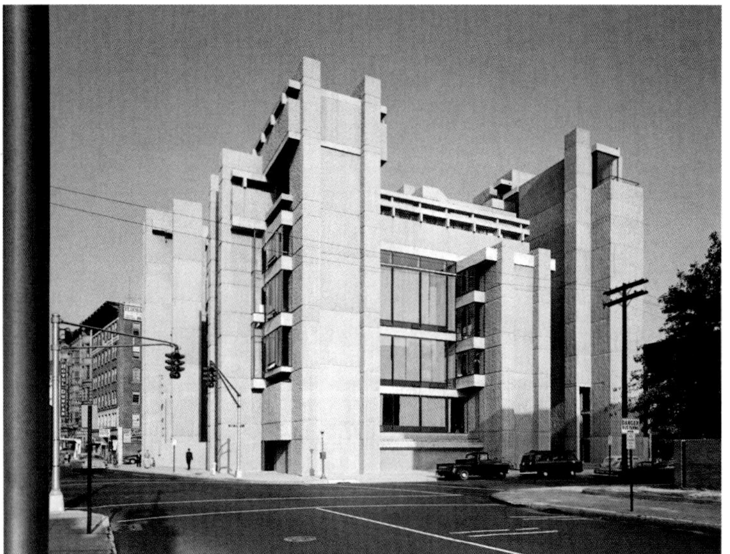

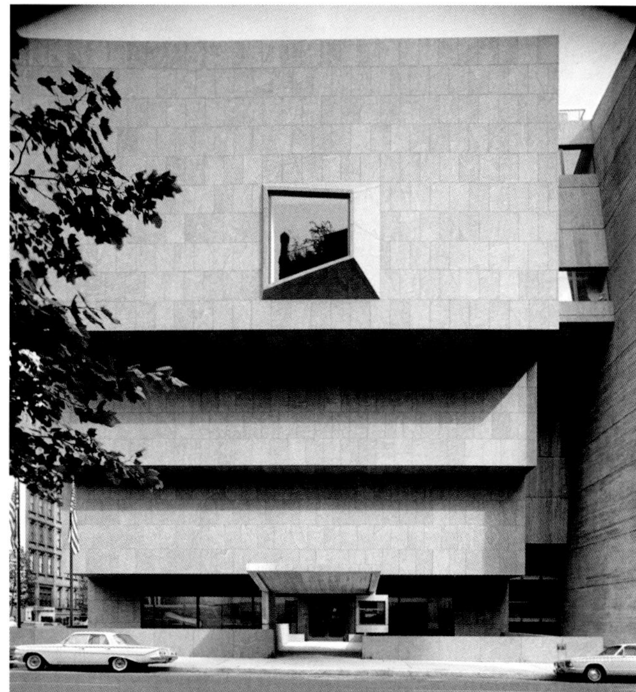

Fig. 7. Yale Art + Architecture Building, New Haven, Connecticut. Paul Rudolph, 1963.

Fig. 8. Whitney Museum, New York. Marcel Breuer, 1966.

Timelessness and Context

Louis Kahn, arguably the greatest American architect of the generation following Frank Lloyd Wright, made the competitive design statements of his contemporaries virtually moot. His work aspired to be timeless—with considerable success. It combines some of the classical attributes of regularity and symmetry with a subtly modulated stress on exposed structural elements. Stoller's photographs eloquently record two Kahn landmarks that have long drawn architectural pilgrims from all over the world: the Salk Institute in La Jolla, California, and the Kimbell Art Museum in Fort Worth, Texas.

By the late 1960s, Modern architects had largely abandoned their mission of replacing the entire built environment as their hero Le Corbusier had once proposed for the whole center of Paris. They were realizing that much of the older built world was here to stay—and even to be appreciated. Respect for context became the watchword for increasing numbers of architects. Stoller had always recorded something of the physical contexts of the works he photographed, but now each new urban building was expected to complement, not simply intrude on, its setting.

Some leading architects had begun to take cues from surrounding buildings, as revealed in a Stoller photo taken from the lobby of Mies van der Rohe's Seagram Building. This handsome composition shows how the symmetrical design of Mies's tower and plaza echoes that of the early twentieth-century Racquet and Tennis Club, which survived the 1950s transformation of Park Avenue and remains the plaza's far wall. While Stoller's black-and-white image shows clearly how Mies integrated the club facade into his plaza design, it doesn't show how his beige granite and bronze mullions match the colors and textures of that older building. More overt efforts to echo historic design followed. Eero Saarinen's early-1960s Stiles and Morse Colleges at Yale University display an unabashed intention to shape buildings and open spaces to resemble the medieval townscapes that once surrounded Gothic monuments.

Stoller and Postmodernism

While the definition of Postmodernism tends to vary from writer to writer, characteristic Postmodern architecture involves the ironic juxtaposition of historical forms and details with Modern design elements, sometimes throwing in shapes, colors, and textures from Pop culture. Participating as he did in the ascendancy of Modernism, Stoller could not have accepted this essentially mischievous new mode very warmly. Nor could most of the architects for whom he shot. Then too, Postmodernism didn't fit well into Stoller's career trajectory. Pioneering Postmodernism from the 1960s tended to be too modest to rate a Stoller assignment, and when the movement became more dominant in the 1970s and 1980s, he was beginning to retire from the field.

One of his subjects, however, was a notably ambitious early example of proto-Postmodernism: the New York State Pavilion at the World's Fair of 1964. Although its architect, Philip Johnson, had once been committed to the purest International Style, he had been quick to try his hand at subsequent approaches, and in this structure he incorporated aspects of Postmodernism. Its major space was an elliptical volume defined by massive cylindrical columns in the Italian Baroque manner. Spanning the vast space was a cable-supported canopy, with conspicuous steel connections emphasizing its Modern aspects and translucent plastic panels in gaudy colors making reference to pop culture. The overhead allusion to the pop world was echoed in the pavilion's floor, which reproduced in terrazzo a Texaco road map of the state.

In 1985, Stoller visited a later landmark of Postmodernism, the Staatsgalerie museum in Stuttgart, Germany, designed by the London architect James Stirling and his partner Michael Wilford. Since this was just a brief visit, not an assignment, Stoller couldn't document the entire intricate complex. But by using a handheld camera he skillfully captured the geometry, scale, and textures of its central circular courtyard, with a half-sunken classical pavilion at its center and a distinctly Modern ramp spiraling around it.

Realities of Color

Stoller shot in color on some of his early assignments, notably to record the buildings of Frank Lloyd Wright and their settings. But his use of color film over the years evolved more or less in sync with the use of color photos in architectural publications. Color printing in the profession's magazines increased gradually during Stoller's active years, from virtually none around 1940 to a color page or two in a typical 1960s issue, after which color became more widespread. Use of color by architecture firms and clients shifted more or less in parallel with that of magazines. Books on architecture varied more widely; they were—and still are—priced largely according to their size and the proportion of color printing.

The cost differential for color film, processing, and printing, which was very steep during Stoller's career, decreased sharply as the technologies involved advanced. By the 1980s all of the pages in a typical architecture magazine—and many books—were running on color presses, even if the color potential was not exploited. Concurrently, these latter-day color presses often yielded rather dingy reproductions of black-and-white photos. For a prominent black-and-white image art directors would sometimes enhance reproduction by superimposing all of the press's ink colors to generate rich four-color black-and-white images.

For photographers of Stoller's generation, color film posed new challenges. When black-and-white reigned, its neutral tones could be manipulated with relative ease in the developing and printing process. Color photography, on the other hand, was recorded on transparencies that were not as amenable to manipulation after exposure; accurate color had to be recorded in the original image. For any photography involving artificial light, the differing color temperatures of the light sources could produce eerie effects. Tinted gels, originated for stage lighting, were often adapted to "correct" light sources to conform to the sensitivities of the film. Split exposures might be used to balance daylight and artificial light. Photographers who had mastered the art of portraying the world in black and white responded somewhat reluctantly to the special demands of color. Today, color in digital images can be manipulated to produce any desired effect, but Stoller used only film.

Besides the technical factors that led to the greater use of color photos there lies a deeper question: Does color always provide a more accurate interpretation of the actual subject? We see reality in color, of course, but we see it in three dimensions. Color in a two-dimensional image can, in fact, distract from the composition of forms and spaces the photographer wants to portray—the forms and spaces on which architects focus their efforts. A patch of green grass in a foreground can stop the eye; bright chairs or artworks can jump out at the viewer; vividly colored carpets can dominate over equally important surfaces. Two photos of the TWA terminal interior illustrate the issue. One could question which one represents the space most accurately (figs. 9, 10).

Even the blue of a clear sky—far different from the neutral backdrop of a sky in black and white—can draw attention away from the architectural subject. A pattern of white clouds on blue can be even more distracting. Of the color photos in this book with large areas of sky, many of them show the soft colors of dusk. But sometimes clouds on a blue sky can contribute to the composition and message of a photograph (fig. 11). Given all these considerations, the photo composition that works best in black and white is not necessarily the best one for color.

Of course, if color is integral to the architectural concept as a whole, color photography is invaluable. Modern architects of the mid-twentieth century conceived and executed their works largely in neutral tones. But occasionally, inherent color was essential to the character of the work. An instance is the Seagram Building, whose bronze and amber-colored glass envelope set it apart from its generally grayish neighbors when it was built—and decades later helps it maintain its uniqueness among the colorless behemoths that grew up around it (figs. 12, 13).

Atypical Subjects

Although Stoller's architectural commissions generally were for work within the evolving mainstream of Modernism, he occasionally photographed buildings almost universally disdained by Modernists. His archives include shots of work by the architect Morris Lapidus, who was widely noted—or notorious—for his 1950s Miami Beach hotels. Other subjects Stoller took on only occasionally were showrooms and shops, some of them significant design achievements at a smaller scale. And photography for his regular architect clients sometimes included models of architectural projects, among them examples of radical proposals that never attained reality.

While Stoller was generally more than busy photographing buildings, houses, and industrial sites, he did find time for some perceptive photographs of noted architects. Even though most of these were taken on assignment, some of them look as if Stoller

Figs. 9 and 10. TWA Terminal at Idlewild (JFK), New York. Eero Saarinen, 1962.

Fig. 11. Taliesin West, Scottsdale, Arizona. Frank Lloyd Wright, 1951.

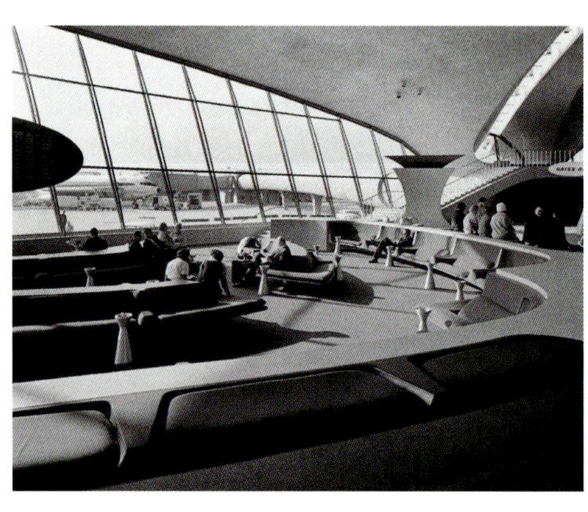

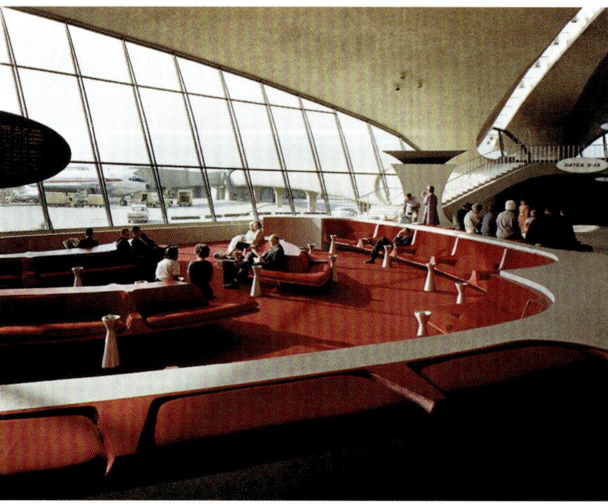

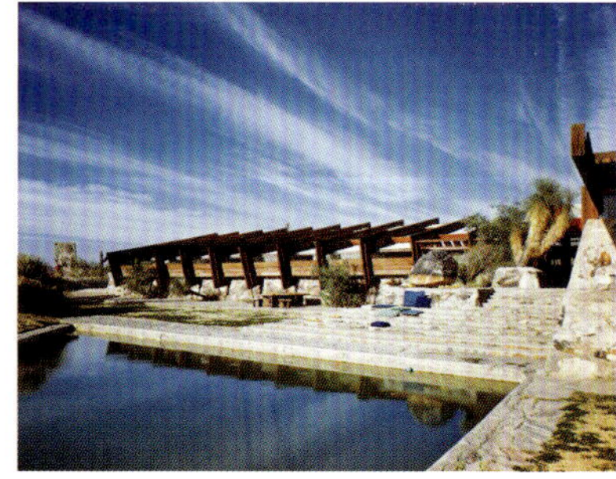

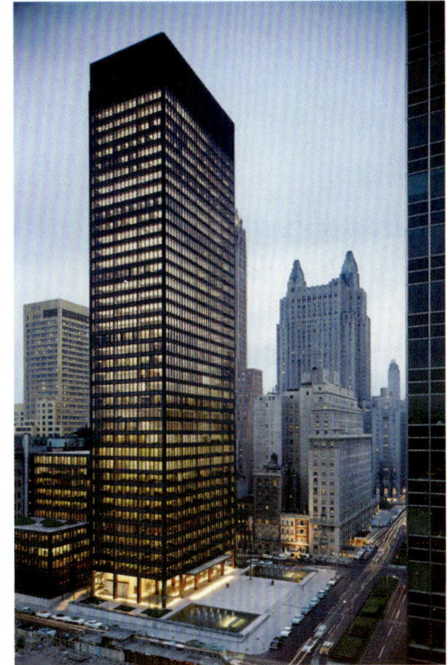

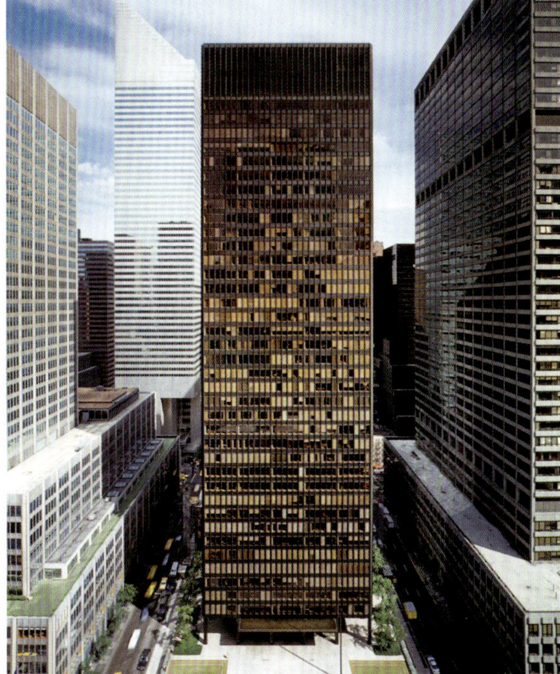

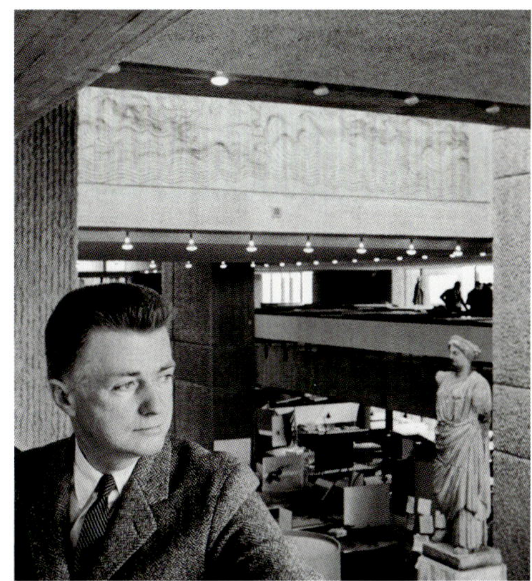

Fig. 12. Seagram Building, New York. Mies van der Rohe with Philip Johnson, 1958.

Fig. 13. Seagram Building, New York. Mies van der Rohe with Philip Johnson, 1991.

Fig. 14. Paul Rudolph at Yale Art + Architecture Building, New Haven, Connecticut. Paul Rudolph, 1963.

had casually encountered the architect during the shoot or during a preparatory walk-through. There is, for instance, an image of Paul Rudolph juxtaposed with a classical figure he had installed in the central void of his Yale Art + Architecture Building (fig. 14). Marcel Breuer is seen against the distinctive rhomboid of one of his Whitney Museum windows. Richard Meier is seen in his studio in an apt approximation of the traditional portrait.

Summation of an Era

It is our good fortune that Ezra Stoller practiced his art during the heyday of Modern architecture—the years when it evolved from a movement of manifestos and experiments to an expanding inventory of prominent real buildings. His archive of some fifty thousand images encompasses a long procession of distinguished and highly varied twentieth-century design accomplishments.

Stoller's contributions to the culture and knowledge base of architecture have been invaluable. He has been just one of many to point out that what most of us know about architectural design we "know" largely through photographs. Most of us—even those of us who are architectural journalists—have actually seen only a fraction of the landmarks in our mental databank. Through the photographs he took—and through the standards he set for other architectural photographers—Stoller has enabled us to "see" hundreds of works we will never be able to visit and helped us to understand the aspirations of their architects.

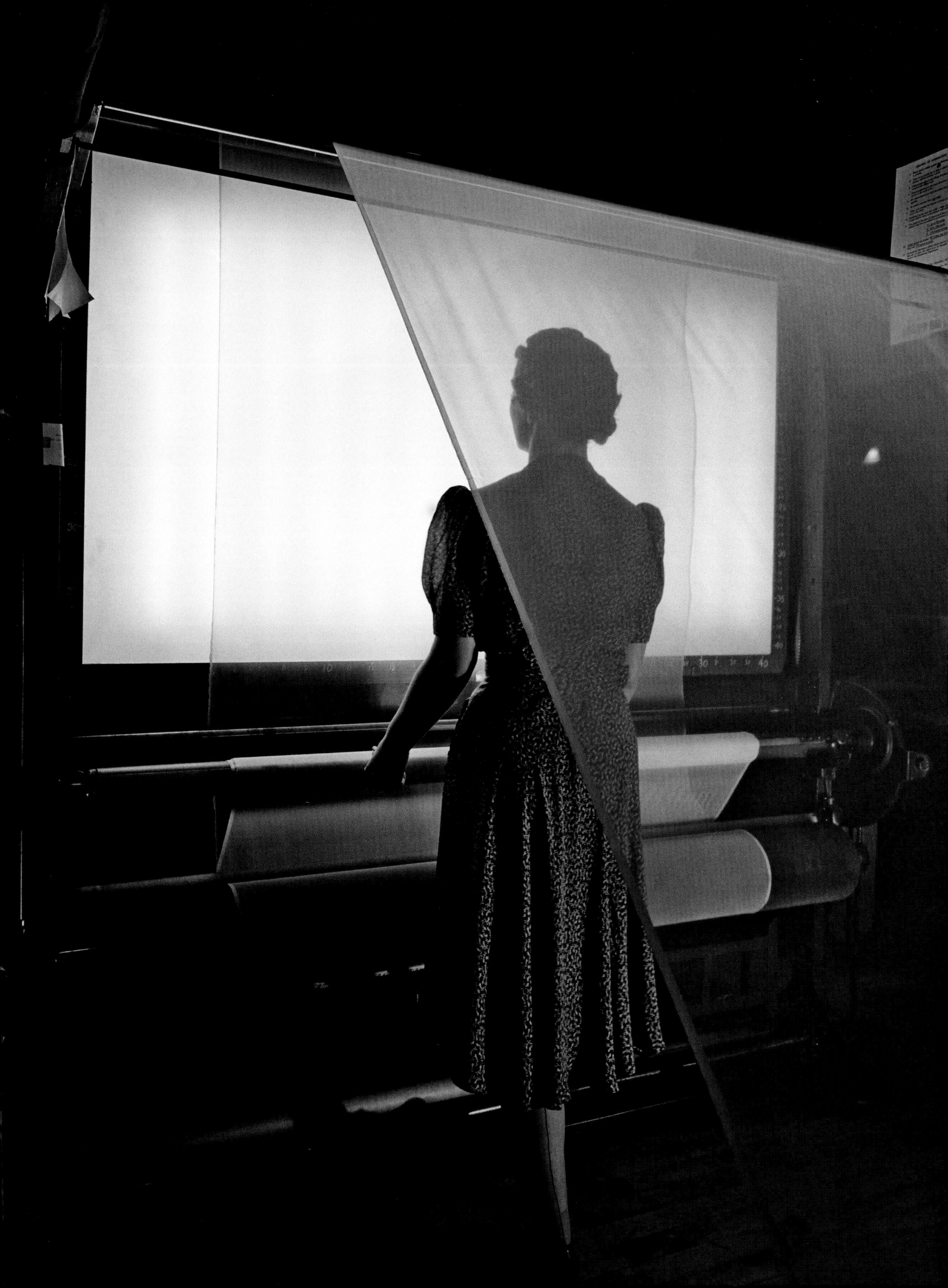

Nina Rappaport

Man and Machine

With the explosive growth of corporations and their factories in the early twentieth century came a focus on commercial and industrial photographs of workers, products, and spaces of production. Photographs that depicted factories, with people making things, and manufacturing processes, revealing an industrious spirit and new marketing efforts, were published in annual reports, in-house magazines, trade magazines, corporate catalogues, and business directories. For a photographer of the time, the challenge was to depict industry and the functional through the abstraction of the two-dimensional surface, and to do it in a way that both revealed what a thing is and also demonstrated its social essence and cultural meaning. The photograph entered as purposeful, useful art that was well aligned—in some practitioners' hands—with the professionalization of commercial photography in the early twentieth century, hastening the industrial narrative and that narrative of "progress." Today, when separated from their original context, these photographs constitute more than a nostalgic look at the past or a historical document. They are works of art. Bertolt Brecht remarked that a "photograph of the Krupp works or the AEG [Allgemeine Elektricitäts-Gesellschaft] tells us next to nothing about these institutions. Actual reality has slipped into the functional. The reification of human relations—the factory, say—means that they are no longer explicit. So something must in fact be *built up*, something artificial, posed."[1] Ezra Stoller participated in this new commercial genre, documenting industry for publicity and promotion and also revealing these industrial landscapes as an art form.

Pictorial photographers such as Clarence White (1871–1925), who founded his own school of photography in New York in 1914 and was part of the Photo-Secession movement, advocated the interdependence of art and commerce despite the dominance of the Pictorialist school of photography, which mimicked painting and featured academic European subjects. White's ideas influenced such photographers as Alfred Stieglitz (1864–1946) and Edward Steichen (1879–1973), who grasped photography's potential as a profession and were interested in real-life subjects, not those that fell

Duplan Silk Mills, Hazelton, Pennsylvania, 1943.

into the category of "fine art." In the case of Steichen's work, "both agency and producer were quick to realize, then, that photography's lineage as art could give prestige to the products or services being promoted and thereby fetishize them as objects of desire."[2] The photographers used the new medium to initiate careers, to make a living photographing products, just as portrait artists had done before them. Psychologist Walter Dill Scott (1869–1955) found that consumers were "open to suggestion" and could be persuaded, through advertising, to buy goods—even unneeded ones. He developed a strategy called "atmospheric advertising" in which he arranged products seductively, sparking consumers' impulse to buy.[3]

The Genesis of Industrial Photography

Industrial photography, like advertising photography, evolved from a profession to an art, following the same transition as early nineteenth-century engravings of factories and their machines used as illustrations. Denis Diderot's *Encyclopédie* (1751–72) and *Days at the Factory* (1843) and magazines such as *Scientific American* and *Harper's Weekly* exposed inventions, machines, and processes that had industrial applications. With the advent of photography in the first decade of the twentieth century, the black-and-white image began to be used for numerous purposes within industry: efficiency analysis, documentation and promotion of the factory within the corporation itself, advertising, and journalistic documentation. Essential to the development of both photography and motion pictures was the work of Eadweard Muybridge, Etienne-Jules Marey, and Frank and Lillian Gilbreth. For their studies of human motion and worker efficiency the Gilbreths would attach lights to workers' hands, then photograph the workers completing tasks. The traces of light would show their movements in the photographs, which would be studied to help develop the most rational and efficient system for manufacturing. These studies were used in Frederick Taylor's 1911 development of Scientific Management (fig. 1).

Despite the seductiveness of the new production technologies and the completed products, it was the *worker* who was of paramount interest, not only for the company's in-house publicity but for the general public. Photography had become not only the appropriate medium, as a new technology itself, but the perfect metaphor for industry—a modern tool revealing modernity, science merging with art.

Companies used photography to document their history and to encourage worker allegiance. This is reflected in the troves of still and moving images in company archives. "Work portraits were featured in the pages of corporate employee magazines, where their photographic meanings were over determined by a post-corporate family harmony over independent union organizing."[4] Lewis Hines, whose child labor photographs of 1910 not only exposed the difficult working conditions, but prompted social reform, later worked as a photographer for Western Electric to promote the company's welfare capitalism in its in-house magazines. "Managers actively worked to create a visual culture of dignified labor as a means of increasing job satisfaction and discouraging unionization, and Hines's work was useful toward these ends."[5] Or, as David Nye, who has so thoroughly researched the archives of General Electric, notes, "corporate photography contains a latent ideology" depending on the reason for the photography assignment.[6]

Manufacturing as a process was usually invisible to the consumer. Factories were often sequestered, in separately zoned districts removed from everyday urban life, and thus became secrets to unfold. This made their off-limit interiors enticing and mysterious to outsiders, while insiders found life in the factory mundane and an oppressive quotidian reality. Worker portraits showed to the outside world the conditions inside (whether real or a bit staged), elevating the worker to heroic status. Margaret Bourke-White (1904–1971), the first female photojournalist for *Fortune* and *Life* magazines, was commissioned to create a portrait of Otis Steel in 1927, for

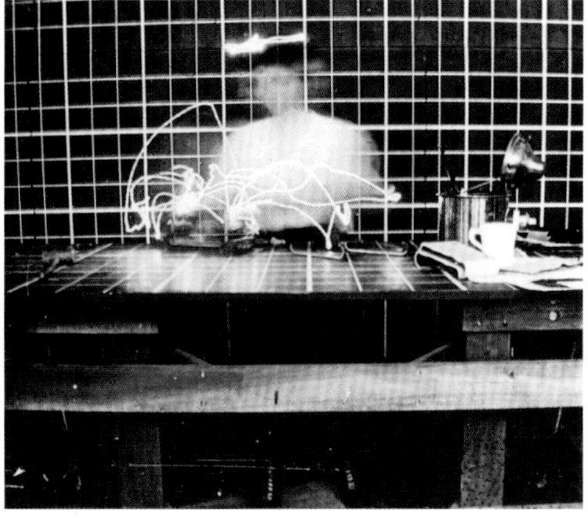

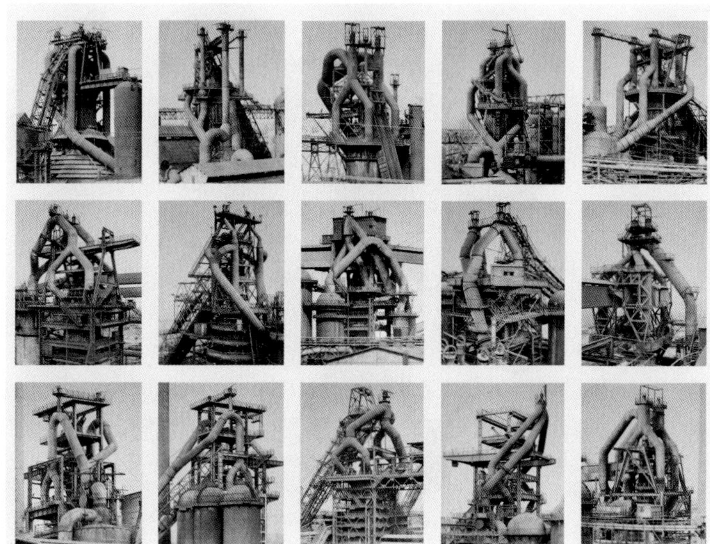

Fig. 1. Frank Gilbreth, motion study, c. 1910. Photograph. Frank and Lillian Gilbreth Collection, Archives Center, National Museum of American History, Smithsonian Institution.

Fig. 2. Bernd and Hilla Becher, *Blast Furnace,* 2003. Fifteen black-and-white photographs, 68 1/4 × 94 1/4 in. (173.4 × 239. 4 cm). Courtesy of the Sonnabend Gallery, New York.

example. She convinced management at Otis to allow her to cover the assignment, and she lived at the mills in her blue jeans, photographing the hot metal and the workers, using new kinds of flash lighting to capture the fire and liquid on film to show that "art must have flesh and blood." [7]

Industrial subjects also became the subjects of a new genre and art form. The German Albert Renger-Patzsch (1897–1966) was influential in the Neue Sachlichkeit (New Objectivity) photographic movement. Like Ezra Stoller, he never considered himself an artist, and he deliberately distanced himself from the categorization. He tended to photograph objects in groupings, capturing their industrial power and robust physicality without sentimentality. He was straightforward in his approach, wanting to call his book *Things,* not *The World Is Beautiful,* as it was later titled. With that book he confronted readers with everyday objects that they normally would overlook. "Unwittingly he made photography a method of phenomenological reduction involving an intuition of the thing in its essential givenness."[8]

Also in this phenomenological approach is the collaborative work of the Bechers—Bernd (1931–2007) and Hilla (b. 1934)—who photographed the industrial landscapes of Germany. They compiled typologies of functionalist architecture of the vernacular and everyday infrastructure, such as water towers, mineshafts, smokestacks, and coal furnaces. They photographed straight ahead, always from the same angle; their images were crisp and precise, without shadows or workers. They considered their photography documentation but ended up monumentalizing the industrial object, as an artifact and an art. Photographed with an attention to detail as rigorous as the functionality of the machines they portrayed, their composite studies parallel guidebooks by horticulturists: each specimen, in a series or a grouping, became significant for its minute and grand variations in black-and-white grids (fig. 2).[9]

Ezra Stoller's Industrial Project

Ezra Stoller photographed industry from the mid-1940s into the 1960s, when America was developing peacetime technologies and the nation was at the forefront of industrial progress. His industrial photography falls into the categories mentioned above: journalistic assignments for the then-new color magazines and photographs for annual reports, internal corporate communications, and advertising. He also used his architectural expertise to photograph factory buildings for clients and their architects.

Within these unique but overlapping themes Stoller excelled at photographing man and machine. He captured the energy of the factory floor and the people who worked

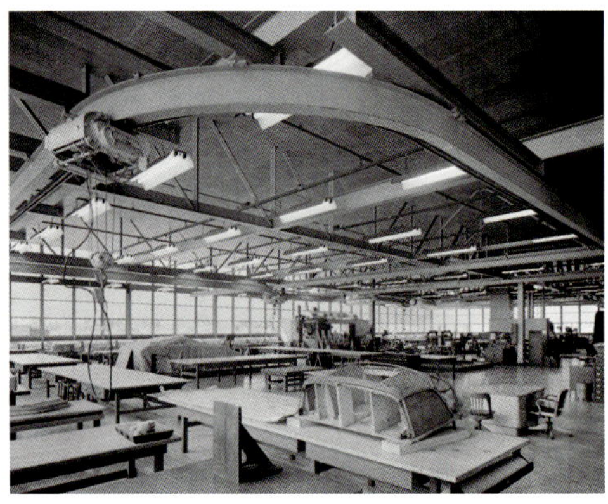

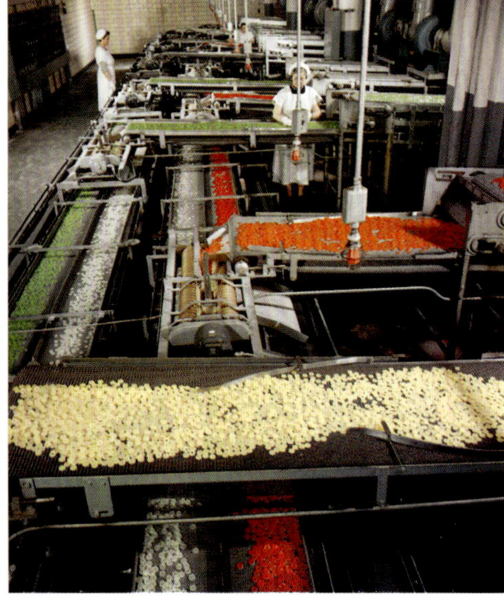

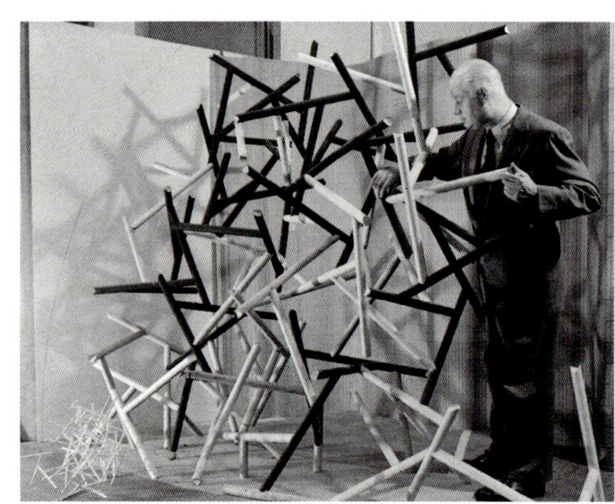

Fig. 3. General Motors Technical Center, Warren, Michigan. Eero Saarinen, 1951.

Fig. 4. Life Savers Factory, Port Chester, New York, 1956.

Fig. 5. Twenty-four-foot cell model with William Burtin, designer, 1957.

there. In depicting the intricacy of American industry he also conveyed the transformation of raw materials into finished products, complete with mechanical details. His depictions of industrial architecture contributed to a new narrative, making American manufacturing appear attractive and worth investing and working in (fig. 3).

Stoller's architectural photographs are striking for their stillness. In comparison, his industrial photographs, done on assignment, reveal a quite different sensibility. In a trove of previously unexplored images we see him embrace the stop-motion dynamic of products on the assembly line—from paper to vinegar, textiles, silks, engines, and typewriters. From his images of some now obsolete processing methods and products we learn the connections between the paper industry and cigarette manufacturing (paper was made for cigarettes and fed into machines that rolled them), between the manufacture of pills and Life Savers (the pill-punching machines were also used to punch out the center of the candies in a cross-industry technology transfer) (fig. 4). Du Pont's new silicon product was processed to make computer chips at IBM, which Stoller also photographed. Stoller's portraits of the industrial landscape—simultaneously more staged and candid than his other work—emphasize technology and the variable scale of the machinery to achieve it, while other photographs captured the mechanization of the workplace and the relationship of worker to individual task.

Stoller was fortunate to make friends with Will Burtin (1908–1972), the German-born graphic designer who moved to the United States in 1938. Burtin obtained a position designing the Federal Works Agency Exhibition for the U.S. pavilion at the New York World's Fair. Between 1945 and 1949 he was artistic director of *Fortune* magazine, and he often hired Stoller as a freelance photographer. Burtin established the modern field of graphic representation and visual communications—a field today called "information design." His innovative integration of drawing, photography, and collage, combined with text, carefully controlled the relationship between word and image, clearly charting, step by step, how to work a tool or machine. He also designed exhibitions of scientific subjects for Upjohn Pharmaceuticals, including "The Brain" (1958) and "The Cell" (1960), making complex topics legible to the general public (fig. 5). In the 1950s Burtin established his own design firm, working for corporate clients on their graphic identities, in-house magazines, and annual reports (filled with charts and diagrams). Stoller, working closely with him, came to understand how Burtin "brought to his assignment . . . a whole new spatial vision of graphic design. . . . Copy and illustrations were not just neatly organized; they were presented as counterpoint to each other."[10] Stoller emphasized his respect for Burtin: "He would never lay out a story until the pictures were in. He would never suggest pictures for his story before he sent me out on assignment. And when he laid out a story, you could read that story from his pictures, and you didn't need a word of type."[11]

In 1943, for his first assignment for Burtin, Stoller photographed a series at the Duplan Silk Mills in Hazelton, Pennsylvania, showing what the company made during the war. Stoller's images highlight women, who were employed in factories while men were on the front. They are seen operating the large weaving machines, carefully calibrating silk for large swaths of fabric. This also was similar to their production of an early version of an artificial silk—rayon. In one image, a woman worker is herself in silk stockings with a prominent seam. She stands between a sheath of thin silk and large industrial rollers. The image, in which the toughness of the machines is contrasted with the delicacy of the silk, shows a similarity to Lewis Hines's compositions, but in a more refined setting (fig. 6).

In Stoller's 1947 *Fortune* series on the GE Silicone plant in Waterford, New York, one spread shows the silica being formed into high-viscosity seals and gaskets. At the Dow Chemical plant in Midland, Michigan, pipes create abstract patterns while Stoller's tilted camera angle reveals various equipment heights, allowing the public its first glimpse into new, unknown processes. Carefully juxtaposed through a window are laboratory beakers and chemical towers, both bulbous in shape but opposite in scale. The same grouping recurs in photographs of the Heinz laboratory outside London—beakers and towers silhouetted in the landscape (figs. 7, 8).

An October 1949 cover story for *Fortune,* in which Stoller photographed a new offset lithographic printing process in step-by-step detail, uses the magazine itself as a case study. The article indicated that printing lagged behind other postwar industries in industrial efficiency but would soon catch up. Some of the issue's pages were printed using the older gravure method, others with the new offset lithographic process and electronic scanners featured in the magazine. Stoller photographed each step in color, showing how both images and typography were produced. Throughout, workers are integrated with machines: some can be seen working inside and between the printer. Other views of the factory floor embed workers and machinery along strong diagonals. Dramatic framing devices thrust the viewer directly into the picture (figs. 9, 10).

From the pre–World War II period through the 1950s, electronics was one of the largest industries in New York.[12] Skilled workers, some of whom had worked in the lightbulb industry, transitioned into electronics. Stoller was invited to photograph CBS Columbia Records; he roamed their factory floor in Long Island City as he photographed all phases of production—electron tubes being installed in radios and TVs; picture and receiving tubes being connected; wires, knobs, and dials being assembled. In the narrative sequence photographs, men and women on the assembly line adjust television screens and cases on overhead conveyors. They press records and add labels

Fig. 6. Duplan Silk Mills, Hazelton, Pennsylvania, 1943.

Fig. 7. Upjohn, Kalamazoo, Michigan, 1950.

Fig. 8. Heinz Research Center, Hayes Park, Hillingdon, England. Skidmore, Owings & Merrill, 1966.

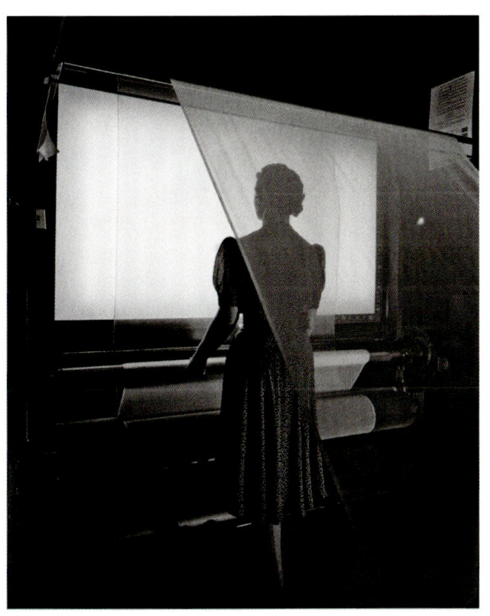

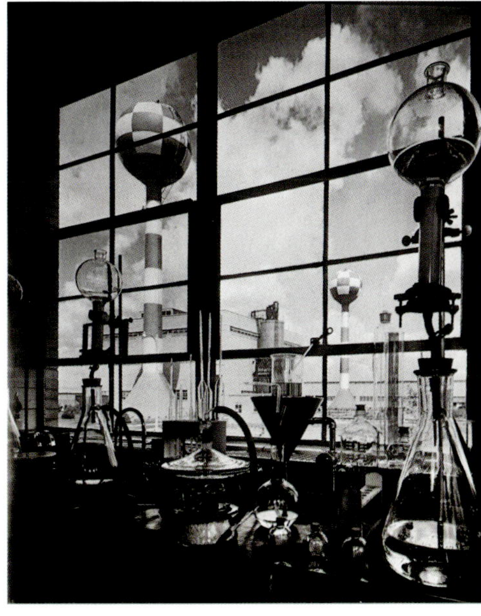

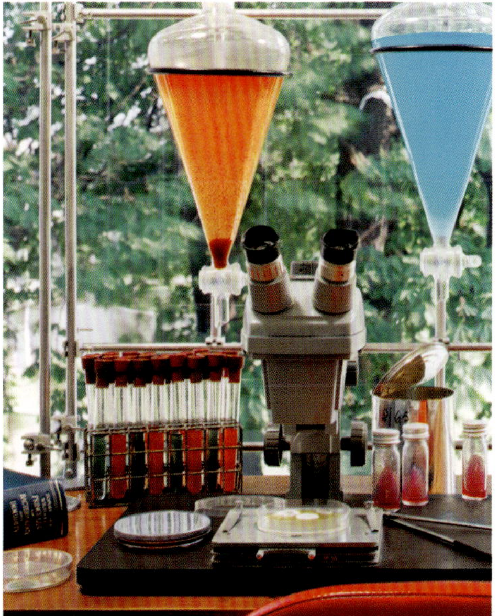

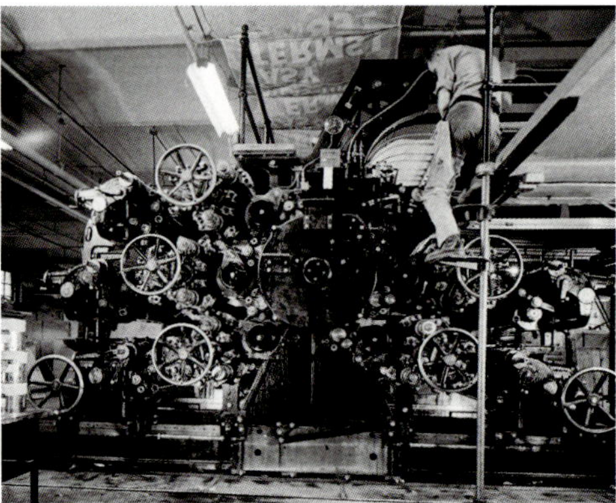

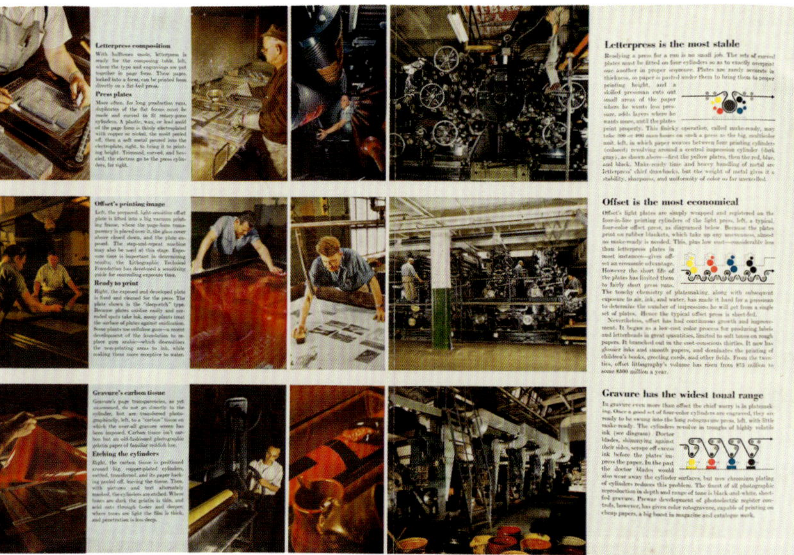

Letterpress composition

Press plates

Offset's printing image

Ready to print

Gravure's carbon tissue

Etching the cylinders

Letterpress is the most stable

Offset is the most economical

Gravure has the widest tonal range

Fig. 9. "Printing," *Fortune* magazine, October 1949.

Fig. 10. Page from "Printing," *Fortune* magazine, October 1949.

as the vinyl disks leave the line. Stoller is empathetic with these workers; they are integral to manufacturing and portrayed as larger than life.

When the photographs are removed from the context of publication, some dramatic shifts in scale occur—from the tiny computer chip photographed in the middle of a man's palm to the scale of the turbine for hydroelectric power and the technologies for astrophysics (figs. 11, 12). Today these photographs also serve the double role of documentation of the new technologies of an earlier era. As Susan Sontag so aptly noted, "Photographs are, of course, artifacts. But their appeal is that they also seem, in a world littered with photographic relics, to have the status of found objects—unpremeditated slices of the world. Thus, they trade simultaneously on the prestige of art and the magic of the real."[13]

Images of larger objects include photographs from a series on hydroelectric power in *Fortune*'s "Power in the West" issue of 1947, in which Stoller followed workers into underground tunnels, where he photographed the turbines and dams. These images celebrate America's power-generating capabilities. Stoller approached the water flooding over the dams and concrete barriers; the white foam is in full view, as is the awesome power source captured on film (fig. 13).

For the essay "Astrophysics & Astronomy" in *Fortune*'s January 1947 issue, Stoller was assigned to photograph "coronographs" and telescopes at Palomar Mountain in California, and Climax, Colorado. These images show his careful calibration of oblique views, use of dramatic angles, and fascination with machines allowing views of nature up close. Space exploration intrigued Stoller in human, photographic, and scientific terms. The opening texts in the magazine discuss the contemplation of the earth and the "vastness of the universe," "rolling back the frontiers of space." They are the first color photographs published of space, and Stoller photographed the observatories from which they were taken; in effect, he was photographing photography equipment of a vast scale (fig. 14).

Stoller roamed Cummins Engine in Columbus, Indiana, much as he did CBS Columbia Records, to photograph the workers. He used close-up views and oblique angles to document their tattoos and protective goggles, and to convey their physical strength. He foregrounded the machinery, showing the scope and breadth of the factory and the employees at work. As a skilled storyteller, he continued to create a pictorial narrative as in his architectural photographs, but here it was of business and technology, men and machines.

In 1941, when Will Burtin became the design consultant for the Upjohn Pharmaceutical Company, he asked Stoller to take photographs for the annual reports and the in-house magazine, *Scope* (fig. 15). The images created for one assignment were also used for the July 1946 issue of *Fortune* and a photographic essay about new technologies and manufacturing titled "Mass Precision Symmetry." In it, Stoller explored the beauty of the abstract patterns created by Upjohn's Kalamazoo, Michigan, plant as workers manufactured pills. Across five pages, seven zoomed-in photographs depict details of the machines used to make molds for pills. The accompanying text noted, "The pattern maybe be observed in the vast, repetitive processes of the chemical plant, or in the fabrication of huge, identical shapes in the aircraft factory. Here the intelligent camera views up close the beauty in the pattern of the small, precise, vivid objects that are the creation for the modern pharmaceutical industry" (fig. 16).

Other commissions with Burtin followed, such as for IBM's in-house magazine *Think*. The December 1958 issue included a cover photograph of a model of a cosmic ray (fig. 17). Stoller thoroughly documented the workings of IBM's factories in a more candid, casual way, photographing the processing and employees *in situ*. On the contact sheets from this series one can see workers looking quickly toward the camera, others looking away; in later shots they are clearly being told how to stand and pose, but naturally. Stoller photographed the internal workings of IBM's machines: the transistors, cores, wires, and chips. He pulled back to document the site, the workspaces, the workers' shoes, even the clocks being set or arranged for installation. In more carefully composed images, those arranged and "styled" by Burtin, he also photographed finished products: Dictaphones and typewriters. From Endicott and Yorktown to New York and Tokyo, Stoller gleaned the specifics of each plant and product. These details subsequently appeared in IBM's brochures and exhibitions, as well as in architectural publications.

Stoller, of course, photographed factory buildings as architecture. He did so for architects such as Skidmore, Owings & Merrill (one of his major regular clients), of their Philip Morris plant in Richmond, Virginia, and their Heinz factory in Pittsburgh, as well as for the Olivetti-Underwood factory designed by Louis I. Kahn in Pennsylvania. In each of these photo essays Stoller emphasized the architecture and the spaces but always included the workers making the goods—how they used the space and the machinery. He often showed the workers at ease. In the Heinz plant the color film enhances the red of the tomatoes from the testing and processing to the final product, ketchup (fig. 18). At Philip Morris, the machines that make the cigarettes are more fascinating than the spaces; and at Olivetti the symmetry of the assembly-line machinery falls into sync with that of Kahn's and engineer August Komendant's structural framework—the building becoming a machine in itself. Stoller captures the architecture of the factories and the atmosphere of the manufacturing spaces with a new perspective implicit in the portrait of a company.

Fig. 11. IBM, cores and transistors, 1955.

Fig. 12. Kitt Peak Solar Observatory, Pima County, Arizona. Skidmore, Owings & Merrill, 1962.

Fig. 13. "Power in the West," *Fortune* magazine, 1947.

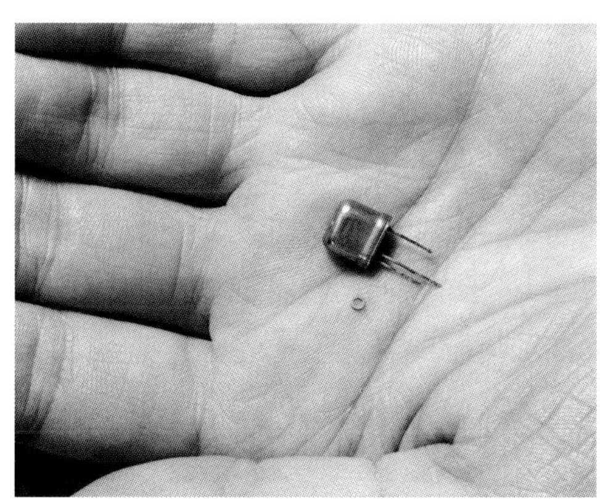

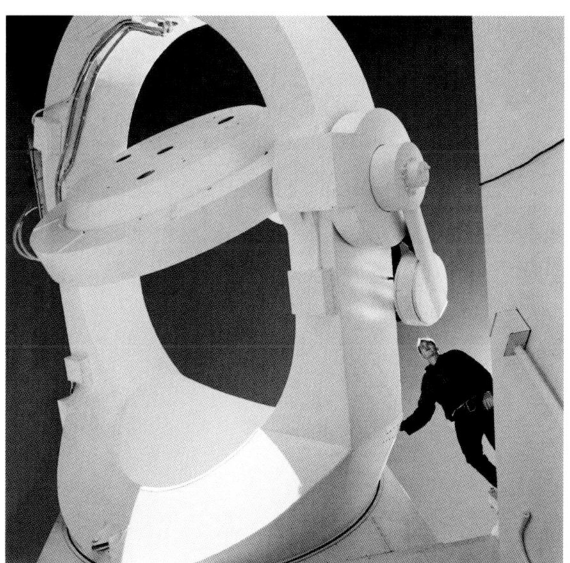

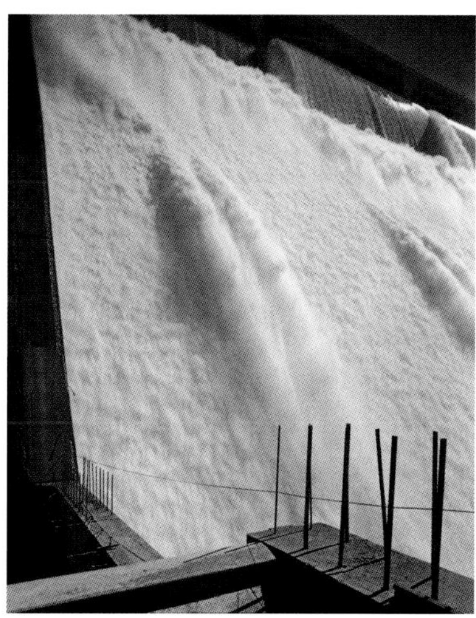

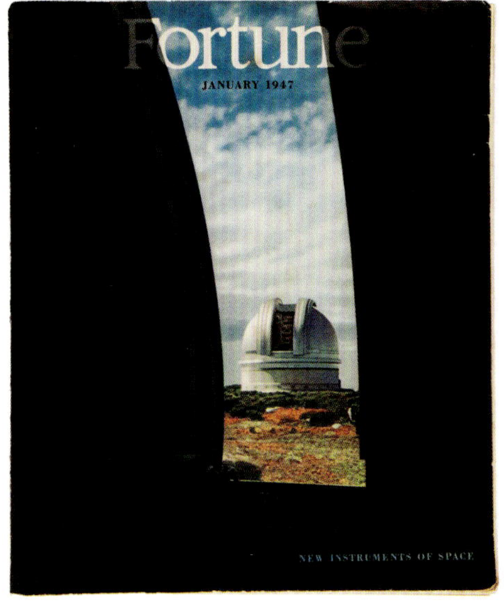

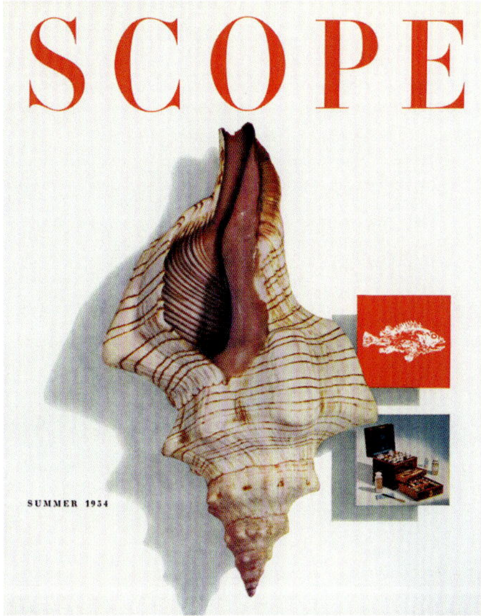

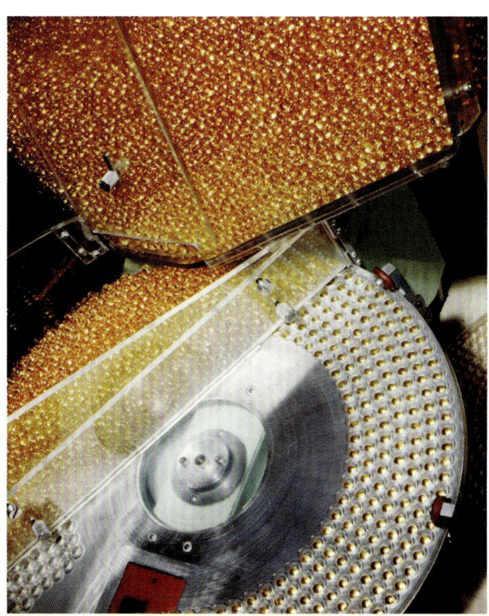

Fig. 14. *Fortune* magazine cover, January 1947.

Fig. 15. *Scope* magazine, Upjohn. Designed by Will Burtin.

Fig. 16. Pill-sorting equipment, Upjohn, Kalamazoo, Michigan, 1942.

Stoller depicts the worker heroically—front and center in many of the images. With the demand for the large-format camera's long exposures, workers are also seen blurred in the background of the TV assembly-line image. In the postwar production frenzy, women are at work alongside men, important to the new workforce. He also captured the transition from individualized handwork to the push-button of total robotic processing. People are pictured loading, feeding, and directing the work (as Charlie Chaplin lampooned in his 1931 film *Modern Times*); eventually they became machines themselves. Stoller's understanding of man's relationship to machine parallels his own relationship to his camera as he innately depicts the object/subject and man/machine.

Occasionally Stoller offered ironic commentaries, such as focusing on towers of insurance papers at Connecticut General Insurance agency in Hartford, Connecticut. The massiveness of the resulting papers resembles factory production, and the stacks of paper mimic buildings. In a photograph of a vast, empty office space at Philip Morris a series of black telephones are plugged into sockets in columns in a grid on the floor. The image is one of sheer "production anticipation."

Stoller's newly discovered industrial genre reveals production: the heroism of the worker at the machine and the precise technologies of the time. The photograph was a fact, a mode in which to capture space and time, transforming both industry into an art and the photographs into art forms—abstract but fluid, comprehensive and specific. They heighten our awareness of making and those who made, mapping a typology beyond the normality of documenting industry. Little could Stoller have known the value of his contribution, both as art and as historical documents of an industrious time of invention and passion.

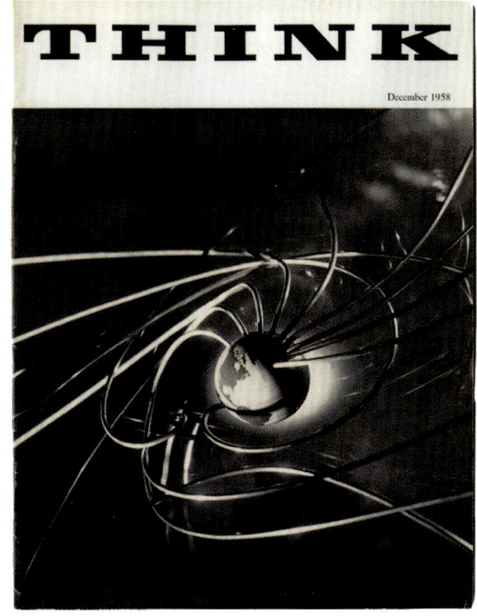

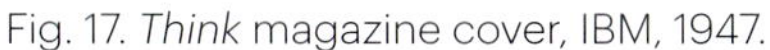

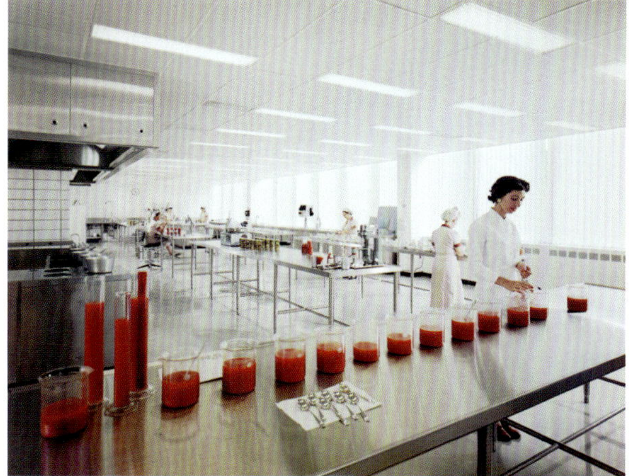

Fig. 17. *Think* magazine cover, IBM, 1947.

Fig. 18. Heinz Factory, Pittsburgh. Skidmore, Owings & Merrill, 1958.

1. Bertolt Brecht, *Brecht on Film and Radio,* ed. and trans. Marc Silberman (London: A&C Black, 2003), 164–65.

2. Paul Jobling, "Real Fantasies: Edward Steichen's Advertising Photography," Patricia Johnson, *Journal of Design History* 2, no. 4 (1998): 349.

3. Walter Dill Scott, *The Psychology of Advertising in Theory and Practice* (Boston: Small, Maynard, 1903).

4. Elspeth H. Brown, *The Corporate Eye* (Baltimore: Johns Hopkins University Press, 2005), 120.

5. Ibid., 146.

6. David Nye, *Corporate Identities at General Electric, 1890–1930* (Cambridge: MIT Press, 1985), 55.

7. Vicki Goldberg, *Margaret Bourke-White* (New York: Harper & Row, 1986), 84.

8. Donald B. Kuspit, *Albert Renger-Patzsch: Joy Before the Object* (Malibu: Aperture/Getty Museum, 1993).

9. "As much as we might want them to be, the photographs 'are not illustrations,' notes one observer flatly, but instead render their subject 'by means of the network of photographs'; when the images are viewed together they provide, he continued, 'an anatomy lesson,' that is an account of the relations between constituent parts." http://www.tate.org.uk/research/tateresearch/tatepapers/04spring/stimson_paper.htm

10. Letter from Ezra Stoller to Chris Mullen, October 5, 1984, Will Burtin Papers, RIT Libraries Graphic Design Archives, RIT.

11. Ibid.

12. *Made in New York,* ed. Max Hall (Cambridge: Harvard University Press, 1959).

13. Susan Sontag, *On Photography* (New York: Dell, 1973), 69.

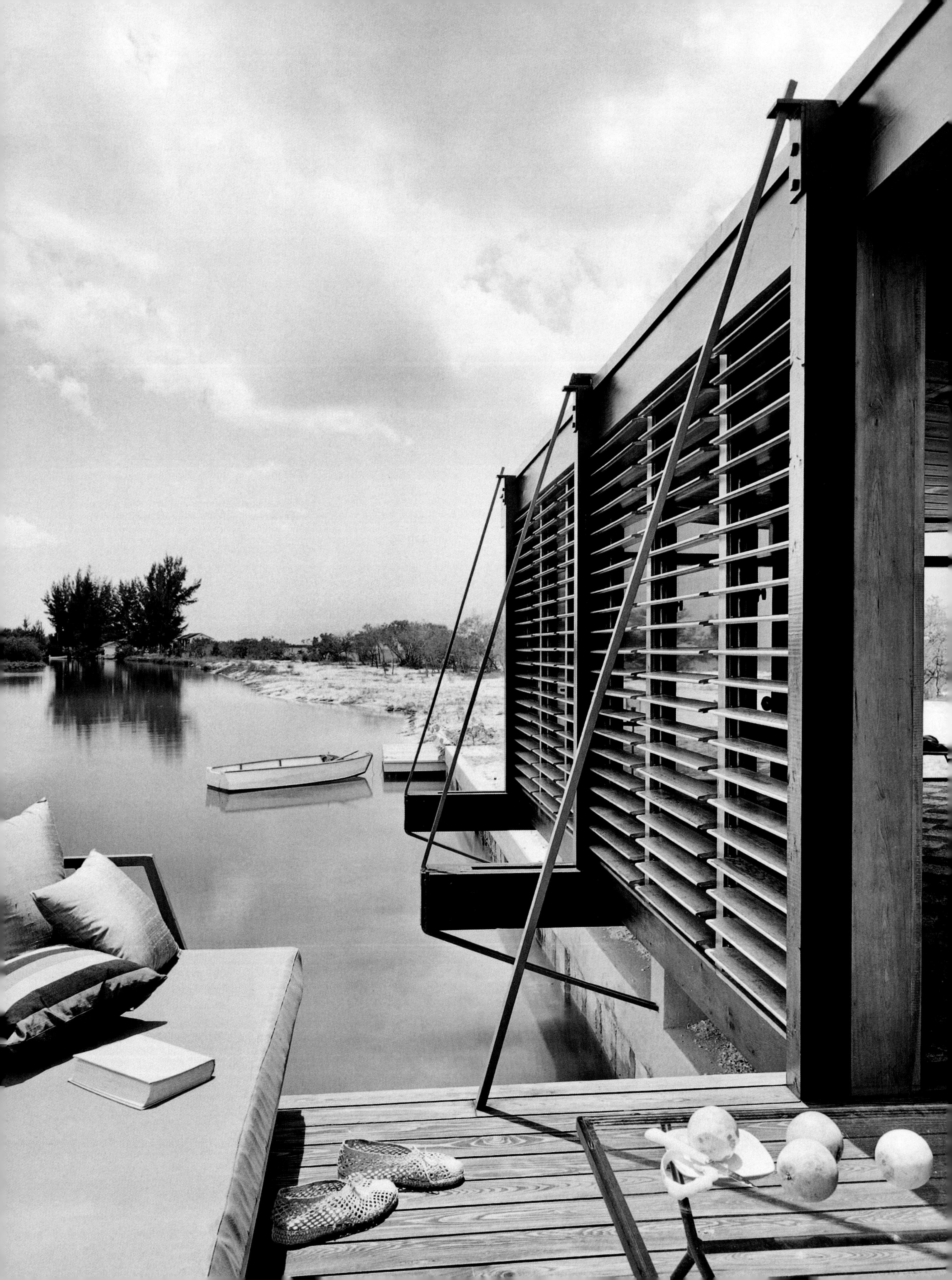

Akiko Busch

Capturing House and Home

Many of us are familiar with the landmarks of Modern architecture not by having seen the buildings themselves but through Ezra Stoller's iconic images of them—the Seagram Building, the interior of the Ford Foundation, the chapel at Ronchamp, the TWA Terminal. Less celebrated have been his vast archives of residential photography. Stoller himself was of the mind that an architect's value was proven in the design of houses, once proposing that work to be "as fundamental a test for an architect as the female nude is for a painter."[1]

That the postwar American house could invite such a manner of devoted attention made sense. It was a time of economic prosperity and a place where the optimism of the era could play itself out in full. The American home was suddenly affordable, and the ingenuity, work ethic, and dogged determination that had been directed toward the war effort could now be turned toward the structures and patterns of ordinary domestic life. A sensibility of functionalism, convenience, and efficiency surfaced. And while it may have had its roots in both the poverty of the Depression and the frugality of wartime shortages, postwar affluence gave it a more creative outlet. As Beatriz Colomina points out in a discussion of the postwar house, "It is difficult not to think of the war. Domestic life could no longer be taken for granted. It became an artform carefully constructed and marketed by a whole new industry. A form of art therapy for a traumatized nation, a reassuring image of the 'good life' to be bought like any other product."[2]

Edgar Kaufmann, Jr.'s, "Good Design" exhibitions at the Museum of Modern Art in the early 1950s further advanced that reassuring image. Including everything from floor coverings and kitchenware to furniture, wallpaper, and appliances, these were intended to show the consumer that Modern design could bring beauty and function into the American home at a reasonable price.

It was a design sensibility made all the more possible by the resources of new materials. Glass, plastics, metal alloys, plywood, synthetic resins, and glues used in the aircraft industry that generated a host of laminates all invited a different way to think about

Guest cottage, "Cocoon House," Sarasota, Florida. Paul Rudolph, 1951.

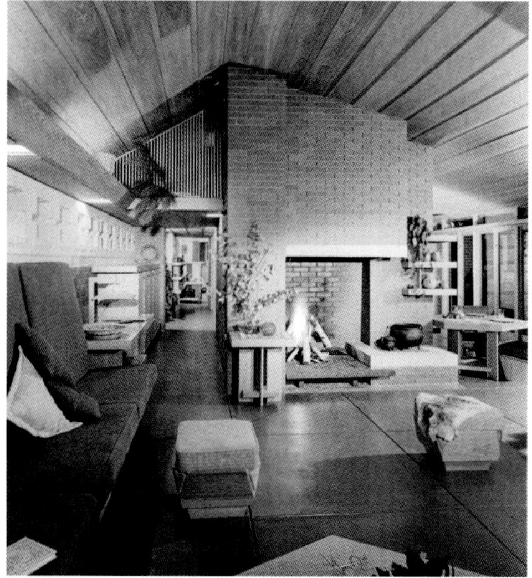

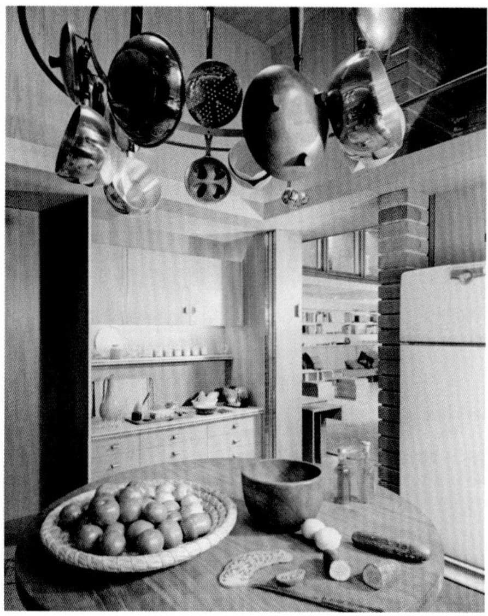

Fig. 1. Zimmerman House, Manchester, New Hampshire. Frank Lloyd Wright, 1952.

Fig. 2. Usonian House at the site of the future Guggenheim, New York. Frank Lloyd Wright, 1953.

construction. Developers, designers, architects, and manufacturers, along with the general public, recognized the opportunities therein, and with changing views toward comfort, convenience, security, and nature, the new American house invited a new way of living, stripped not only of the clutter of the past but of its tired routines and habits as well. In the words of Esther McCoy, "During the period of waiting, paper designs flourished like wild mustard in the fields after the first winter rains. Fresh approaches to plan, to form, to structure lay on paper ready to be tested. The day of the architect was in sight. His fortunes, which sag with each drop in the economy, were bright for the first time in a decade and a half."[3]

If the glass and steel skyscrapers of Modern urban architecture conveyed structural clarity, efficiency, and economy, such qualities all had an equal place in the home, whether derived from Wright's Prairie style, with its strong horizontal lines, casement windows, and overhangs, or from the poured concrete, brickwork, and stone favored by Paul Rudolph. But even the modest split-level, the raised ranch, the California ranch, and all their variations on the domestic landscape reflected a similar rationality and functionalism. These too could be well-organized, simplified, and often literally transparent; these too could offer their residents, a family with all its attendant chaos, a sense of clarity. For all the casual freedom of the open floor plan, it was also about a sense of order—not in any sort of compulsive, controlling sense but rather with the idea that it is possible for the home to convey a sense of efficiency, composure, lucidity.

Editors at consumer magazines such as *House & Garden, House Beautiful,* the *Ladies' Home Journal,* alongside those at such publications such as *Architectural Forum,* were all eager to cover and catalogue the accessories to the modern home, and the manufacturers of new materials and products complied by buying ad pages. Stoller was often the photographer of choice; the houses he documented, frame by frame, from the late forties through the seventies, give us a record of this radically new perspective on American domestic life.

Part of that new sense of order was that things be visible, that the anatomy of the building, whether framed with wood or steel, be clear, the craft of construction exposed—the joinery in woodwork, the placement of beams, the millwork, the brickwork, the stonework revealed. How things fit and how this sense of fit could be made evident spoke to the integrity of design. And just as materials might be used to reveal structure, Stoller's photographs revealed architecture. Stoller preferred black-and-white film to color, convinced that the "most effective method of communication is always the most economical one," and the economy of his photographs spoke to the economy in construction of his subject.[4] His 1952 photographs of Frank Lloyd Wright's Zimmerman house reveal the entire material narrative of the low, single-story Usonian house,

Wright's version of the modest house that could be made affordable to all middle-class Americans (figs. 1, 2). Its chief characteristics were its inexpensive materials and construction, flat roof, concrete slab floor, carport, lack of ornamentation, and built-in furniture. The texture of the Georgian cypress woodwork and ceiling, the rhythm of the board-and-batten walls, the weight of the massive central brick fireplace, the precision of the cast concrete window casings, and the transparency of the plate-glass doors all demonstrate the simple beauty that could result from such a straightforward formula.

And never before did kitchens have such pristine elegance. For all their sensuality, the rounded white cabinetry and appliances in the Quincy Shaw McKean kitchen gleam with capability (fig. 3). In Ulrich Franzen's Beattie House, the precise rectangles of the cabinetry, the stainless steel front of the dishwasher, the square of illumination from the skylight overhead all suggest a sense of supreme alignment between object, material, light (p. 264). And such appliances were as essential to the building technology of the home as plywood and plasterboard. Stoller photographed the mechanics of a house, the furnace, boiler, the sinks, refrigerator, washing machine and dryer, the entire catalogue of sparkling amenities, as though they were fine furniture, even seizing the opportunity to confer a sense of elegance on something so small as a brushed aluminum switchplate. His images convey the popular fascination with these machines. All of them, he knew—and made us know—were the systems that made domestic space, and the lives within it, hum along serenely and efficiently.

These photographs capture the reasoned coherence of mid-century residential design. Implicit is the suggestion that this material repose might carry over into the lives around it; the clarity, economy, and efficiency in these residences have to do not only with their design and construction but with the very act of living in them as well. That said, order and logic are two different things. Stoller's photographs also manage to convey idiosyncrasies of that time. This was, after all, an era when the bedrooms were chaste but the laundry rooms voluptuous; a blender, vase, and handful of eggs on the kitchen counter all but read as an erotic still life. Stoller was as attuned to the shadows of these houses as to their light, and his compositions sometimes nod to the noir sensibility in films of that period. Consider his photograph of the bedroom of Edward Durell Stone's House of Ideas (fig. 5), commissioned by *Collier's* magazine in 1940 to exhibit new furniture and materials; the light is such that the white pillow glows with an eerie luminescence, suggesting that Hitchcock might step into the room for a sinister interior shot.

And then there is the parked automobile. Stoller's thankfully brief youthful aspiration to be an auto mechanic shows up here in the sumptuous curve of a fender or the

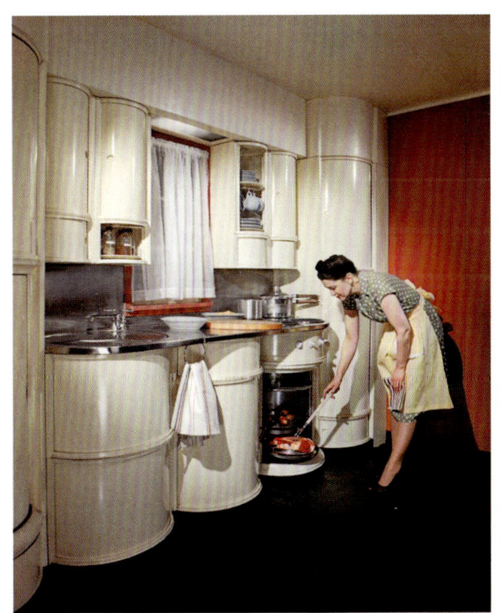

Fig. 3. Quincy Shaw McKean House, Prides Hill, Massachusetts. Quincy Shaw McKean, 1941.

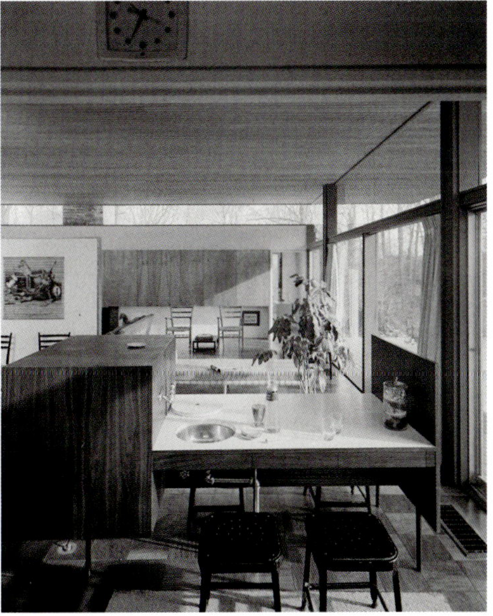

Fig. 4. Beattie House, Rye, New York. Ulrich Franzen, 1957.

angle of a fin inevitably positioned against the stern linearity of the house itself. In his photograph of Harry Weese's Brenner House, the bulbous roof and rounded trunk of an old Chrysler underscore the rigorous geometry of the carport's beams and grille work (fig. 6). The photograph was taken at night, the front door and picture window glowing rectangles. The Emerson Fehr house images suggest even greater repose (fig. 7). The Chevrolet is parked in a carport with a raised floor; on the deck over it, in silhouette, two deck chairs have momentarily perched to present themselves as spindly insects. The raised floor, the rooftop furniture, the head-on elevation shot all suggest a stage set for stillness. The buildings may all have been about shaping space, but the car was what traveled through space, and, as such, was often a cherished accomplice in the photograph; temporarily stilled in its garage, carport, or driveway, it nonetheless continued to resonate with motion, distance, speed, space.

The question of visual accomplices is raised from time to time elsewhere—the kitchen table set for breakfast, the bowl of fruit placed precisely on the counter, the robe thrown across the foot of the bed. One suspects such posing, mandated by magazine work, may not have been entirely to Stoller's taste. But as most people who have ever lived in a house would likely admit, domestic life often requires just such posturing; it just as often presents our image of ourselves. And in the bright confidence of postwar America, especially, these houses reflected a new pattern for domestic life.

Likewise, these rooms are noticeably without that imprint of disarray that family life leaves on whatever space it touches. And for being photographs of residences, there are remarkably few children's rooms here. "Where are the kids?" one is tempted to ask. One might also be tempted to say that these are the views of men of a certain generation; while the images were often viewed by women in women's magazines, the houses were largely designed by men, and certainly they were photographed by a man. But they are also images of their time, when ideas about domestic life followed a different imperative. For whatever it has come to mean today, aspirational design in the mid-twentieth century considered a new protocol for domesticity that included efficient appliances that reduced housework, affordable furniture, a connection to the outdoors, a sense of openness, and those vast plate-glass doors and windows that led out onto the patio and straight into the future itself. If these rooms are posing, then there remains something authentic in the pose.

While these rooms are largely unoccupied, they are clearly inhabited. Often, it is on account of a chair, whether it is a Saarinen womb chair, a slat-back chair, or an outdoor webbed chaise. Even those hanging at random angles from the ceiling in George Nakashima's studio speak to a human presence (fig. 8). More than any other piece of

Fig. 5. Collier House of Ideas, New York. Edward Durell Stone, 1941.

Fig 6. Brenner House, Champaign, Illinois. Harry Weese, 1952.

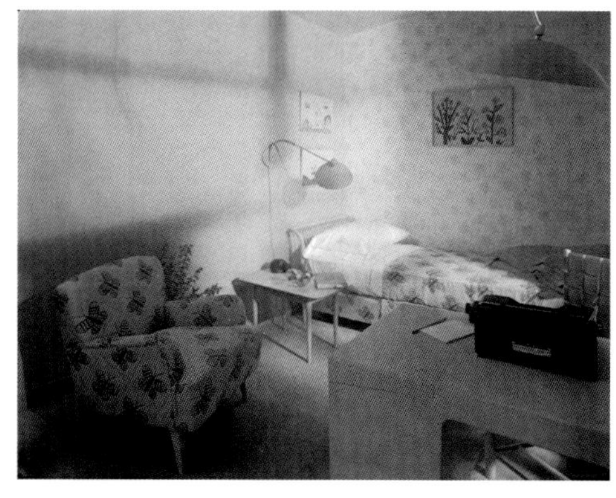

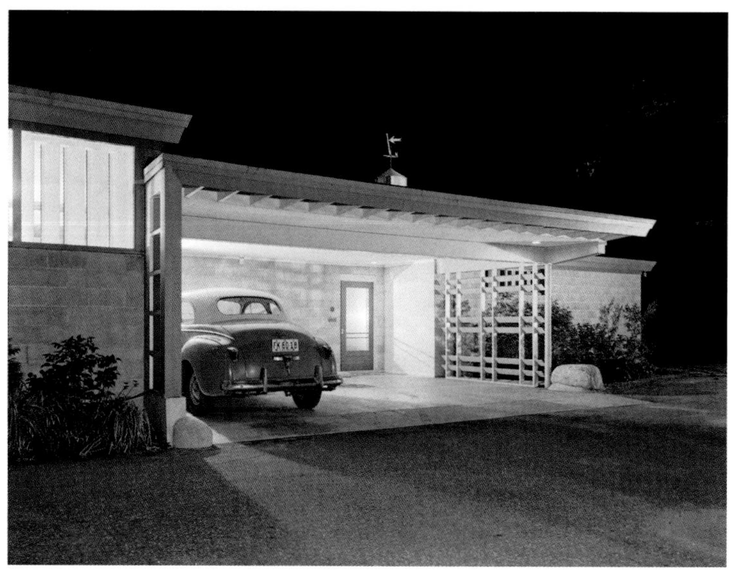

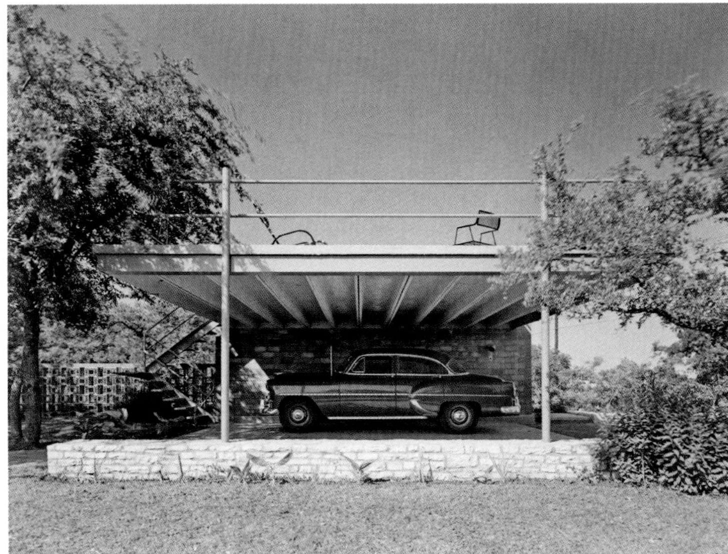

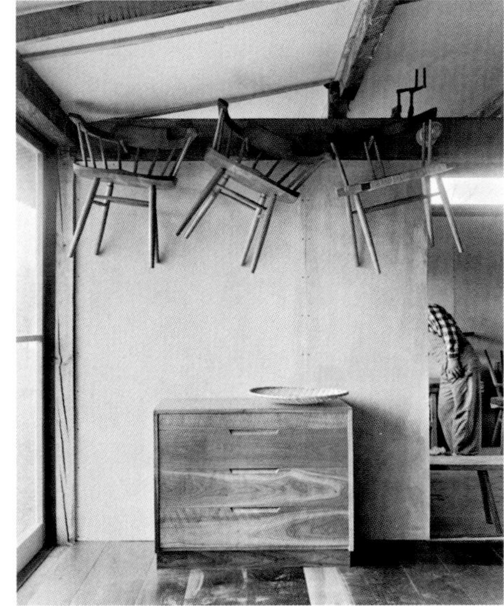

Fig. 7. Fehr House, Austin, Texas. Emerson Fehr, 1953.

Fig. 8. Nakashima Showroom, New Hope, Pennsylvania. George Nakashima, 1952.

furniture, an empty chair invariably conveys a human presence. A chair has arms, legs, a back; its very form suggests a human body in repose. Stoller knew that the absence implied by the empty chair speaks just as clearly to presence.

If Stoller got this, if he got the respect for efficiency, the clarity, the convenience, along with the moments of humor, it may have been because his engagement with mid-century domestic architecture was not confined to his photographs. Stoller was himself trained as an architect, and *McCall's* magazine in March 1950 featured his own house, explaining that "as he went around the country snapping a kitchen here, a dining counter there, an ingenious storage wall or play cupboard, he made notes of good ideas he was going to use some day in his own house." The ad from General Electric accompanying the spread advocates "A New Freedom in Living . . . A New Pleasure That Means Better Living." Translated here, that better living included a kitchen that flowed into a laundry room that doubled as his children's playroom, built-in cabinetry, and ribbon windows with a view to the dense greenery outdoors. Stoller's daughter, Erica, talks of cabinetry that was ideal for small children to hide in but recalls that it was the siting that distinguished the house most: "He understood light in a very real, not hypothetical, way, how an overhang could shield the sun from coming in, or where it could warm the house when you wanted it to. And maybe best of all, you could take a bath in the sun; what better place really for a picture window than the bathroom."[5]

This grasp of site, this connection to the outdoors, this sense of flow between interior and exterior space and how one continually frames the other, surfaces repeatedly in these views of home. Whether it is a body of water, the boughs of a tree, or the wisp of a cloud, components of landscape continually inform and engage with the language of the building. The decks, patios, and yards, the outdoor living heralded by Modernism, are all recorded here. It was Le Corbusier who advocated reinstalling "in our machine society, the conditions of nature which have been disrupted. That is, sun, space, and greenery, which are the cosmic factors of life and without which we would die."[6]

Strong talk, but certainly it captured the growing mistrust in urbanism and the idealism with which so many mid-century architects viewed the suburban model as a place that could reconnect residents to the natural world. Houses, whether they were in southern California or eastern Connecticut, should reflect some essential connection to their climate, site, vegetation—a sense of exchange between indoor and outdoor space. In these photographs, then, water, clouds, stone, the bend of a tree may all serve as pictorial elements, but far more importantly they suggest the natural forces that the built world contends with; it is the configuration of the natural world and the structure of the built world that together make the whole.

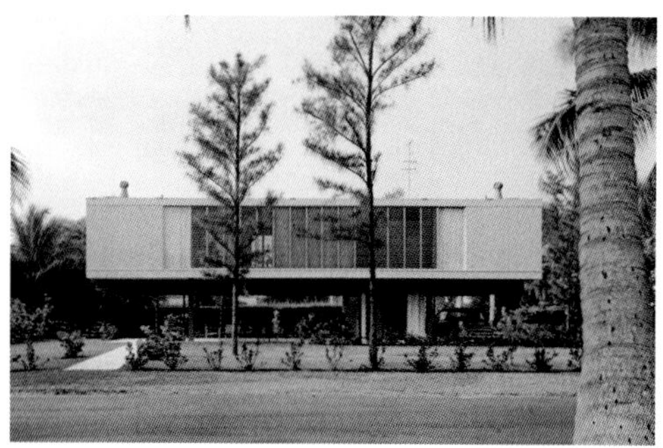

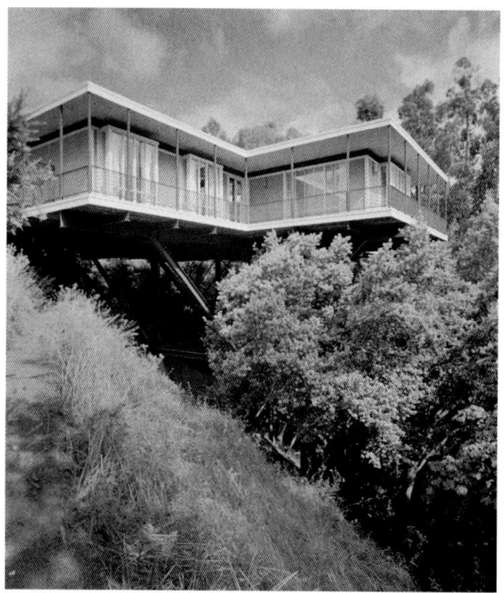

Fig. 9. Biggs House, Delray Beach, Florida. Paul Rudolph, 1956.

Fig. 10. Wilmarth House 2, Colusa, California. Lawrence Lackey, 1963.

Stoller documents this mutual engagement in all its variations. In the photograph of Paul Rudolph's Biggs house, the palms riff on the vertical supports and linearity of the house itself (fig. 9). In the photograph of Rudolph's Coward House, the Spanish moss dripping from serpentine branches overhead speaks to the angularity of the carport. And unless one looks closely into the shadows in the photograph of Lawrence Lackey's Wilmarth House, it is easy to believe that the leaves of the shrubbery and tall wild grass are the soft scaffolding that support the house on its embankment (fig. 10). Richard Meier's Douglas House seems to spring from its hillside of dark conifers like some exotic ice palace (fig. 11).

But these are exterior views, and time and again, interior views take us outdoors as well. In the bedroom of Rudolph's Haskins House a window opens to the view of a chaise, neatly aligned to face the opposite direction from the beds indoors, and there is an almost dreamlike quality to the way the chaise and the thin grove of trees just beyond suggest some remote but parallel retreat (fig. 12). In the interior of the Nakashima Studio/showroom we find one iteration after the other of Shoji screens, broken here and there with a clear view to the woods or sky. Hanging in the foreground is a Japanese paper *koi*. The composition is a dazzling play of translucence and transparence and the subtle visual rhythms that can be suggested by geometric construction and organic form.

Elsewhere and everywhere in Stoller's photographs of houses, we are drawn up the stairs, down the hall, past the window to the sycamore tree, through the living room to the patio and a view to the sea, or past the formal dining table to the canopy of leaves just beyond. Understanding architecture as a spatial experience, Stoller observed that an "architectural photograph can never do more than suggest a part of that space in a segment of time."[7] But it is his arrangement of those segments that made the suggestions so strong, transforming them so often to eloquent visual statements.

This is what these photographs do; they offer us this multiplicity of views. And sightlines. Time and again one finds frames within frames within frames; or a view to a view to a view. The eye travels down a hall, beneath a set of stairs, past a cabinet, through the window to a mountain beyond. A tree trunk, a column, a beam, a wall, the edge of a window, the leg of a chair, one small, disparate tableau after another. One thing frames another and that another, and it seems almost dazzling that a single room, hallway, interior can accommodate so many views. But such was the range and such were the possibilities of the mid-century American home, and Ezra Stoller saw them all.

Which is to say, it is not just the camera angle that draws the eye into these visual narratives. One thing leads naturally to another here, as can happen only in an era of confidence and hope. The images often seem elegiac; now, at a time when American

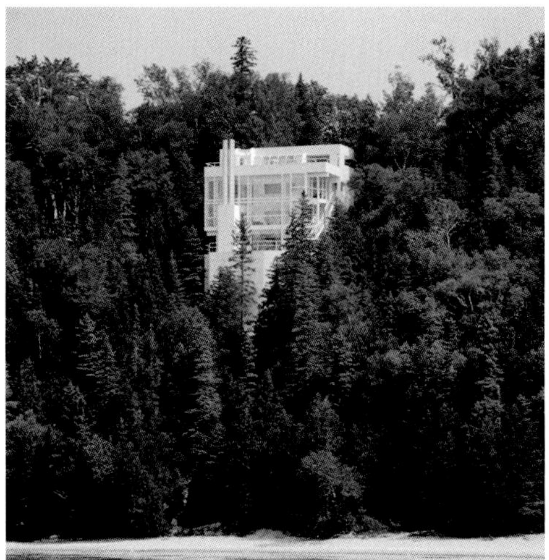

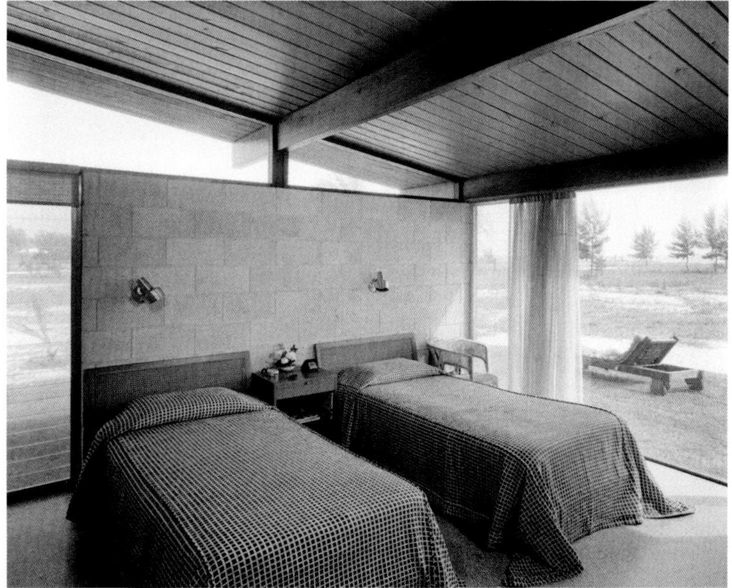

Fig. 11. Douglas House, Harbor Springs, Michigan. Richard Meier, 1974.

Fig. 12. Haskins House, Sarasota, Florida. Paul Rudolph, 1952.

residential architecture has been so compromised, they are especially poignant. Whether it is the fact that home ownership is out of reach for so many, or the sight of so many anonymous subdivisions indifferent to their landscape, or the financial blight of entire neighborhoods shuttered by McMansions in foreclosure, the lessons of the efficient, affordable, flexible postwar Modern house seem to have been forgotten. To be sure, not all of these were inexpensive; some of them were custom-designed or prototypes built at tremendous expense. Still, as their visual record, these photographs convey an idea of home that reflected economy, efficiency, ease. And for all the day-to-dayness of it, for all the ordinariness of the kitchens, bedrooms, appliances, patios, and cars, for all the conventional machinery of everyday life in the middle of the last century, these photographs affirm that there was, in fact, nothing ordinary about any of it. Stoller crafted these images without drama or intrusion. With clarity, respect, and insight, he has given us a portrait not simply of a period in American architecture, but of a way to live that was both human and humane.

1. William S. Saunders, *Modern Architecture: Photographs by Ezra Stoller* (New York: Abrams, 1990), 12.

2. Beatriz Colomina, "Reflections on the Eames House," in Diana Murphy, ed., *The Work of Charles and Ray Eames: A Legacy of Invention* (New York: Abrams, 1997), 132.

3. Esther McCoy, *Case Study Houses, 1945–1962,* 2nd ed. (Santa Monica: Hennessey and Ingalls, 1962), 8.

4. Conversation with Ezra Stoller, October 1984.

5. Conversation with Erica Stoller, March 2, 2010.

6. John Peter, *The Oral History of Modern Architecture: Interviews with the Greatest Architects of the Twentieth Century* (New York: Abrams, 1994), 142.

7. Ezra Stoller, from lecture notes written in Rye, New York, August 1984.

Portfolio
Architectural Photography

In Portfolio captions, year refers to date of photograph

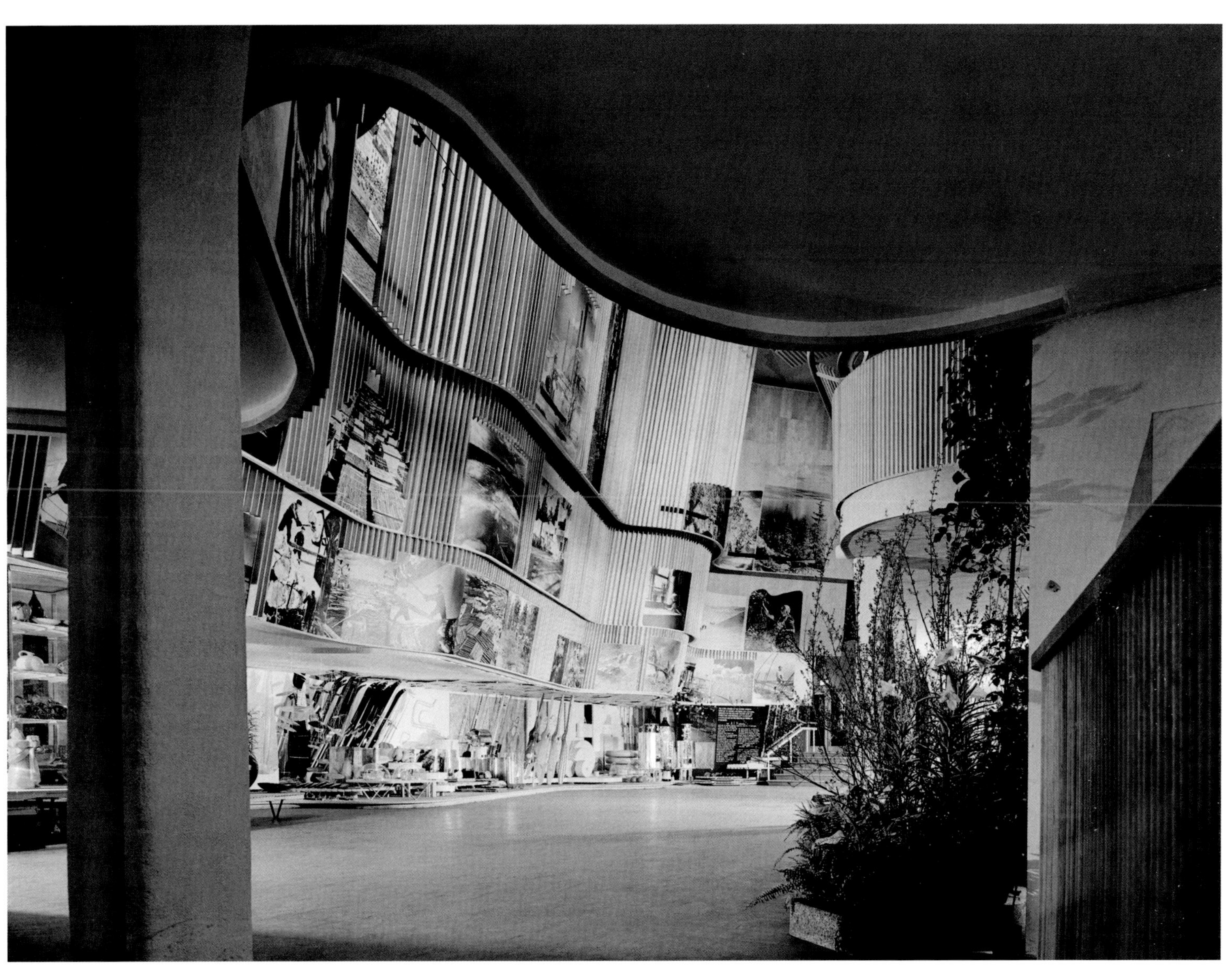

1939 World's Fair, Finnish Pavilion, Queens, New York.
Alvar Aalto, 1939.

Overleaf
Chamberlain Cottage, Wayland, Massachusetts.
Walter Gropius and Marcel Breuer, 1942.

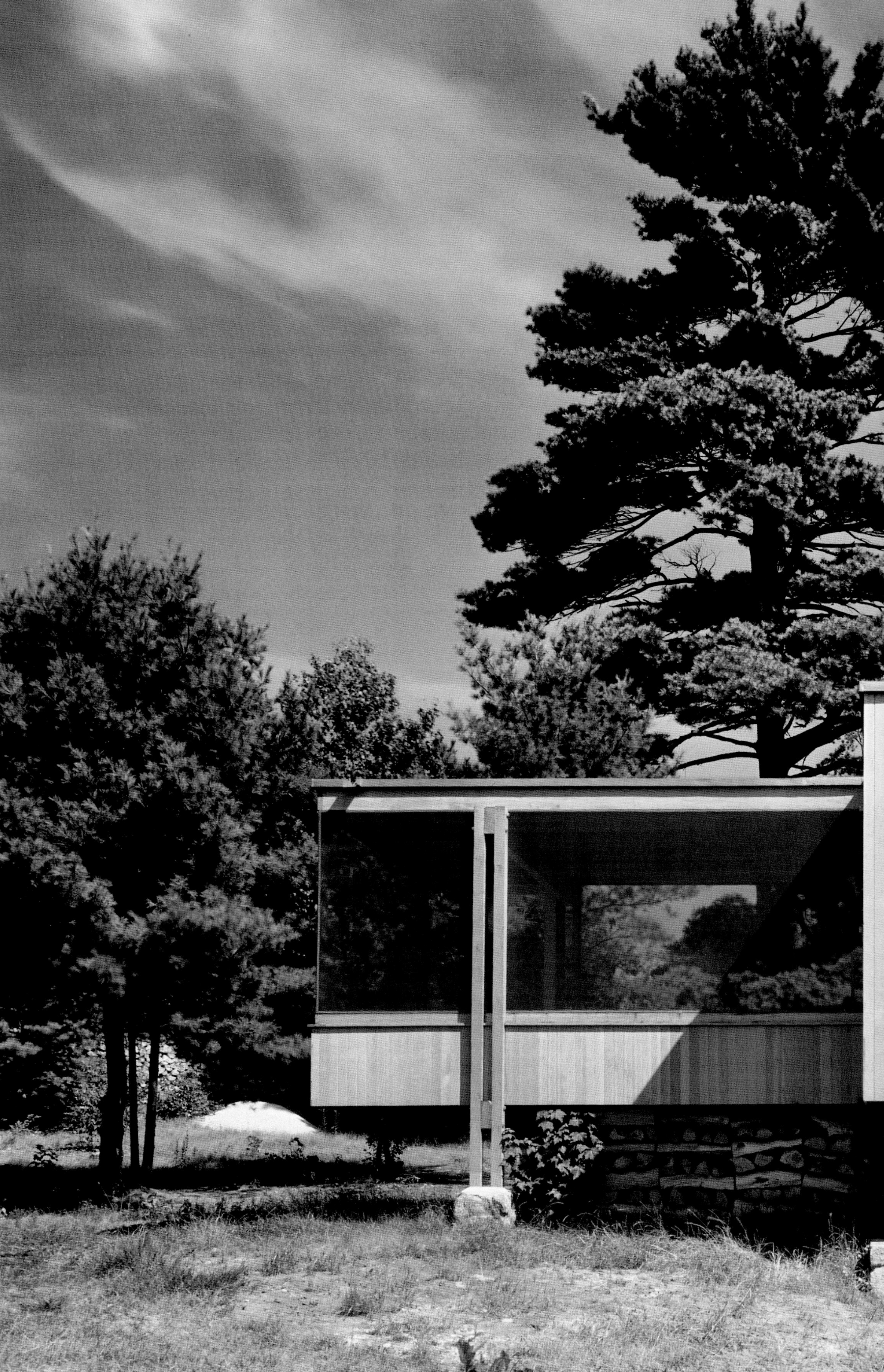

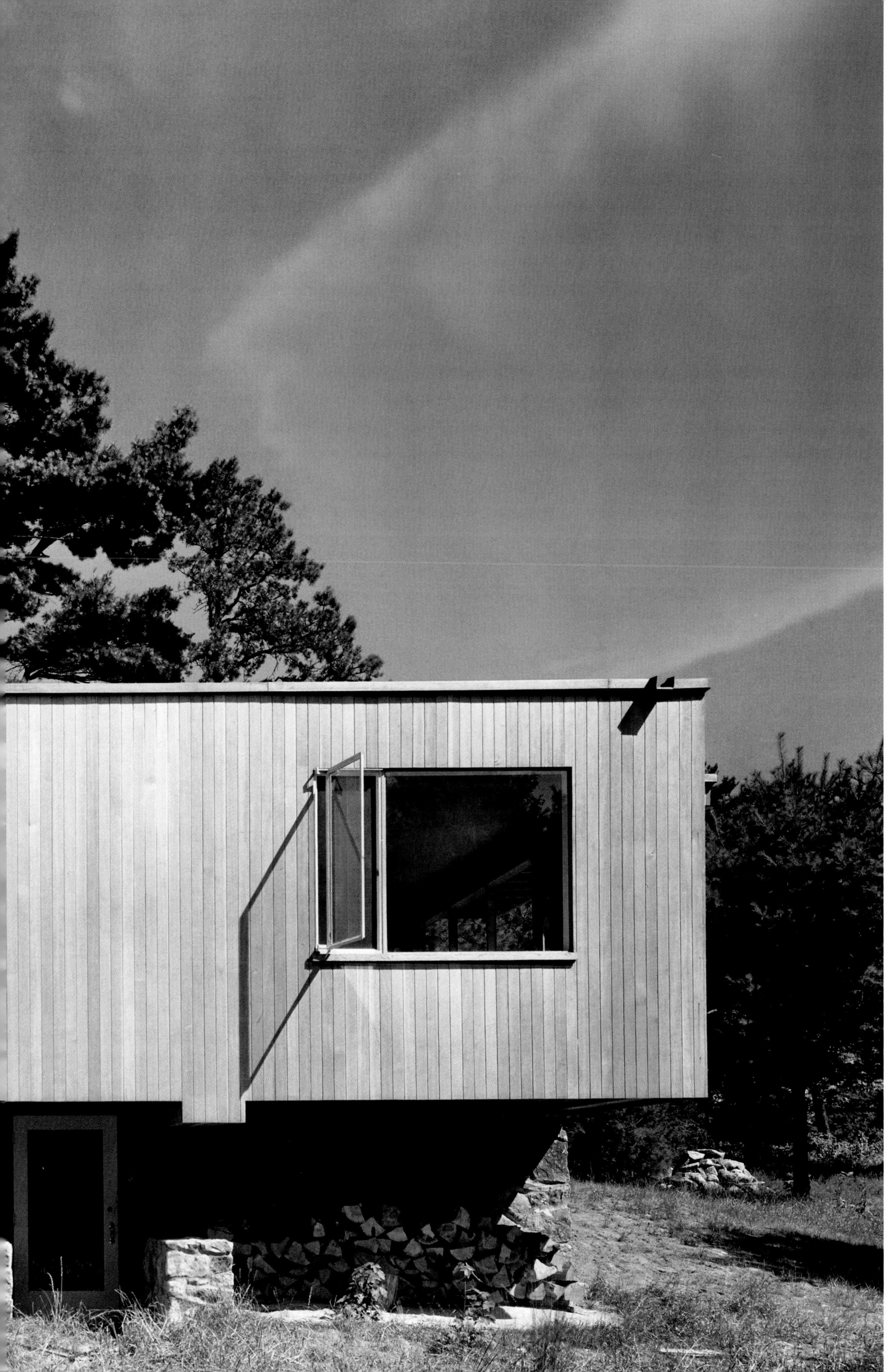

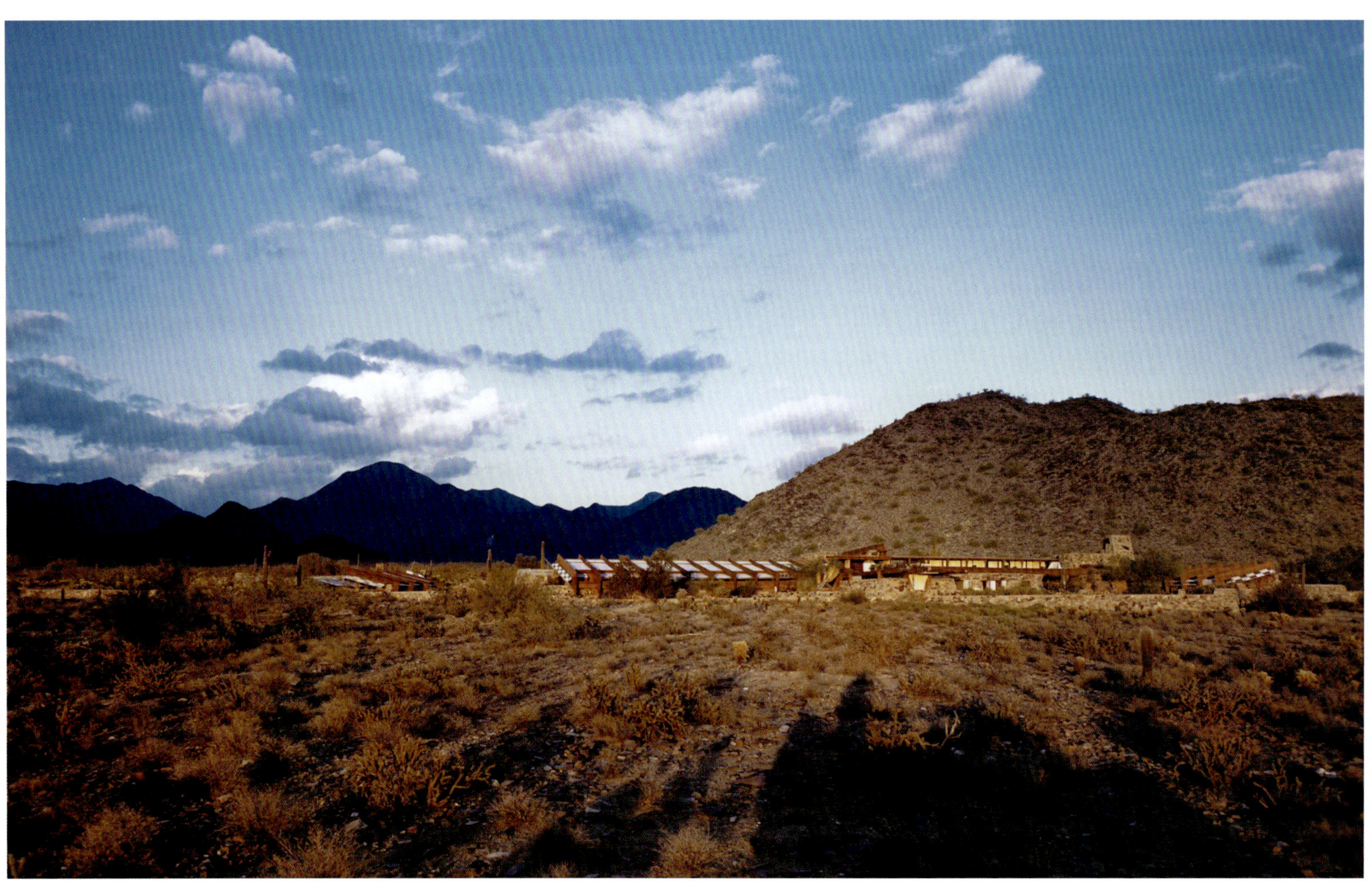

Taliesin West, Scottsdale, Arizona.
Frank Lloyd Wright, 1951.

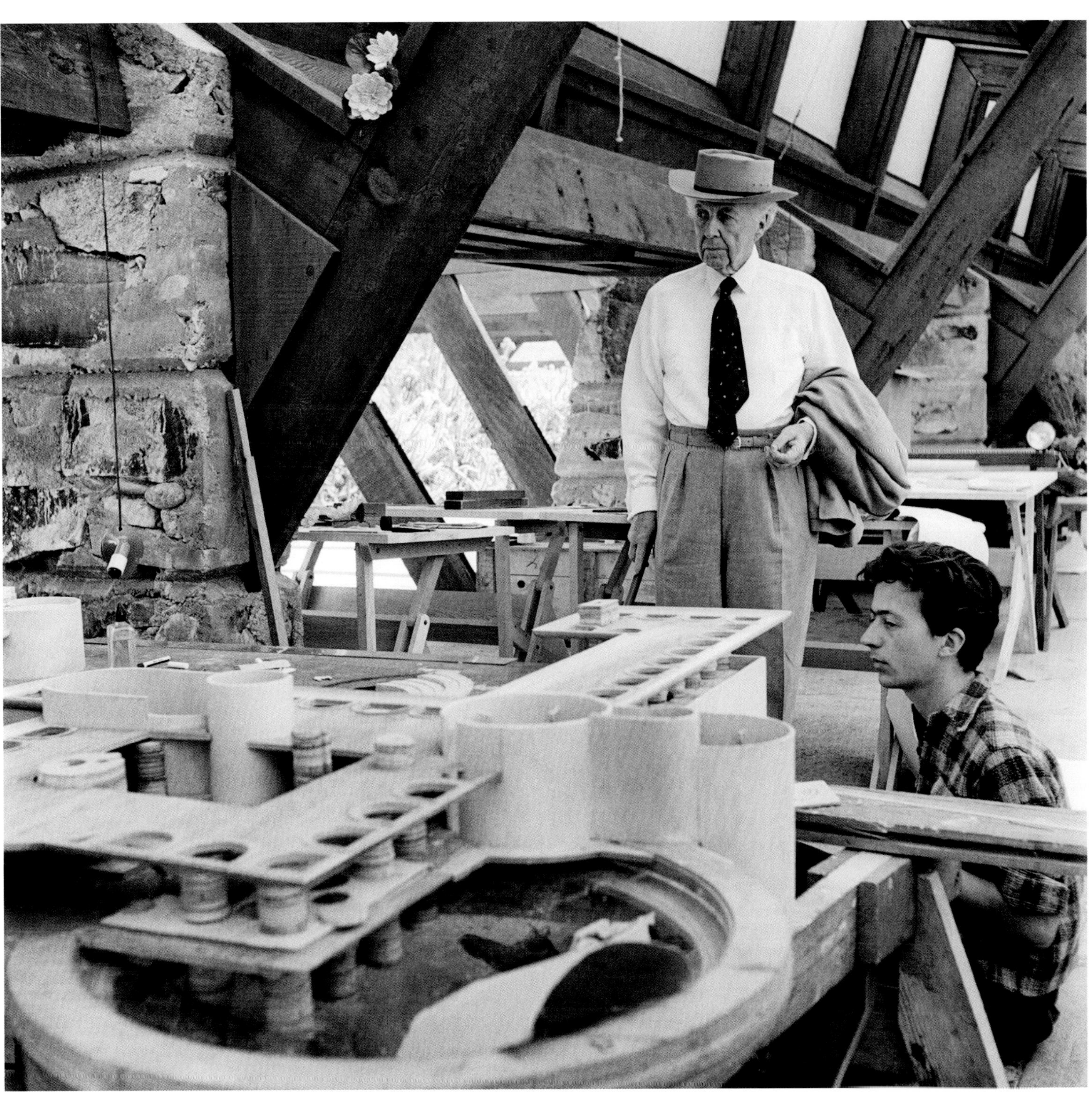

Frank Lloyd Wright, Taliesin West,
Scottsdale, Arizona, 1945.

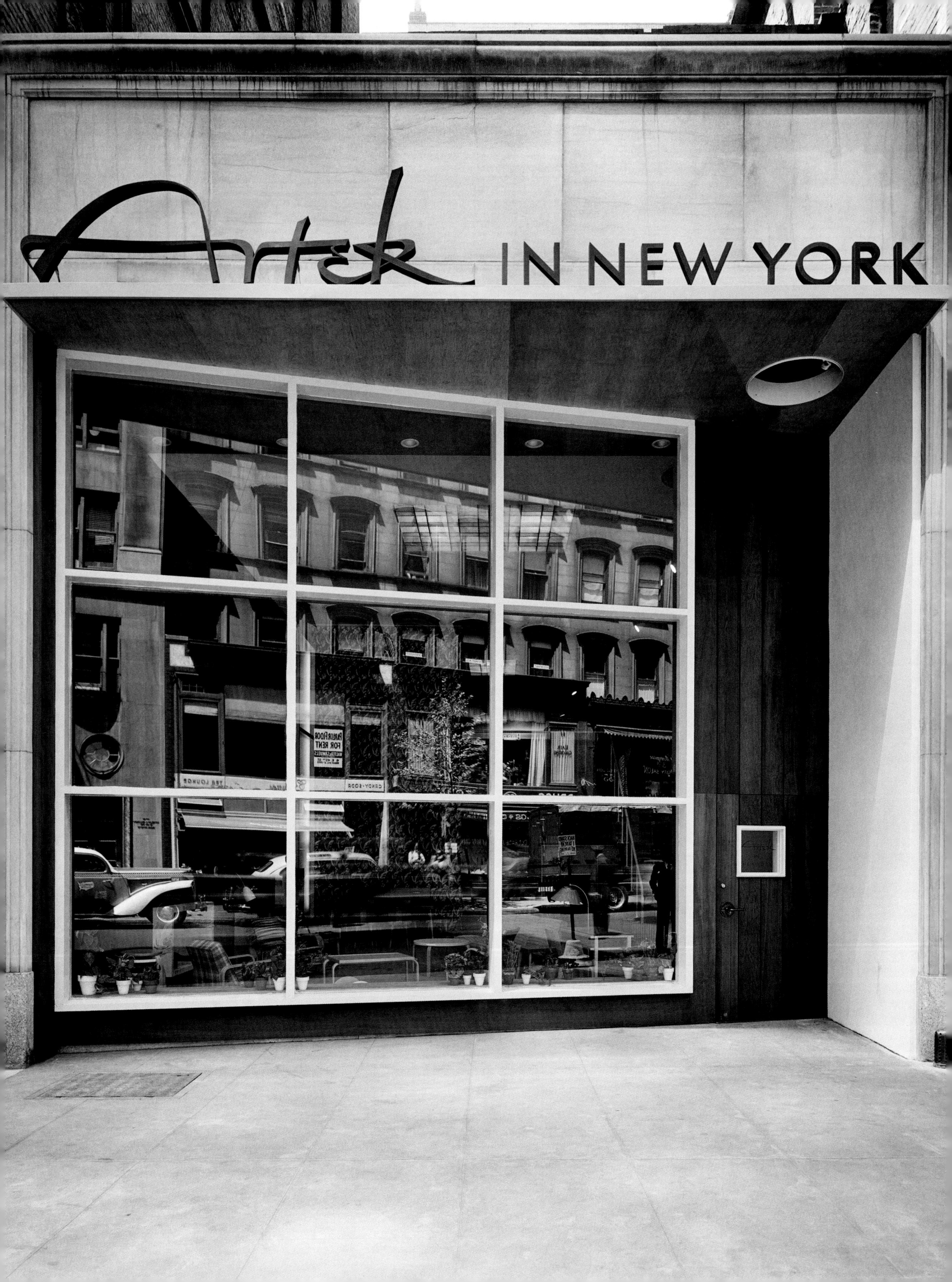

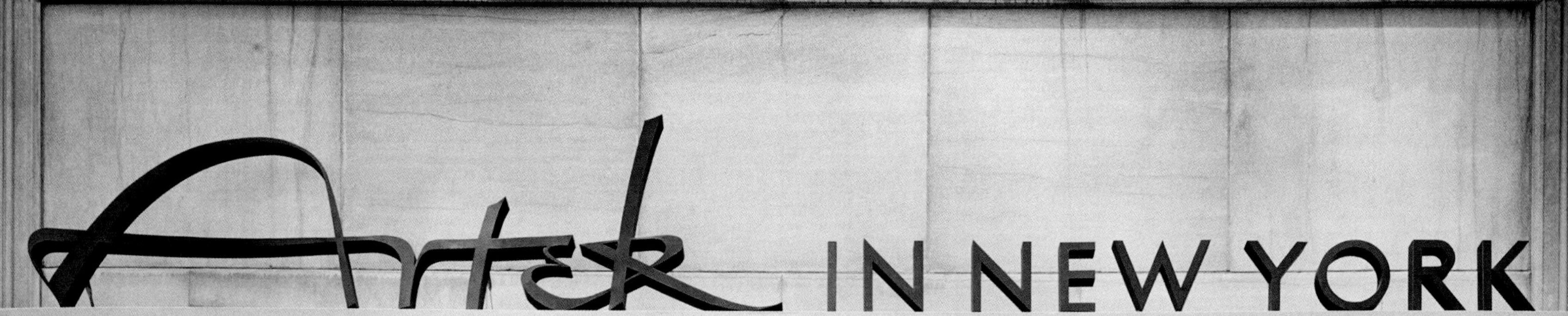
Artek IN NEW YORK

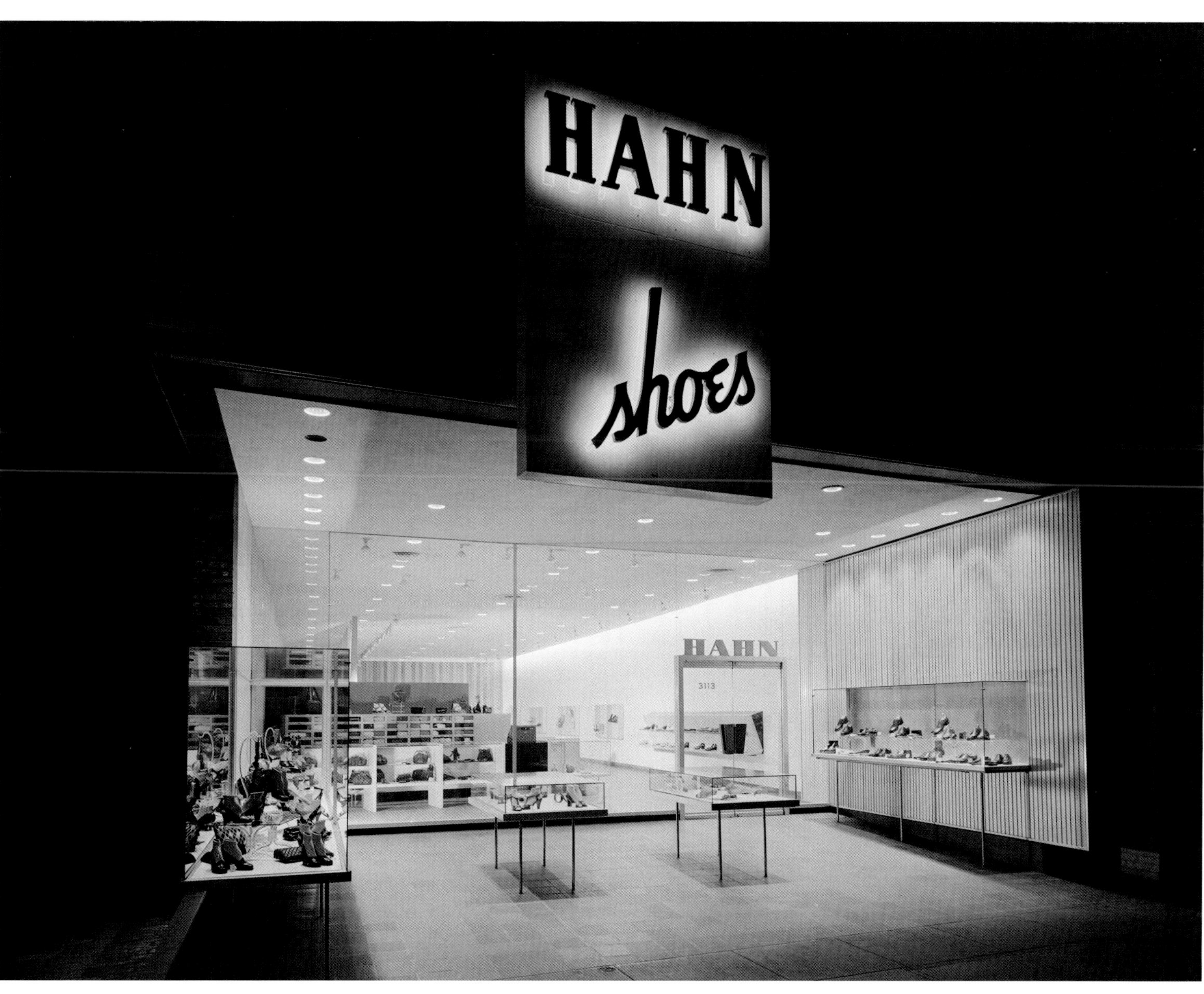

Artek in New York Shop.
Morris Ketchum, 1943.

Hahn Shoe Store, Washington, D.C.
Ketchum, Gina & Sharp, 1947.

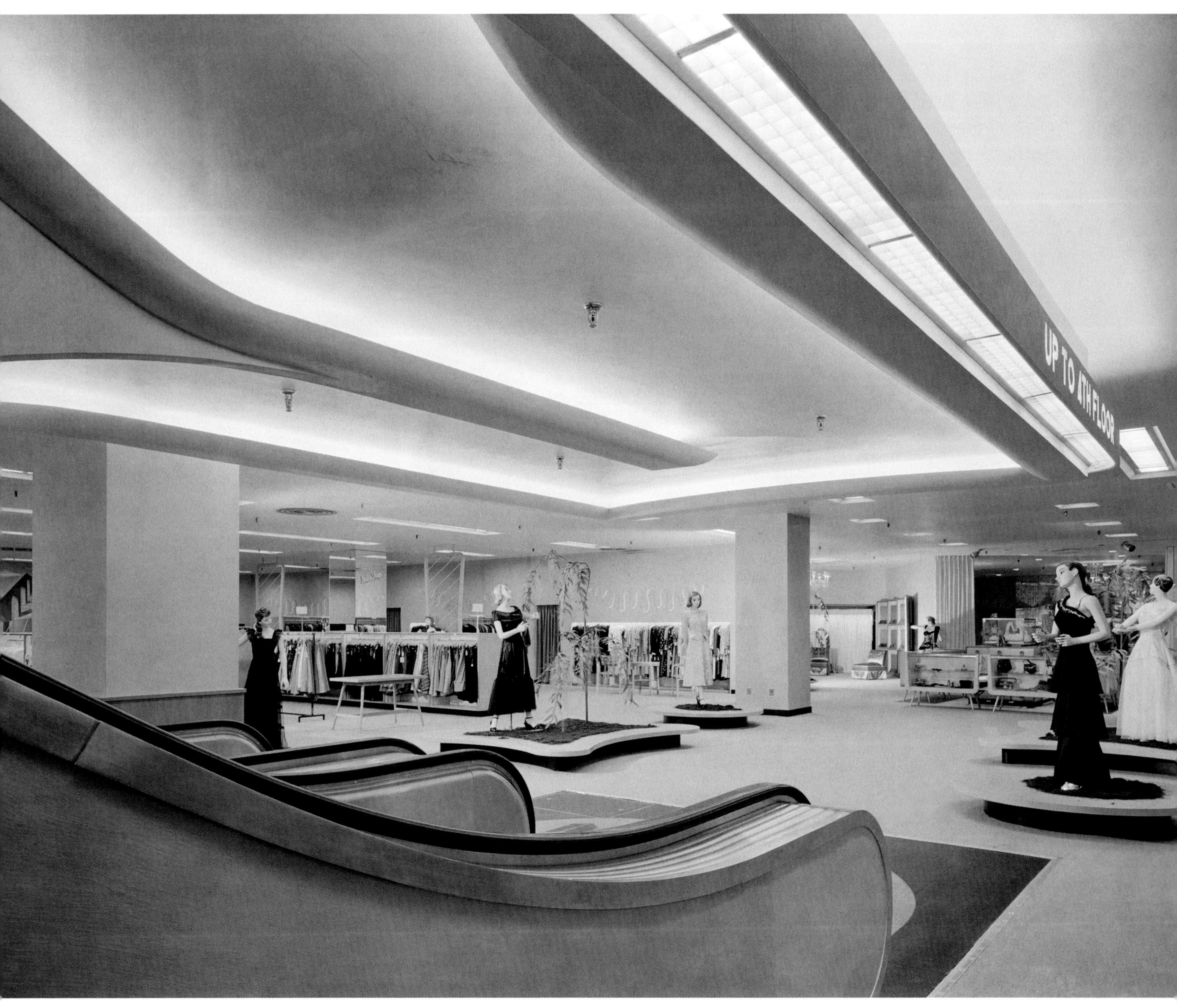

Foley Brothers Department Store, Houston, 1948.

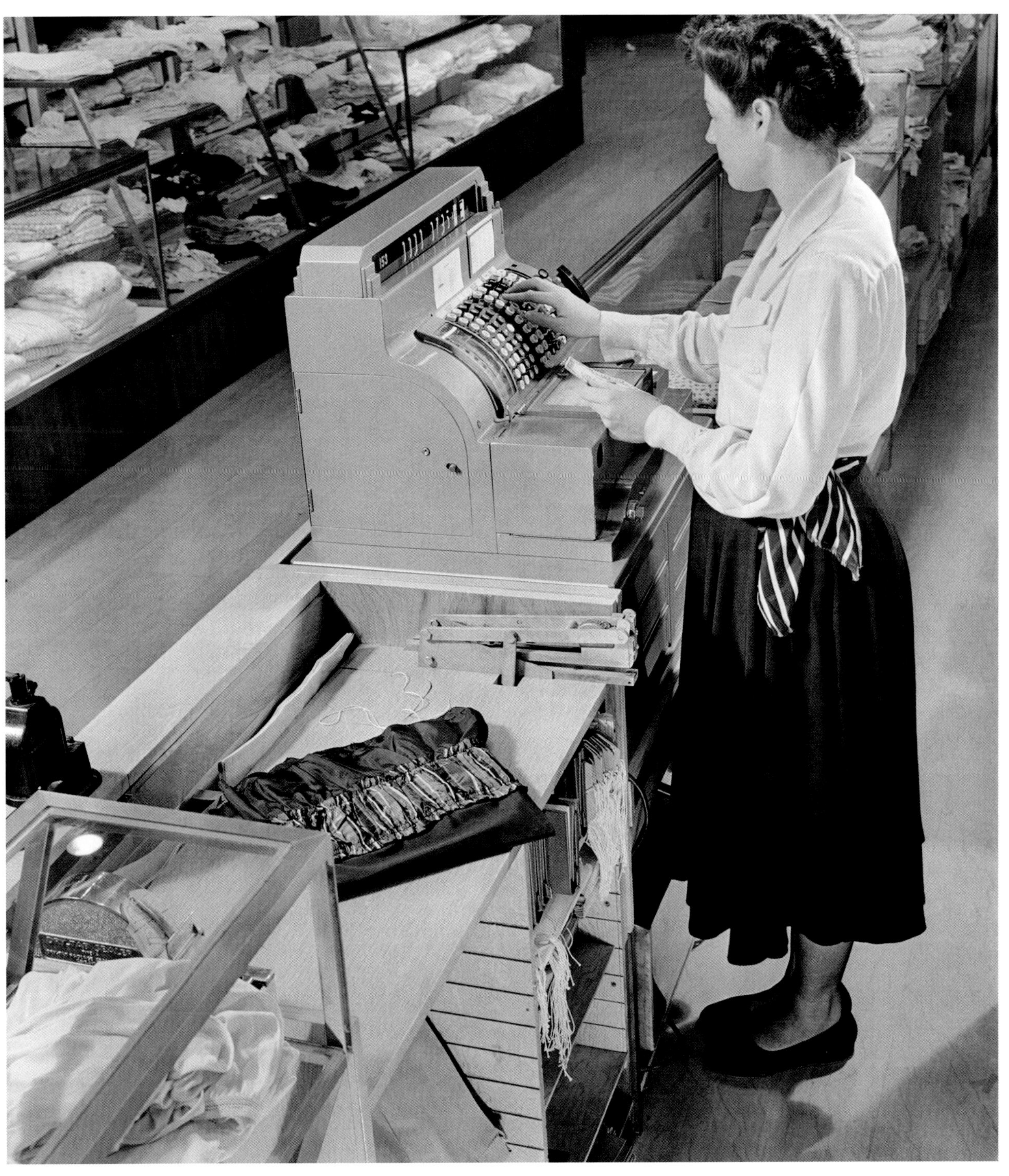

Foley Brothers Department Store,
Houston, 1948.

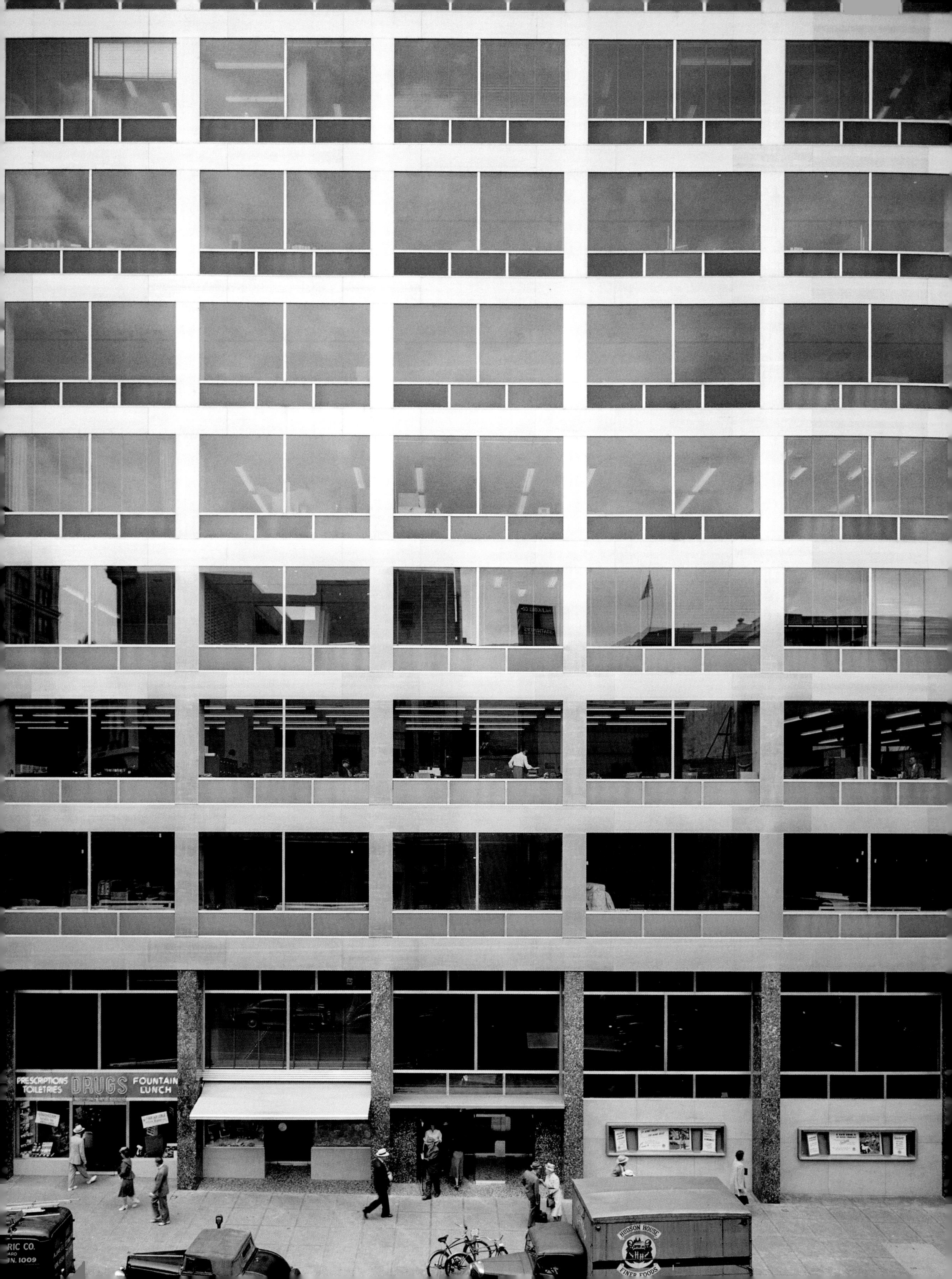
PRESCRIPTIONS
TOILETRIES
DRUGS
FOUNTAIN
LUNCH
HUDSON HOUSE
FINER FOODS

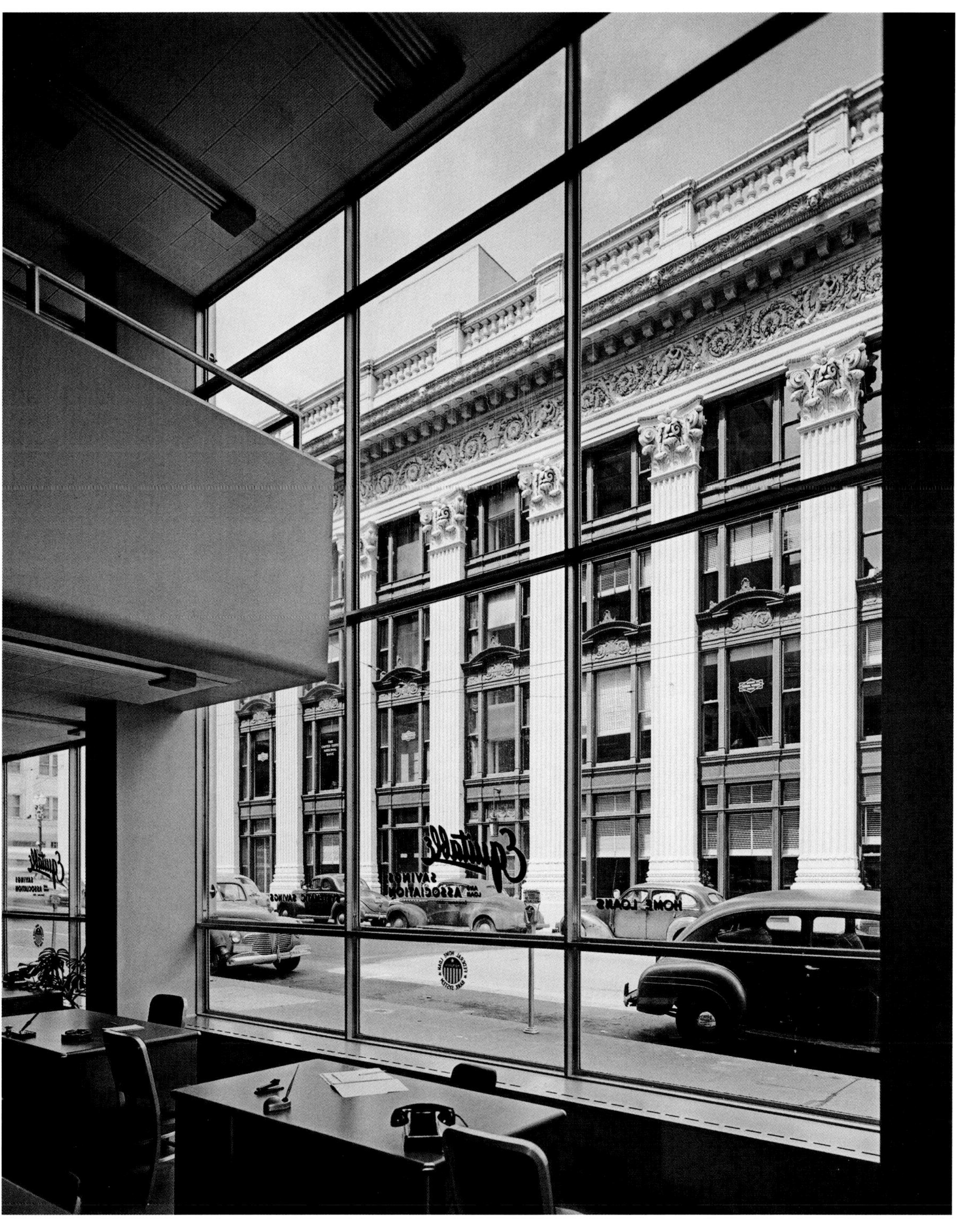

Equitable Building, Portland, Oregon.
Pietro Belluschi, 1948.

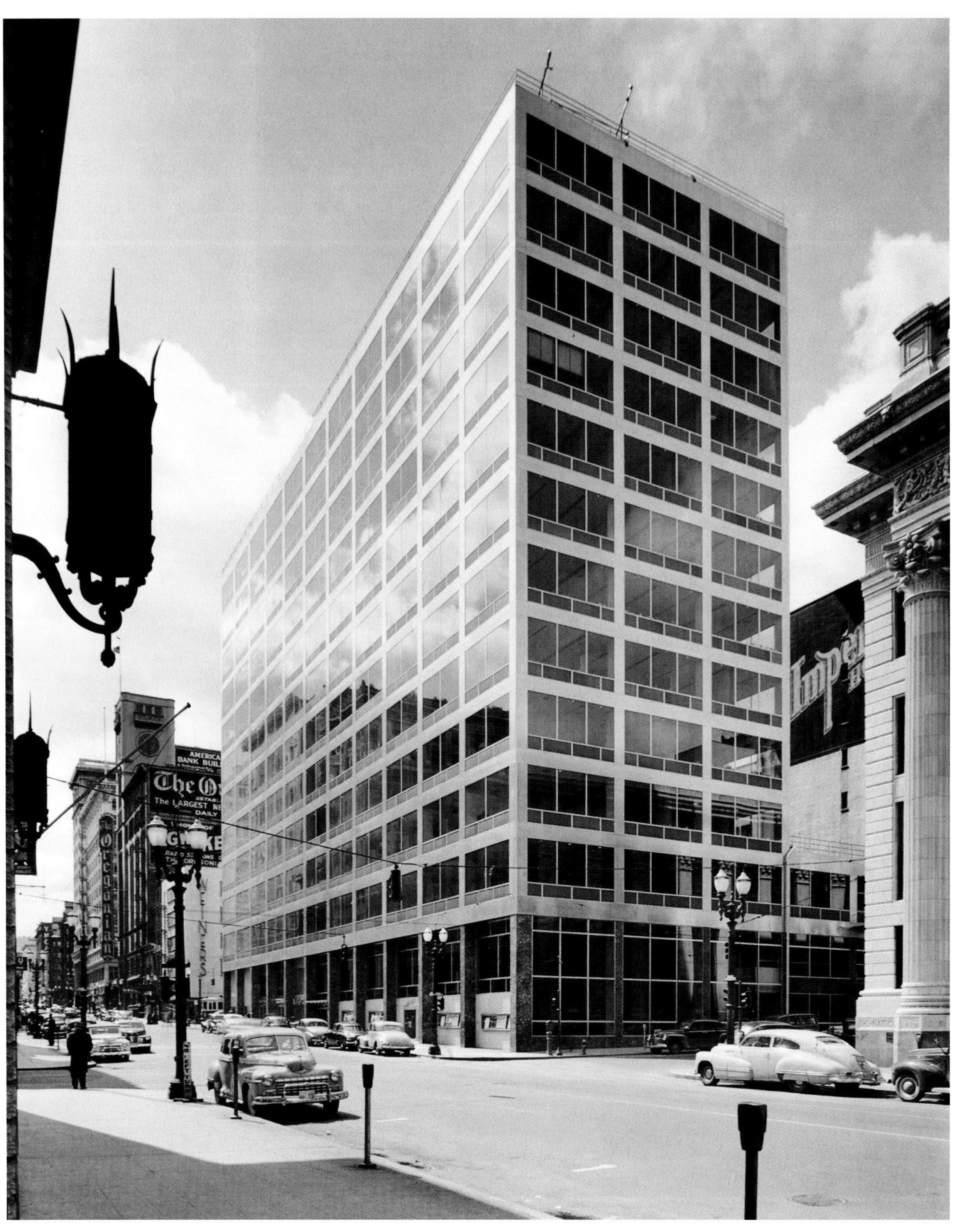

Equitable Building, Portland, Oregon.
Pietro Belluschi, 1948.

Parking garage, Miami.
Robert Law Weed & Associates, 1949.

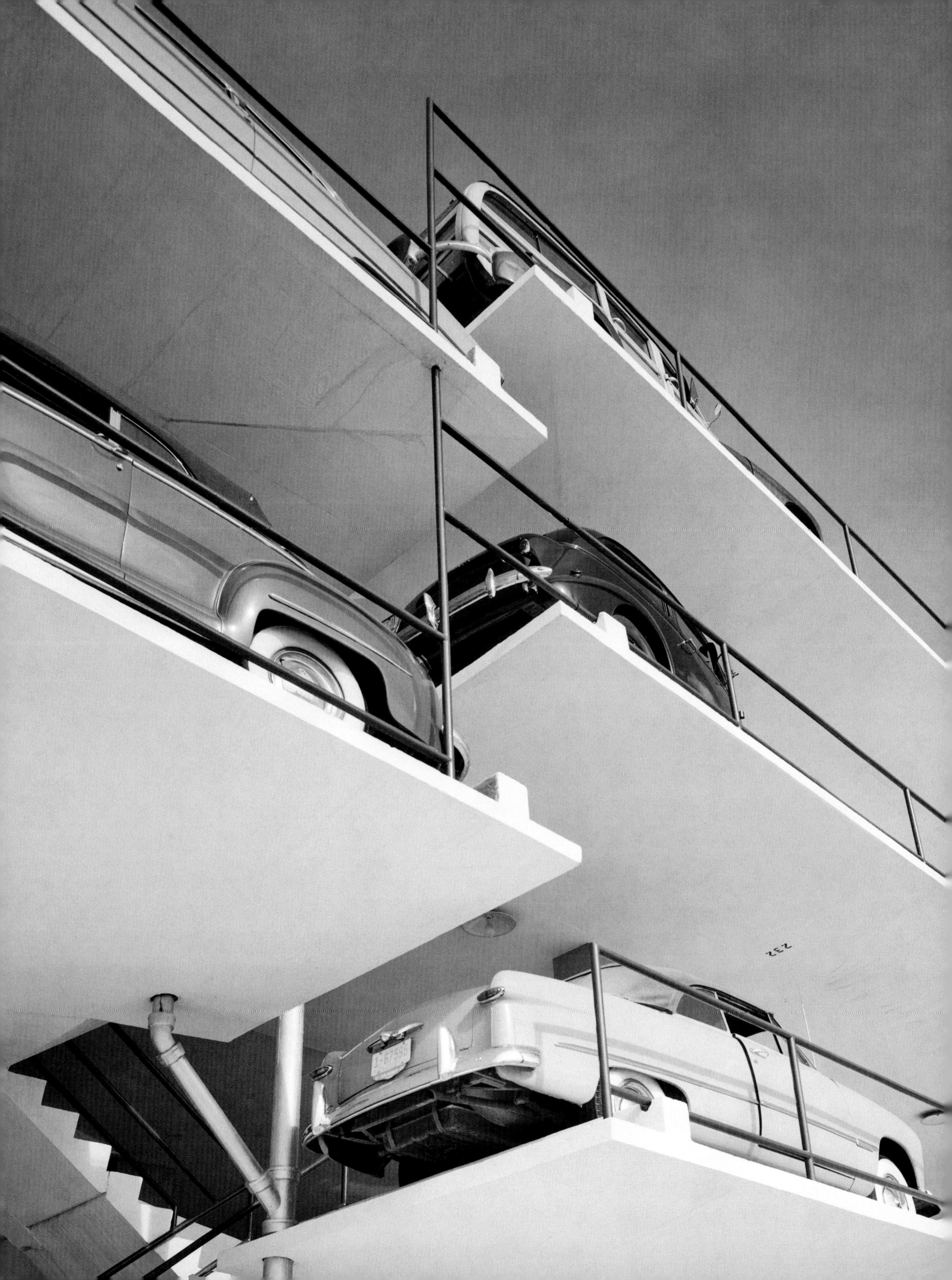

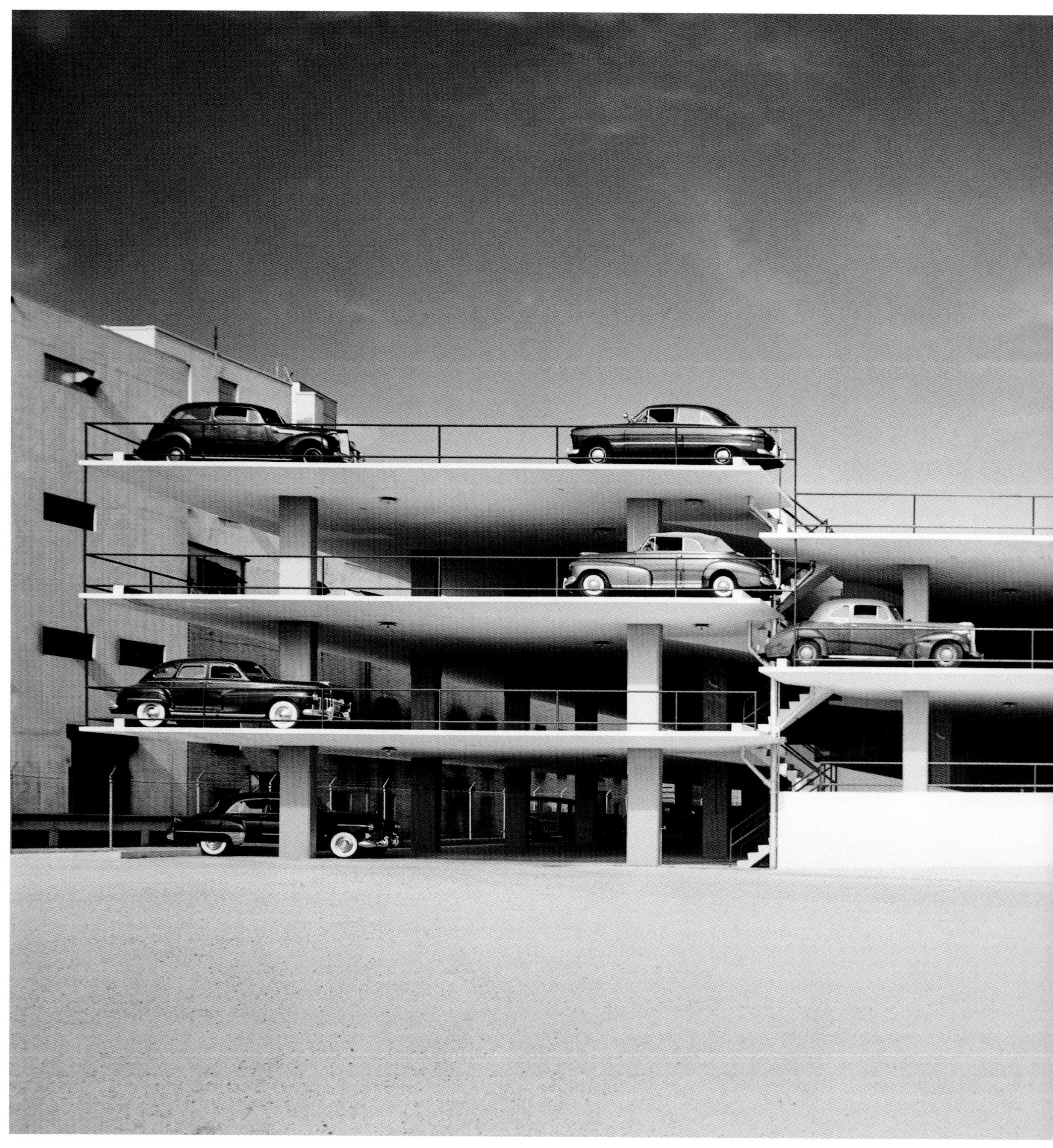

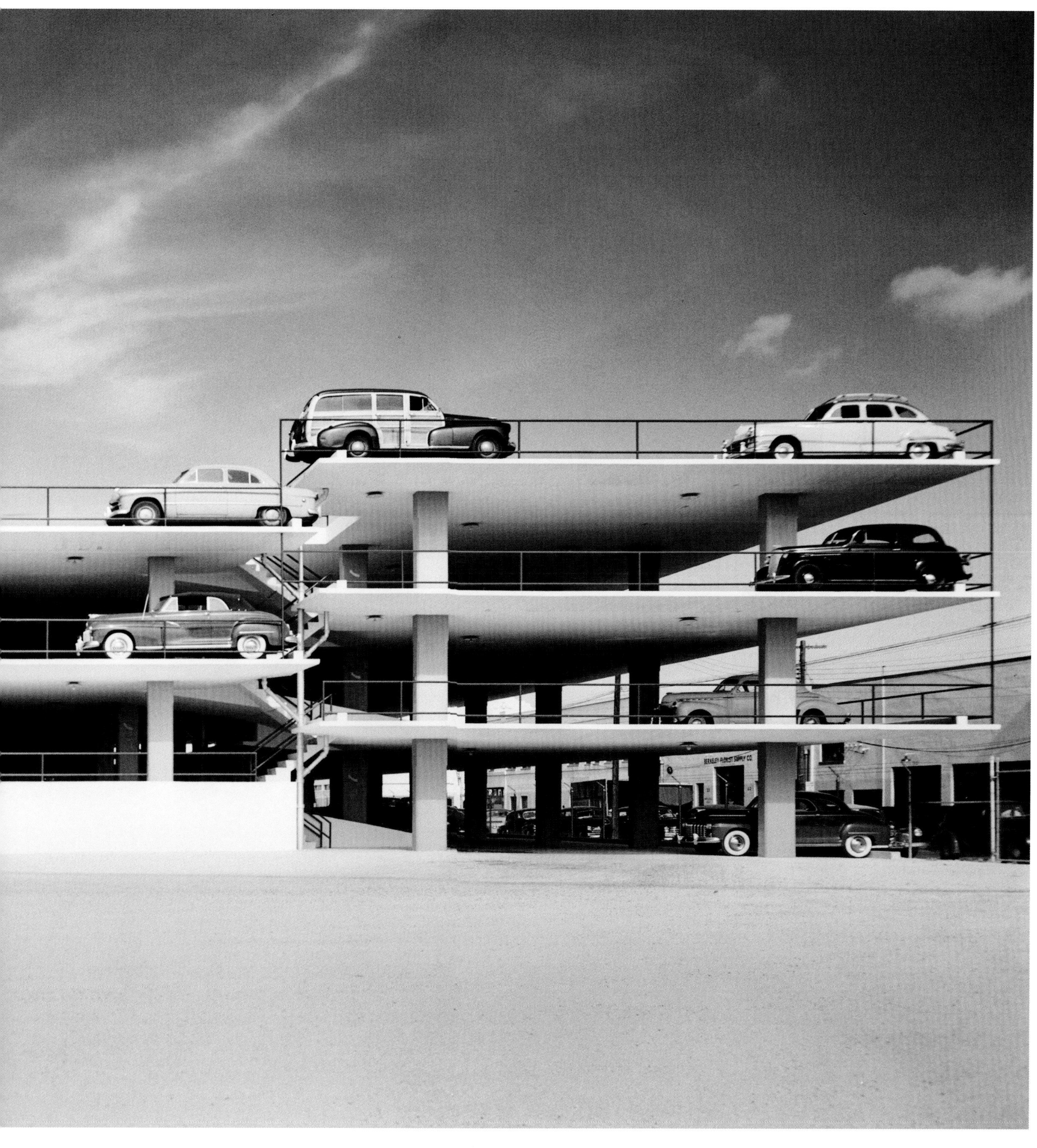

Parking garage, Miami.
Robert Law Weed & Associates, 1949.

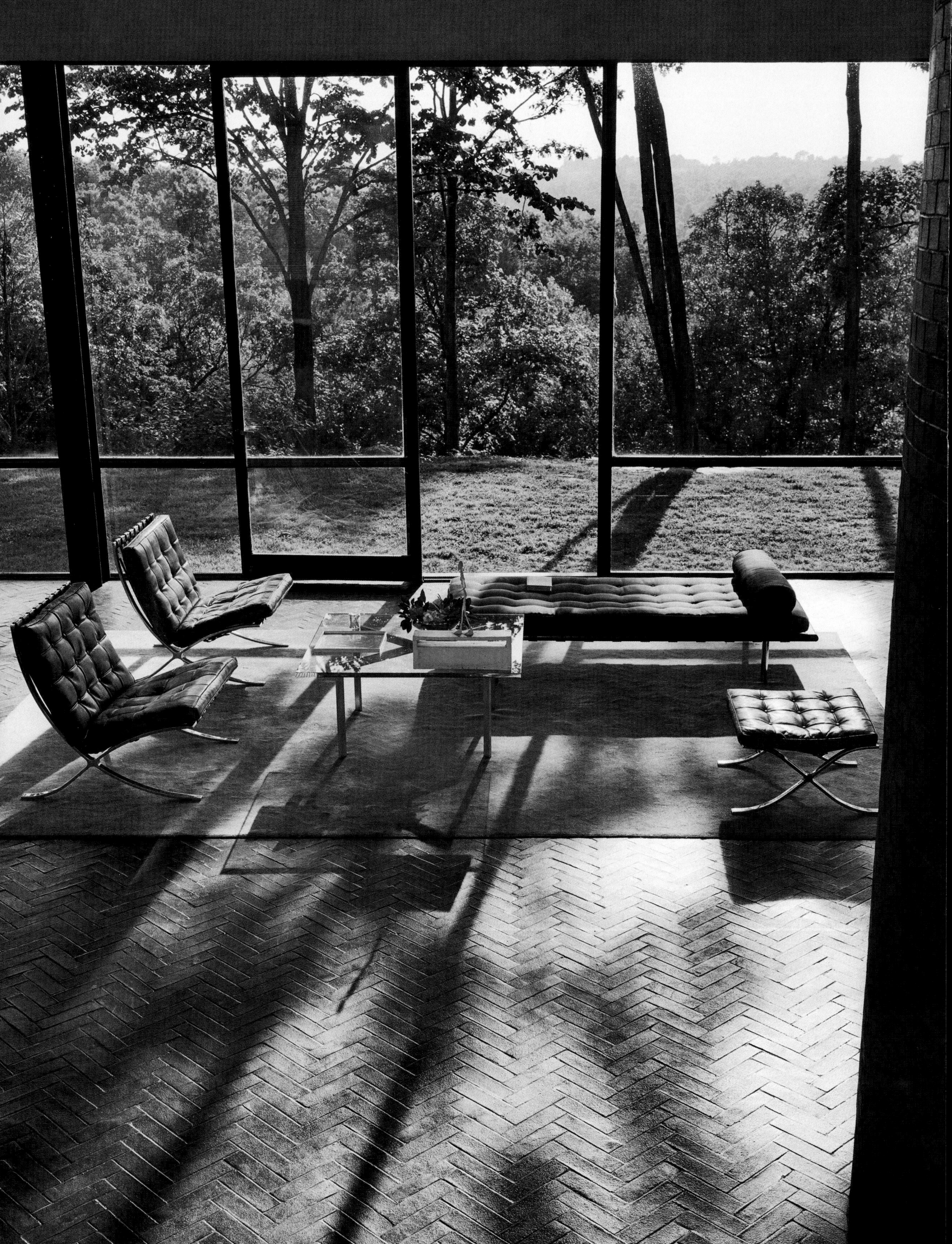

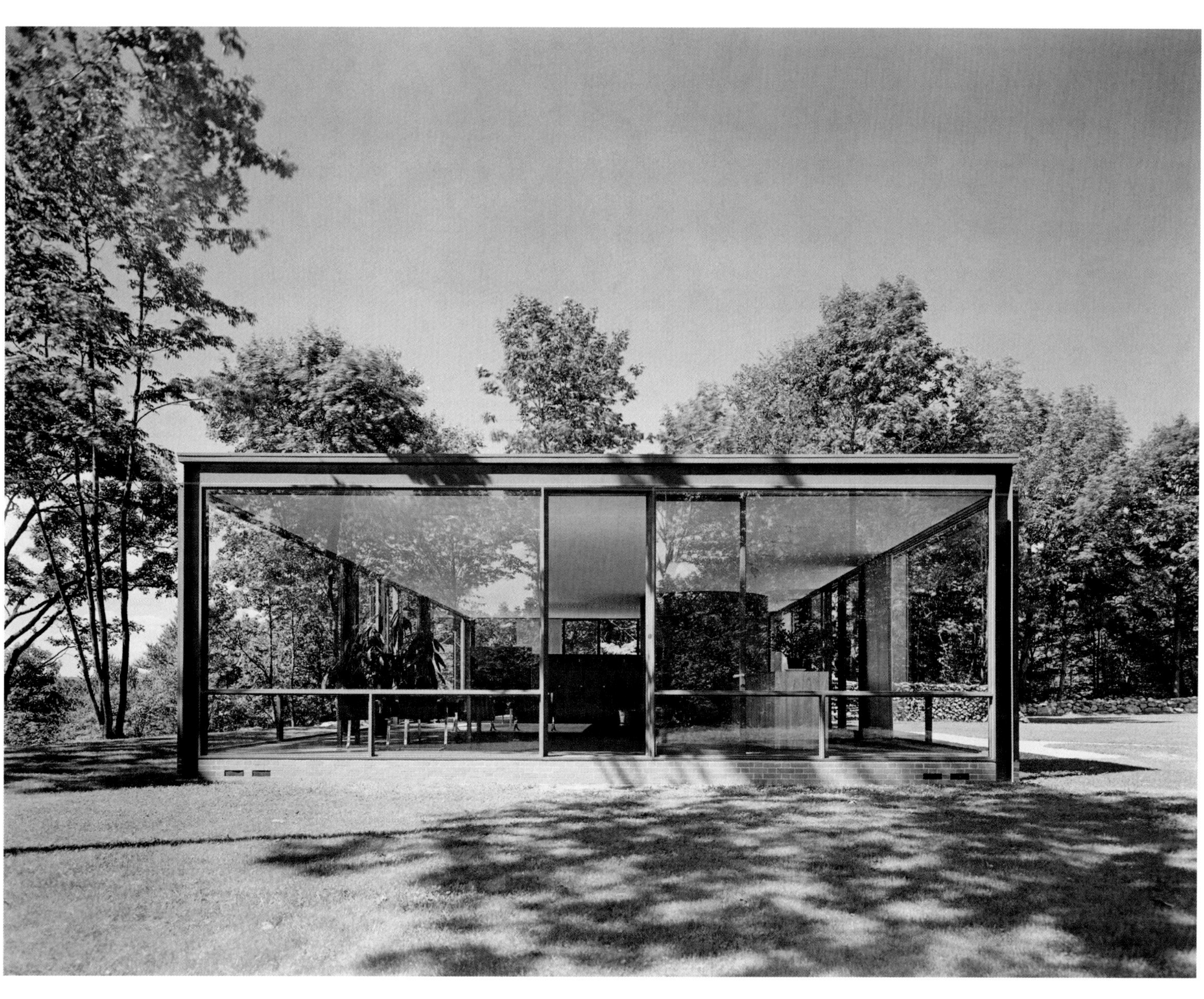

These pages and overleaf
Glass House, New Canaan, Connecticut.
Philip Johnson, 1949.

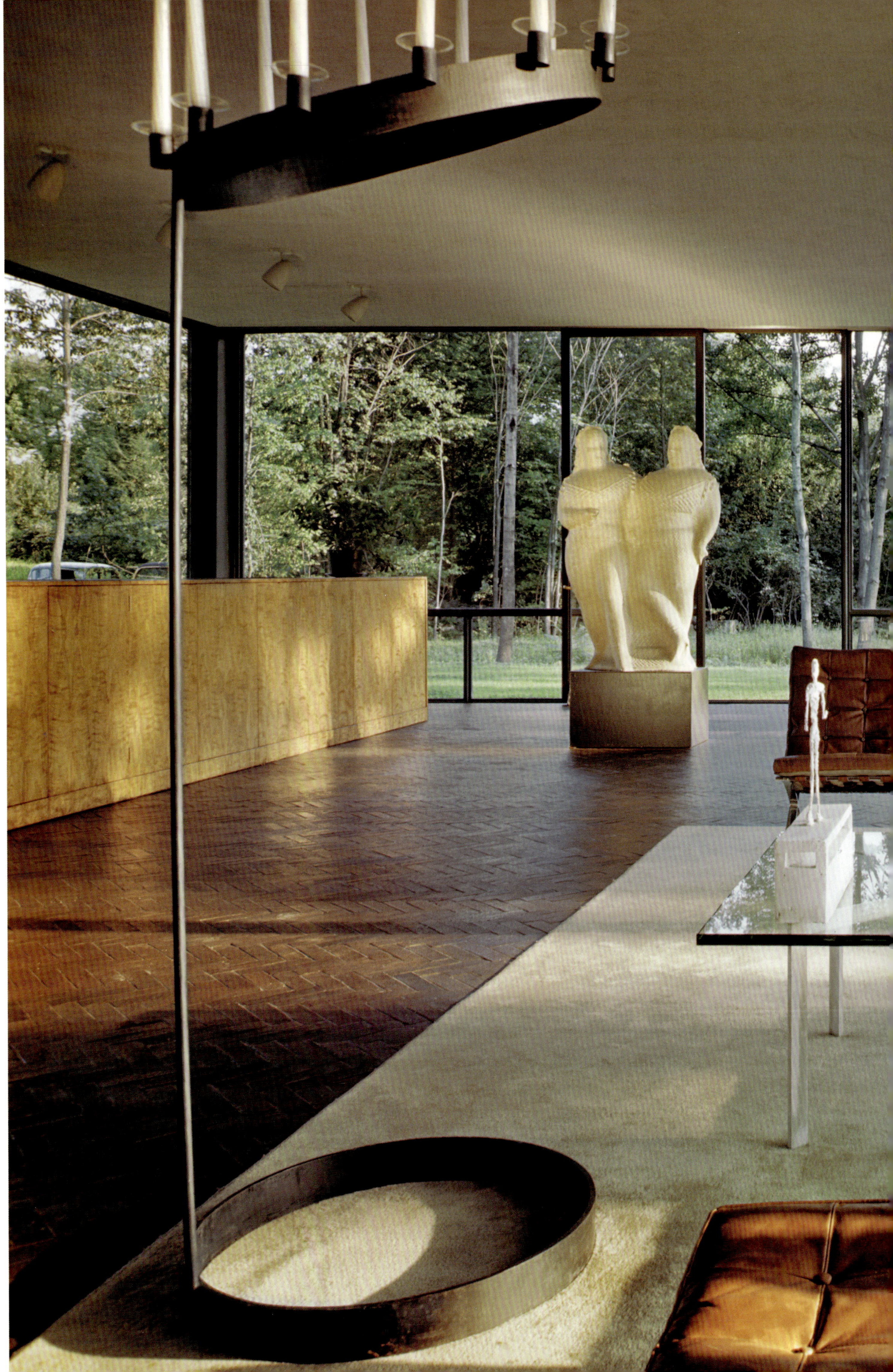

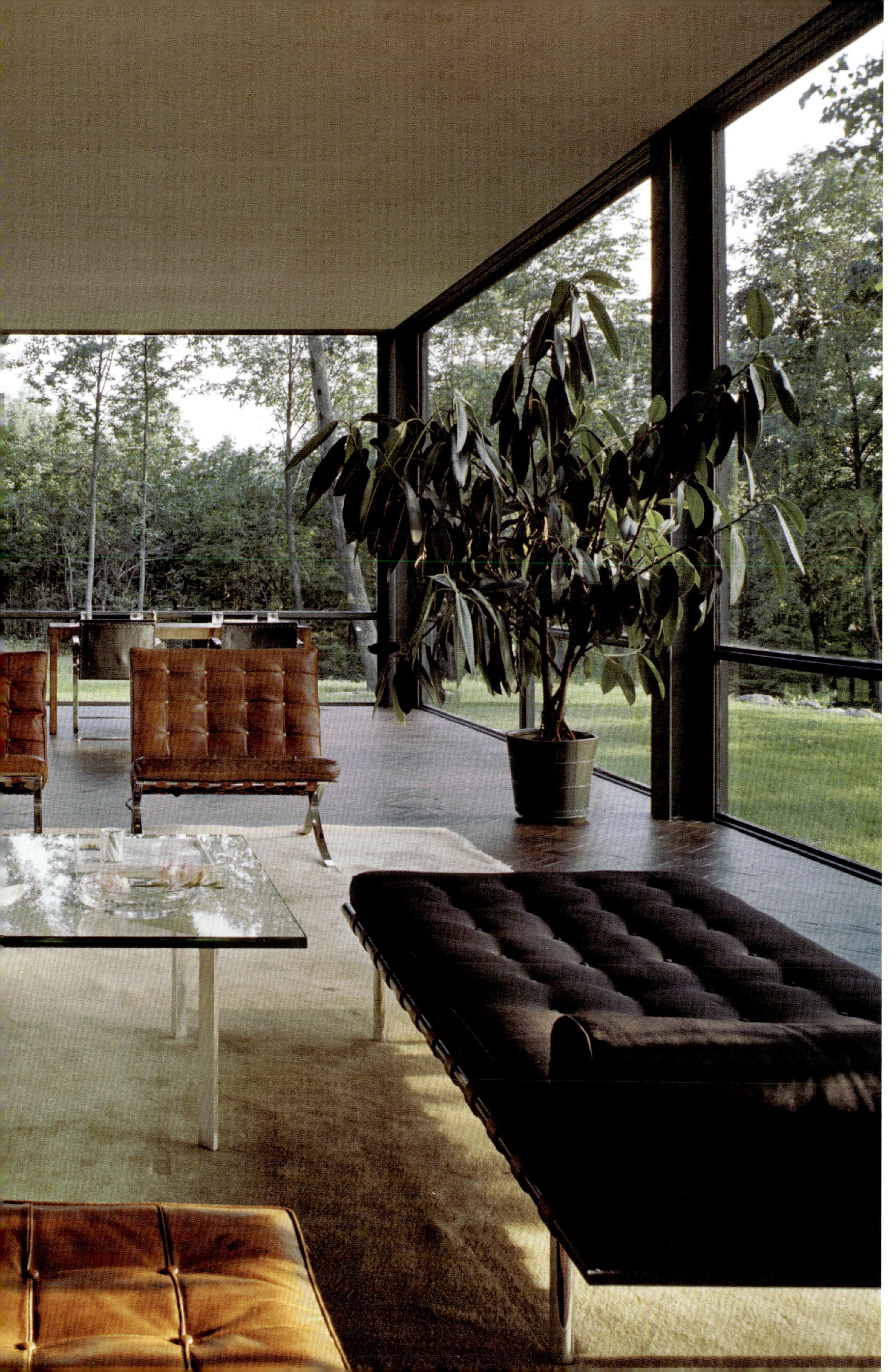

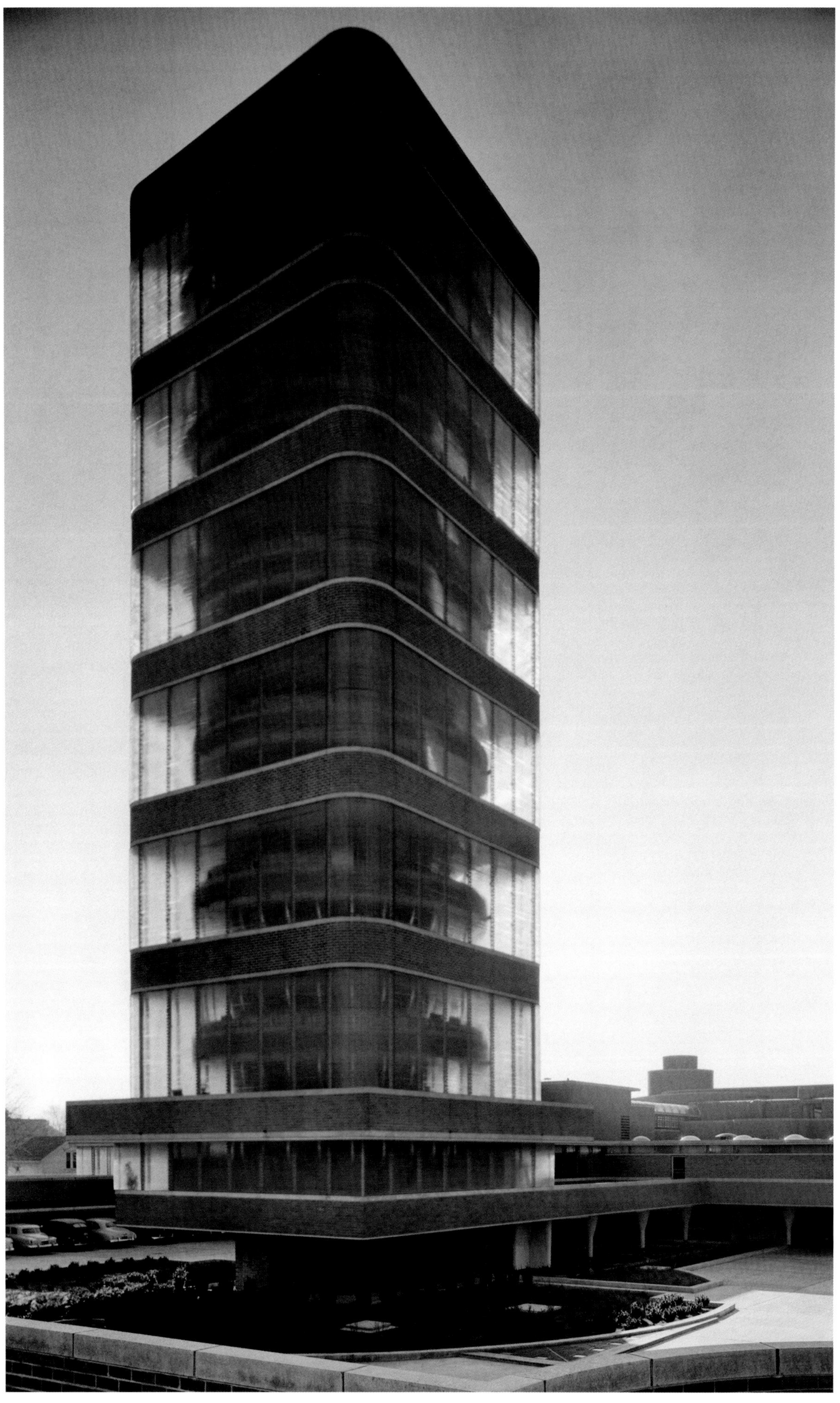

Johnson Wax Tower, Racine, Wisconsin.
Frank Lloyd Wright, 1950.

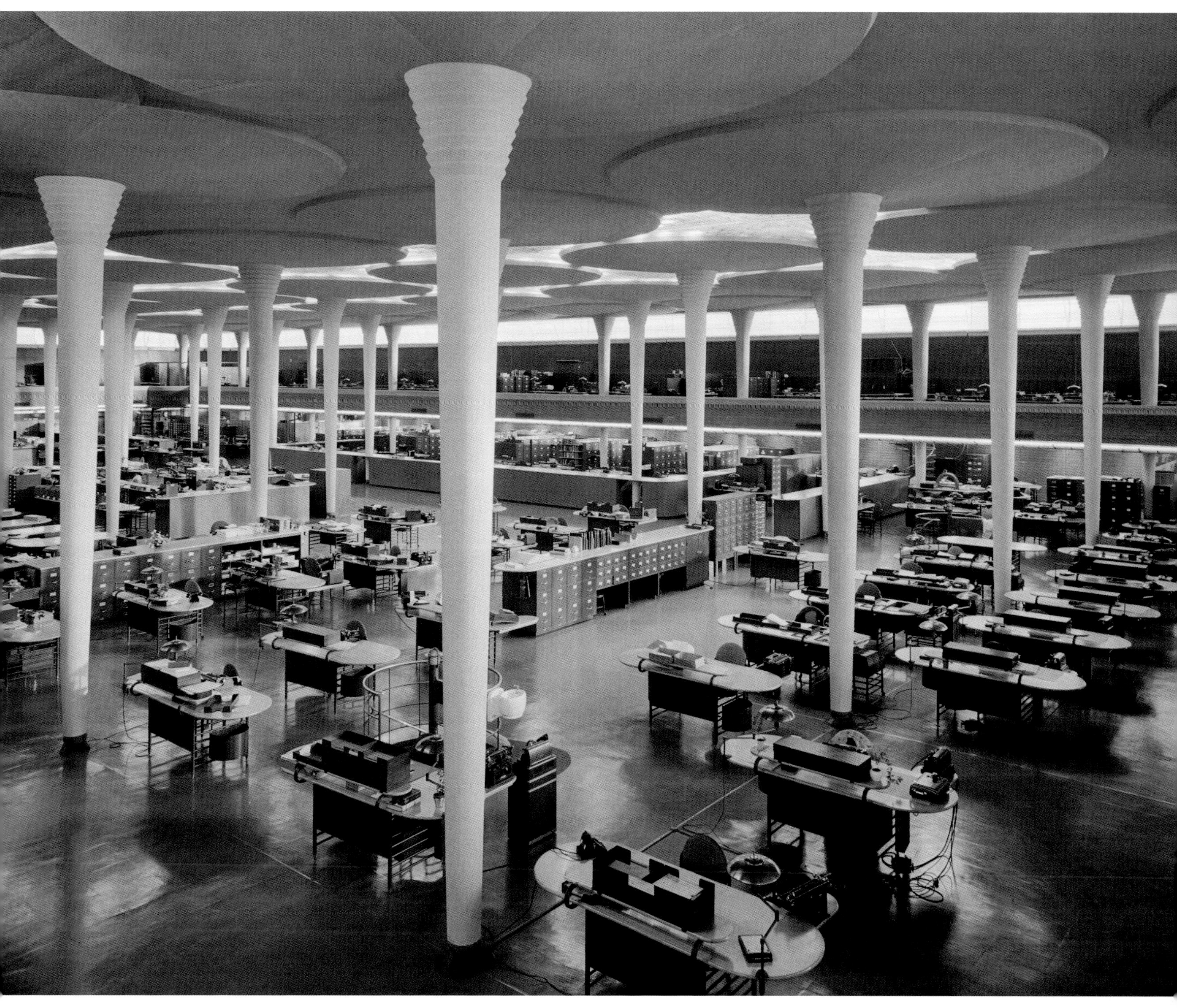

Johnson Wax Tower, Racine, Wisconsin.
Frank Lloyd Wright, 1950.

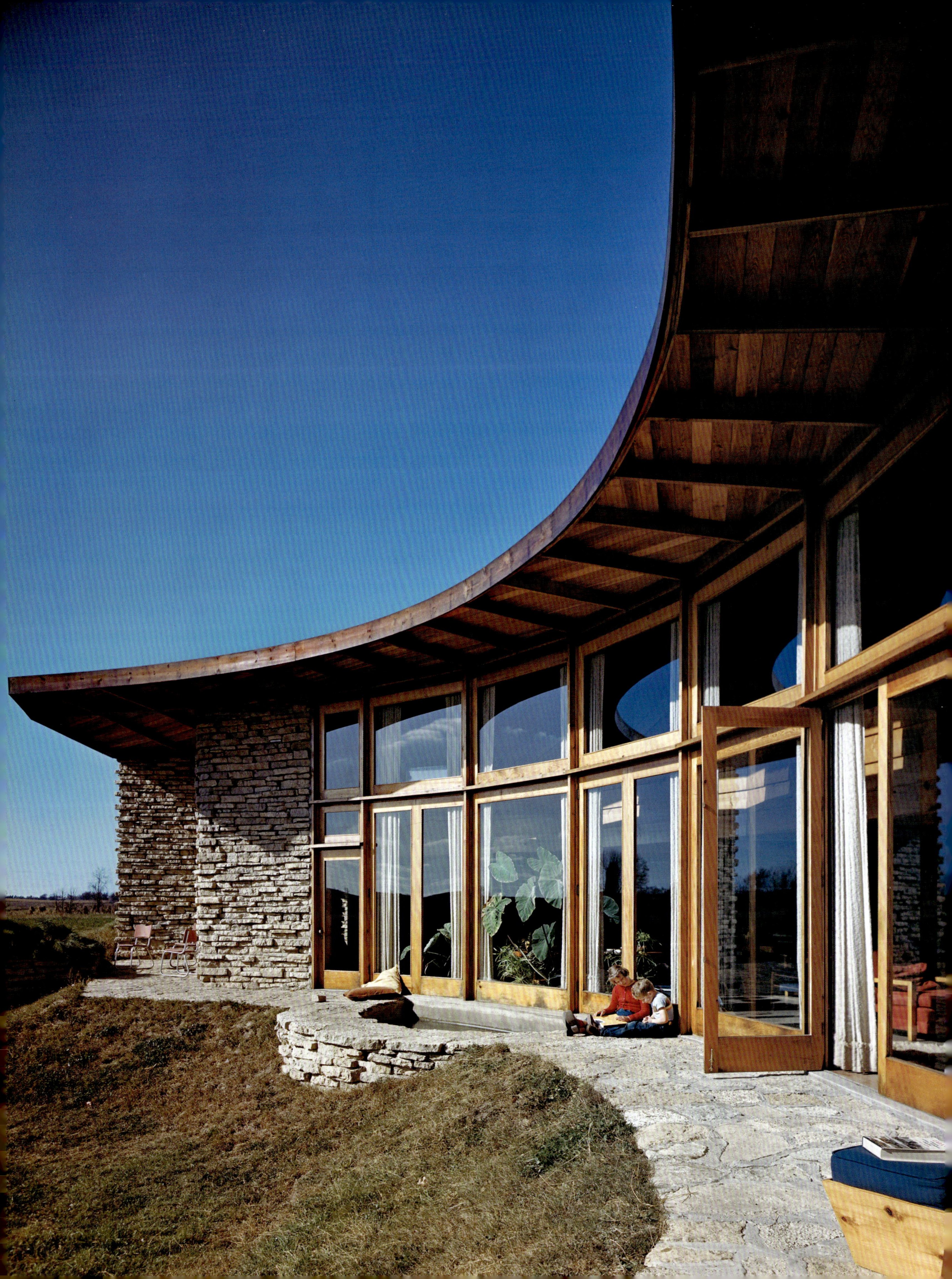

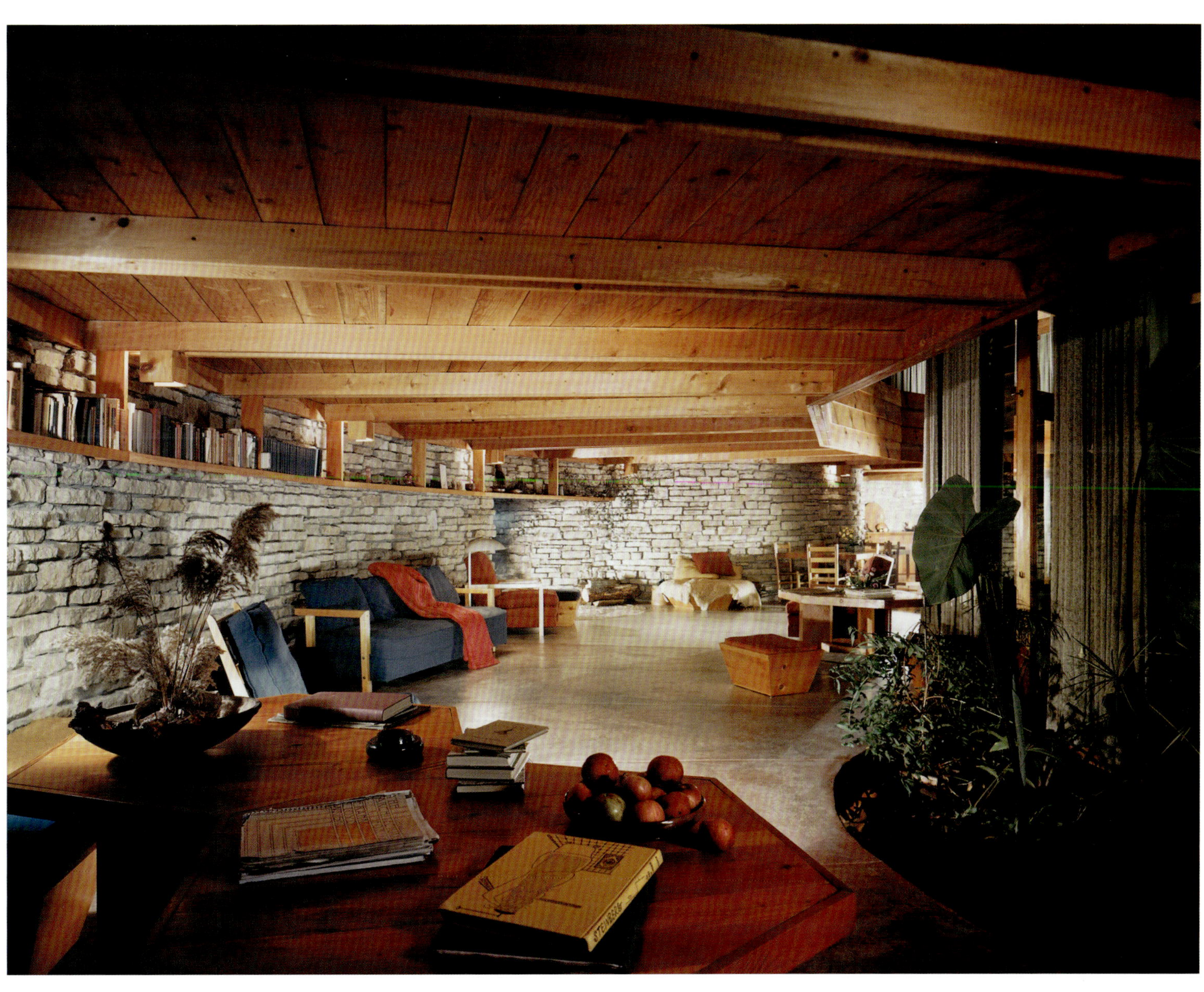

Jacobs II House, Middleton, Wisconsin.
Frank Lloyd Wright, 1950.

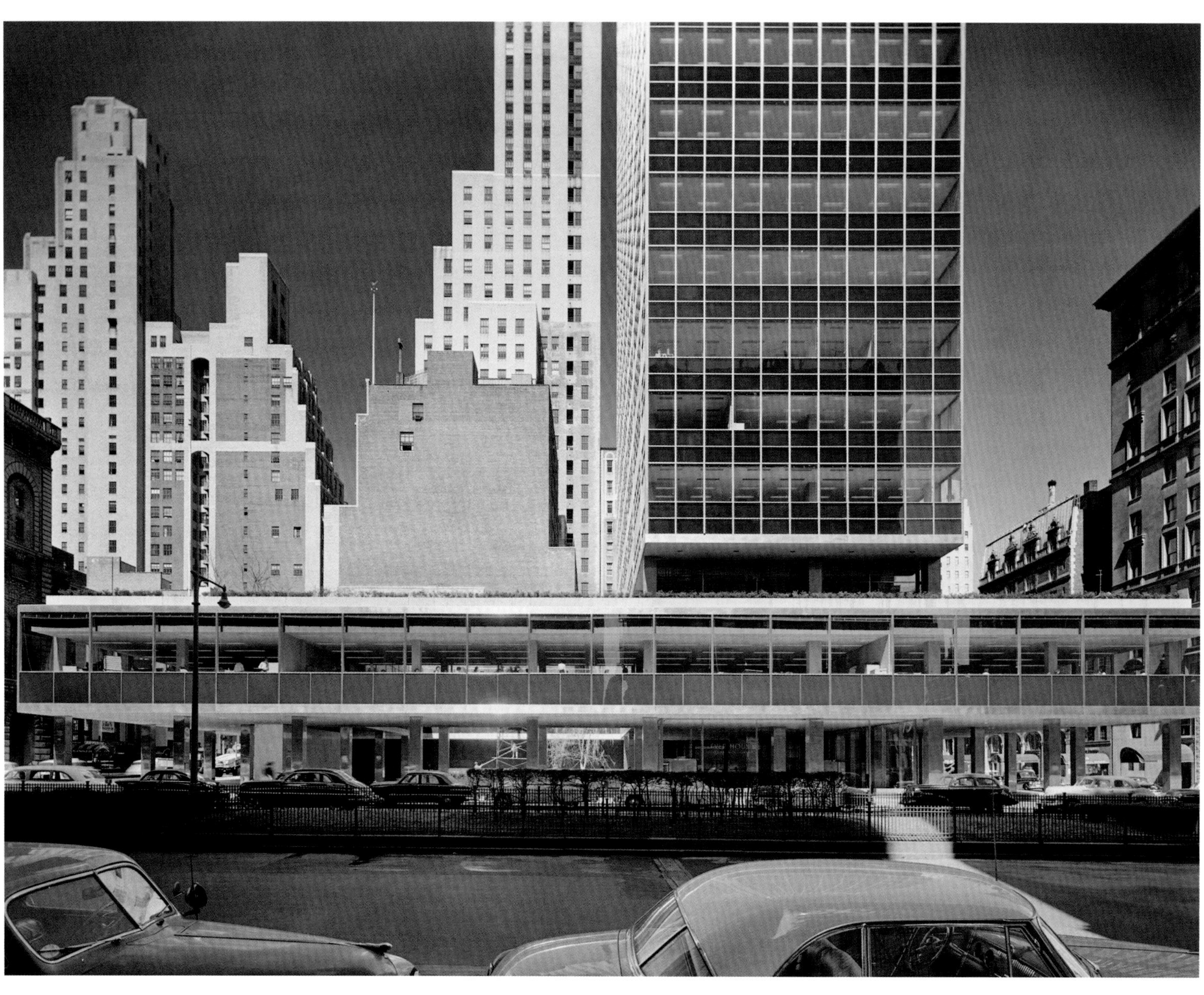

Lever House, New York.
Skidmore, Owings & Merrill, 1952.

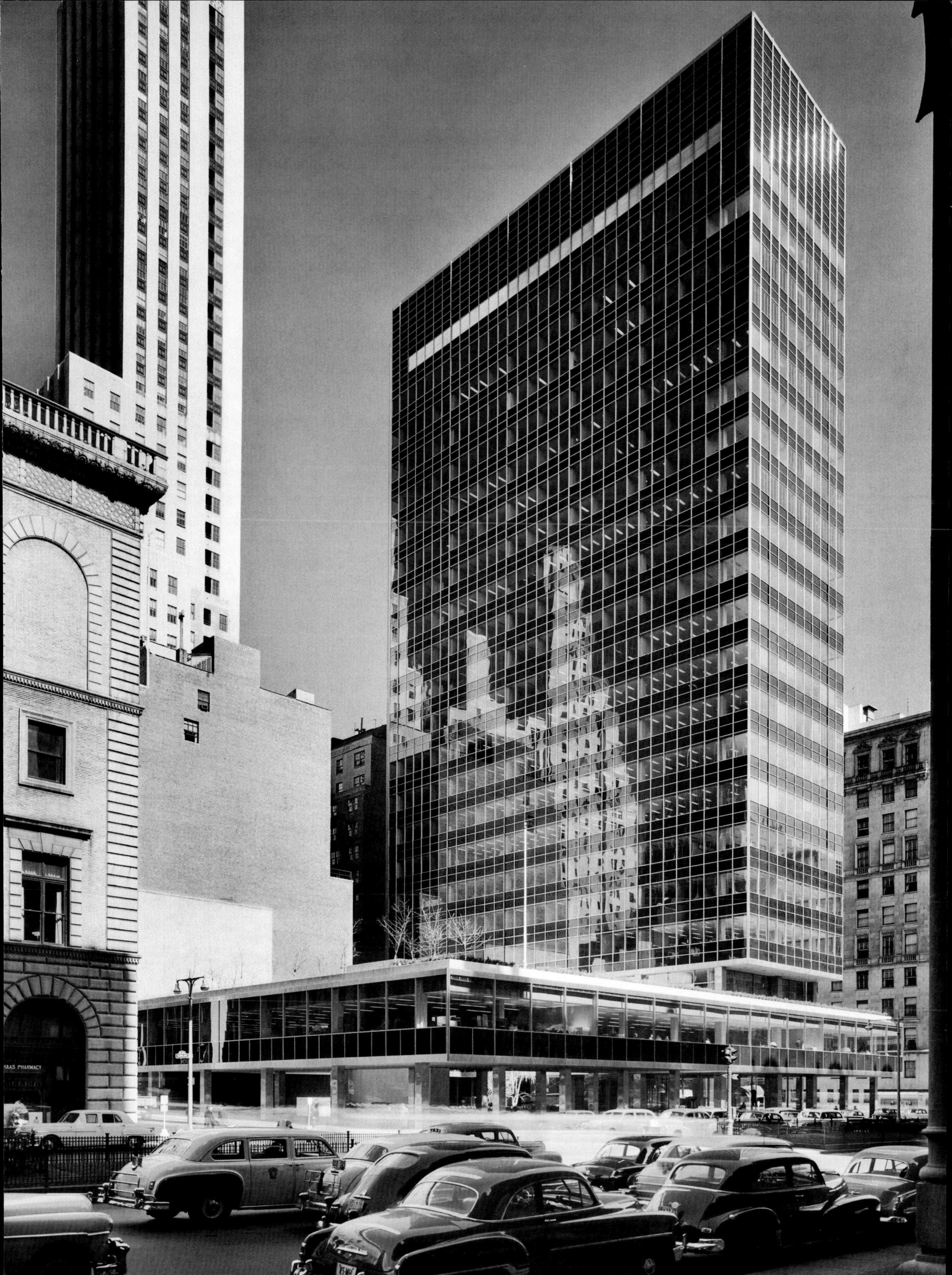
HAAS PHARMACY

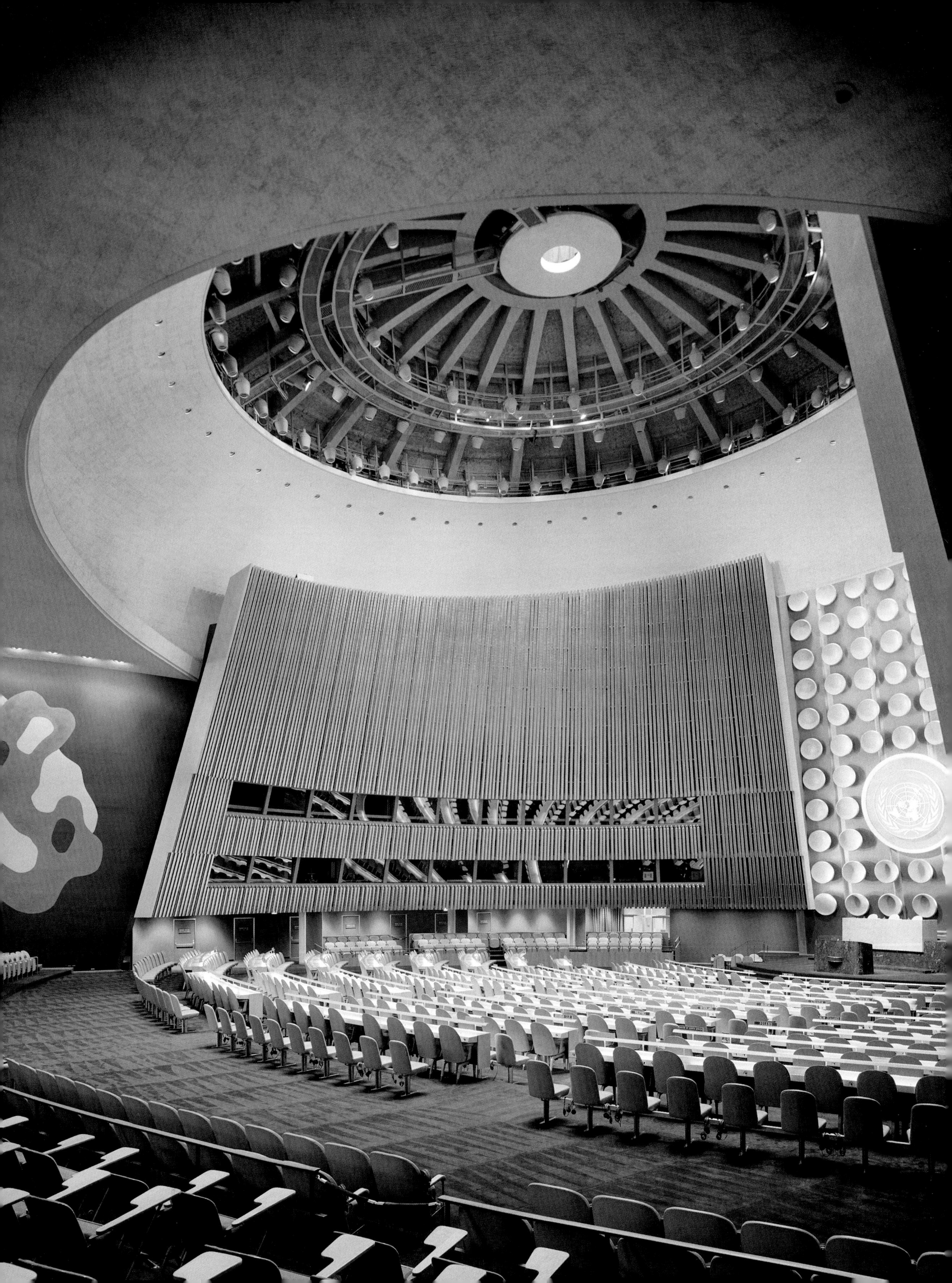

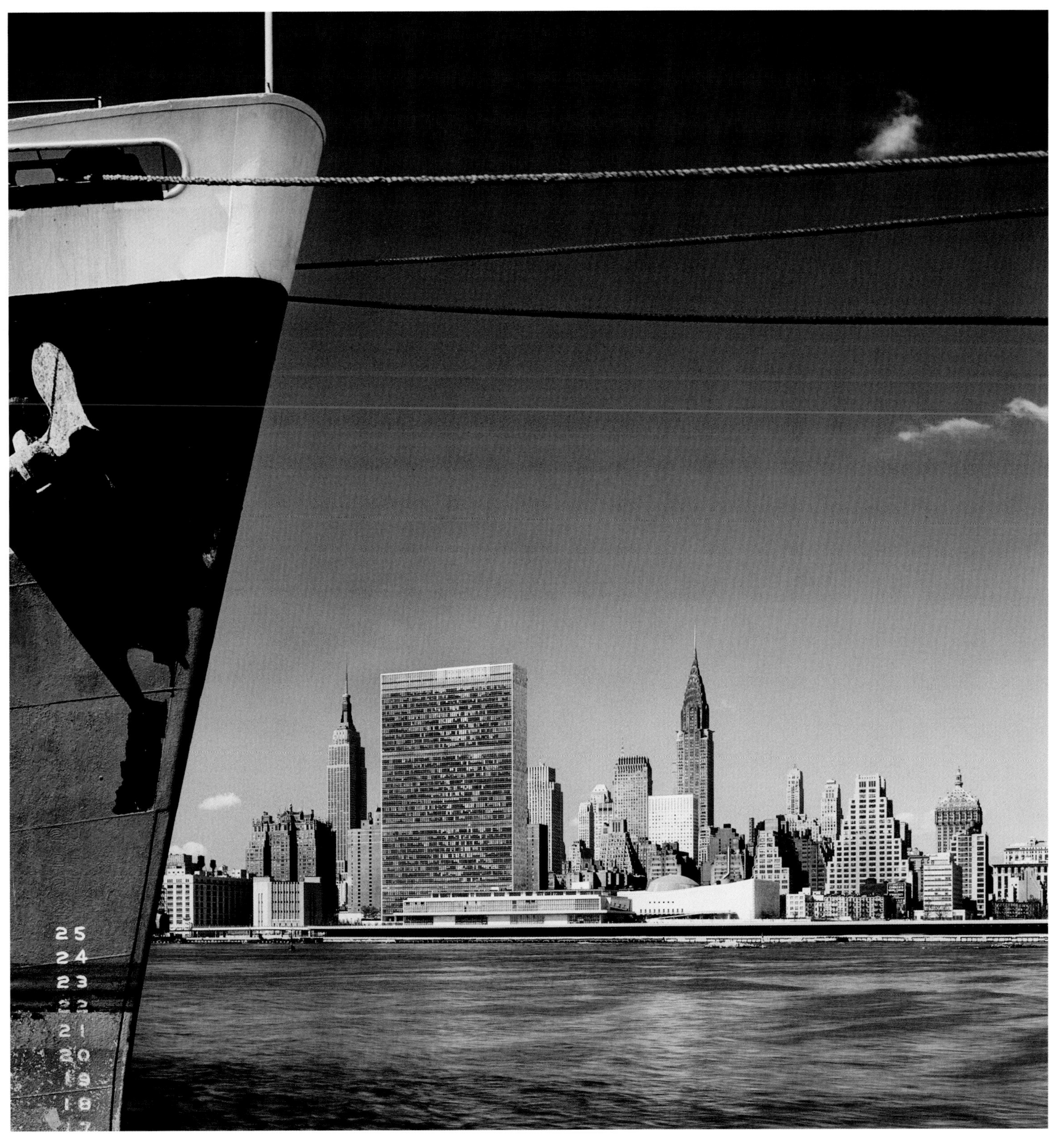

United Nations, New York. International team of architects led by Wallace K. Harrison, 1953. At left, General Assembly.

United Nations, New York.
International team of architects led
by Wallace K. Harrison, 1953.

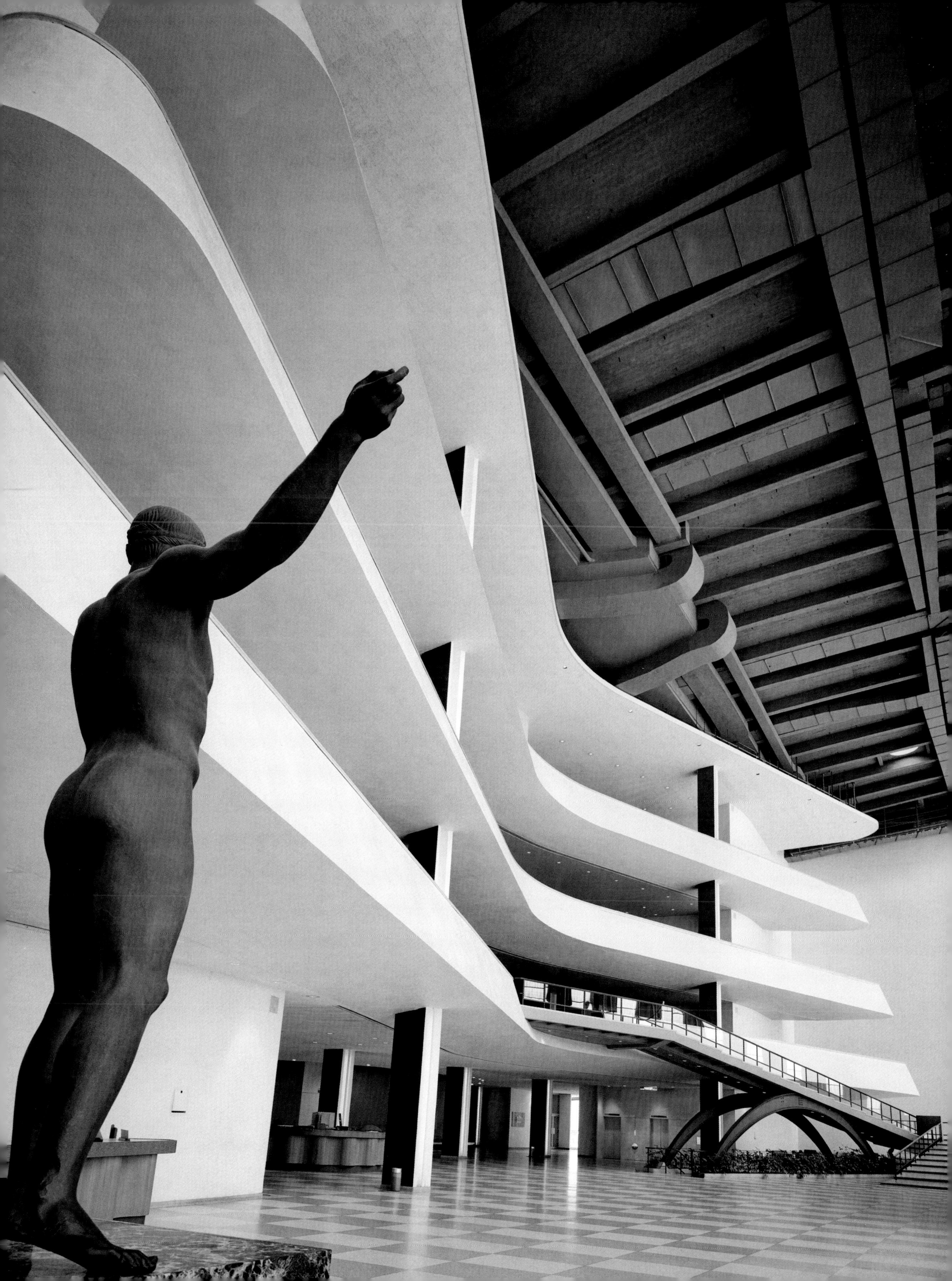

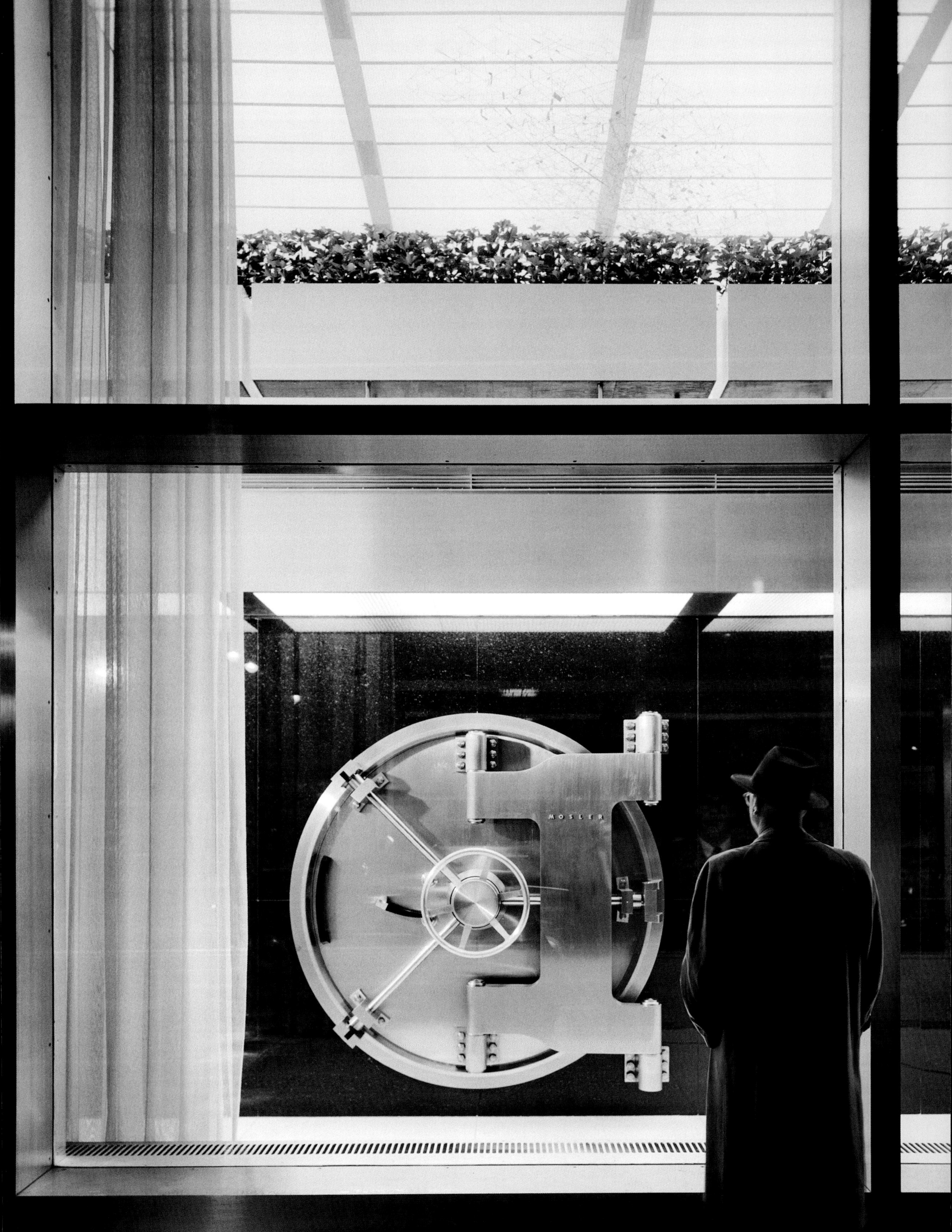
MOSLER

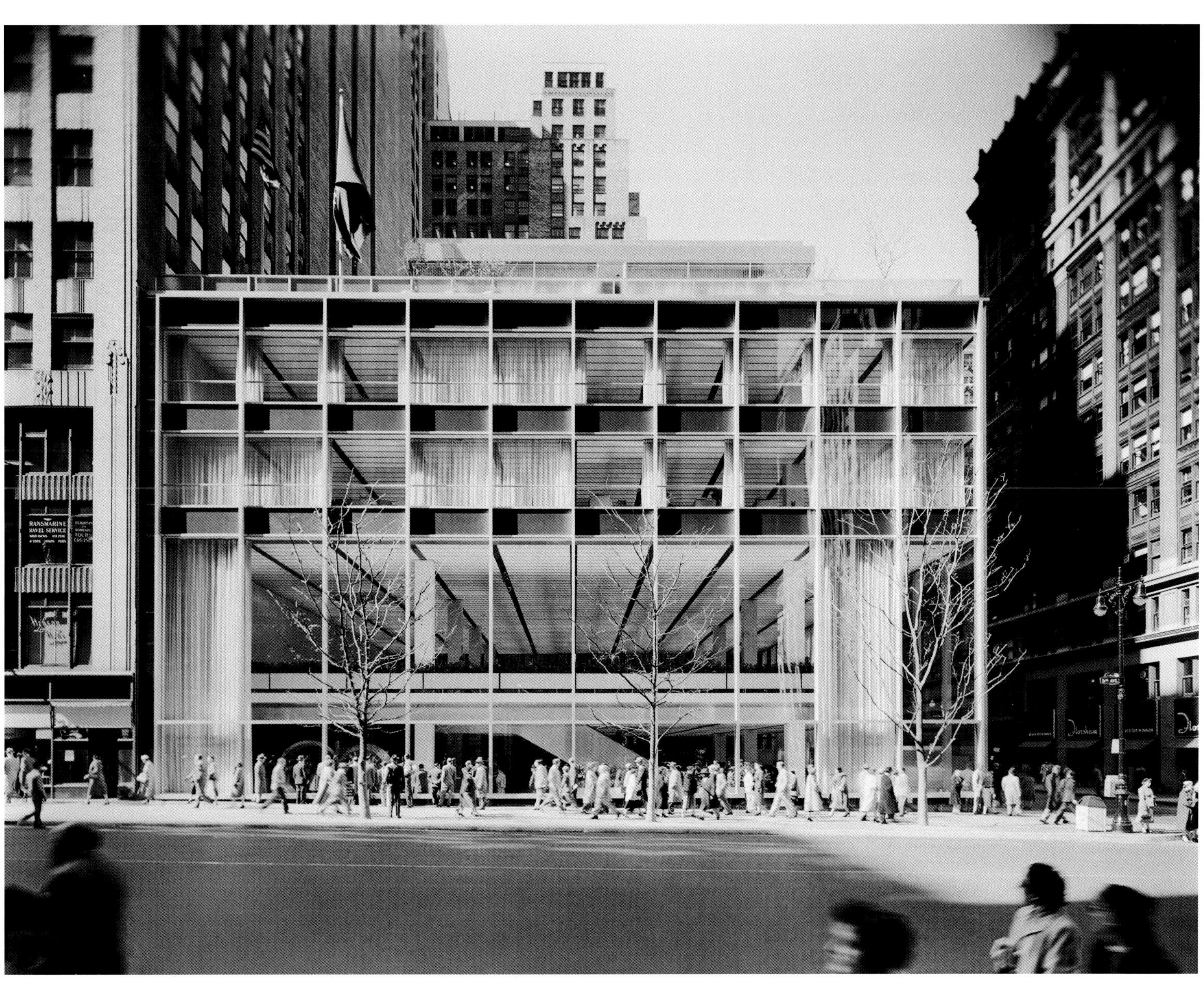

These pages and overleaf
Manufacturers Trust Company, 510 Fifth Avenue, New York. Skidmore, Owings & Merrill, 1954. Bank vault, left, designed by Henry Dreyfus, 1954.

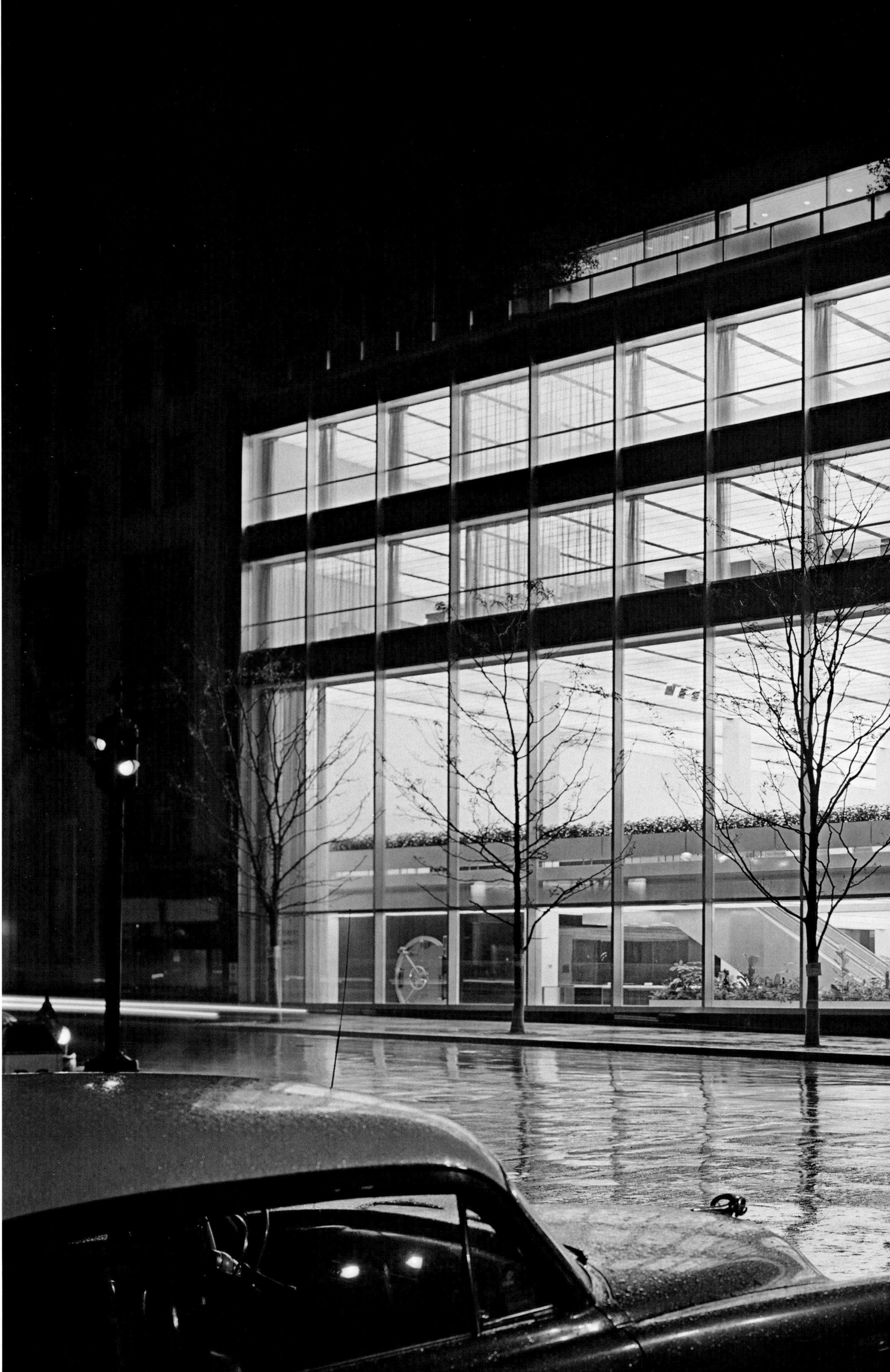

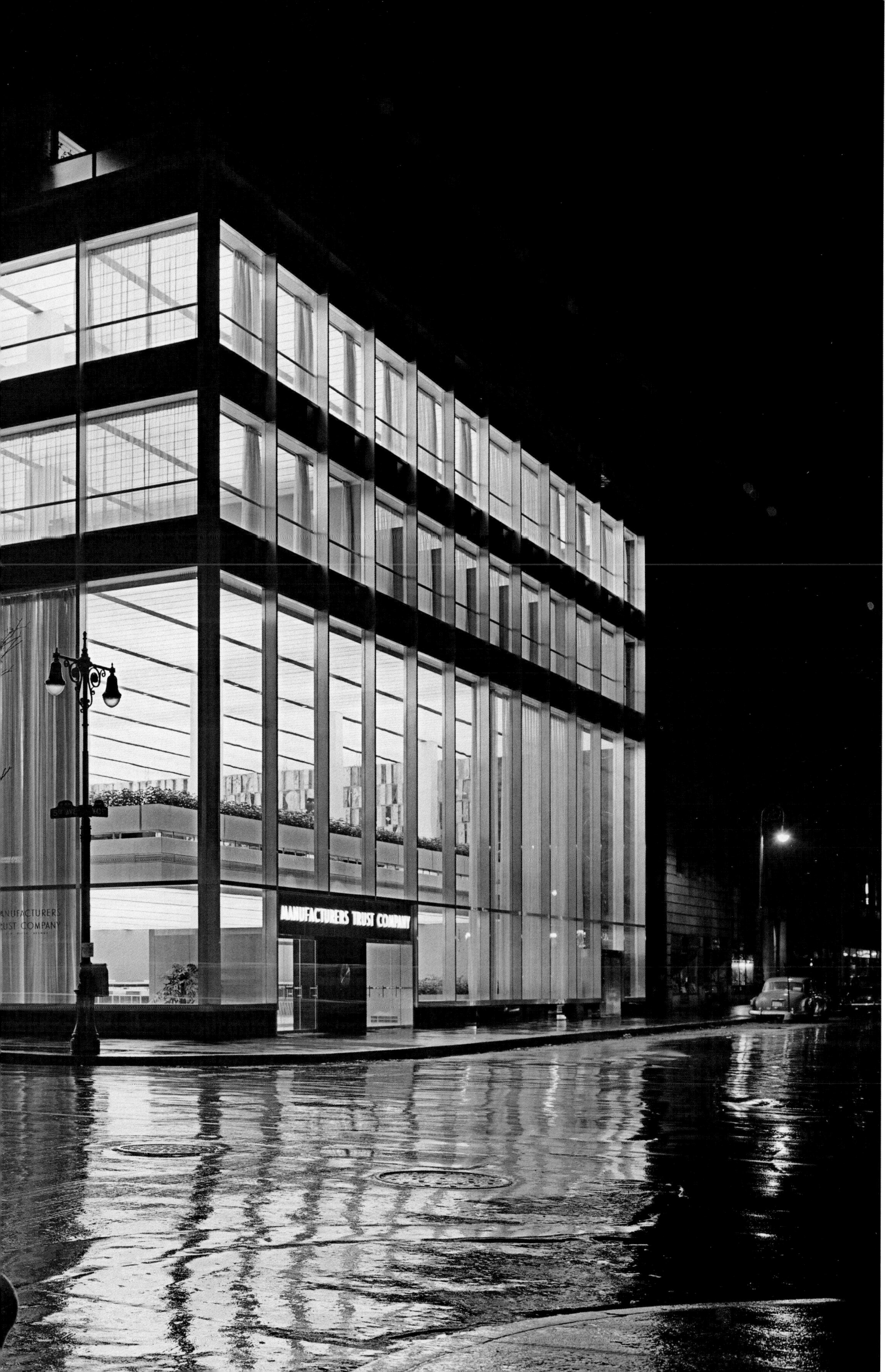
MANUFACTURERS TRUST COMPANY

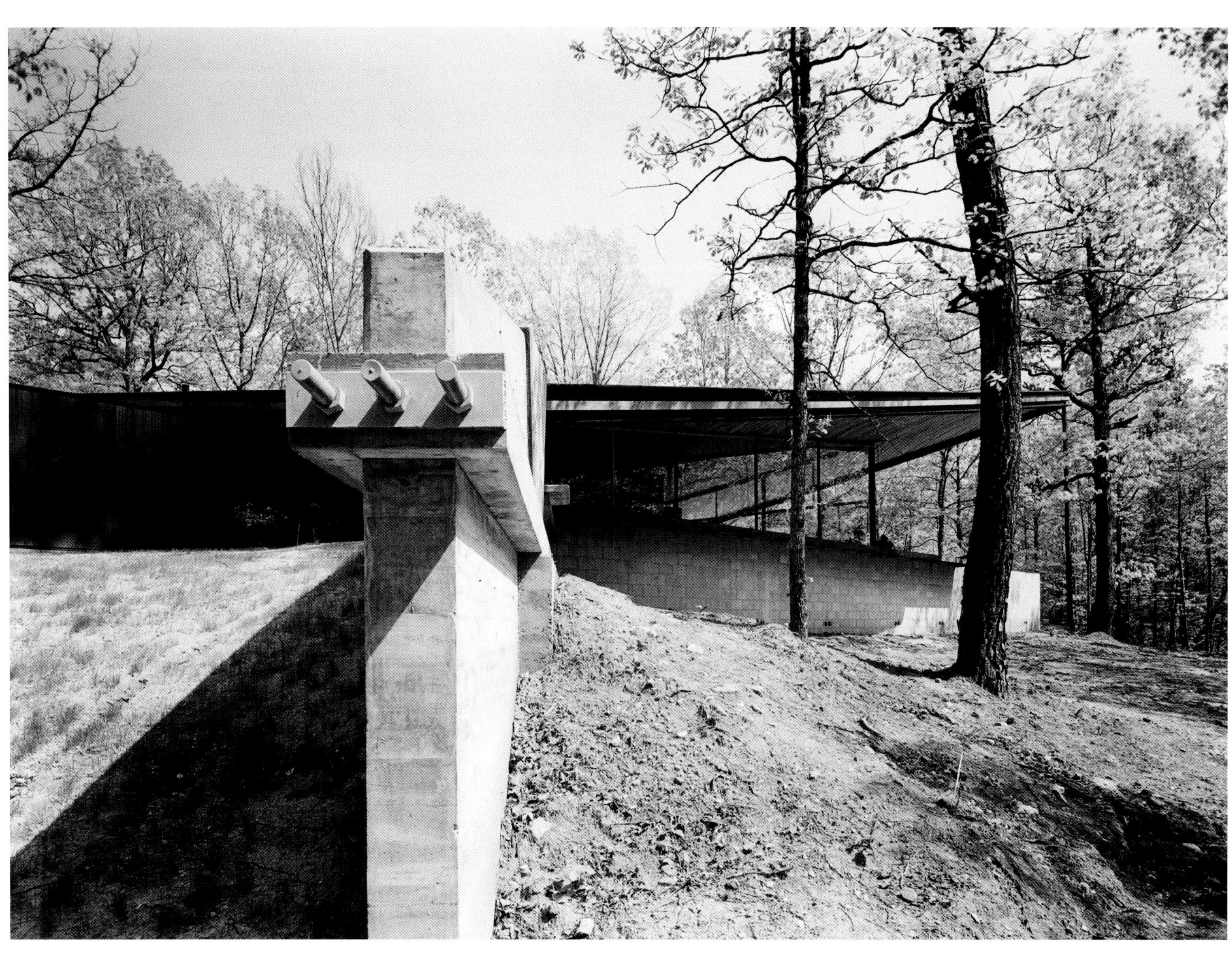

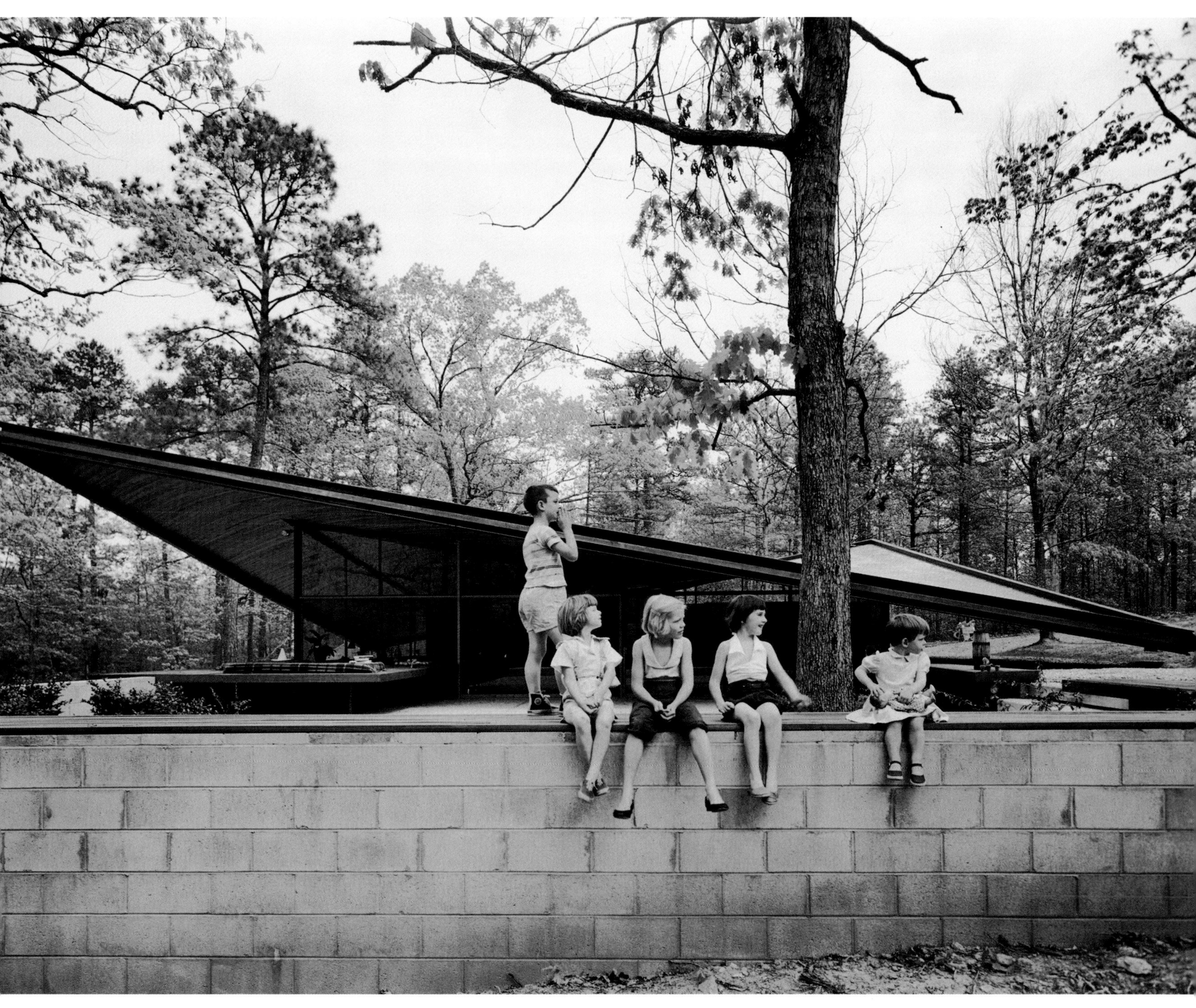

Catalano House, Raleigh, North Carolina.
Eduardo Catalano, 1955.

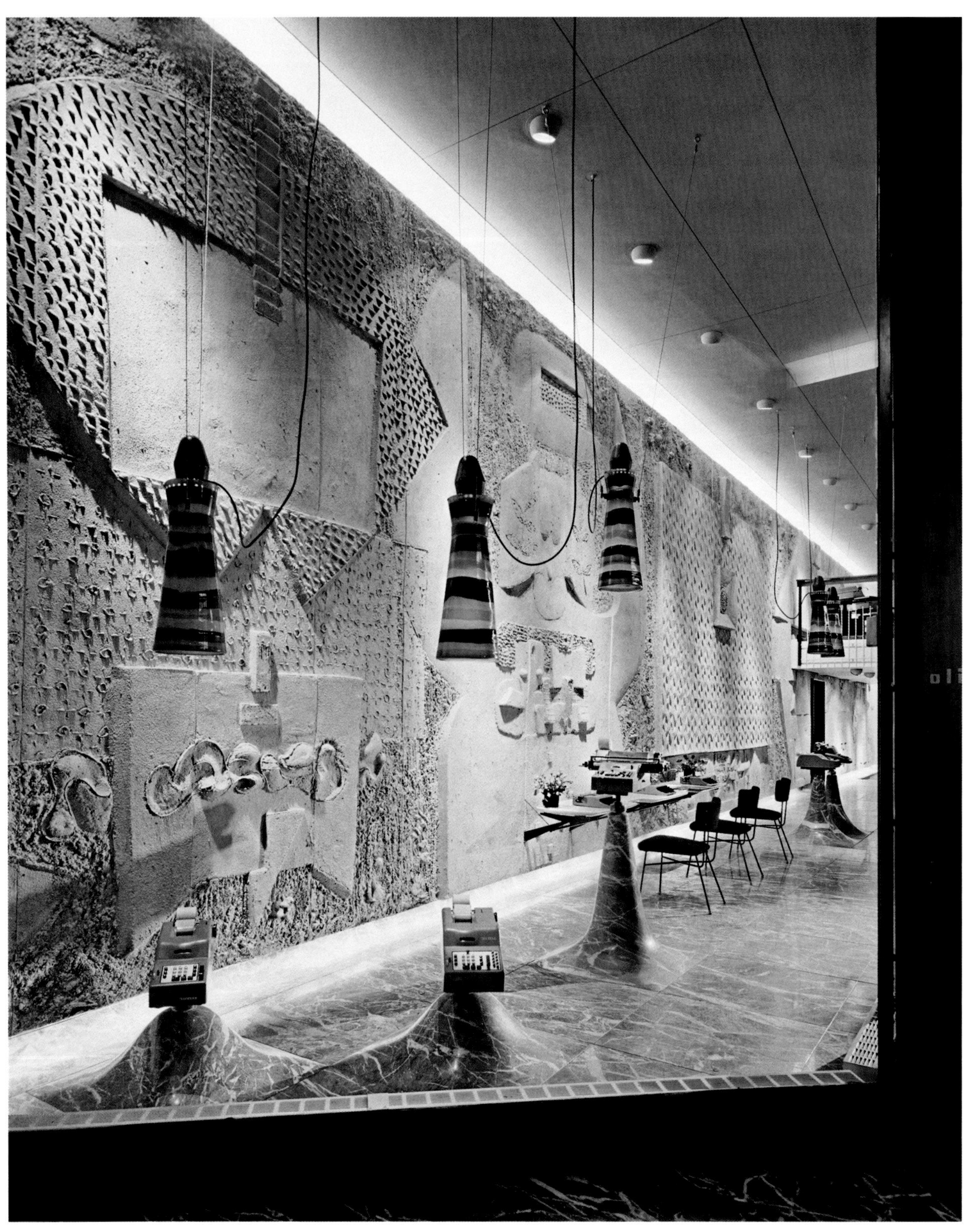

Olivetti Showroom, New York.
Belgiojoso, Peressutti & Rogers;
Constantino Nivola, sculptor, 1954.

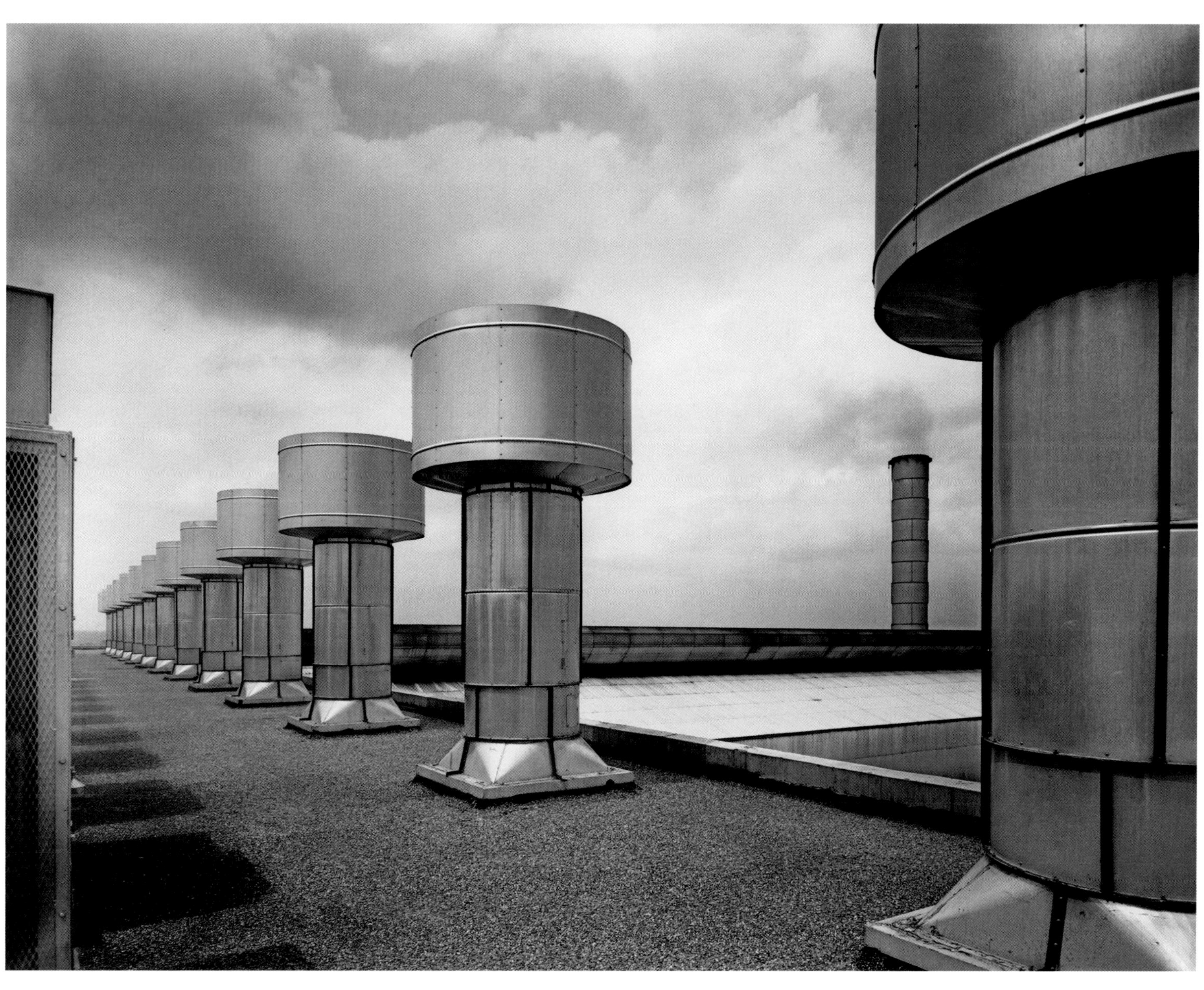

Reynolds Plant, Arkadelphia,
Arkansas, 1955.

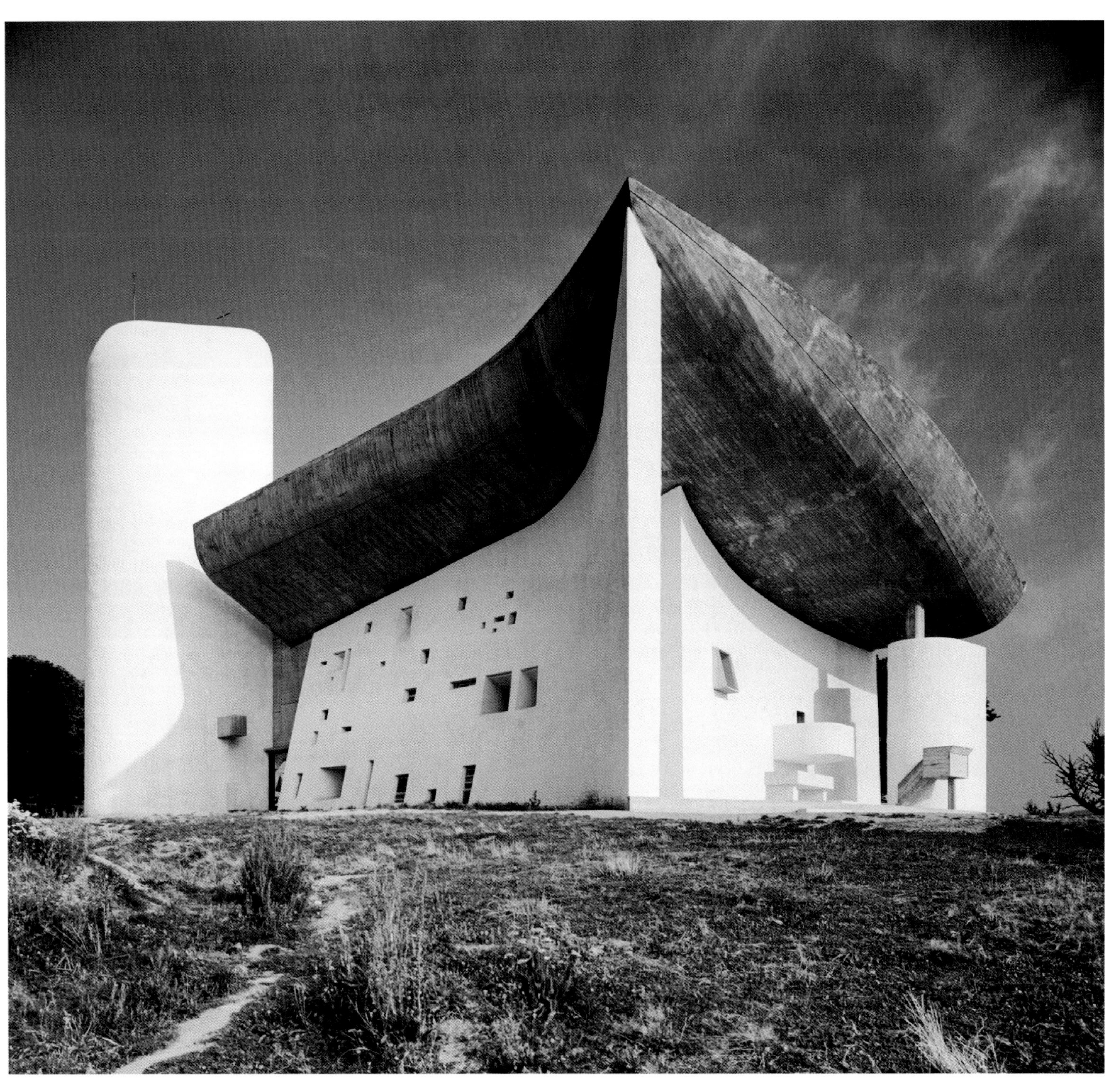

Notre Dame du Haut, Ronchamp, France. Le Corbusier, 1955.

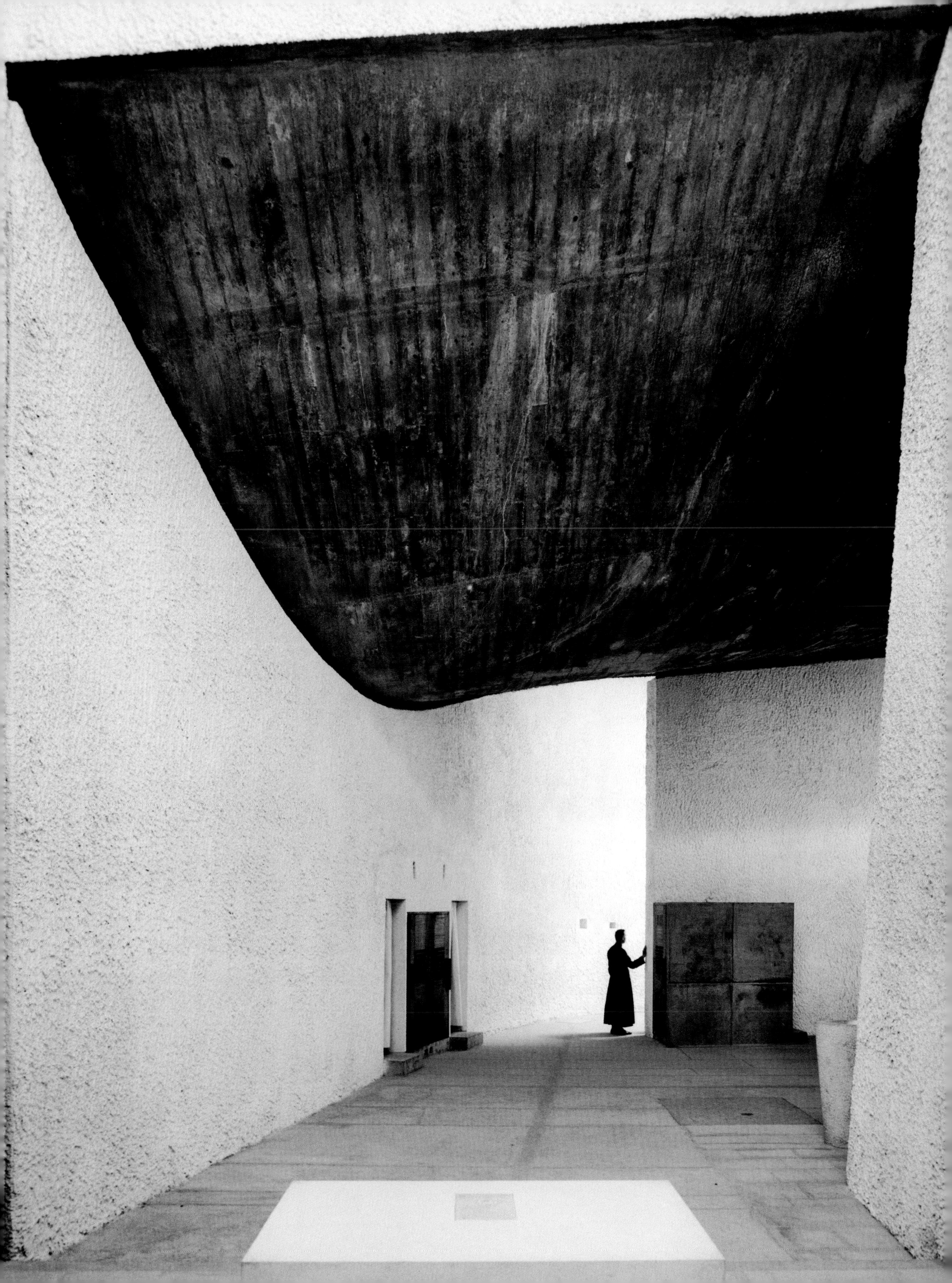

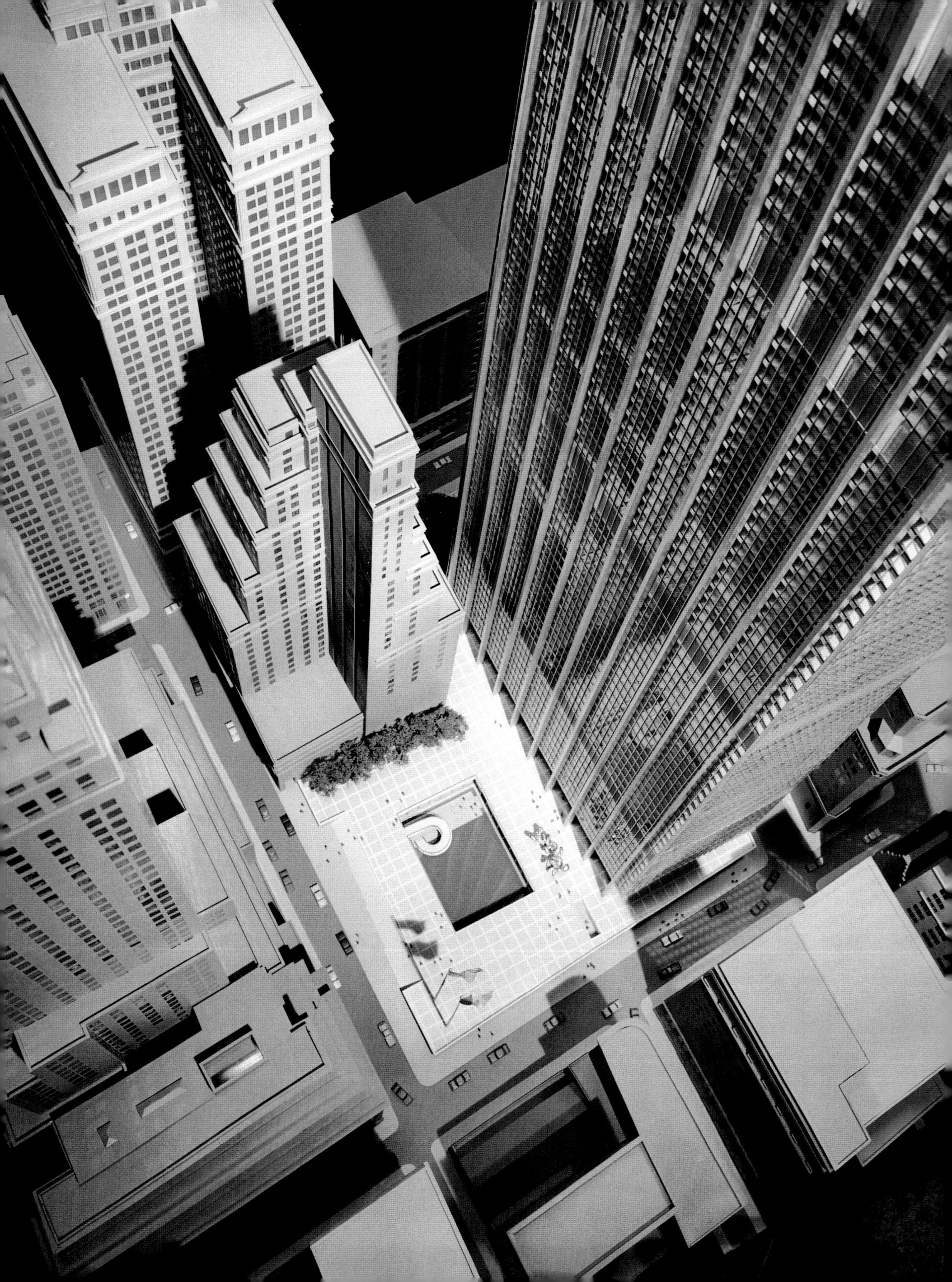

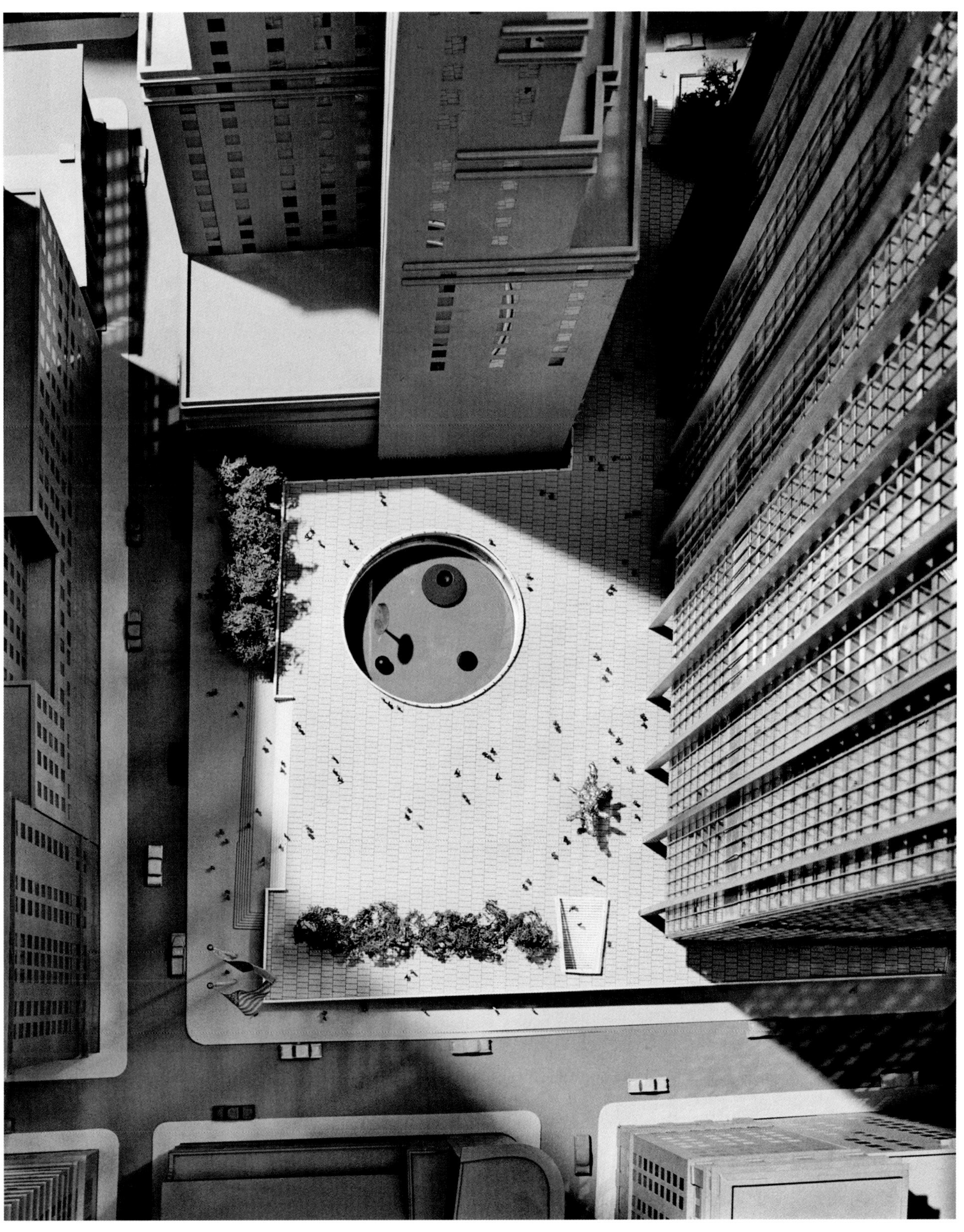

Chase Manhattan Bank model.
Skidmore, Owings & Merrill, 1955.

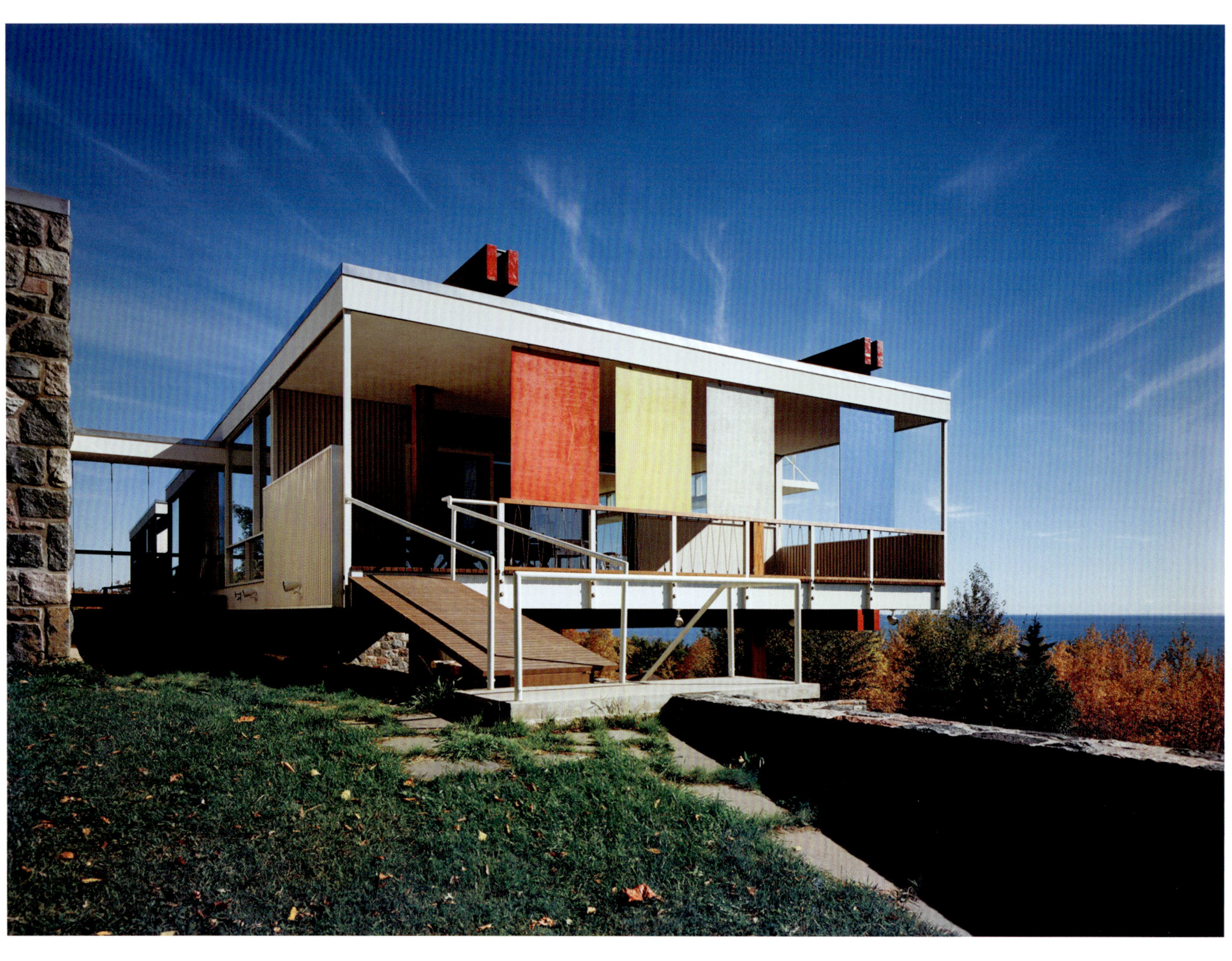

Above and opposite
Starkey House, Duluth, Minnesota.
Marcel Breuer, 1956.

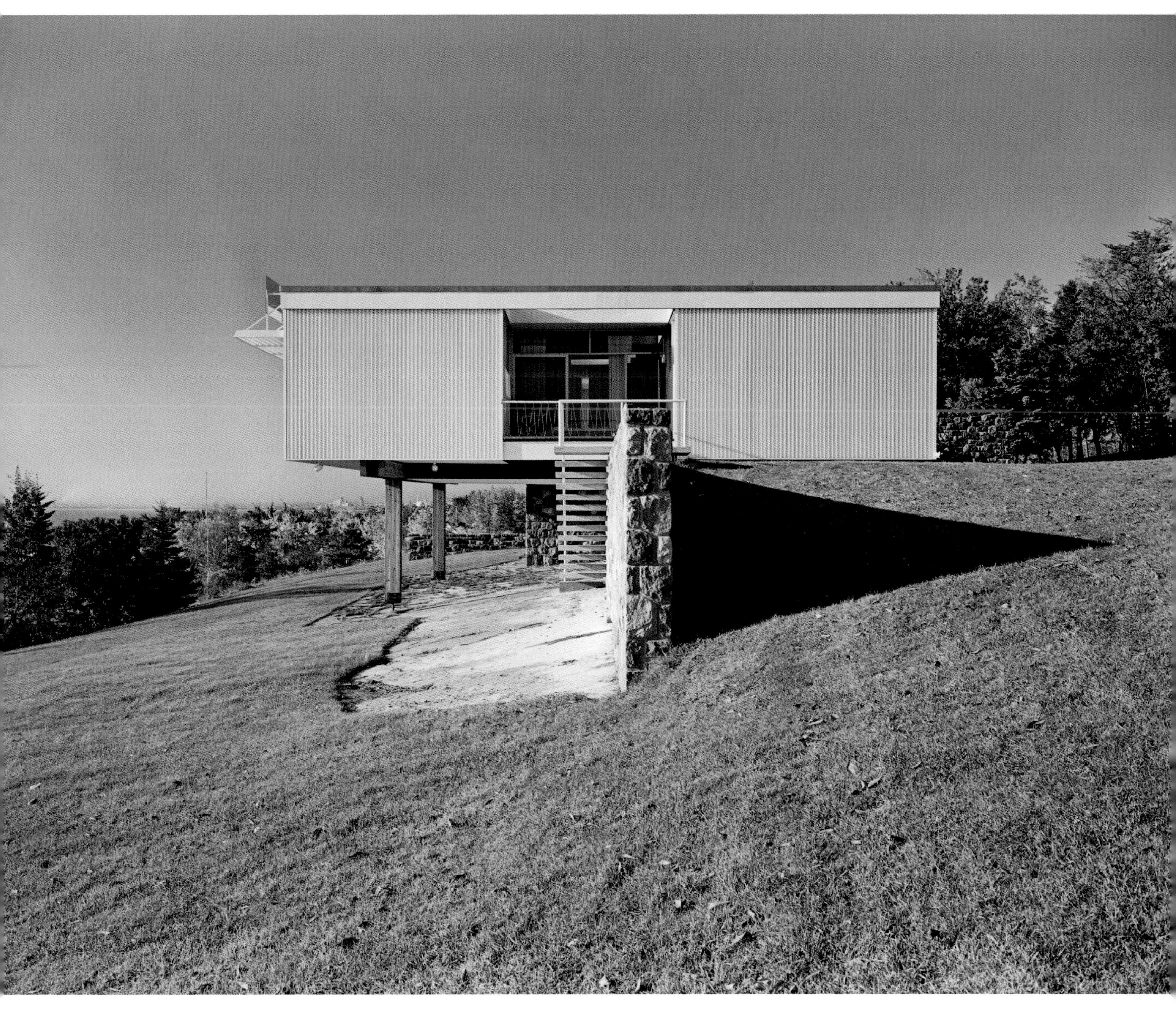

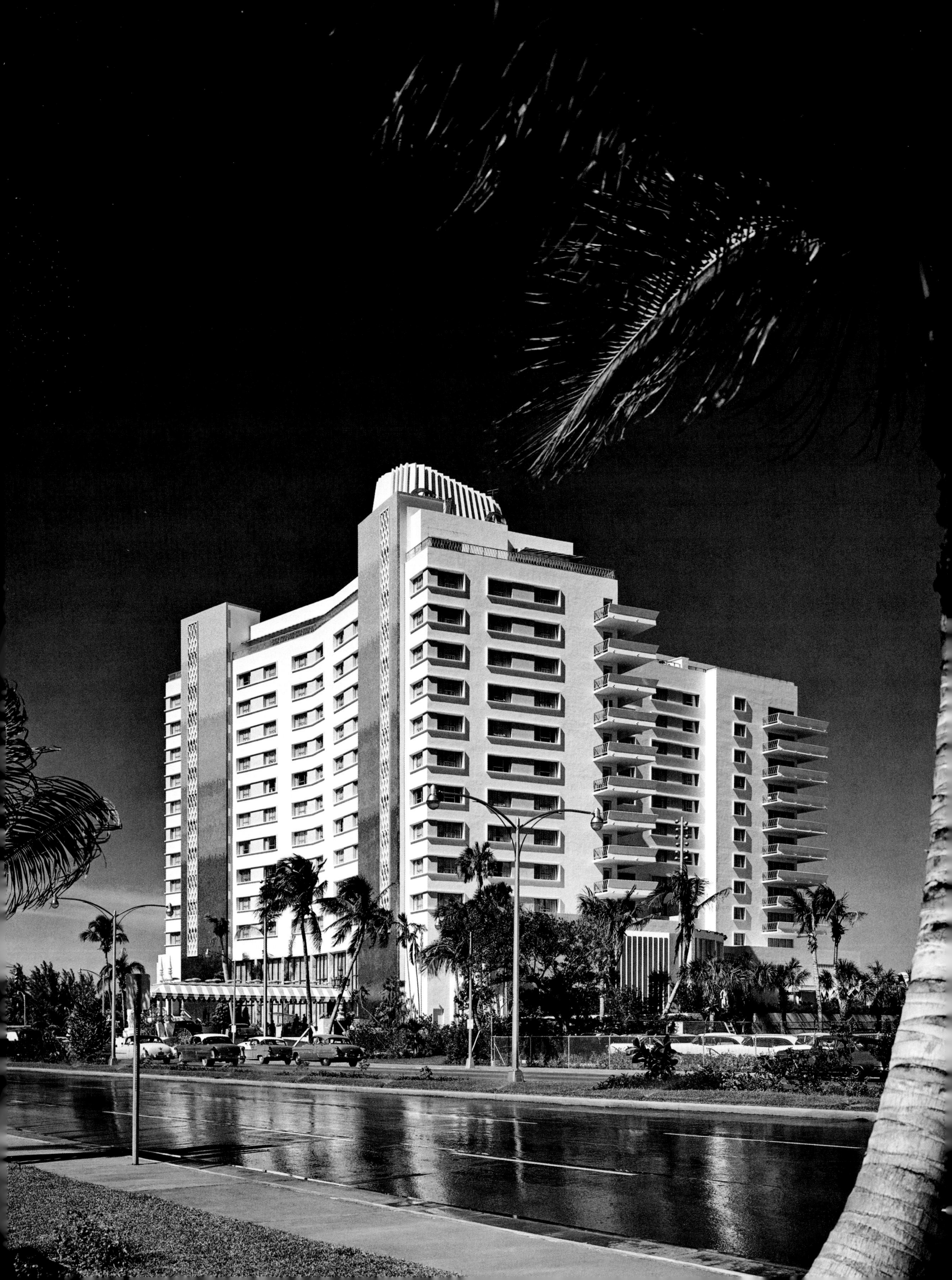

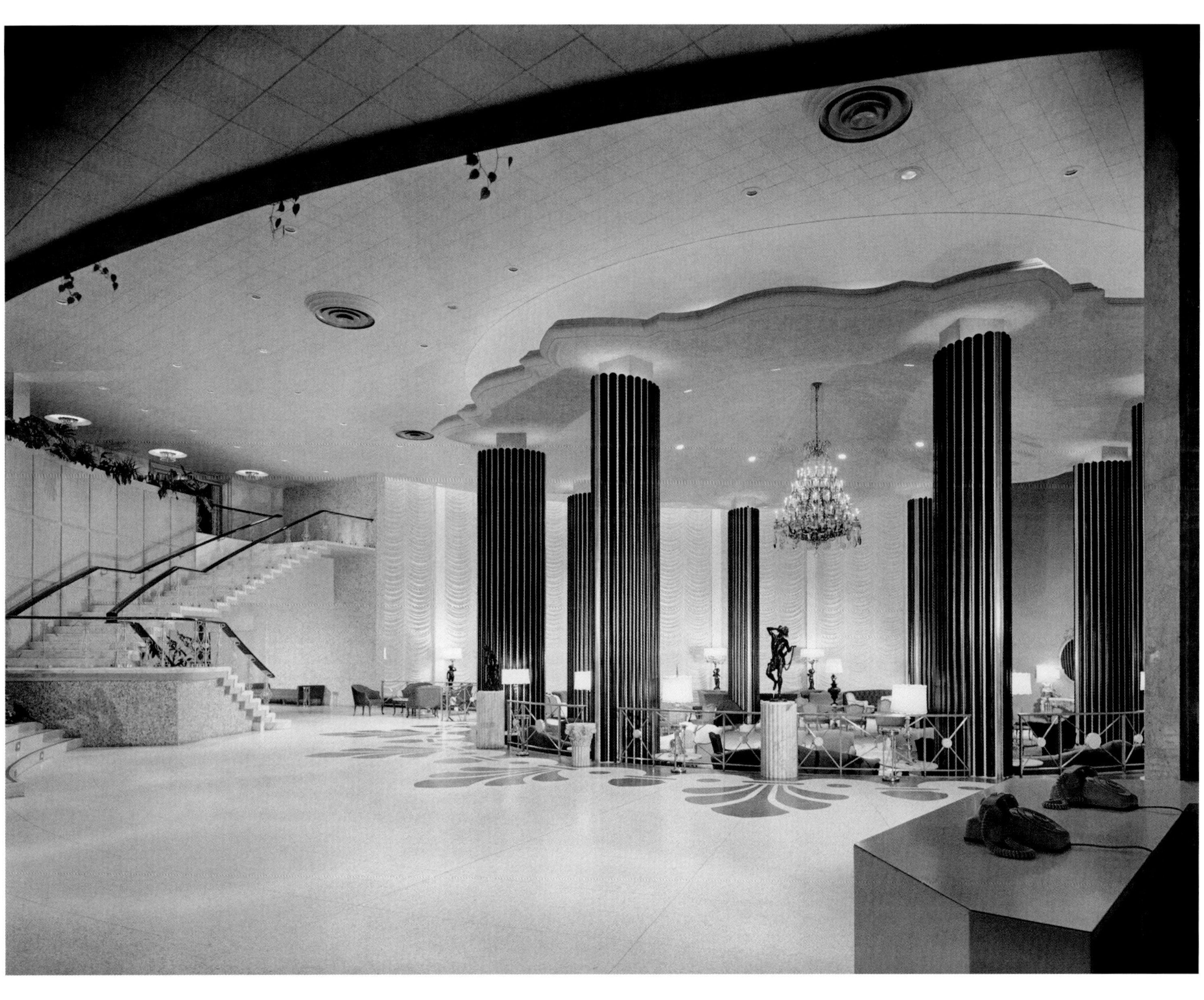

Eden Roc Hotel, Miami Beach.
Morris Lapidus, 1956.

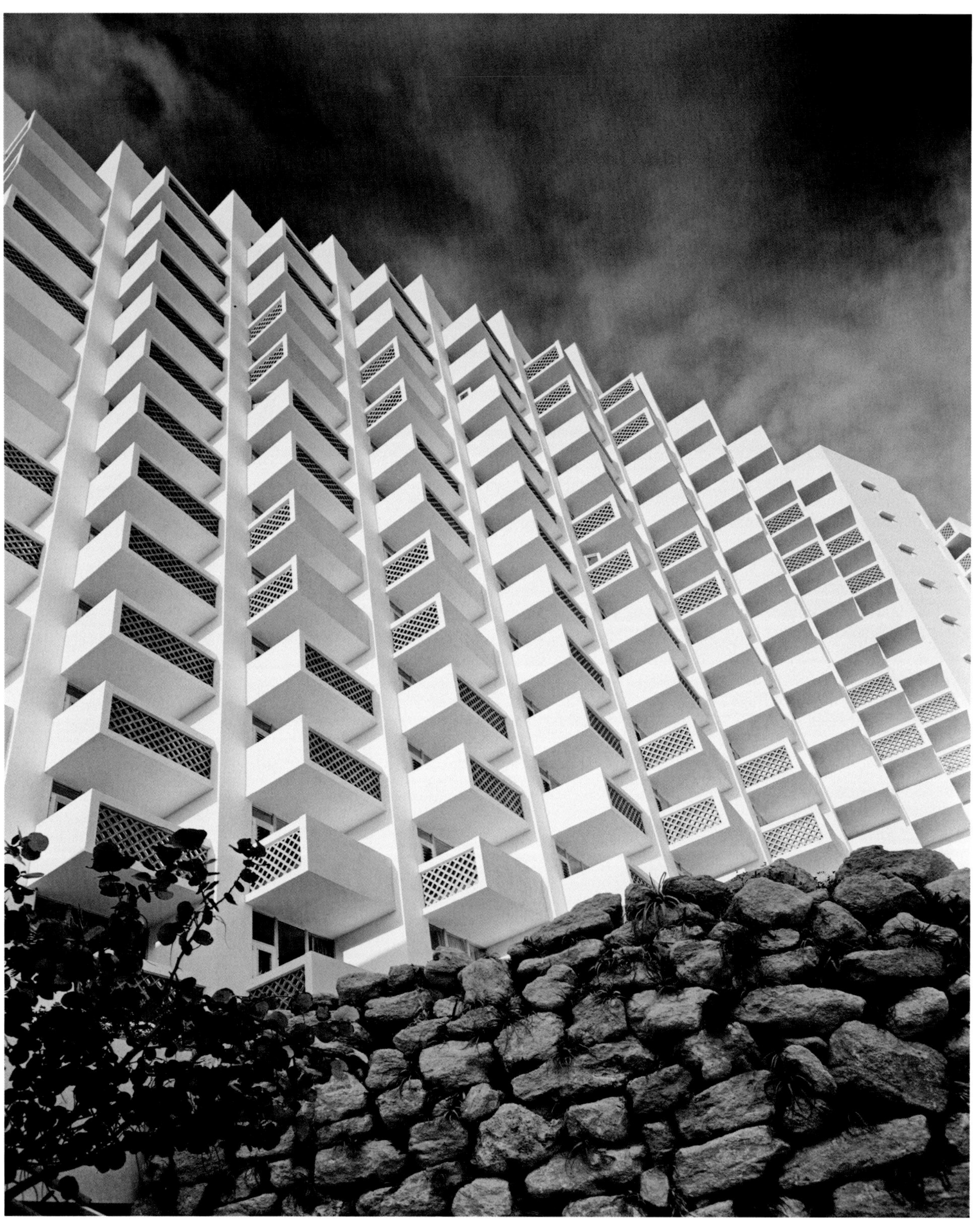

Americana Hotel, Miami Beach.
Morris Lapidus, 1957.

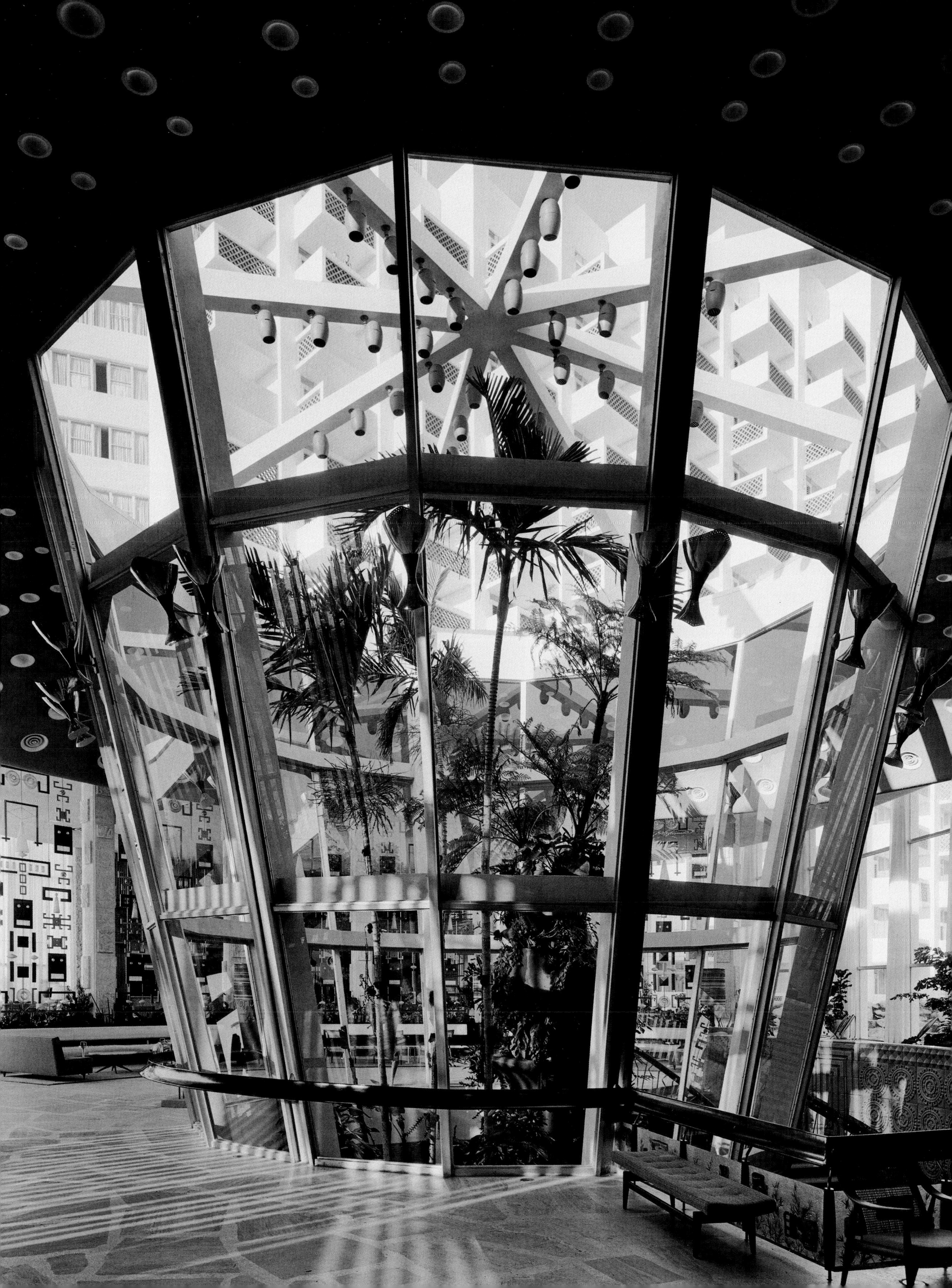

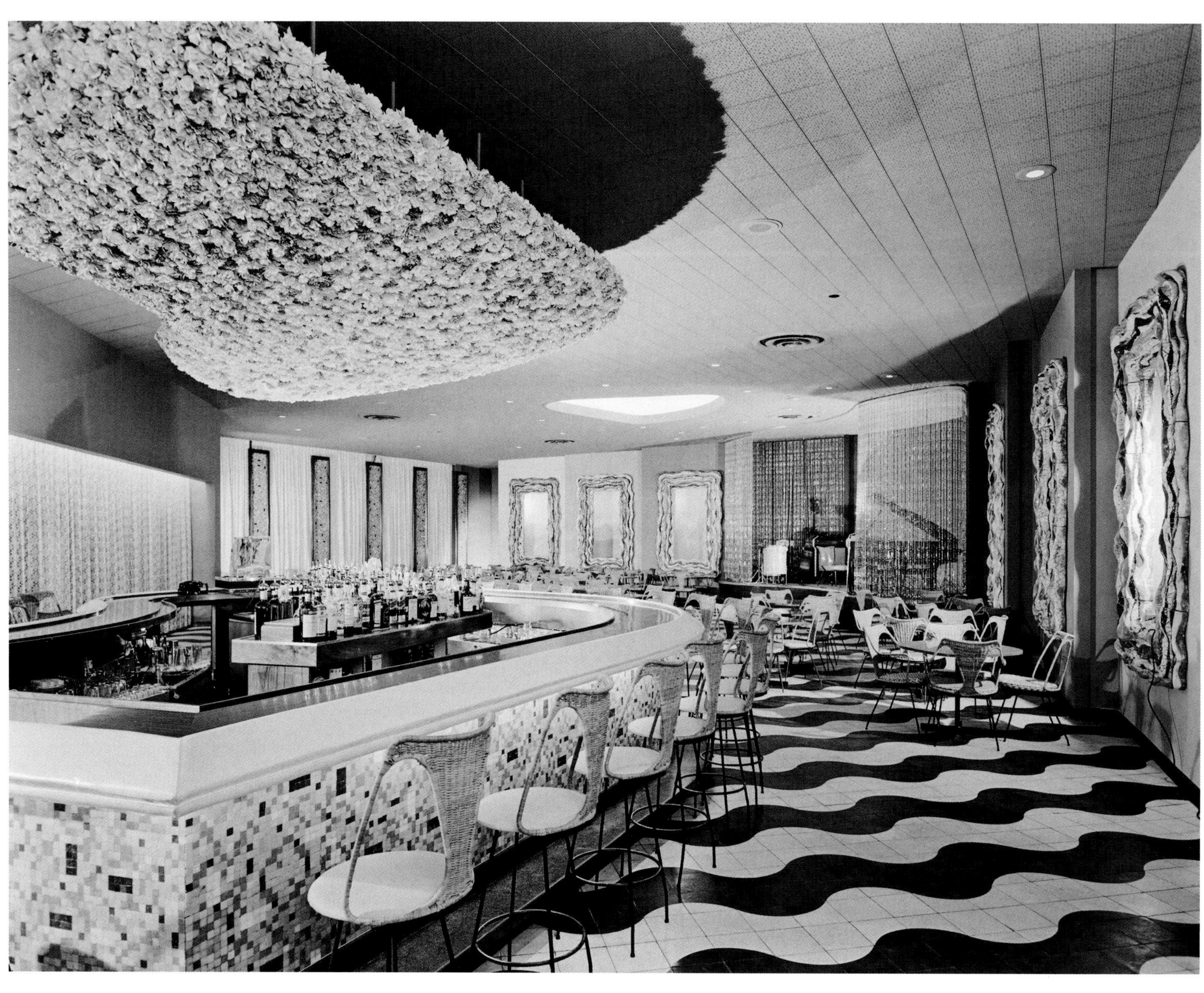

Americana Hotel, Miami Beach.
Morris Lapidus, 1957.

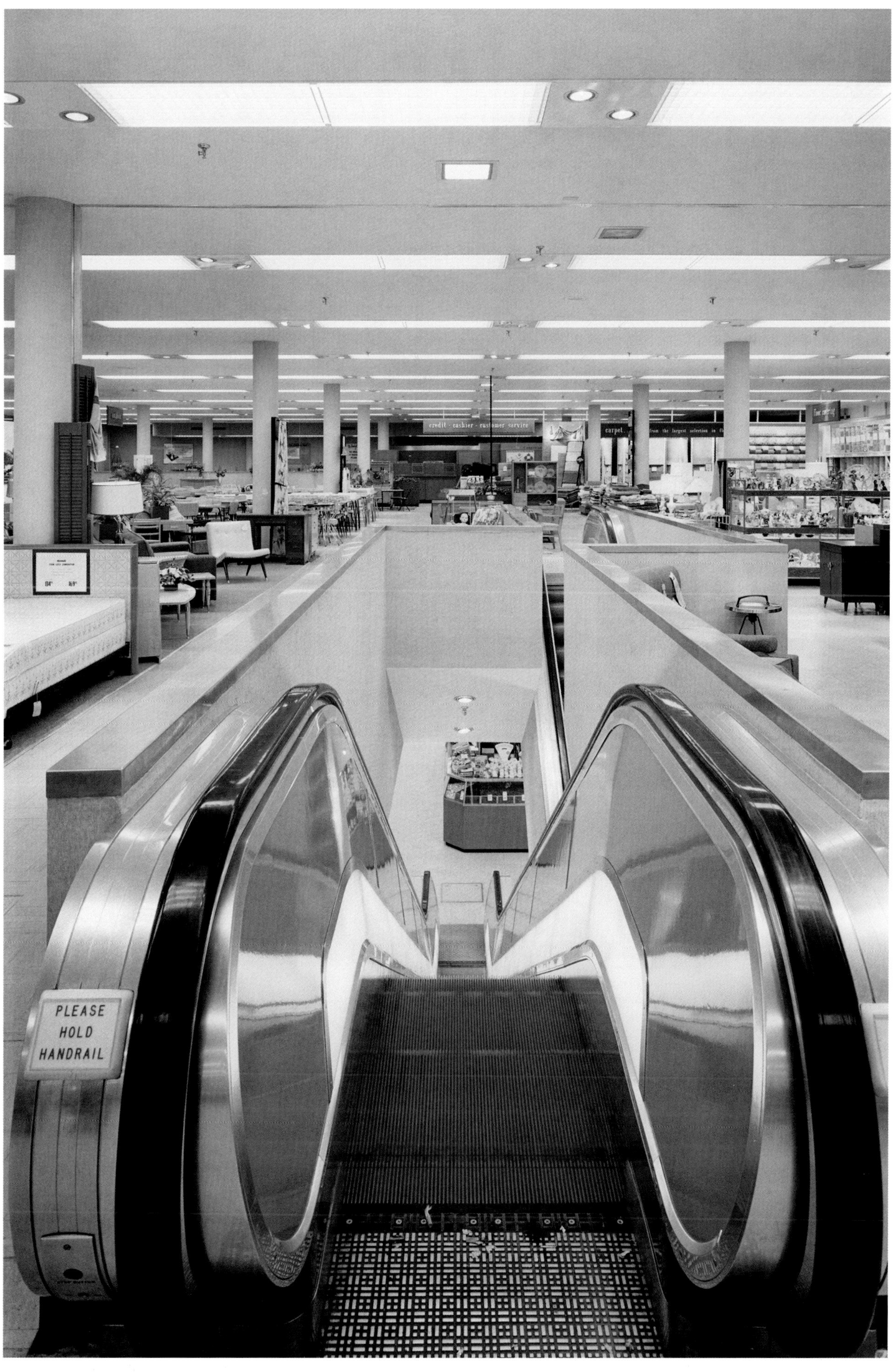

Sears Roebuck & Company, West Palm Beach.
Weed, Russell, Johnson, 1957.

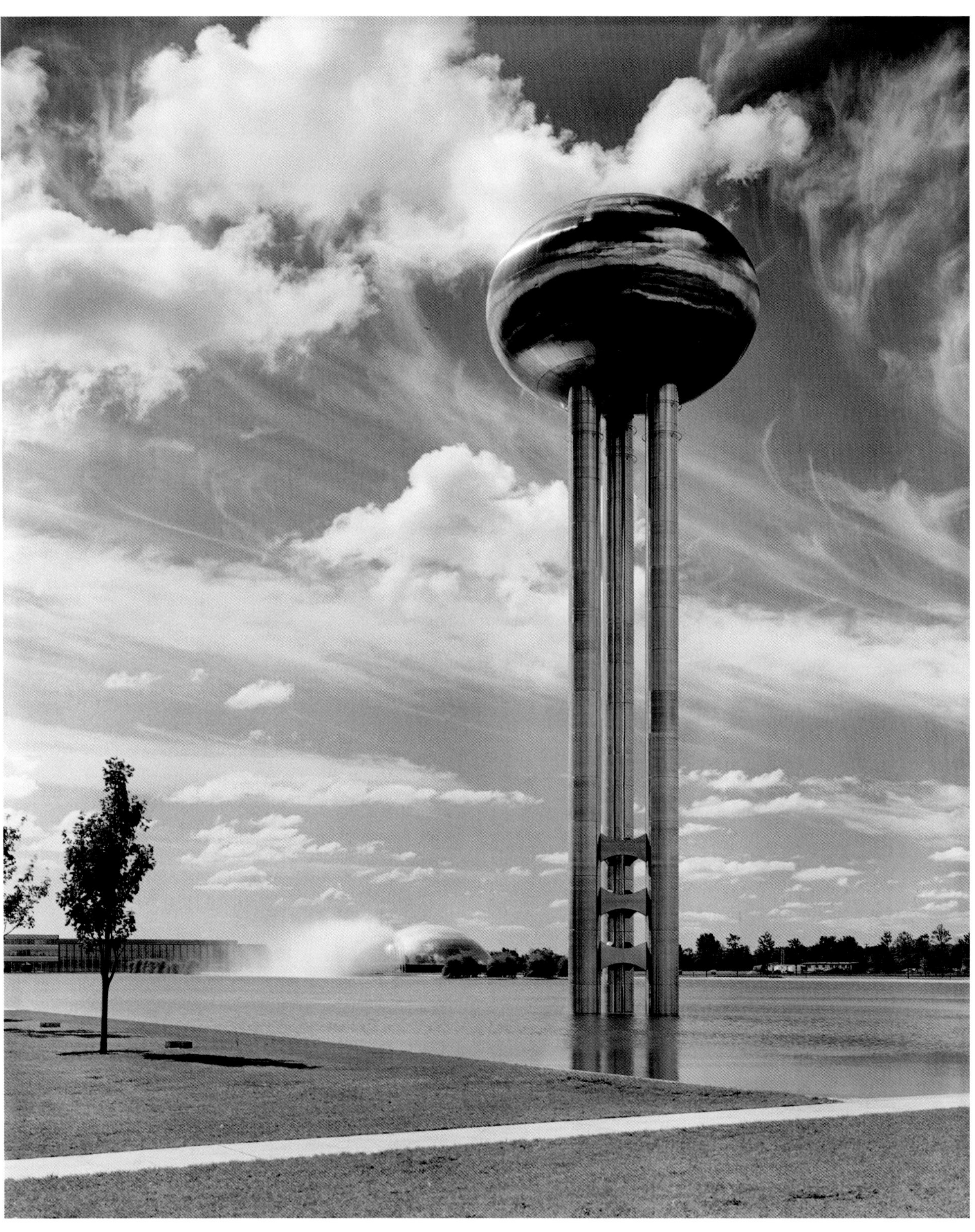

General Motors Technical Center,
Warren Michigan. Eero Saarinen, 1955.

The Family, Isamu Noguchi, sculptor.
Connecticut General Life Insurance Co., Bloomfield,
Connecticut. Skidmore, Owings & Merrill, 1957.

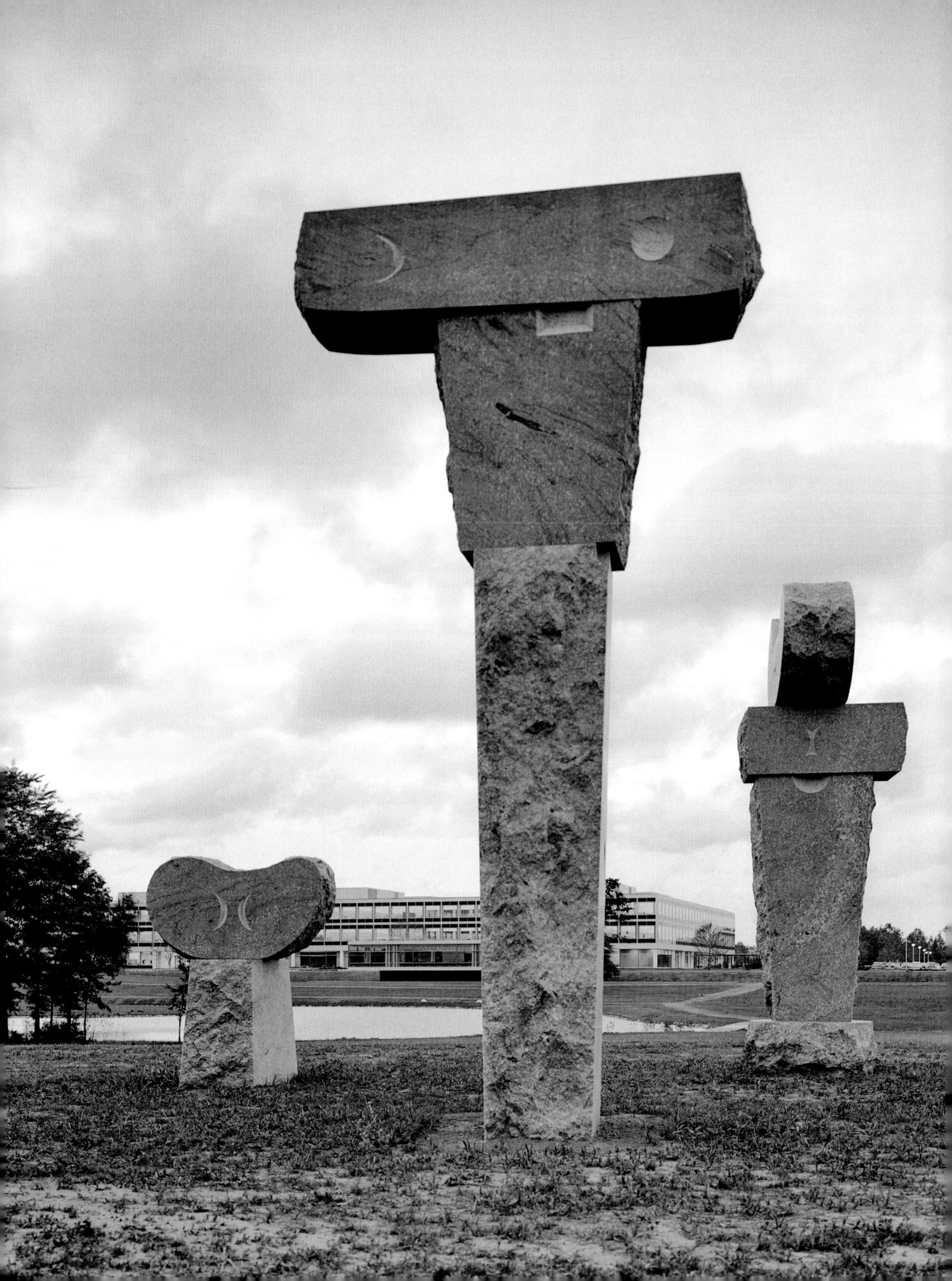

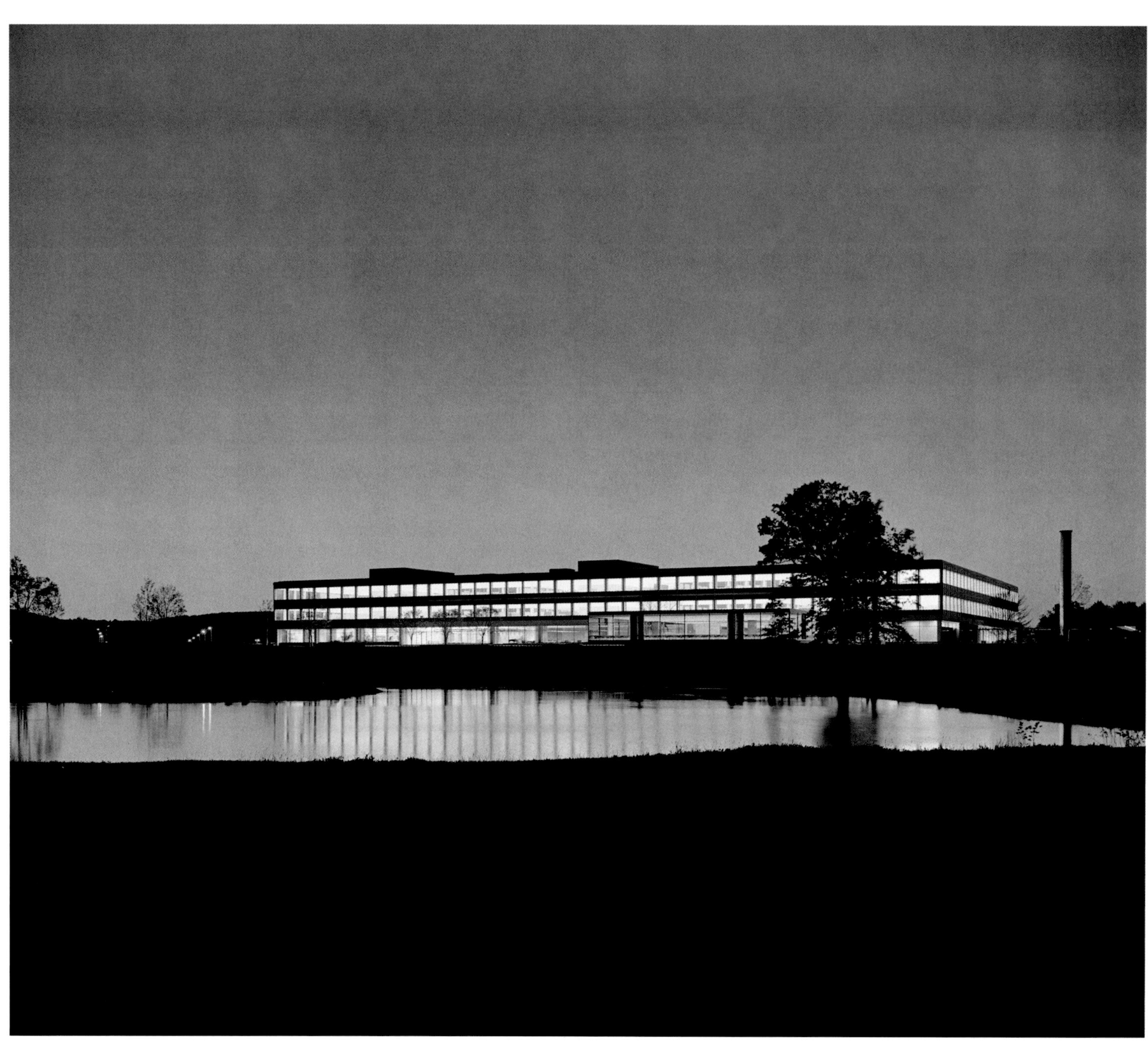

Connecticut General Life Insurance Co., Bloomfield, Connecticut. Skidmore, Owings & Merrill, 1957.

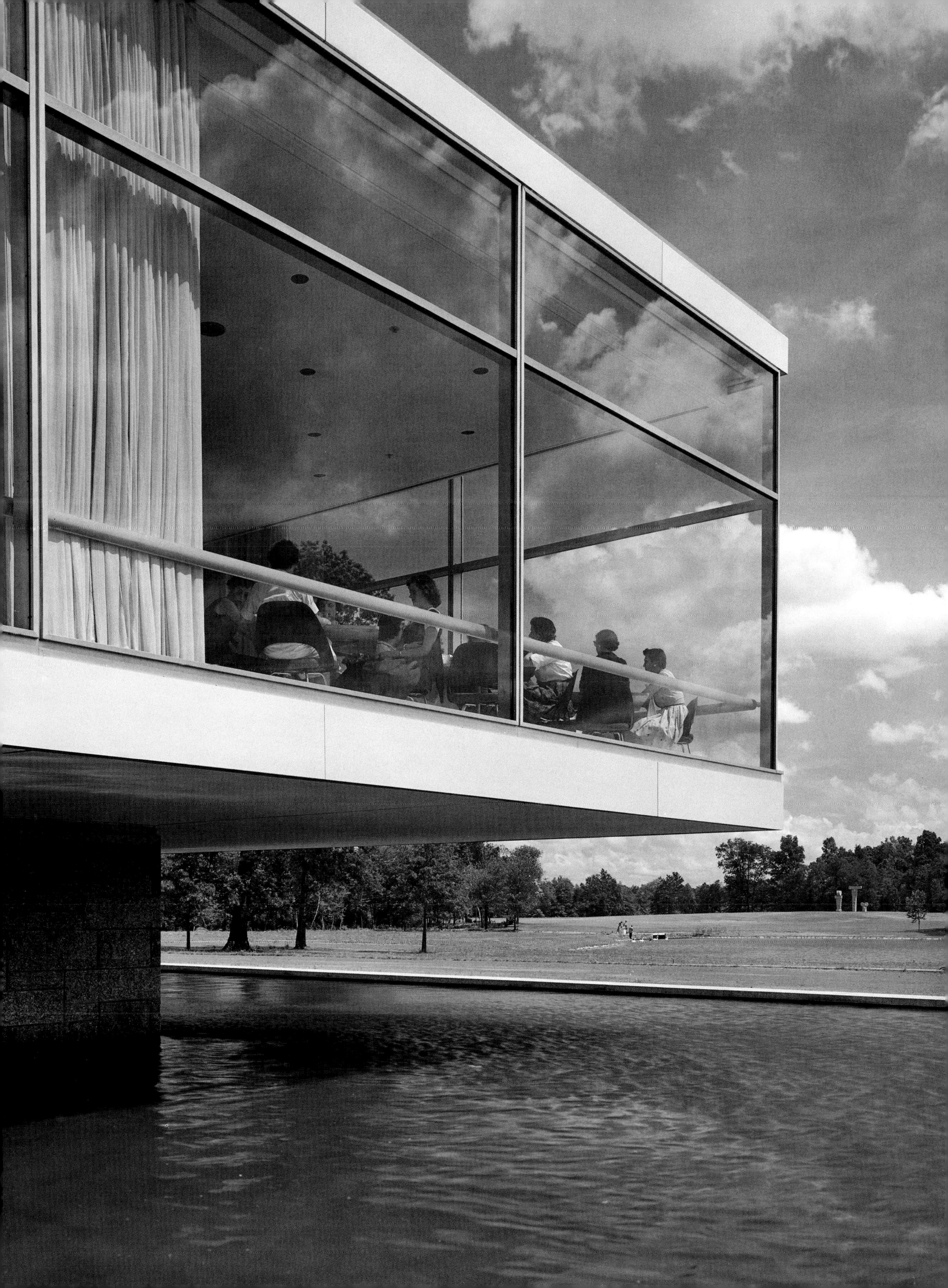

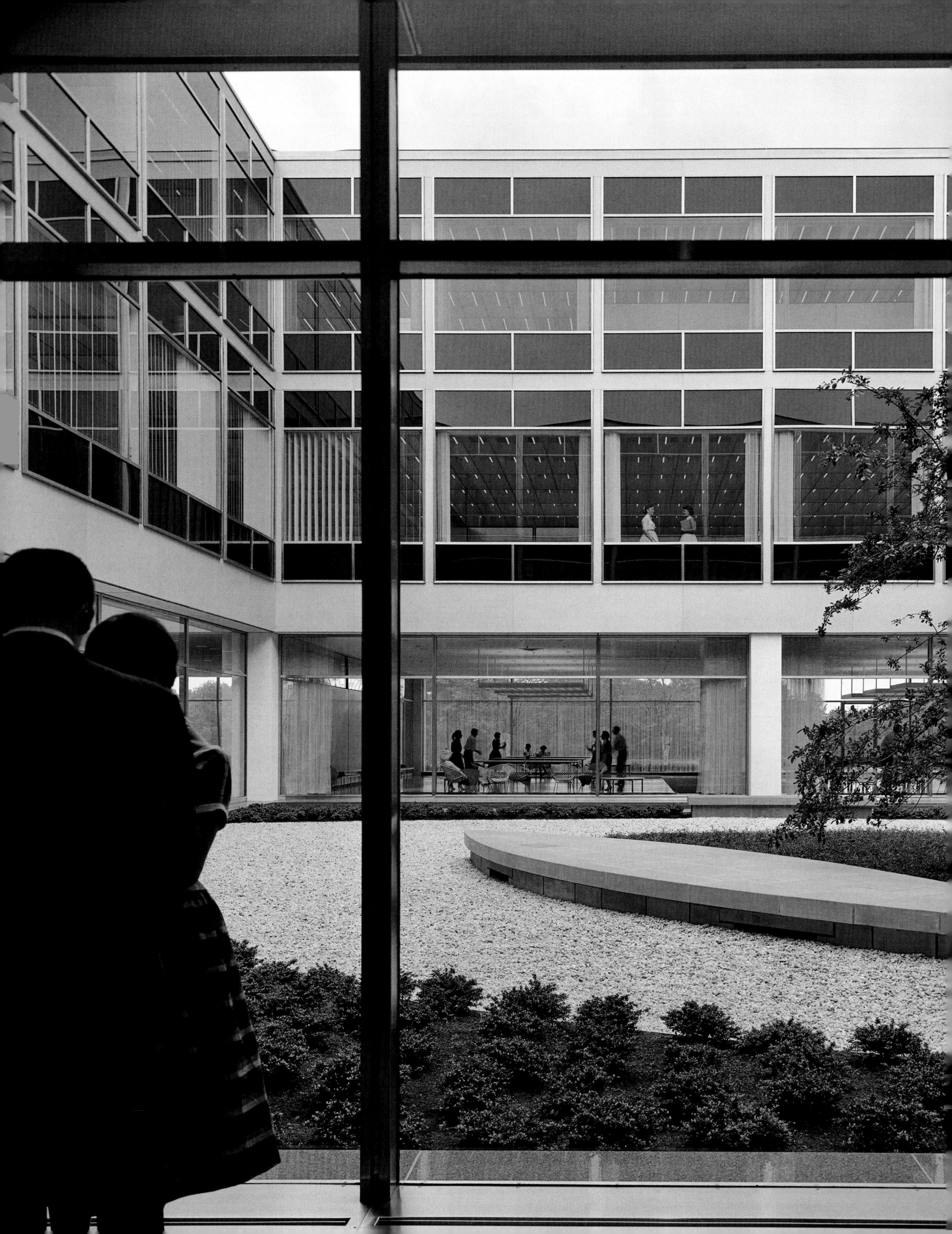

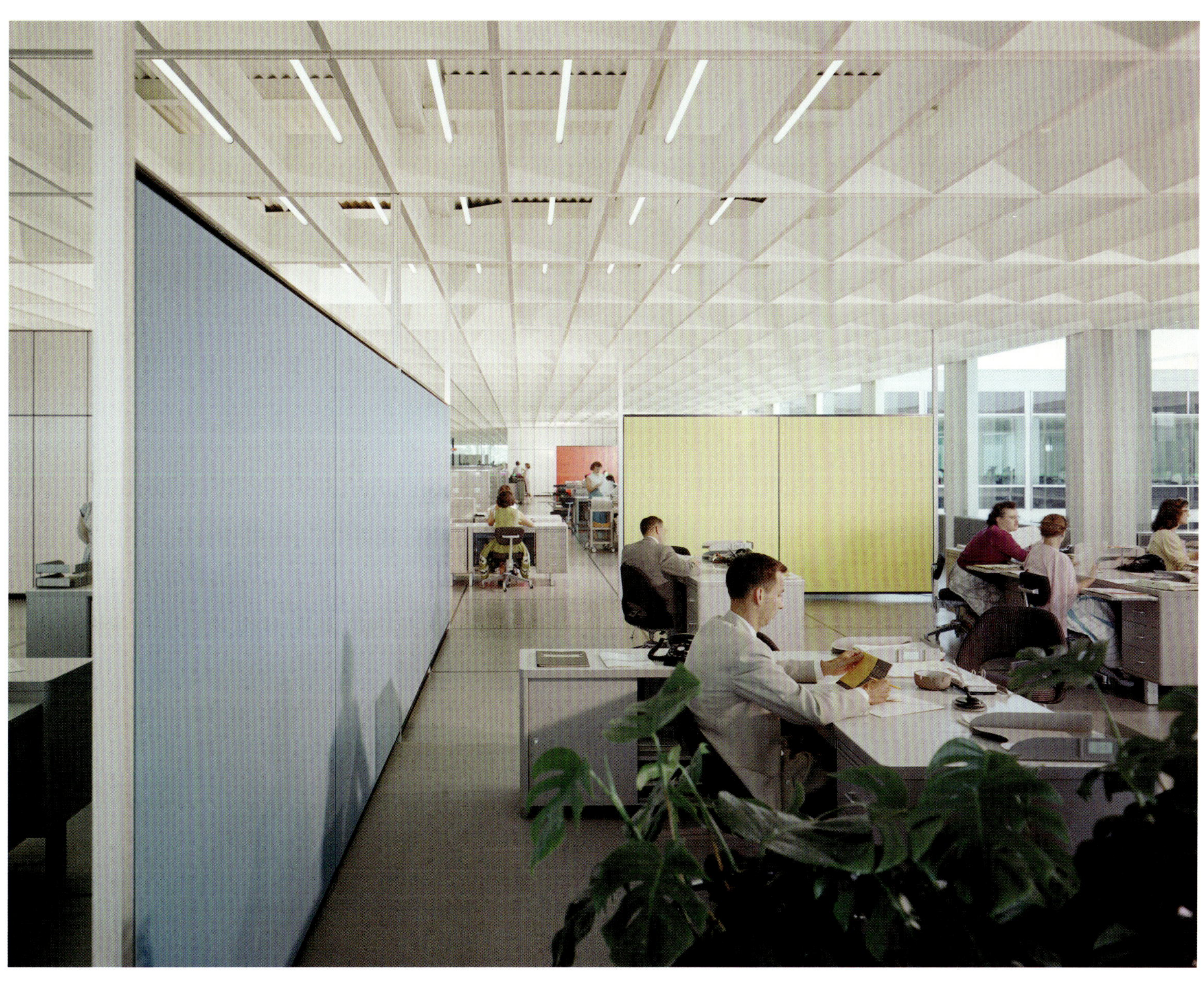

Connecticut General Life Insurance Co., Bloomfield, Connecticut. Skidmore, Owings & Merrill, 1957.

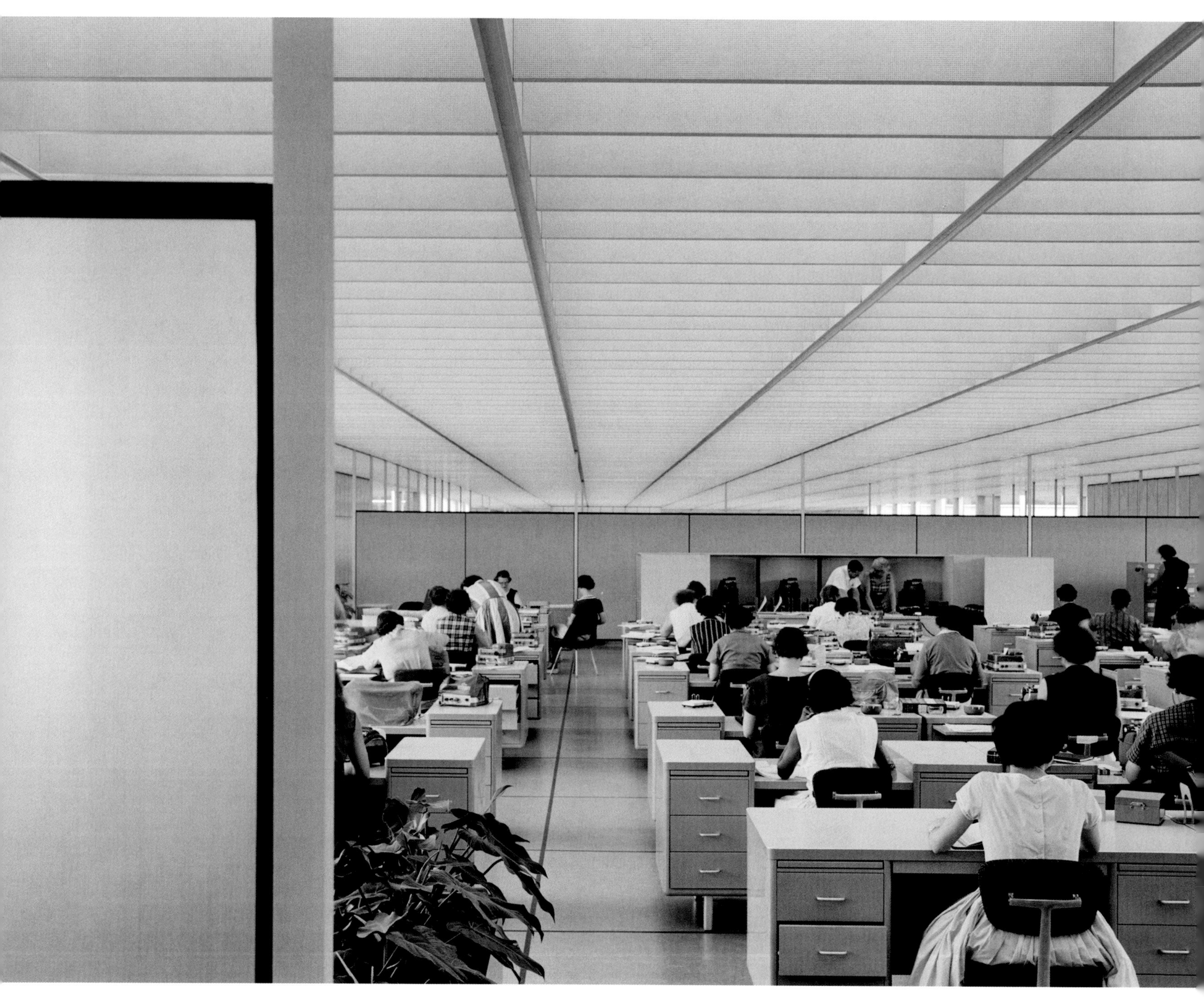

Above and opposite
Connecticut General Life Insurance Co., Bloomfield, Connecticut. Skidmore, Owings & Merrill, 1957.

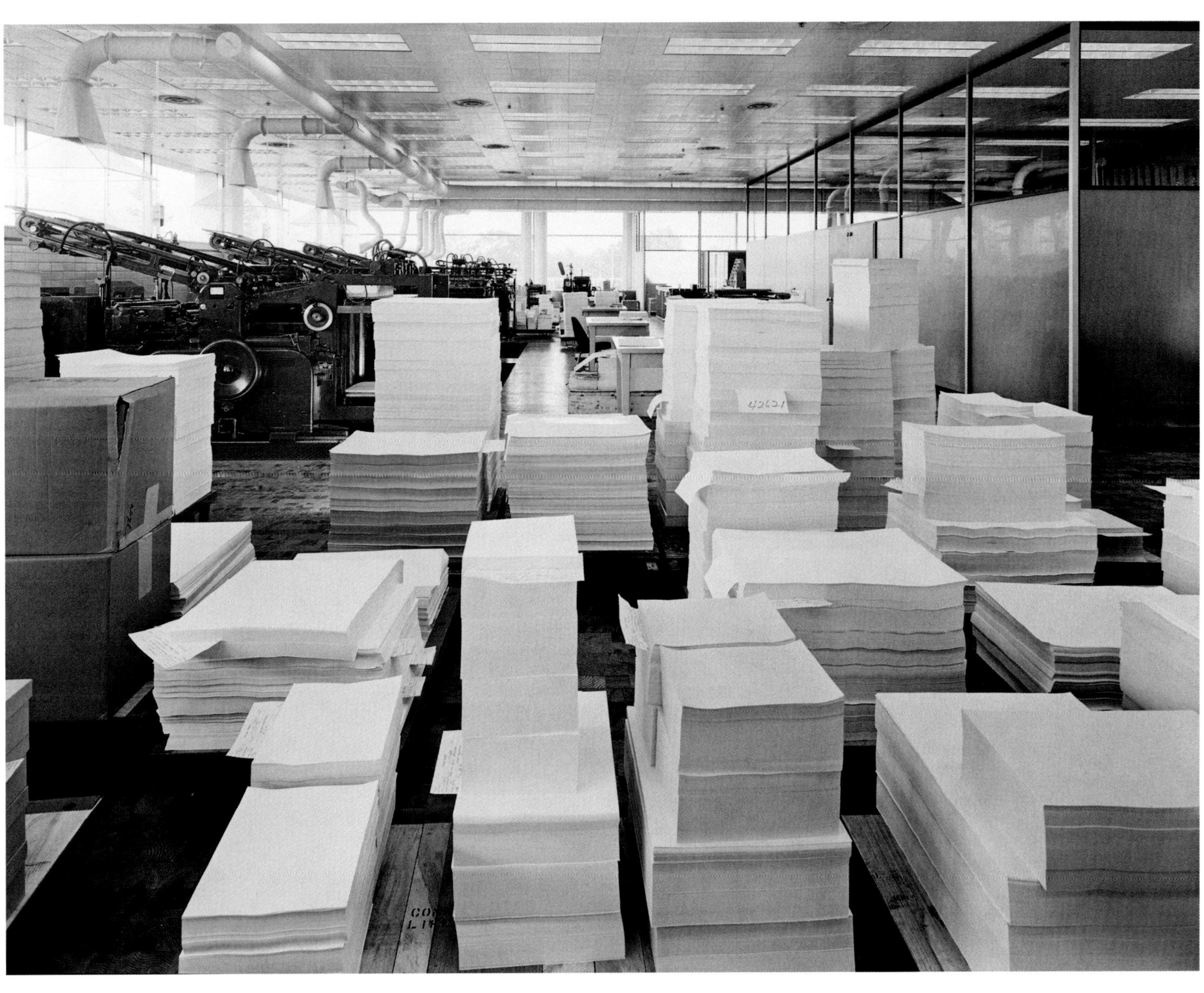

Right and overleaf
Seagram Building, New York.
Mies van der Rohe with Philip Johnson, 1958.

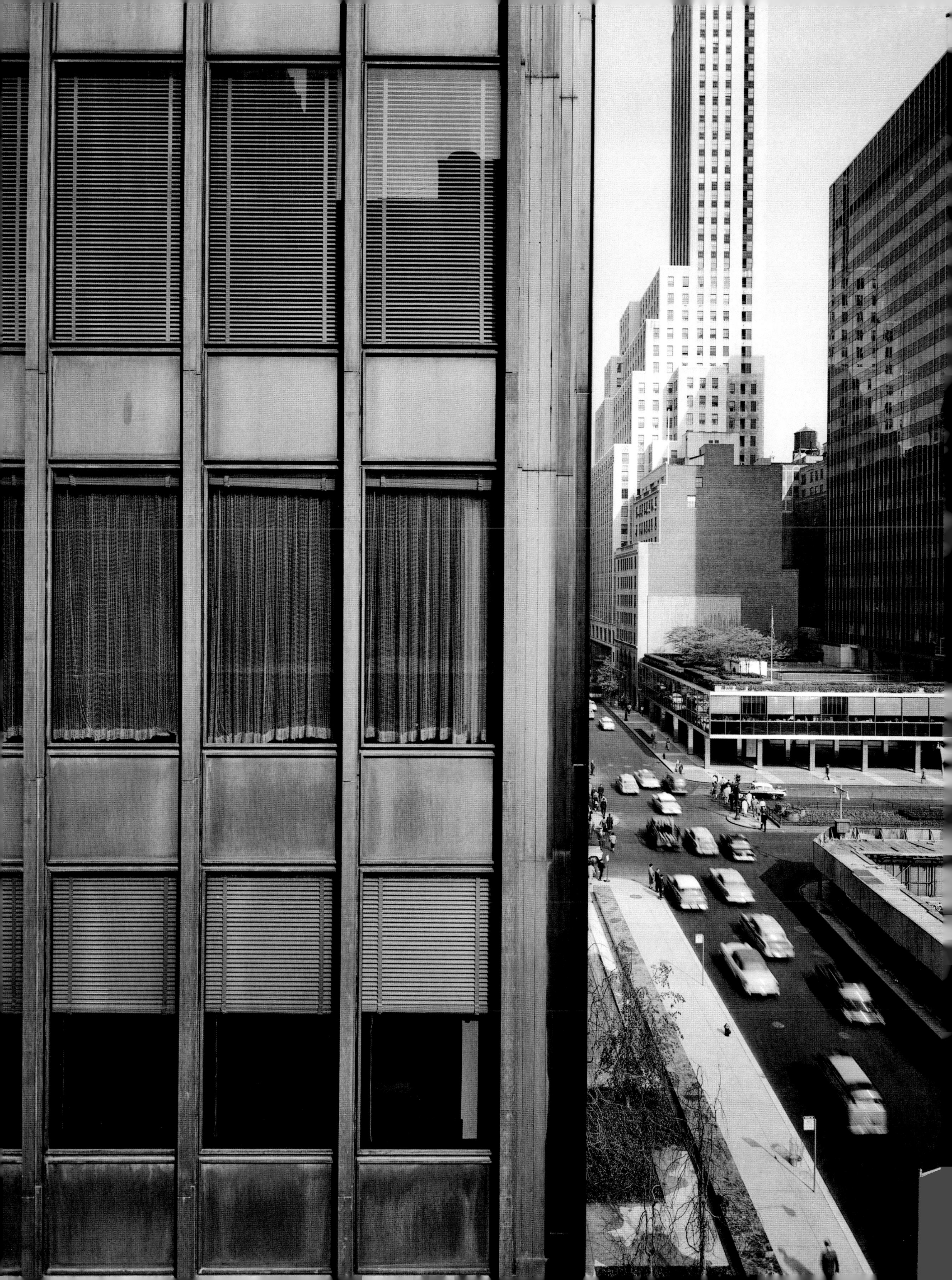

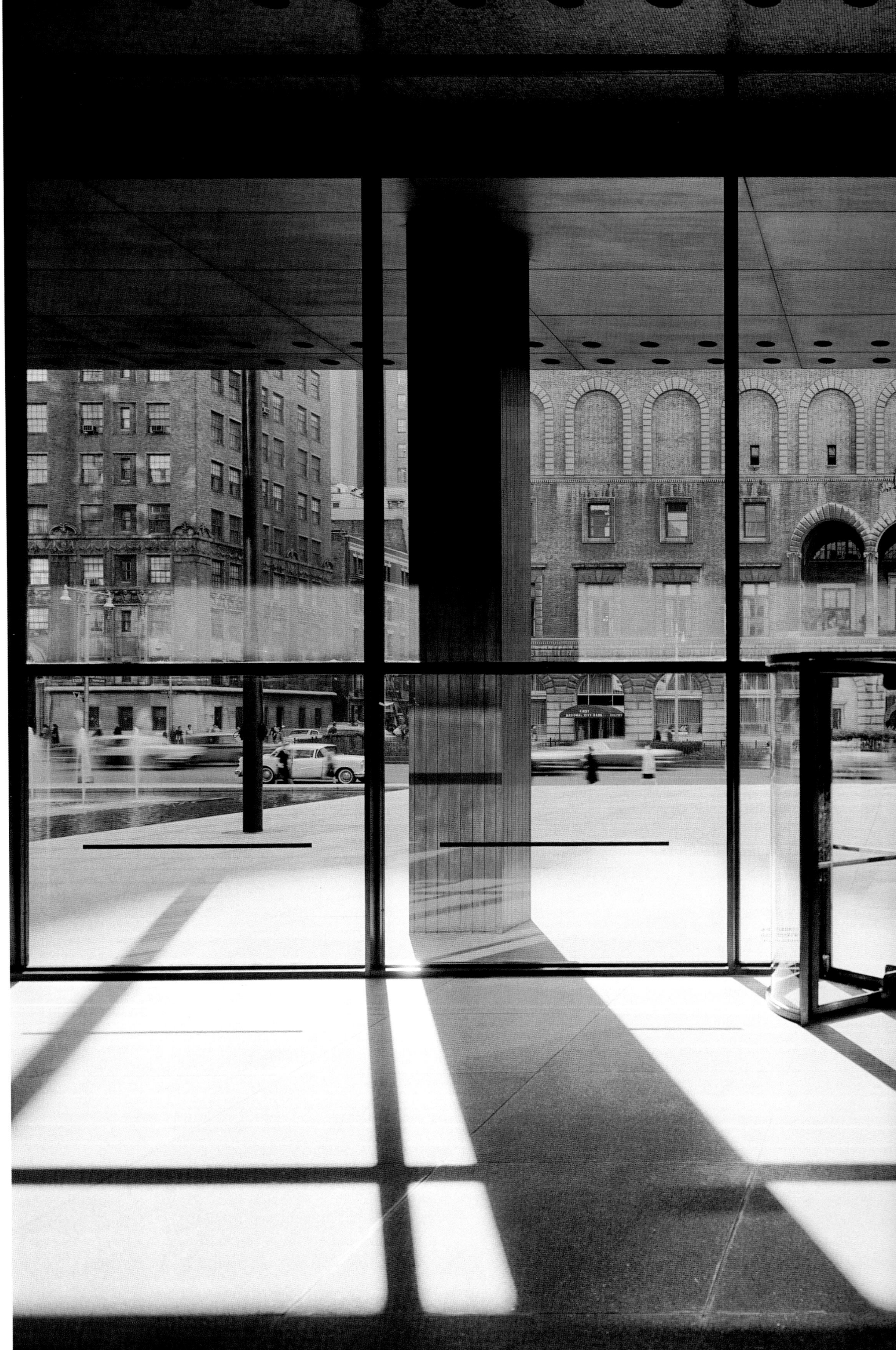
FIRST
NATIONAL CITY BANK

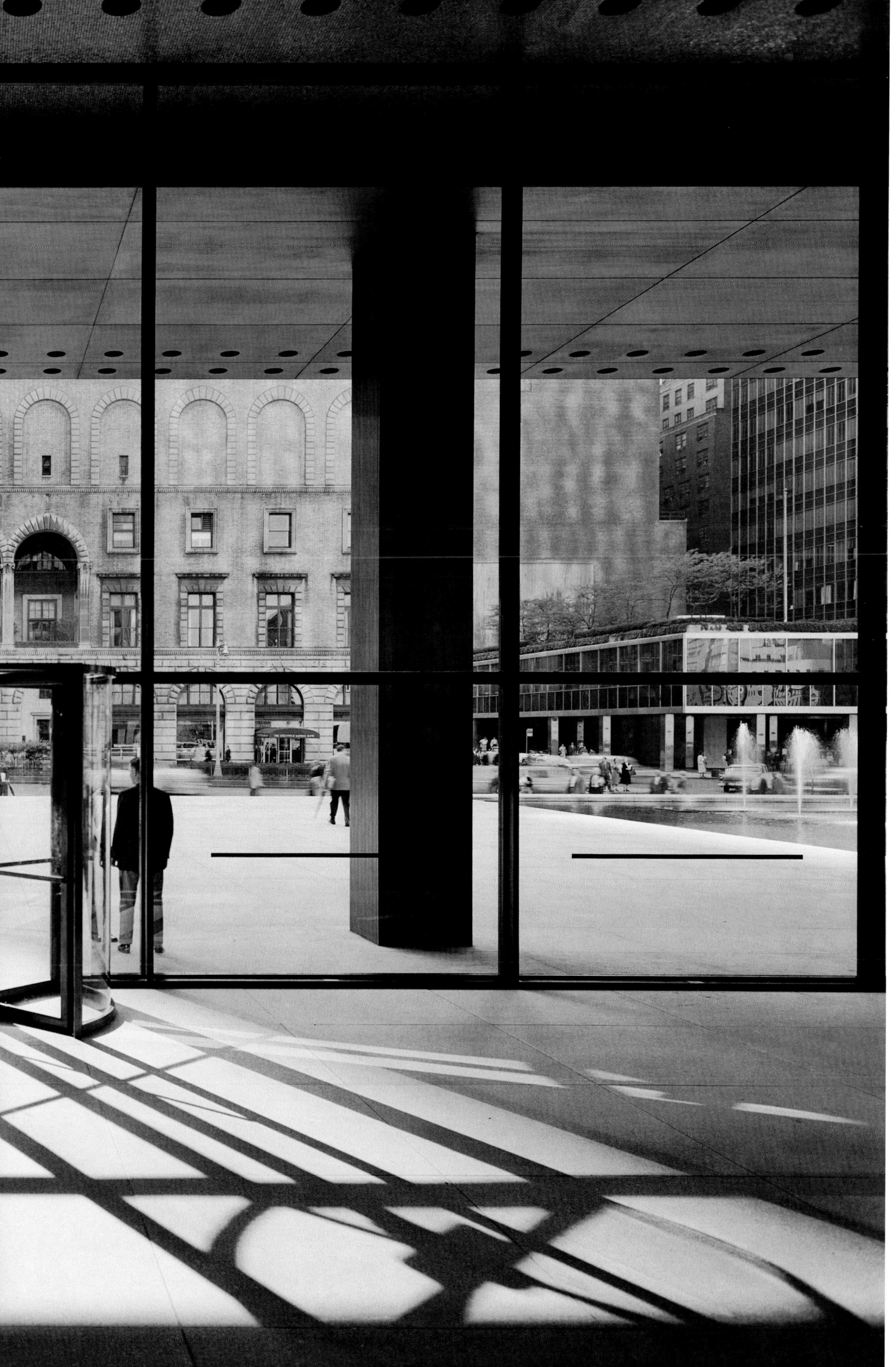

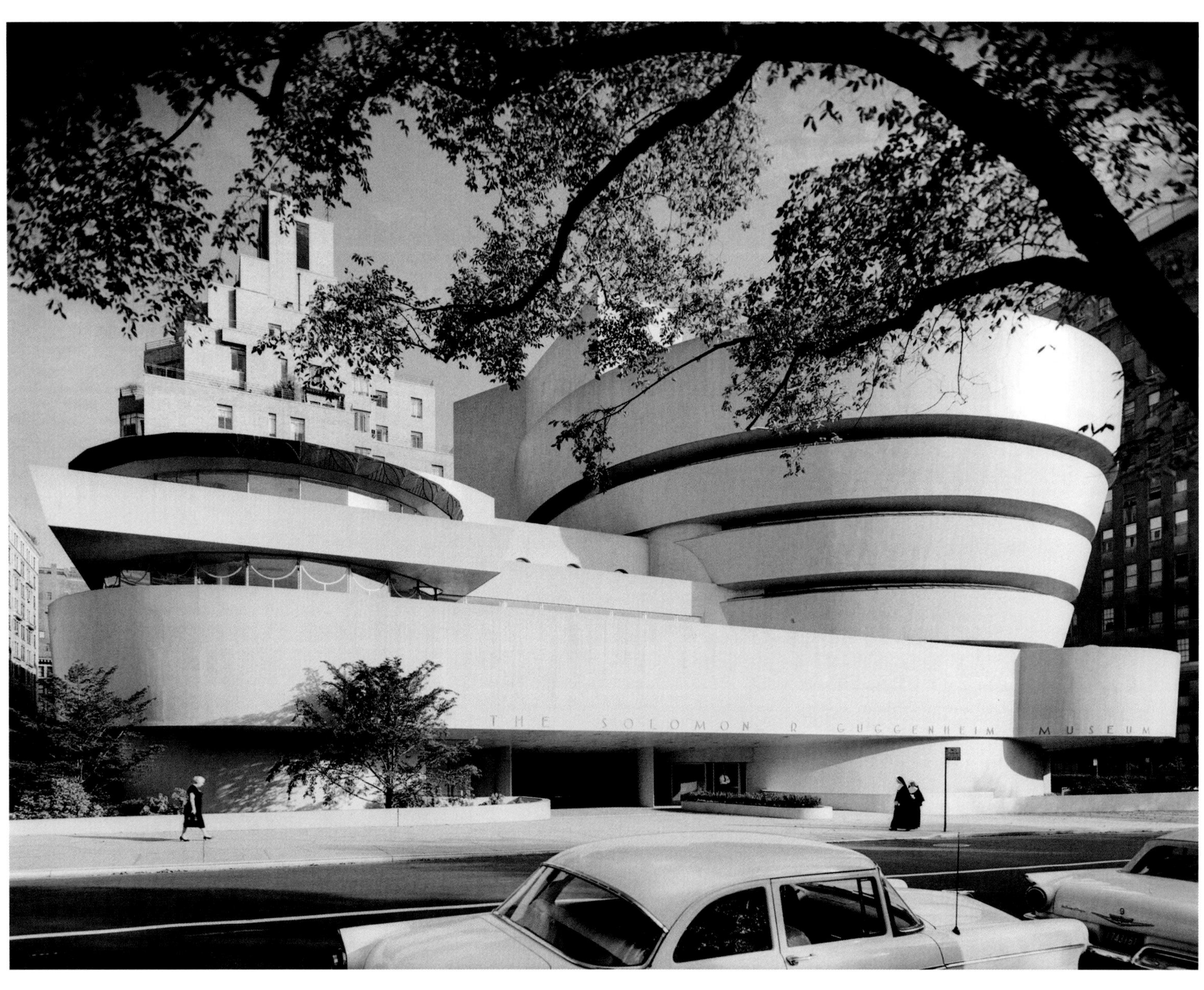

Guggenheim Museum, New York.
Frank Lloyd Wright, 1959.

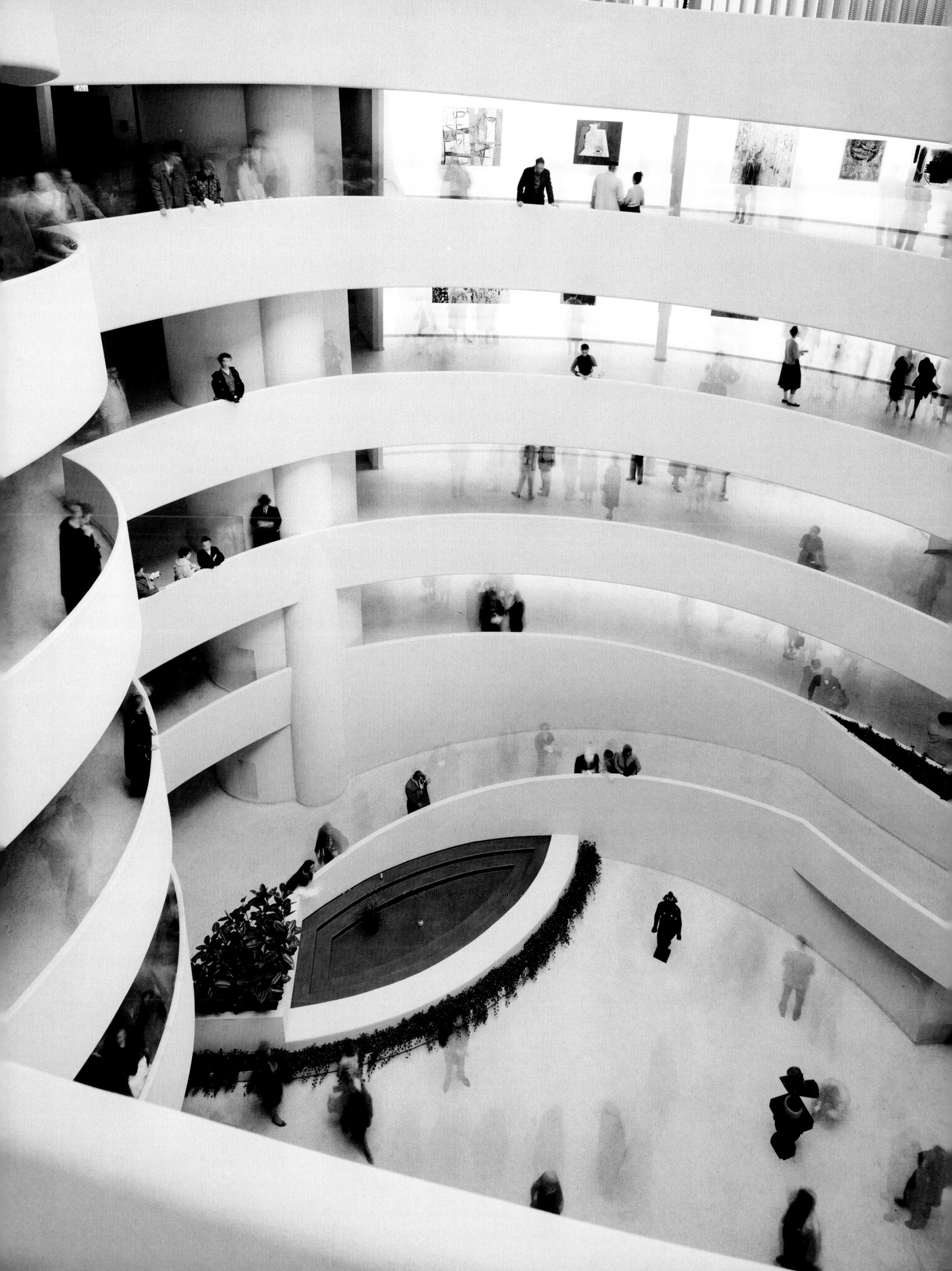

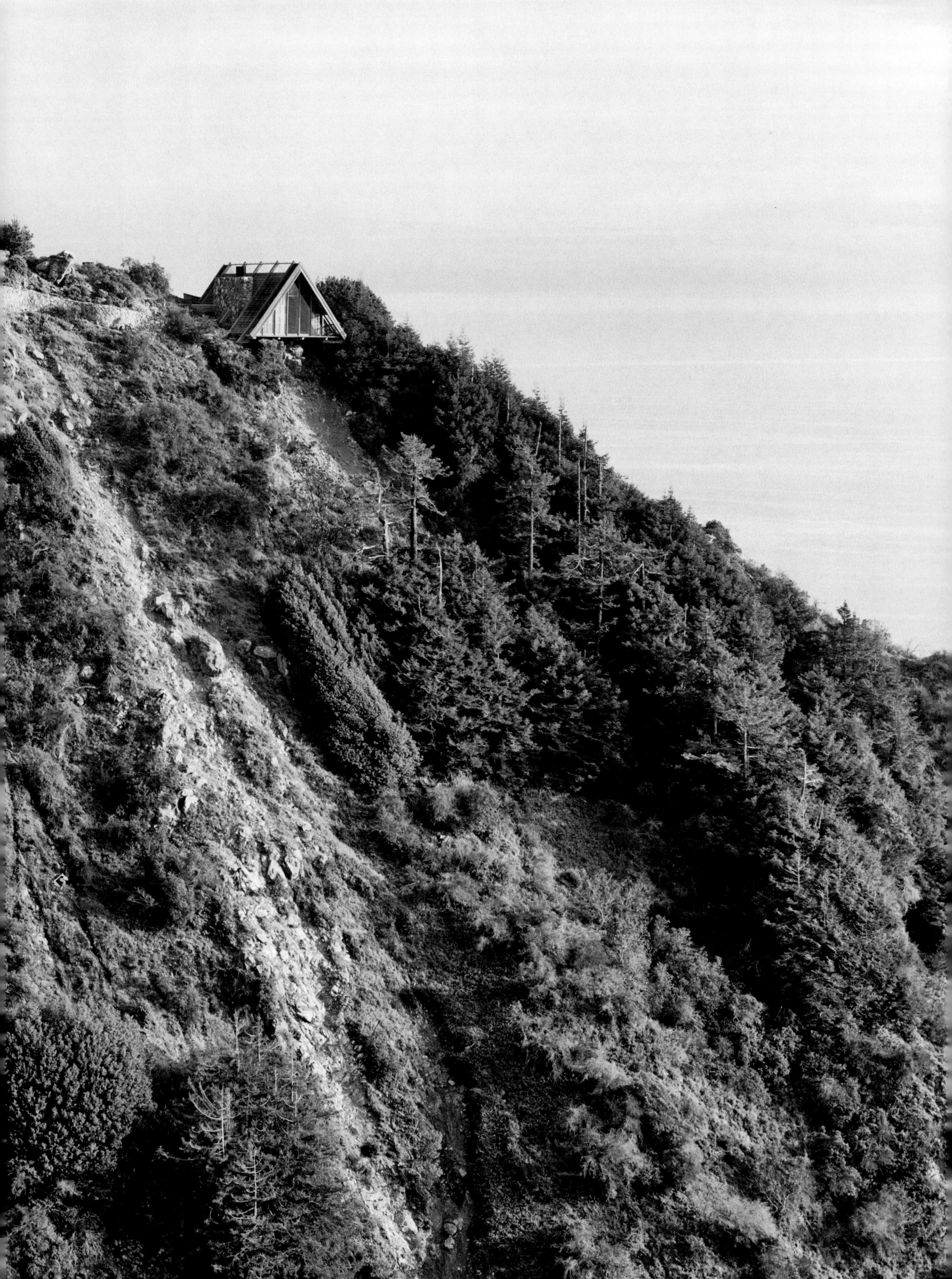

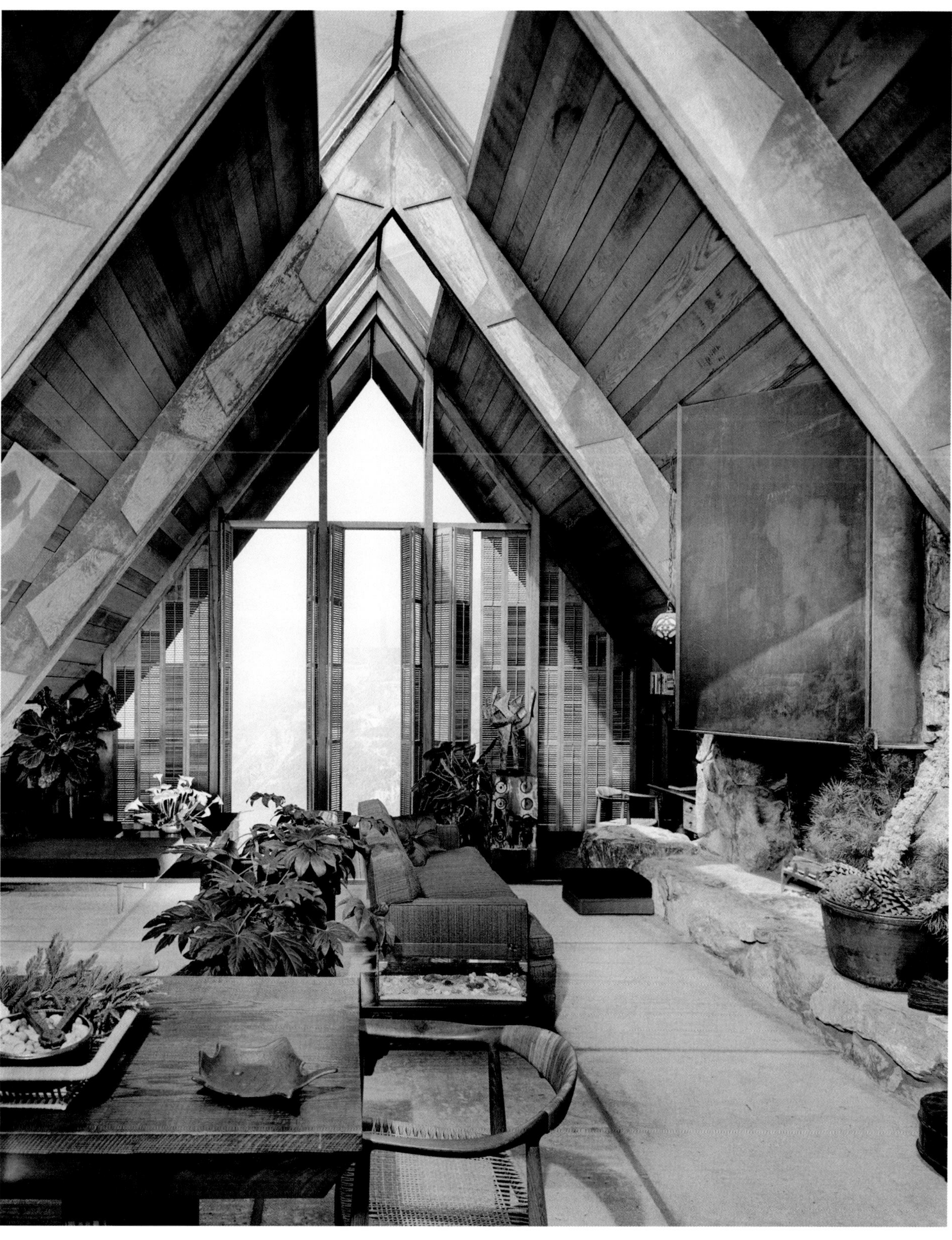

Nat Owings House, Carmel, California.
Nat Owings, 1960.

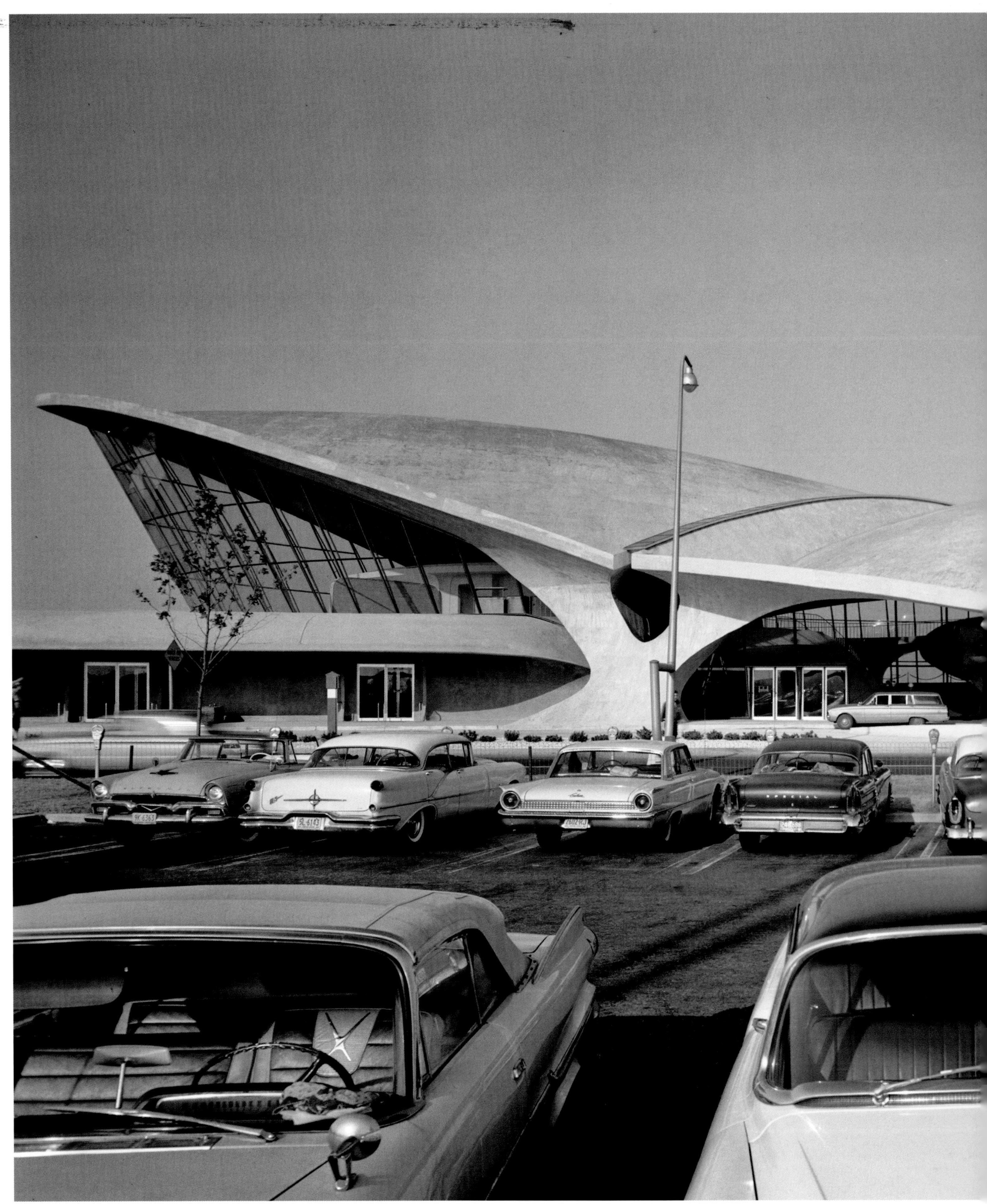

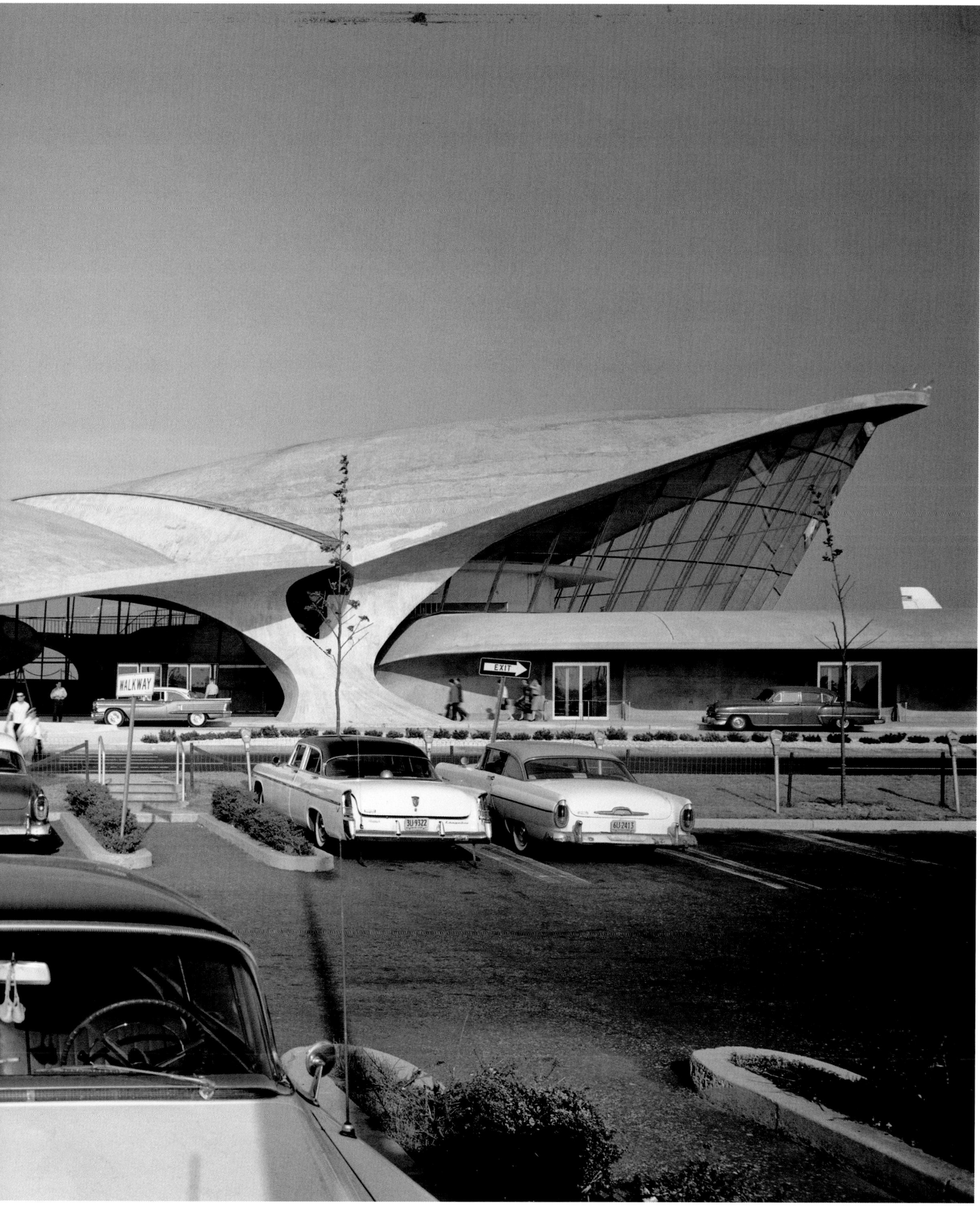

TWA Terminal at Idlewild (JFK) Airport,
Queens, New York. Eero Saarinen, 1962.

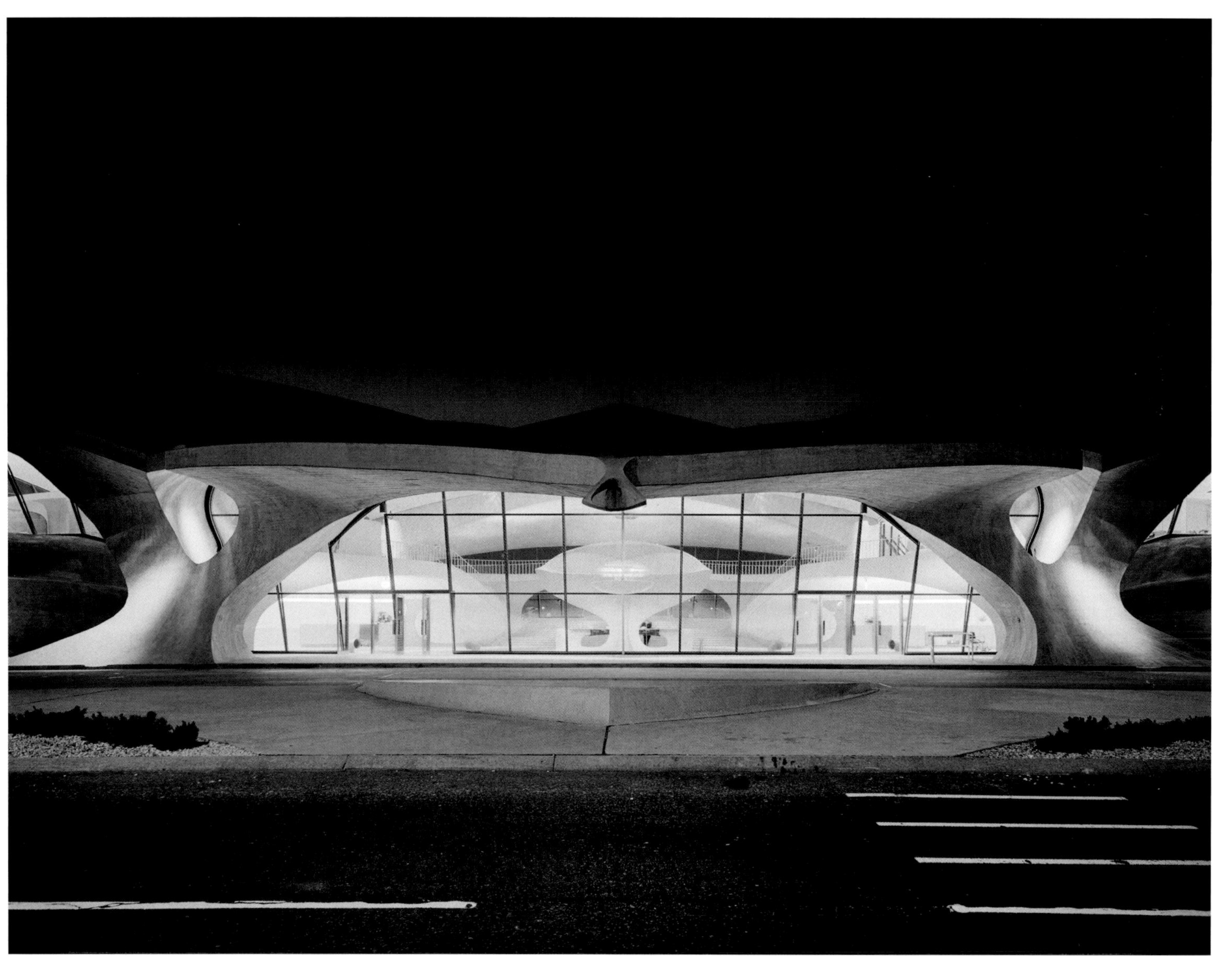

TWA Terminal at Idlewild (JFK) Airport,
Queens, New York. Eero Saarinen, 1962.

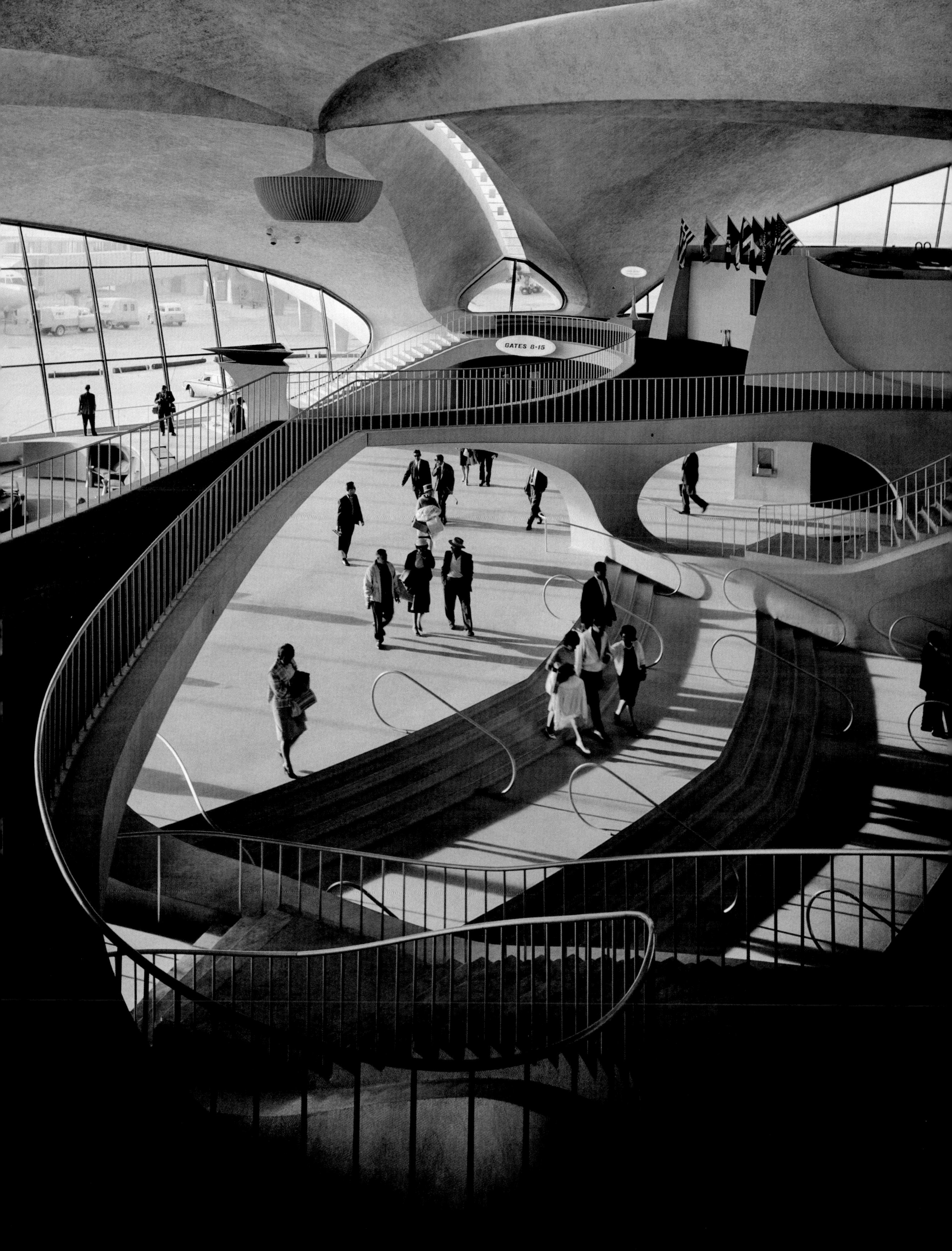
GATES 8-15

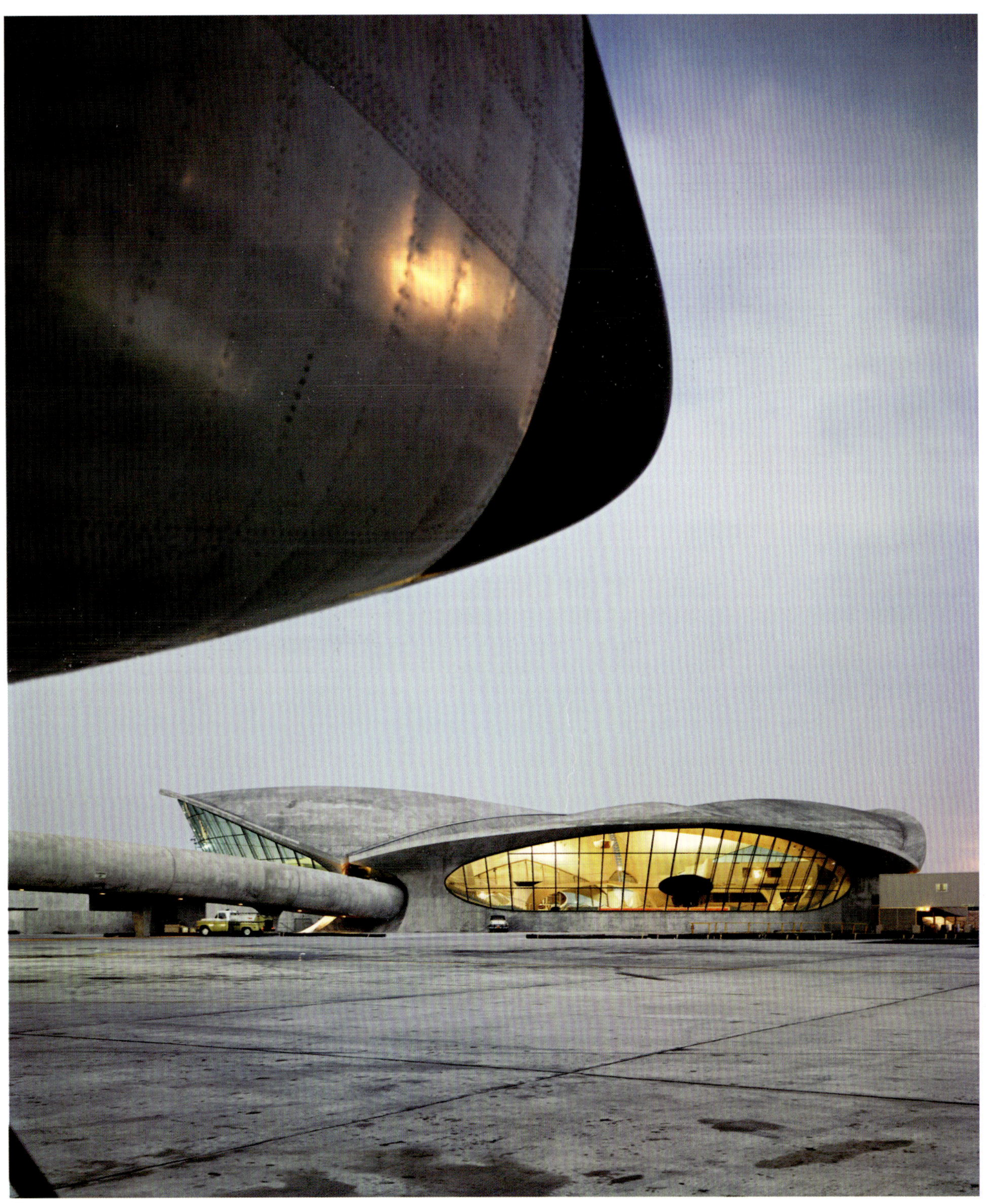

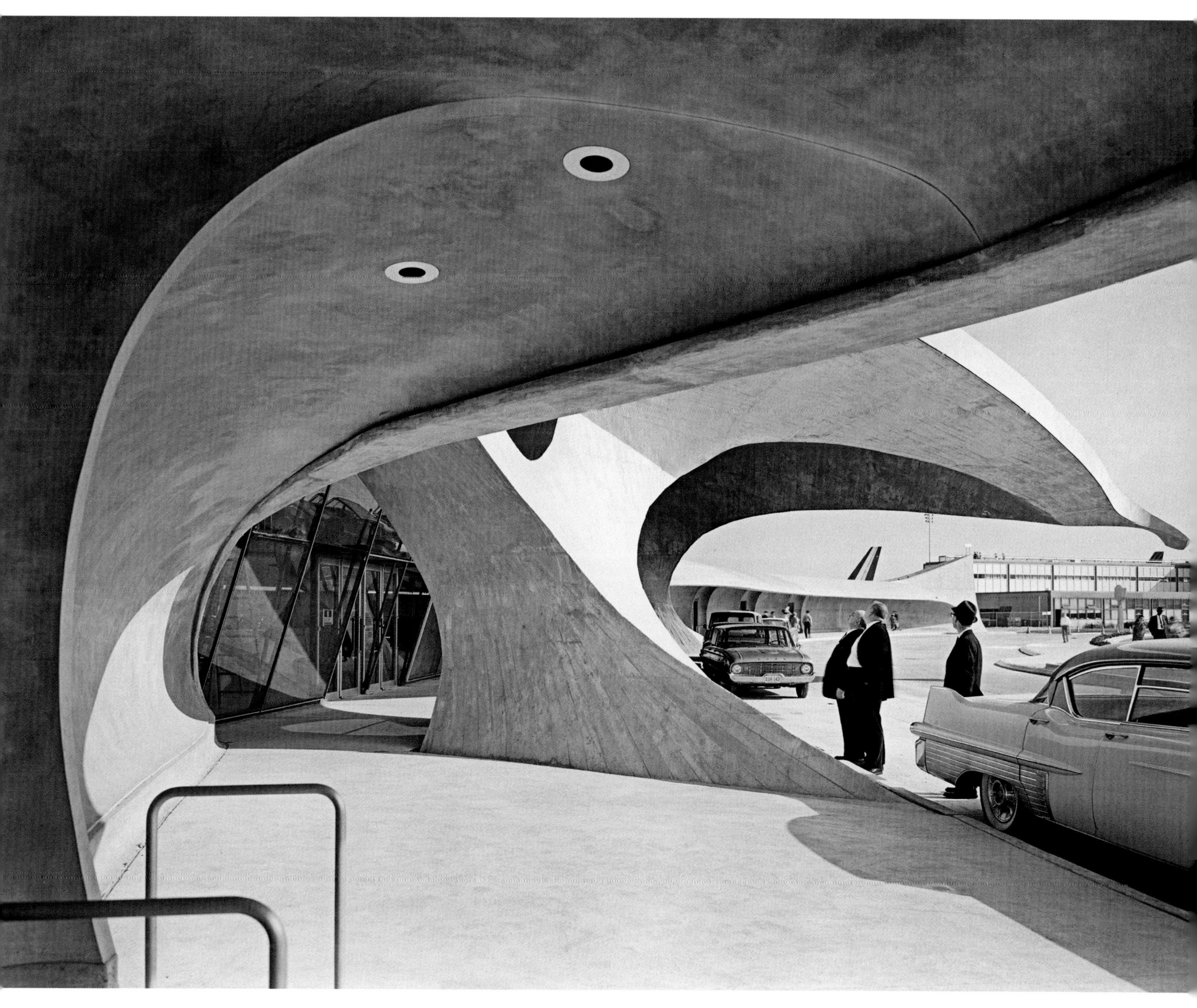

These pages and overleaf
TWA Terminal at Idlewild (JFK) Airport, Queens, New York. Eero Saarinen, 1962.

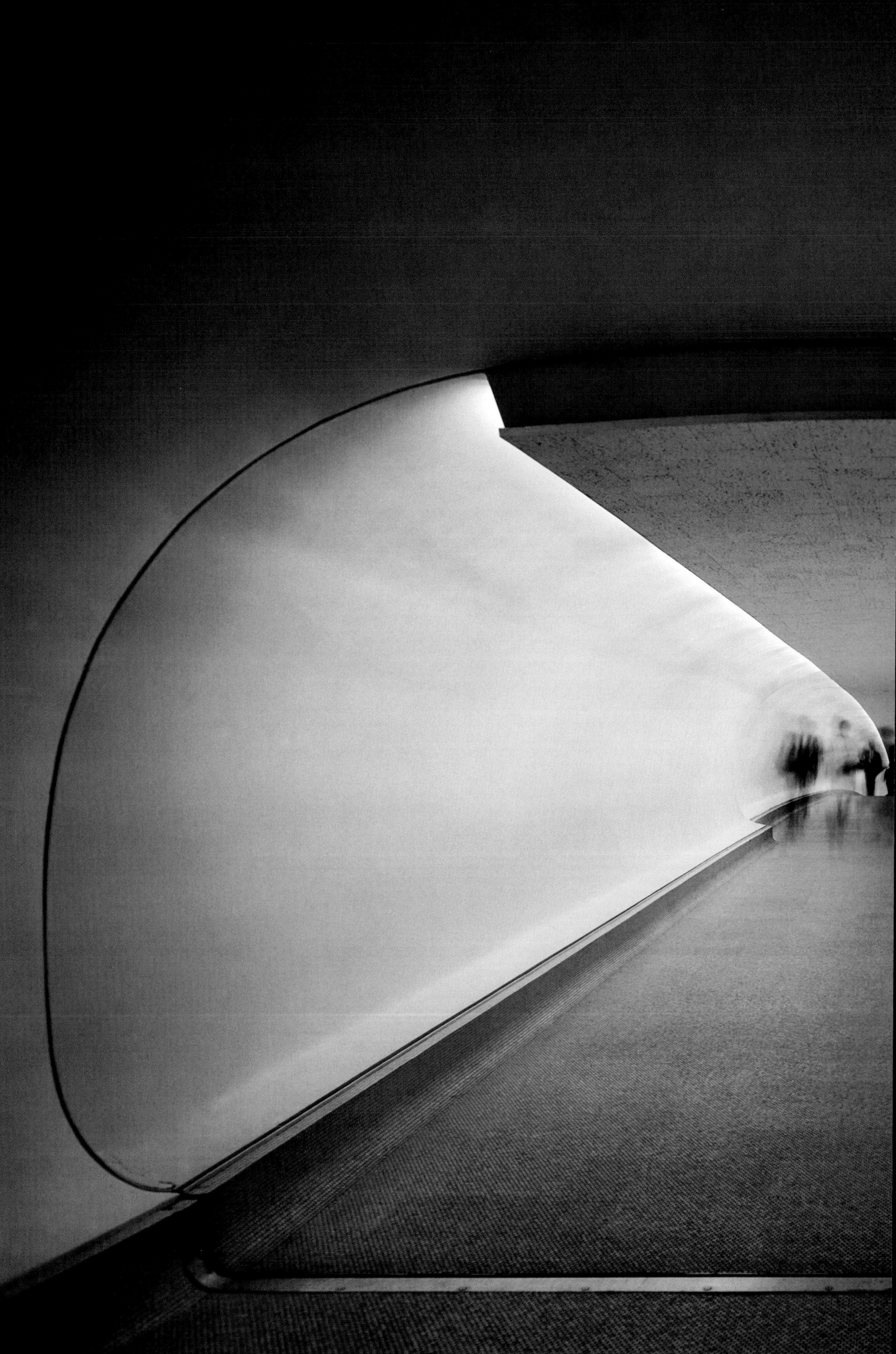

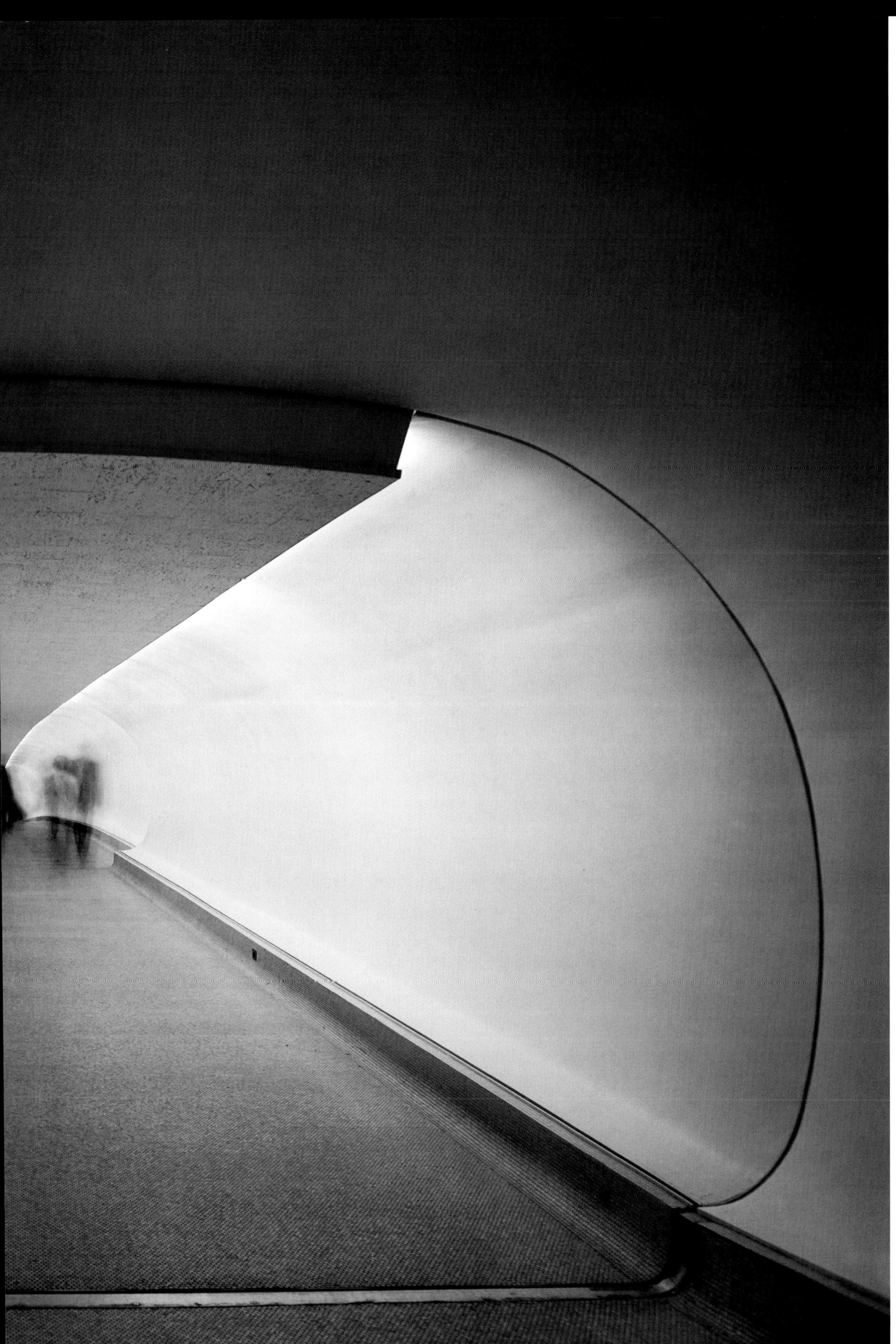

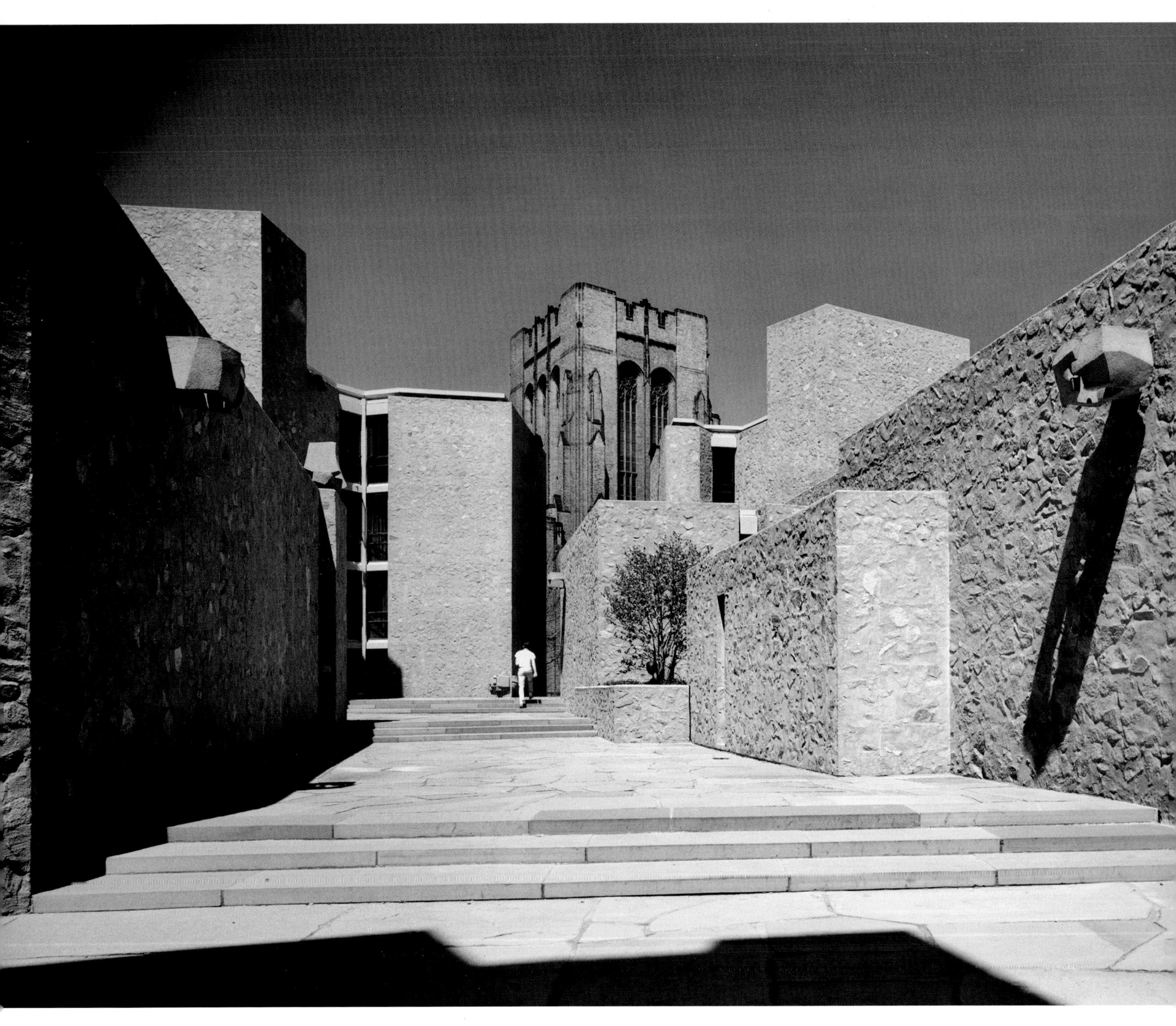

Stiles and Morse Colleges at Yale University, New Haven, Connecticut. Eero Saarinen, 1962.

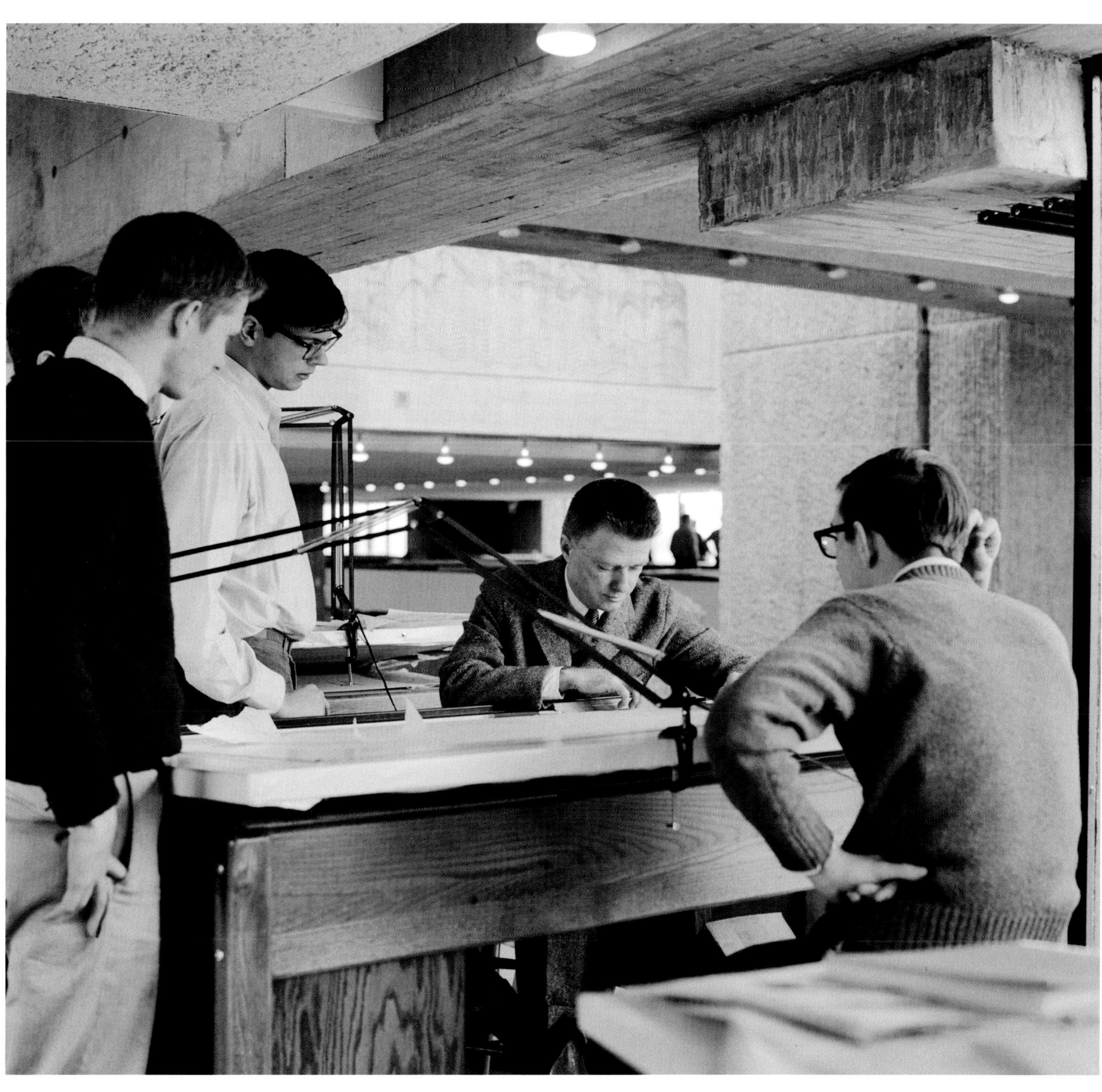

Paul Rudolph with students,
Yale Art + Architecture Building,
New Haven, Connecticut, 1963.

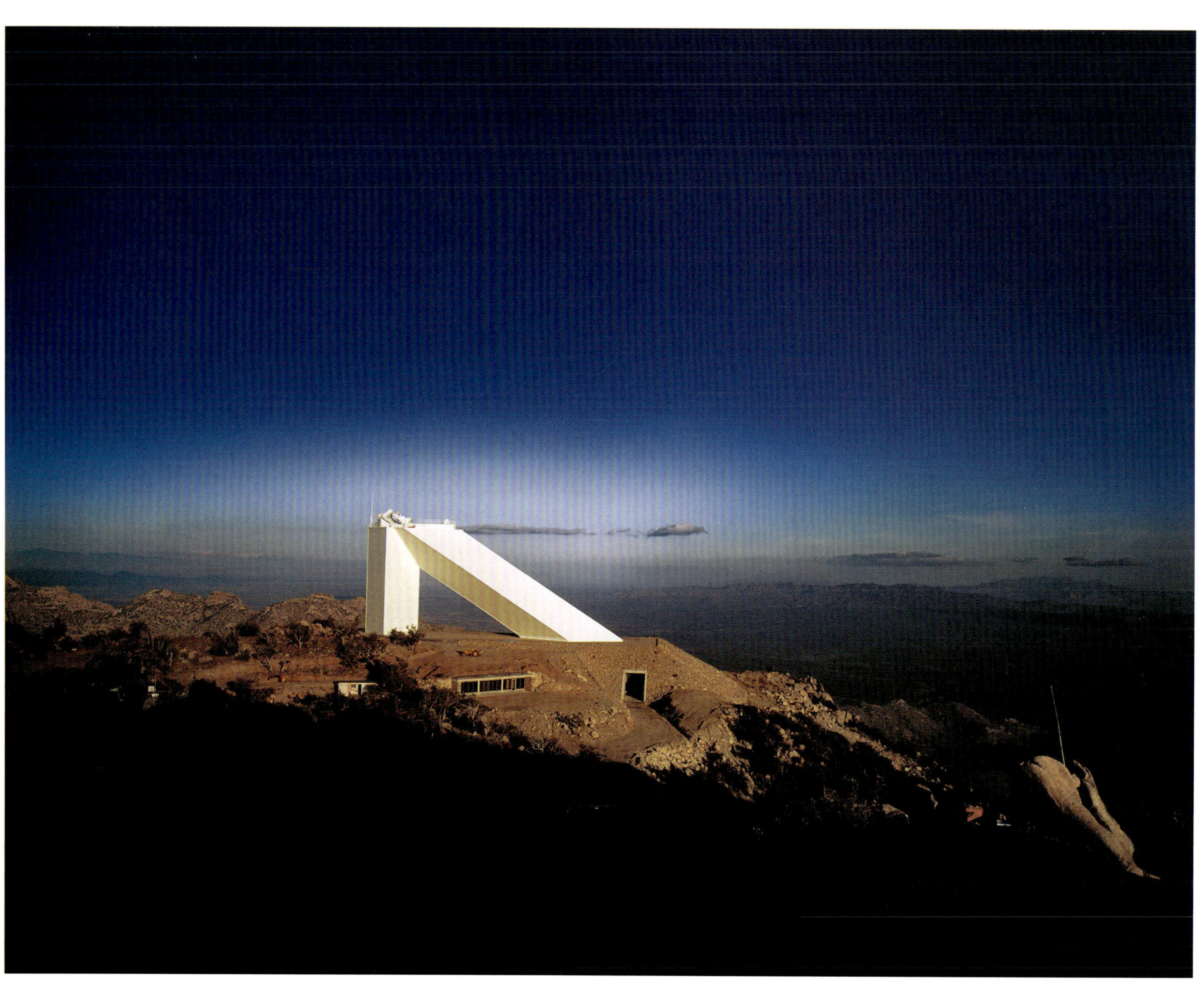

Kitt Peak Solar Observatory, Pima County, Arizona. Skidmore Owings & Merrill, 1962.

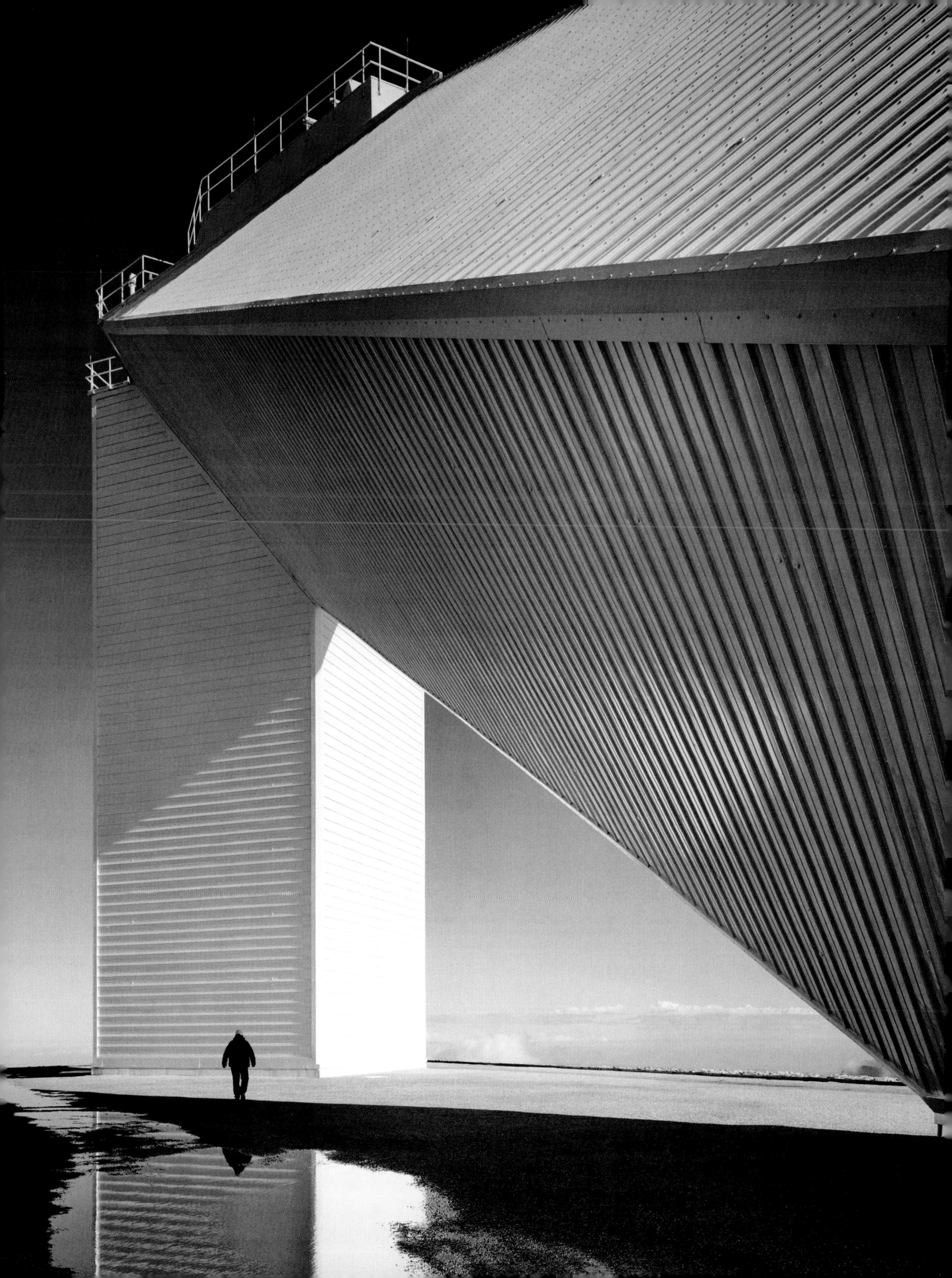

Marin County Civic Center, San Rafael
California. Frank Lloyd Wright, 1963.

Overleaf
Fallingwater, Bear Run, Pennsylvania.
Frank Lloyd Wright, 1963.

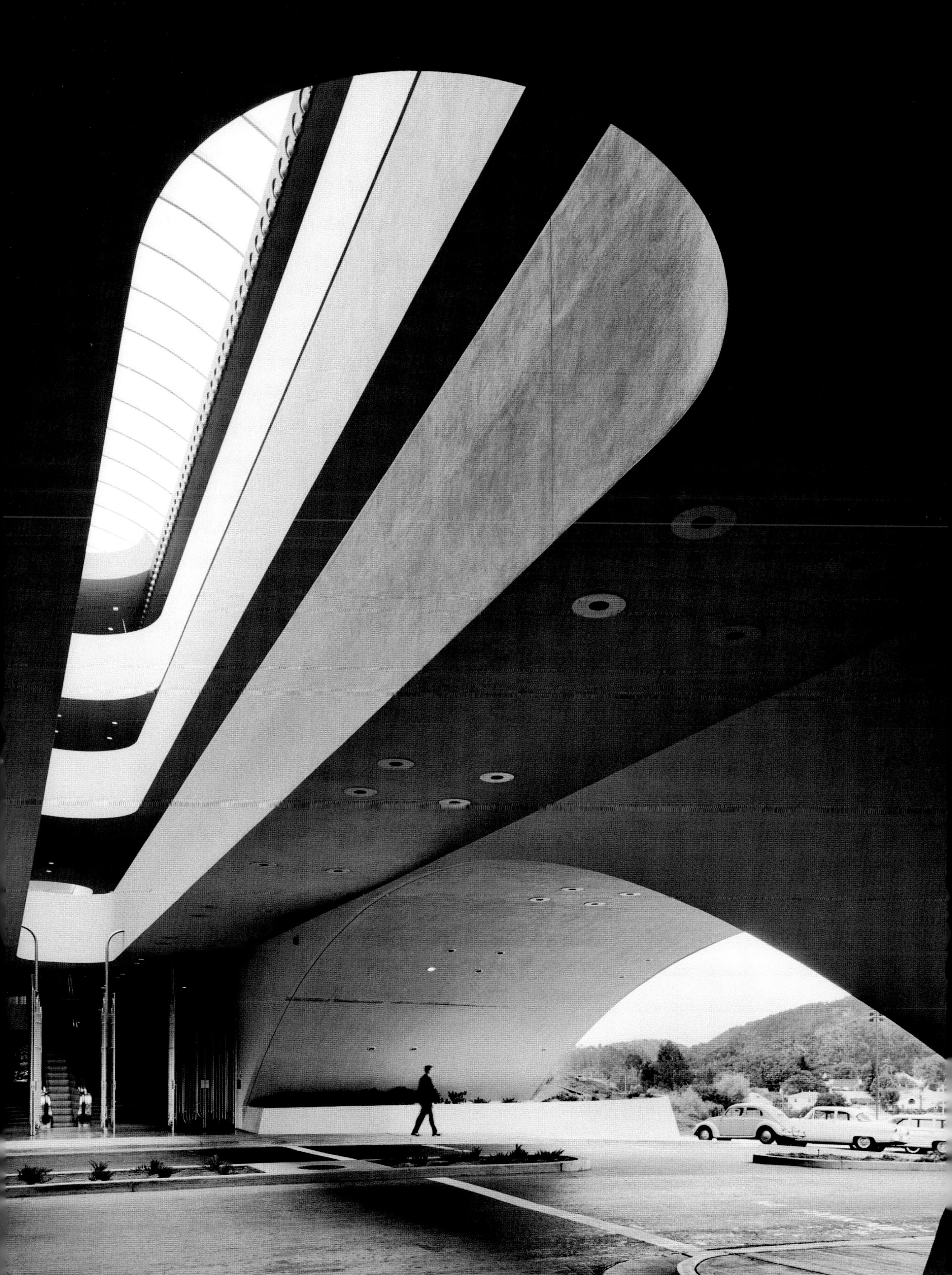

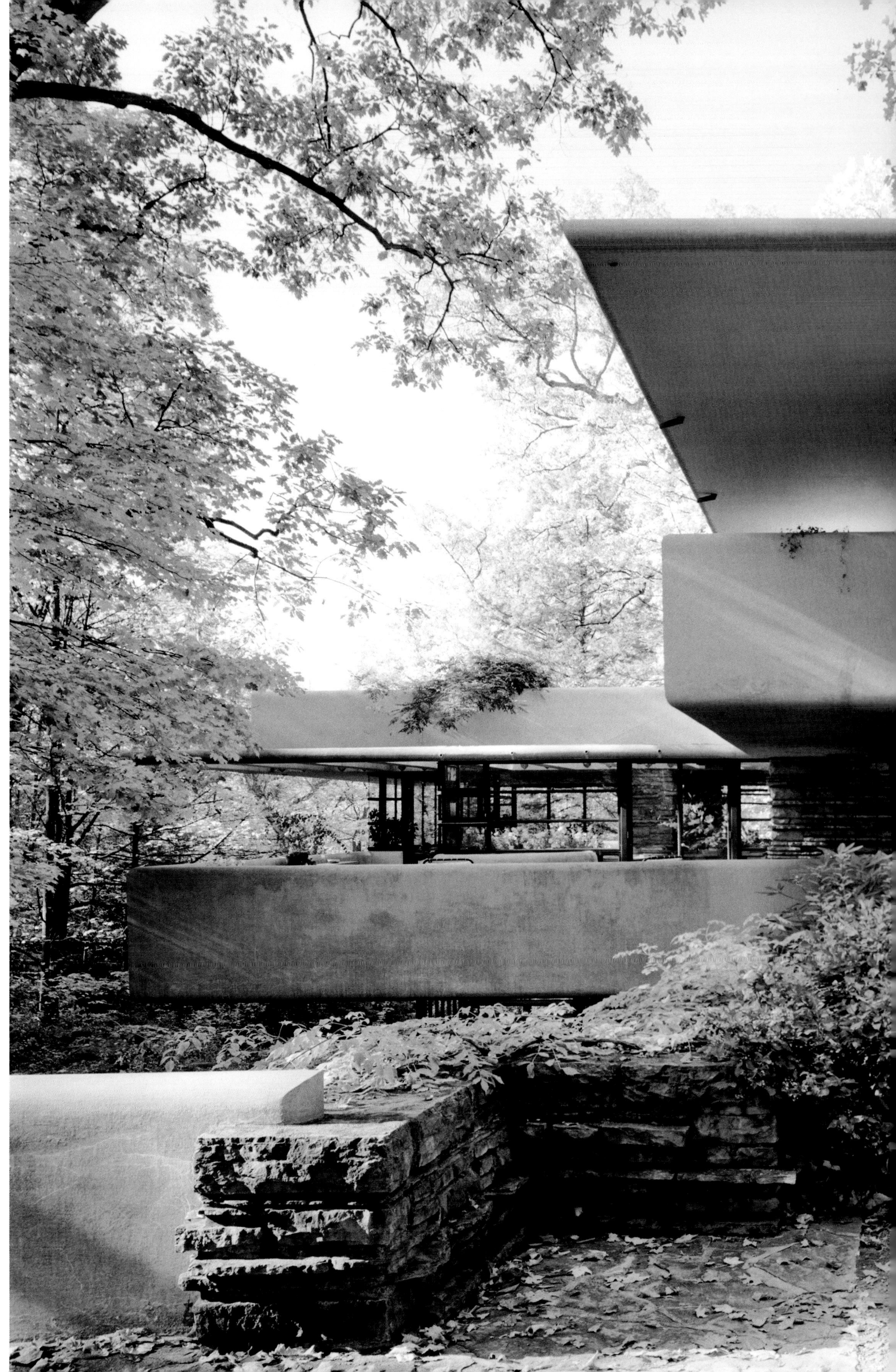

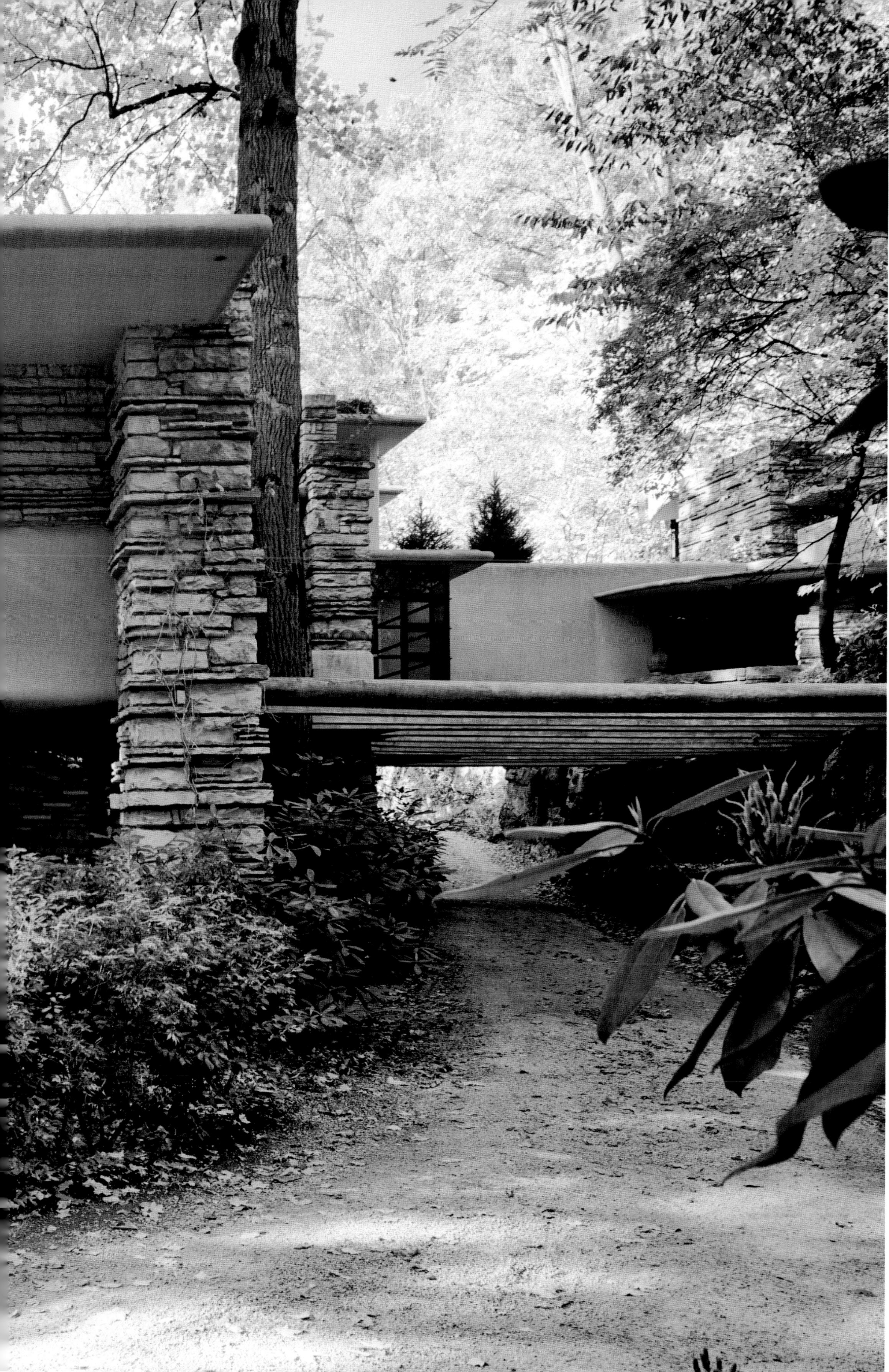

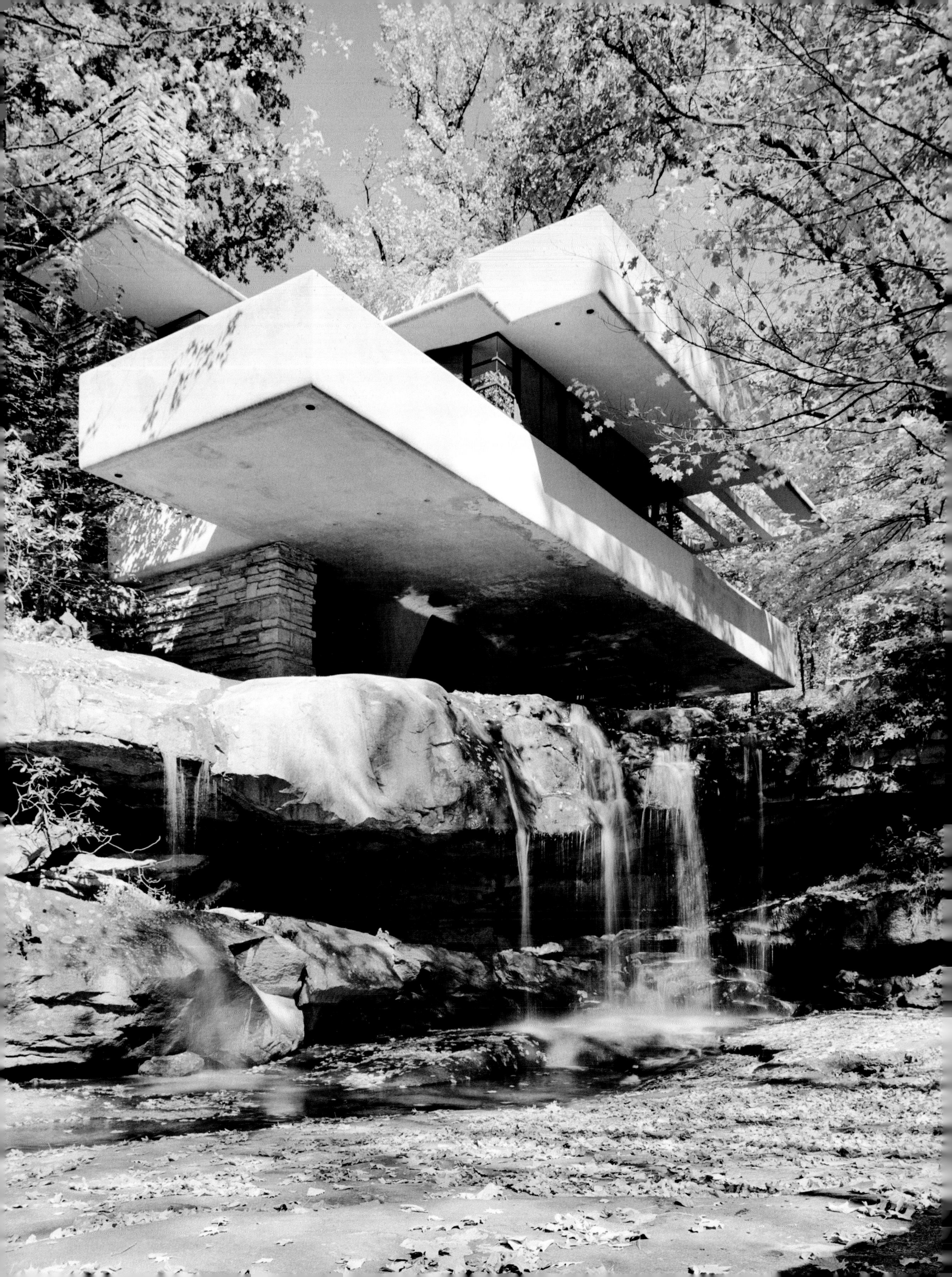

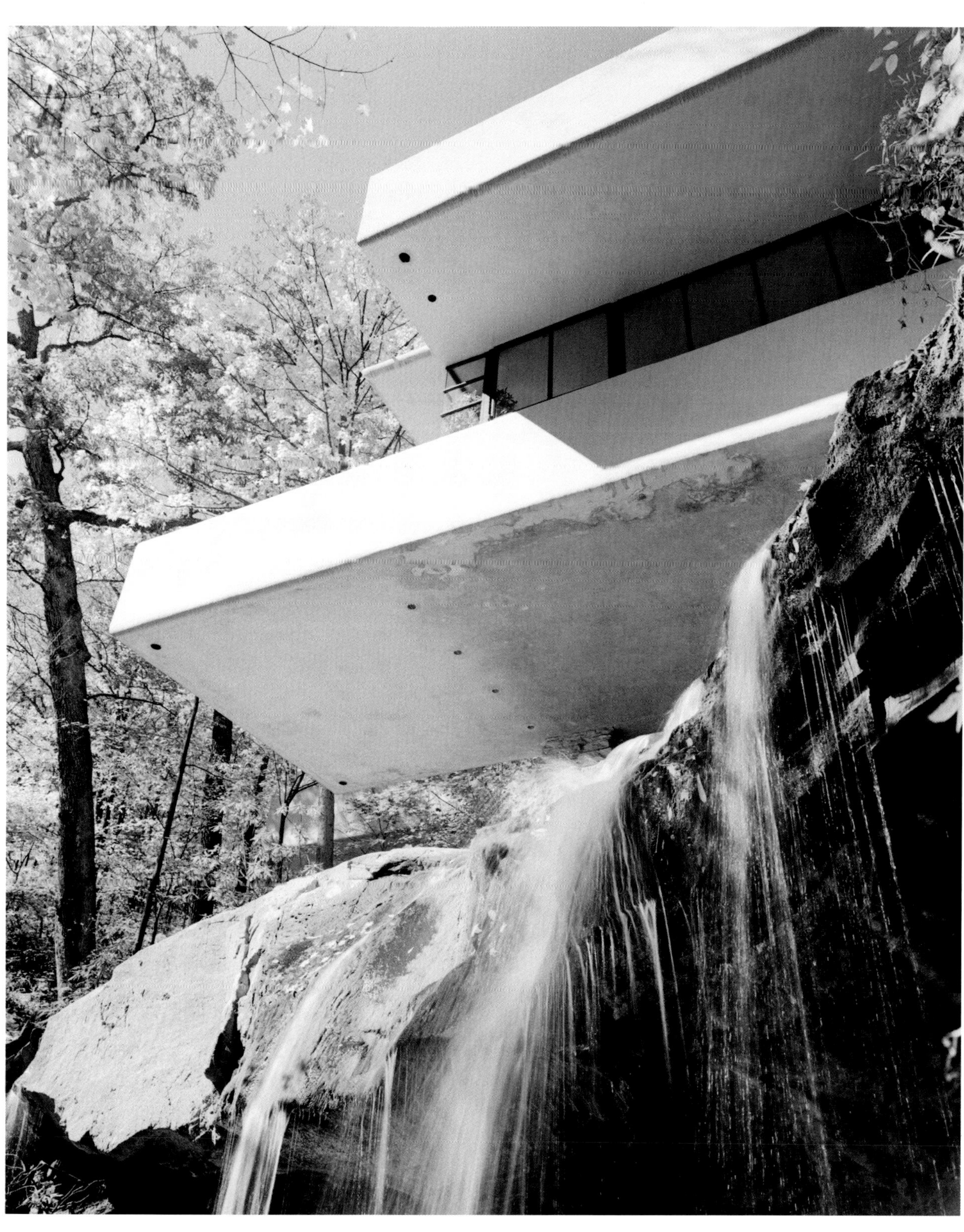

Fallingwater, Bear Run, Pennsylvania.
Frank Lloyd Wright, 1963.

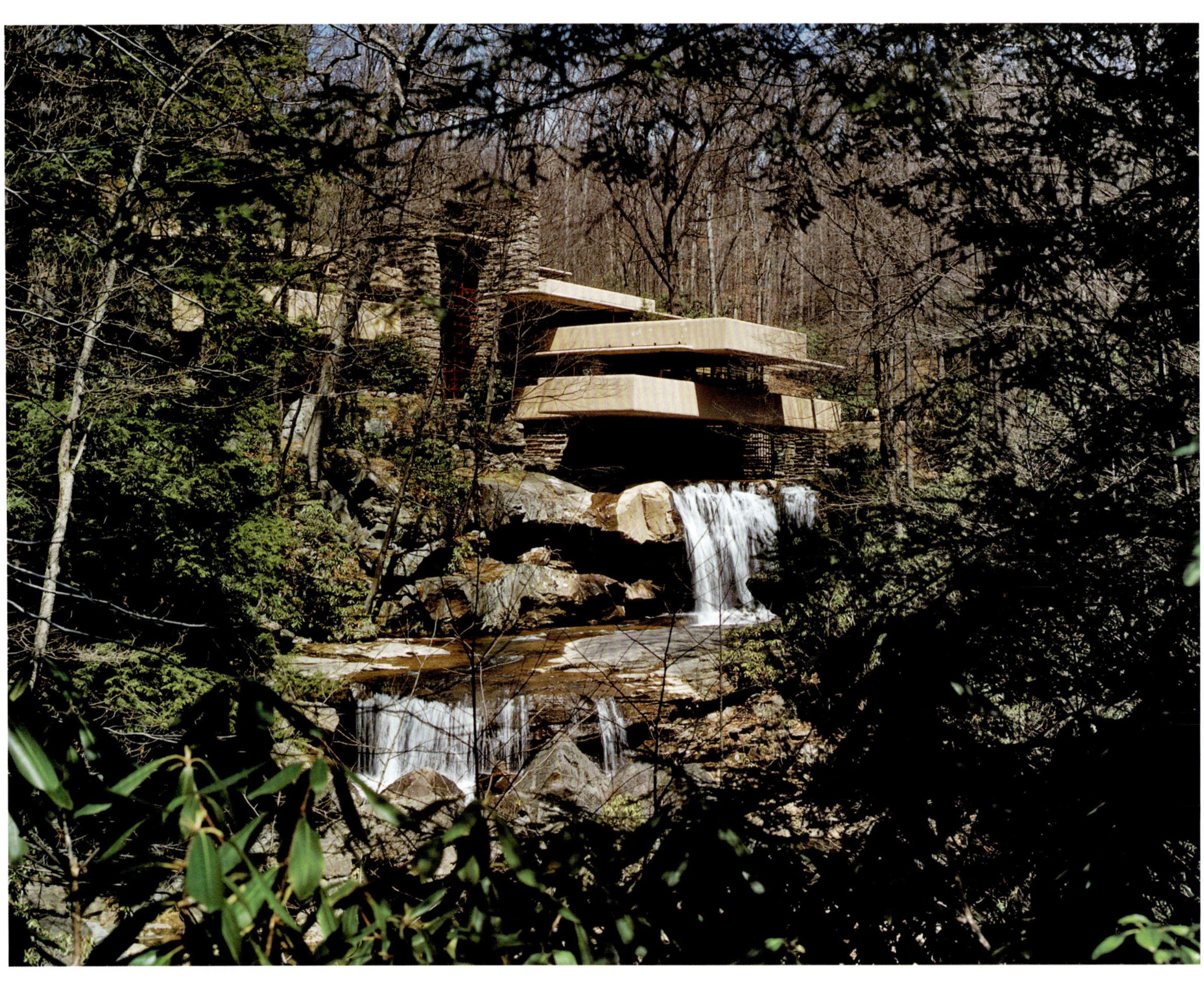

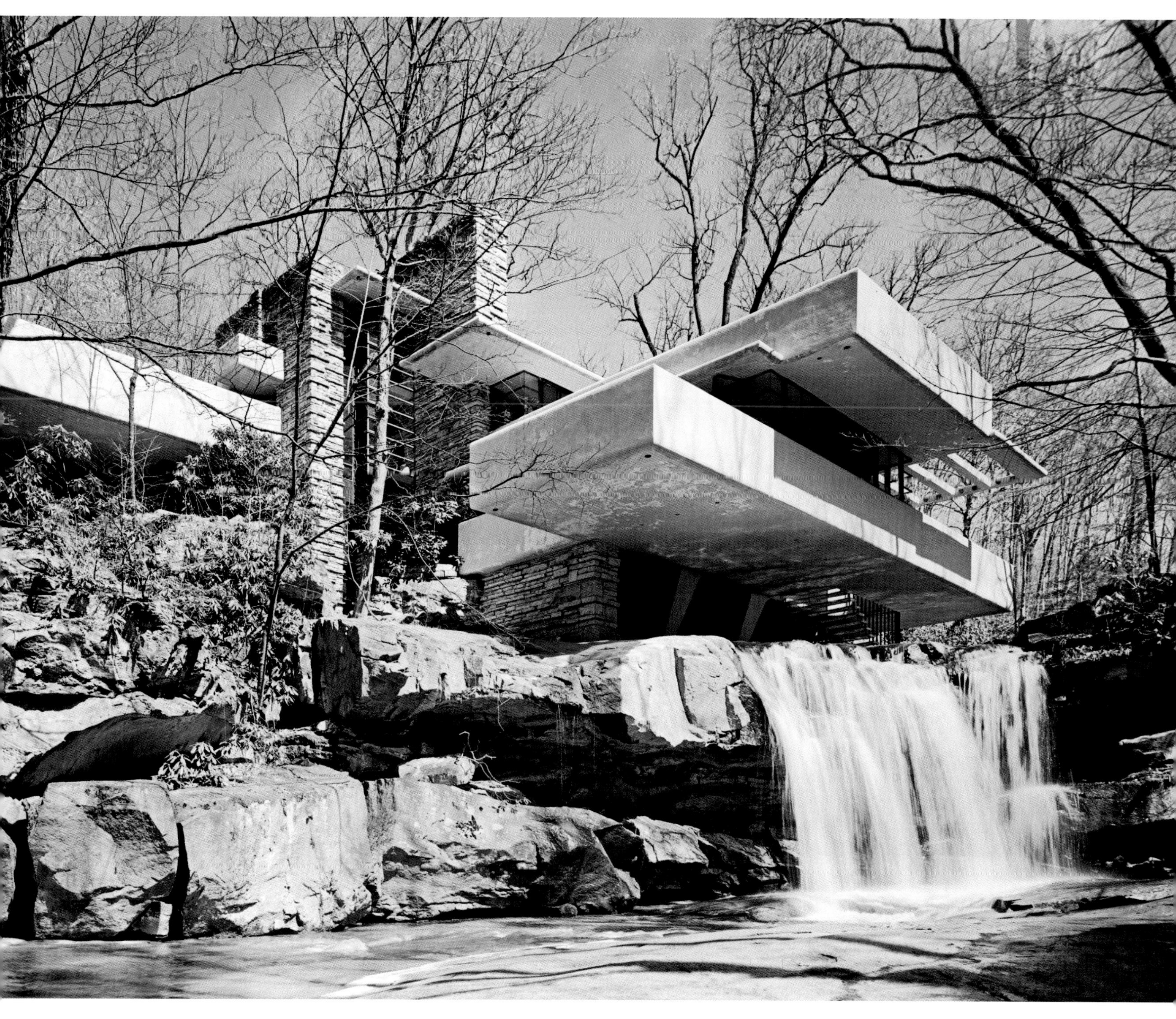

Fallingwater, Bear Run, Pennsylvania.
Frank Lloyd Wright, 1971.

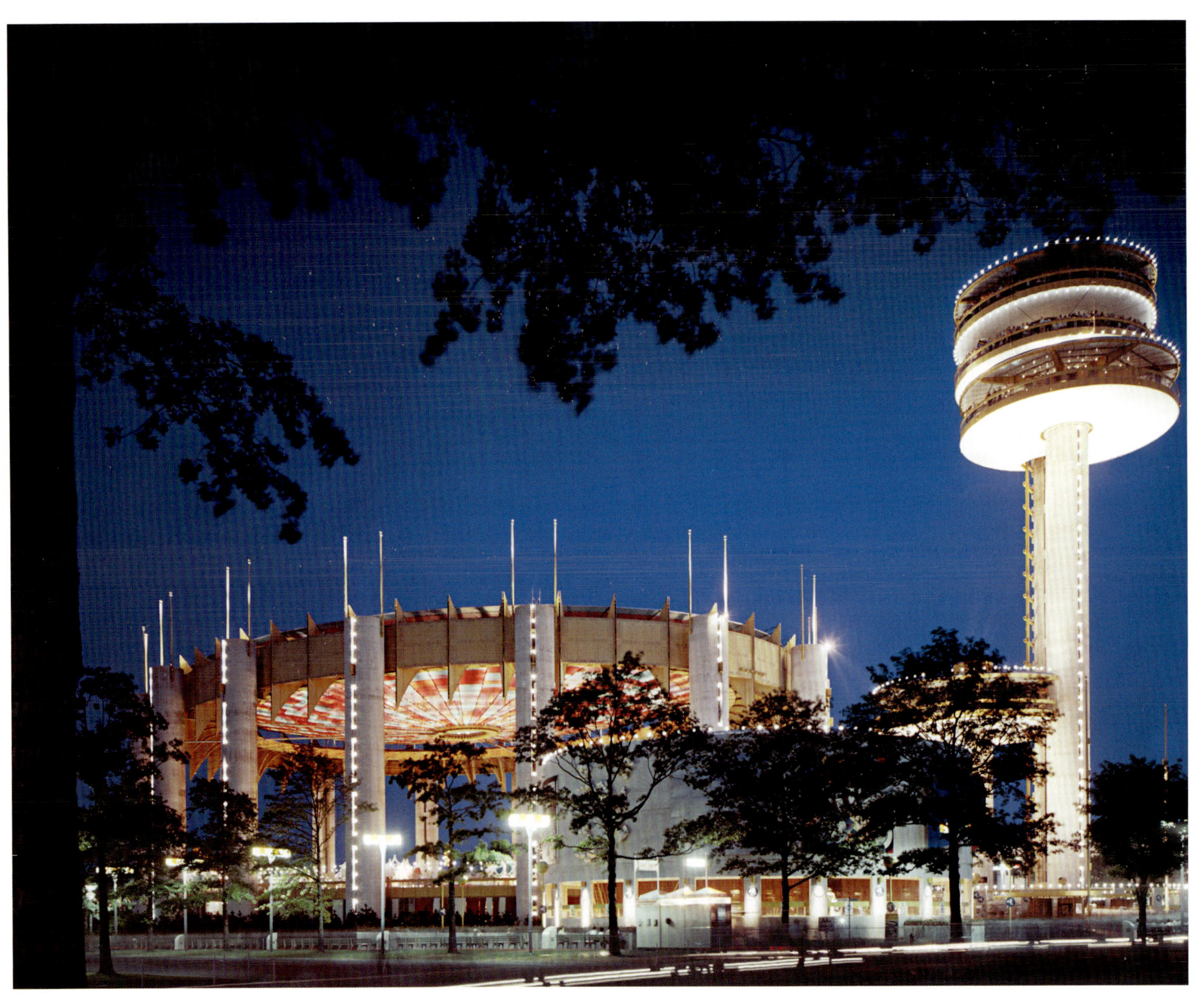

1964 World's Fair, New York State Pavilion, Queens, New York. Philip Johnson, 1964.

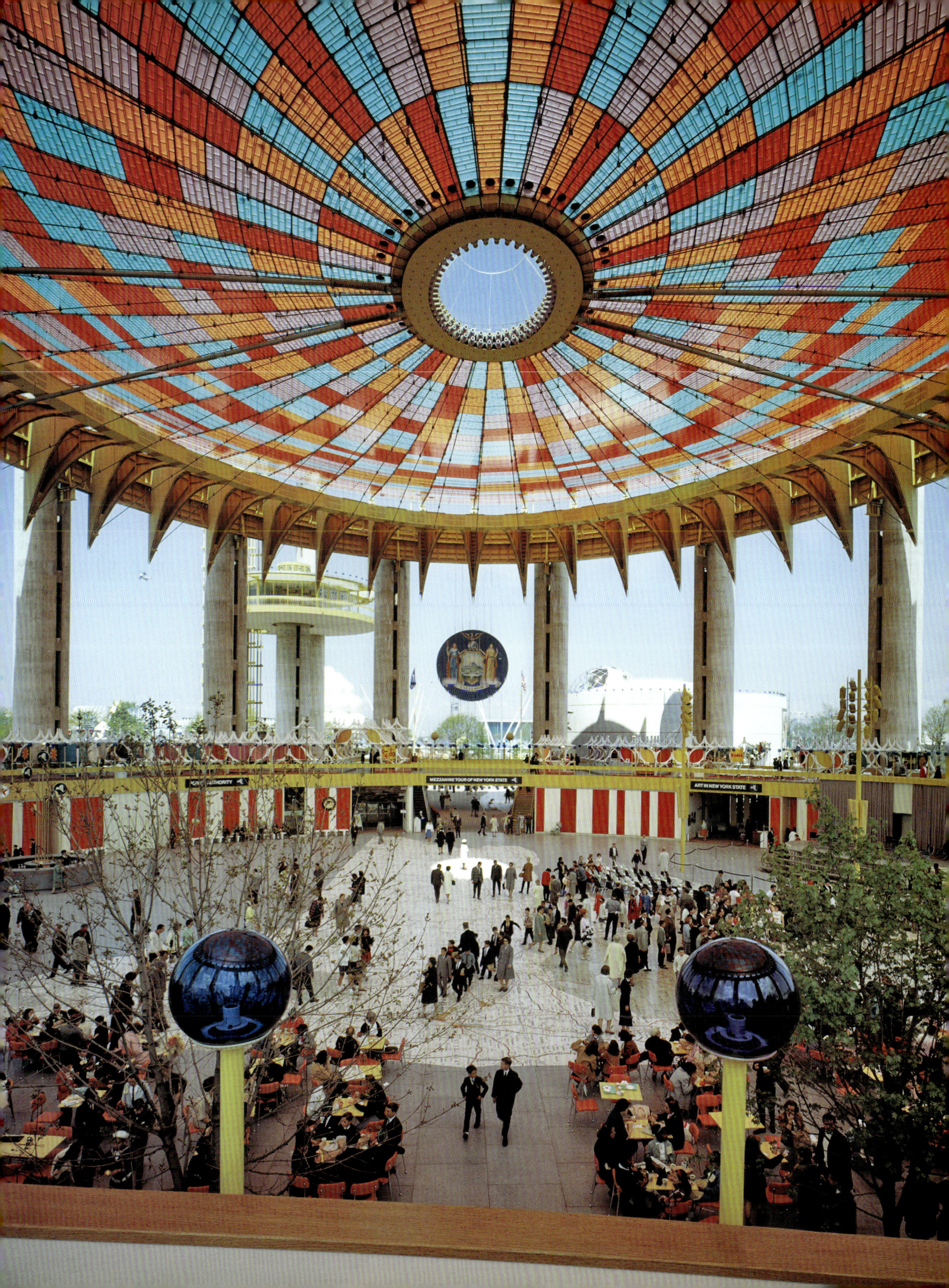
MEZZANINE TOUR OF NEW YORK STATE
ART IN NEW YORK STATE

Right and overleaf
Dulles Airport, Chantilly, Virginia.
Eero Saarinen, 1964.

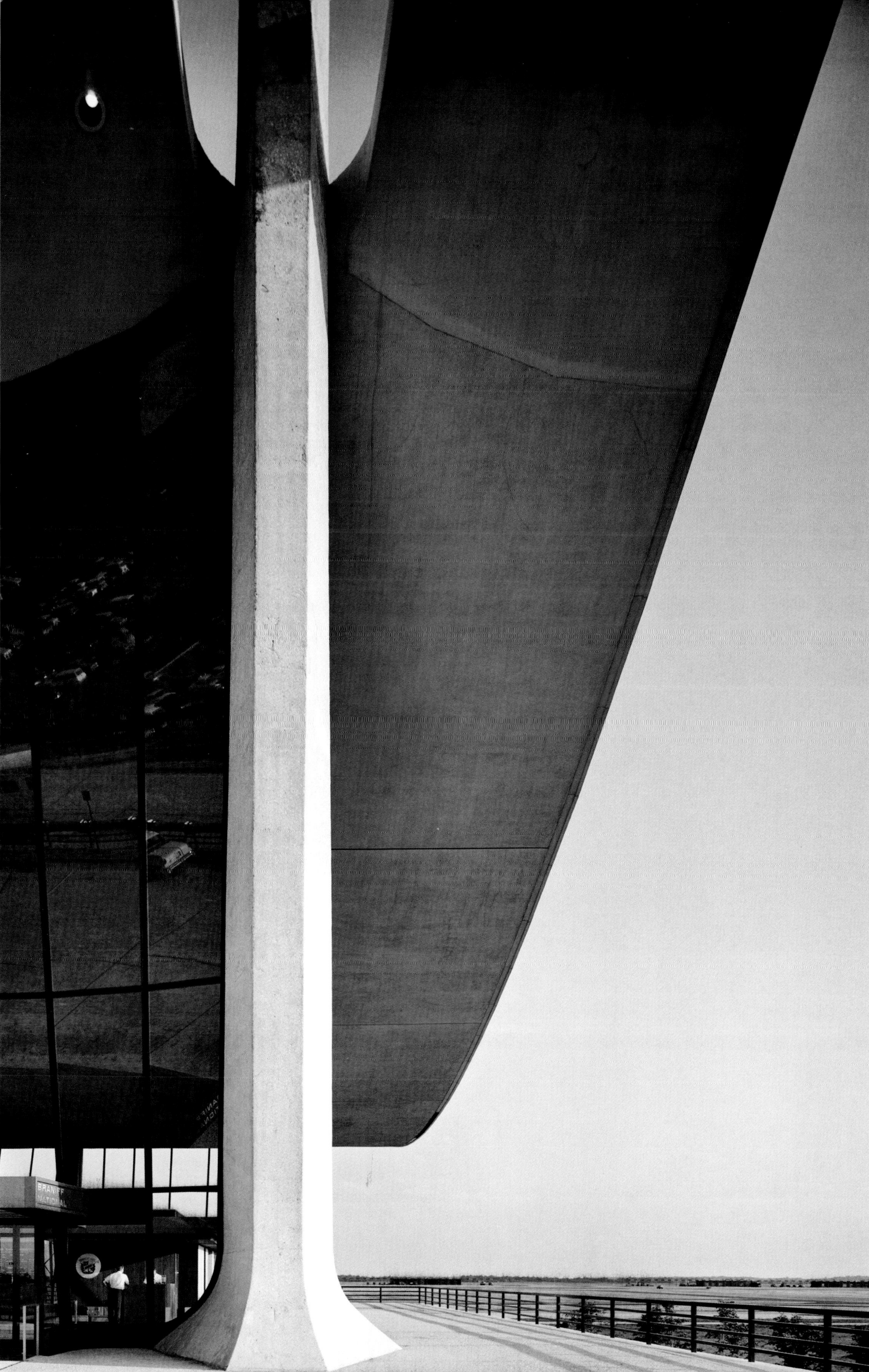
BRANIFF
NATIONAL

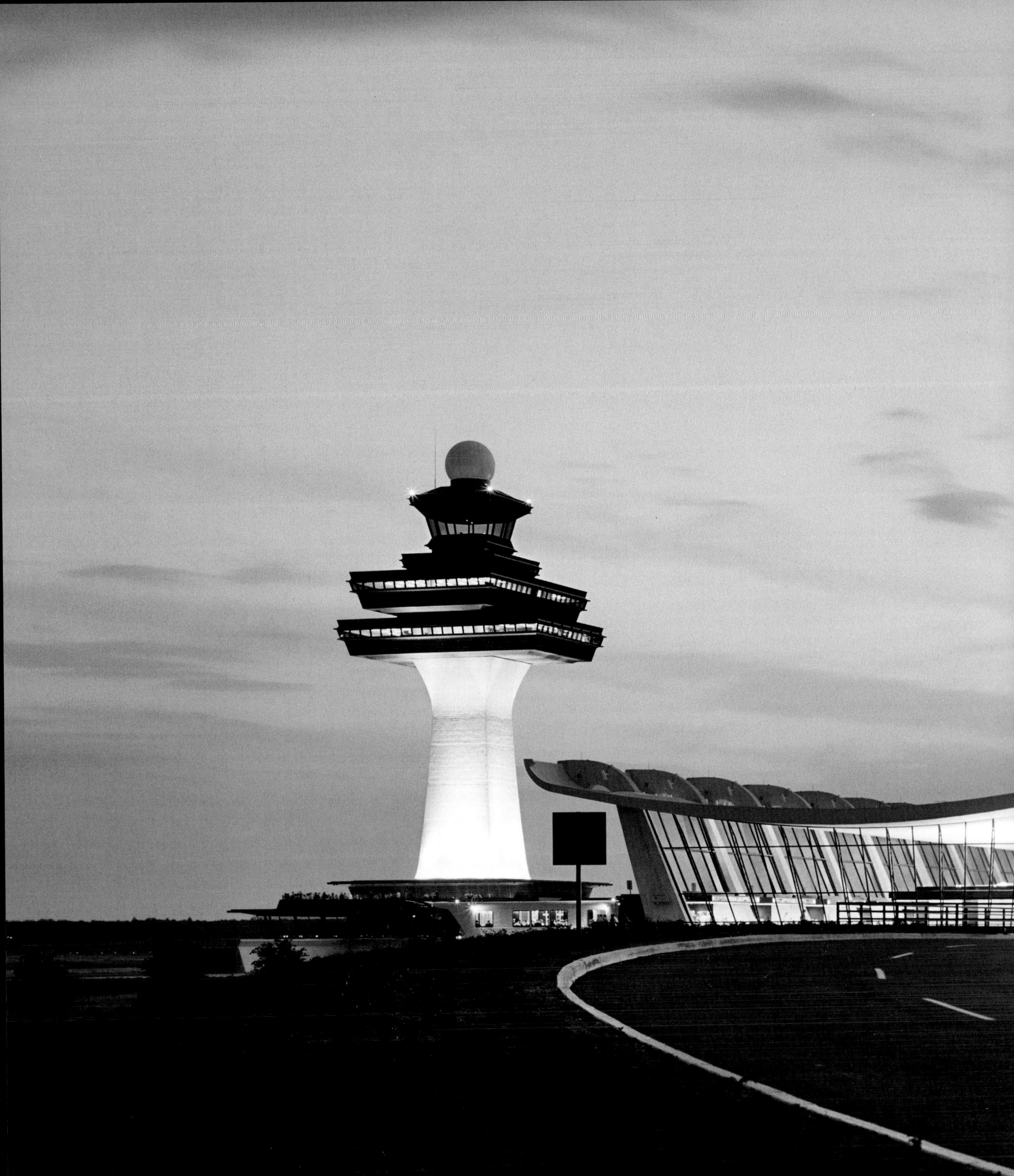

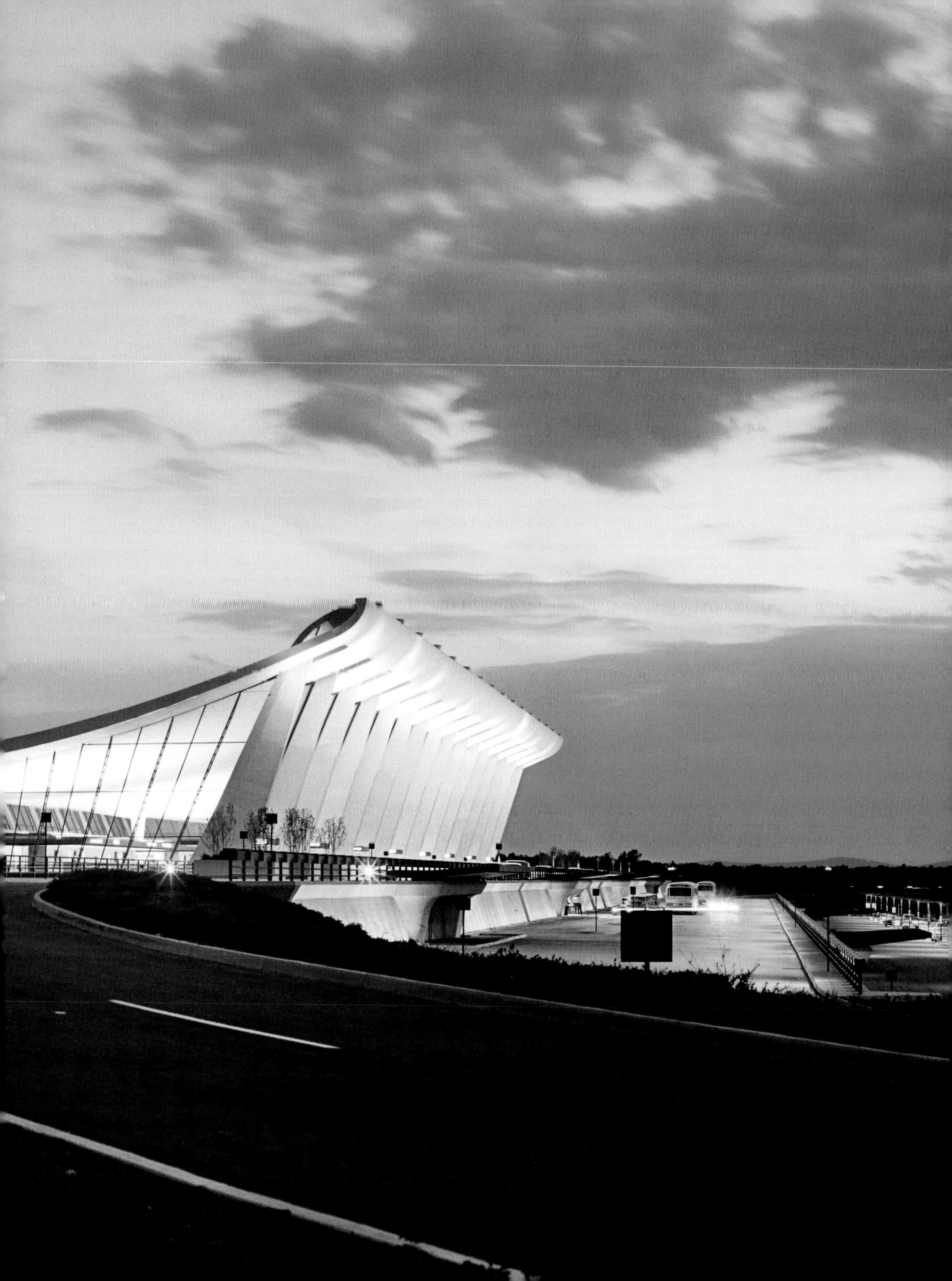

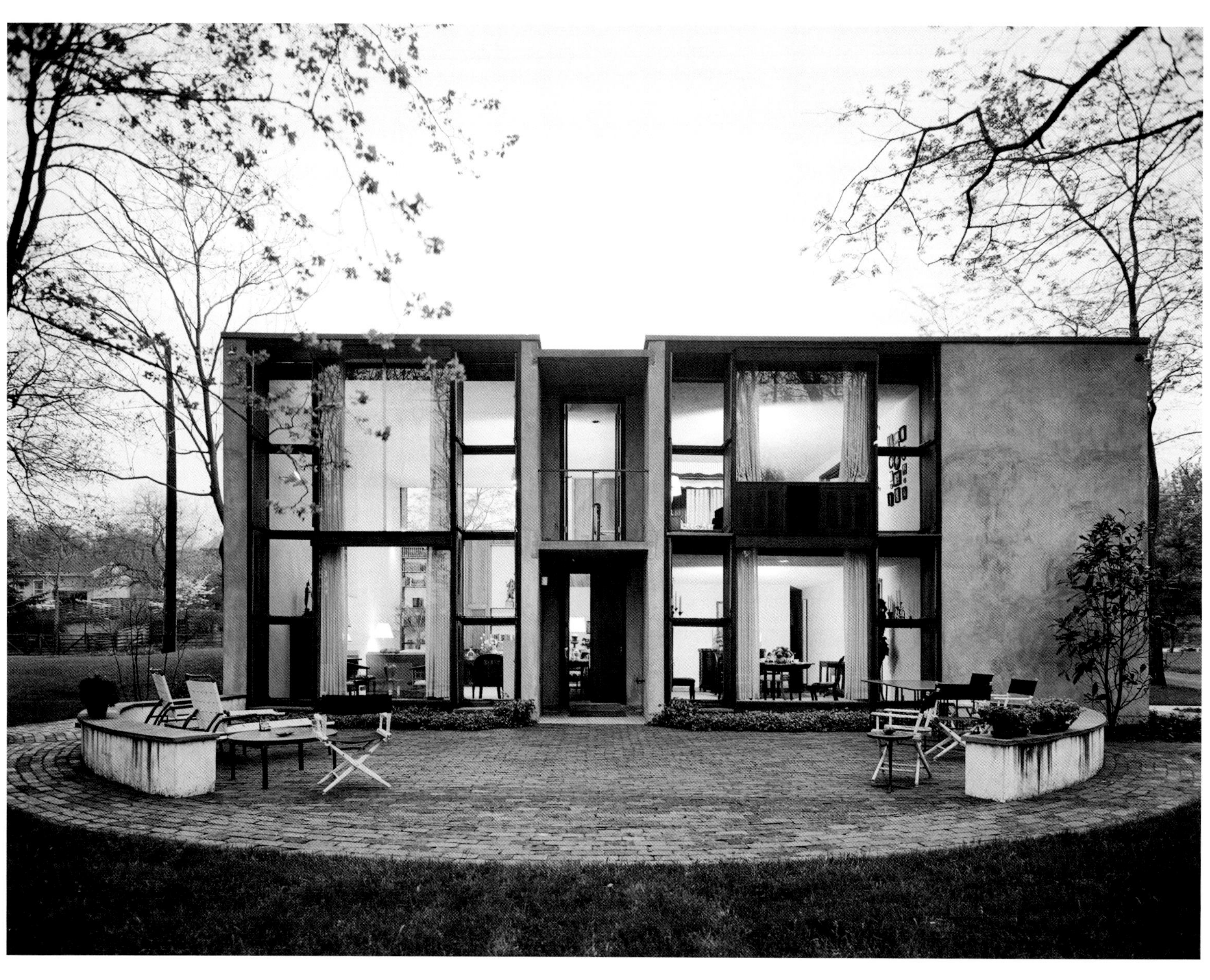

Esherick House, Philadelphia.
Louis Kahn, 1966.

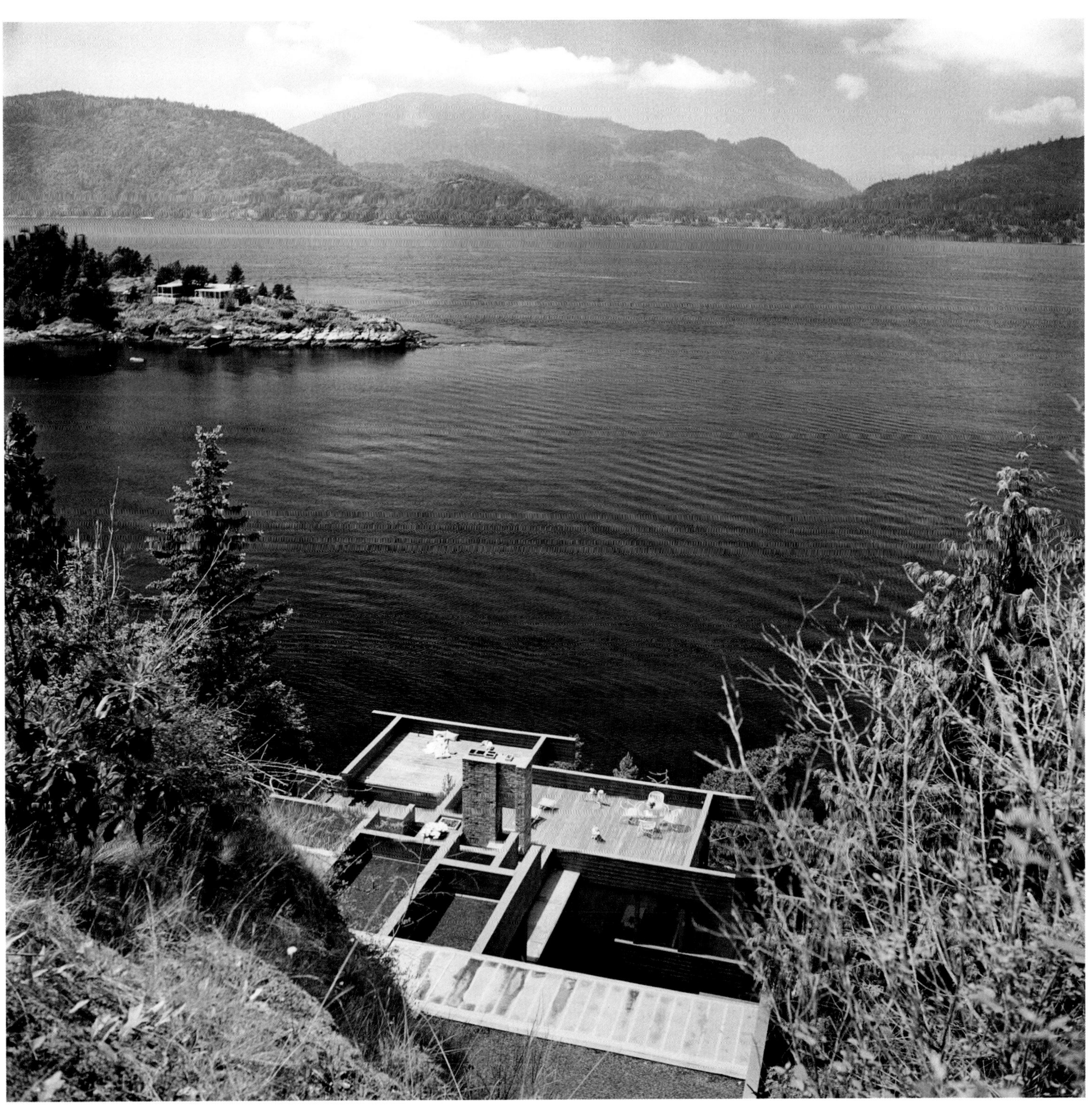

David Graham House, Vancouver.
Arthur Erickson, 1967.

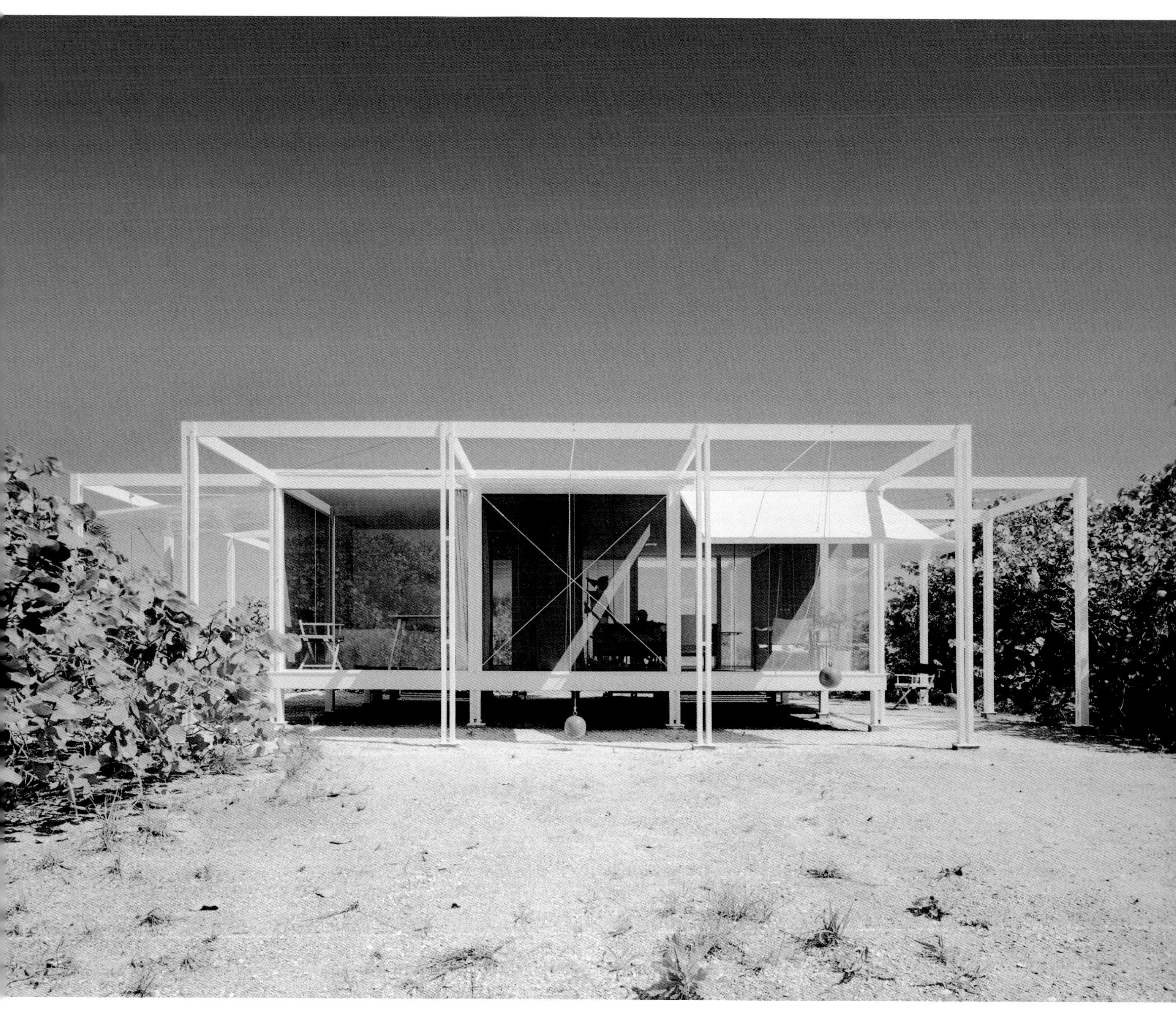

Walker Guest House, Sarasota, Florida.
Paul Rudolph, 1953.

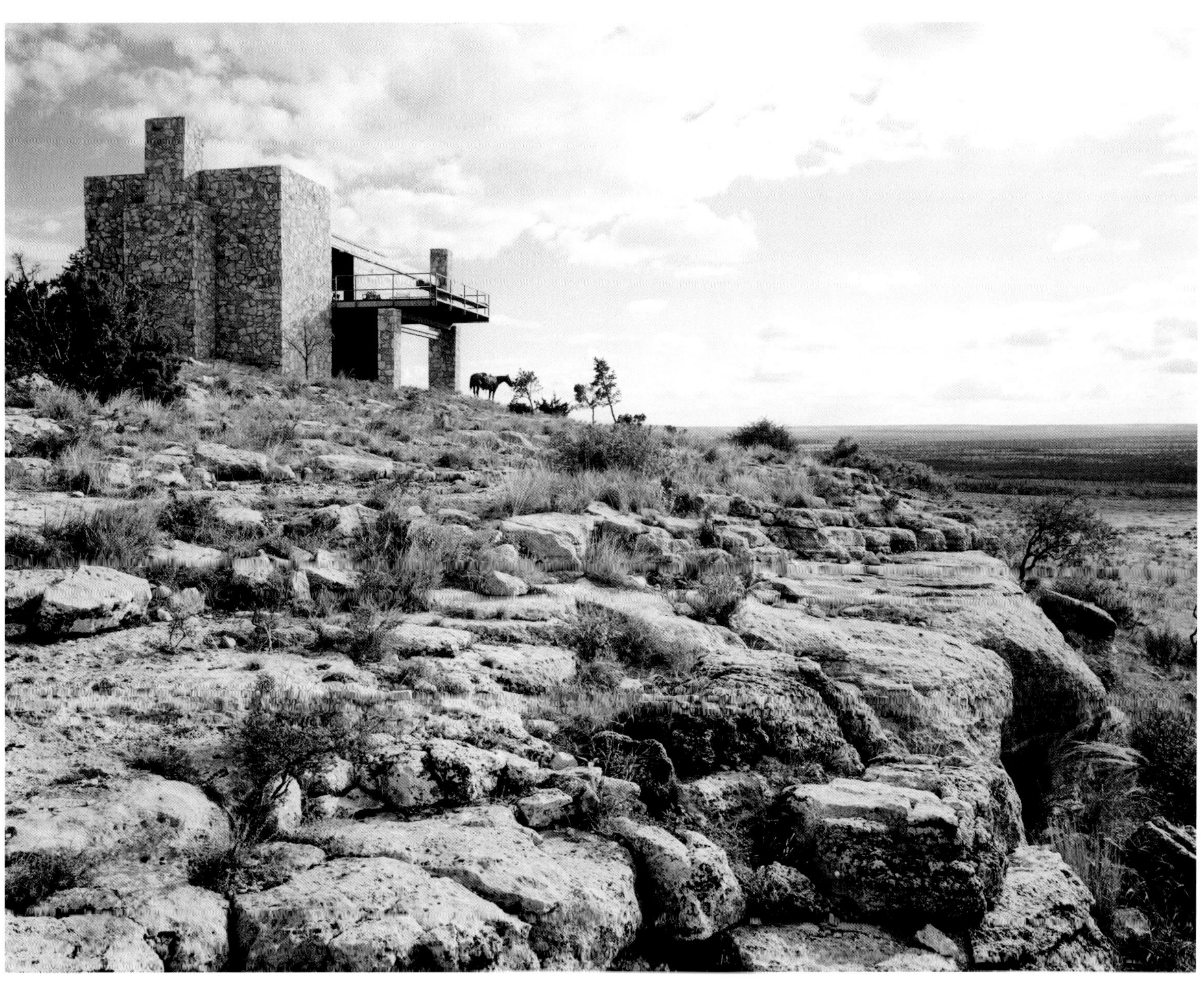

Hunting Lodge, "Birthday House,"
Sterling County, Texas. Frank Welch, 1966.

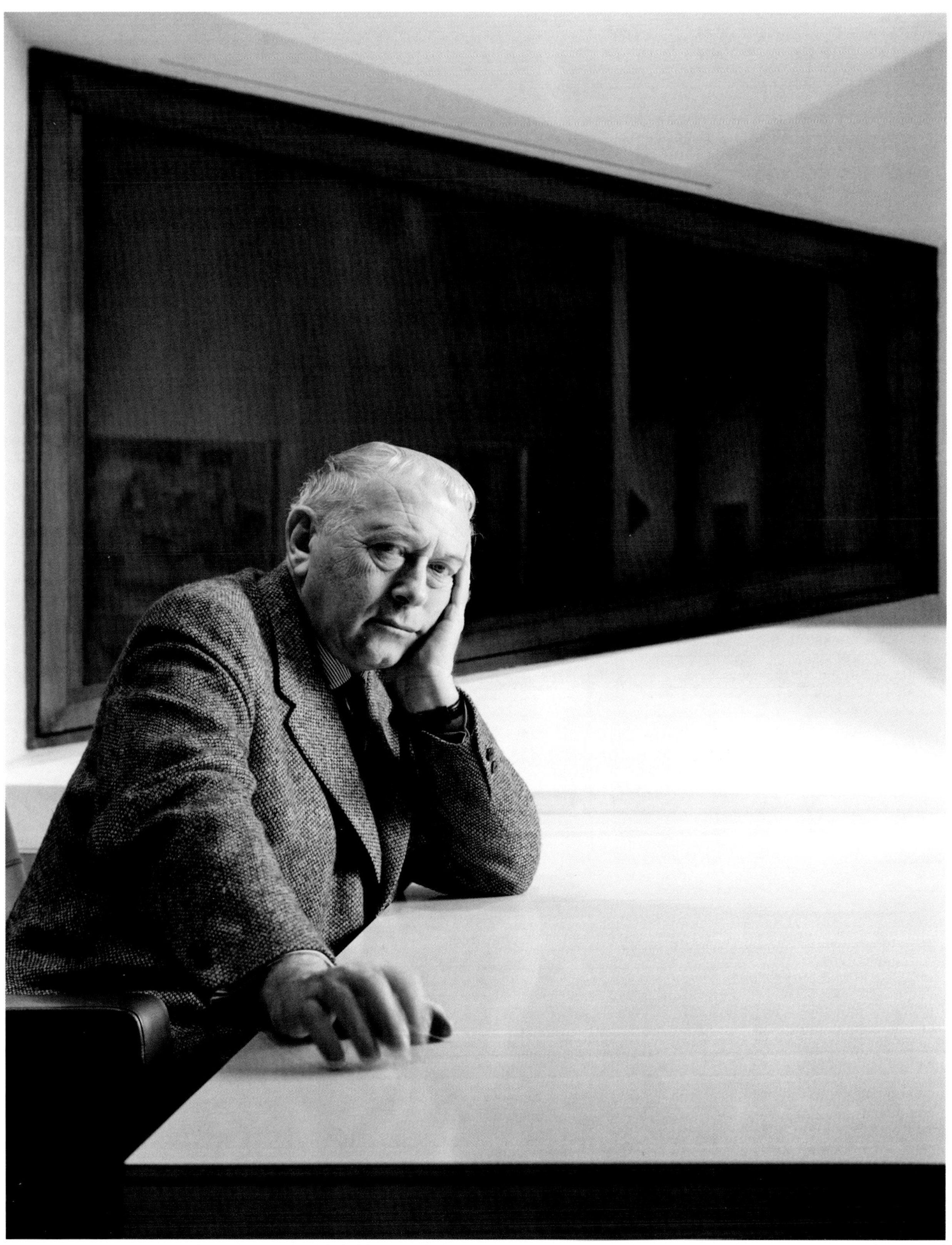

Marcel Breuer at Whitney Museum, New York, 1967.

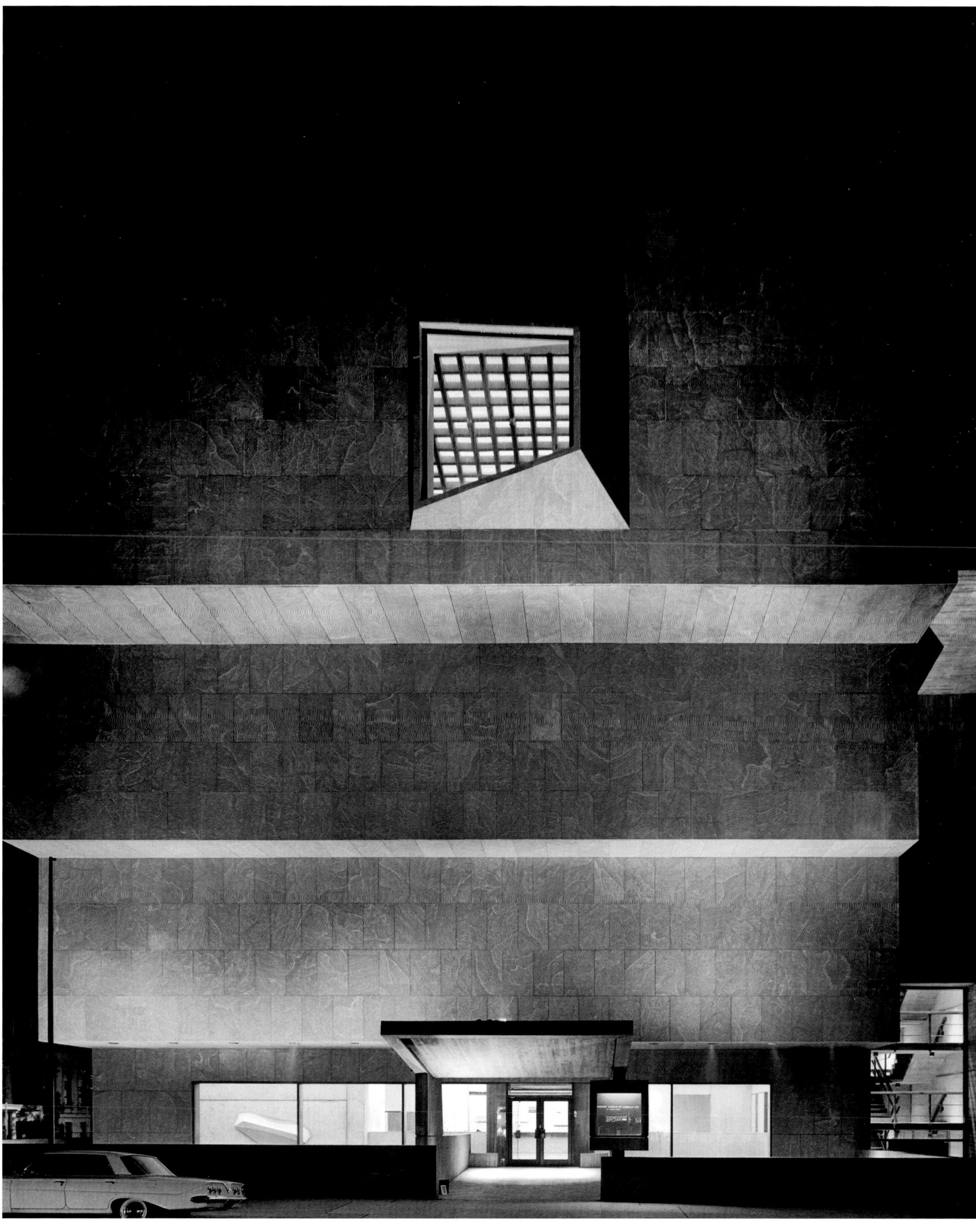

Whitney Museum, New York.
Marcel Breuer, 1966.

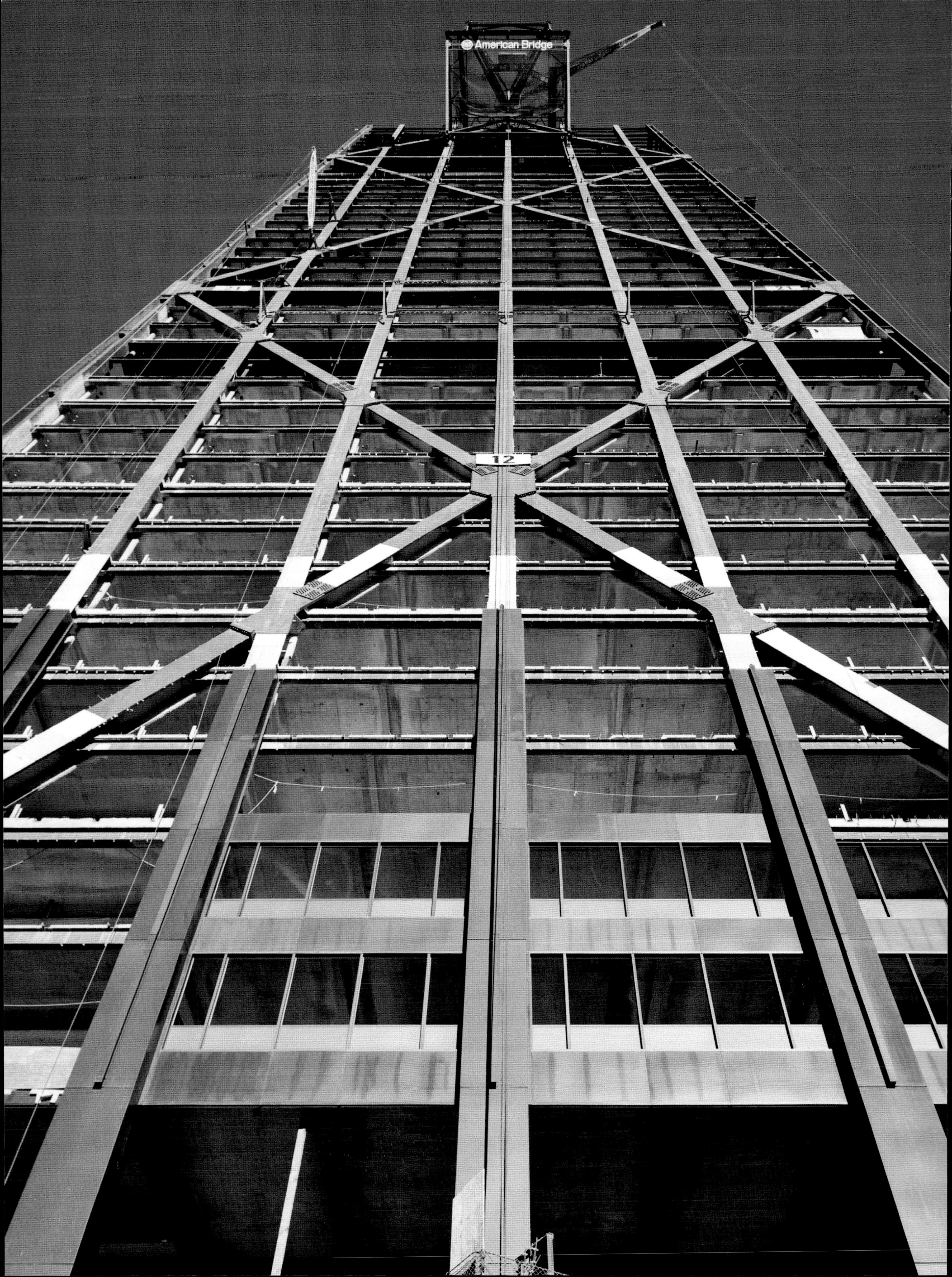
American Bridge
12

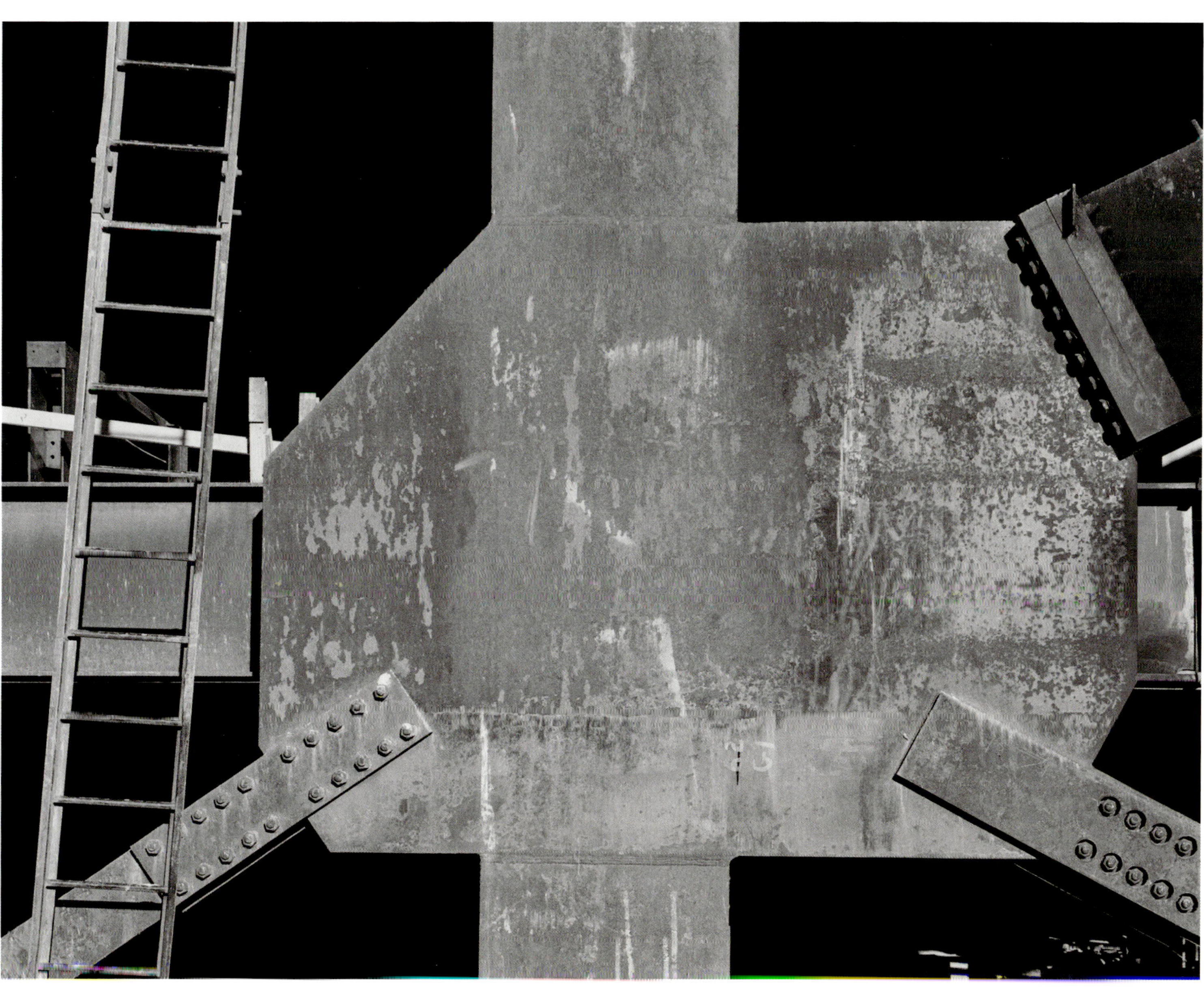

John Hancock Center construction, Chicago.
Skidmore, Owings & Merrill, 1967.

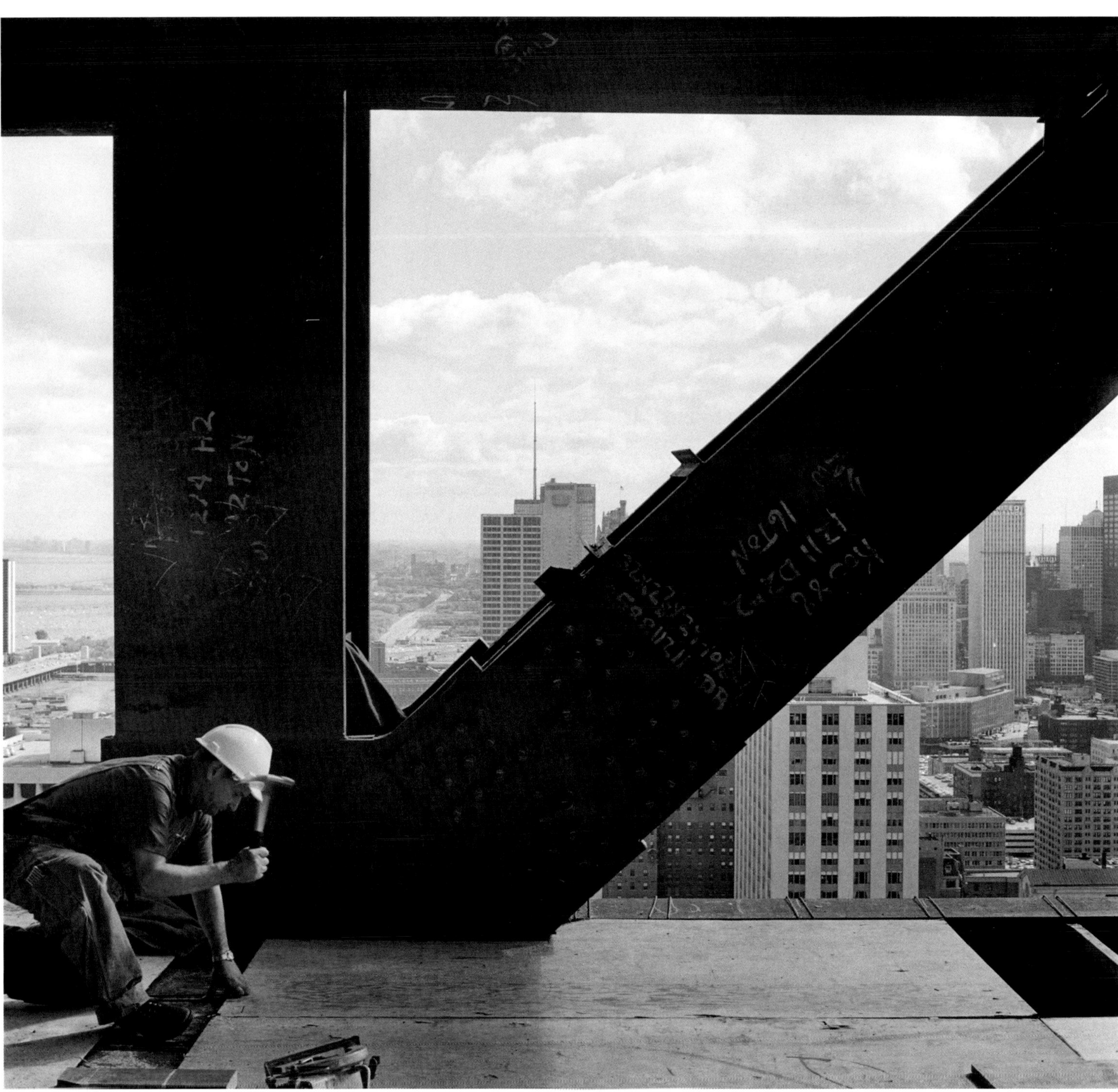

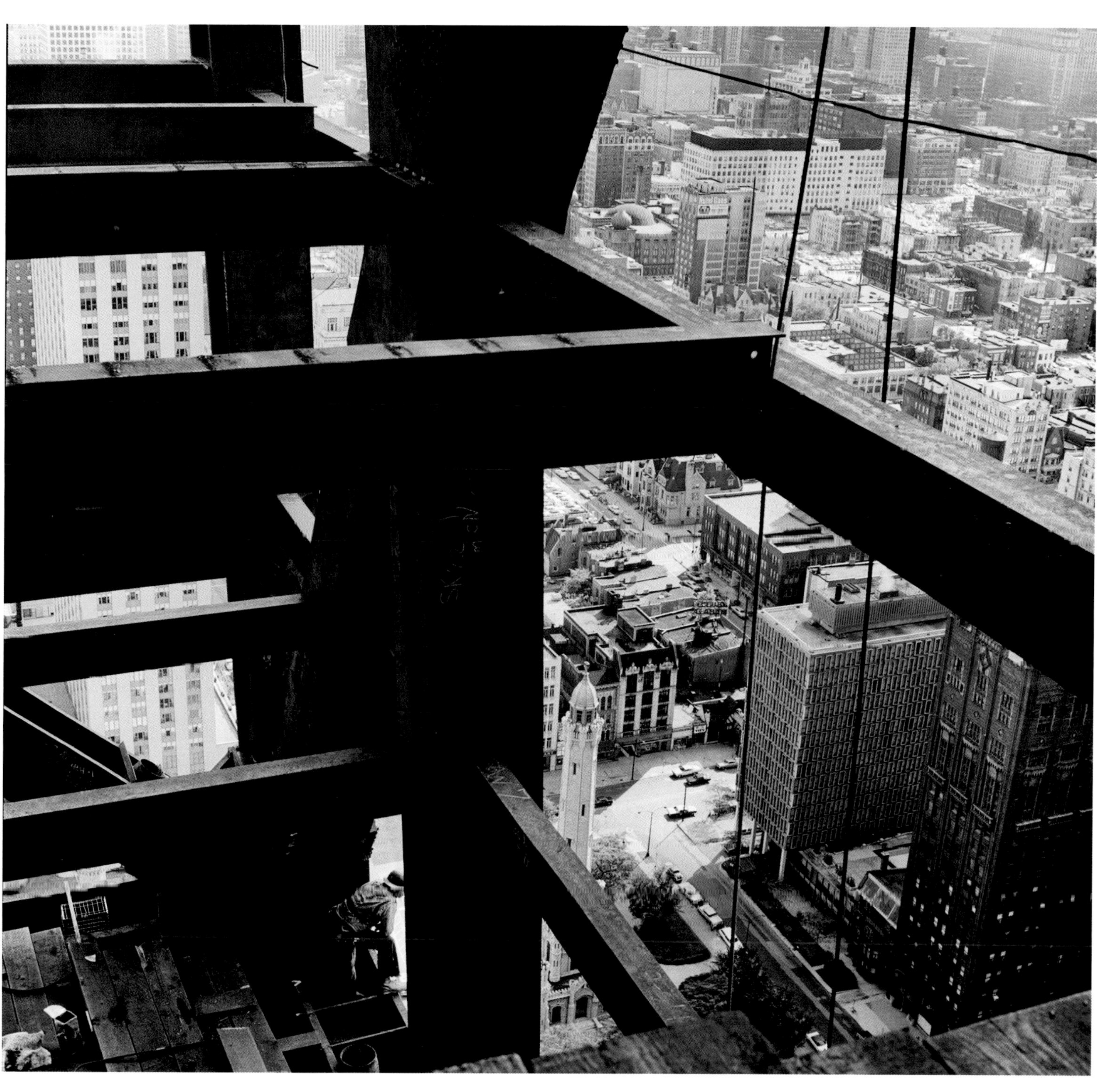

John Hancock Center construction, Chicago.
Skidmore, Owings & Merrill, 1967.

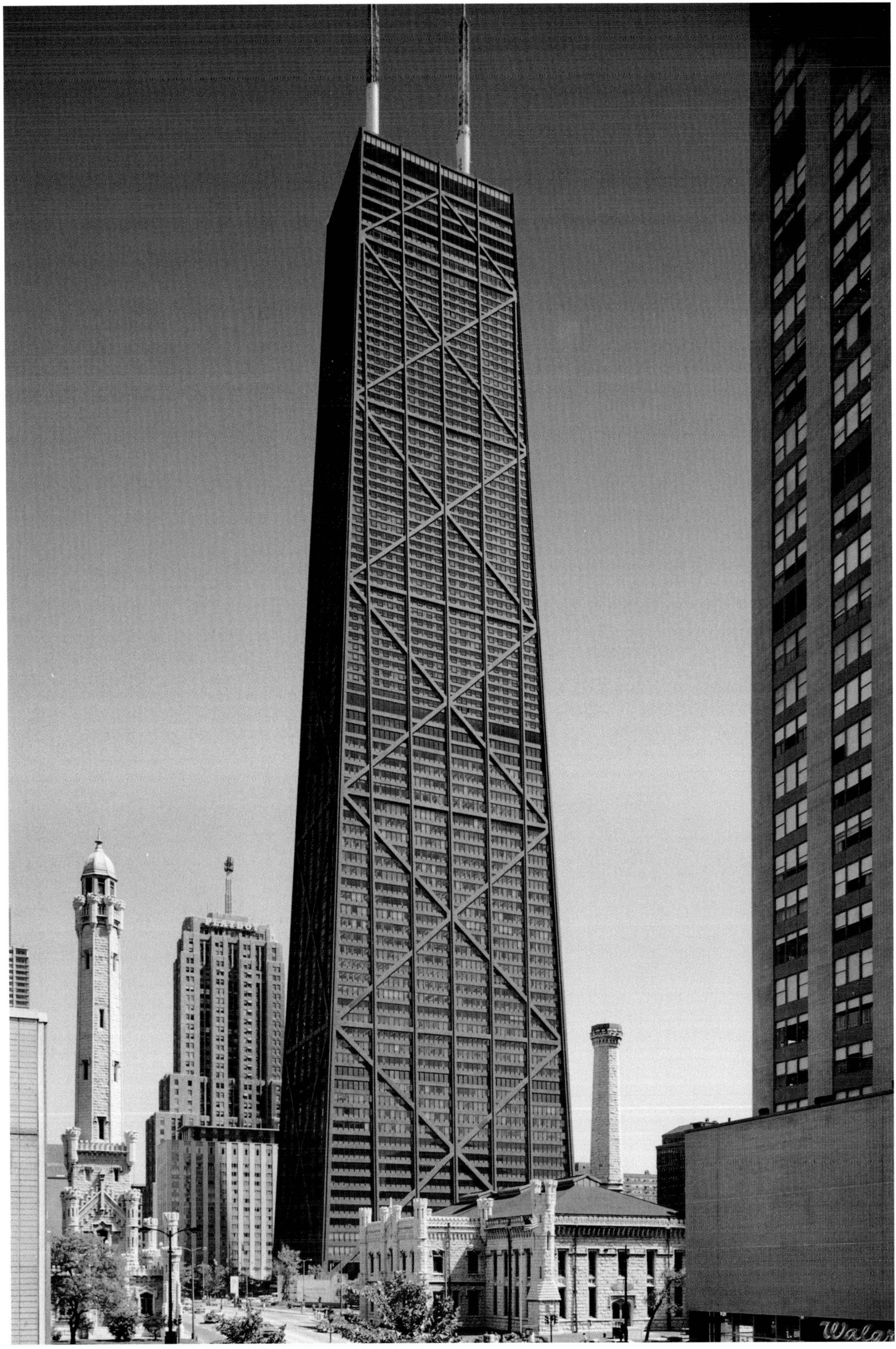

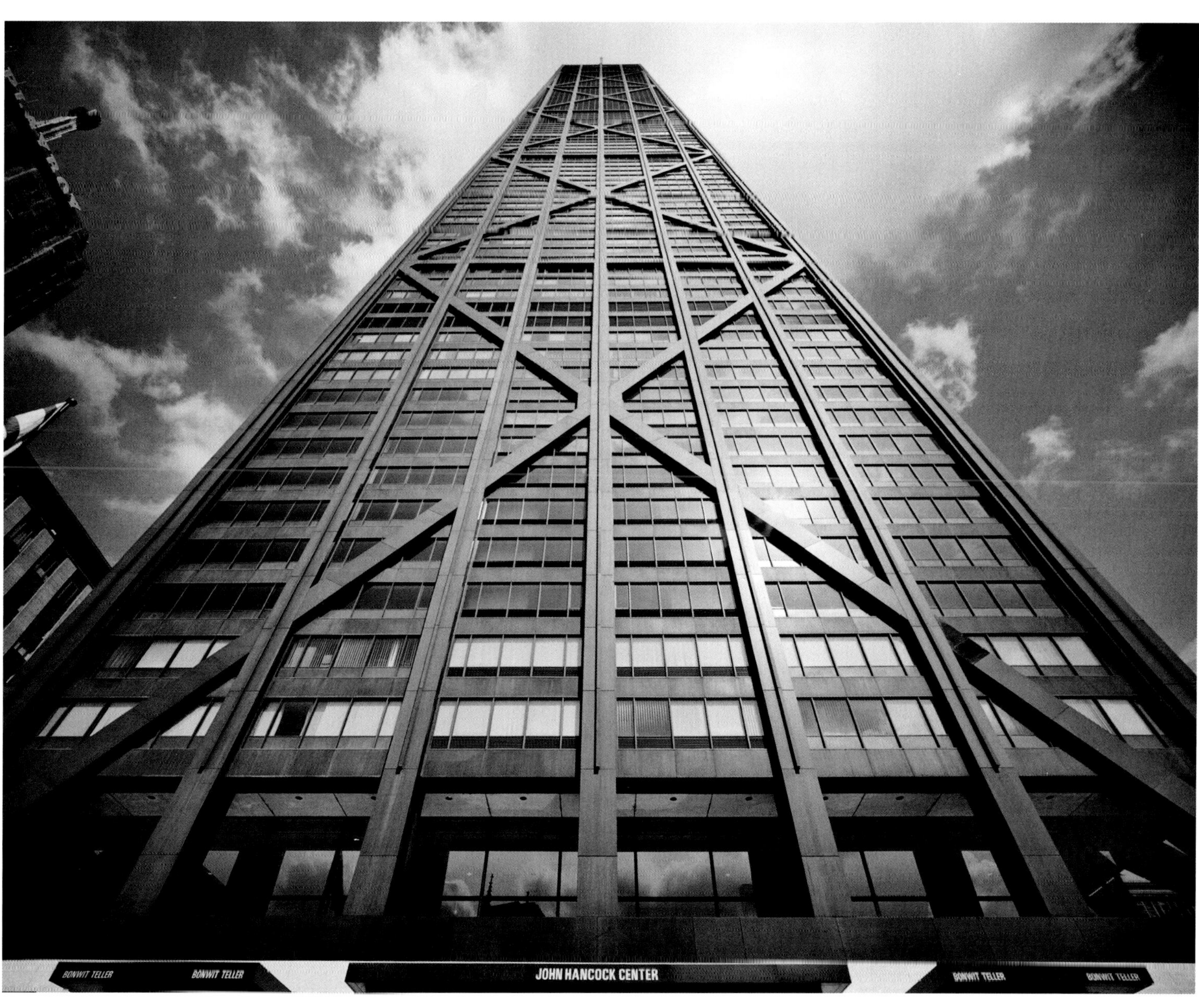

John Hancock Center, Chicago.
Skidmore, Owings & Merrill, 1970.

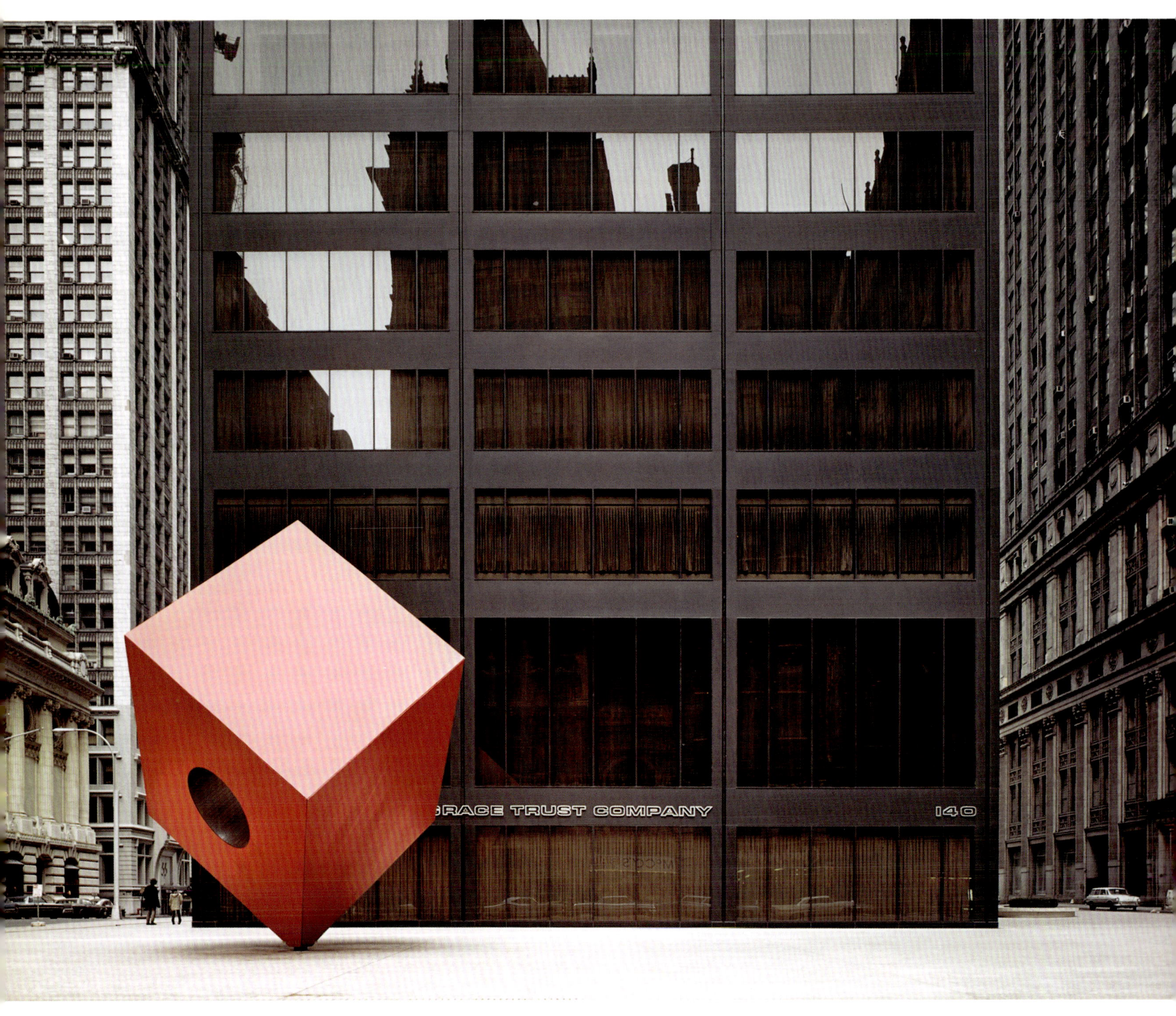

140 Broadway, New York.
Skidmore, Owings & Merrill, 1968.

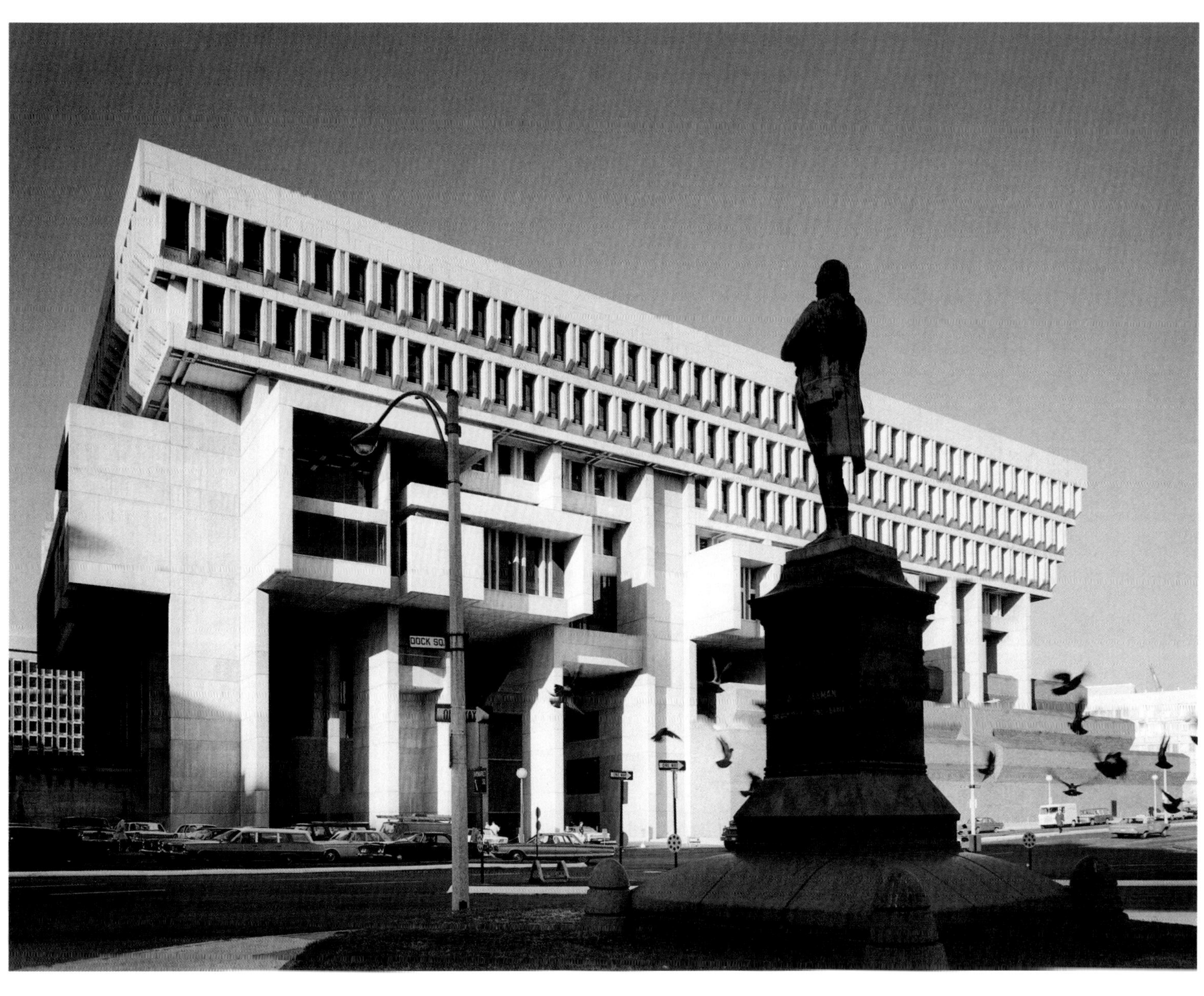

Boston City Hall.
Kallmann, McKinnell & Knowles 1968.

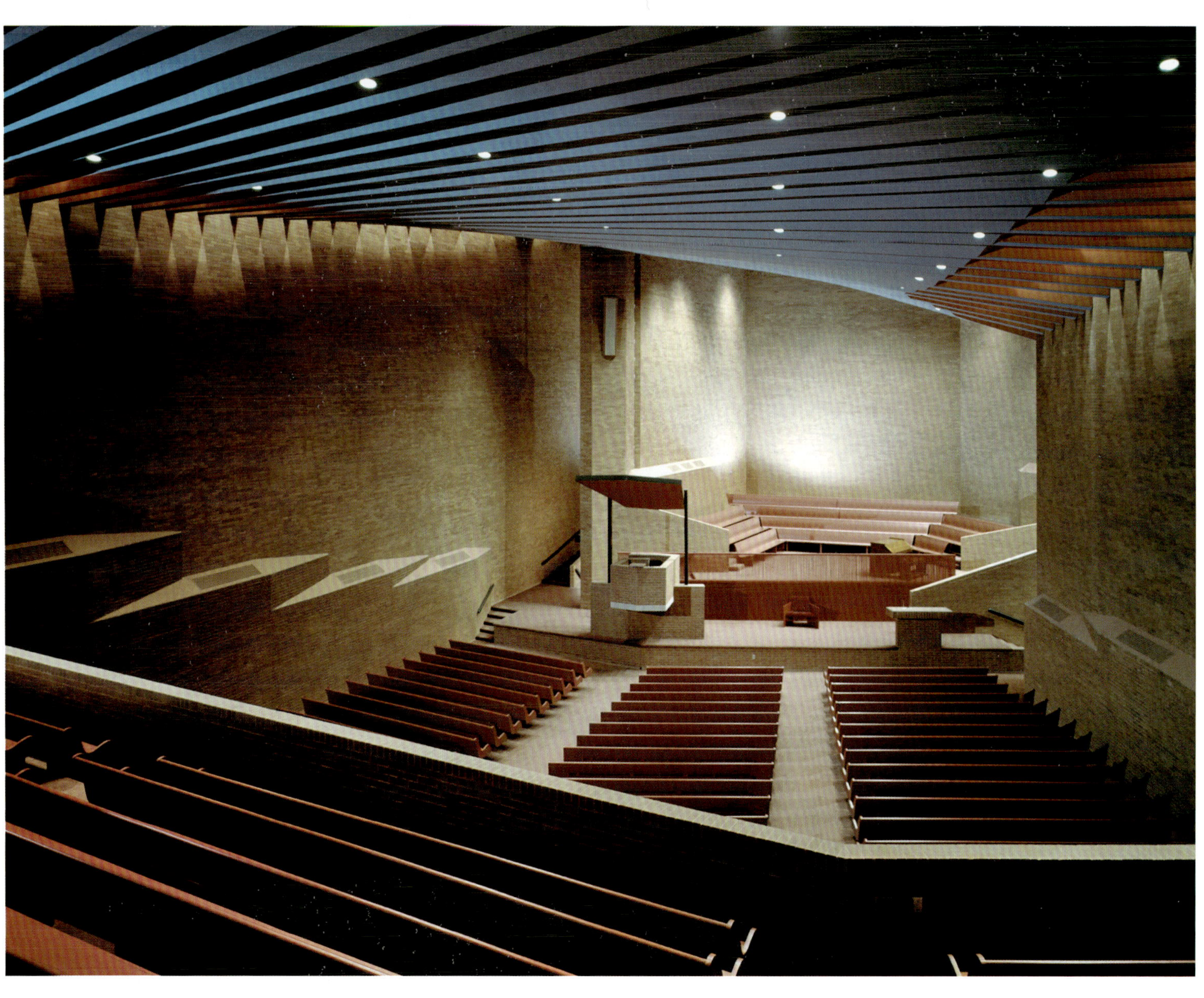

Tuskegee Institute Chapel, Tuskegee, Alabama. Paul Rudolph, 1969.

Overleaf
Weyerhaeuser, Tacoma, Washington. Skidmore, Owings & Merrill, 1971.

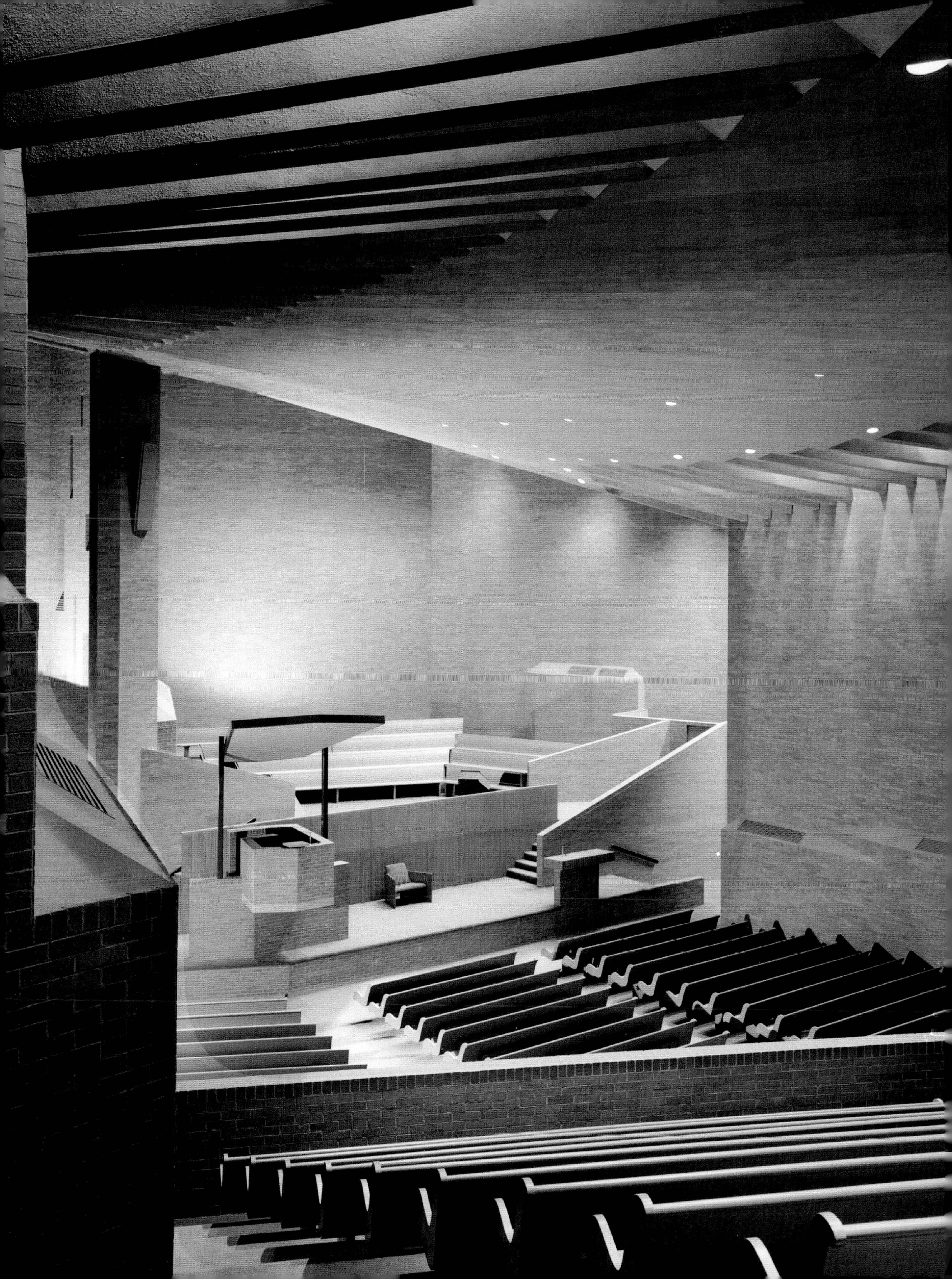

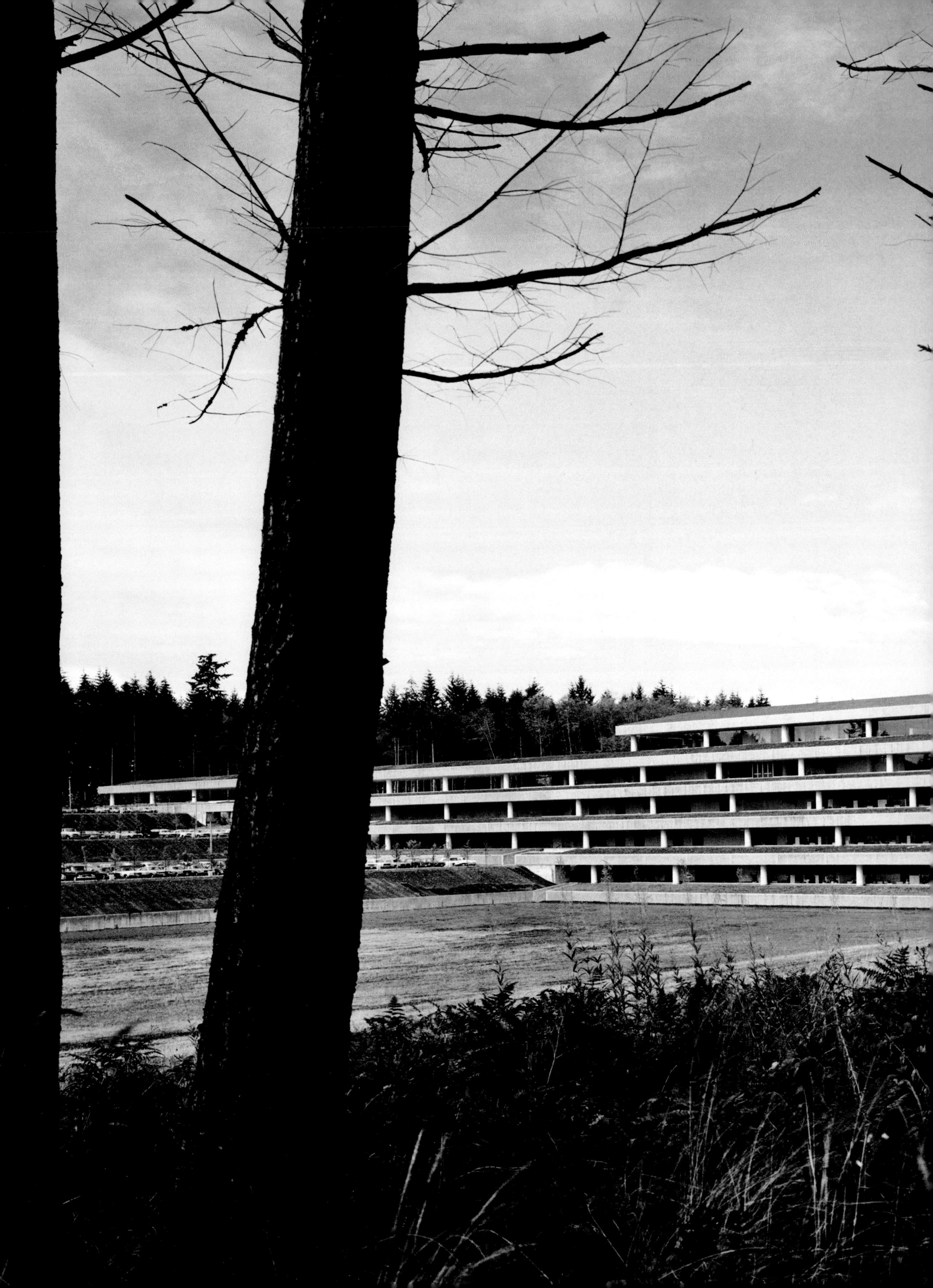

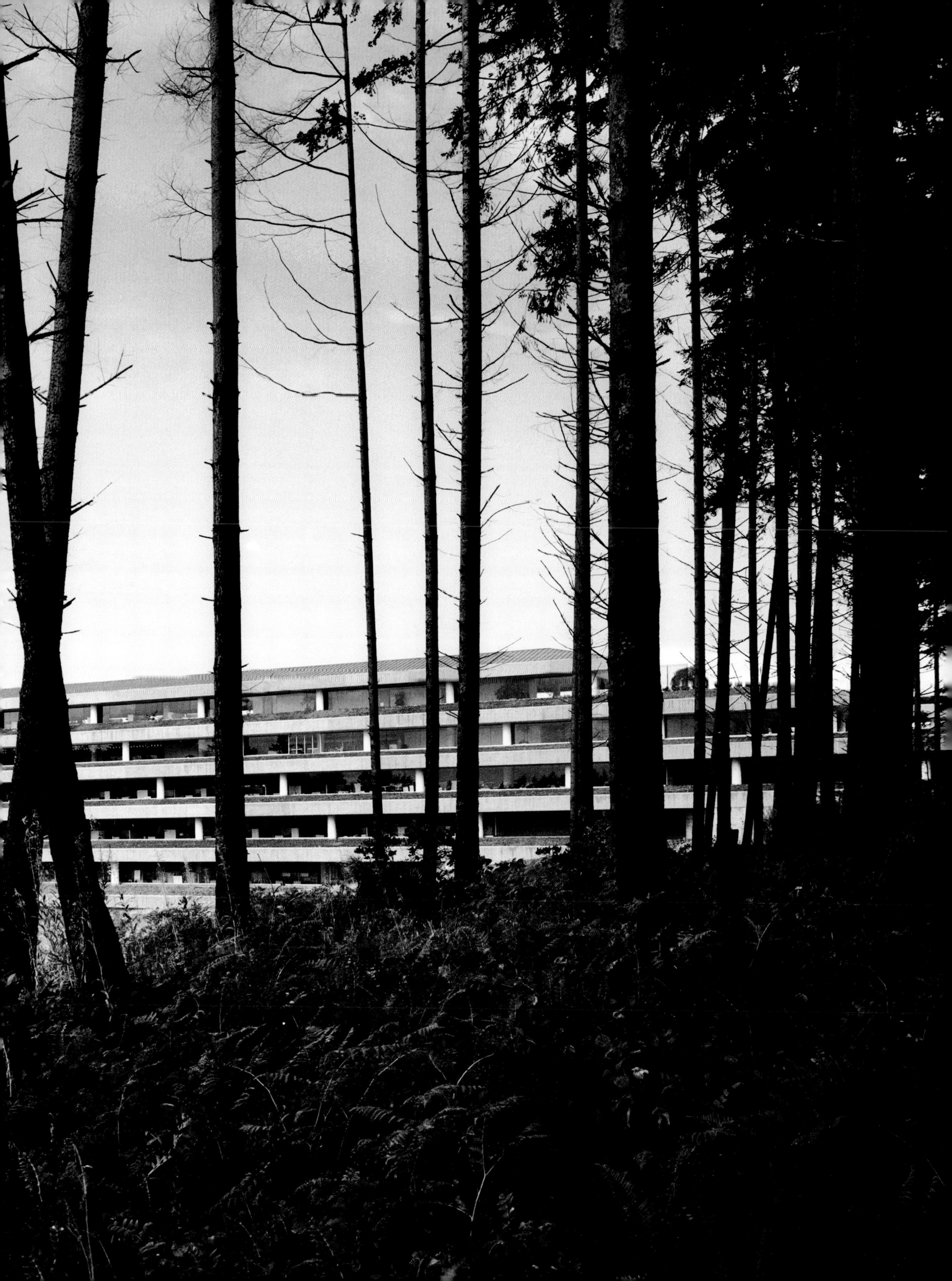

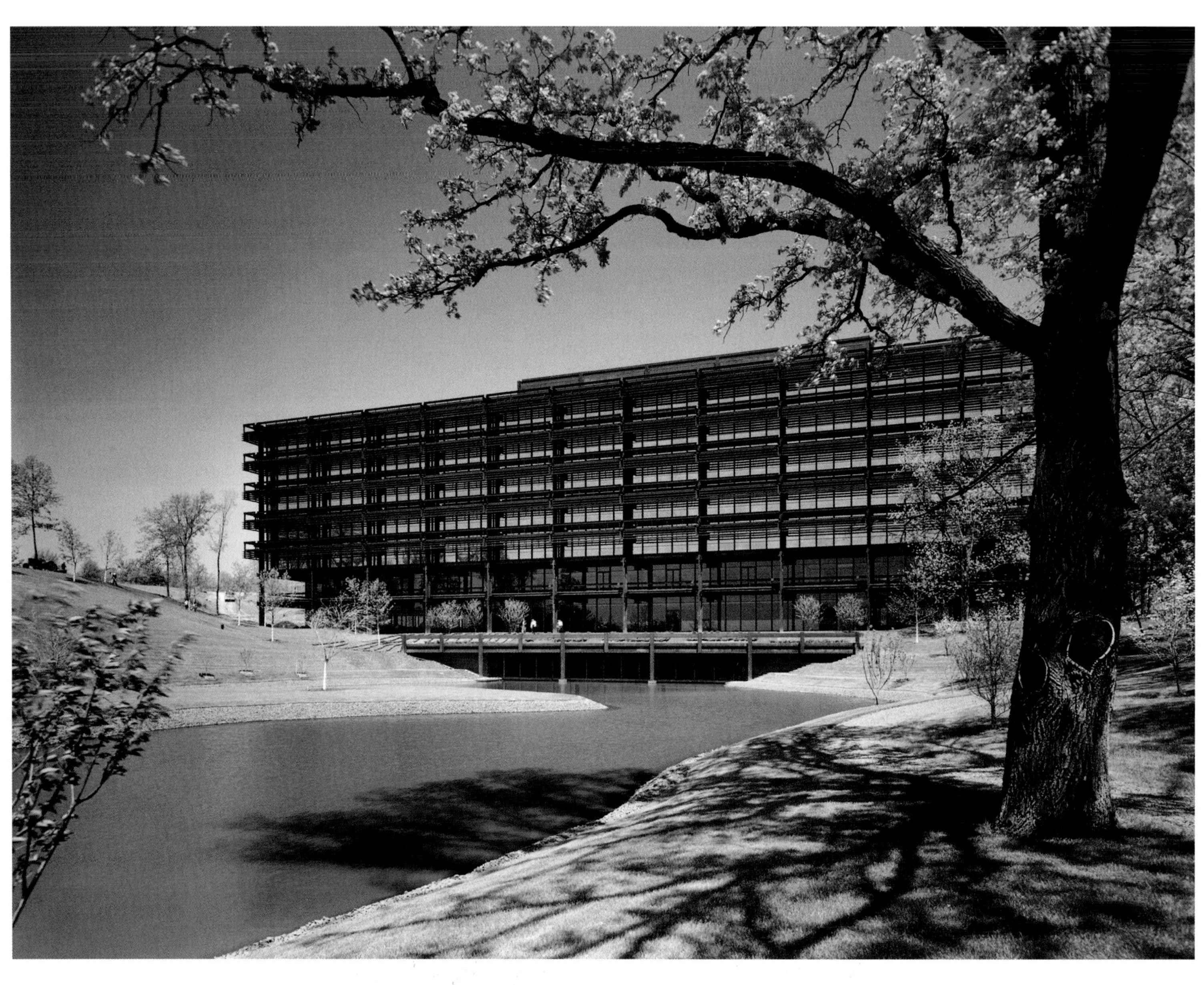

John Deere Company, Moline, Illinois.
Eero Saarinen, 1972.

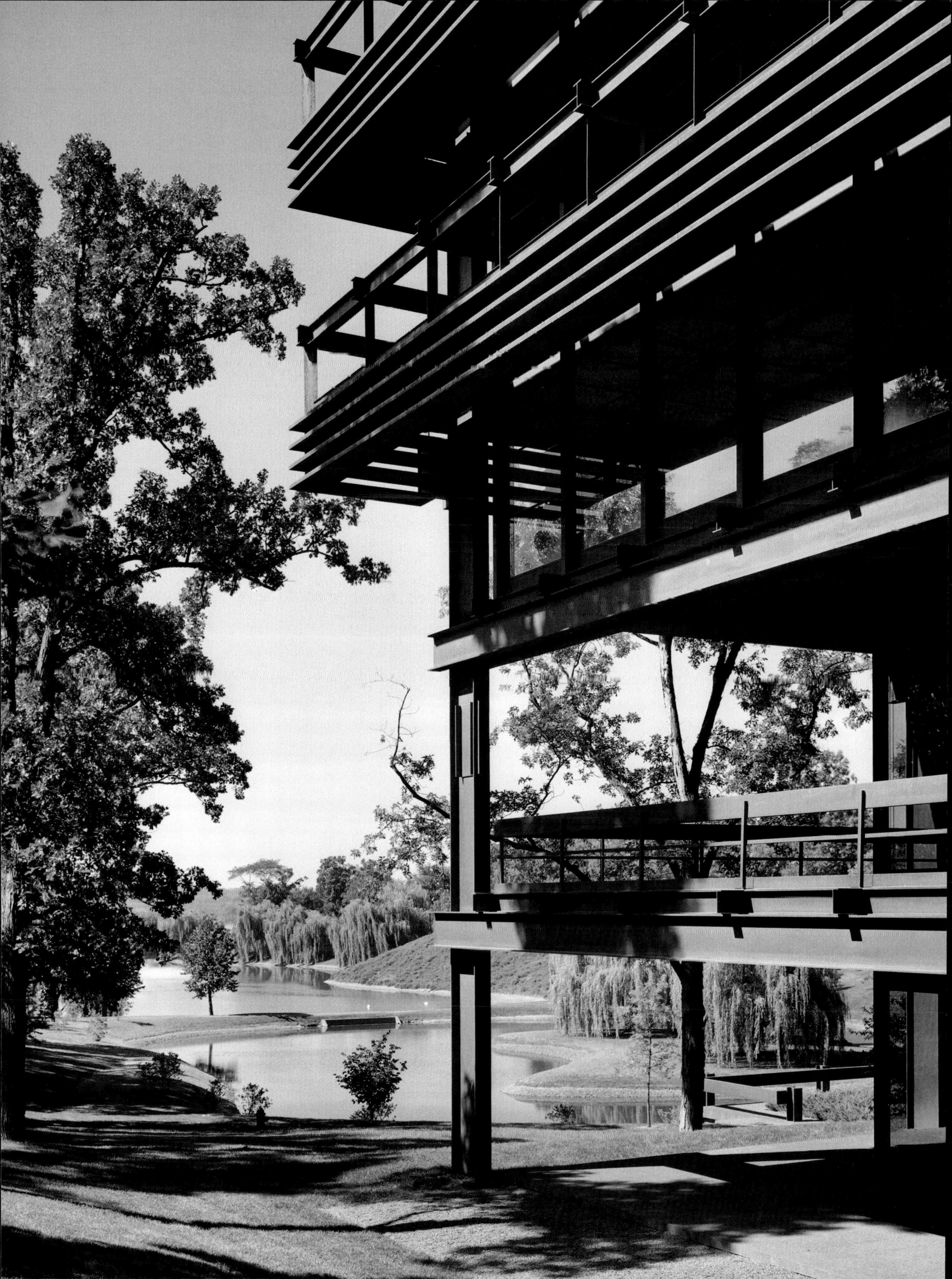

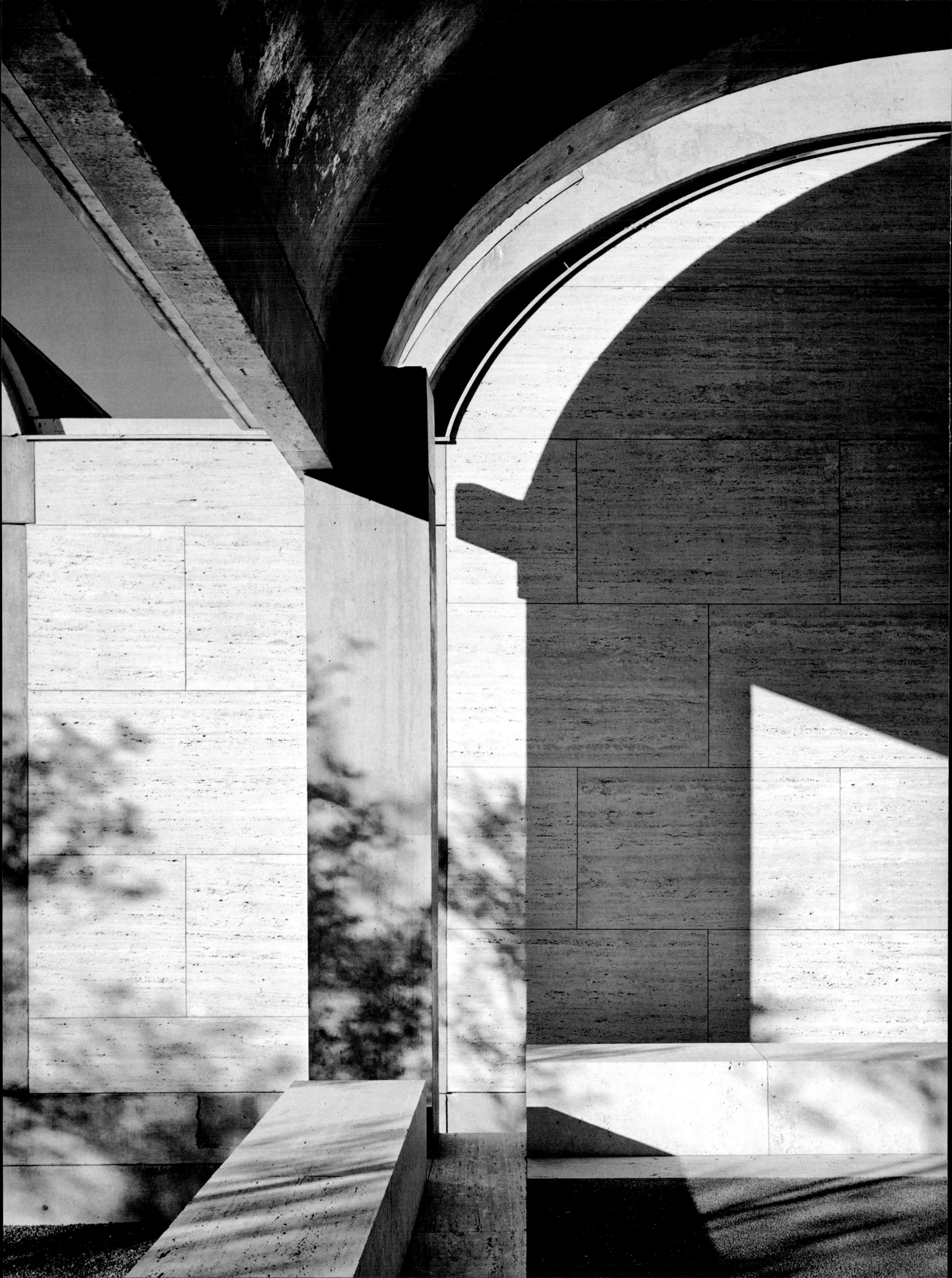

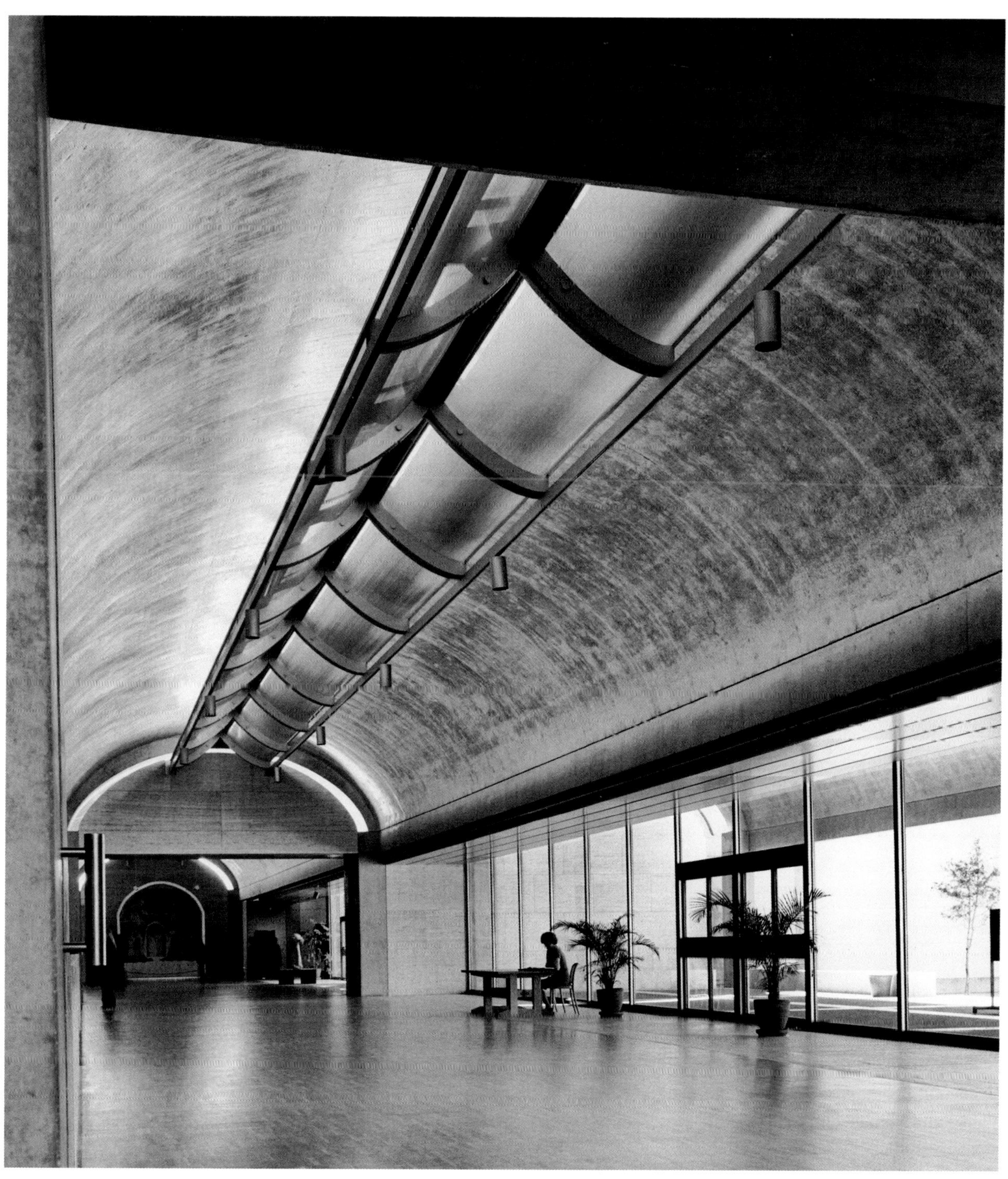

Kimbell Art Museum, Fort Worth, Texas.
Louis Kahn, 1972.

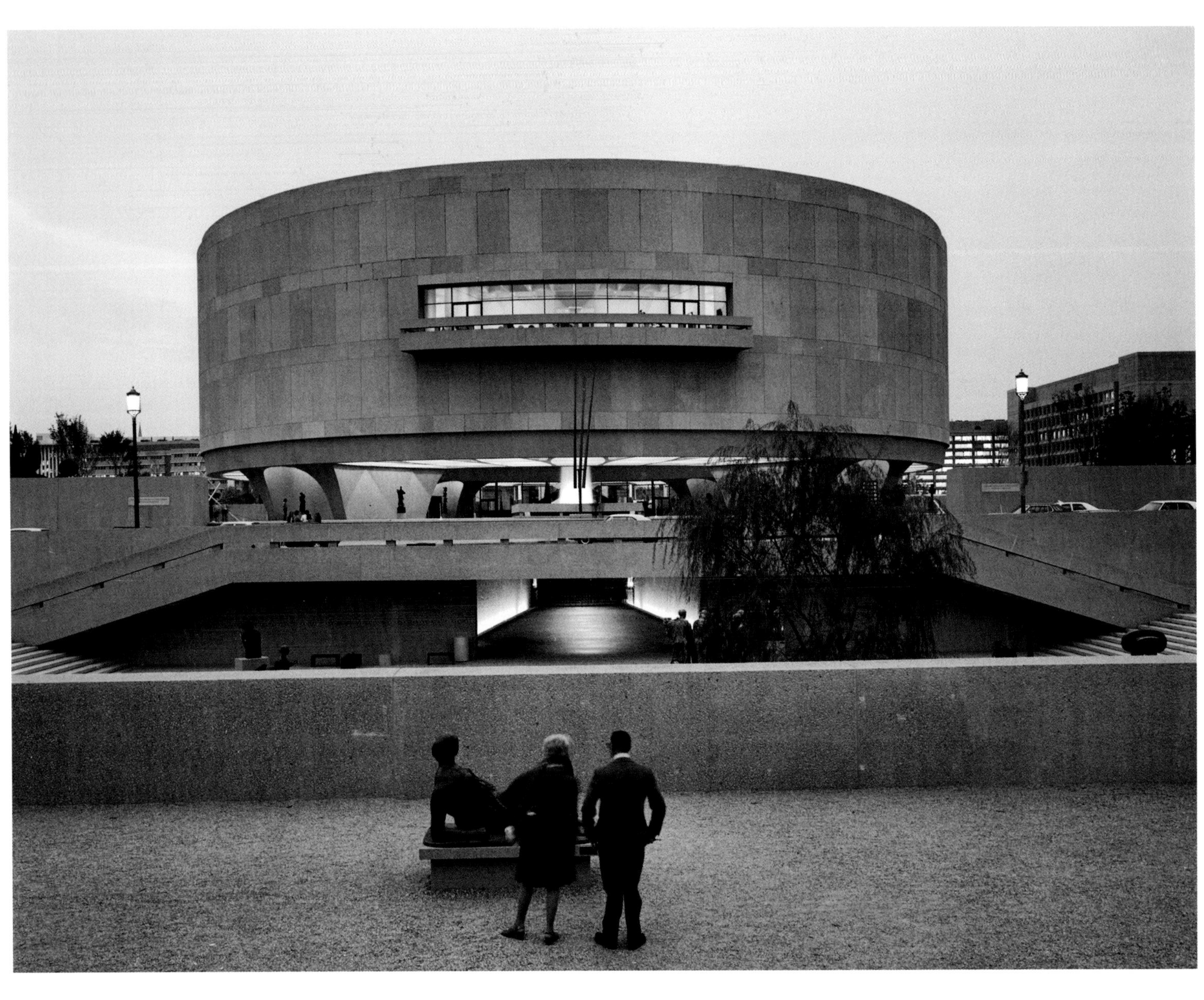

Hirshhorn Museum, Washington, D.C.
Skidmore Owings & Merrill, 1974.

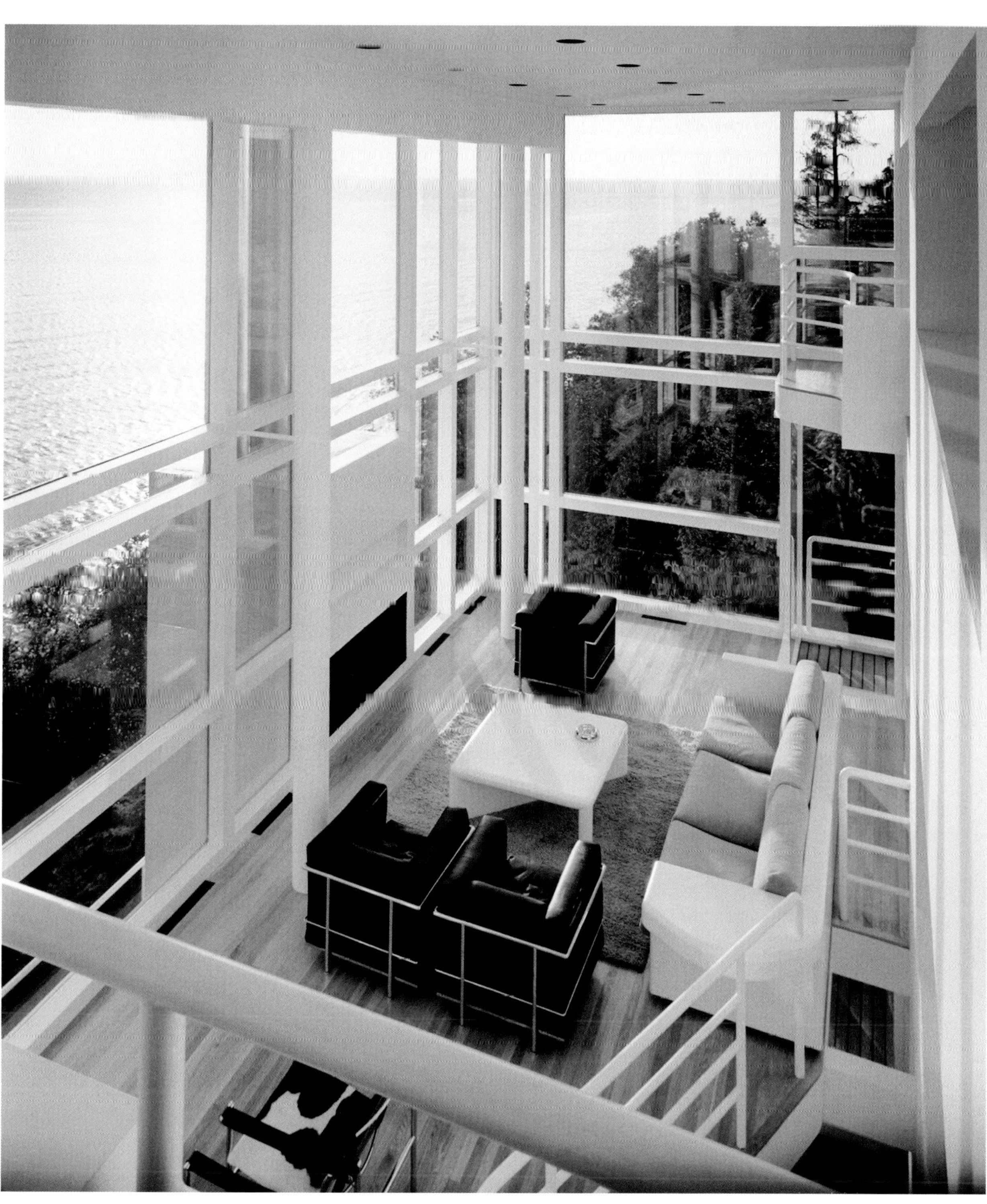

Douglas House, Harbor Springs, Michigan.
Richard Meier, 1974.

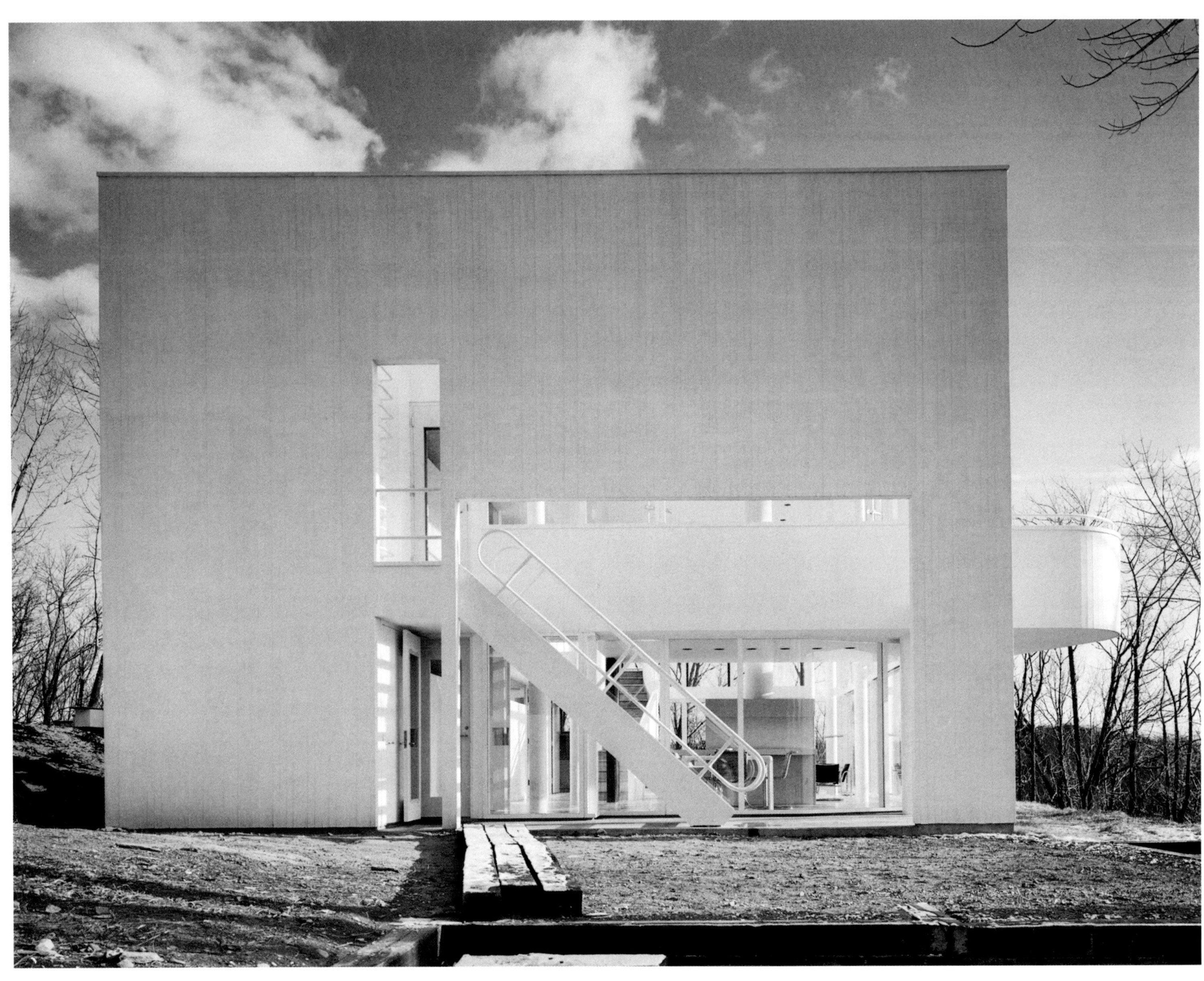

Shamberg House, Chappaqua, New York.
Richard Meier, 1974.

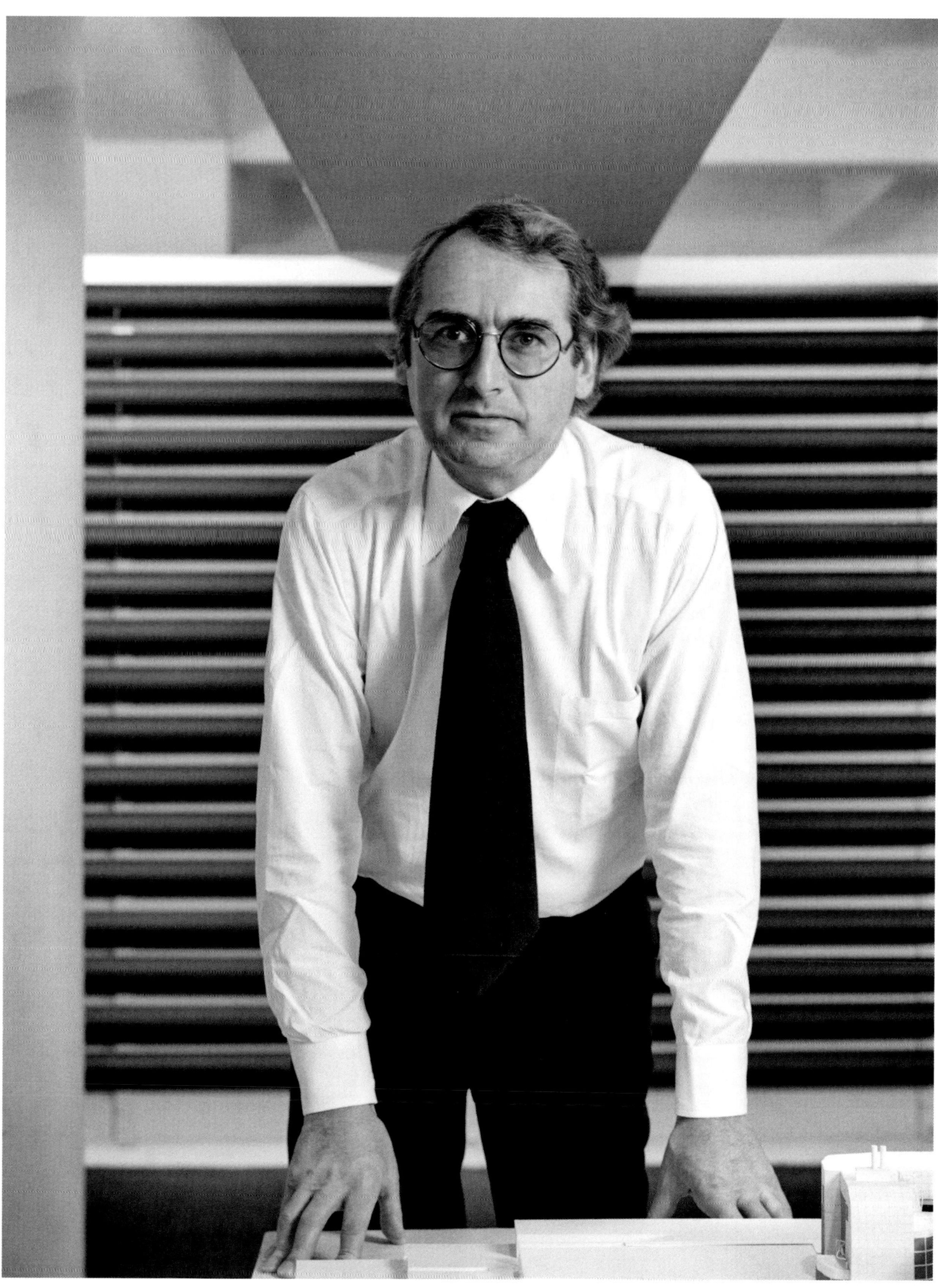

Richard Meier, New York, 1977.

Overleaf
Salk Institute for Biological Research,
La Jolla, California. Louis Kahn, 1977.

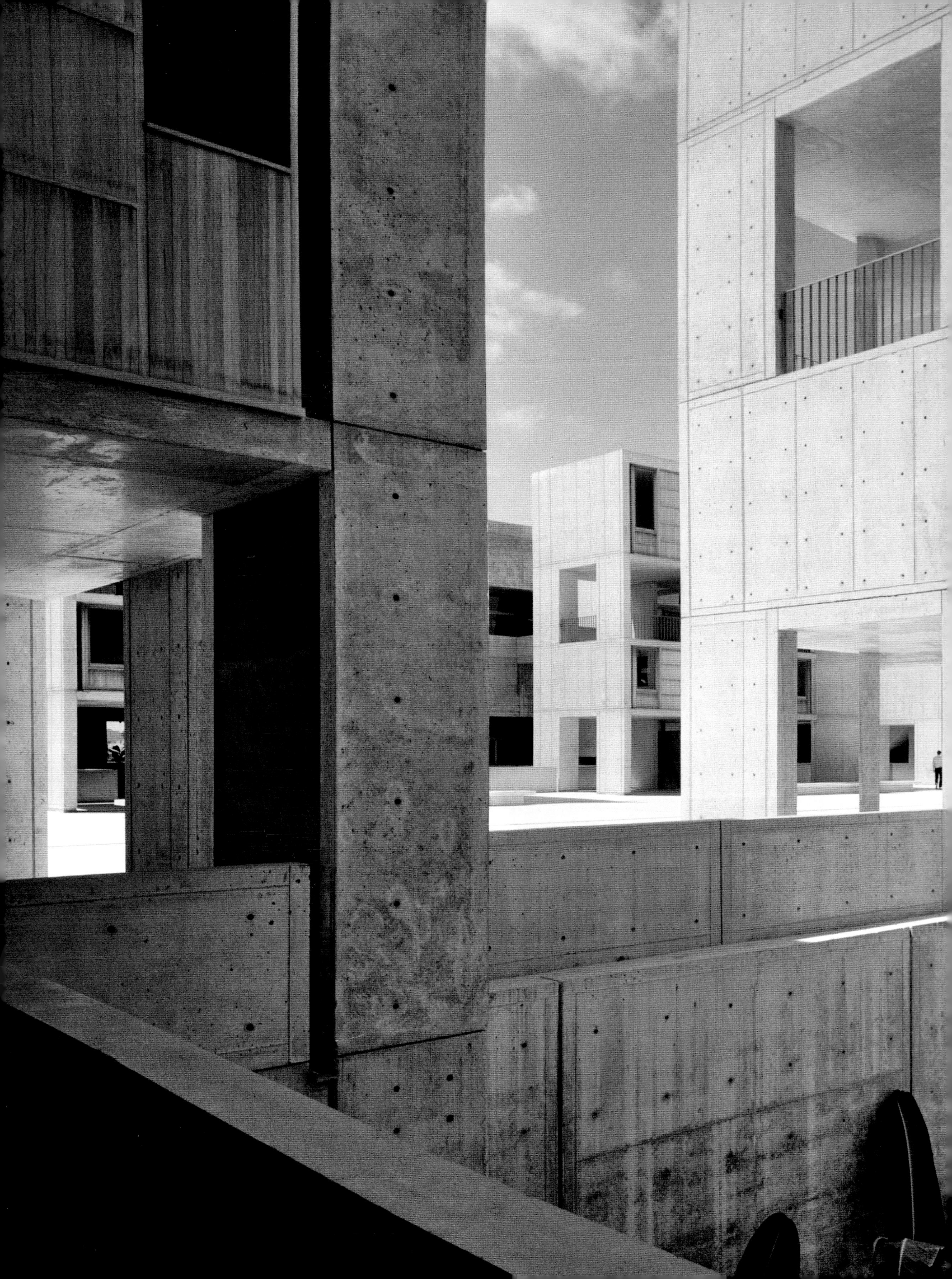

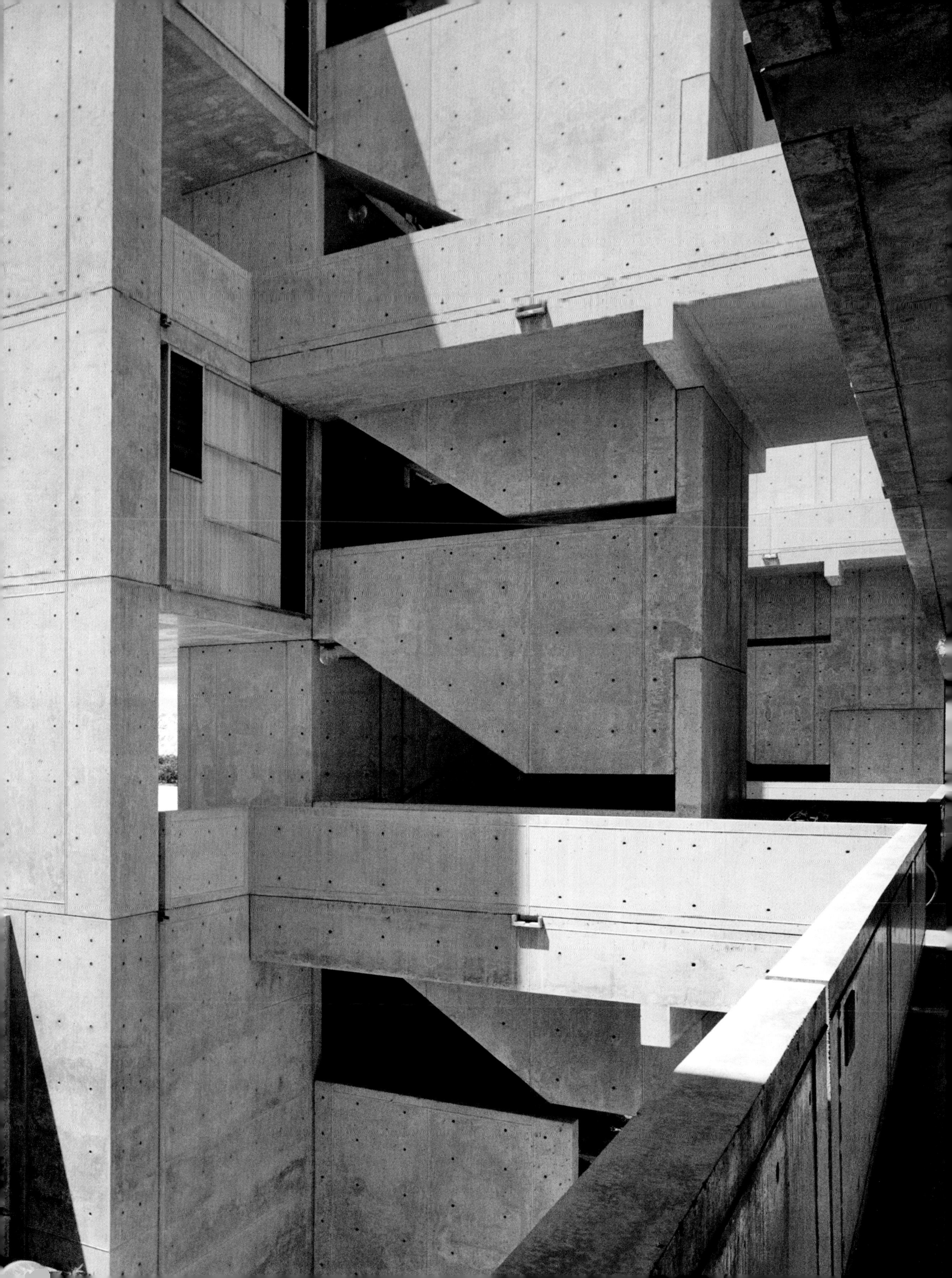

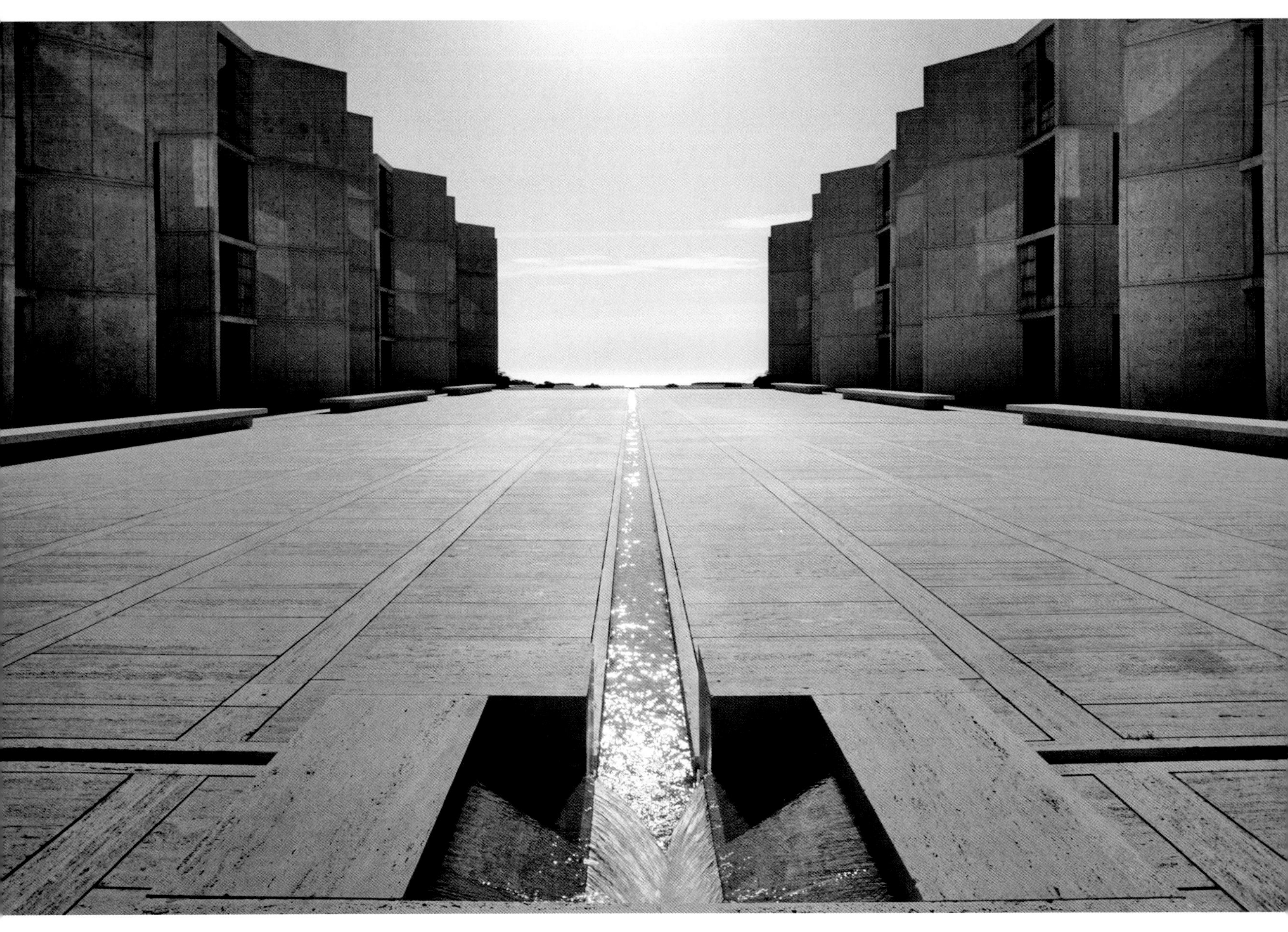

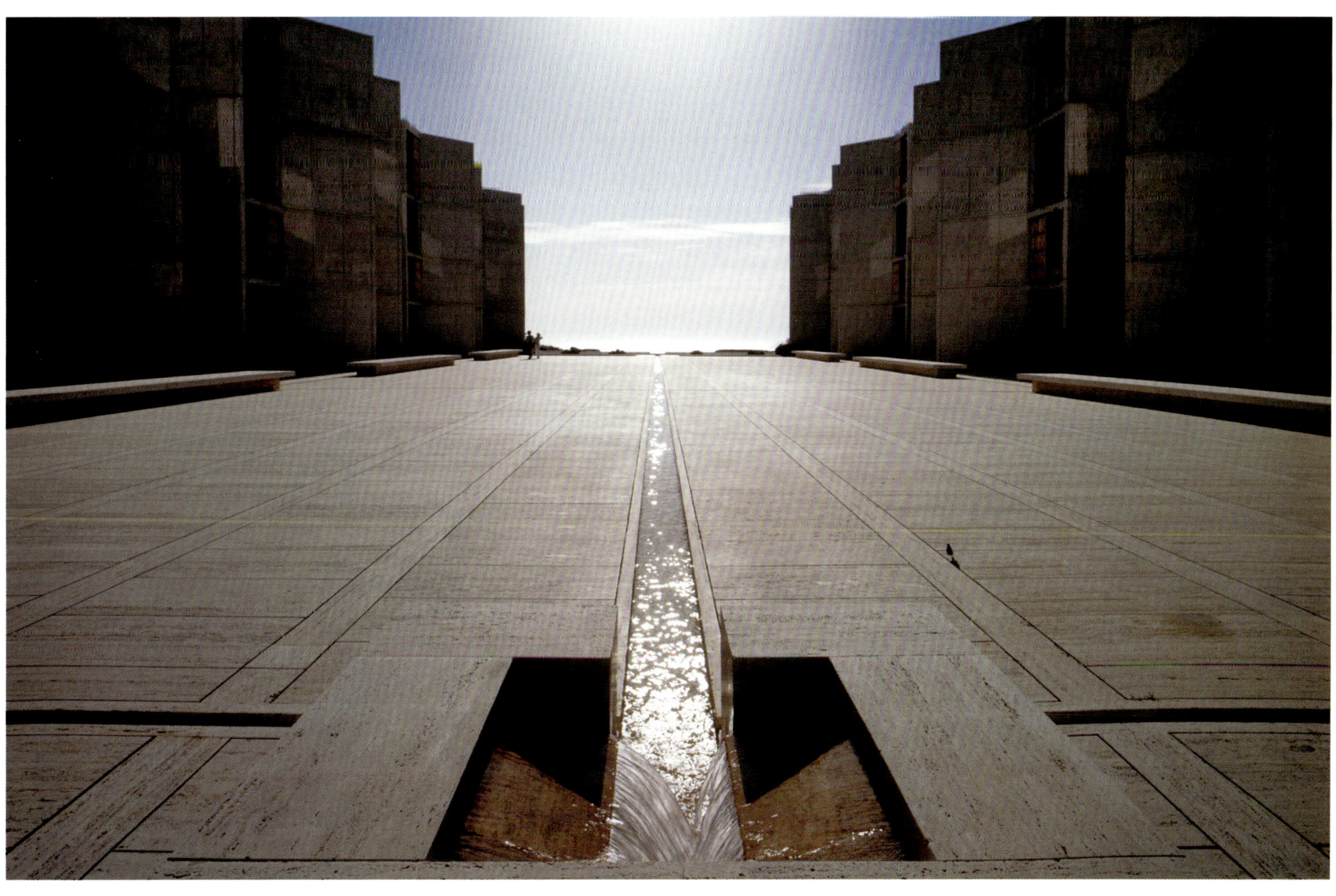

Salk Institute for Biological Research,
La Jolla, California. Louis Kahn, 1977.

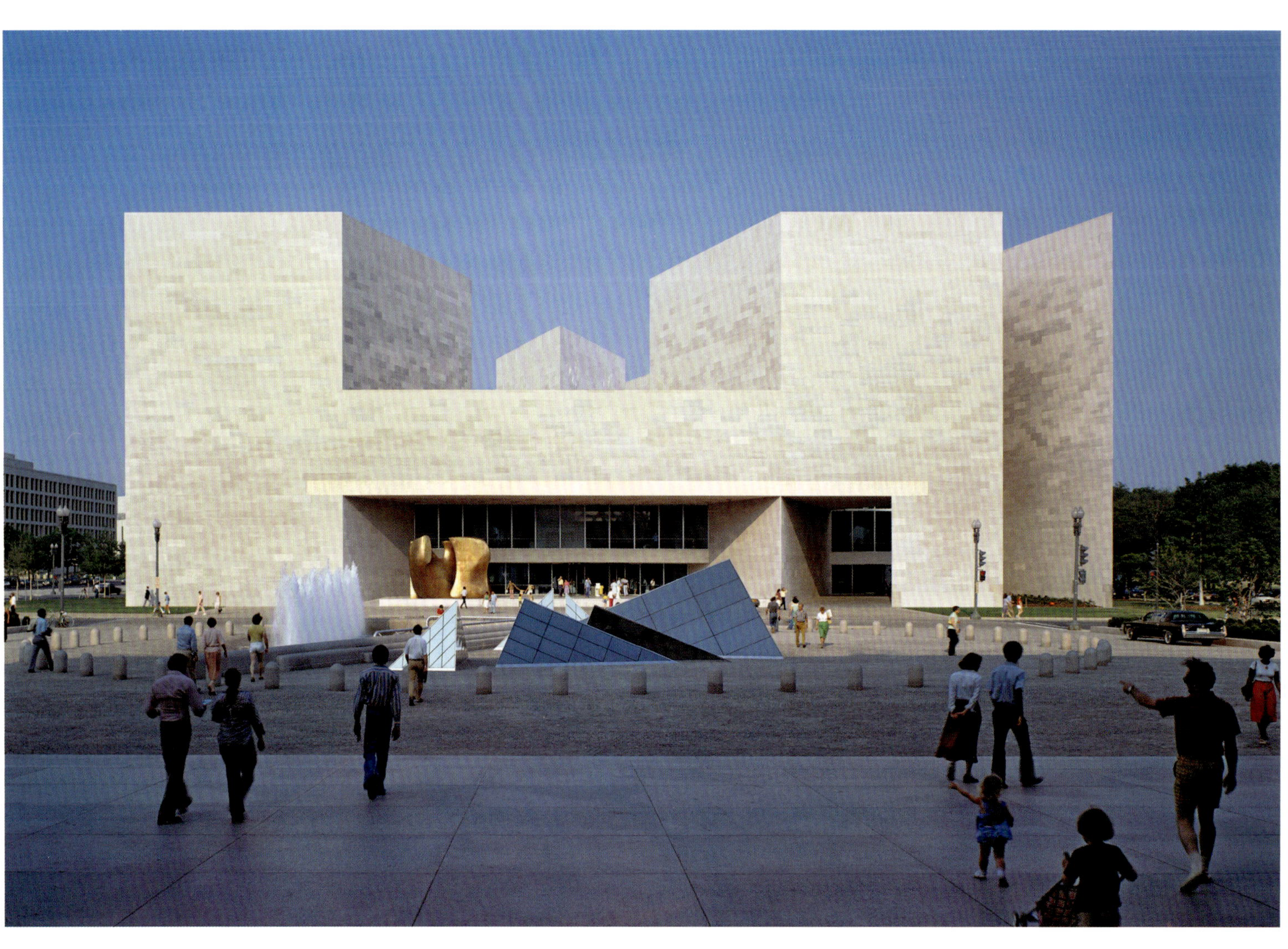

Above and opposite
East Wing, National Gallery of Art, Washington, D.C. I. M. Pei, 1978.

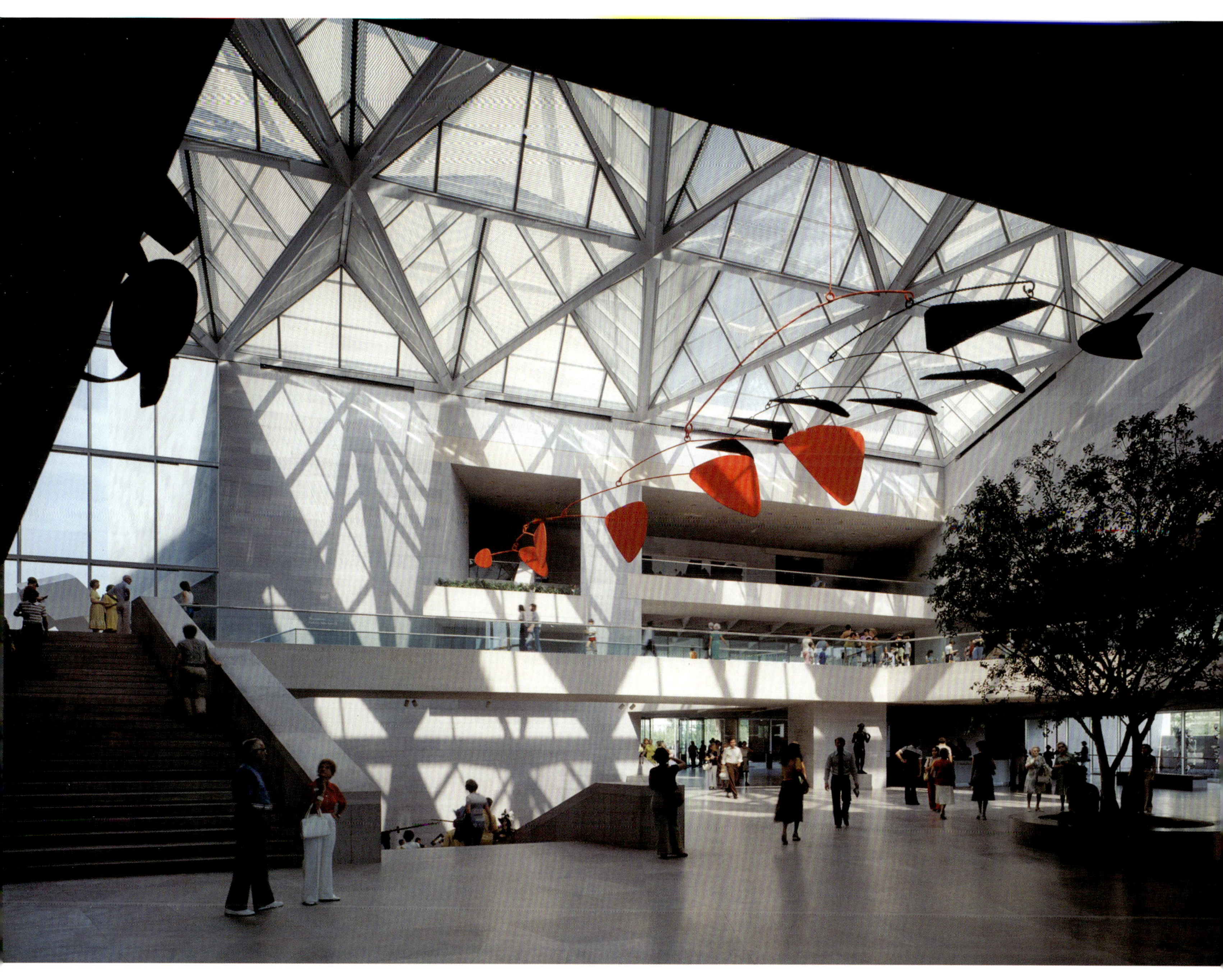

Portfolio
Man and Machine

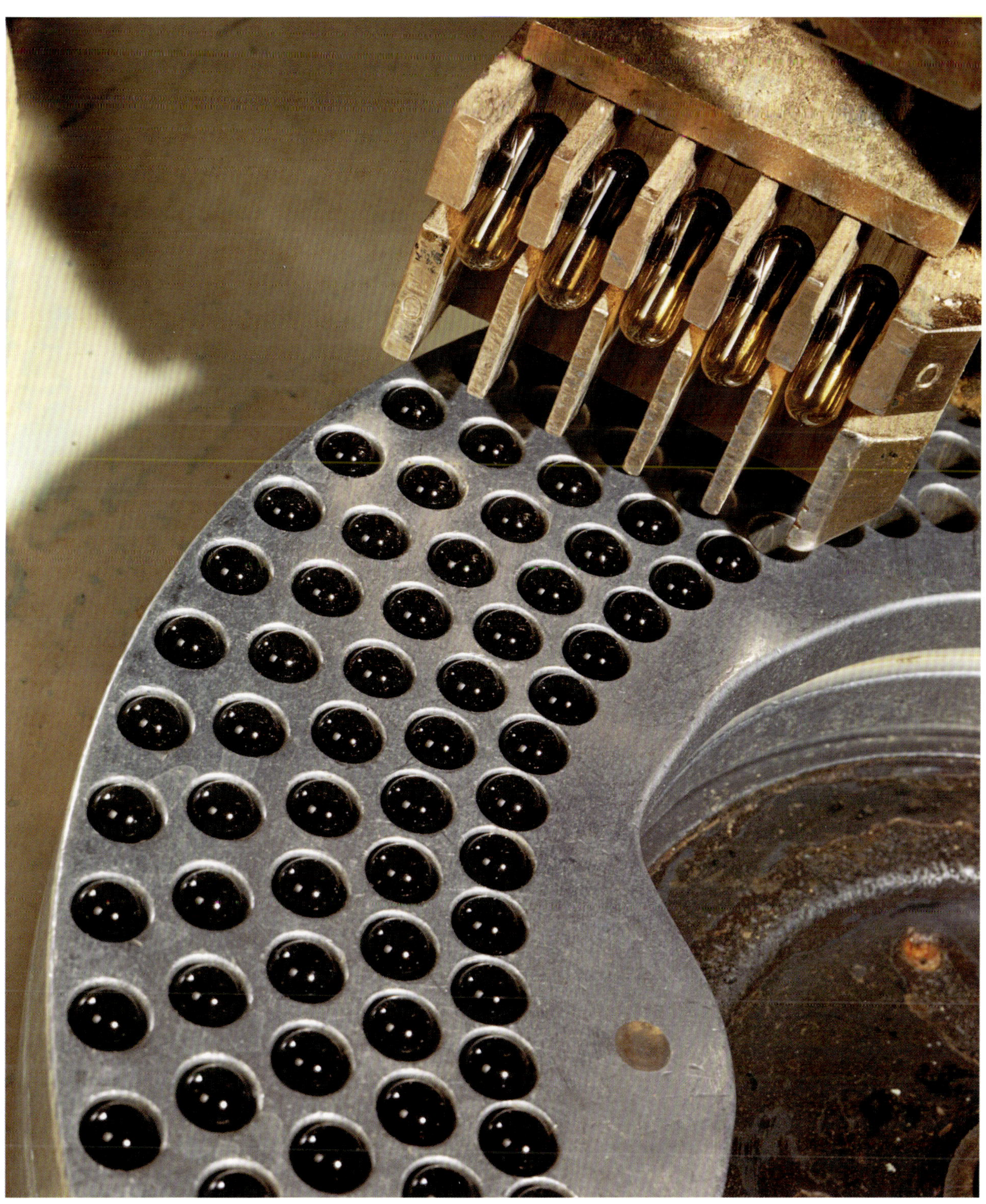

Upjohn pill-making equipment,
Kalamazoo, Michigan, 1942.

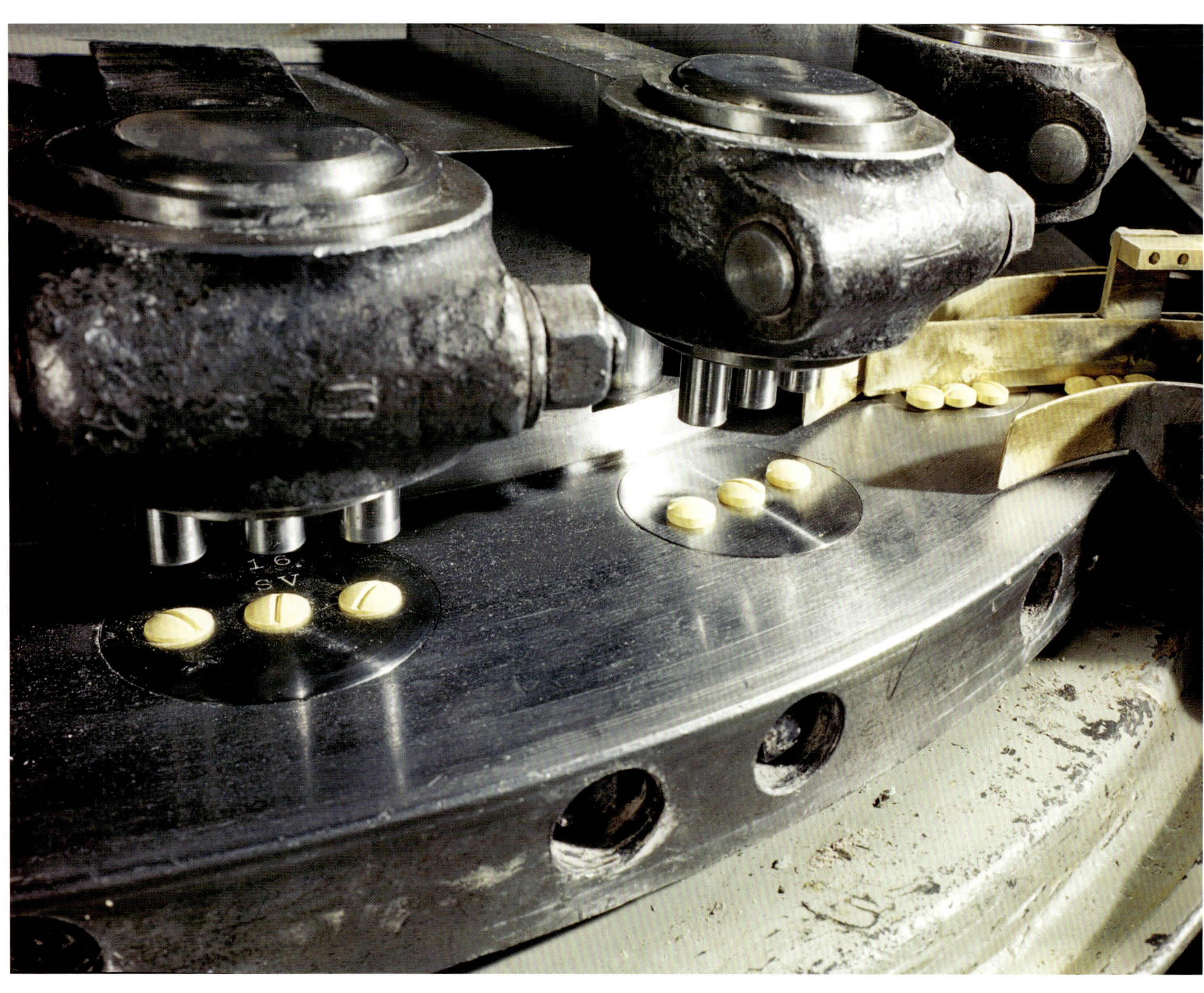

Upjohn pill-making equipment, Kalamazoo, Michigan, 1942.

Upjohn, Kalamazoo, Michigan, 1949.

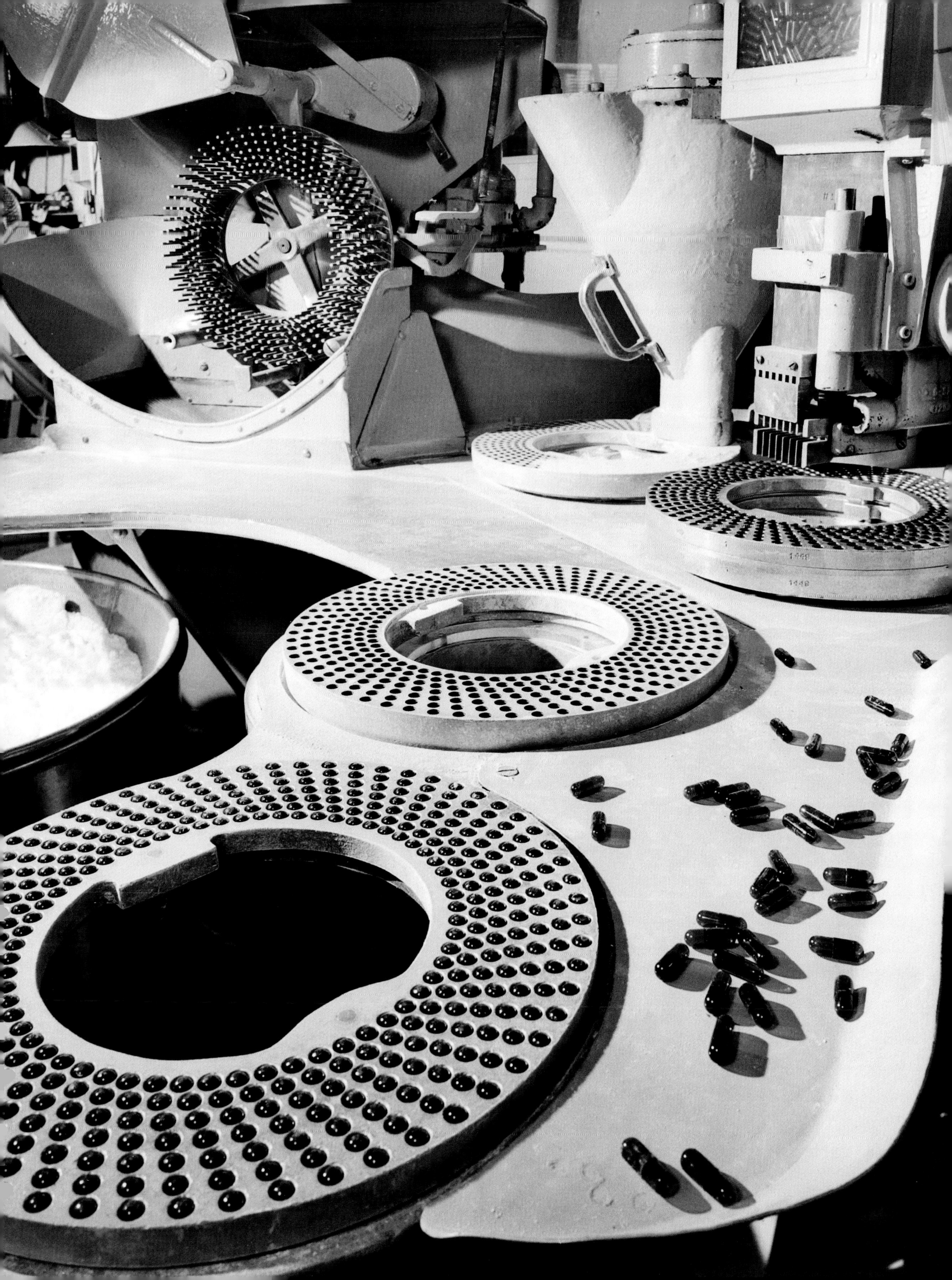

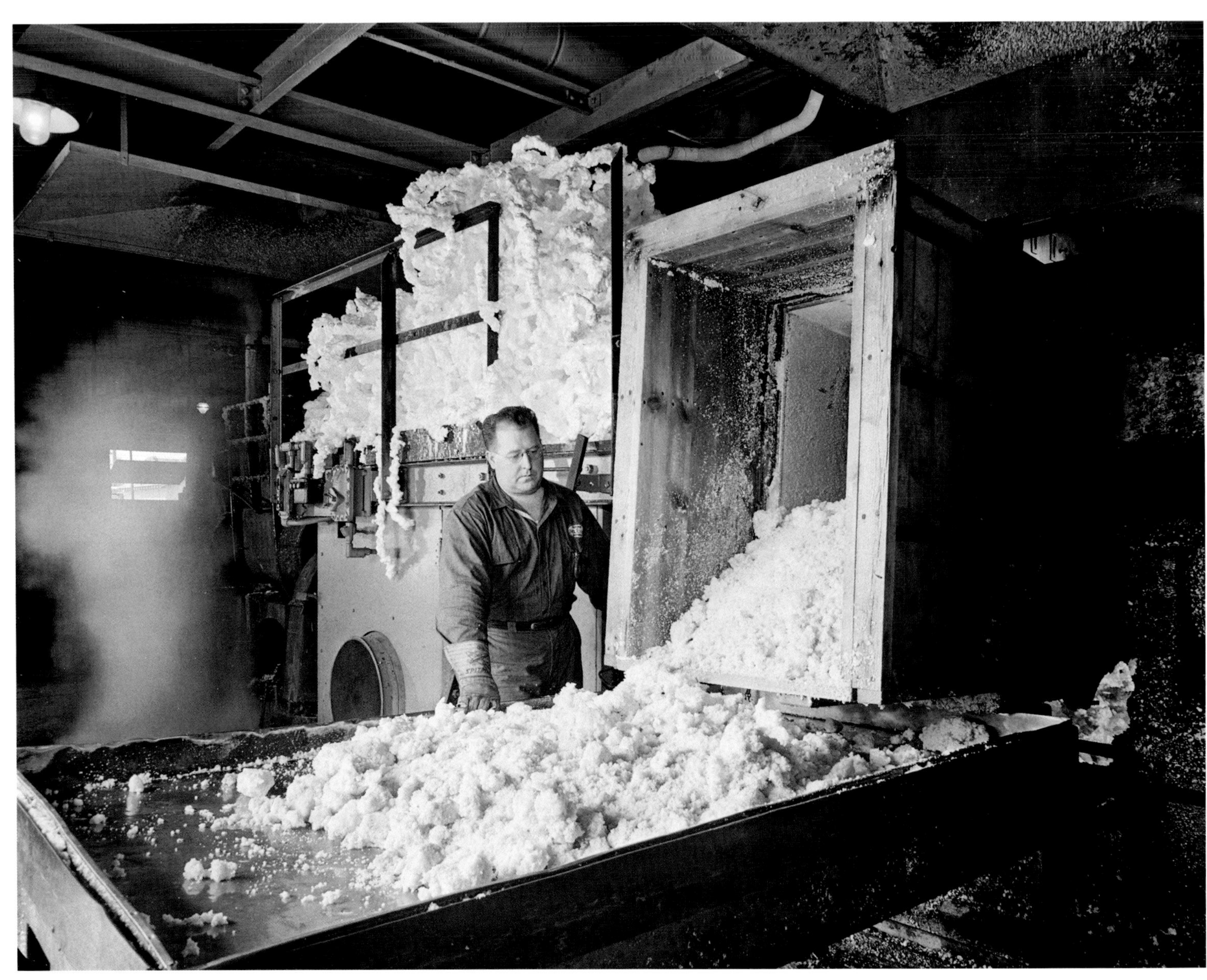

Above and opposite
Standard Oil Bayway Refinery,
Linden, New Jersey, 1944.

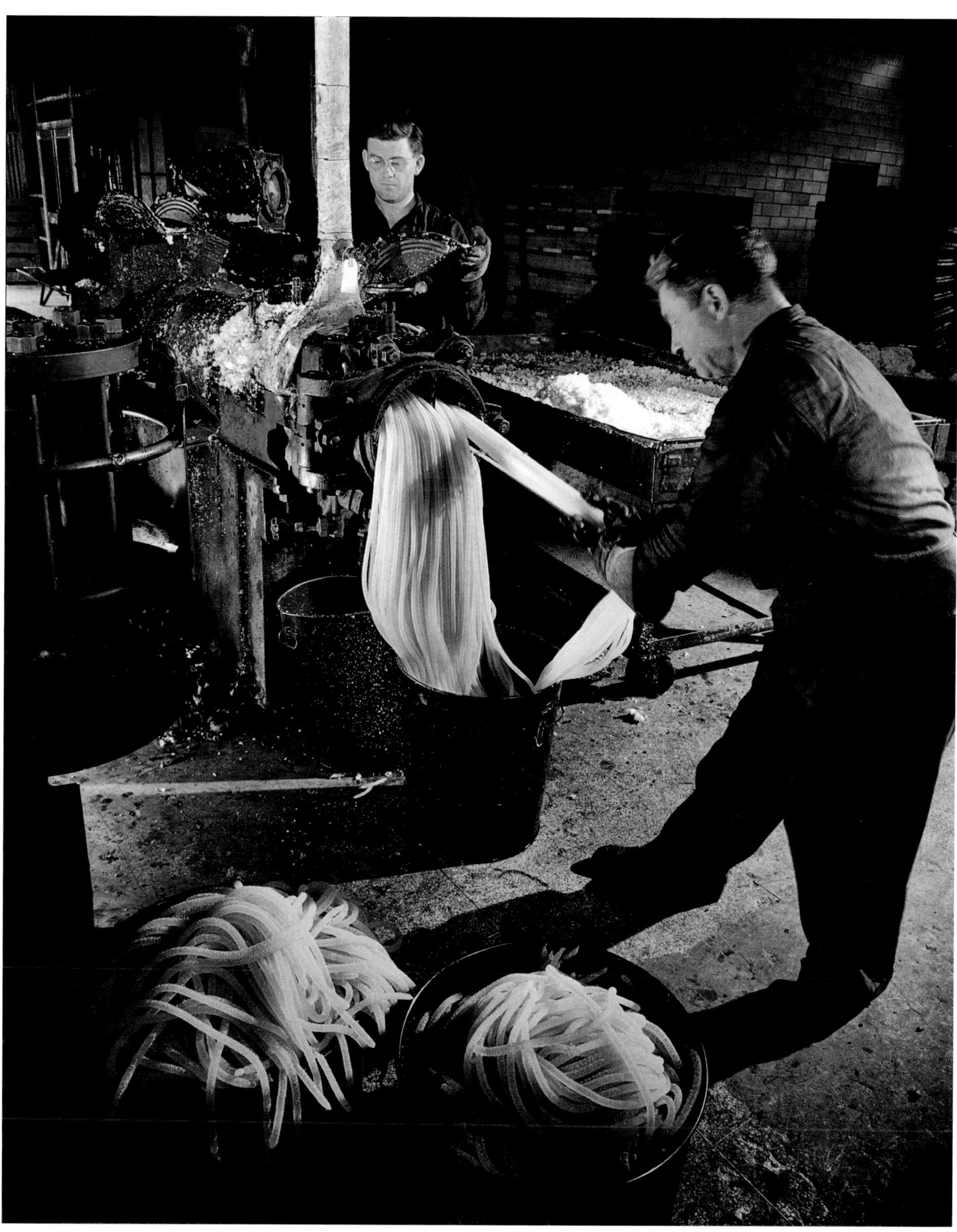

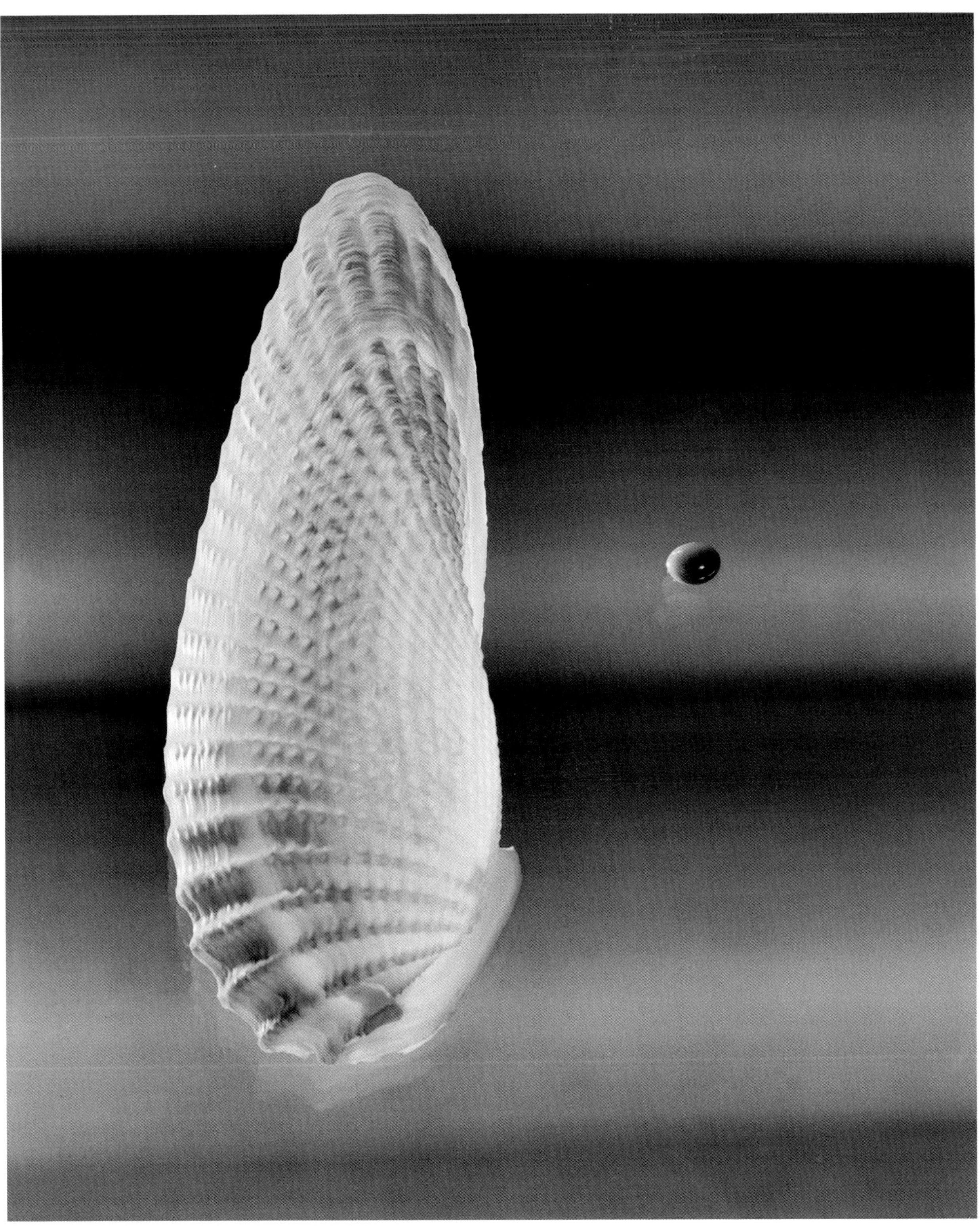

Shell with pill, *Scope* magazine, Upjohn.
Graphic design by Will Burtin, 1952.

Pills for *Scope* magazine, Upjohn.
Graphic design by Will Burtin, 1944.

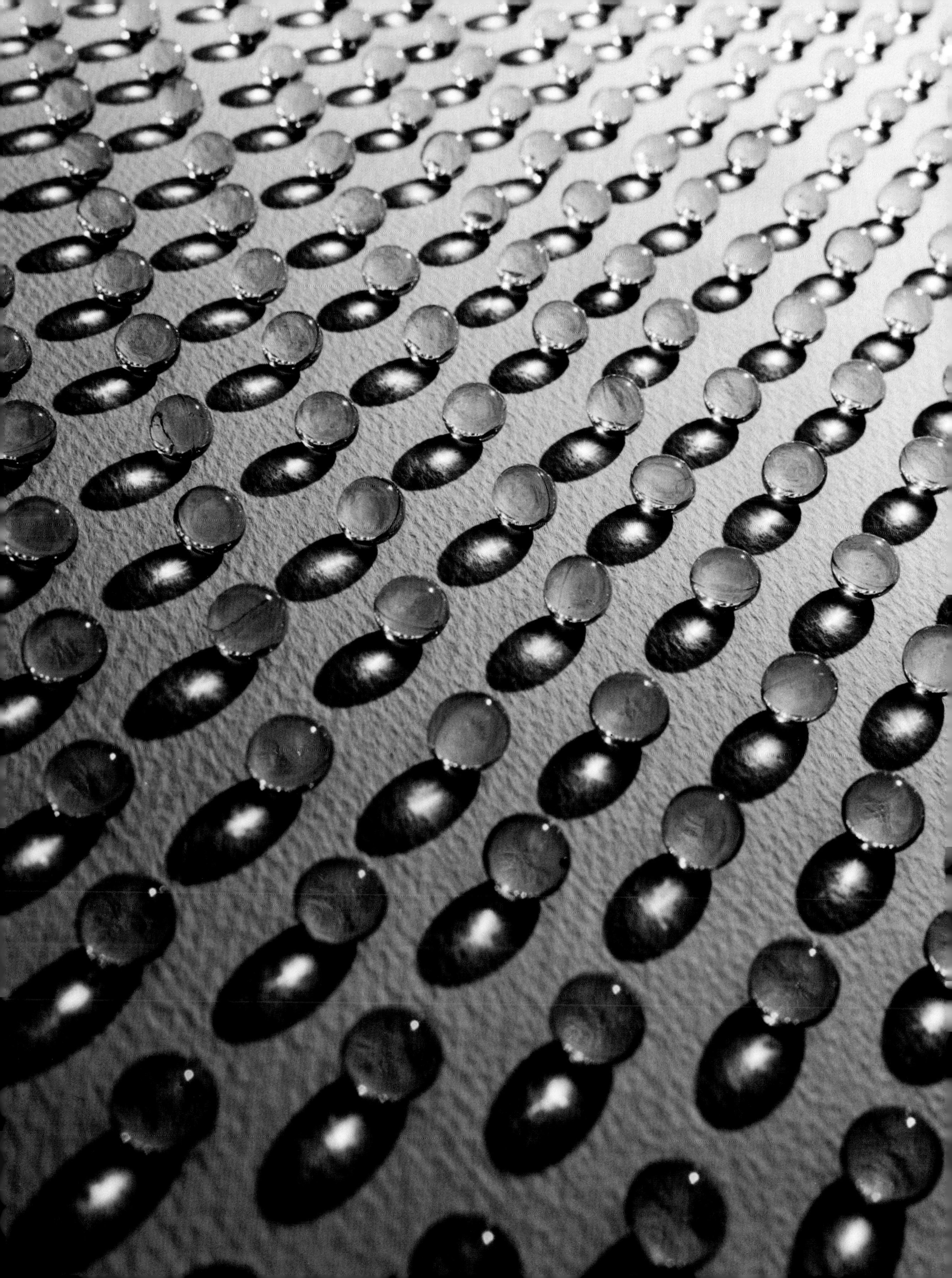

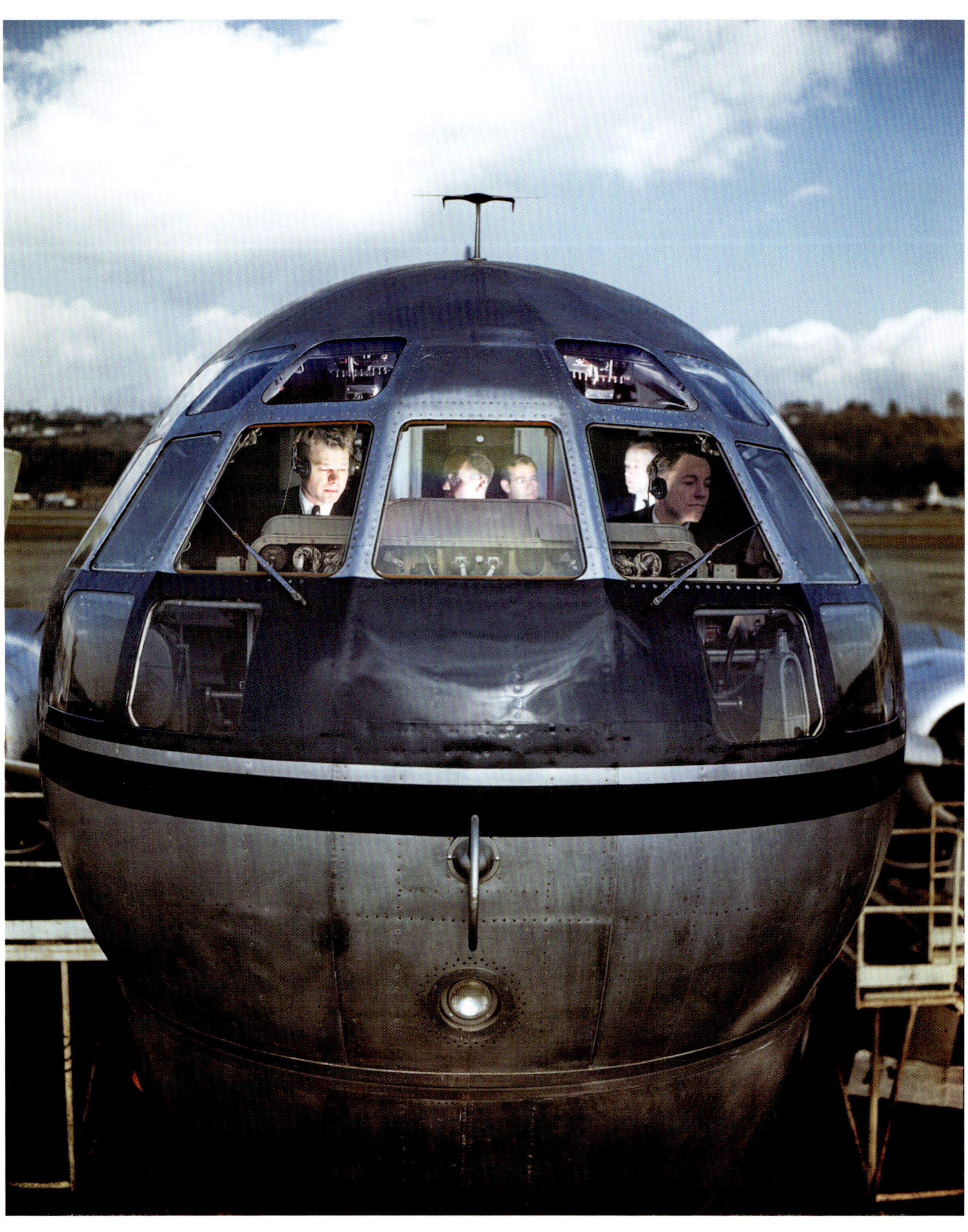

"Astrophysics," *Fortune*, 1947.

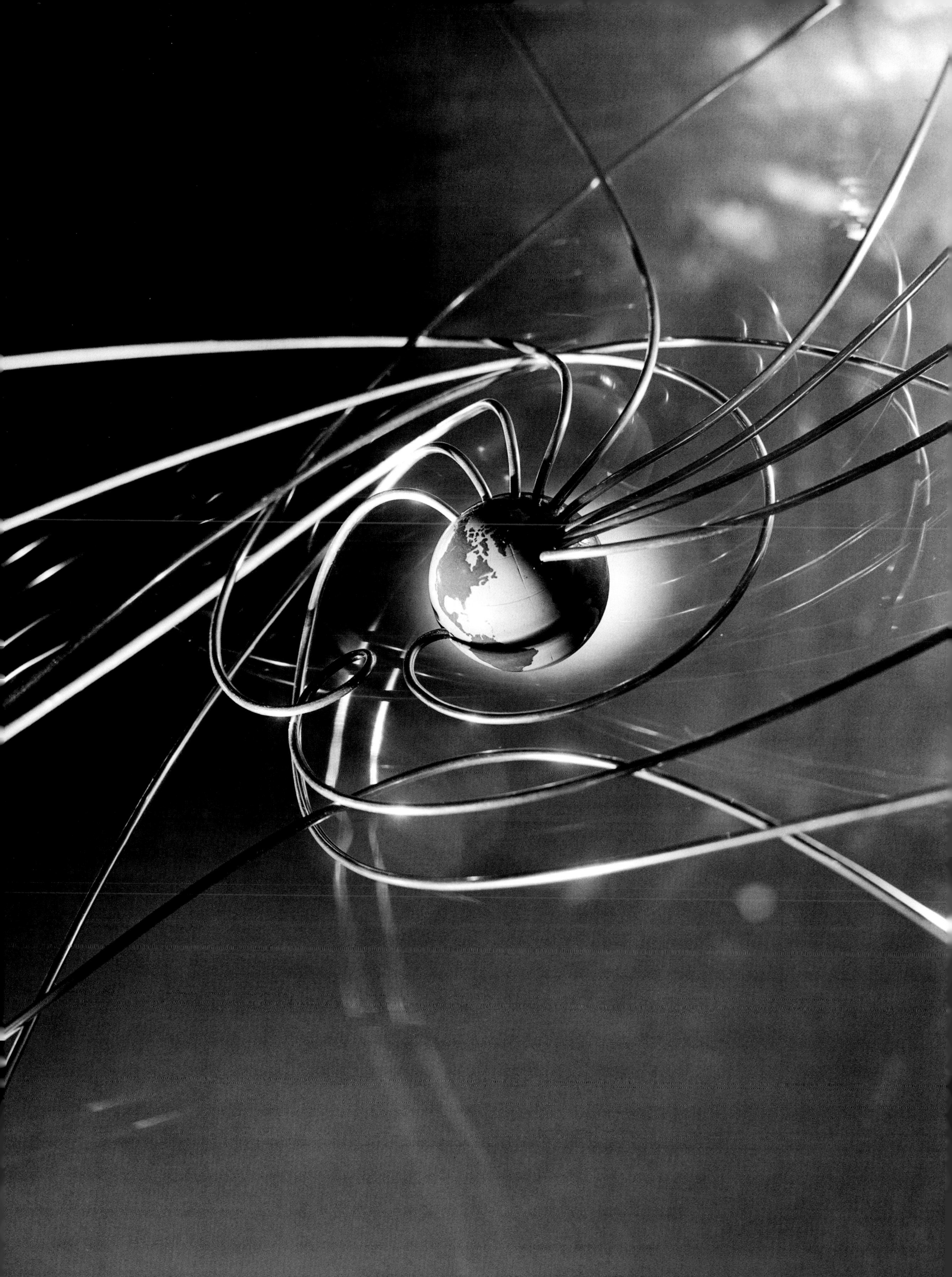

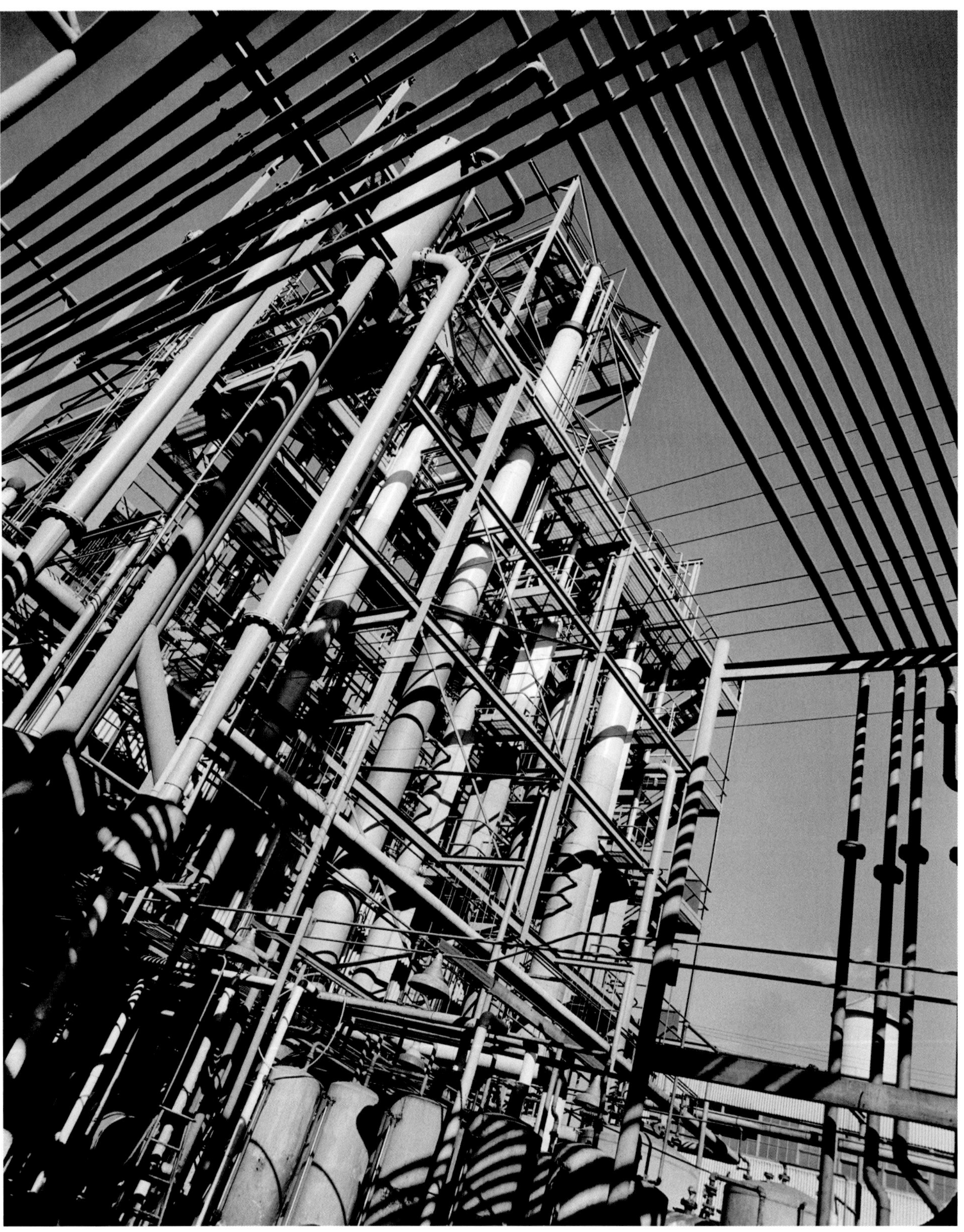

Silicone Plastics for *Fortune*, 1947.

Right and overleaf
"Power in the West," *Fortune*, 1947.

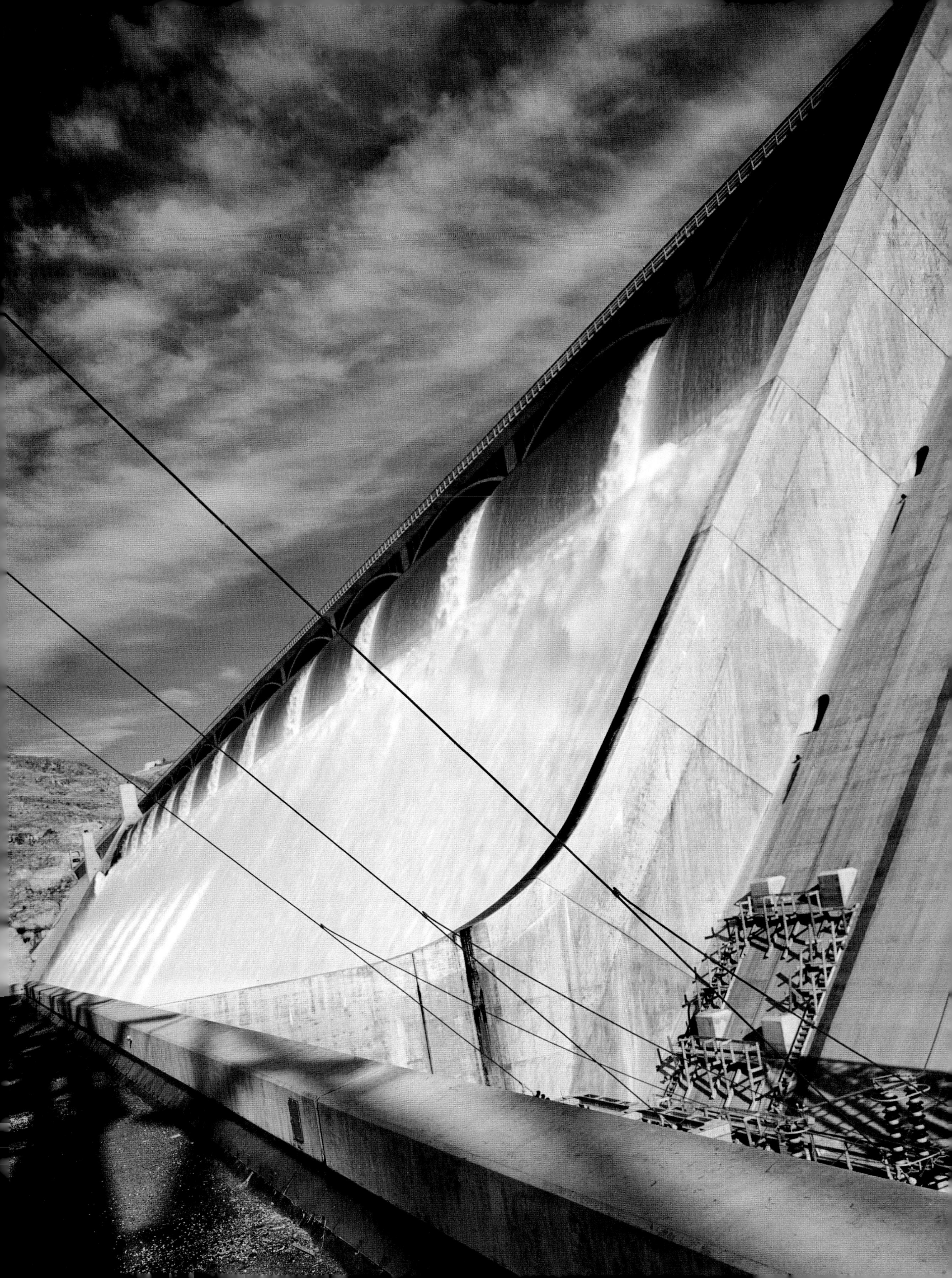

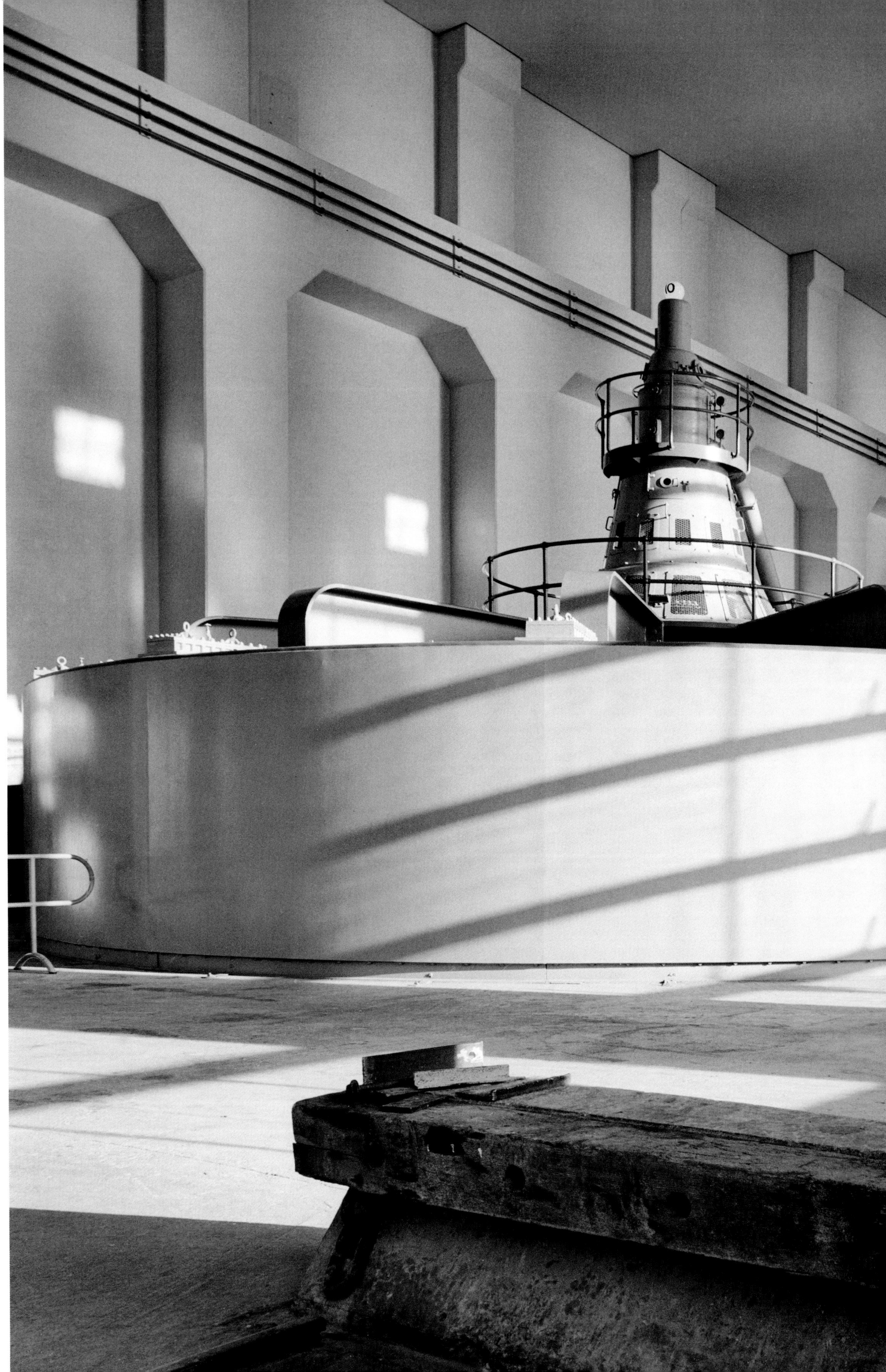

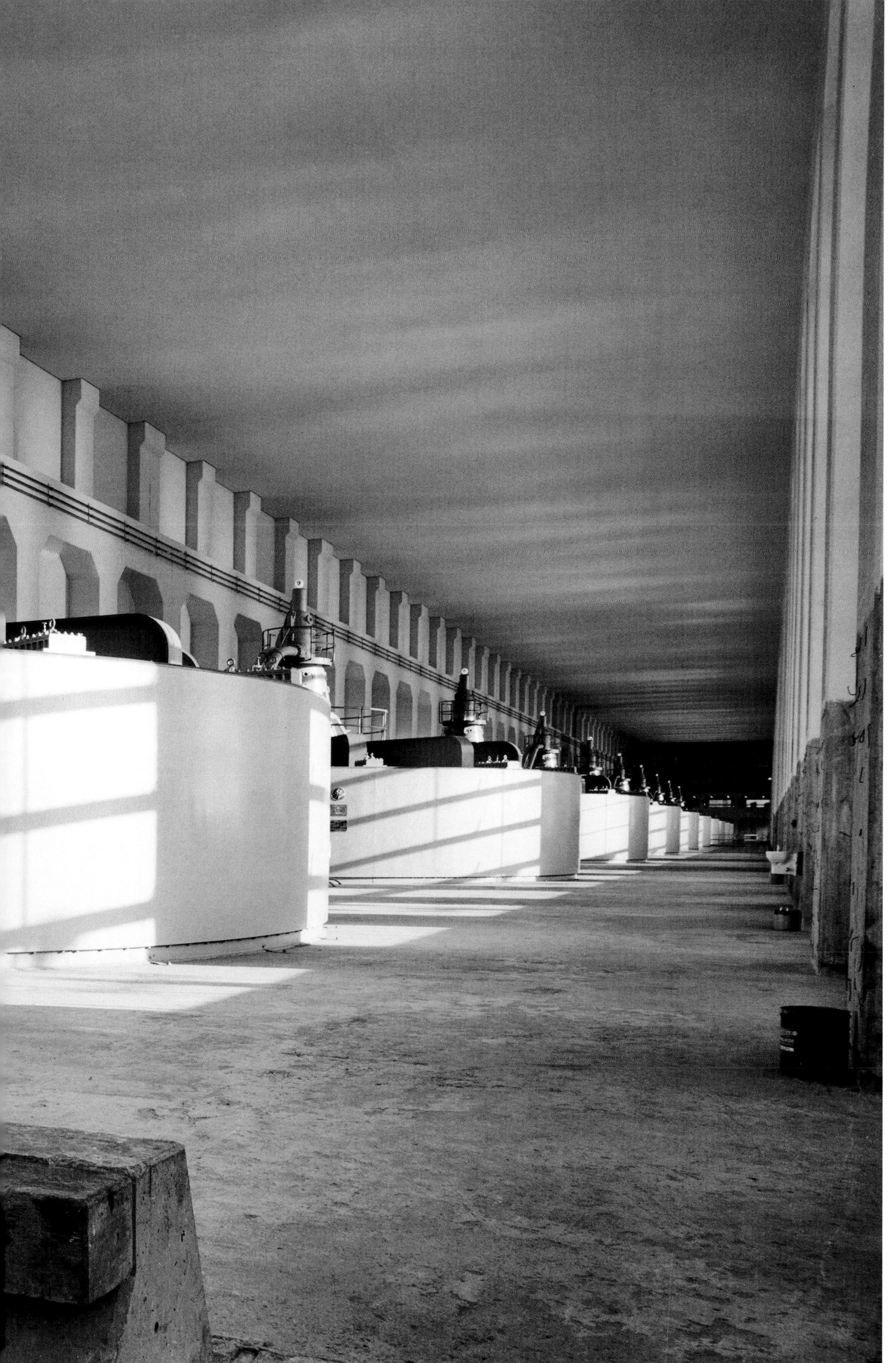

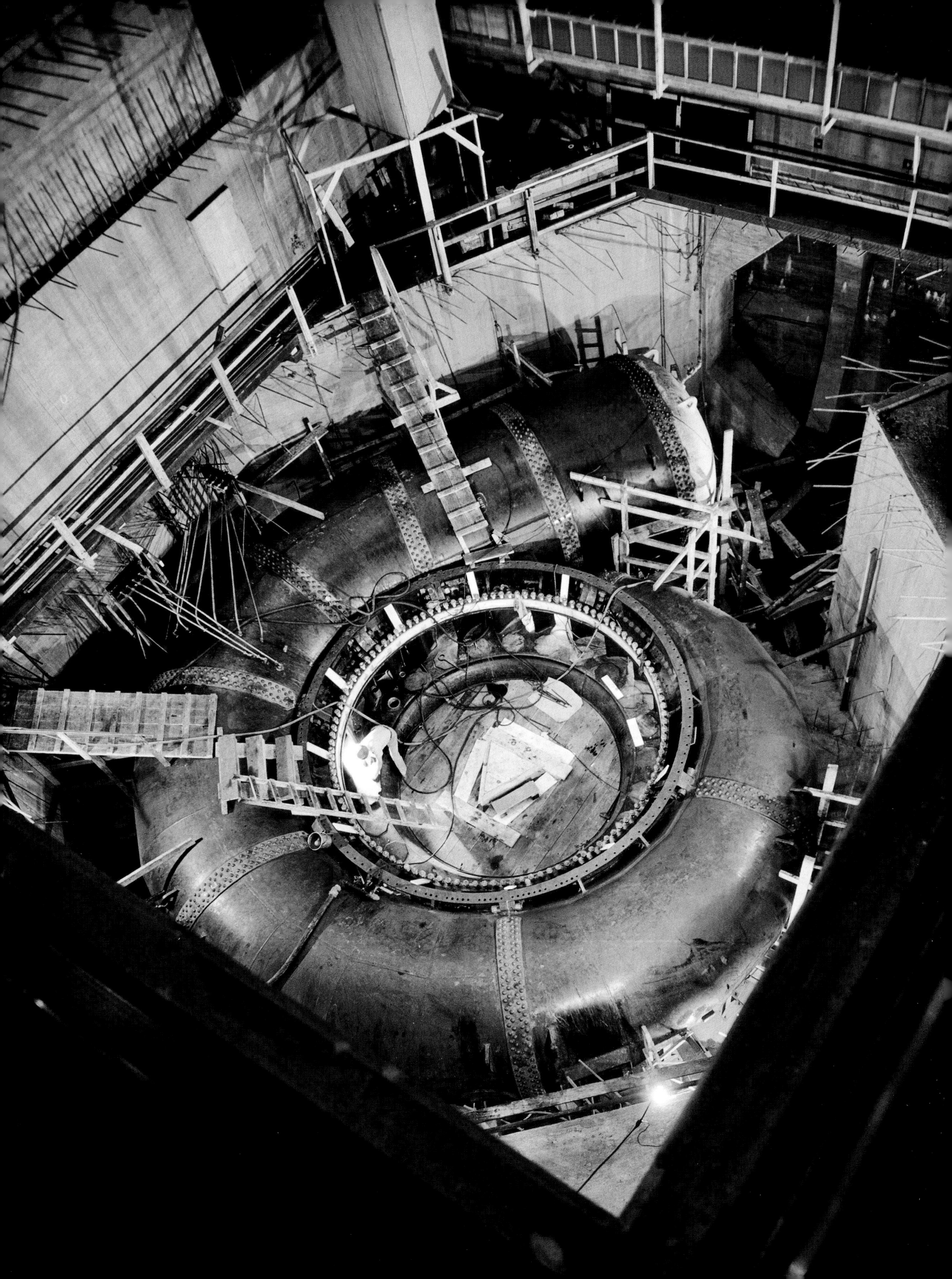

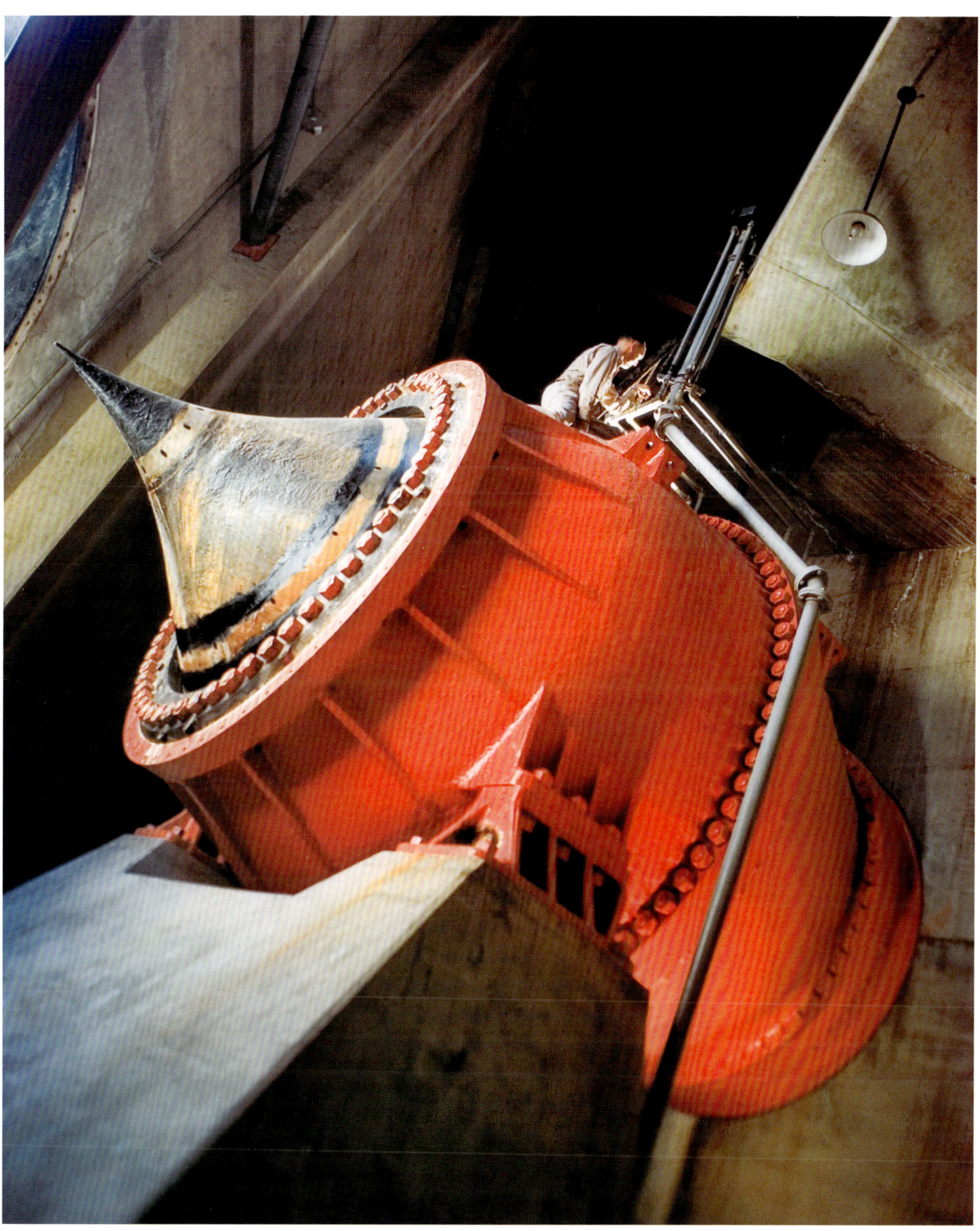

"Power in the West," *Fortune*, 1947.

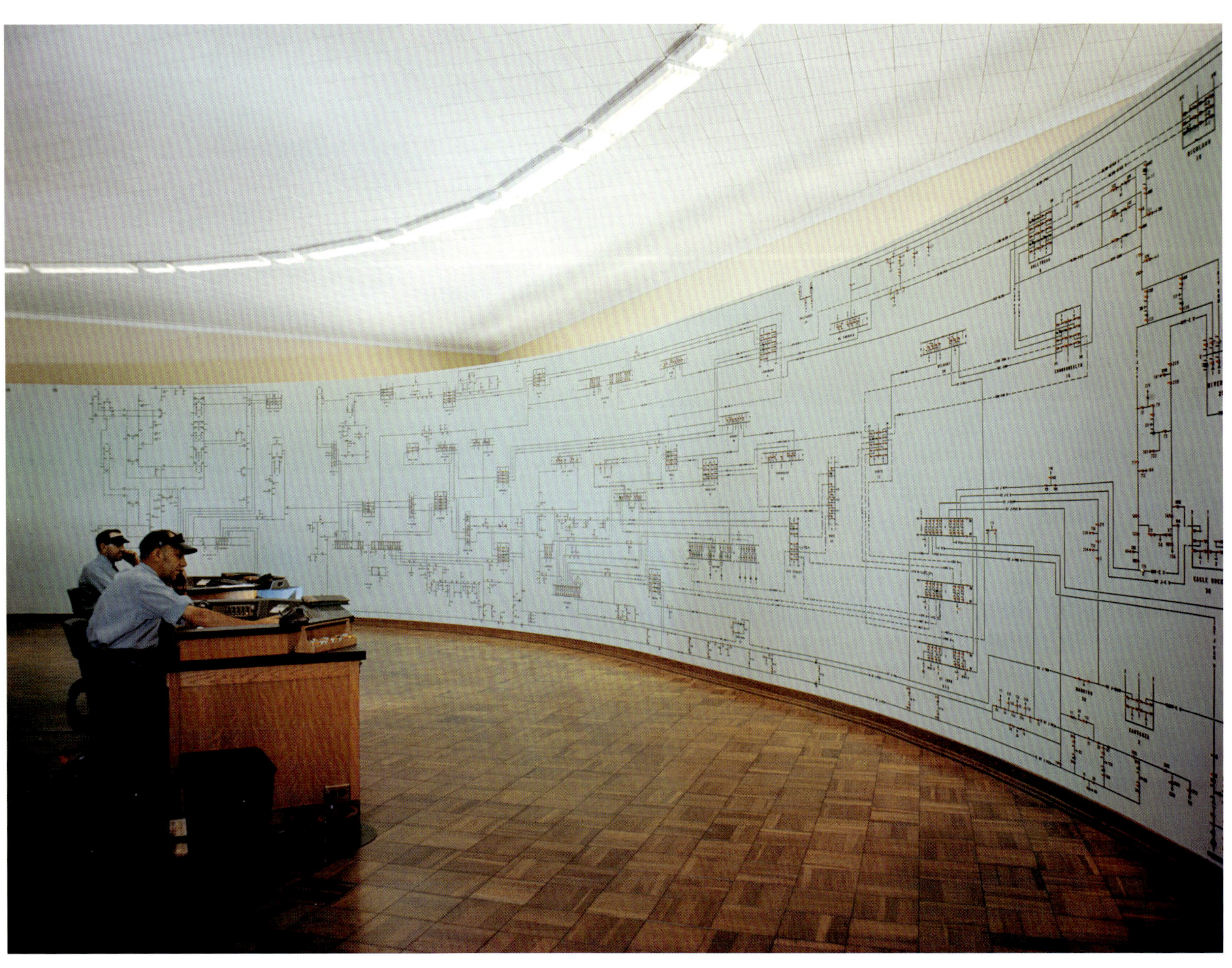

"Power in the West," *Fortune*, 1947.

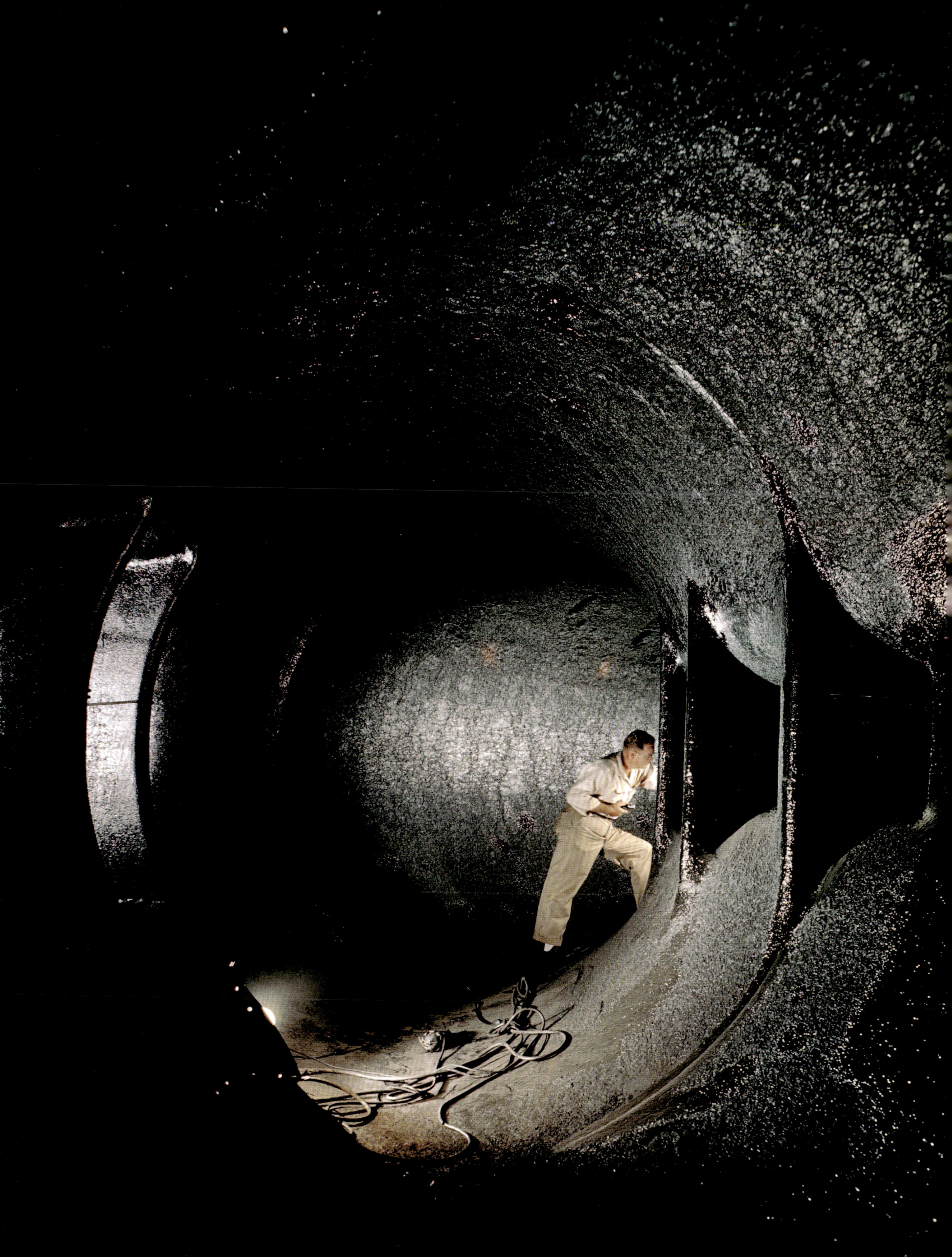

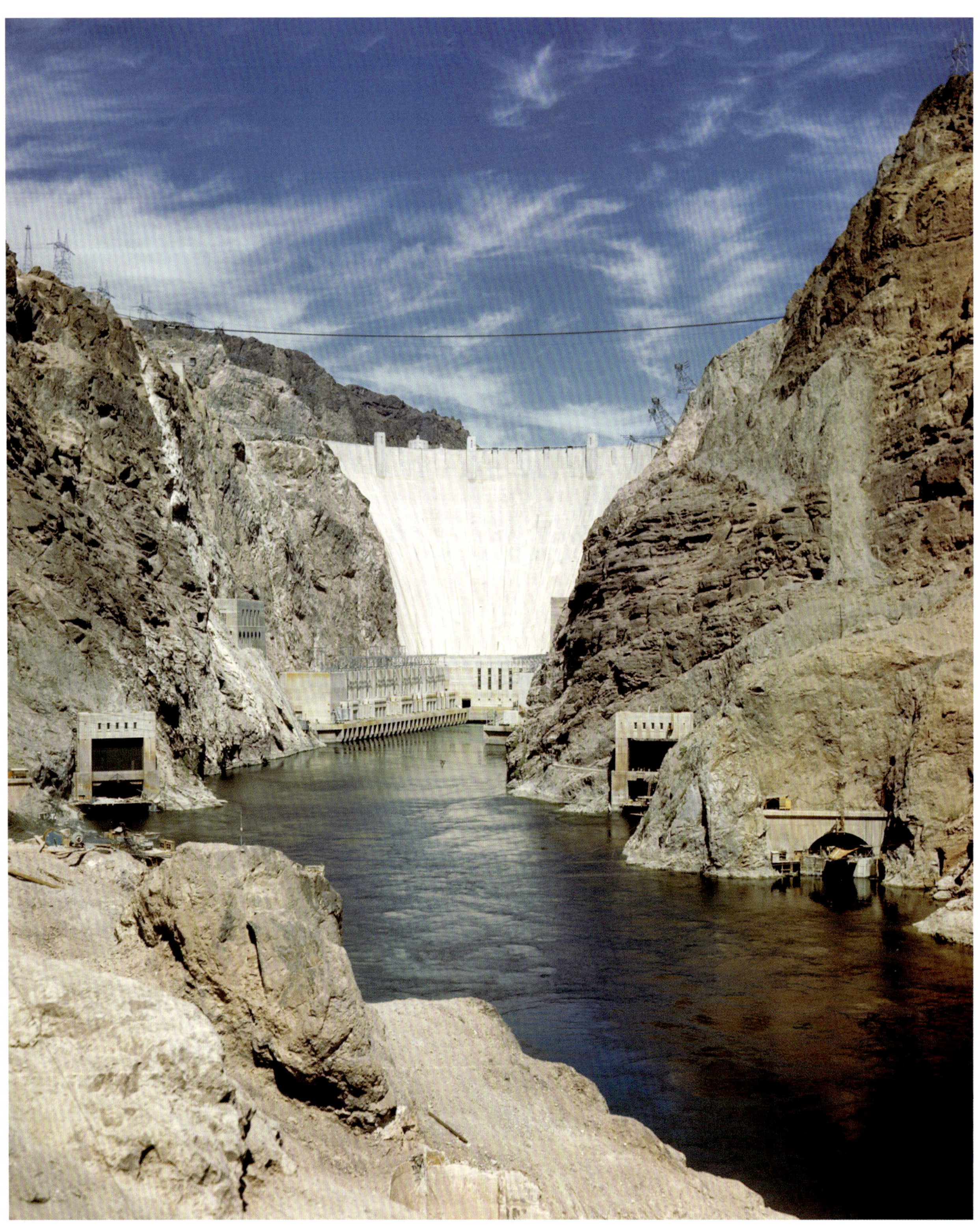

"Power in the West," *Fortune*, 1947.

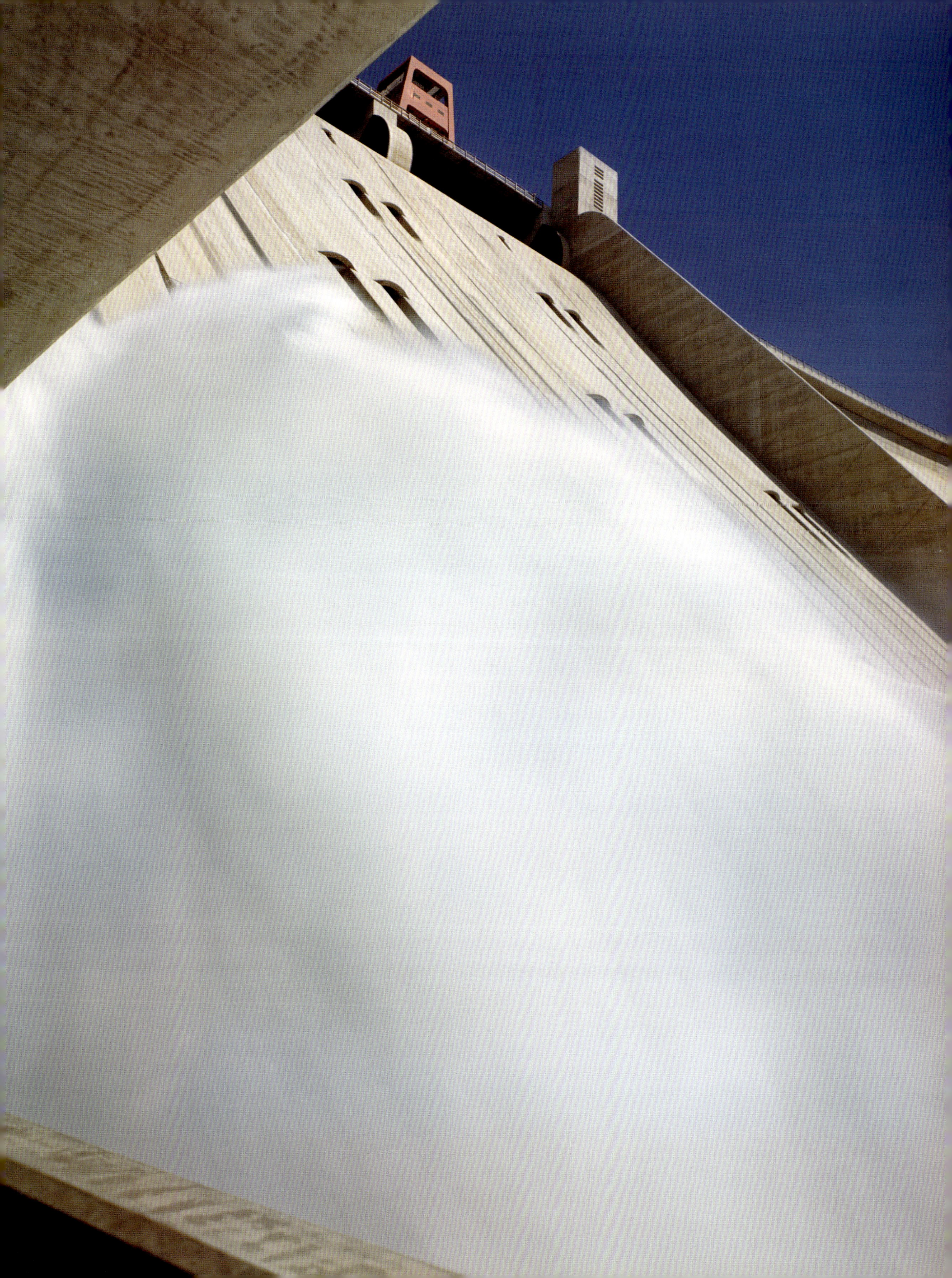

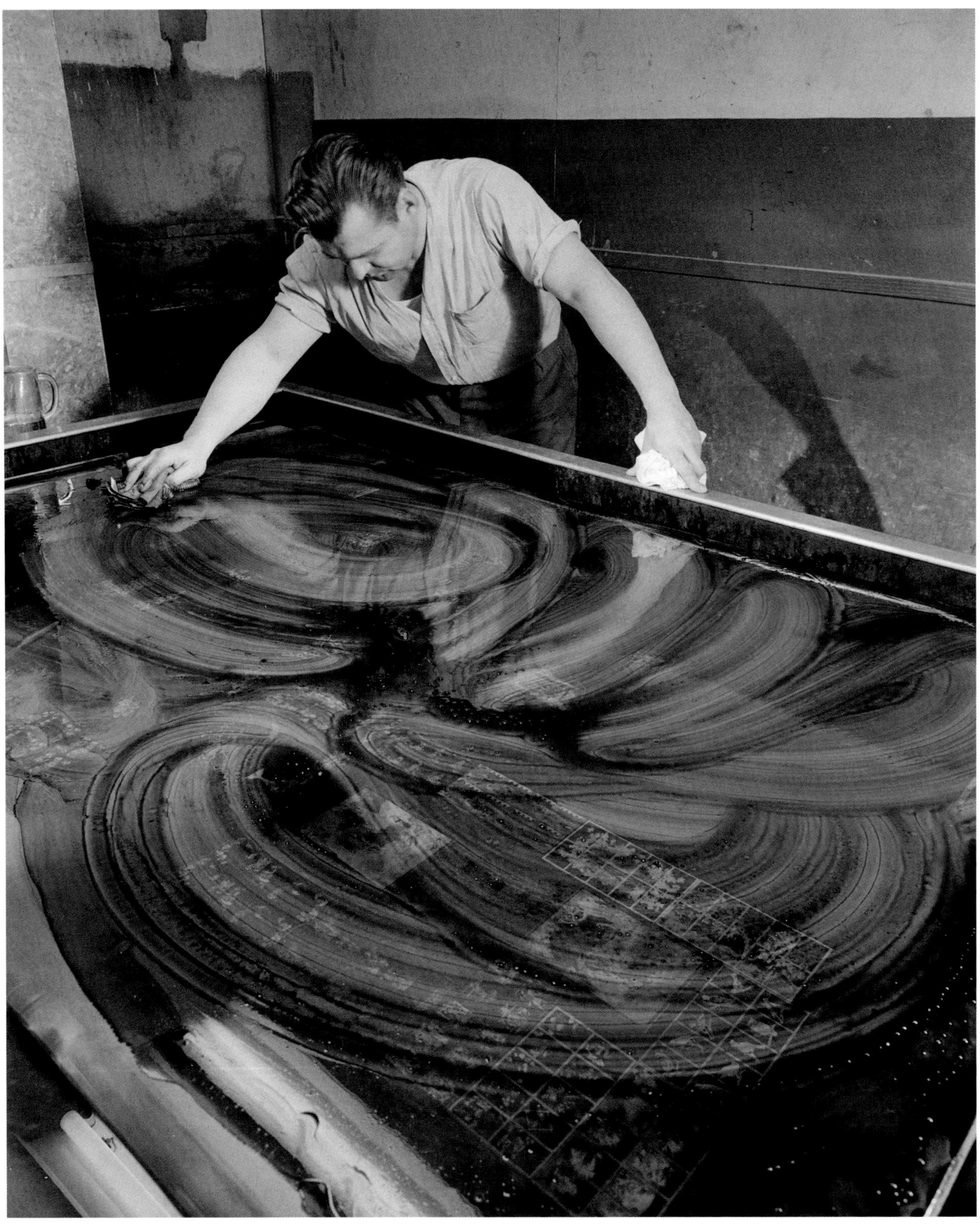

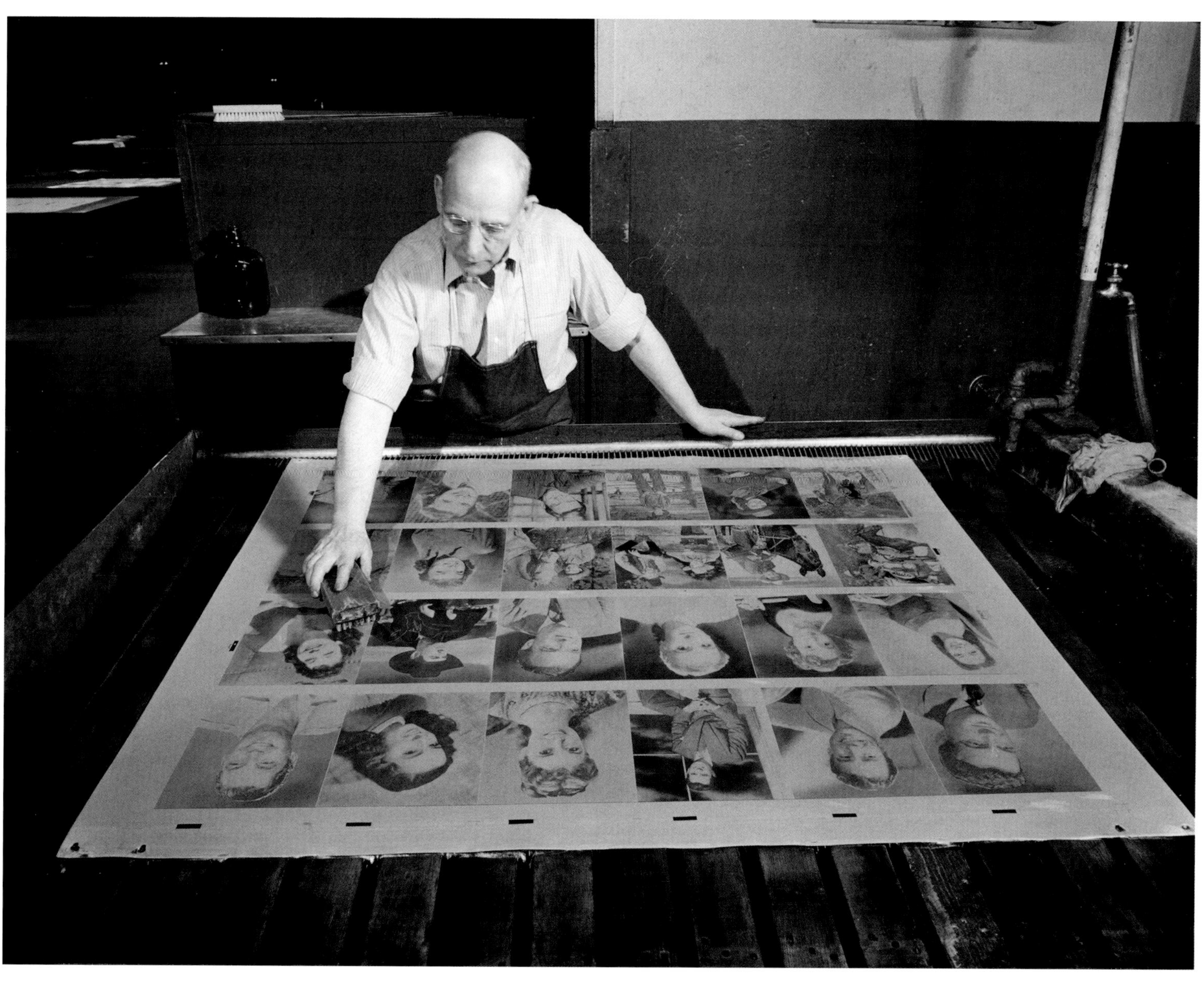

"Printing," *Fortune*, 1949.

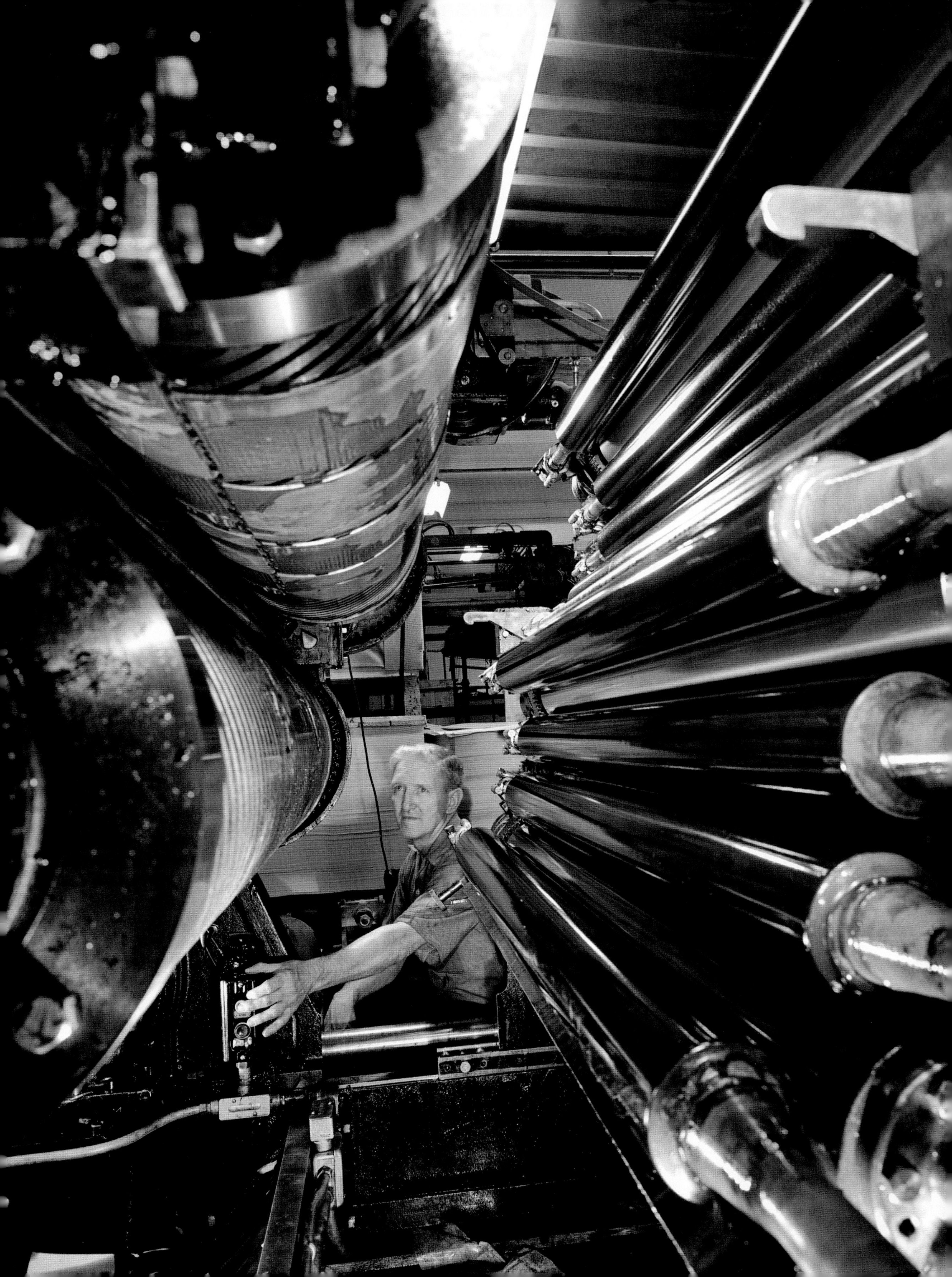

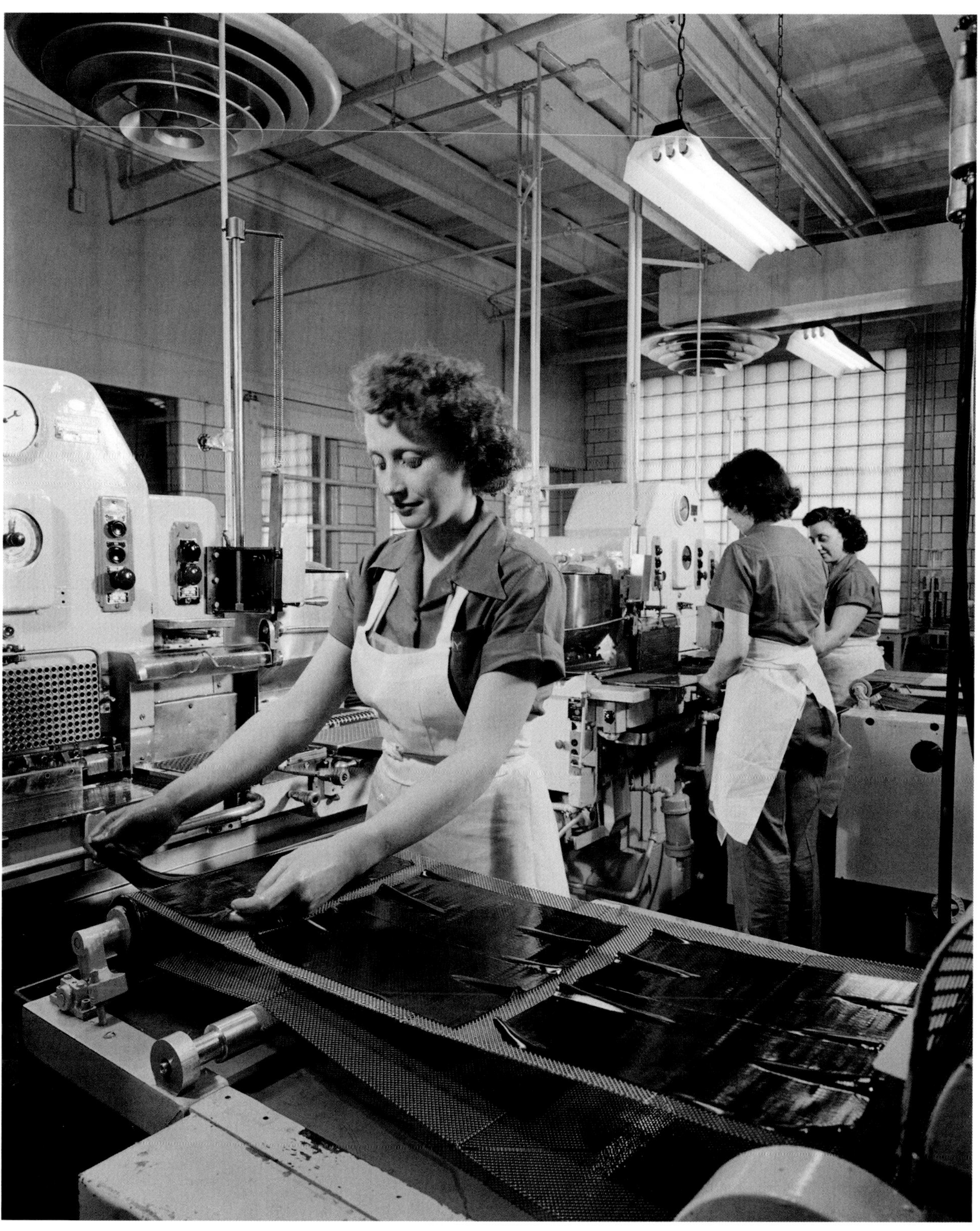

"Printing," *Fortune*, 1949.

Penicillin, Upjohn, 1949.

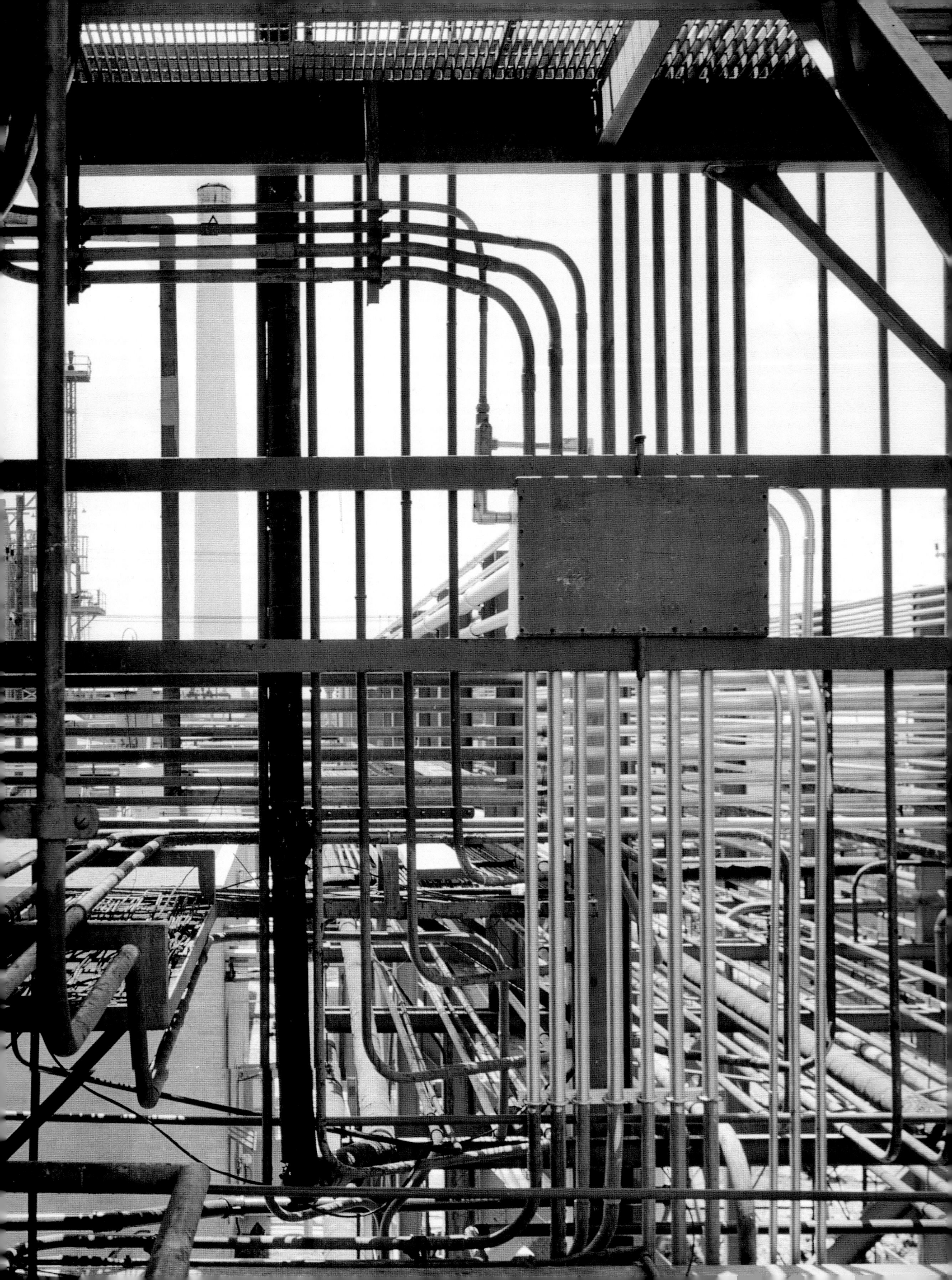

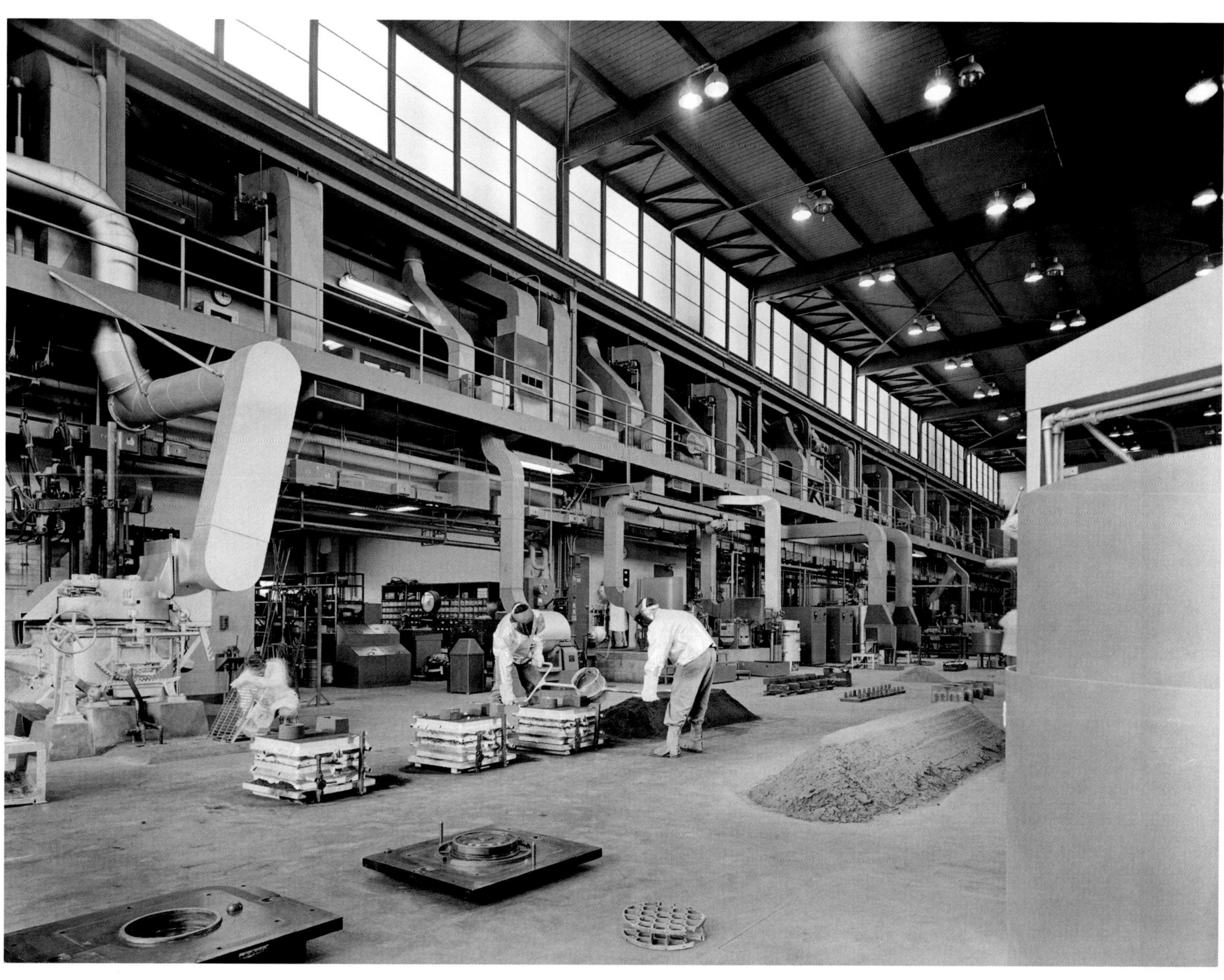

Du Pont article, *Fortune*, 1950.

General Motors Technical Center,
Warren, Michigan. Eero Saarinen, 1951.

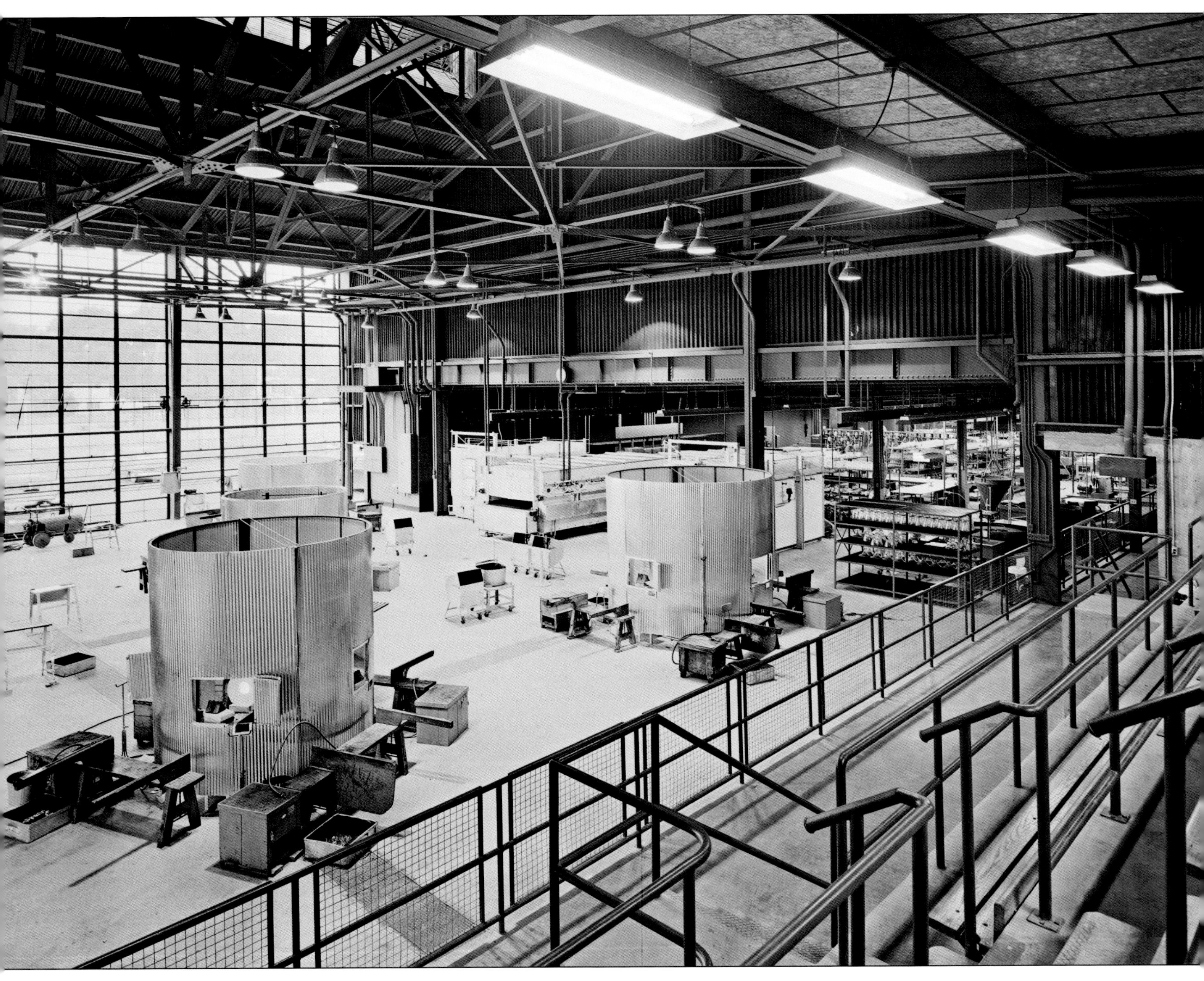

Corning Glass Center, Corning, New York.
Harrison & Abramovitz, 1951.

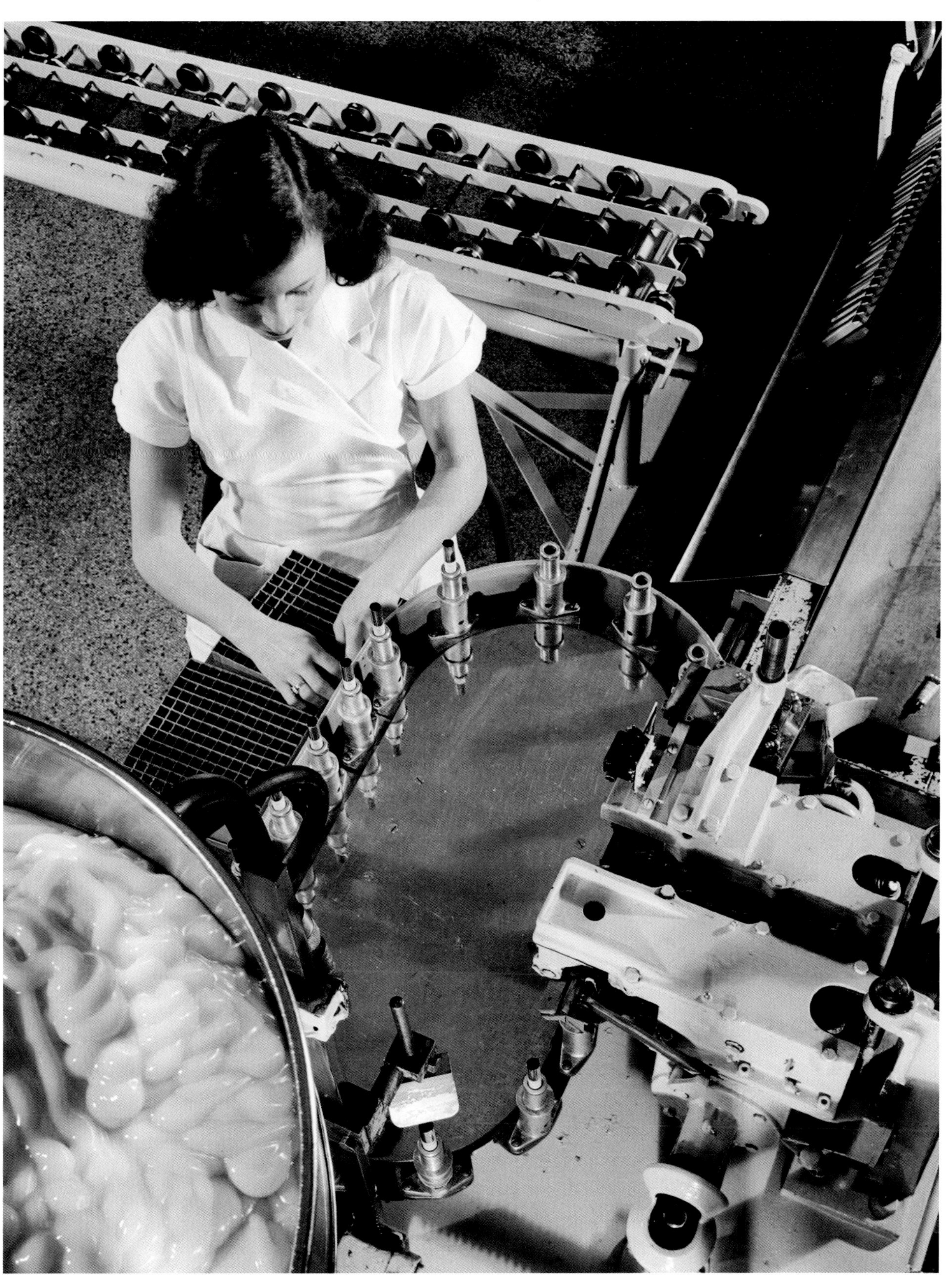

Upjohn, Kalamazoo, Michigan, 1953.

Overleaf
CBS Columbia, Long Island City, New York, 1953.

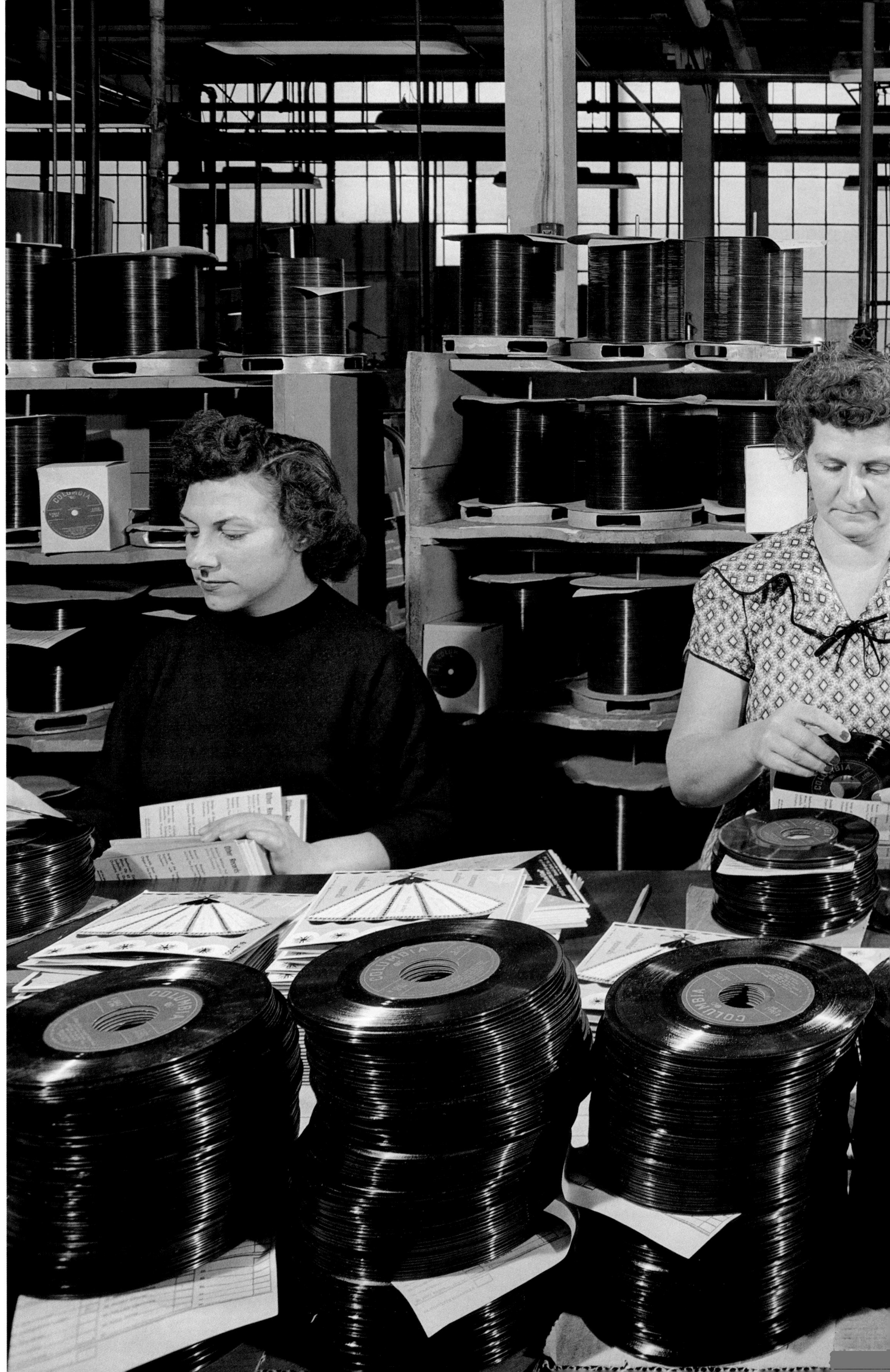
COLUMBIA

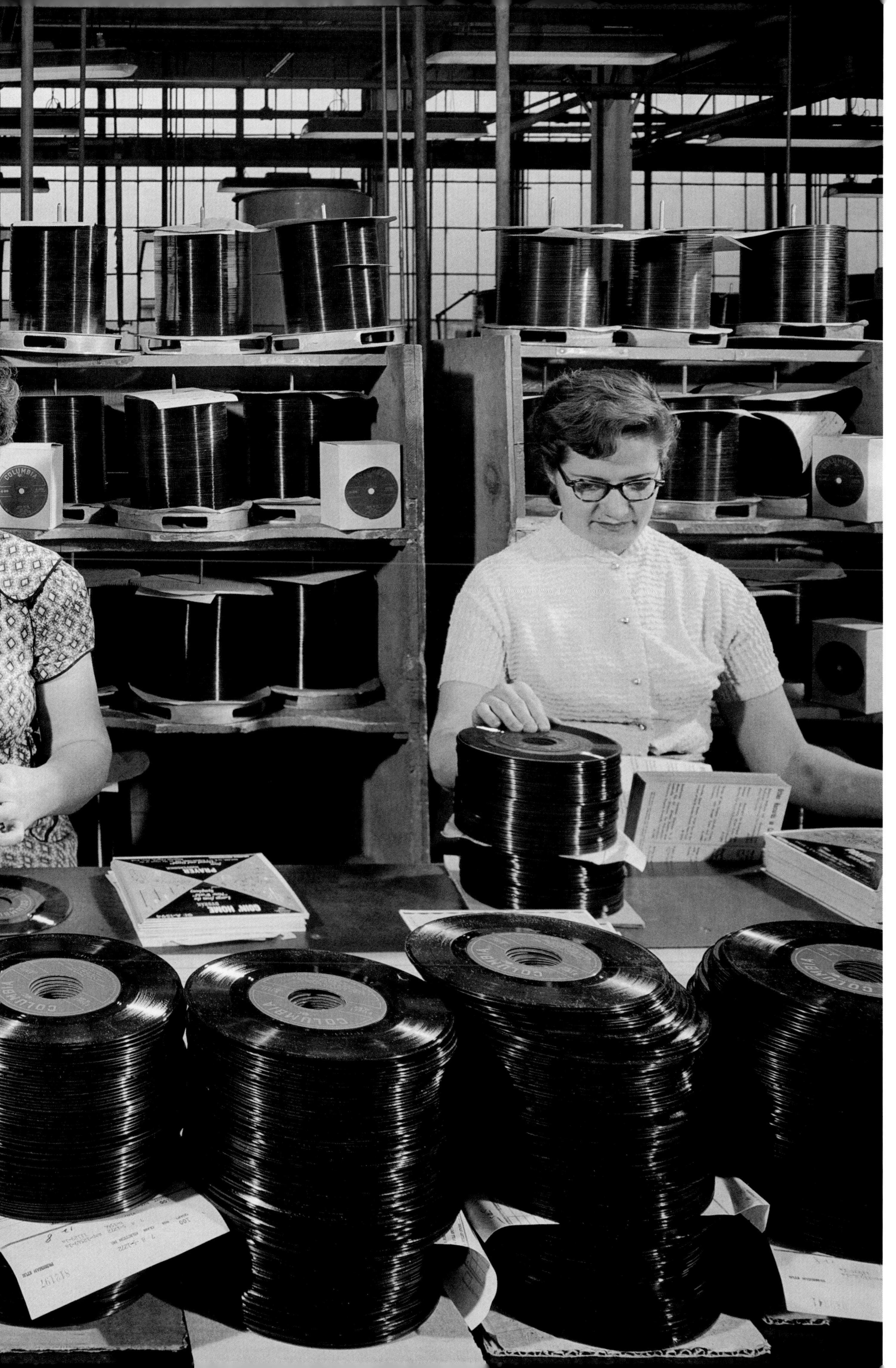
COLUMBIA

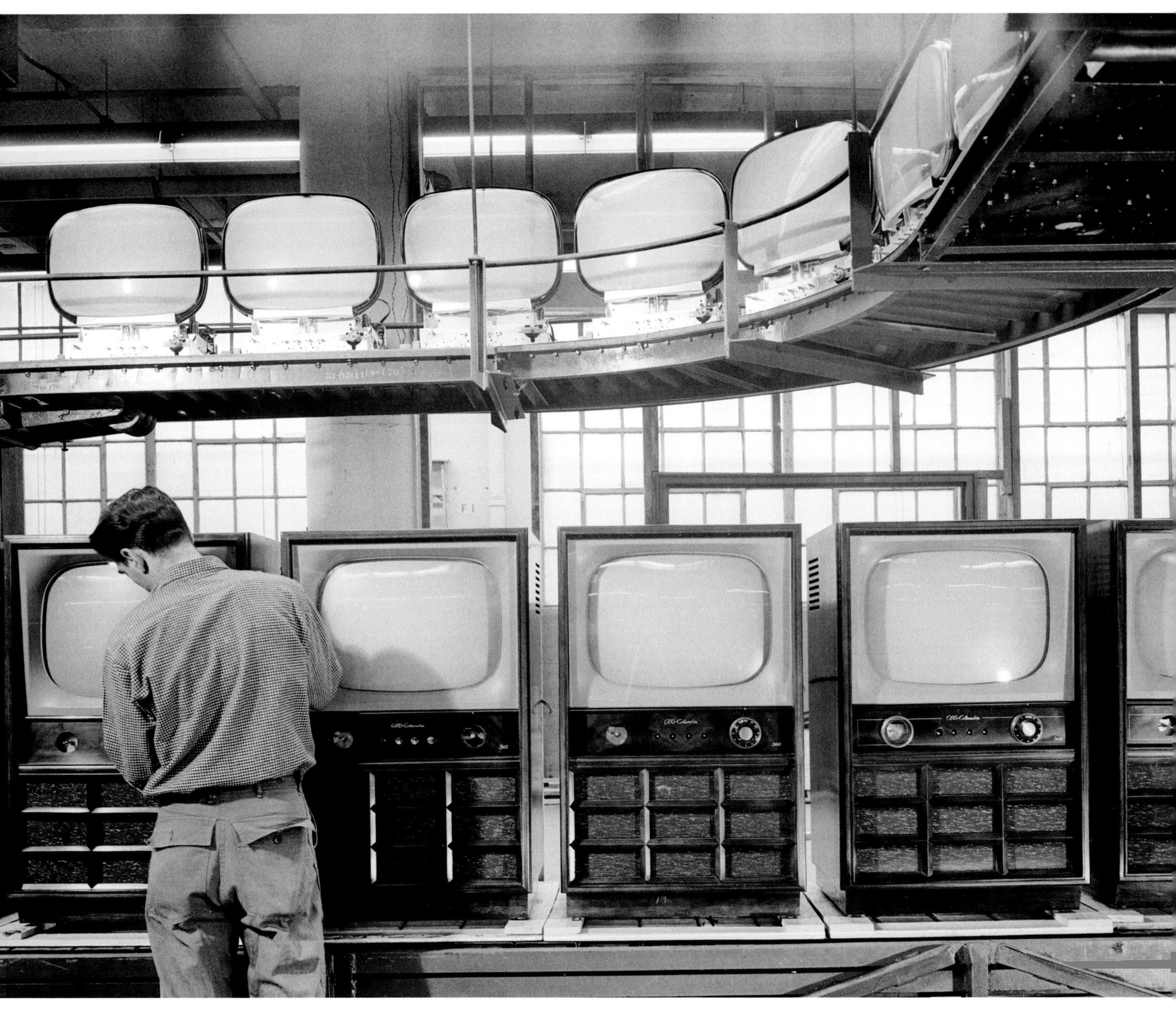

CBS Columbia, Long Island City, New York, 1953.

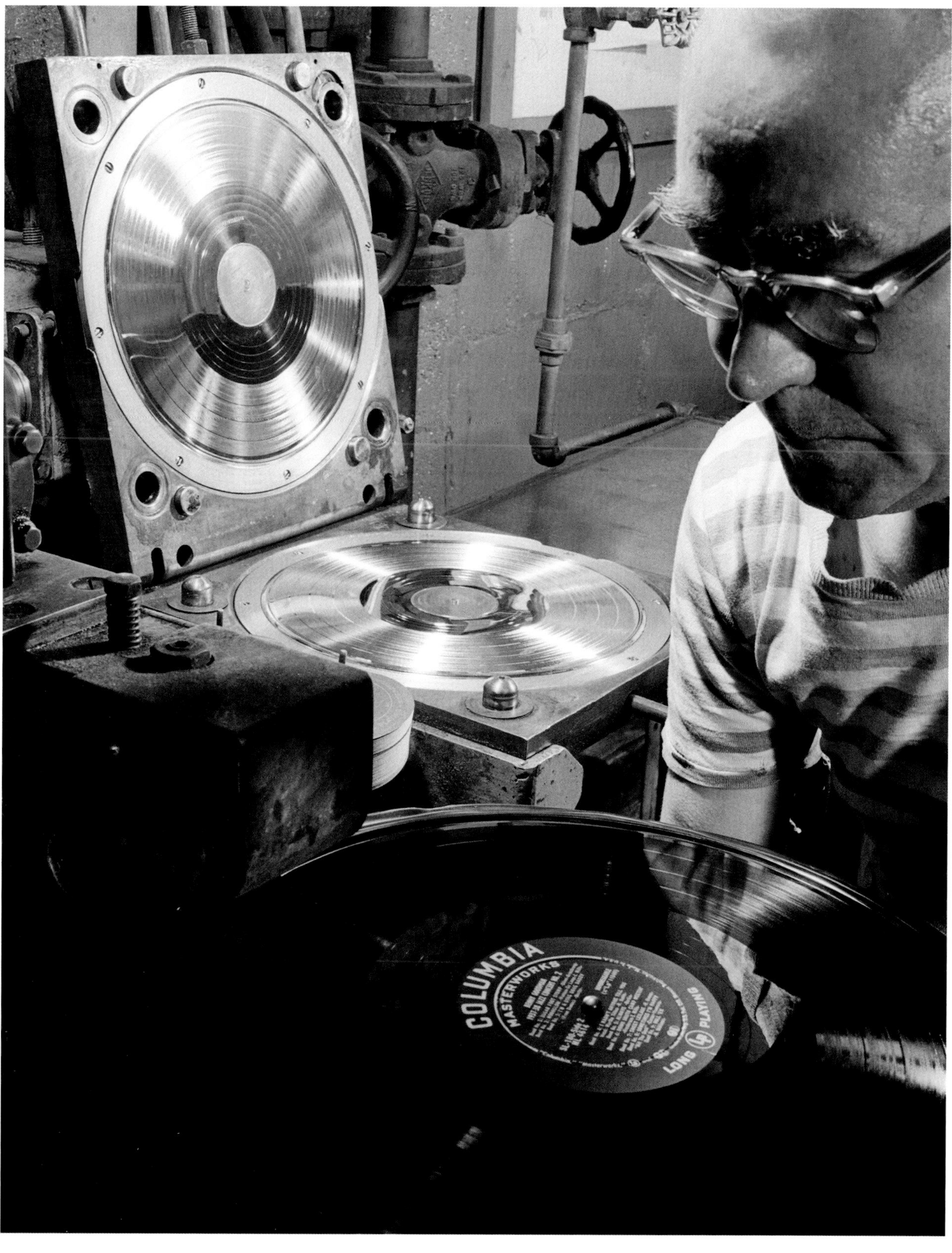

CBS Columbia, Long Island City, New York, 1954.

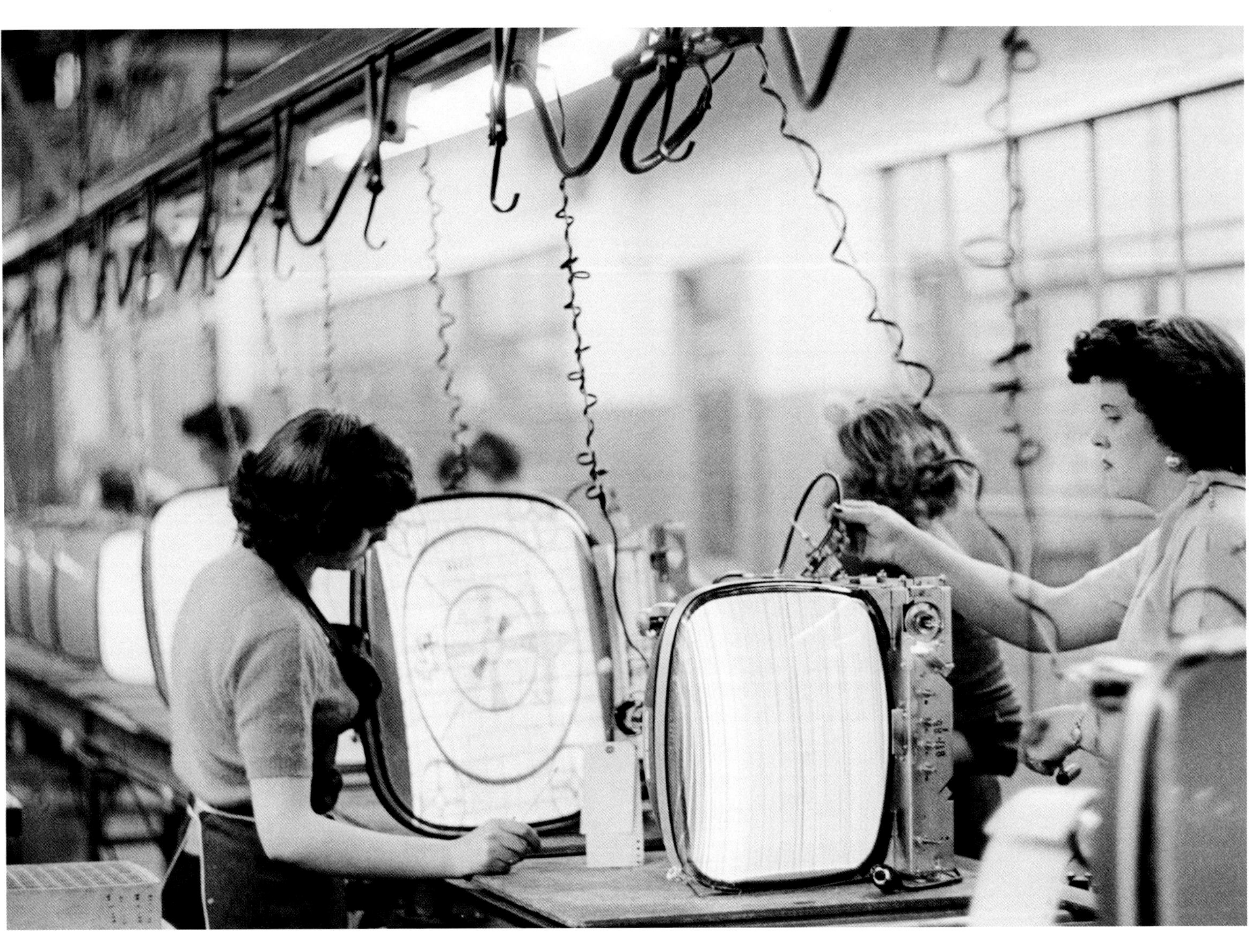

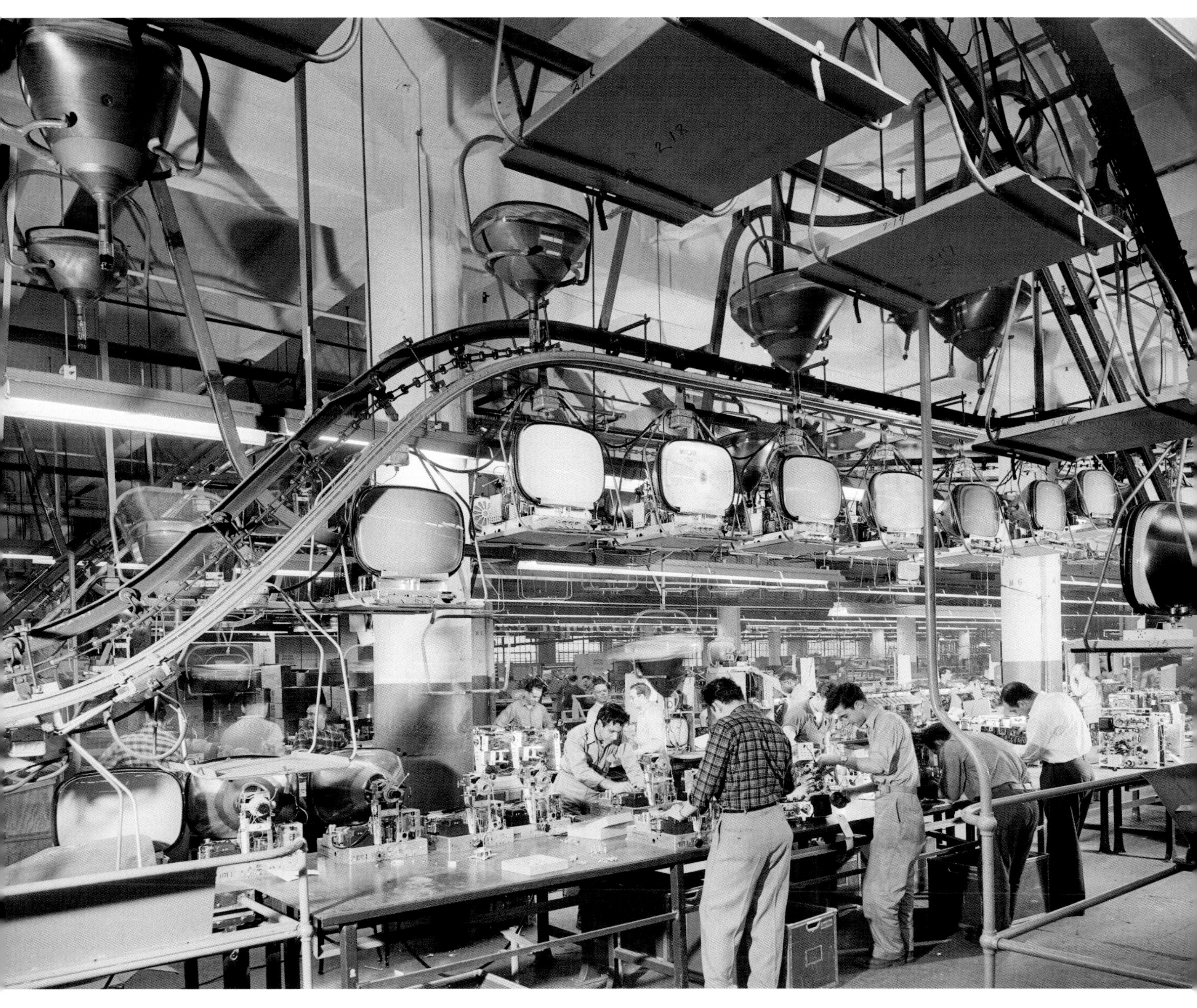

CBS Columbia, Long Island City,
New York, 1954.

Duplan Silk Mill, Hazelton, Pennsylania, 1943.

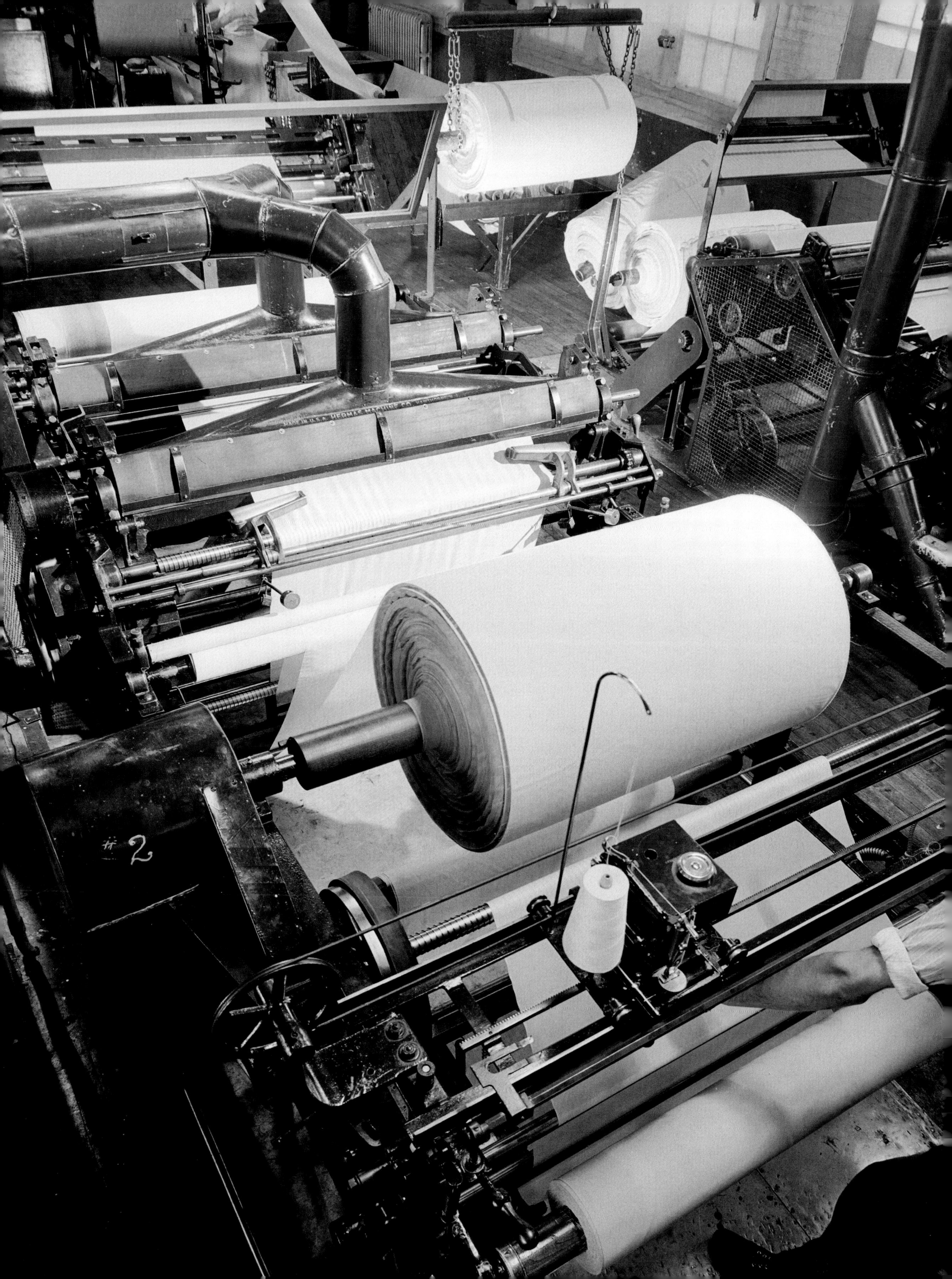
HERMAS MACHINE CO.
#2

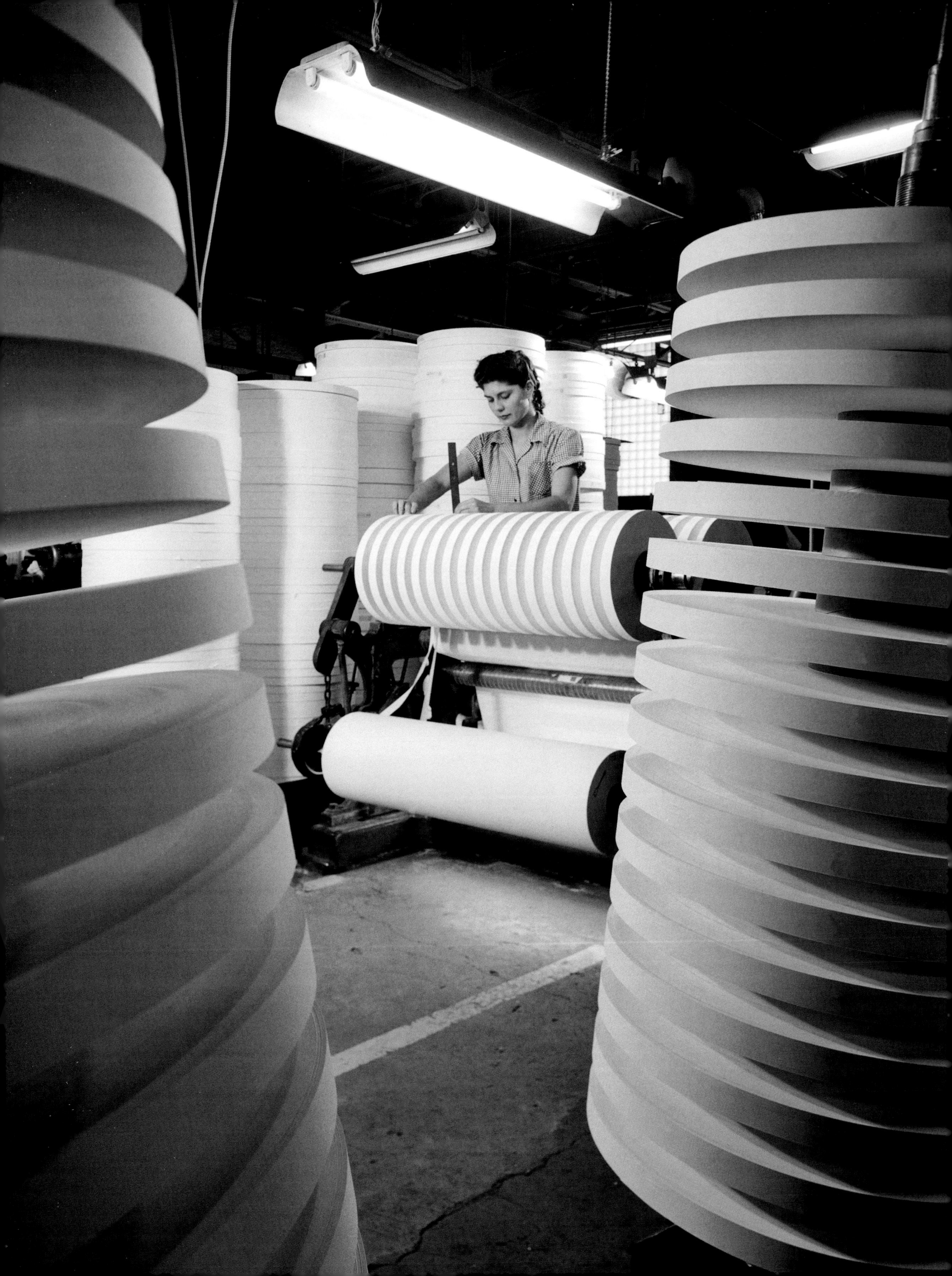

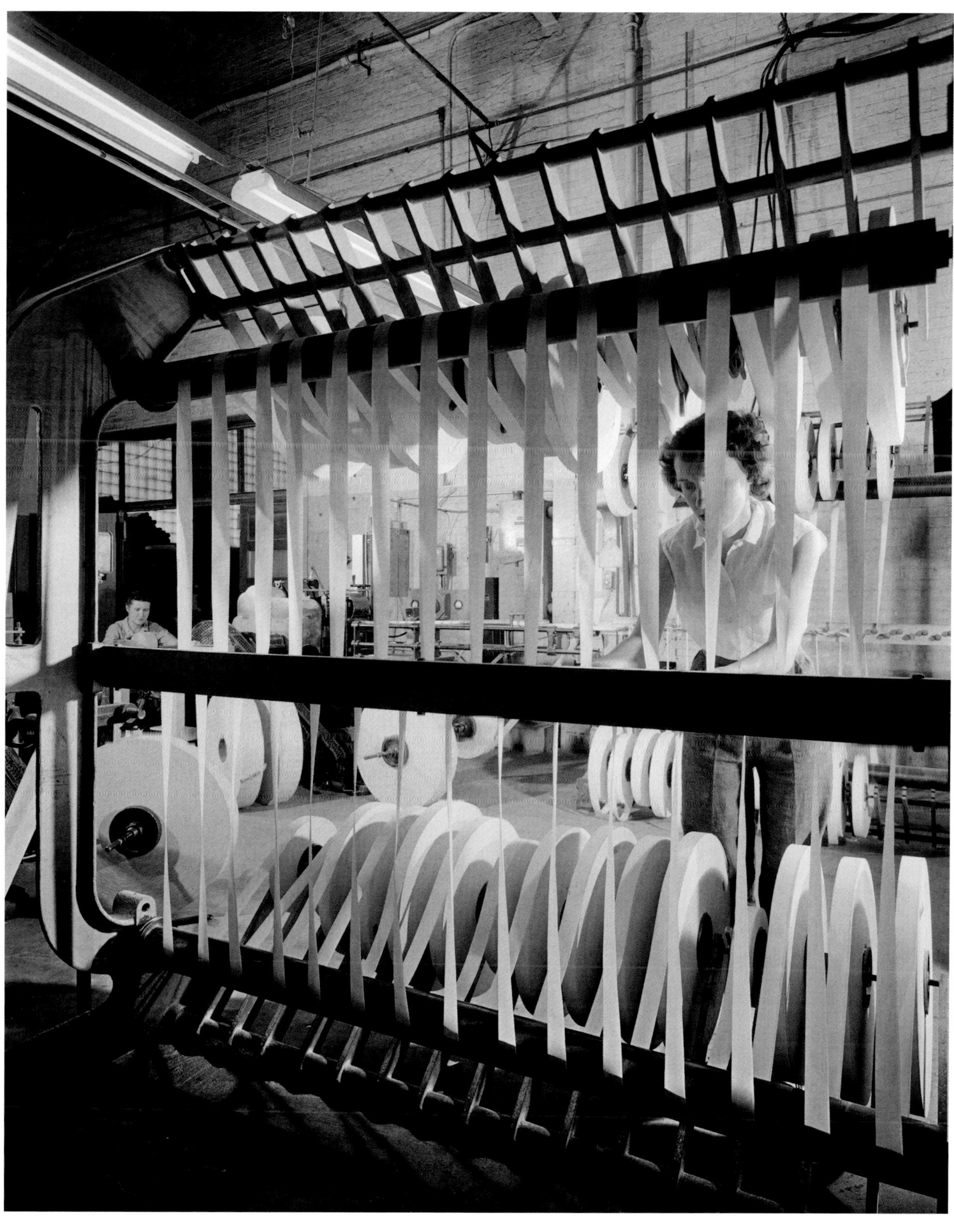

Peter Schweitzer Paper Company,
Spotswood, New Jersey, 1954.

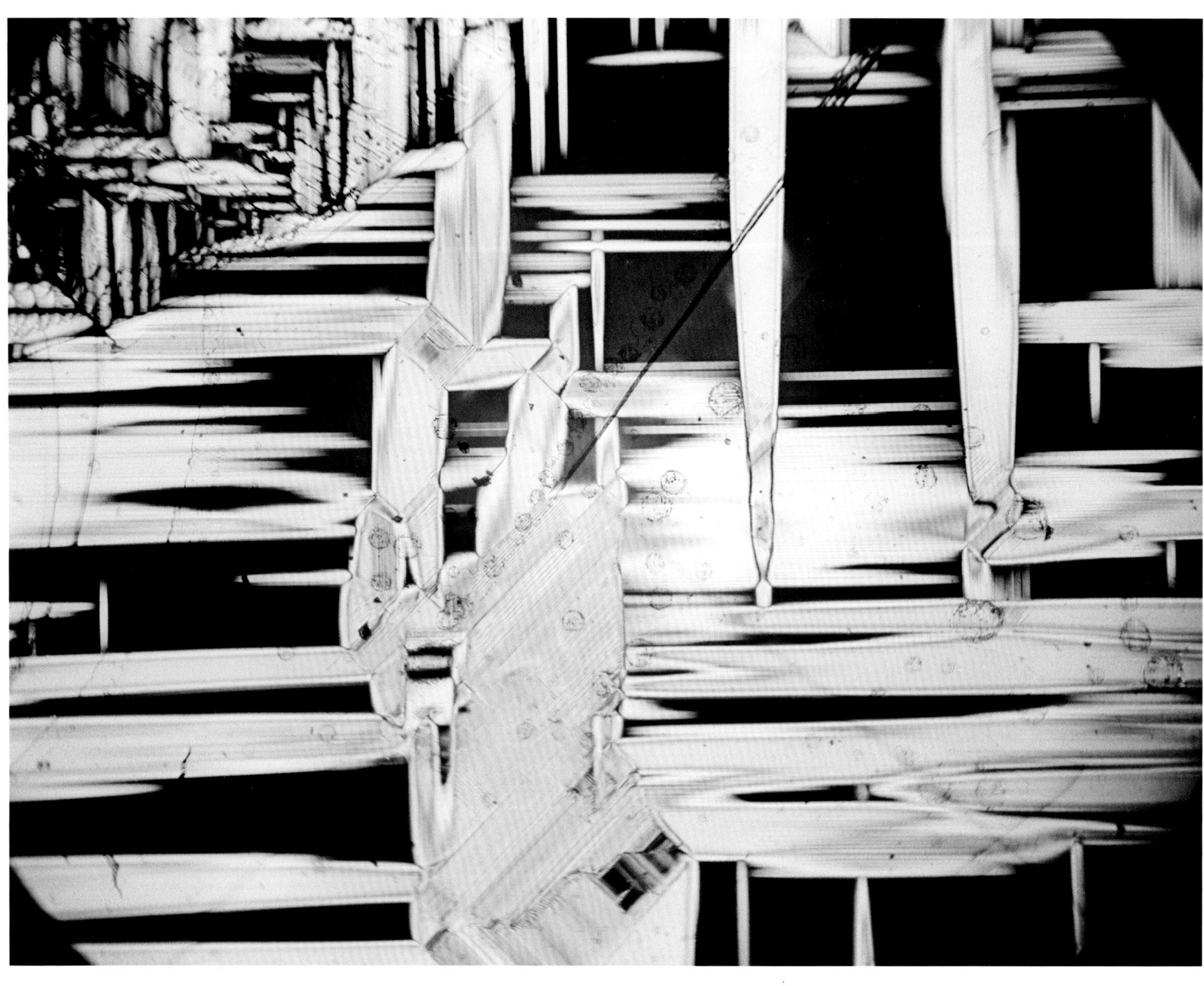

IBM, 1954.

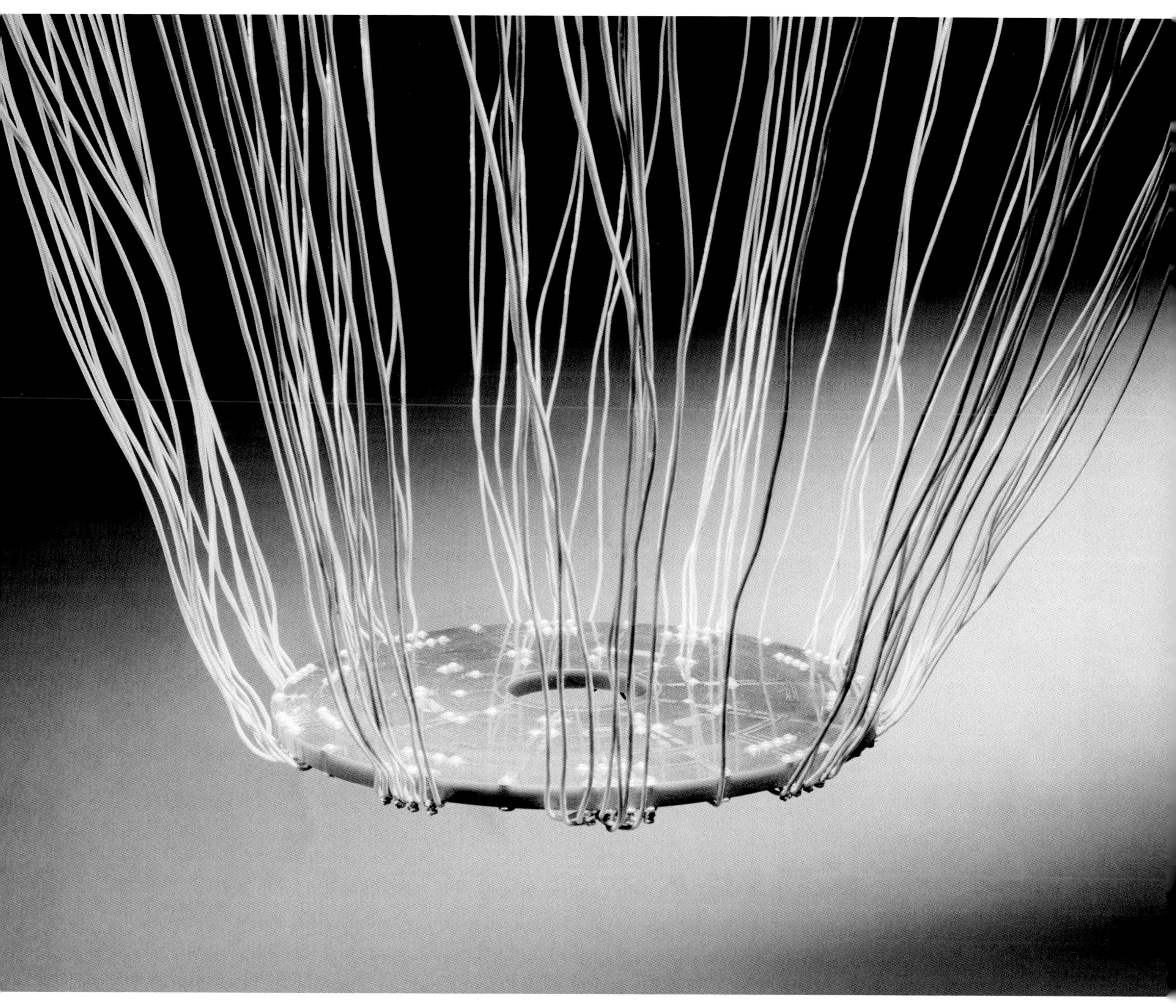

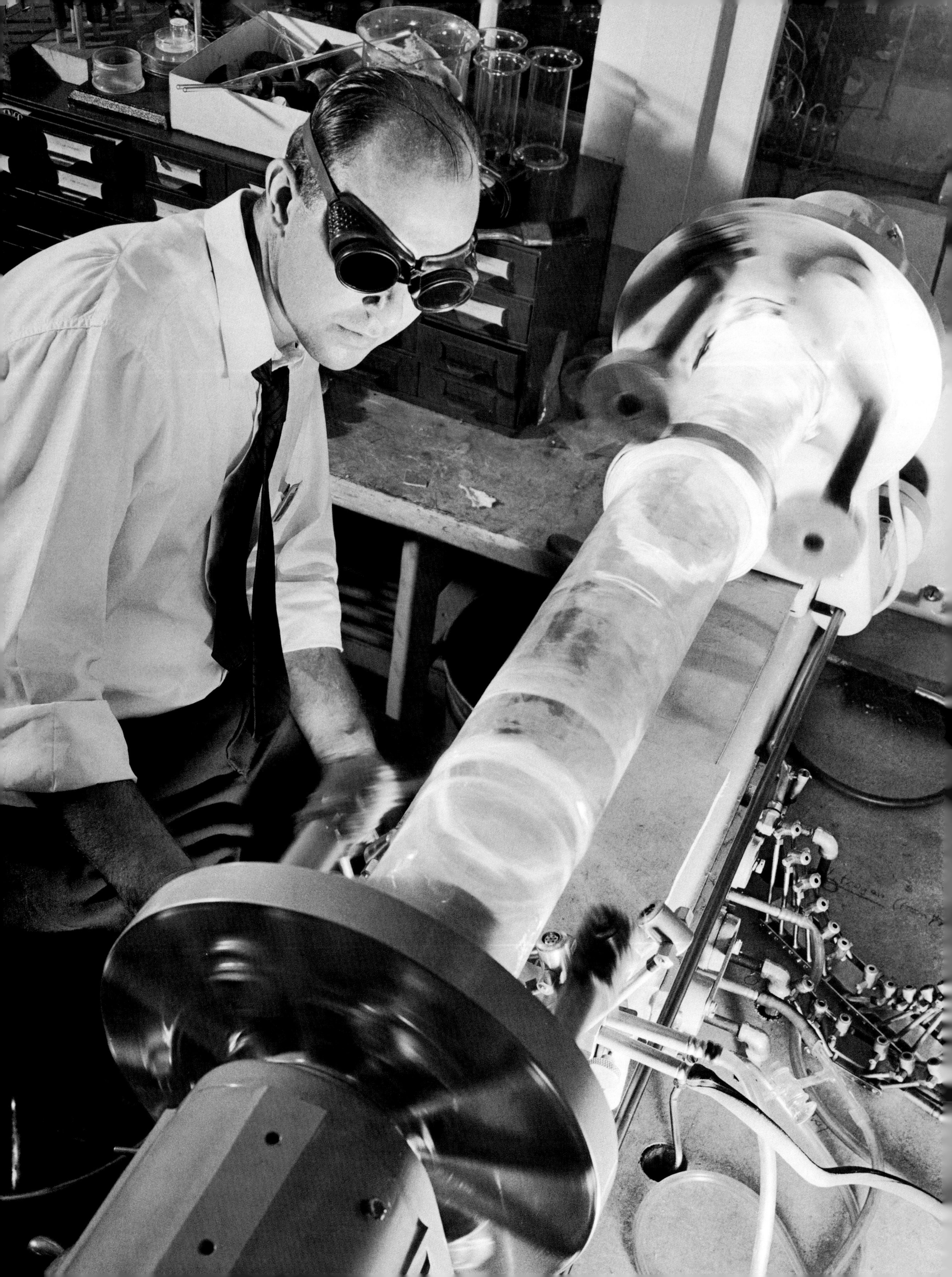

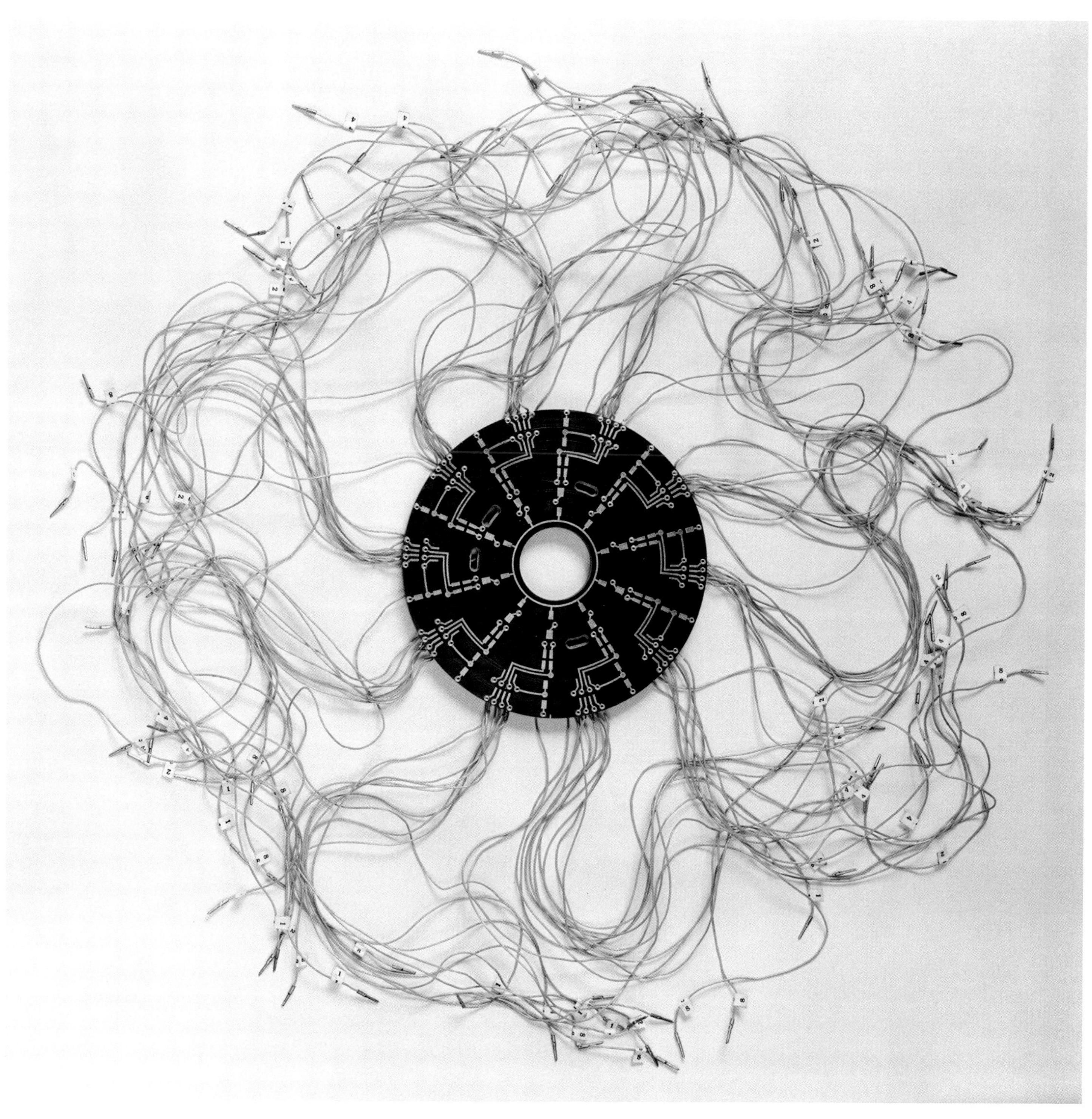

IBM, 1954.

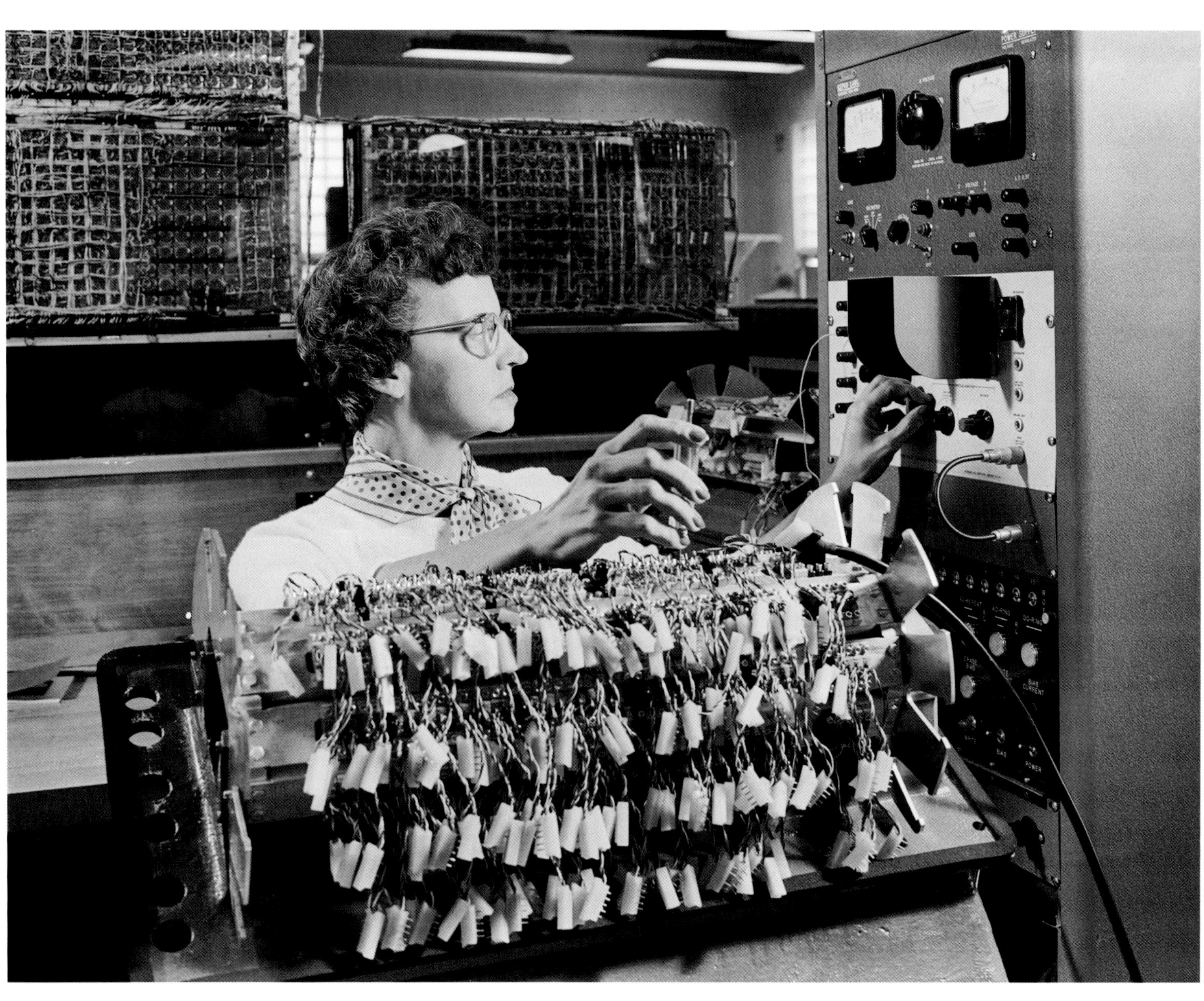

IBM, 1954.

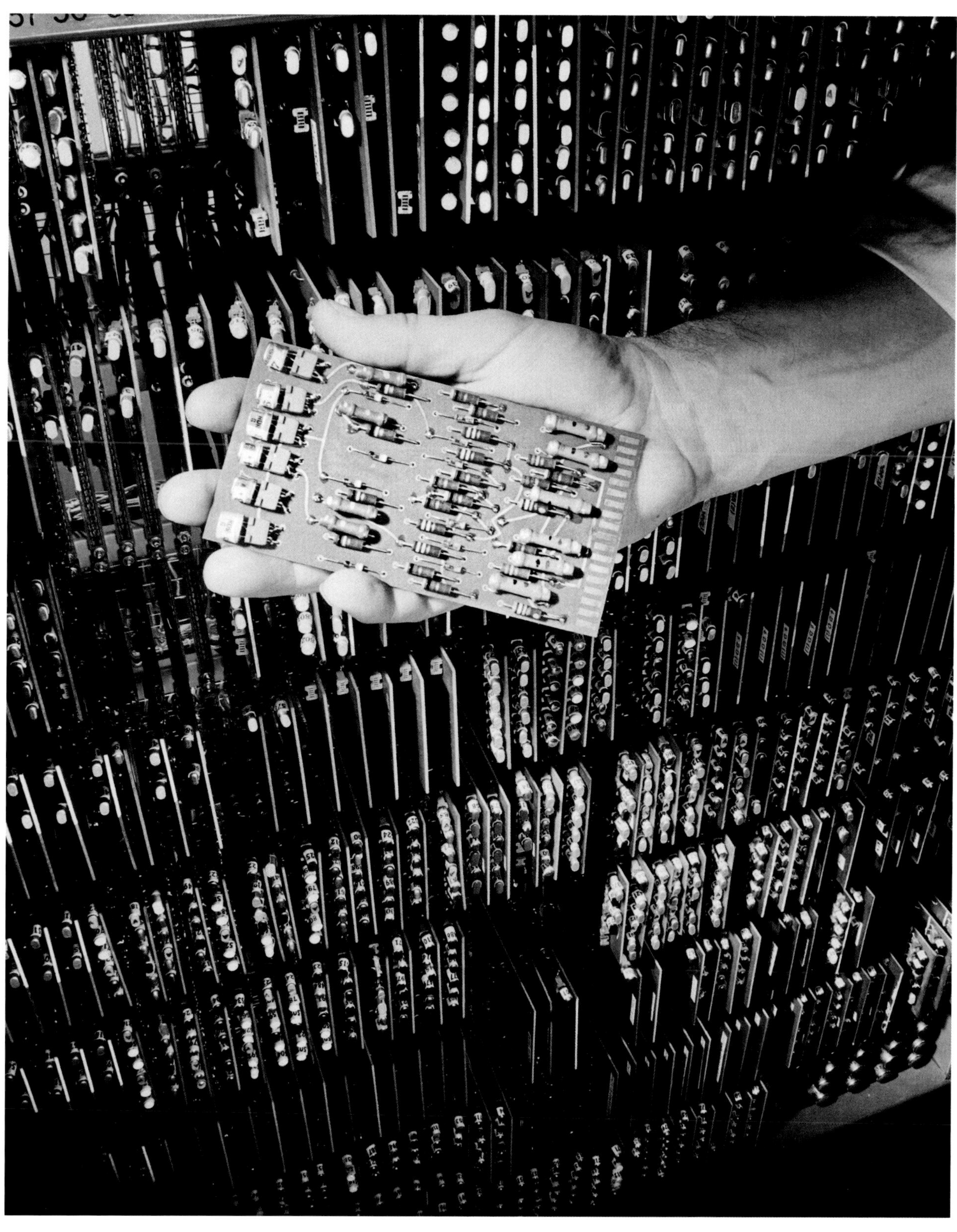

Overleaf
IBM, 702 Machine, 1955.

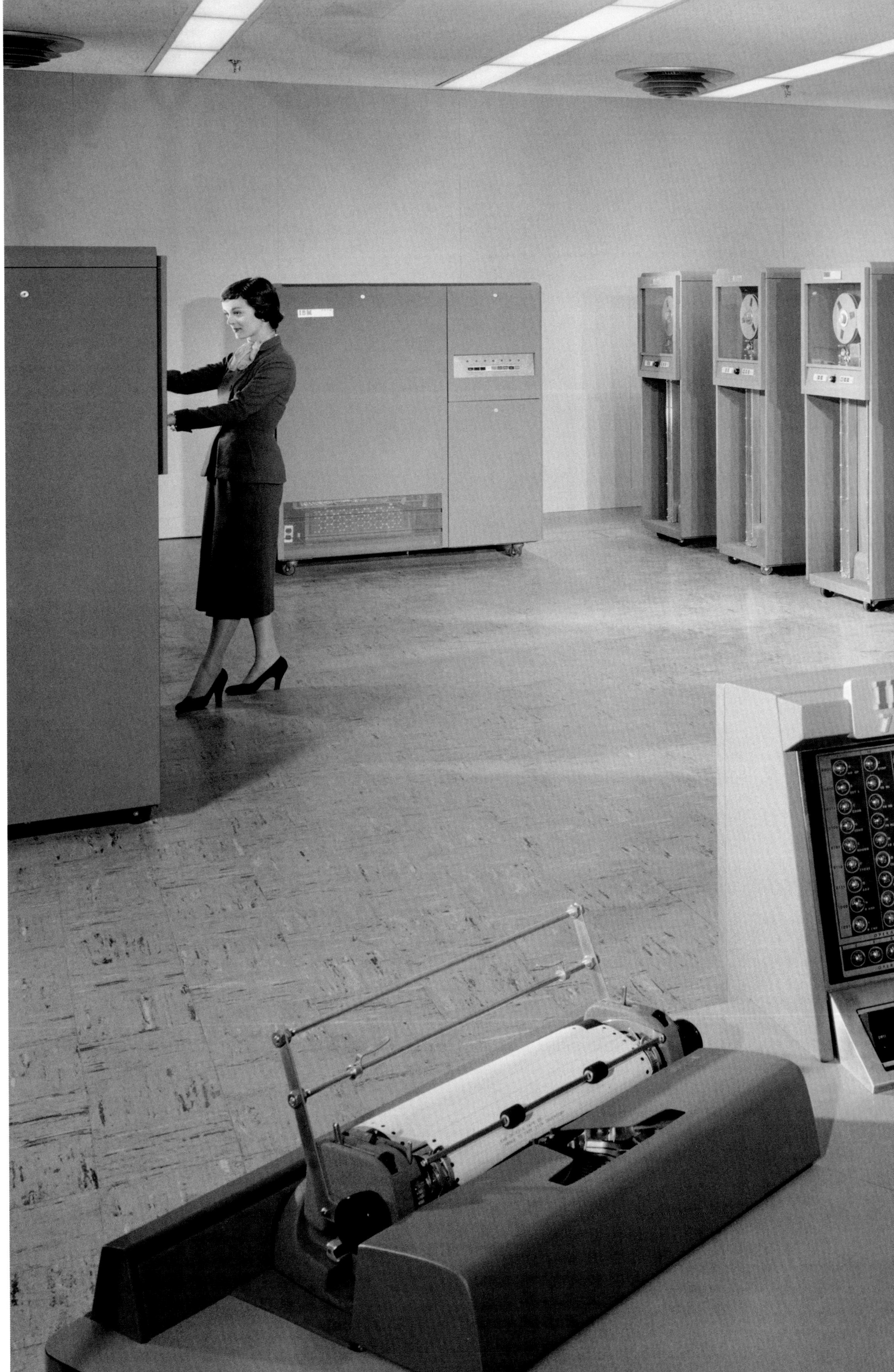

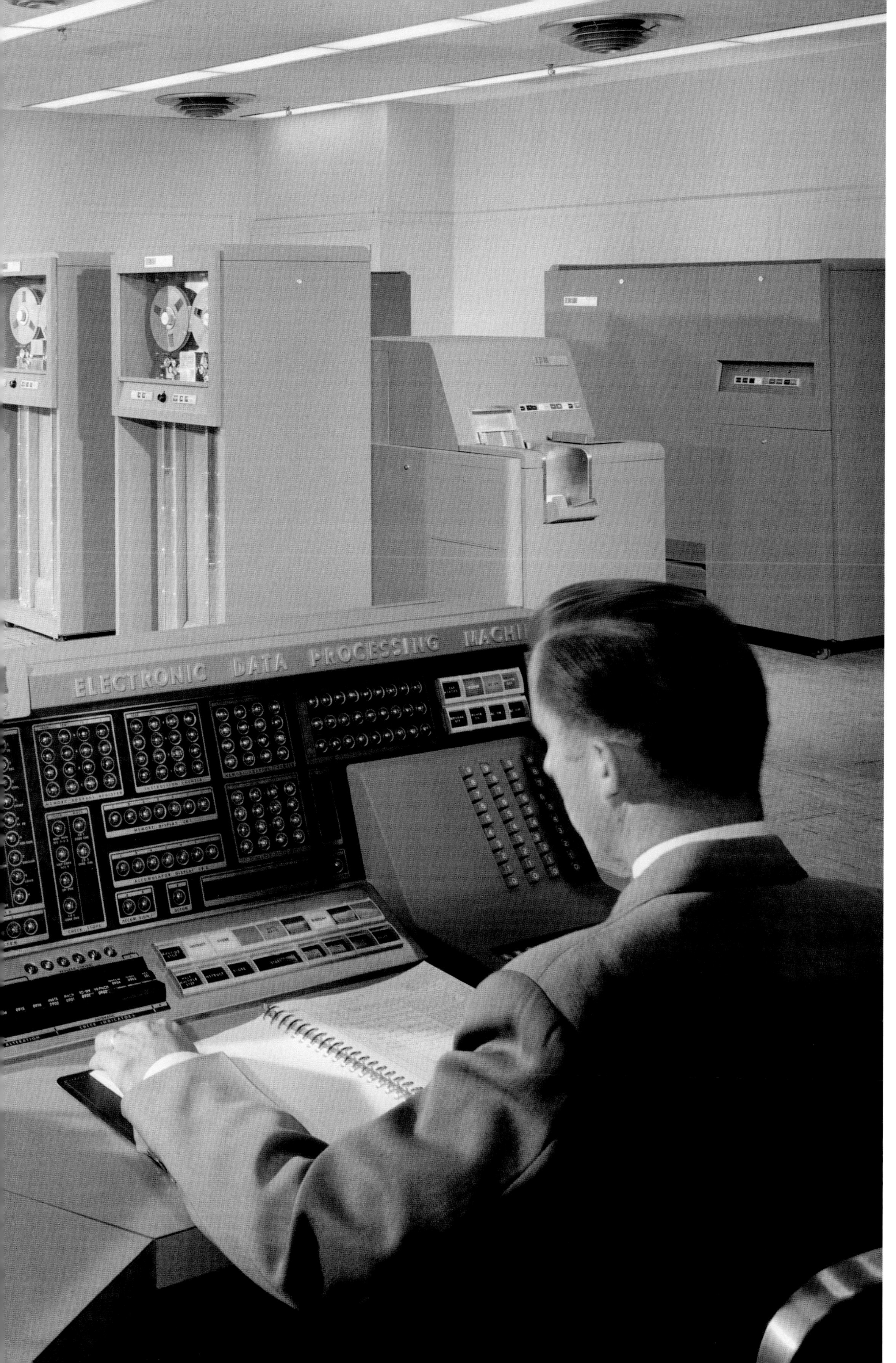
ELECTRONIC DATA PROCESSING
IBM

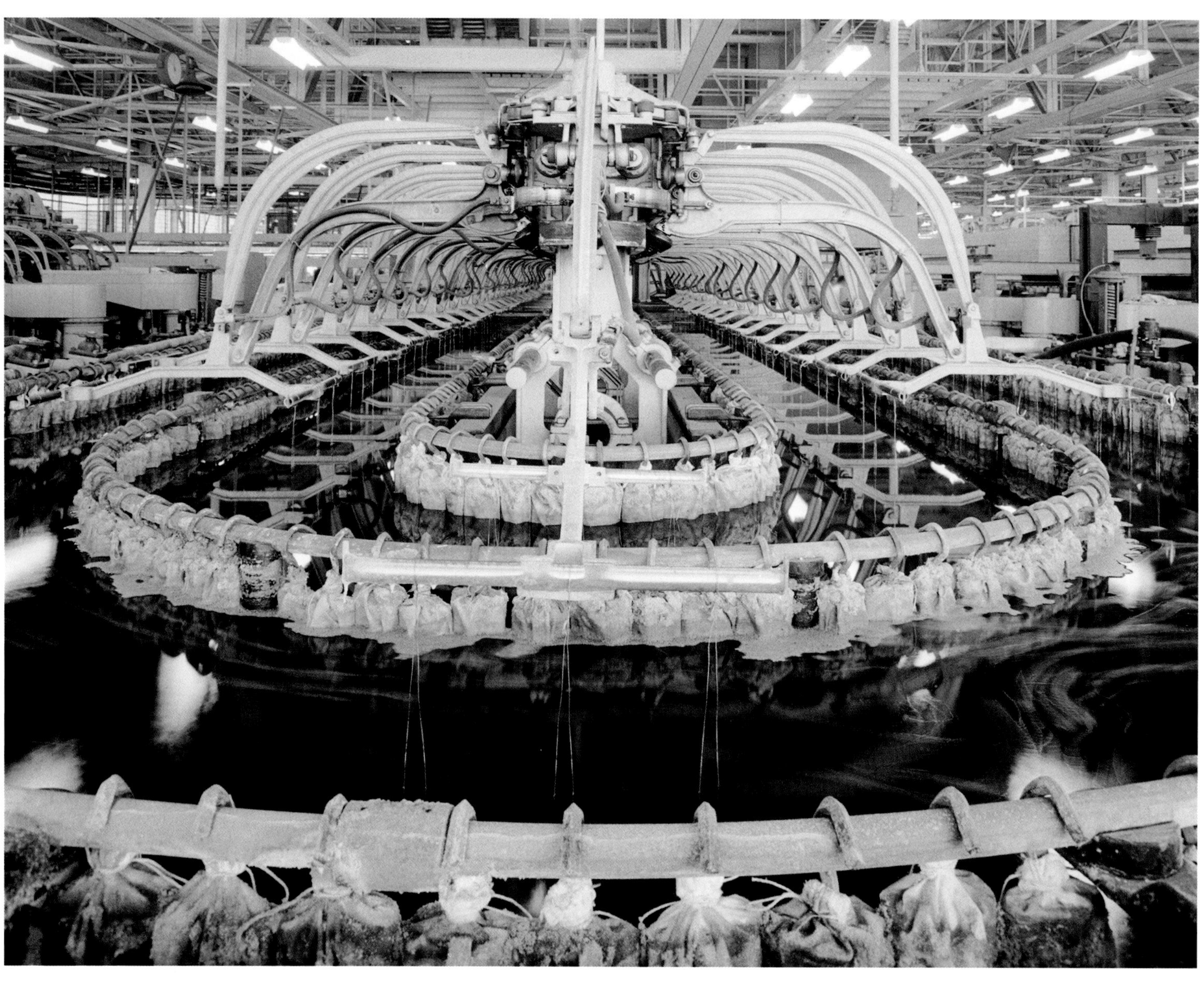

Above and opposite
IBM, Endicott, New York, 1956.

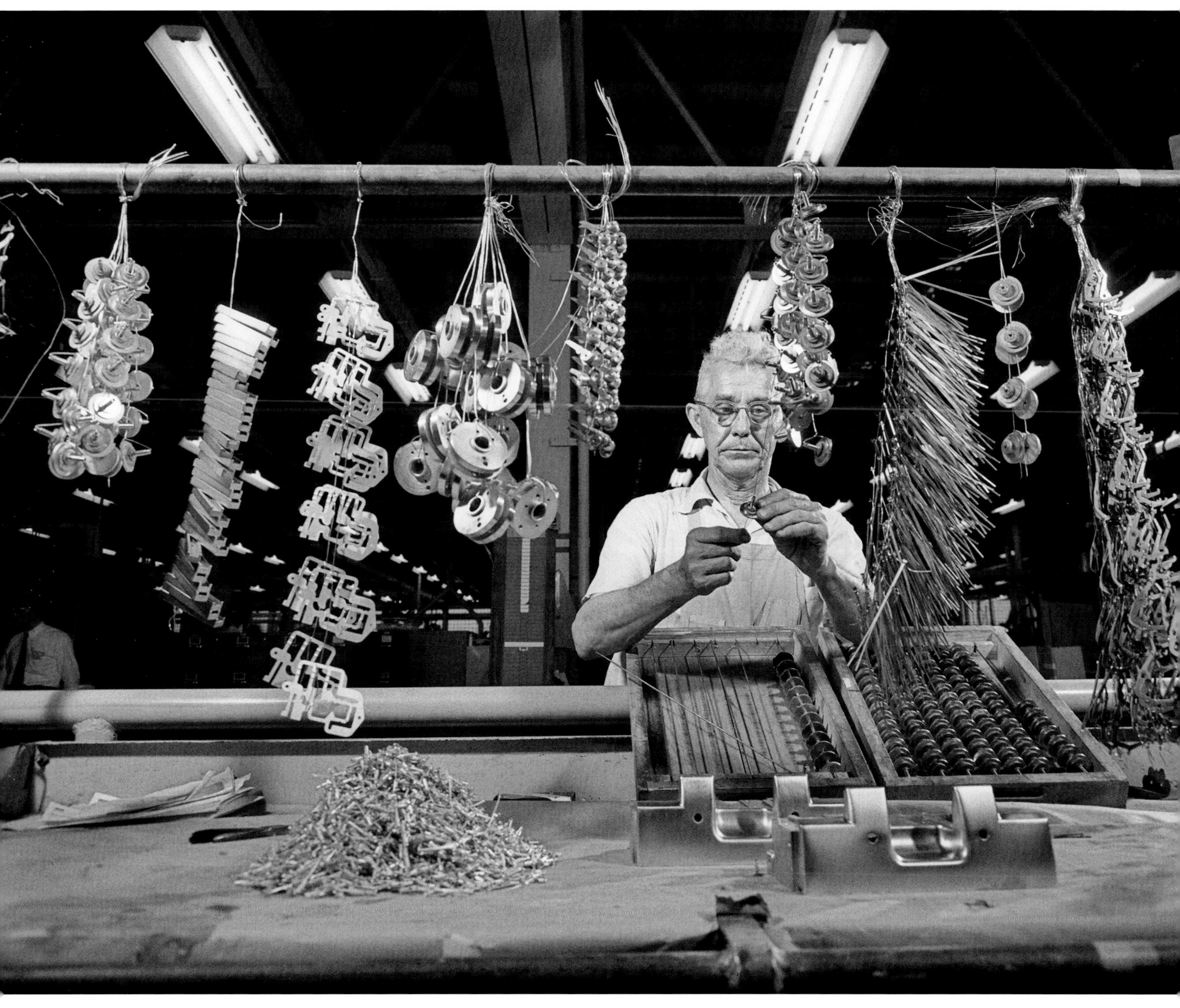

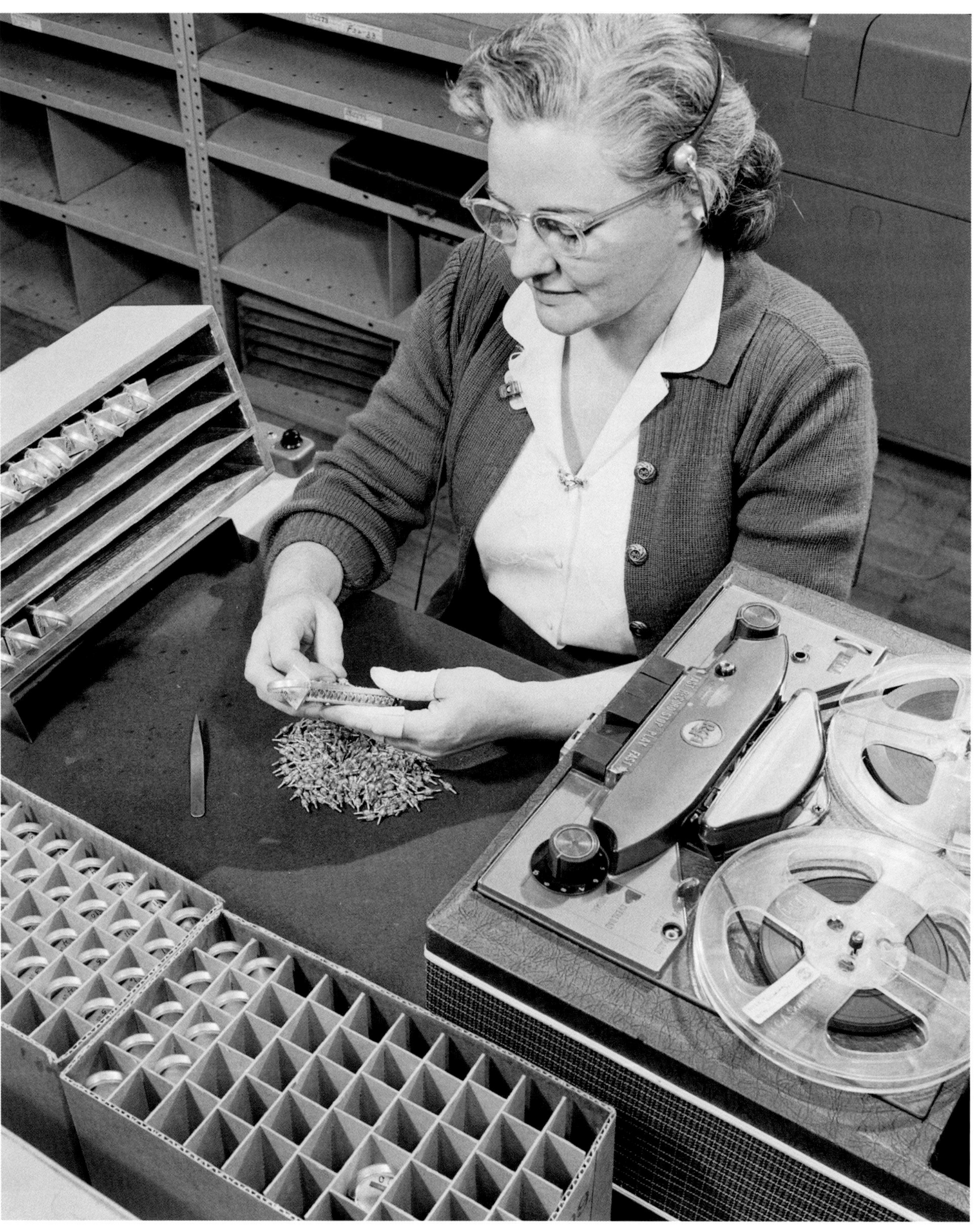

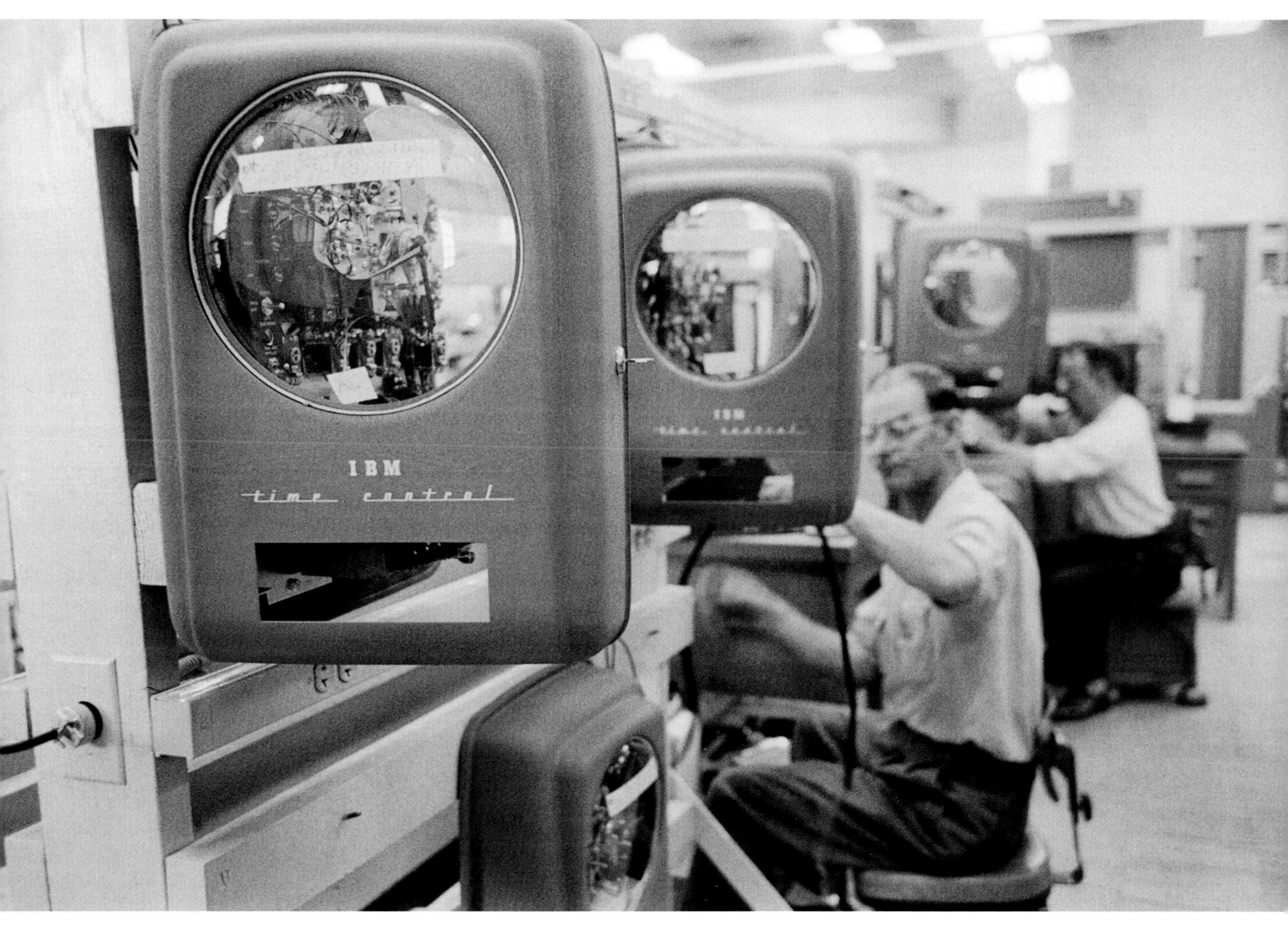

Above and opposite
IBM, Endicott, New York, 1956.

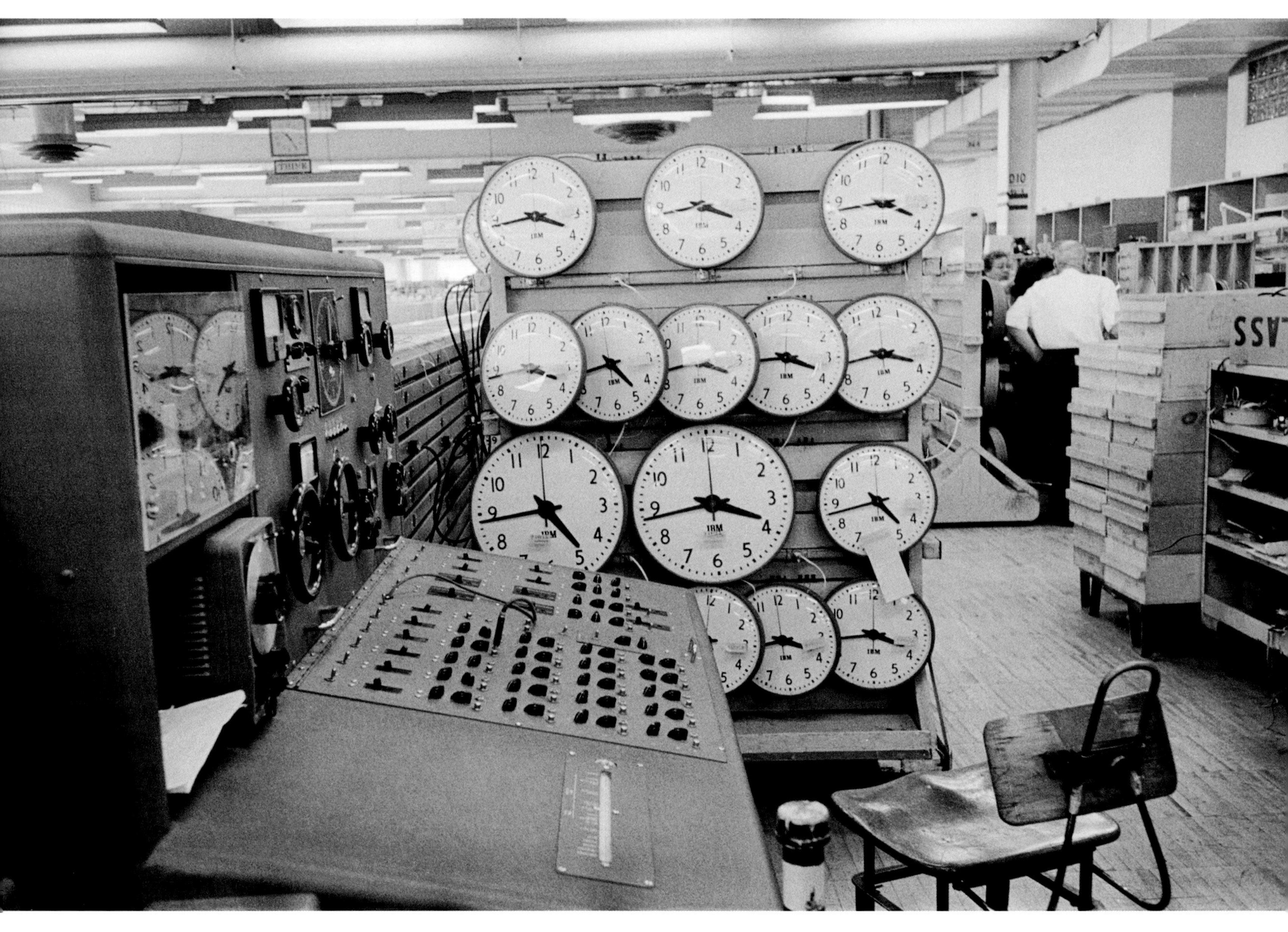

Above and opposite
IBM, Endicott, New York, 1956.

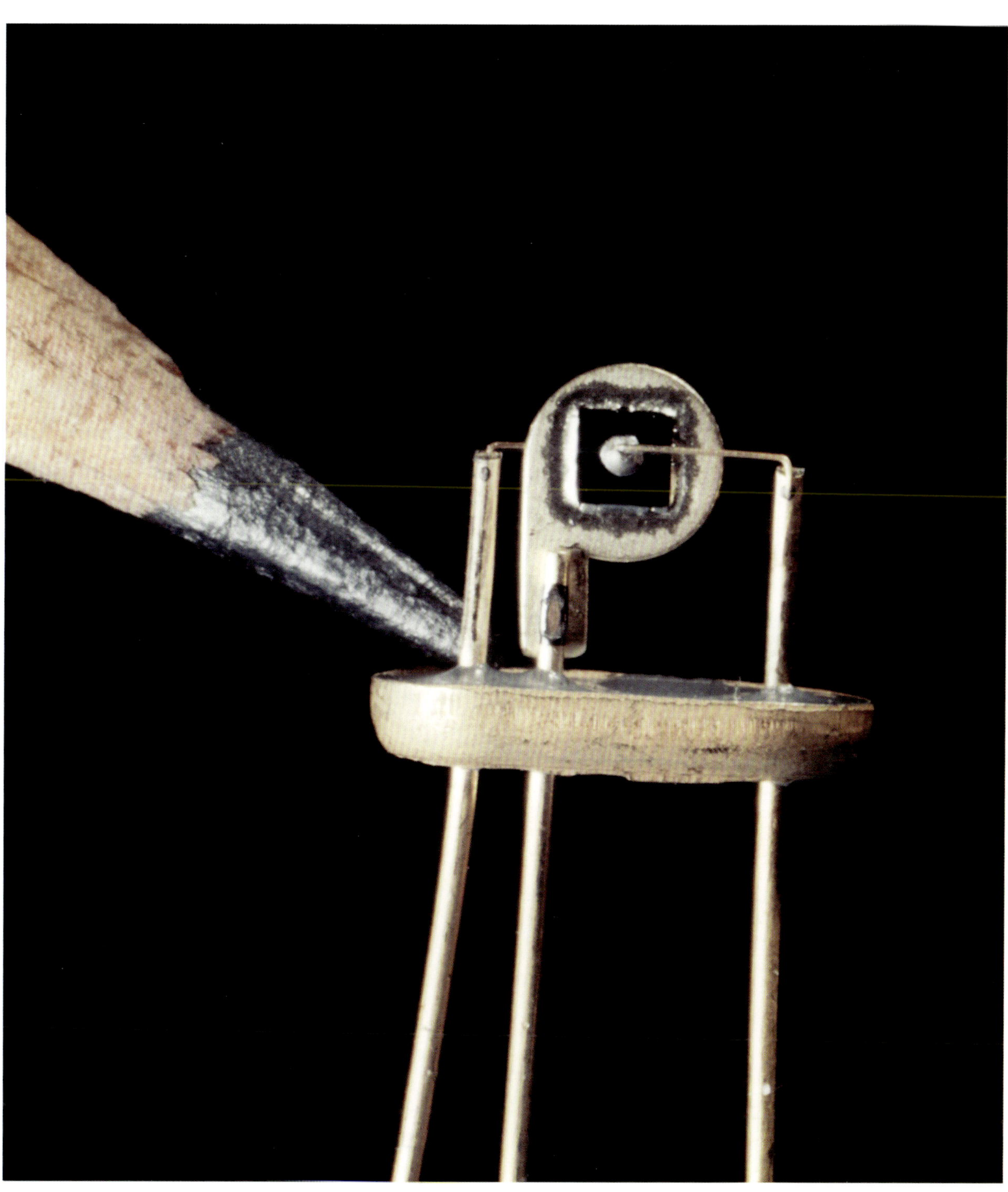

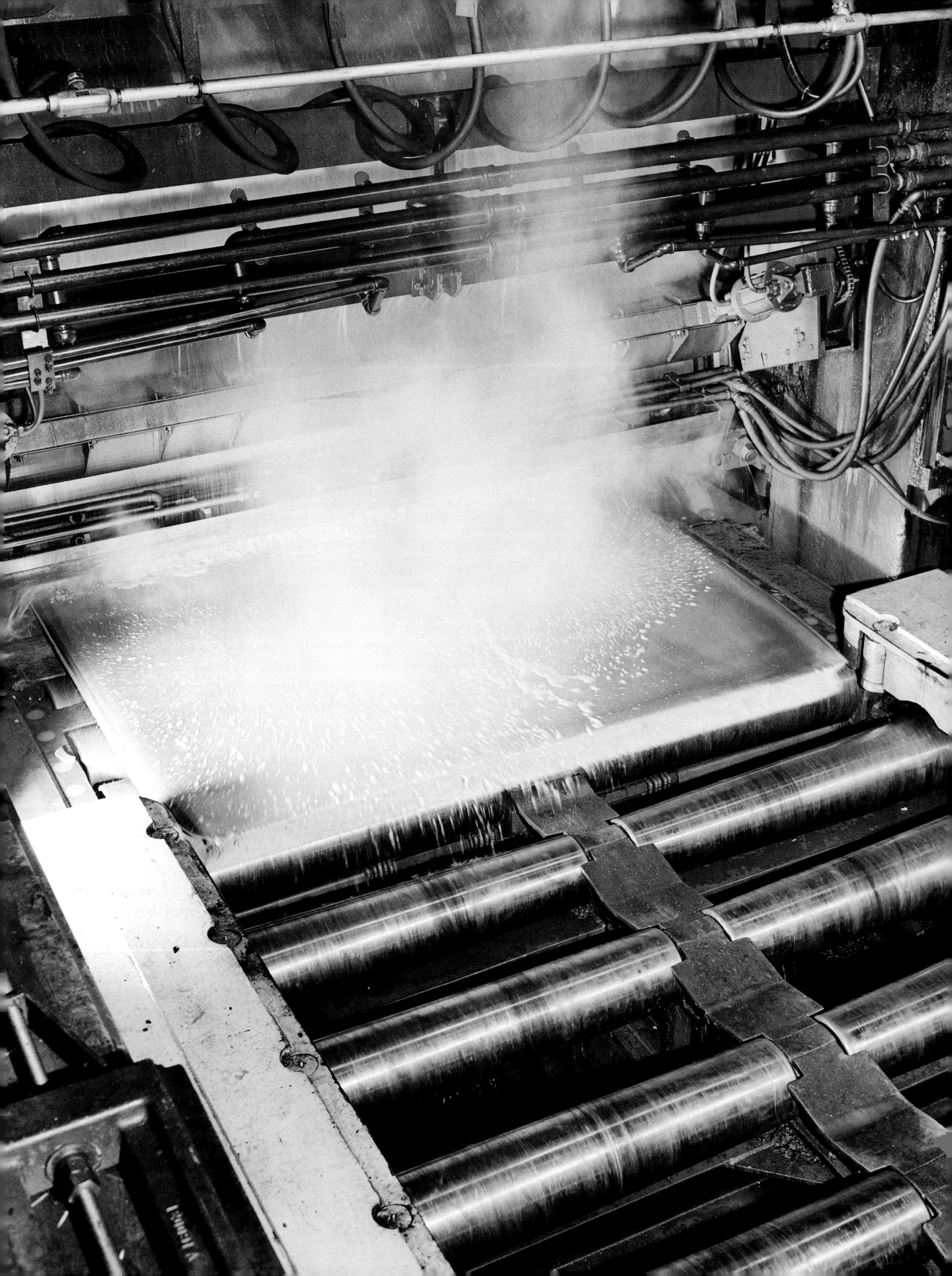

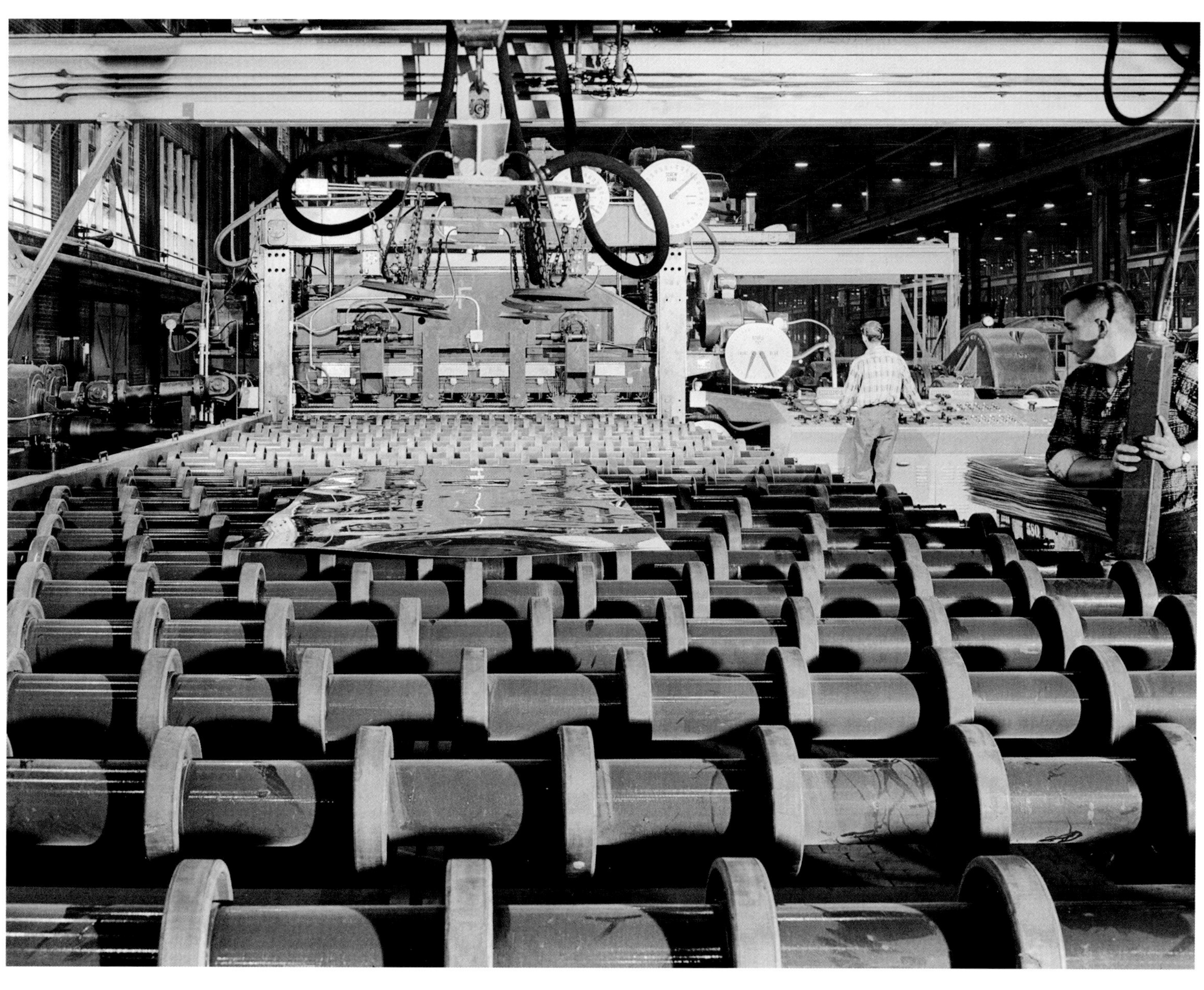

Reynolds Metals Plant, McCook, Illinois, 1956.

Heinz Factory, Pittsburgh, Pennsylania.
Skidmore, Owings & Merrill, 1958.

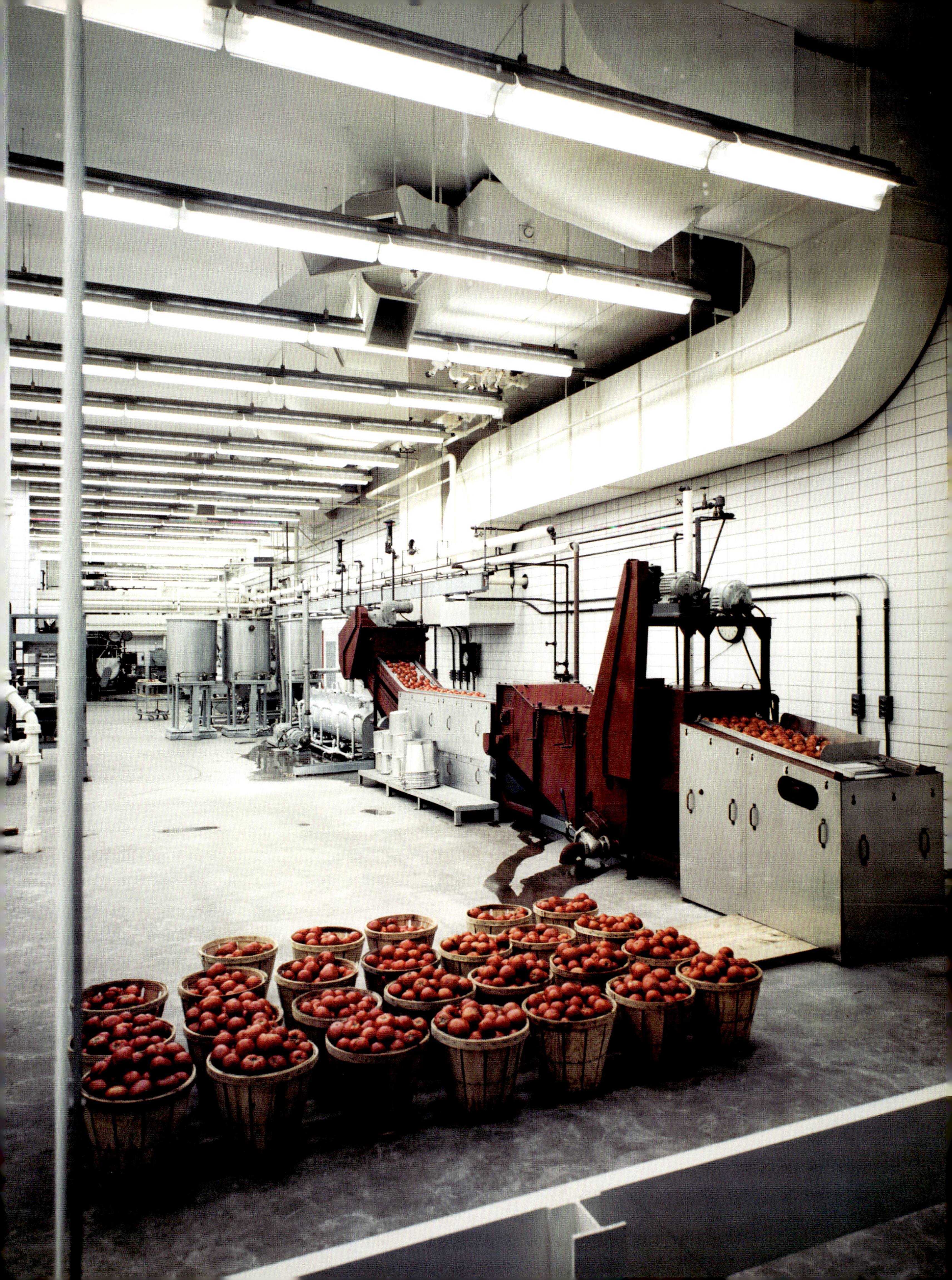

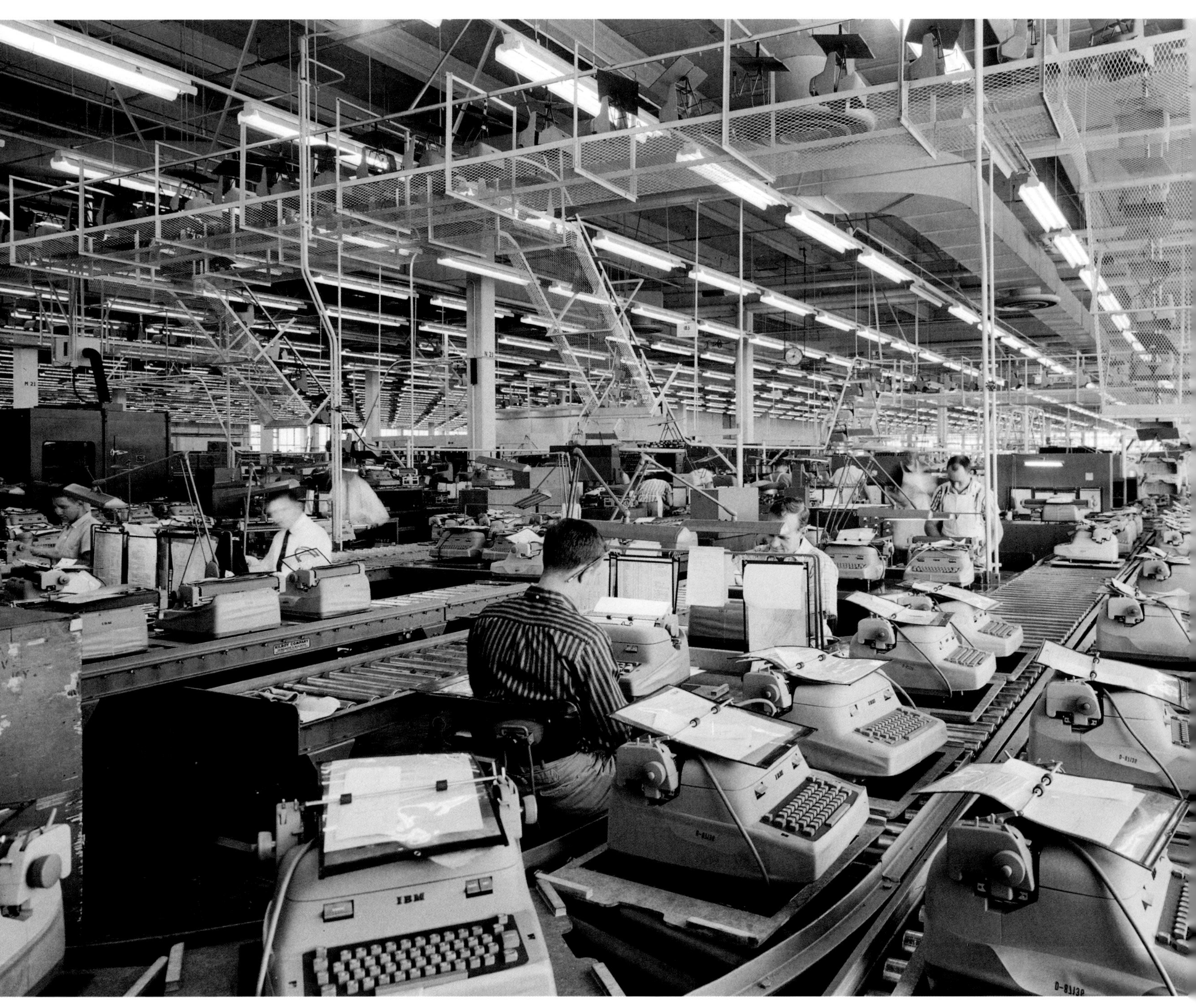

IBM, Lexington, Kentucky, 1958.

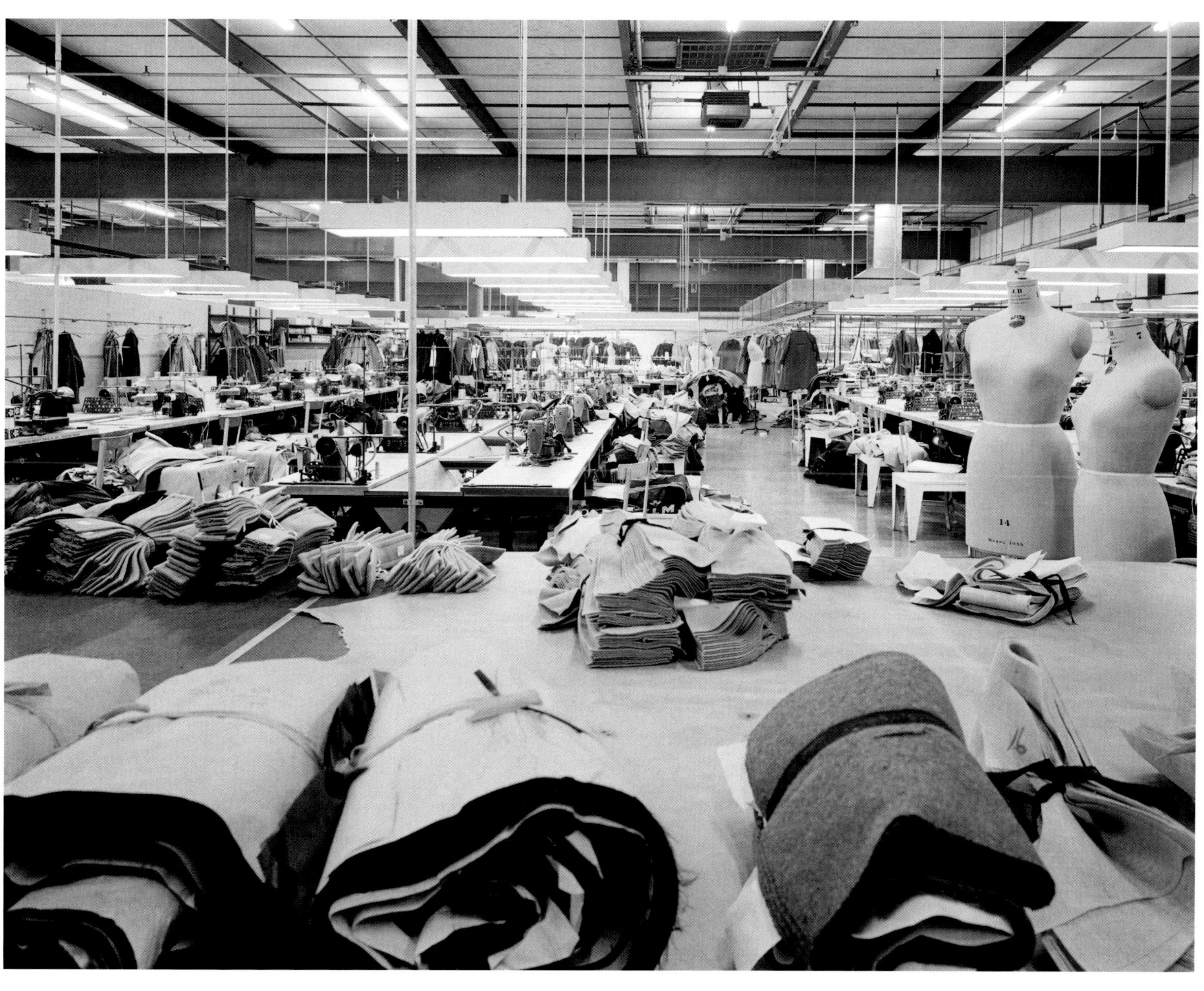

Barkin Levin Plant, Long Island City, New York. Ulrich Franzen, 1958.

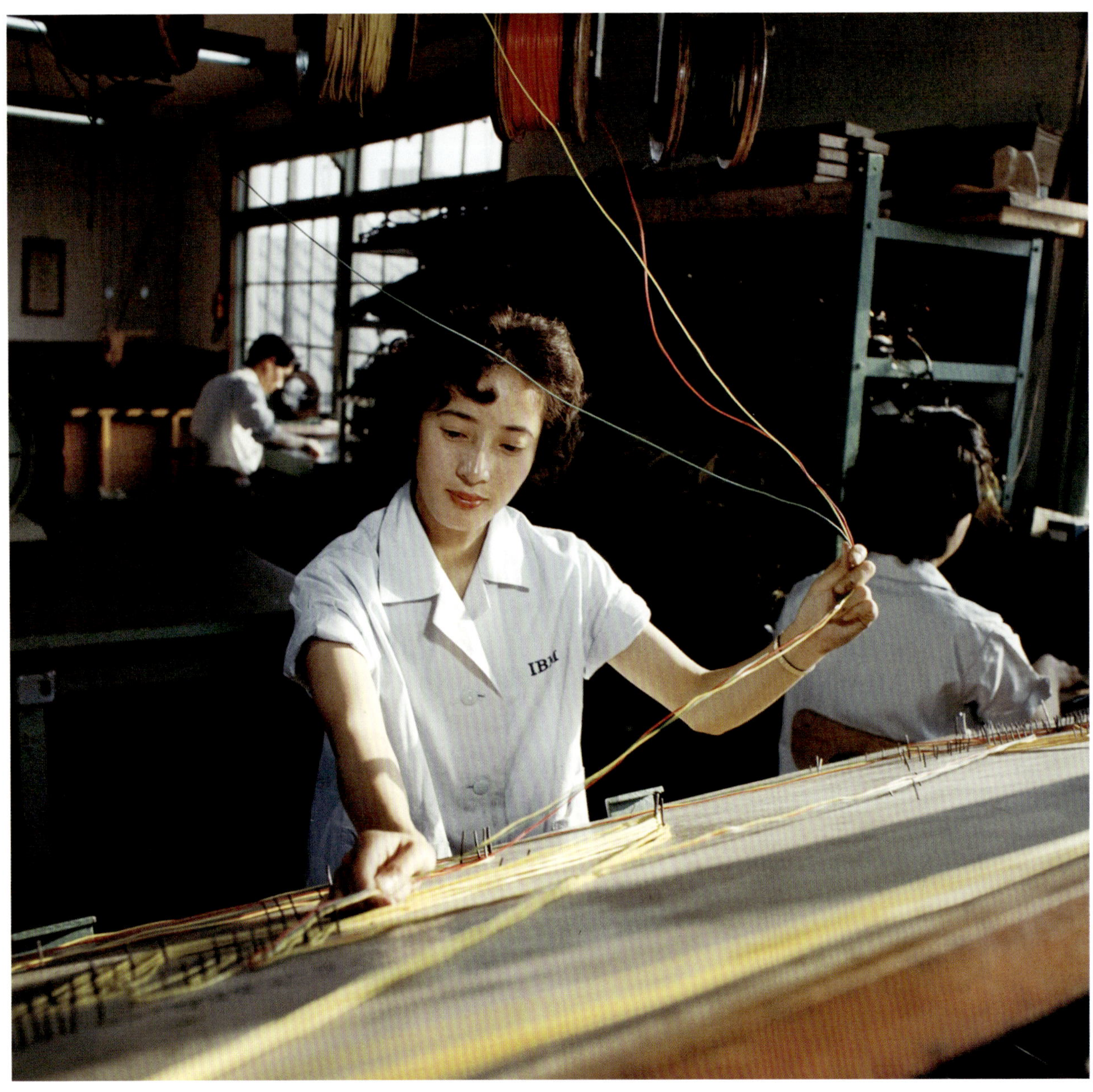

IBM, Tokyo, 1959.

Cummins Engine Company,
Columbus, Indiana, 1962.

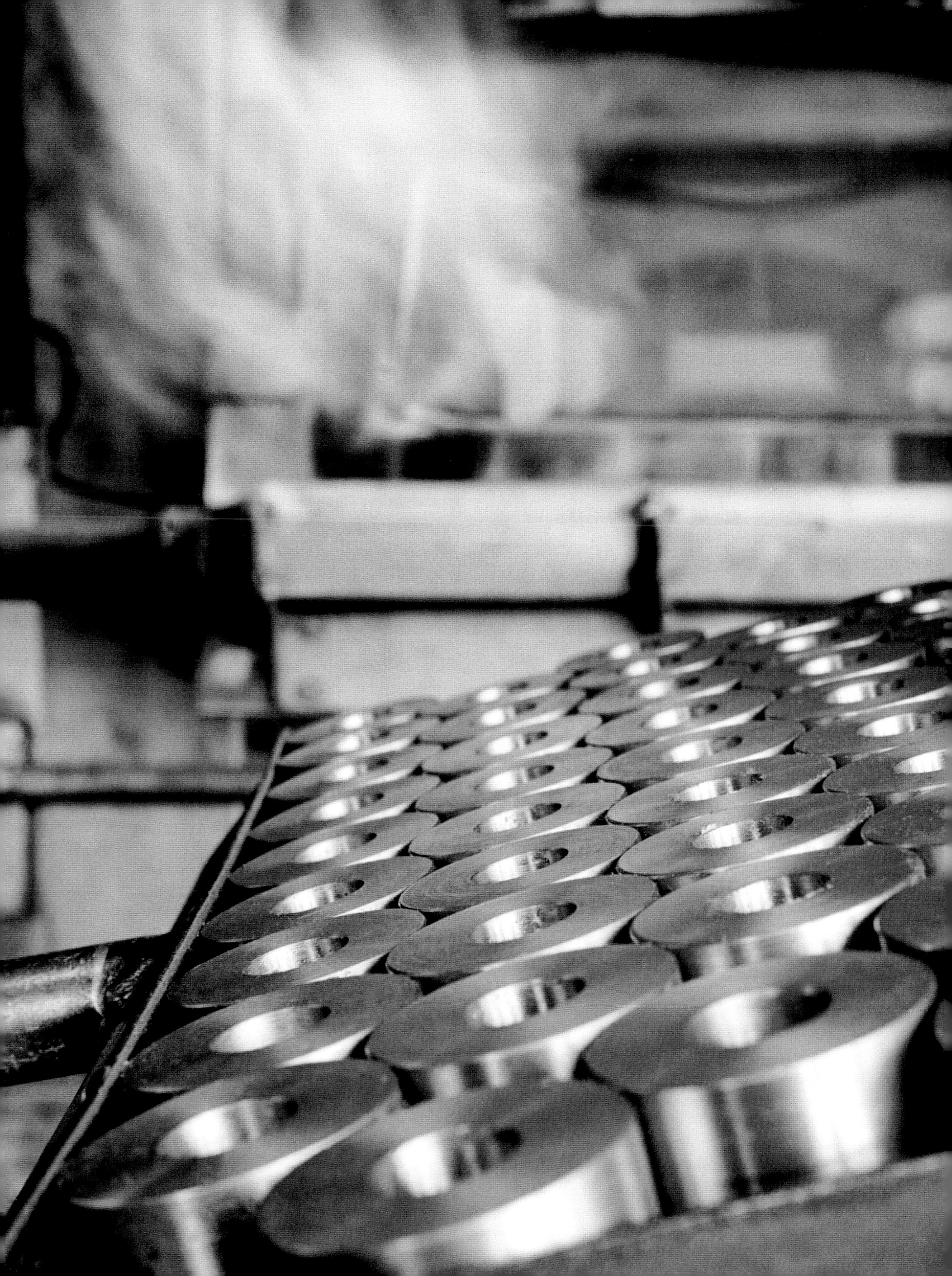

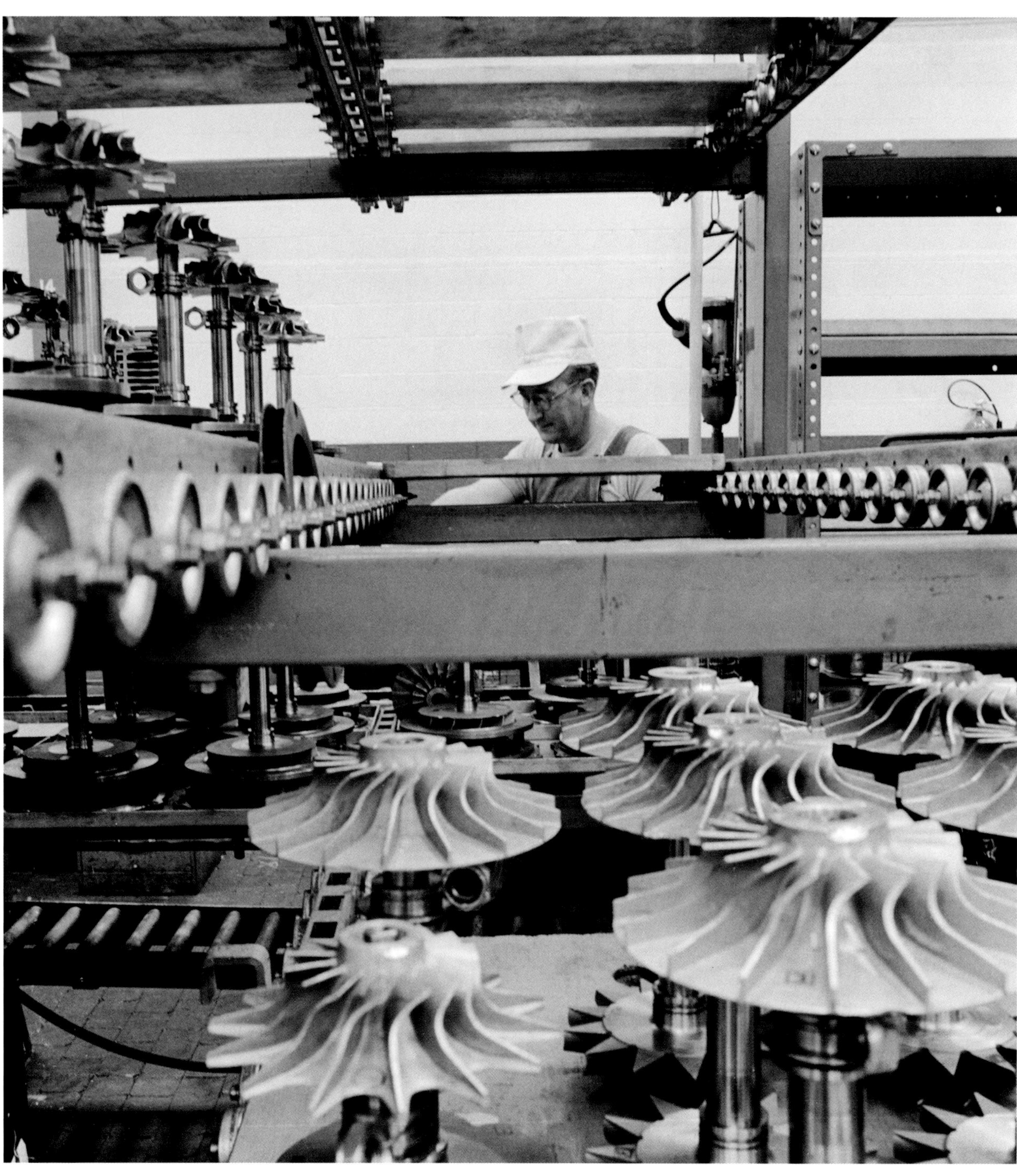

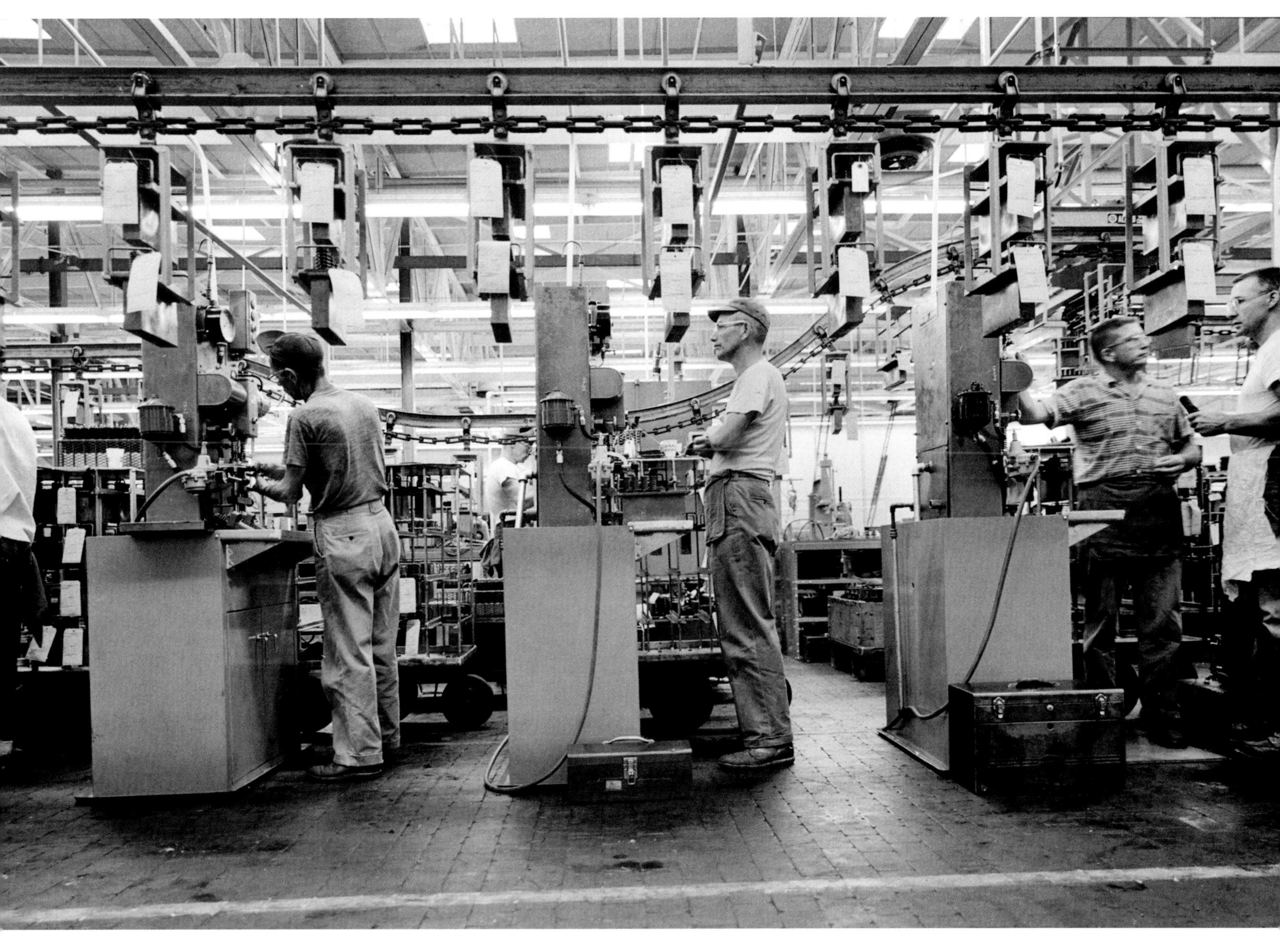

Above and opposite
Cummins Engine Company,
Columbus, Indiana, 1962.

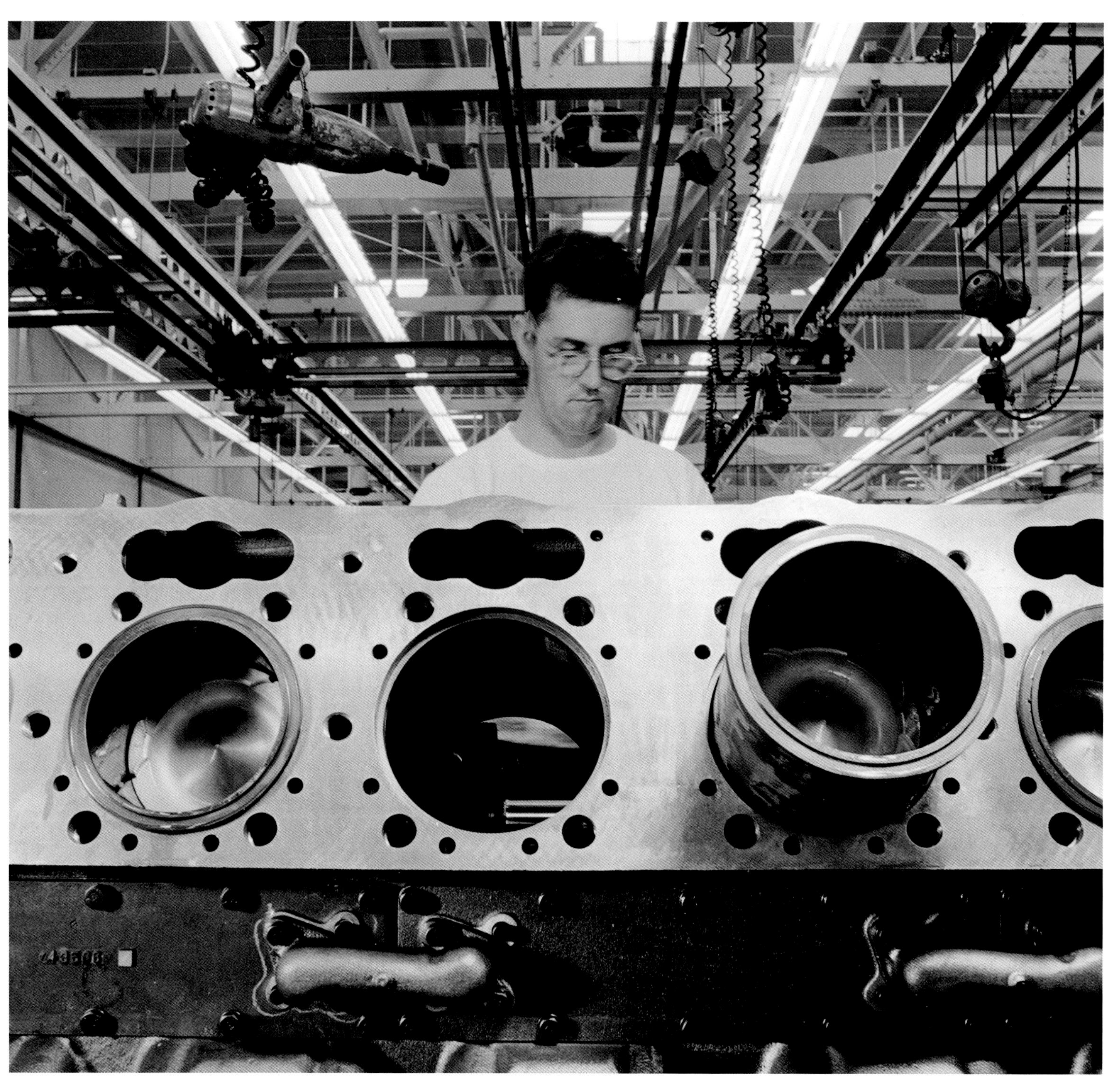

Above and opposite
Cummins Engine Company,
Columbus, Indiana, 1962.

Overleaf
Olivetti-Underwood Factory,
Harrisburg, Pennsylania. Louis Kahn, 1969.

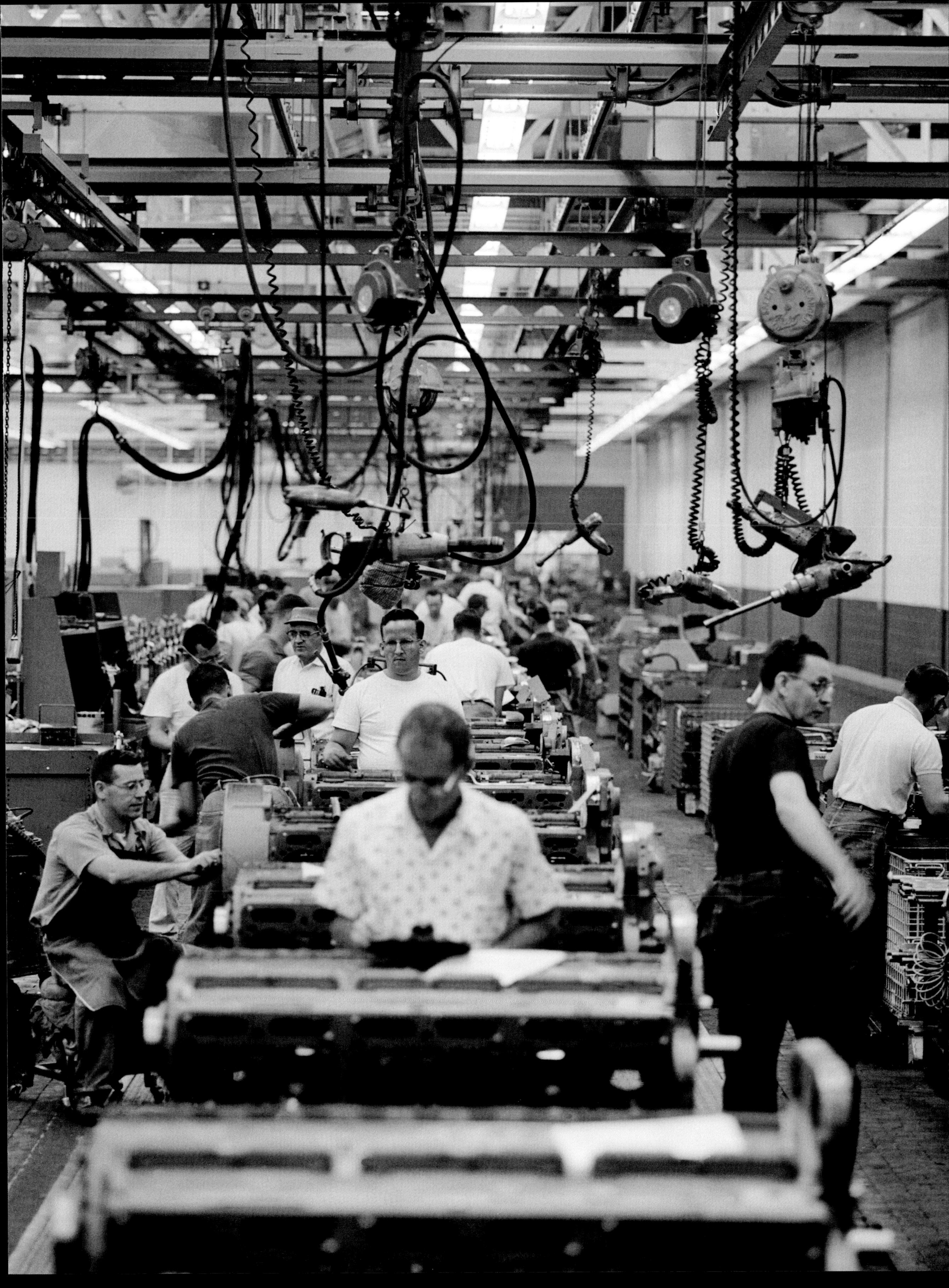

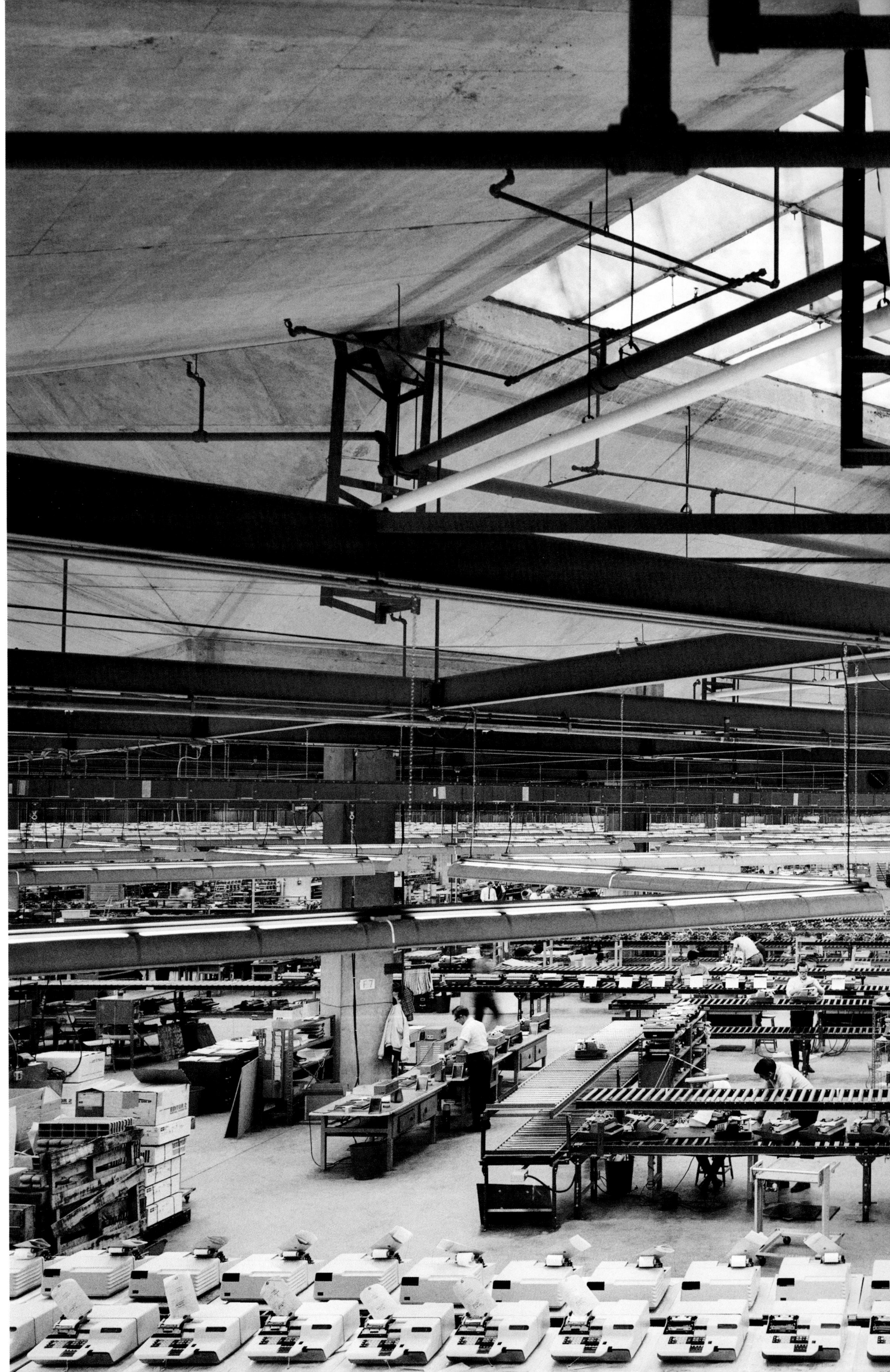
F7
EDITOR 2

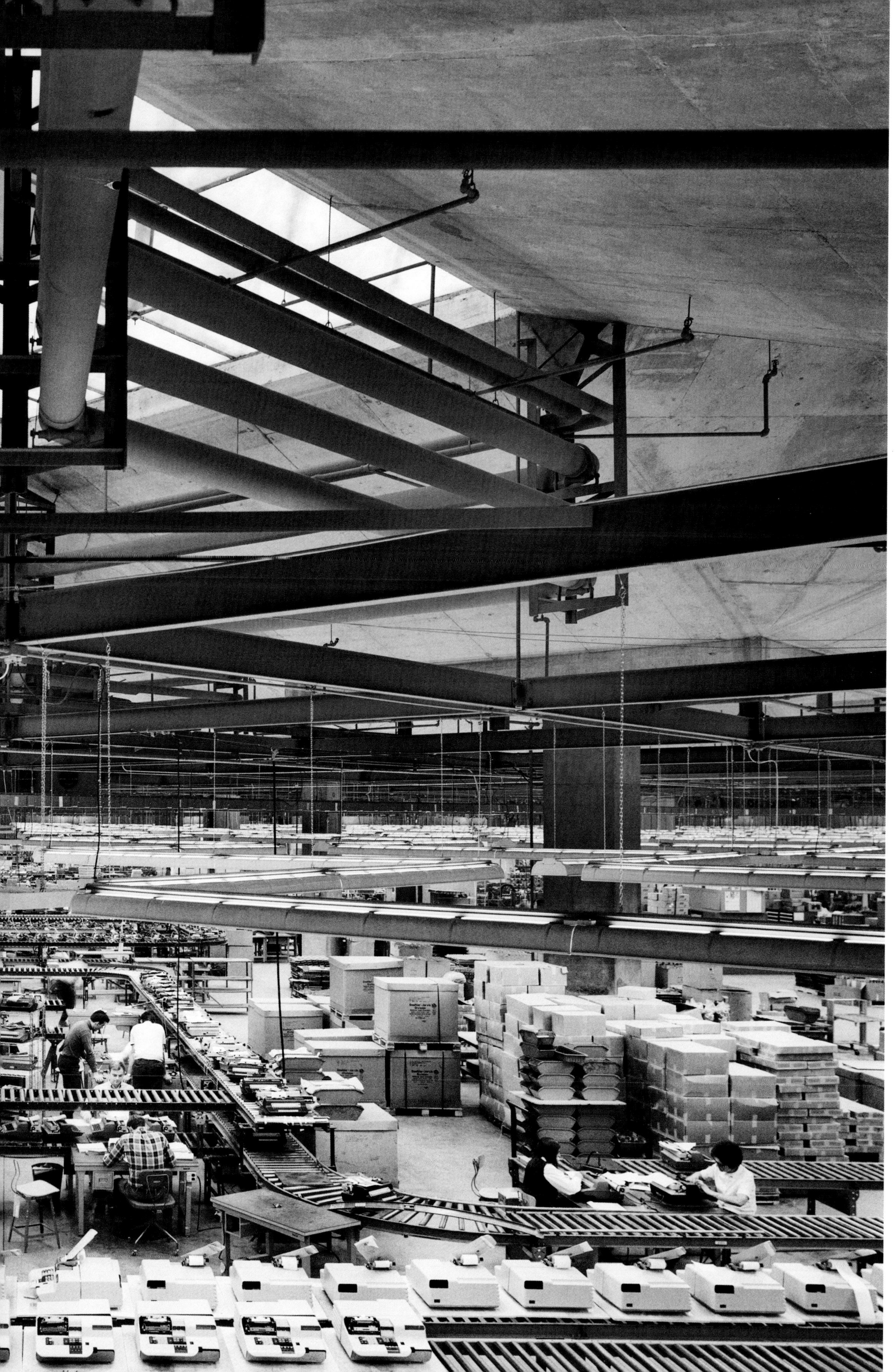

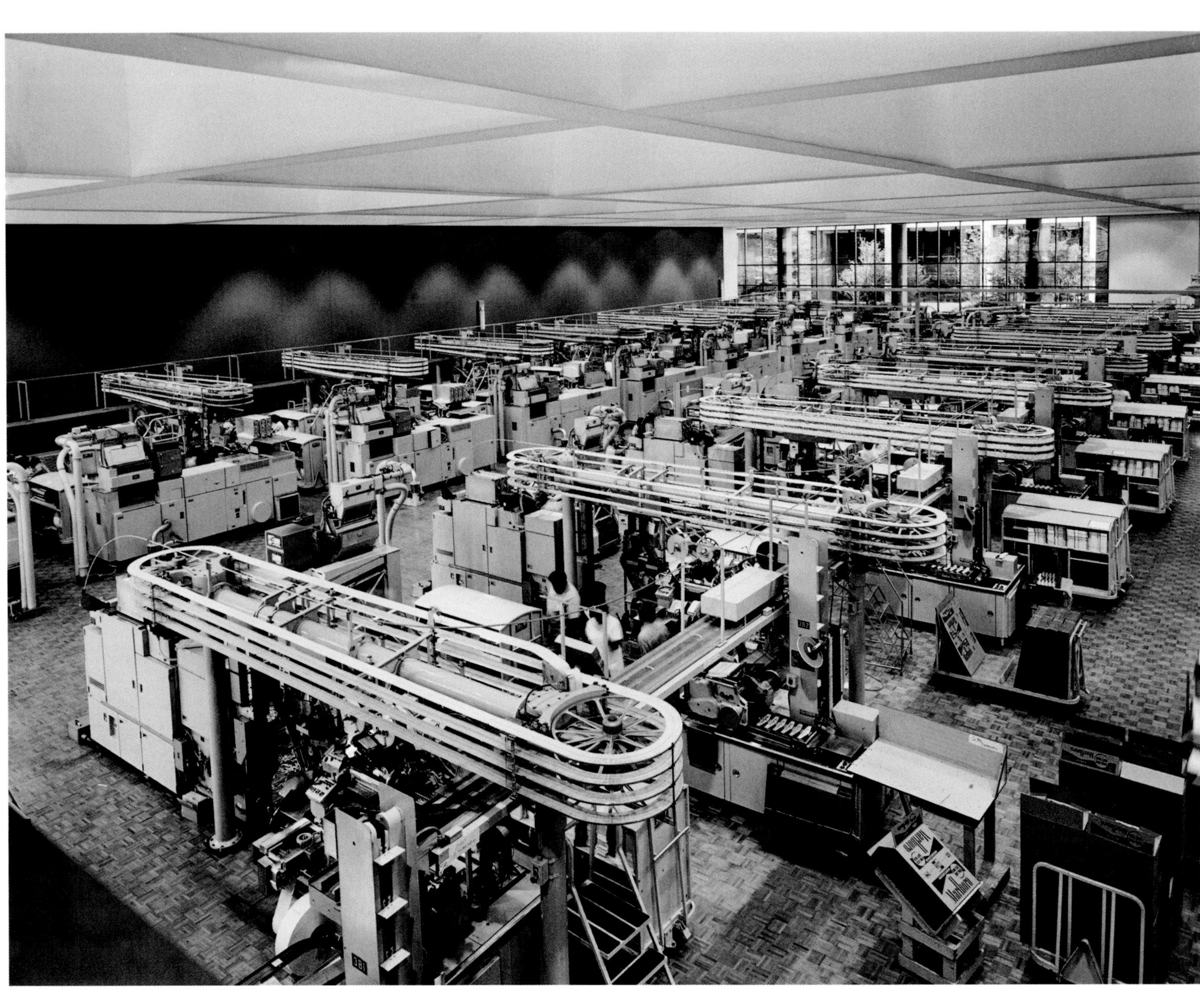

Philip Morris, Richmond, Virginia.
Skidmore, Owings & Merrill, 1973.

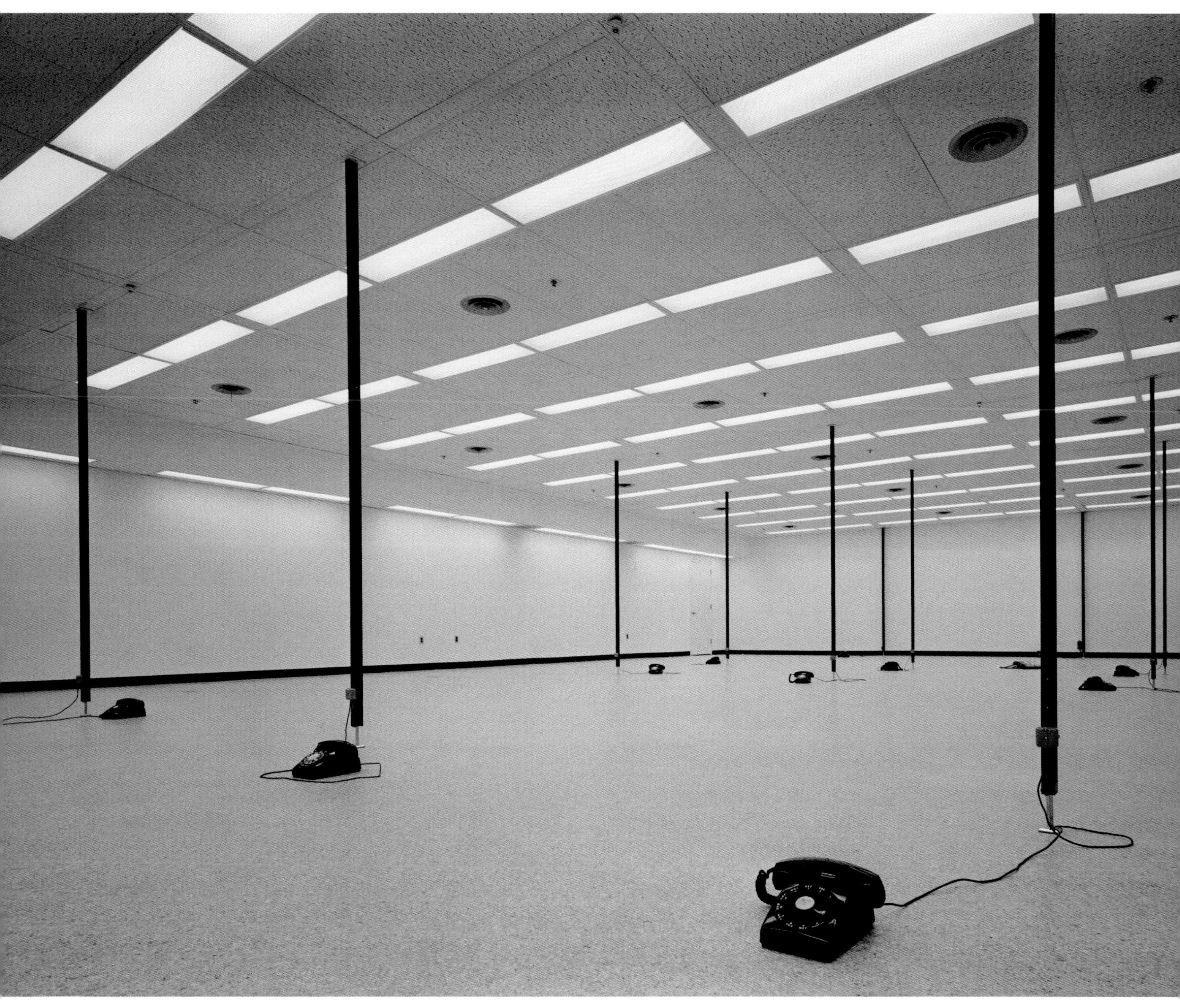

Philip Morris Research Tower,
Richmond, Virginia. Ulrich Franzen, 1972.

Portfolio
Capturing House and Home

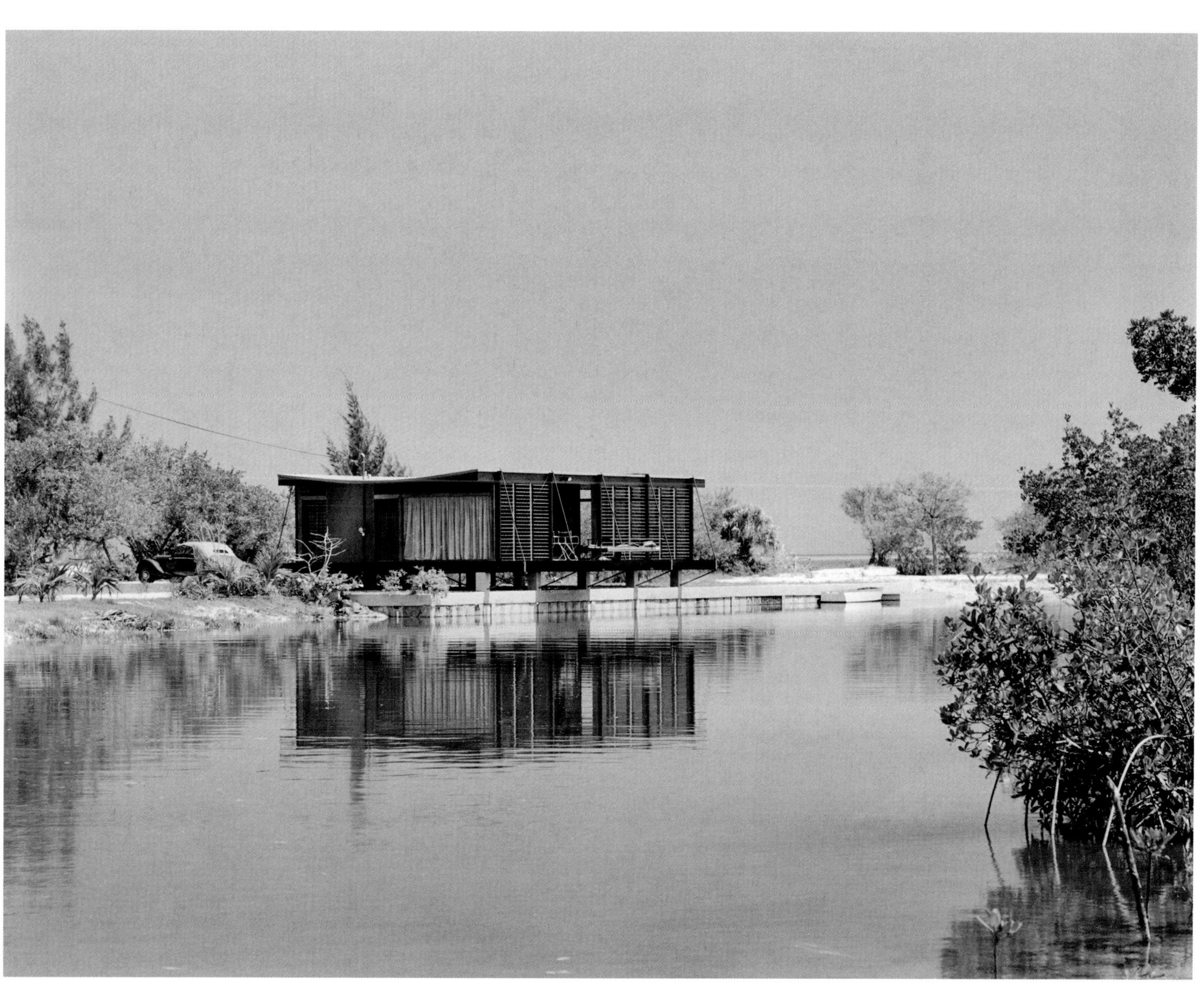

Above and overleaf
Guest Cottage, "Cocoon House," Sarasota, Florida.
Ralph Twitchell and Paul Rudolph, 1951.

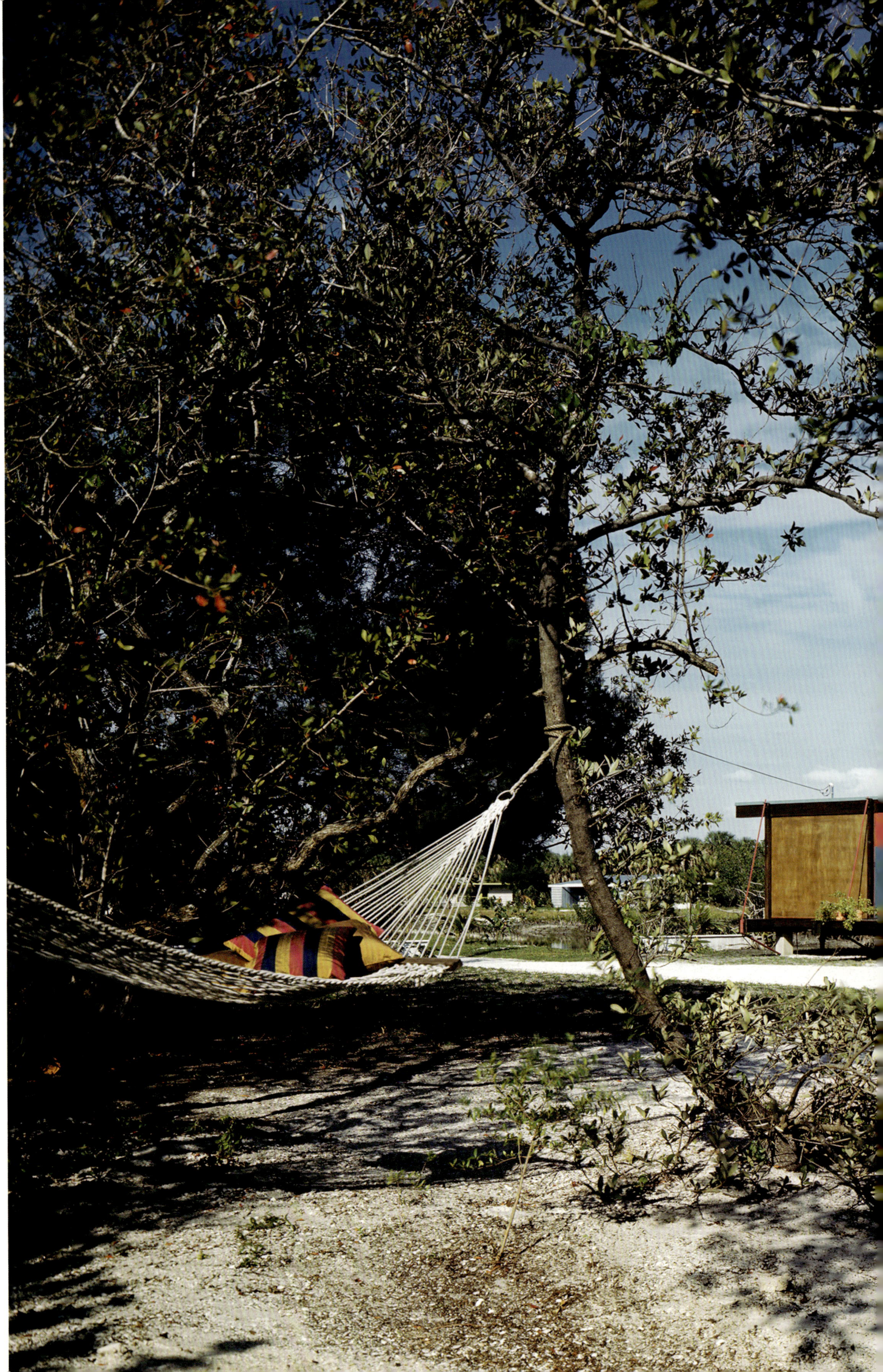

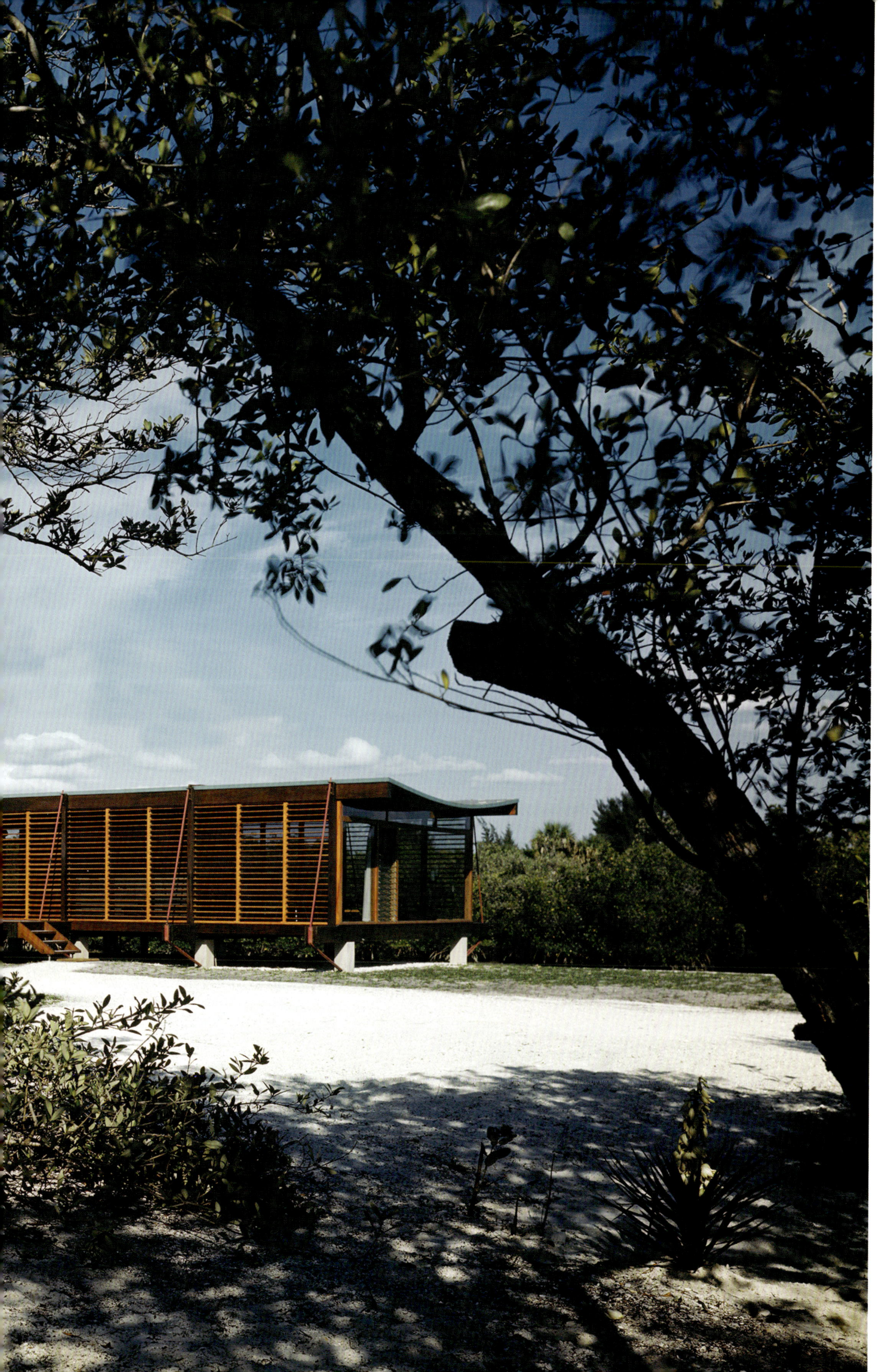

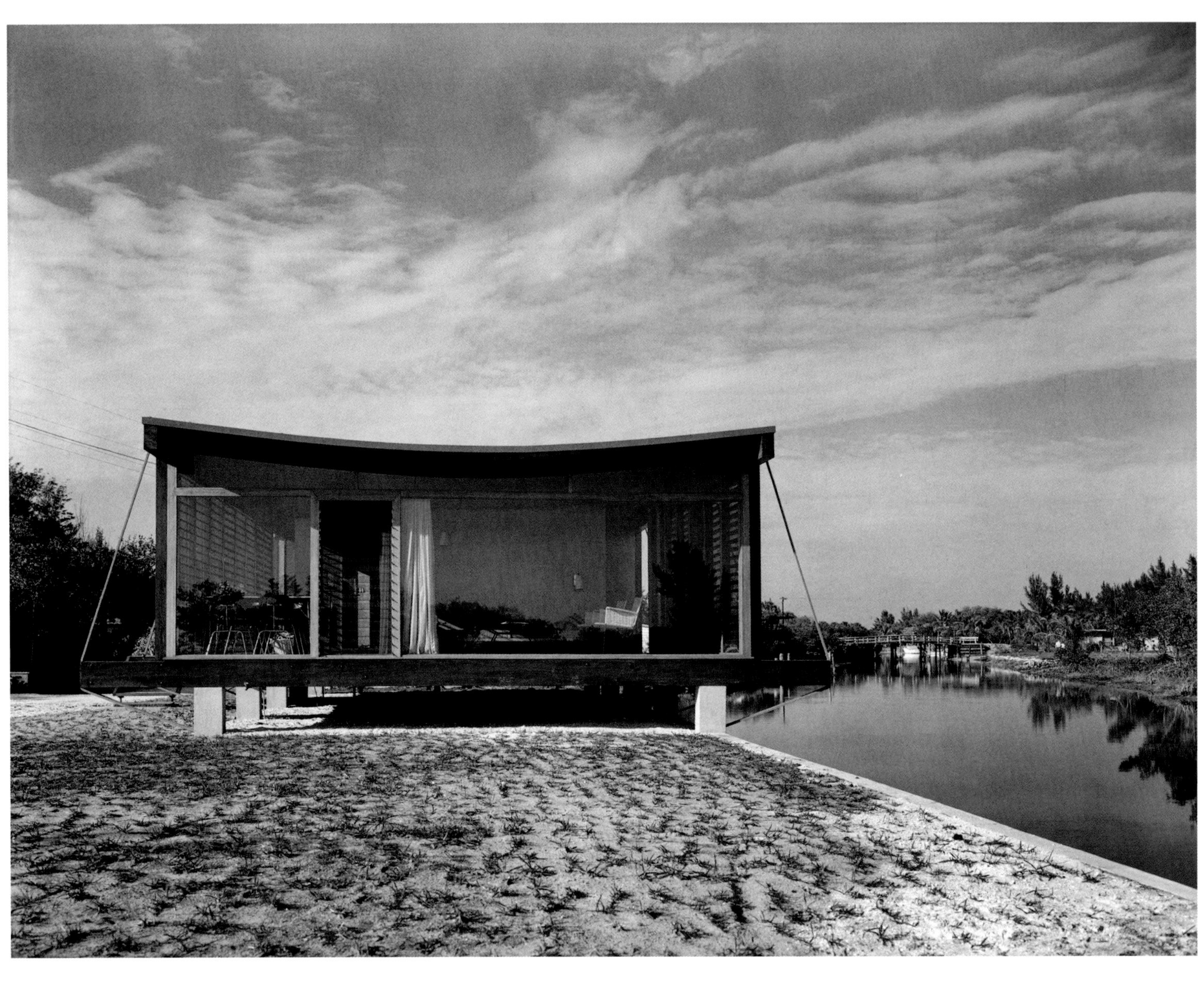

Above and opposite
Guest Cottage, "Cocoon House," Sarasota, Florida.
Ralph Twitchell and Paul Rudolph, 1951.

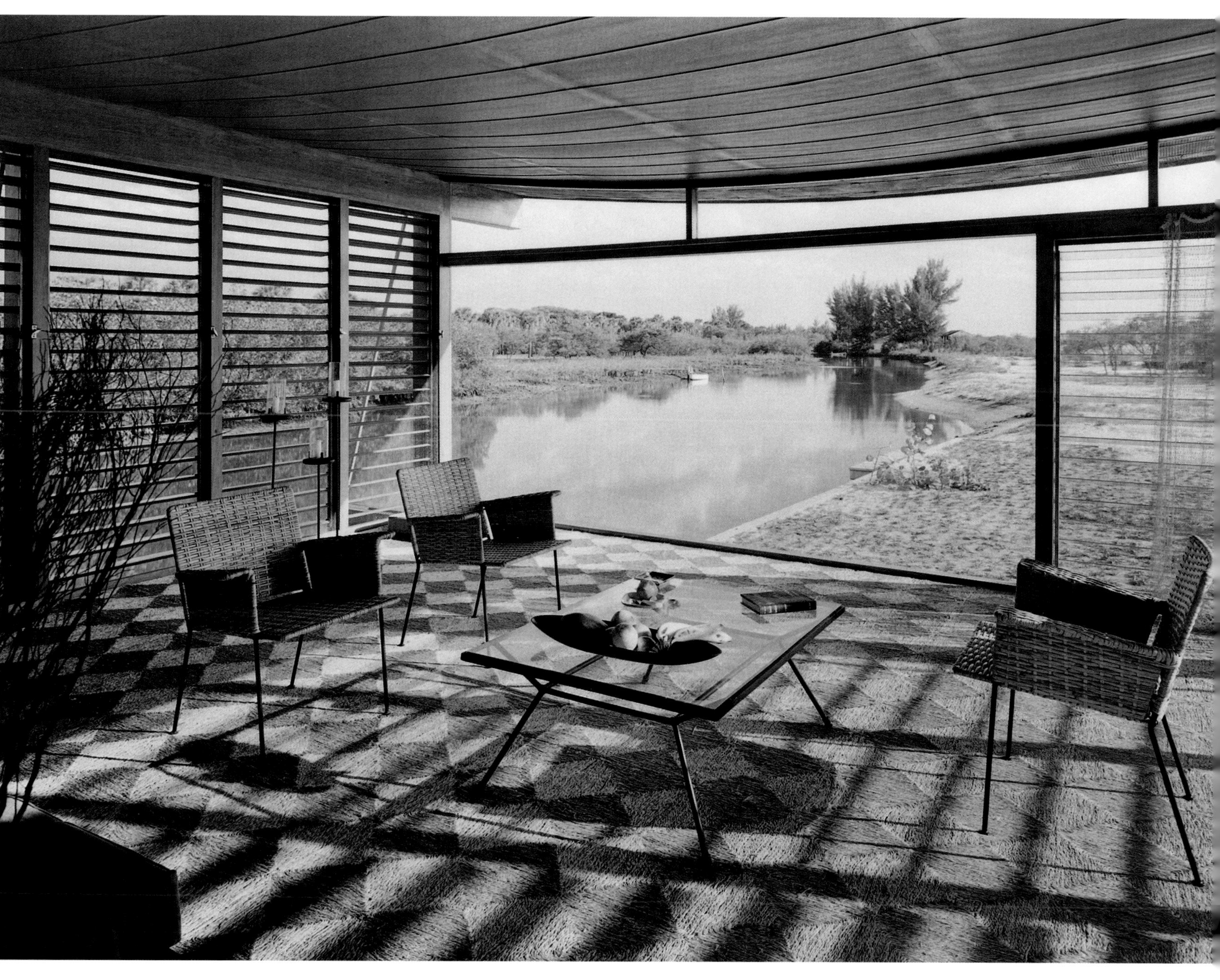

Overleaf
Leavengood House, St. Petersburg, Florida.
Ralph Twitchell and Paul Rudolph, 1951.

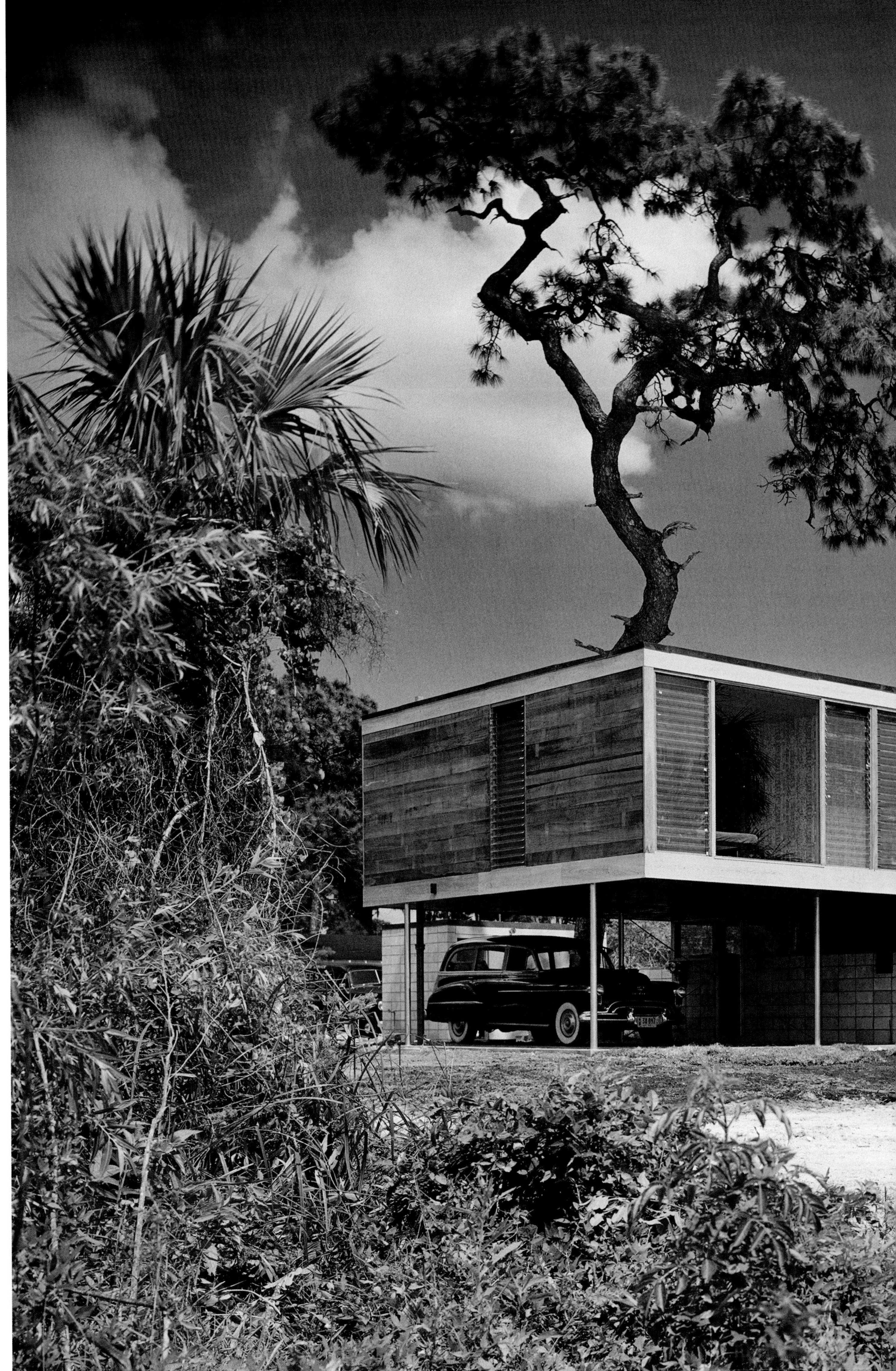

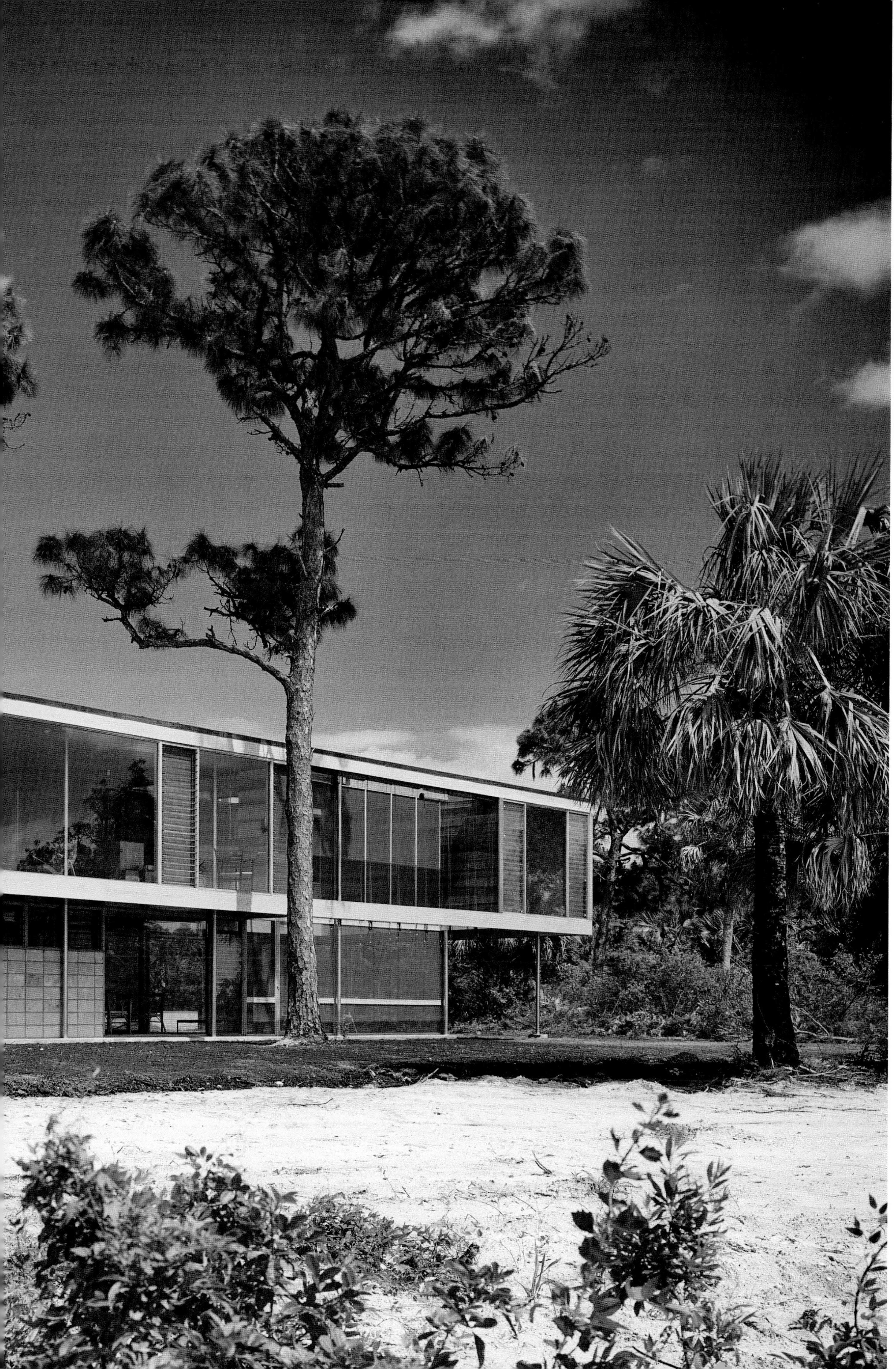

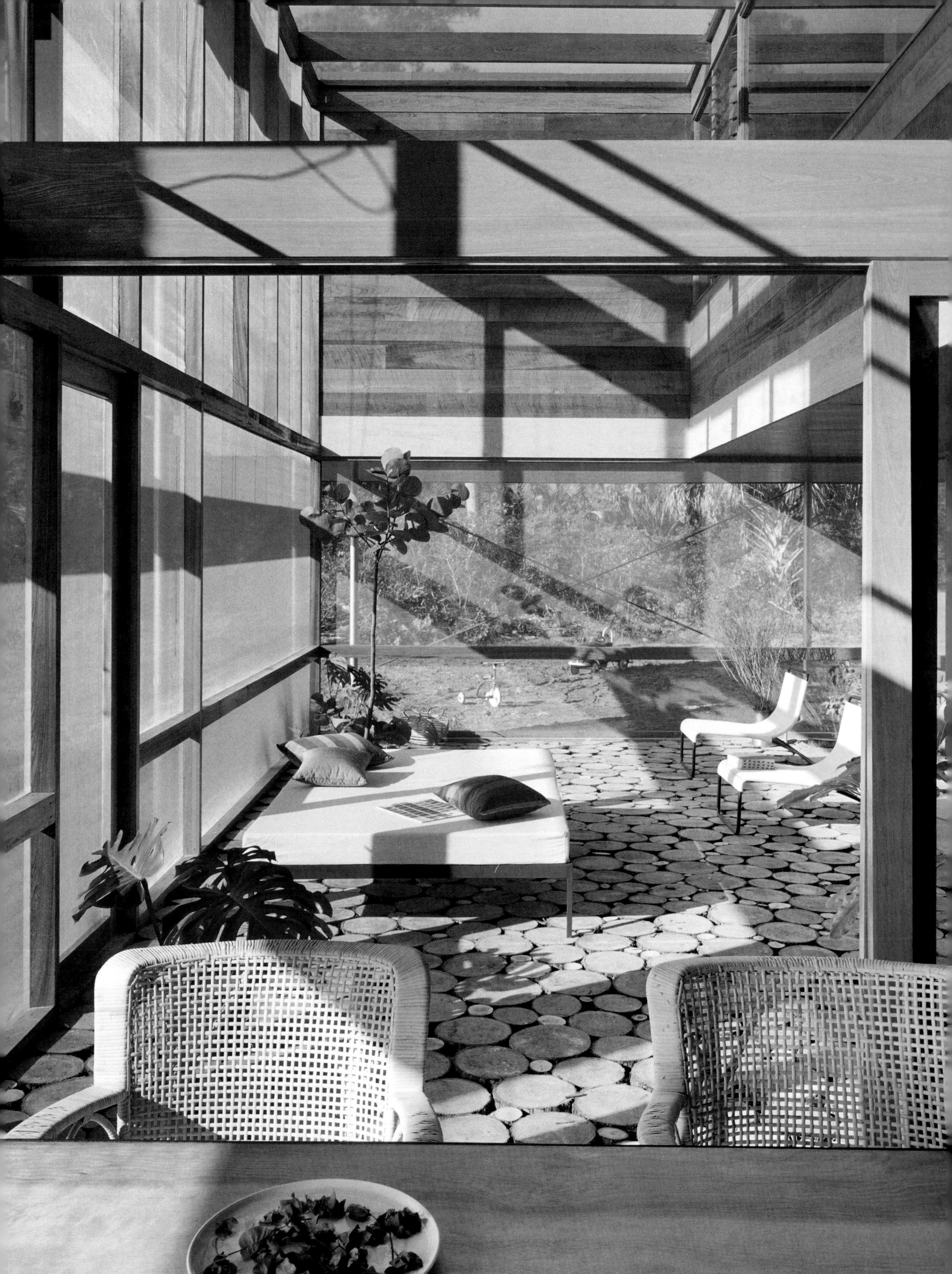

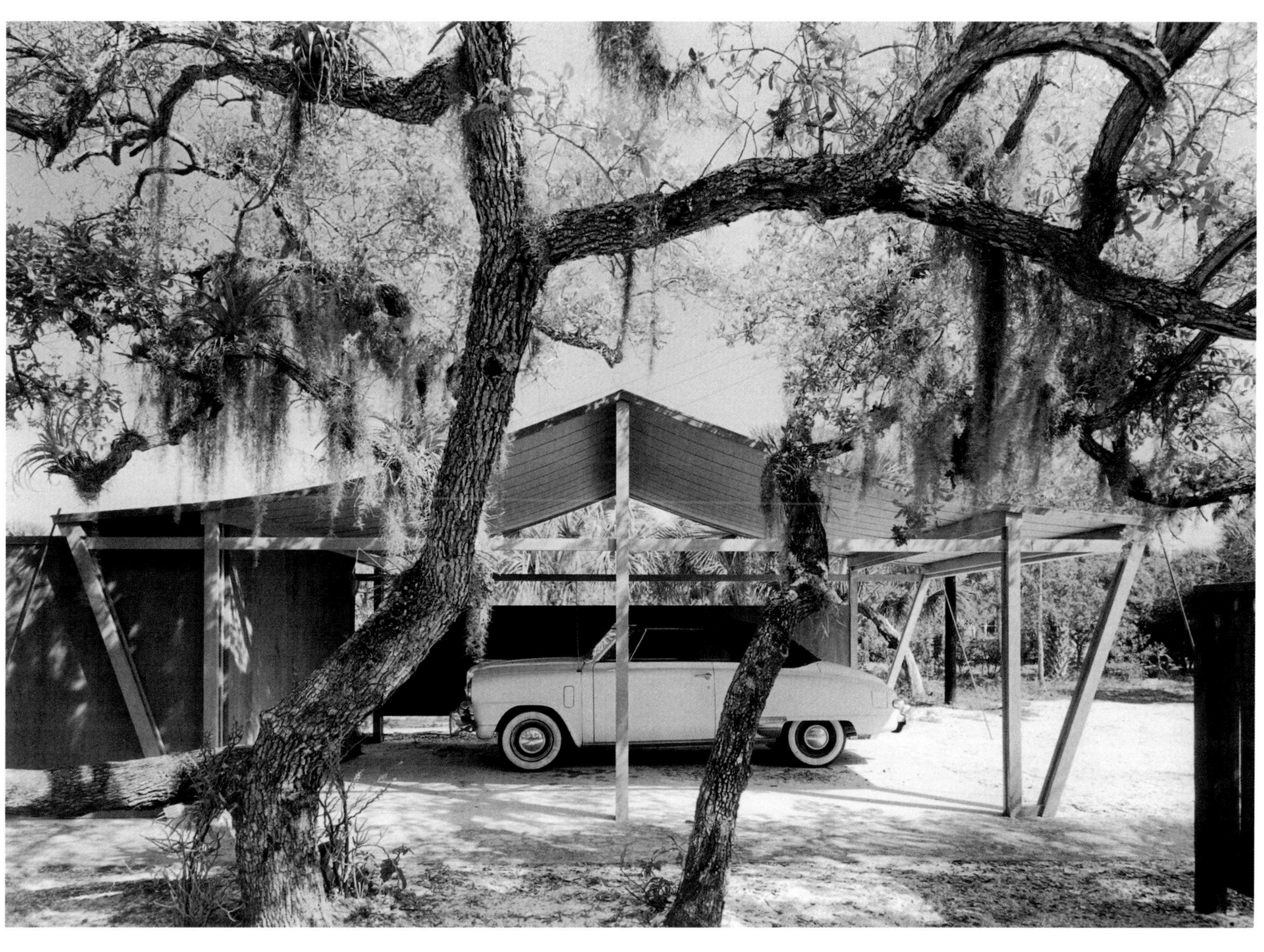

Coward House, Sarasota, Florida.
Ralph Twitchell and Paul Rudolph, 1952.

Overleaf
Usonian House at the Guggenheim Museum, New York. Frank Lloyd Wright, 1953.

Leavengood House, St. Petersburg, Florida.
Ralph Twitchell and Paul Rudolph, 1951.

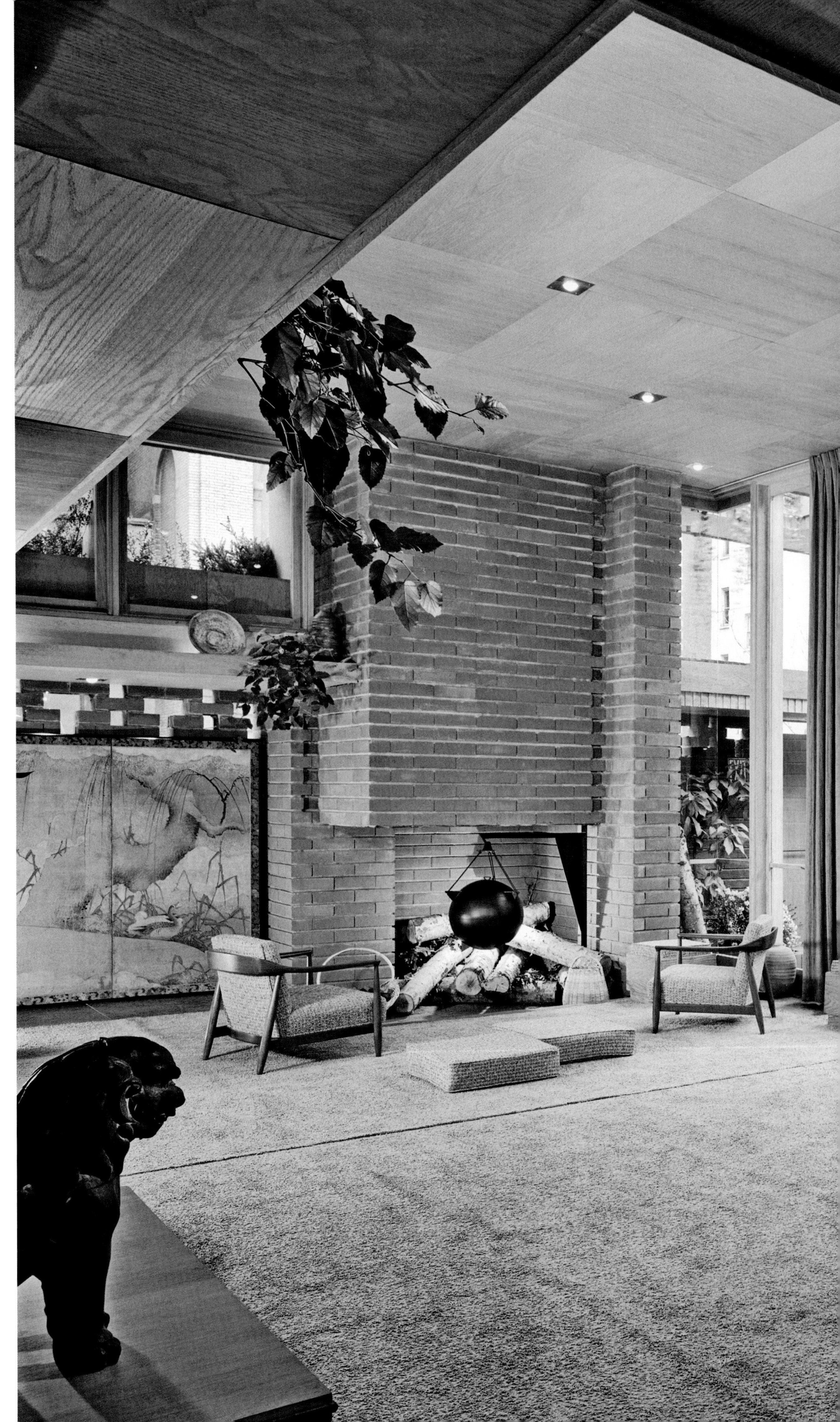

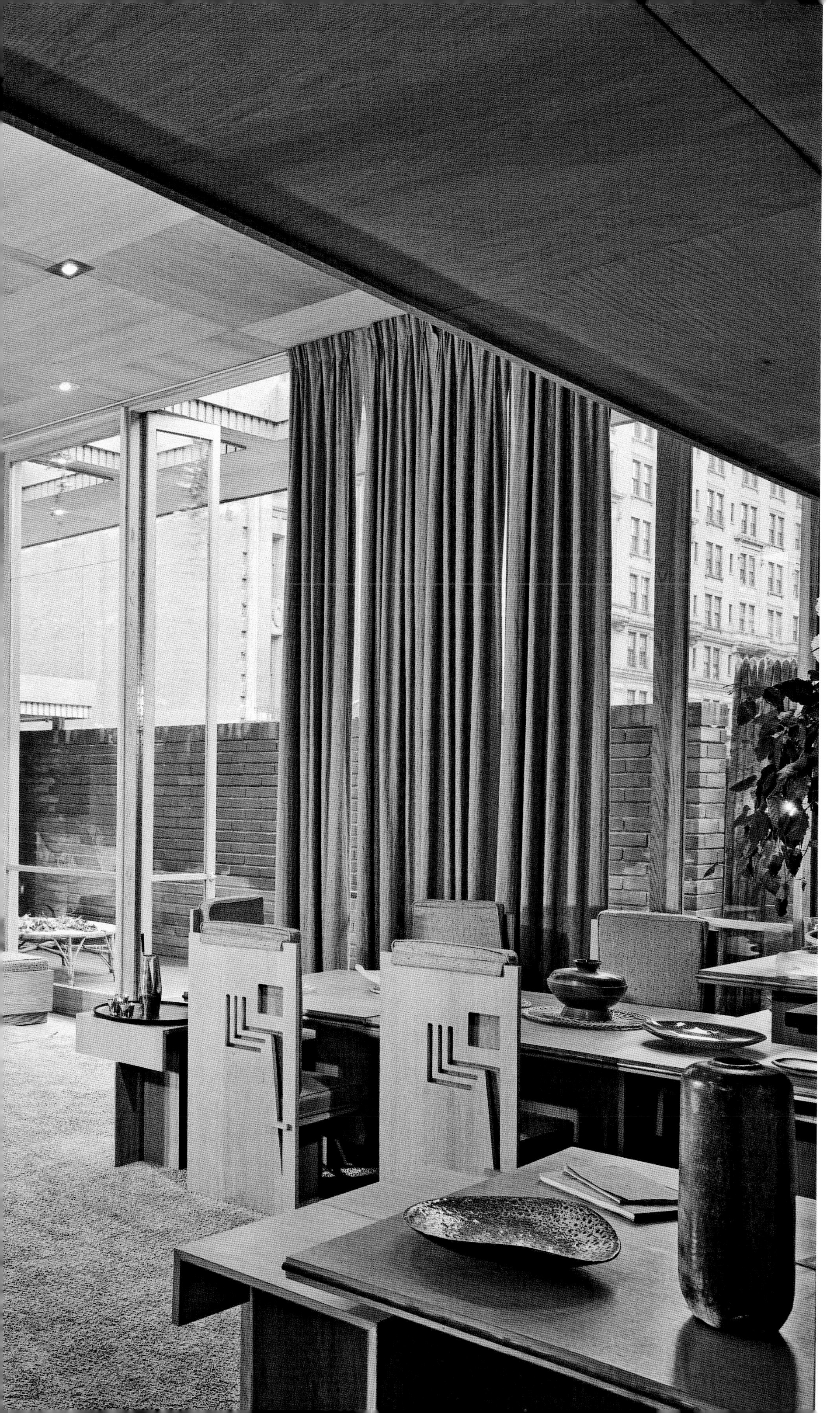

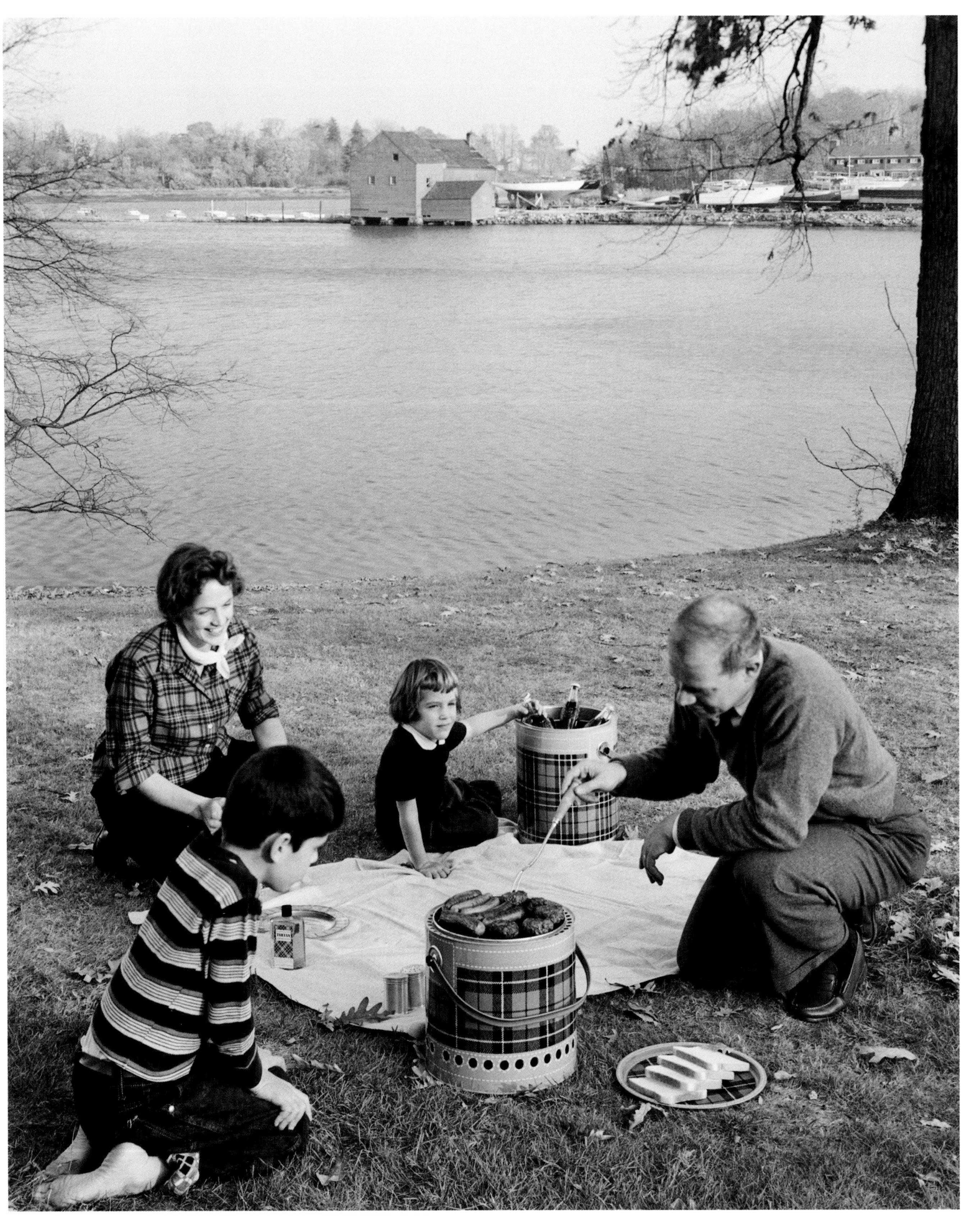

Hamilton Metal Products Grill, Rye, New York.
Designed by Sam Aaron, 1953.

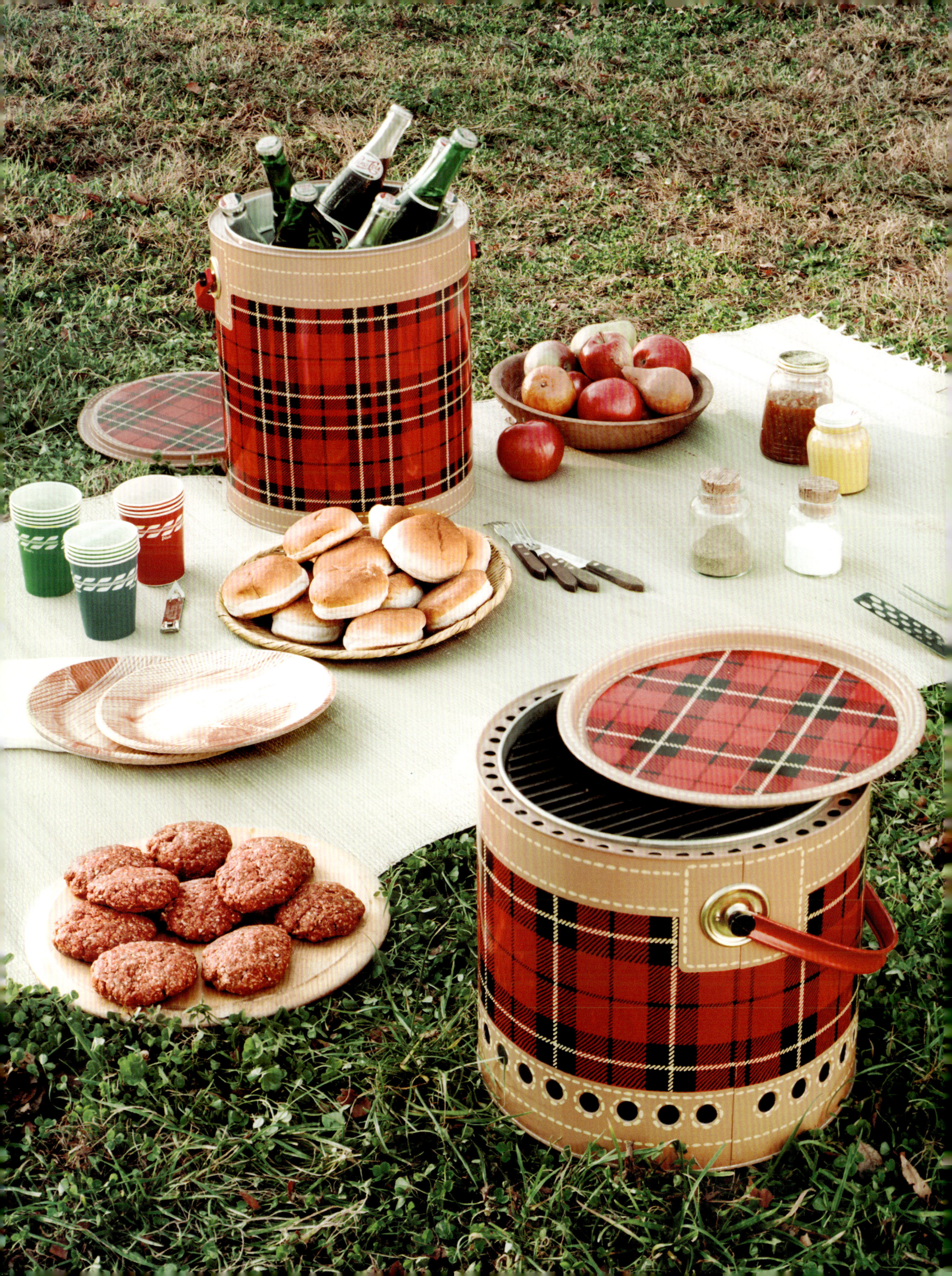

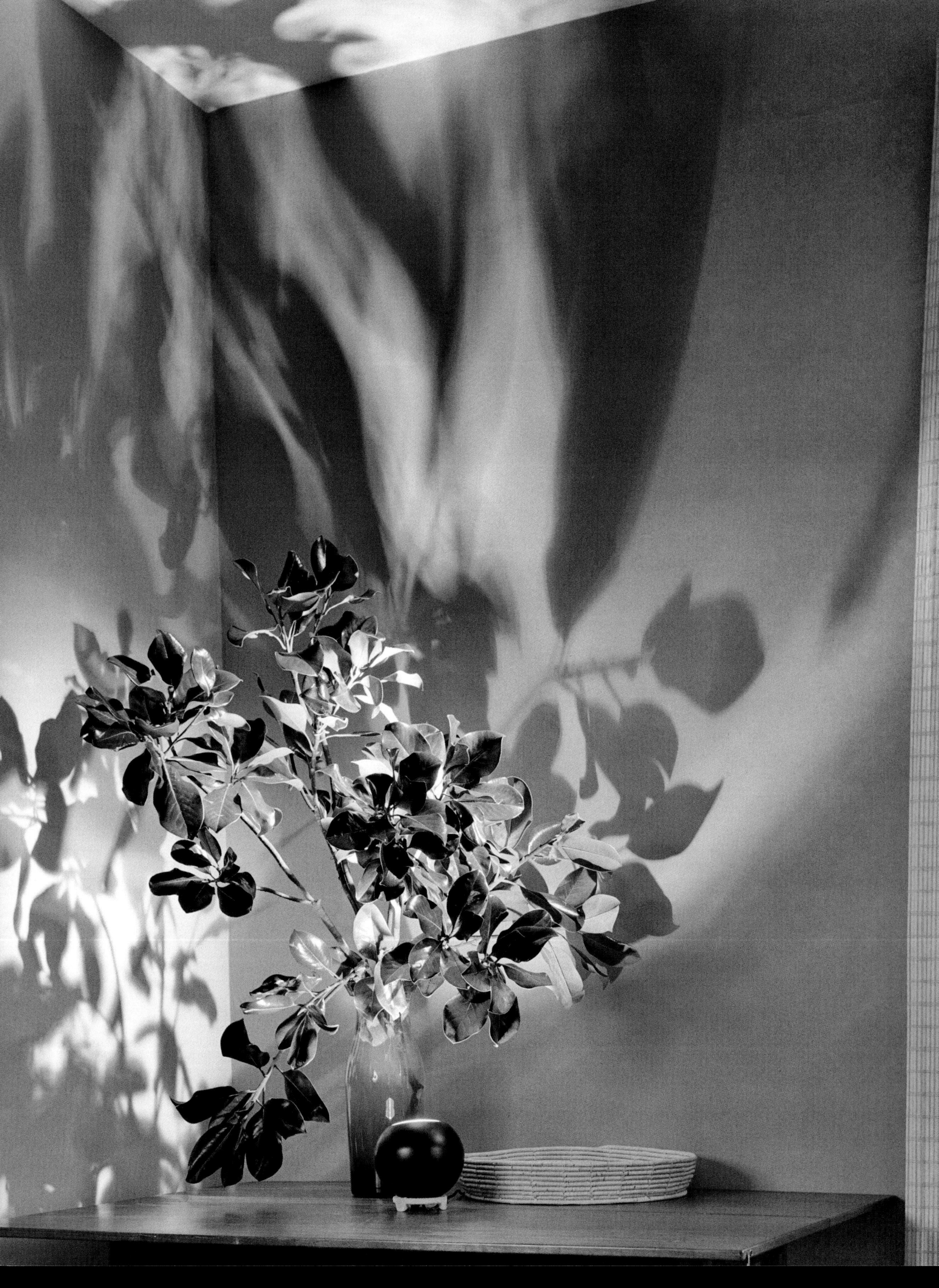

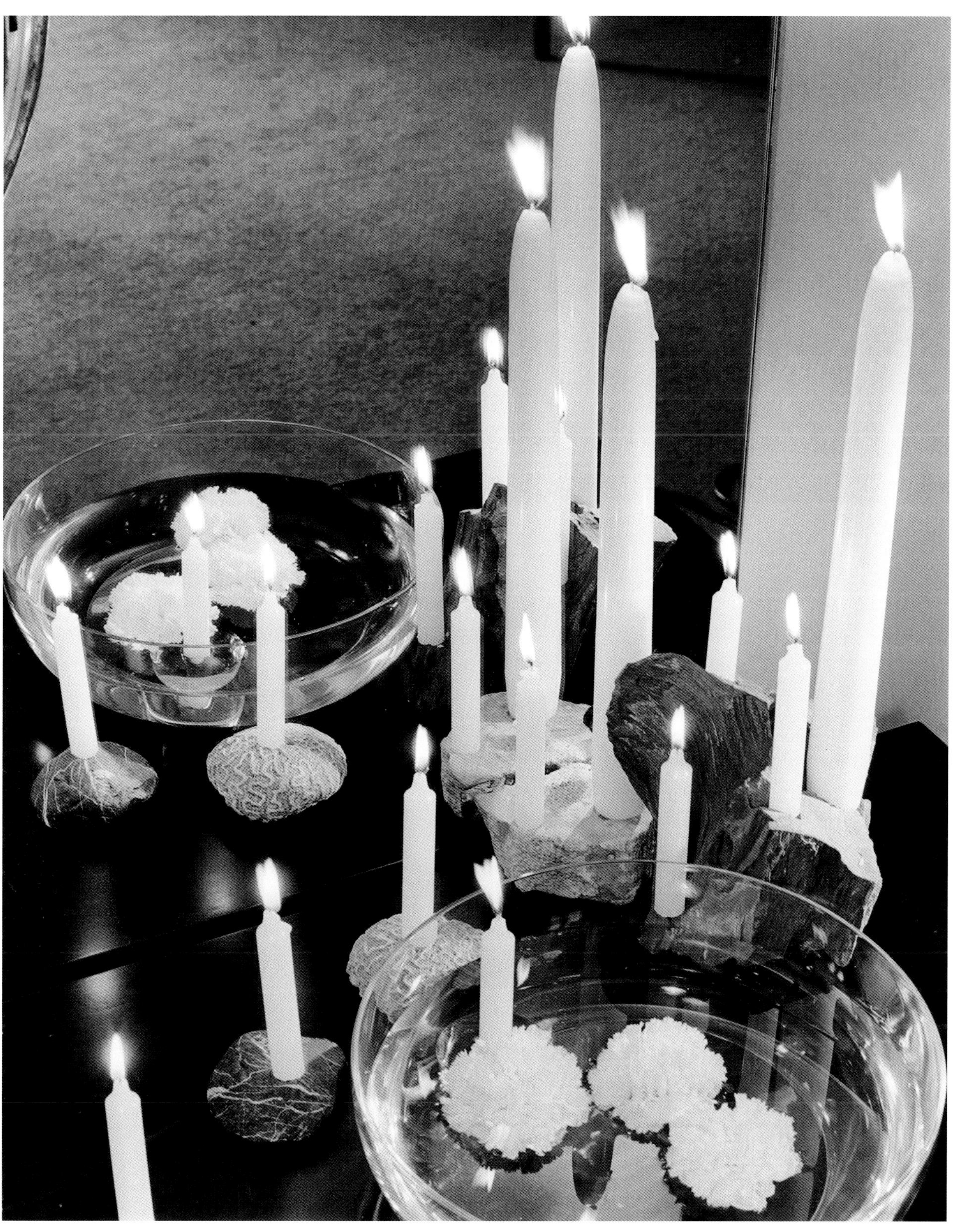

Decorations at Stoller House, Rye, New York.
Photographed for *House Beautiful,* 1958.

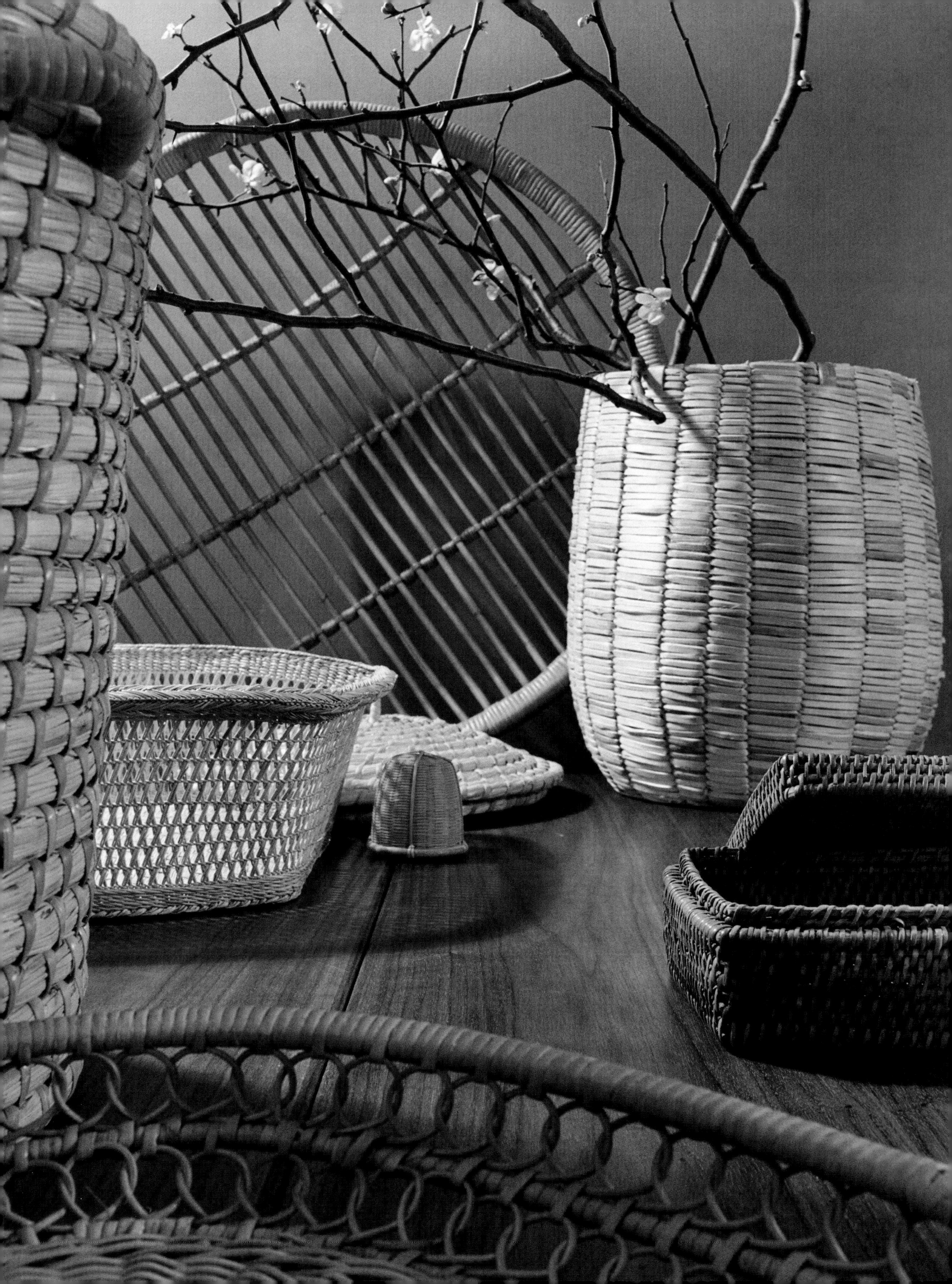

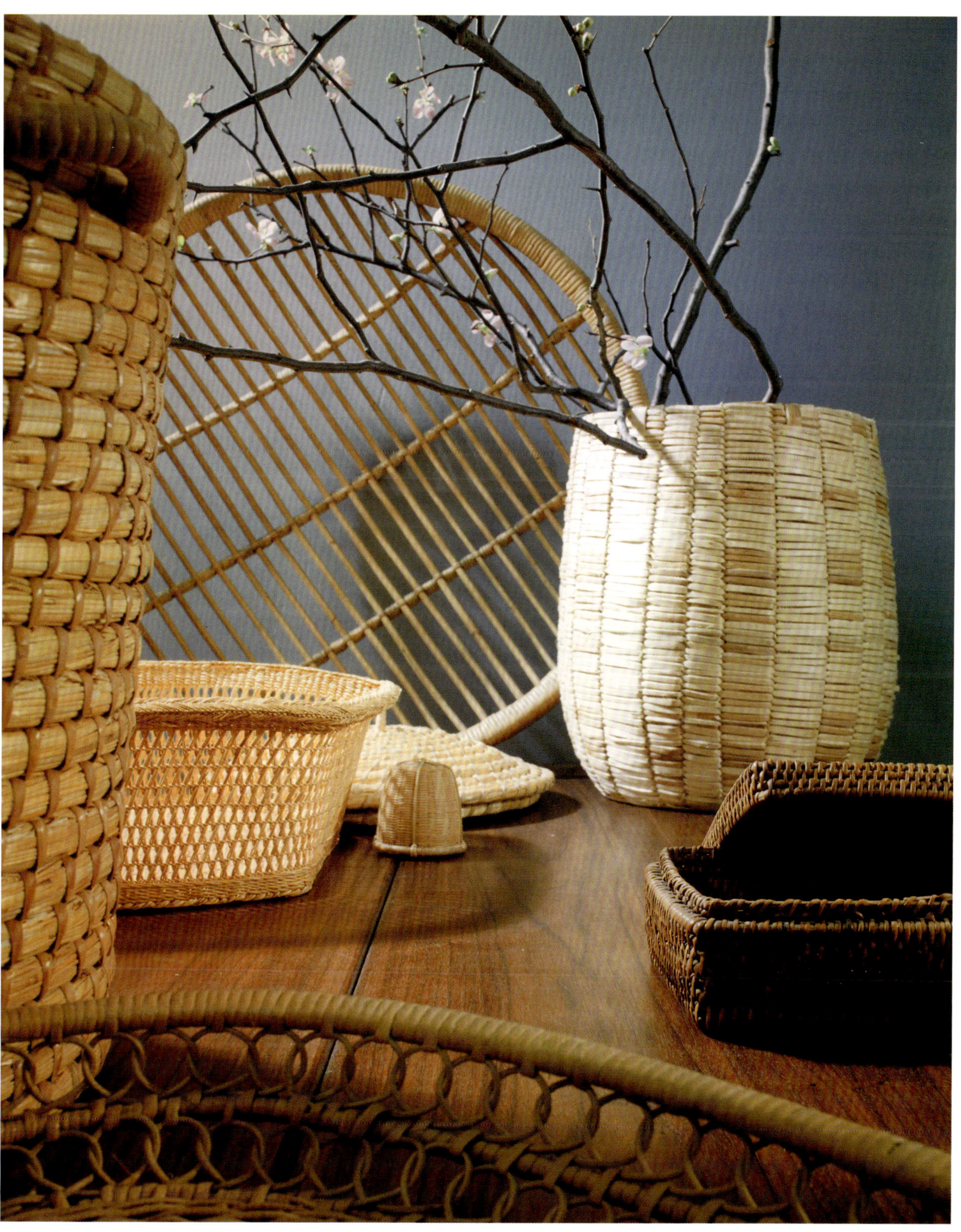

Decorations at Stoller House, Rye, New York.
Photographed for *House Beautiful*, 1958.

Overleaf
Miller House, Columbus, Indiana.
Eero Saarinen, 1958.

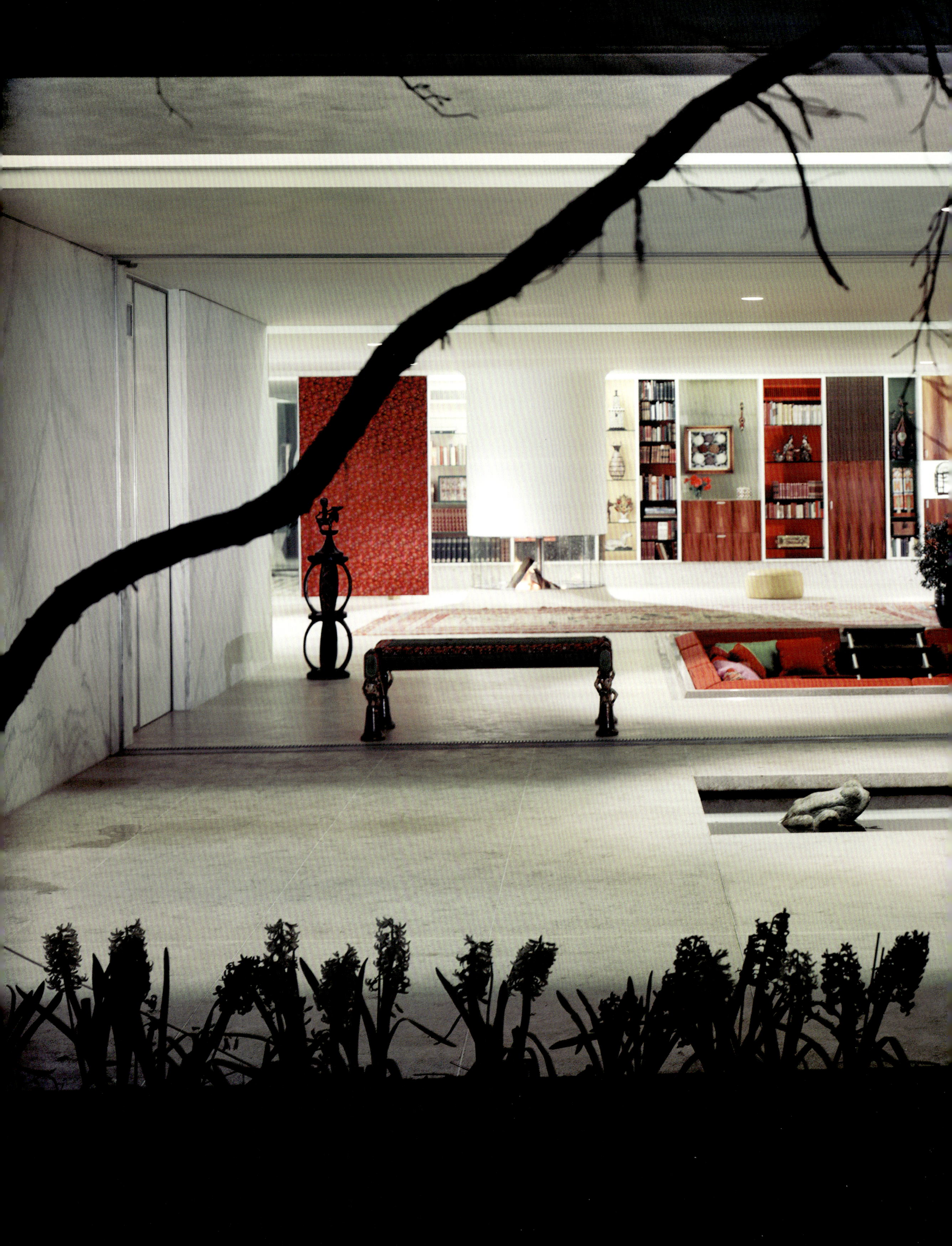

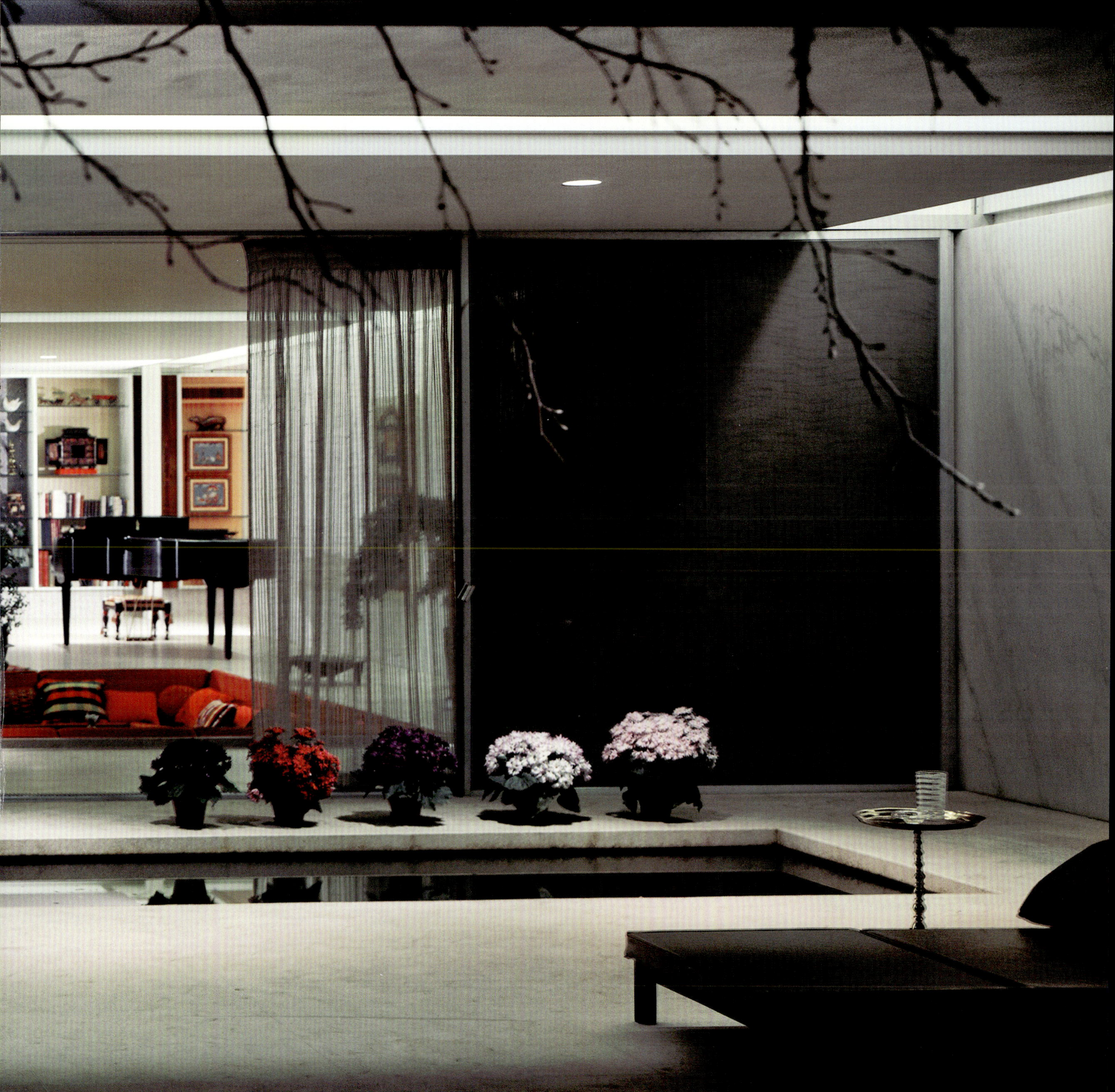

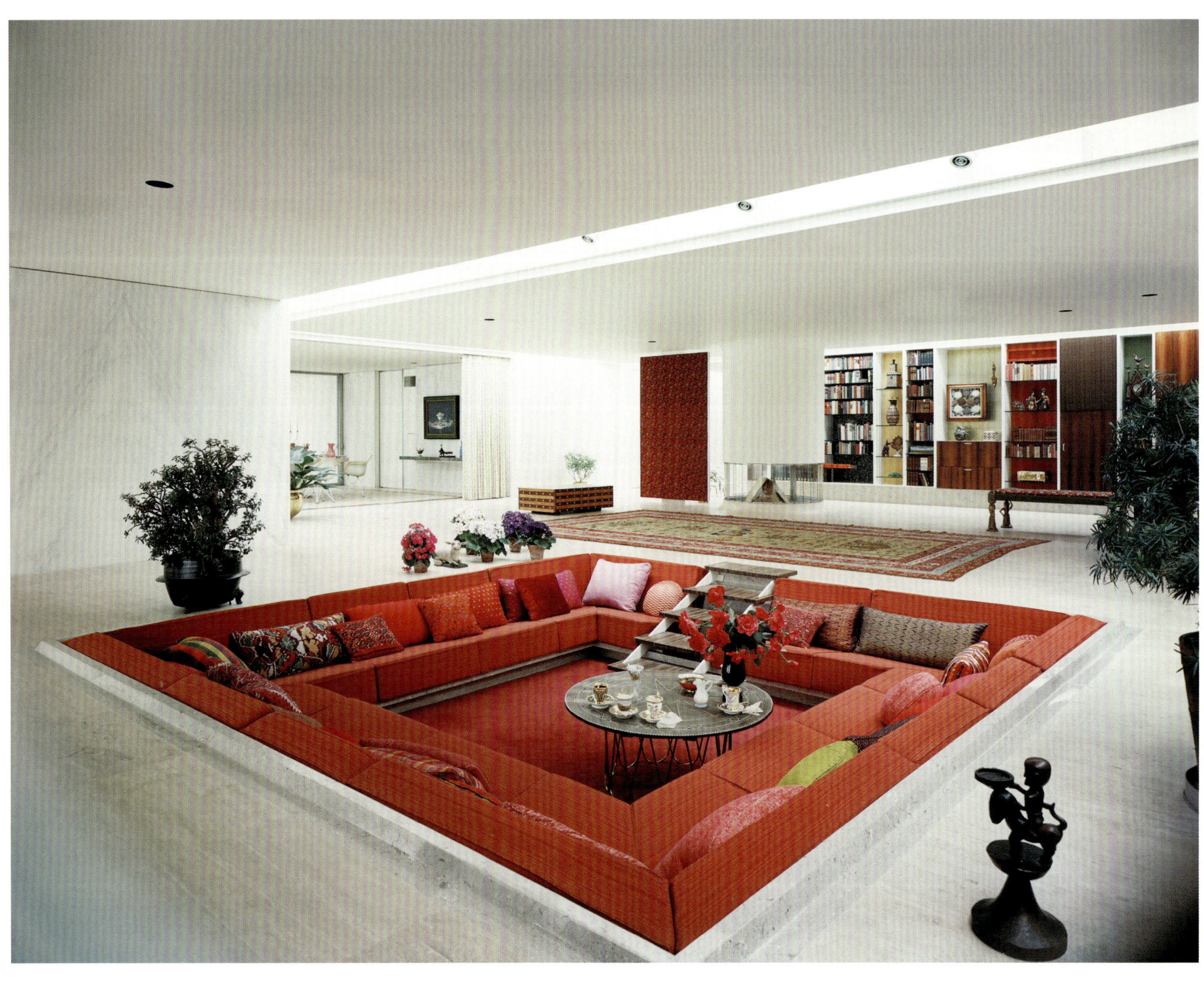

Miller House, Columbus, Indiana.
Eero Saarinen, 1958.

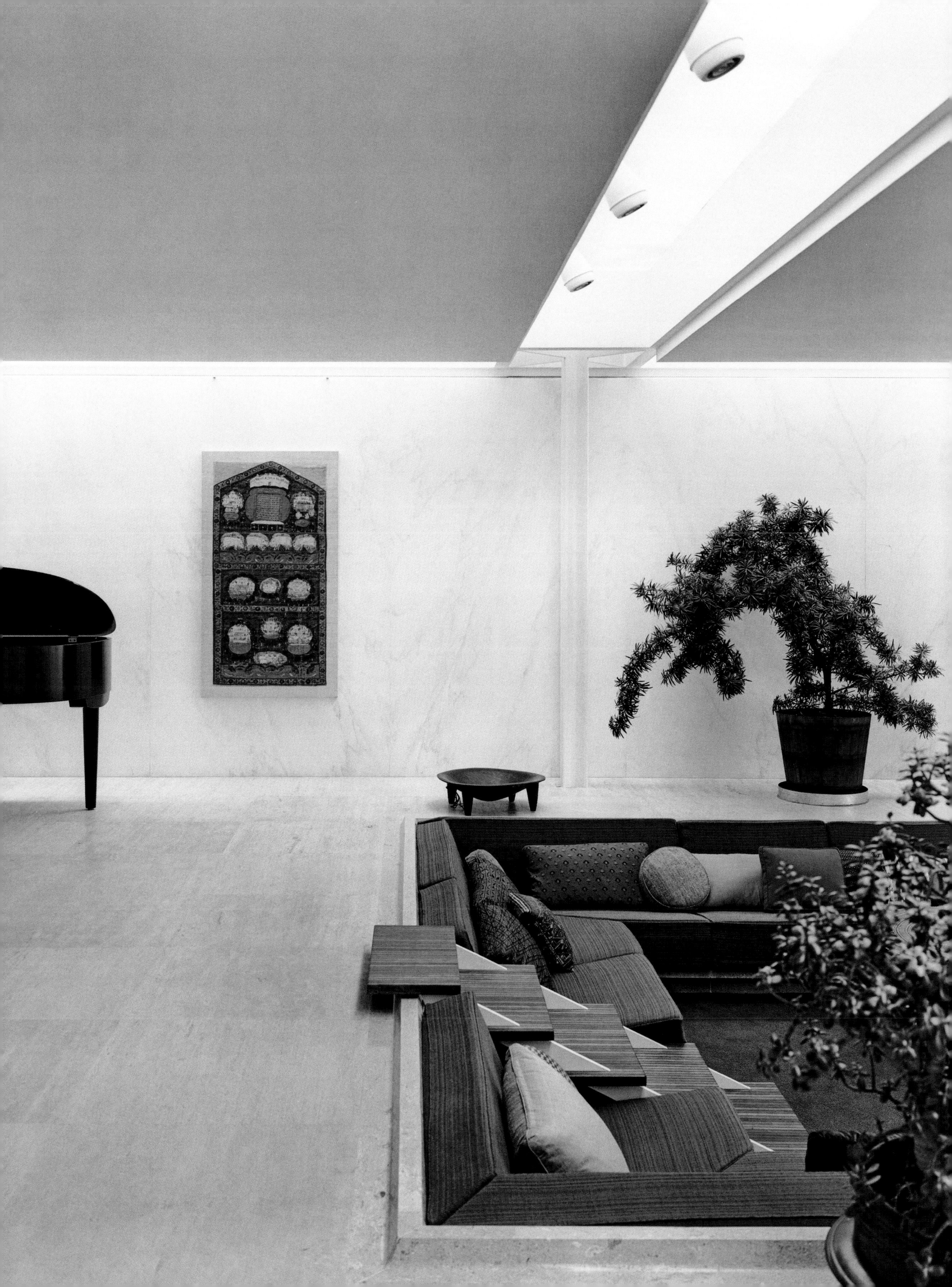

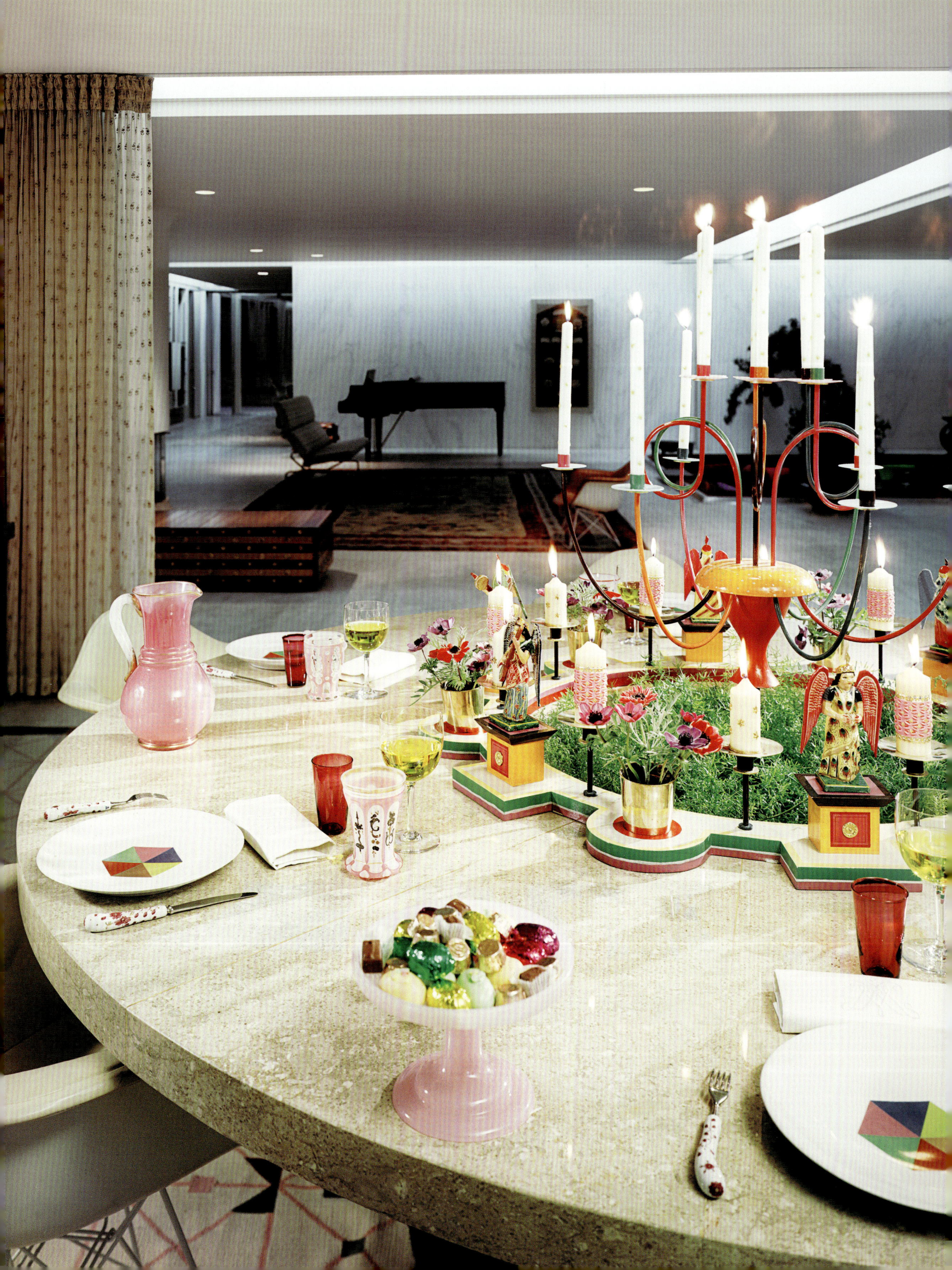

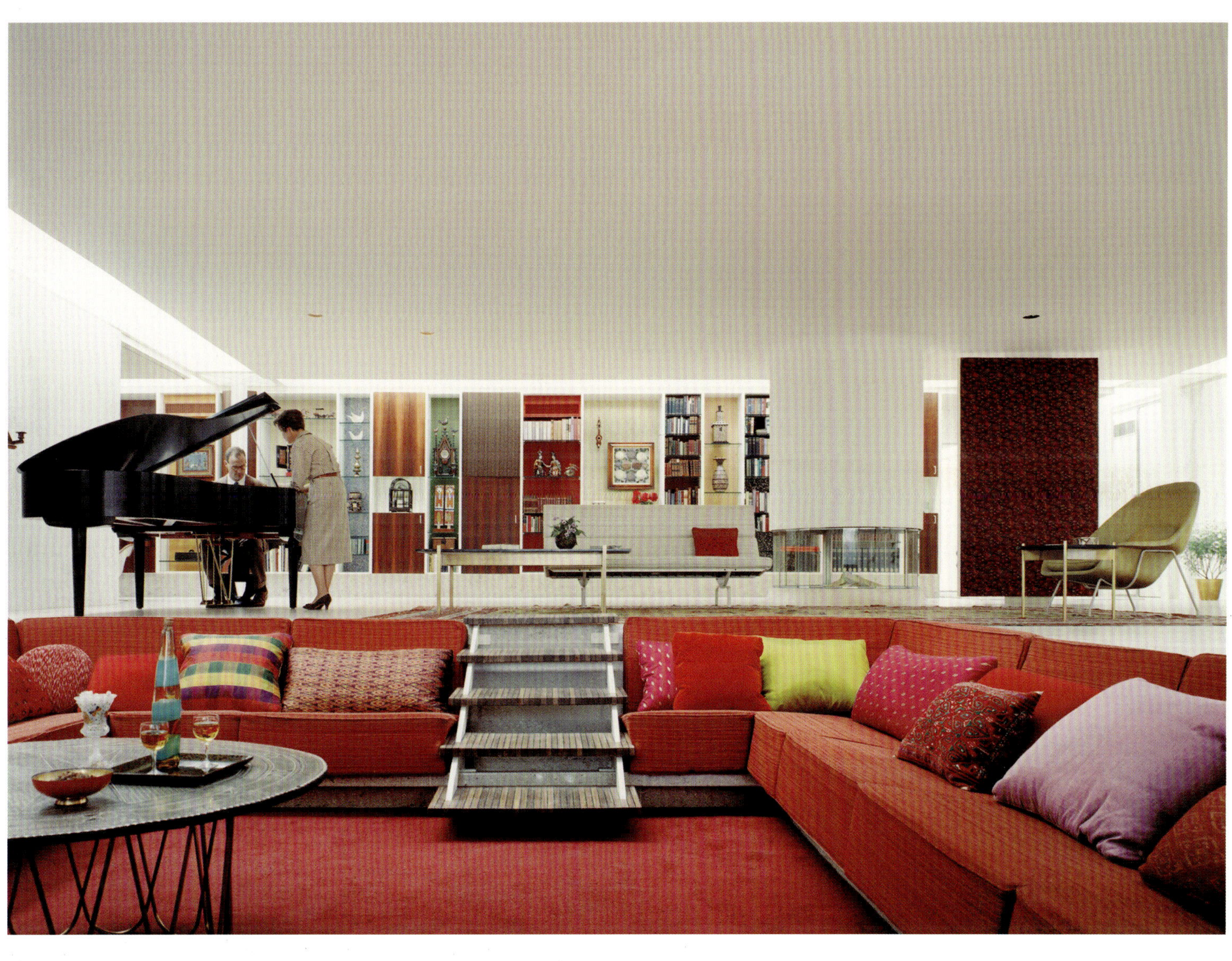

These pages and overleaf
Miller House, Columbus, Indiana.
Eero Saarinen, 1958.

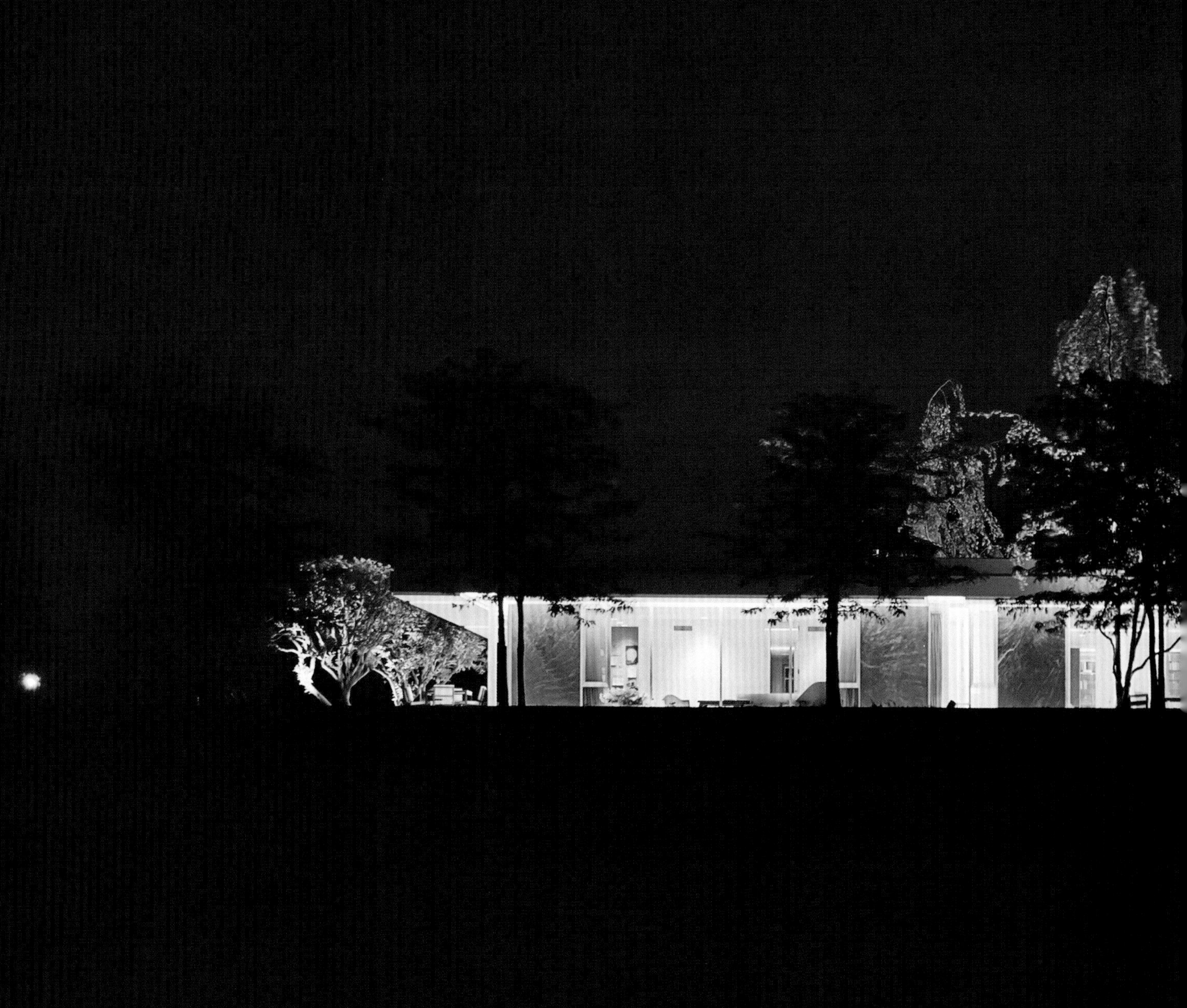

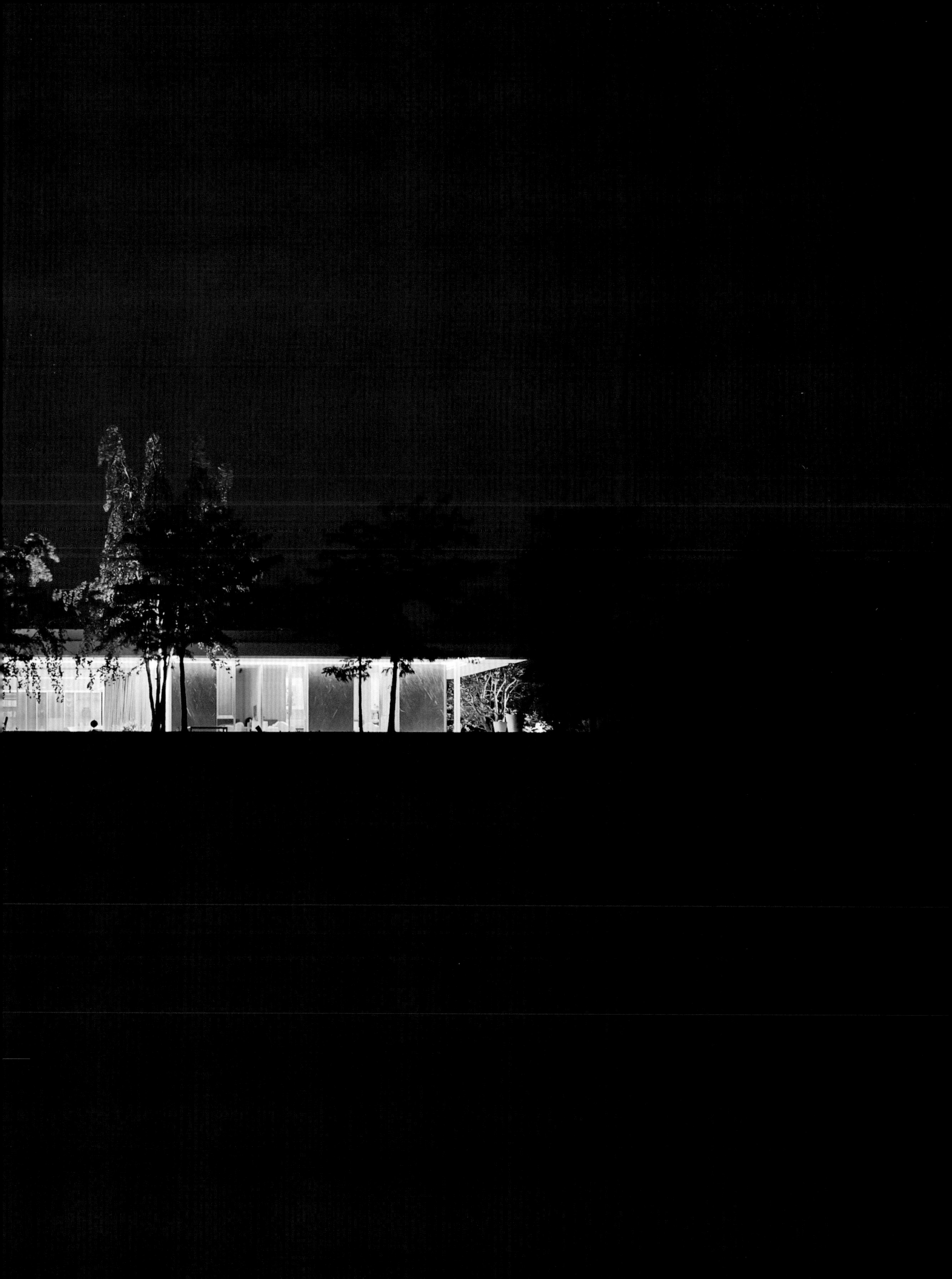

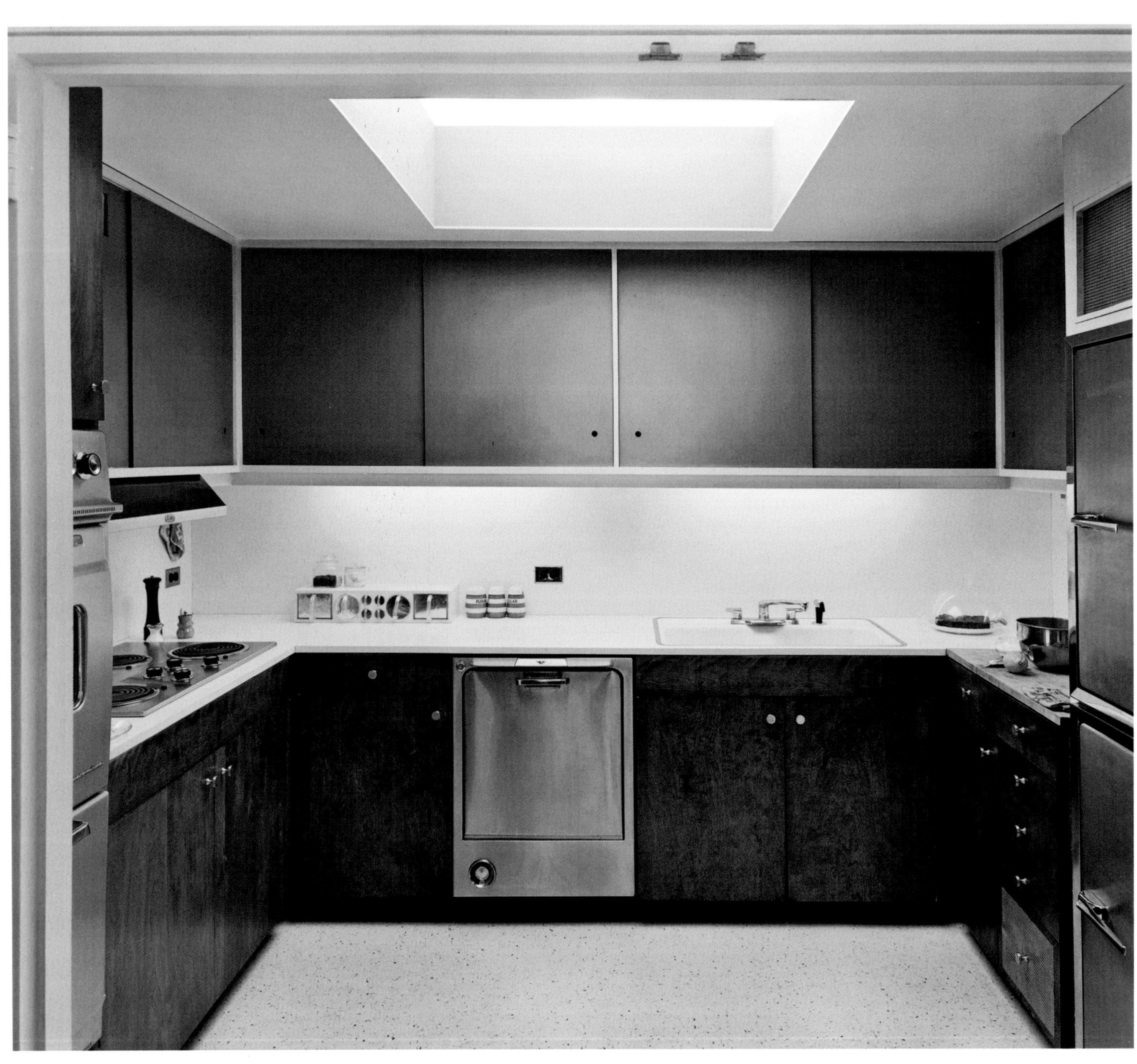

Beattie House, Rye, New York.
Ulrich Franzen, 1957.

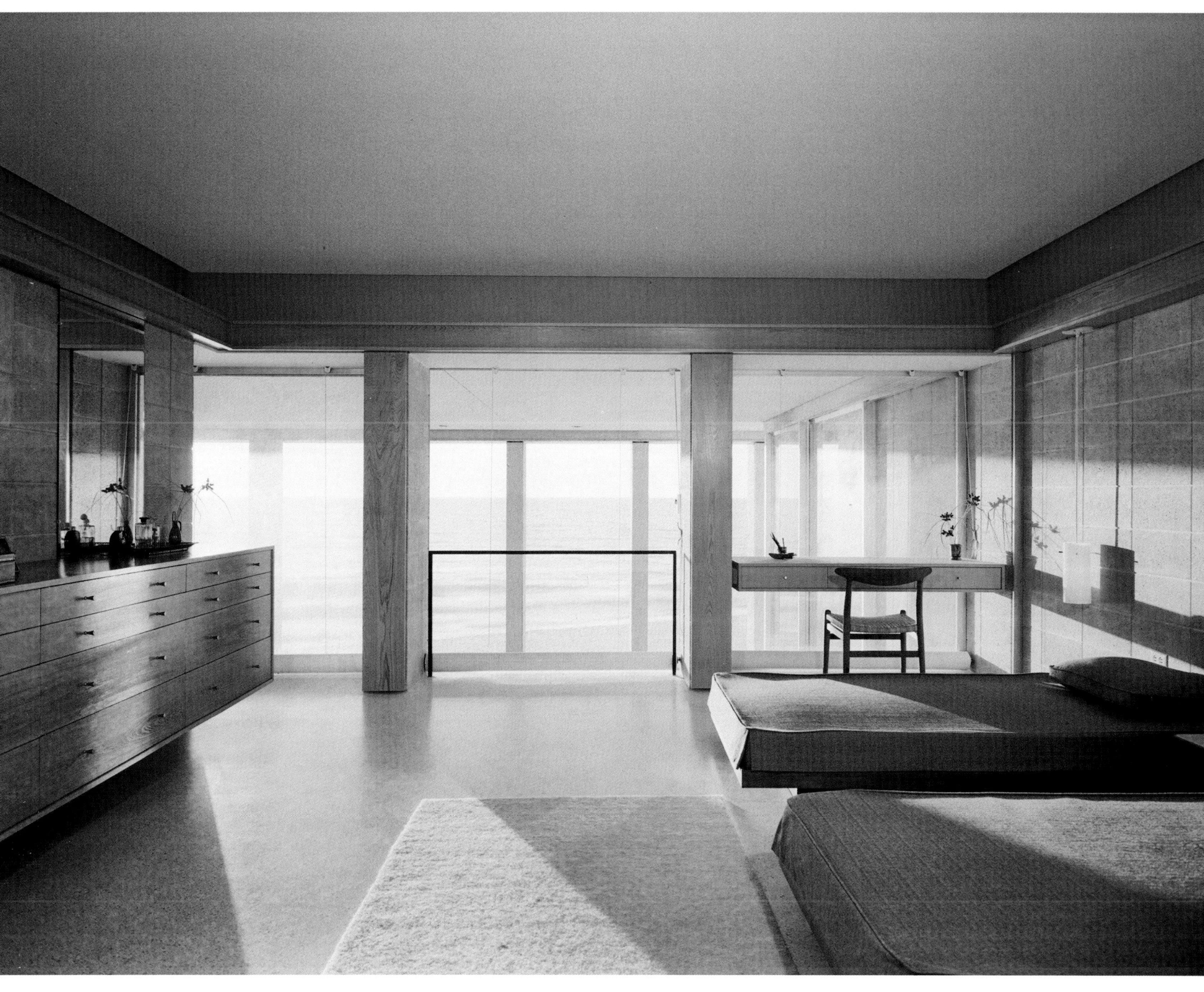

Deering House, Casey Key, Florida.
Paul Rudolph, 1959.

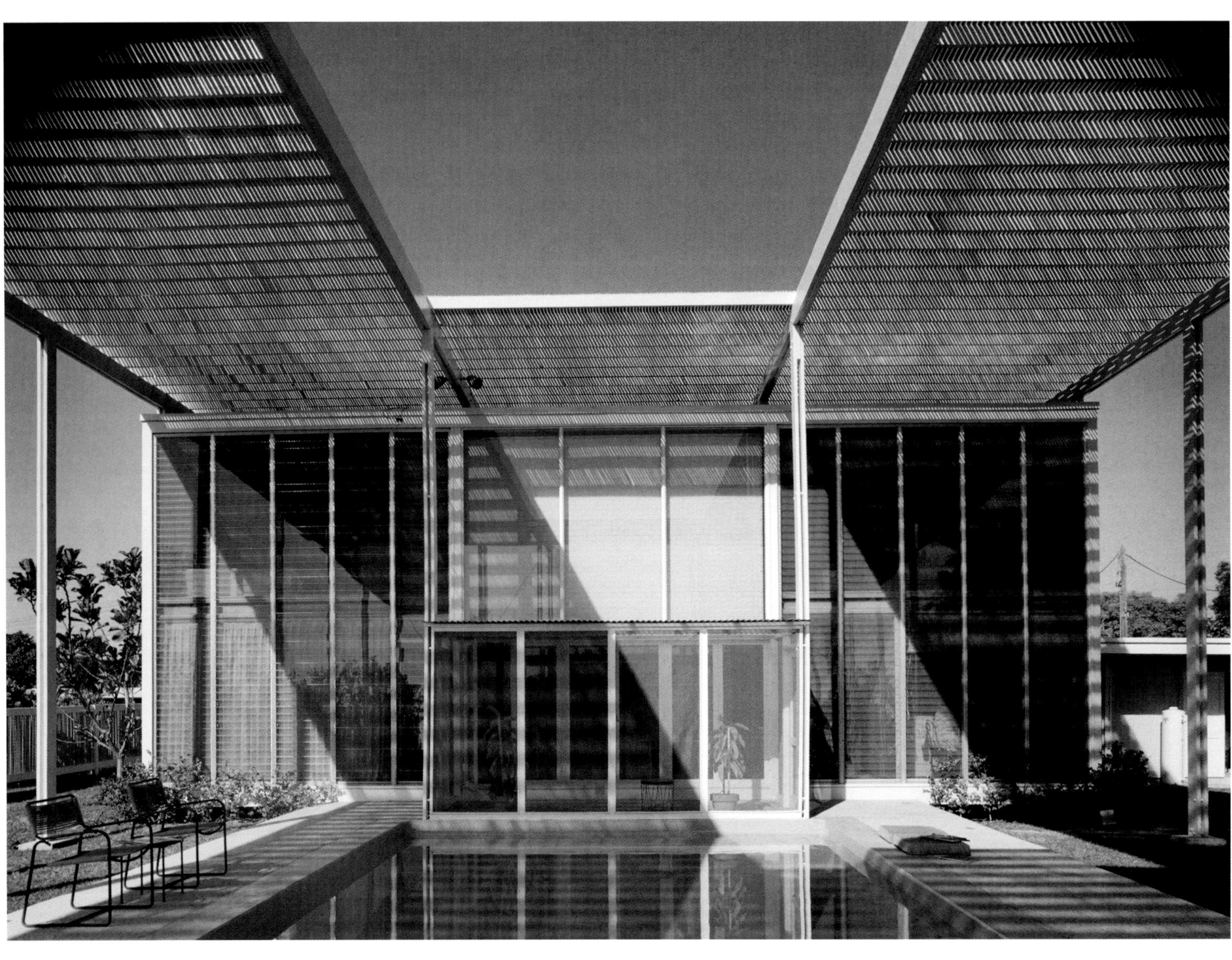

Hiss "Umbrella" House, Sarasota, Florida. Paul Rudolph, 1958.

Castle House, New London, Connecticut. Ulrich Franzen, 1961.

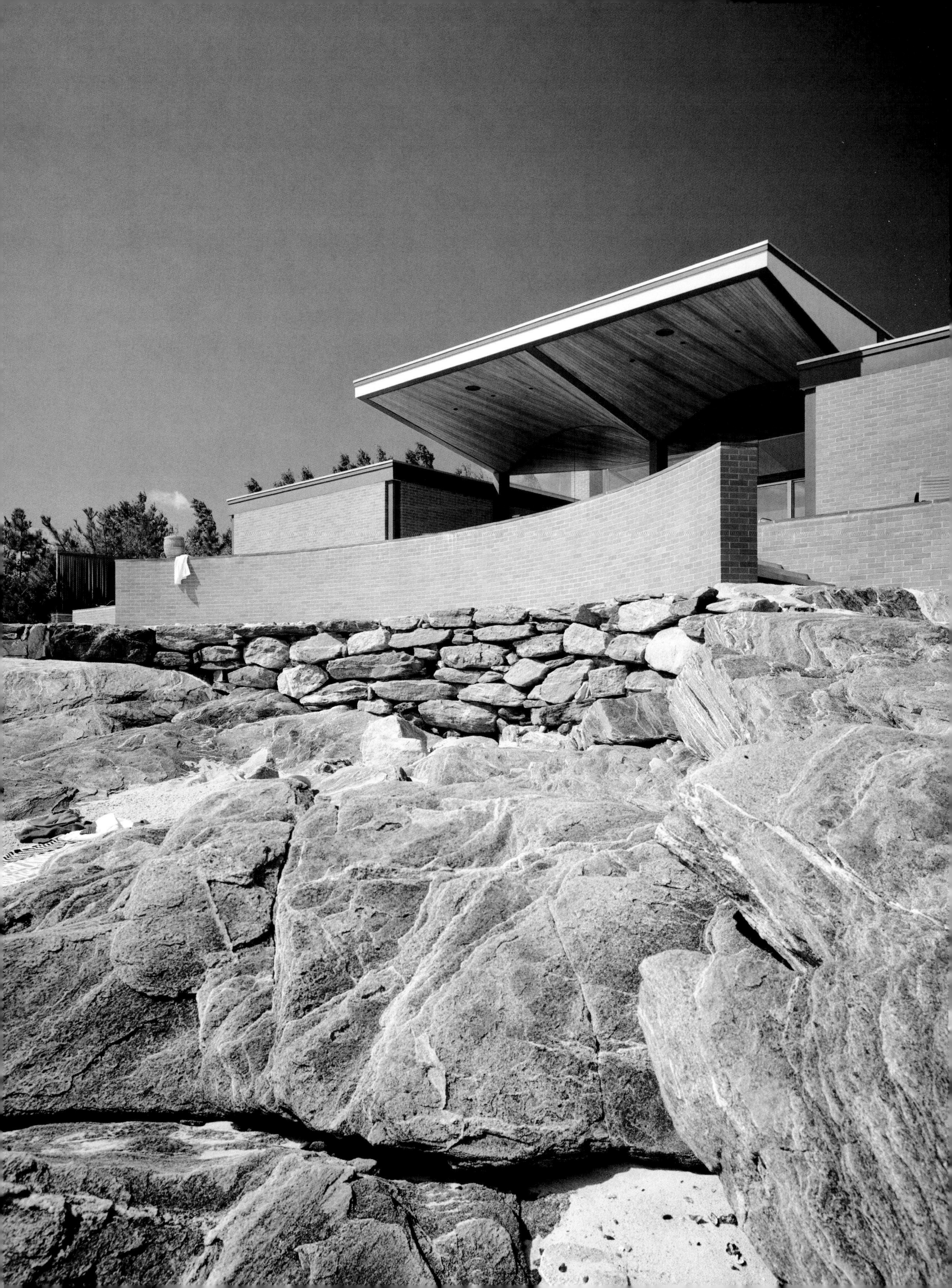

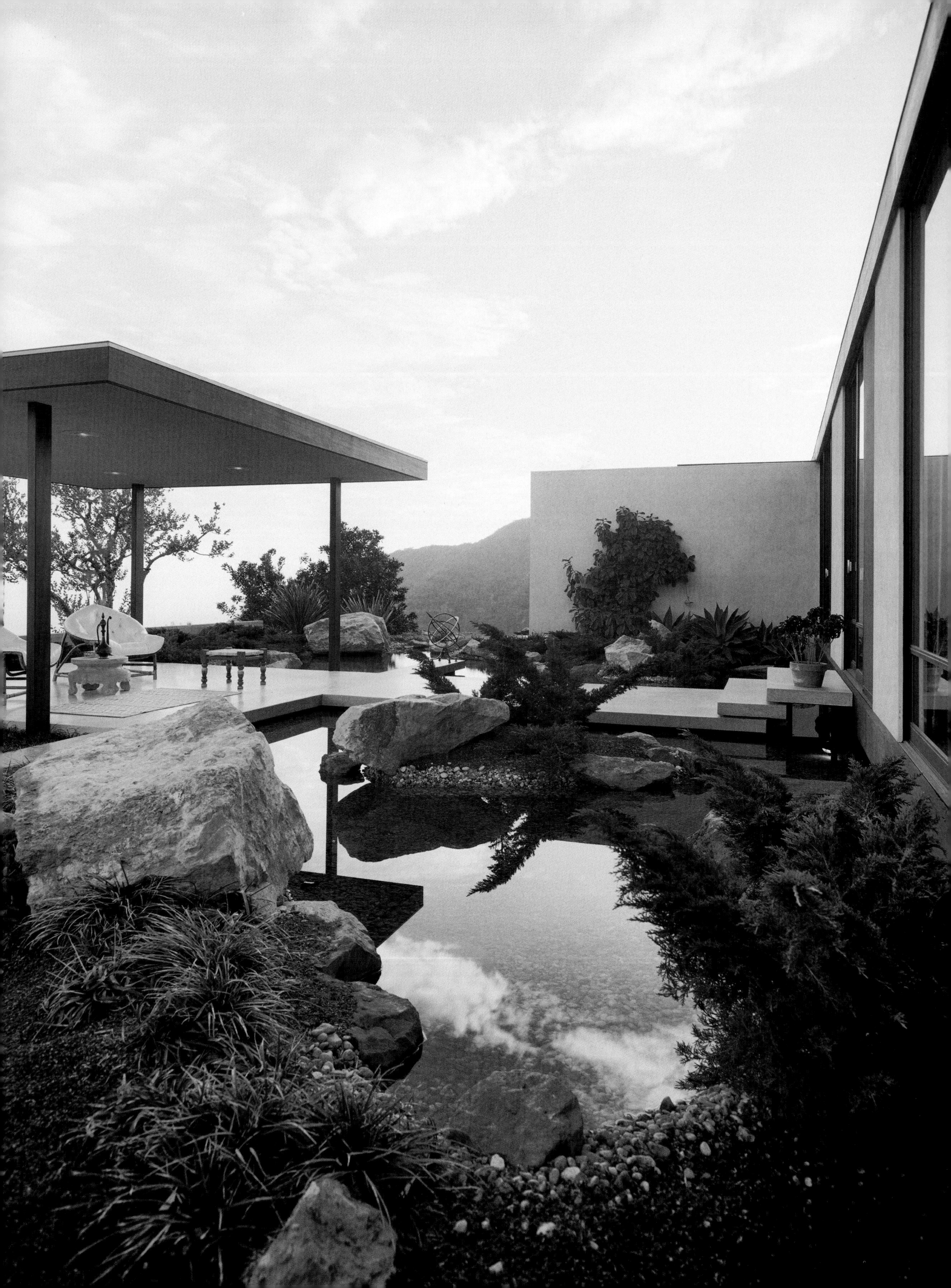

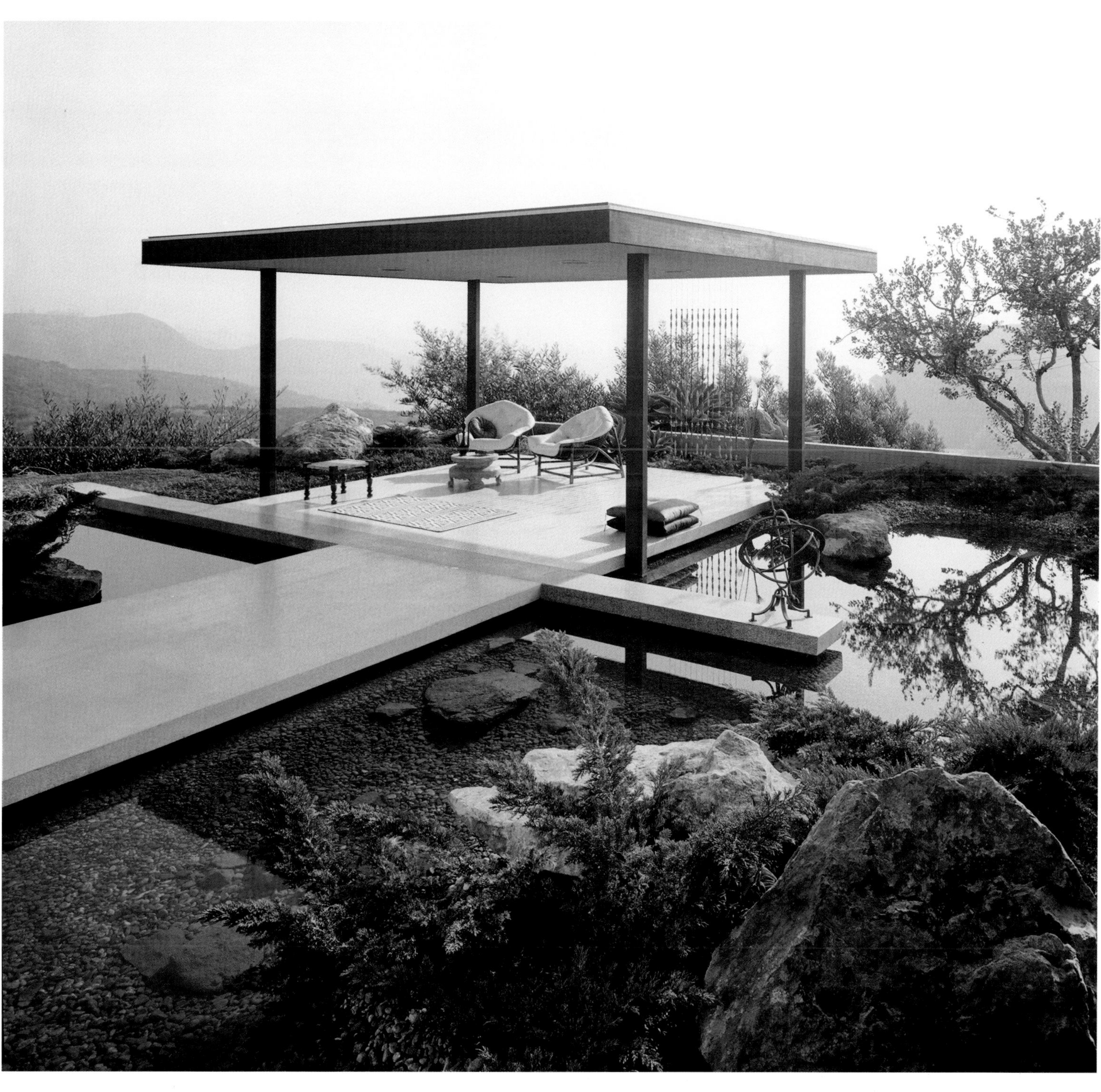

Marco Wolff House, Los Angeles.
Ladd & Kelsey, 1959.

Overleaf
Nakashima House/Studio, New Hope, Pennsylvania. George Nakashima, 1962.

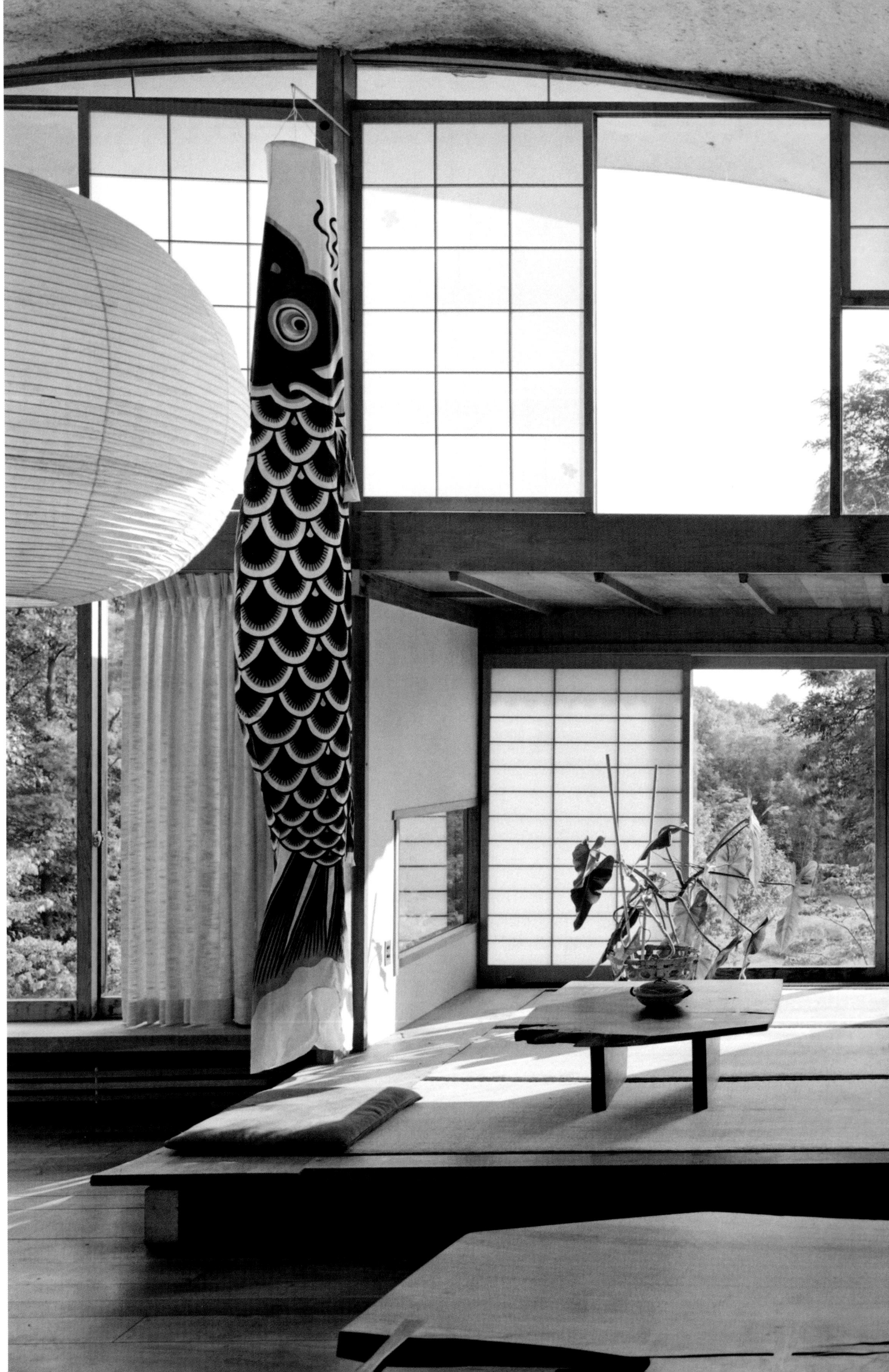

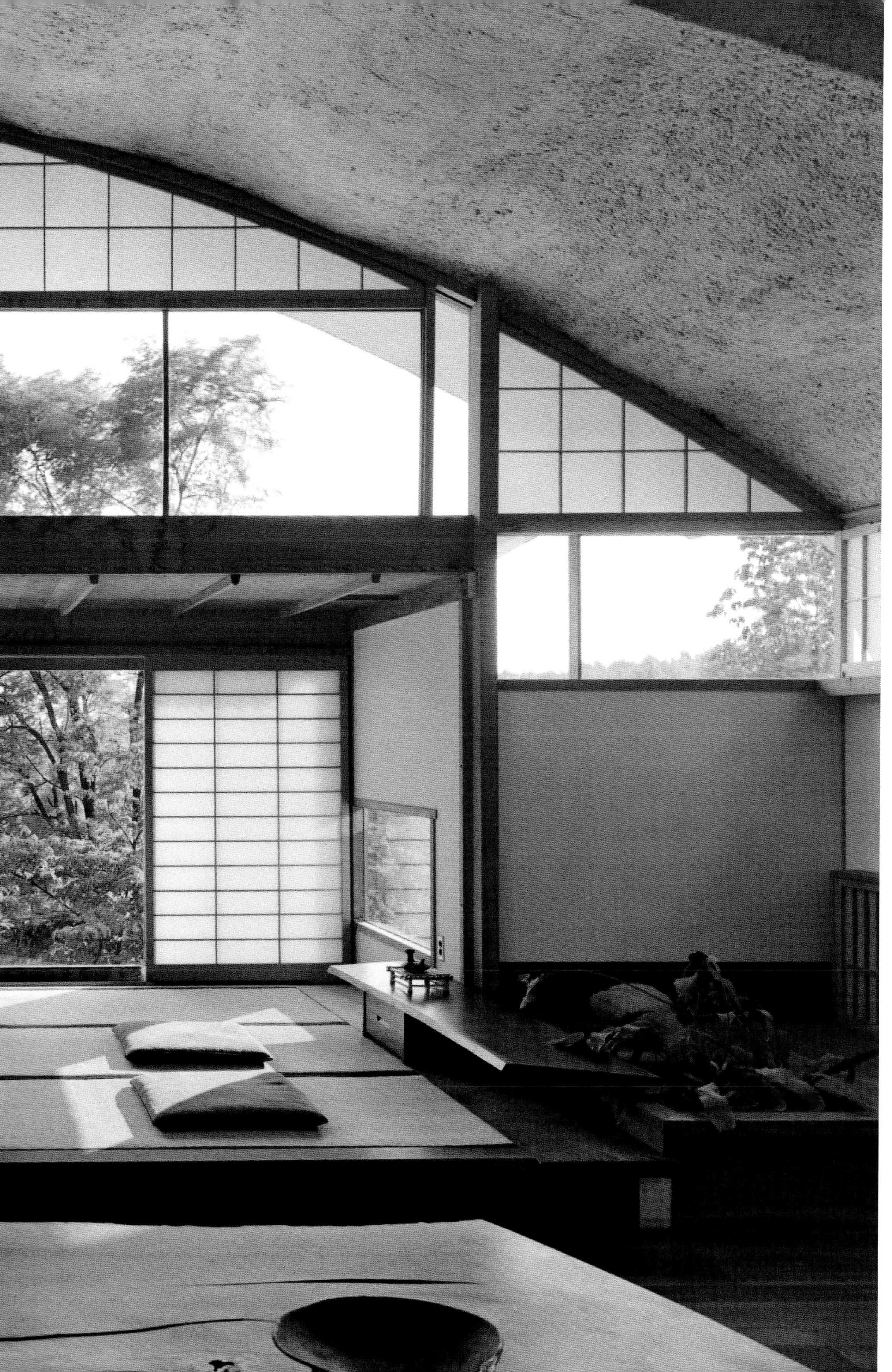

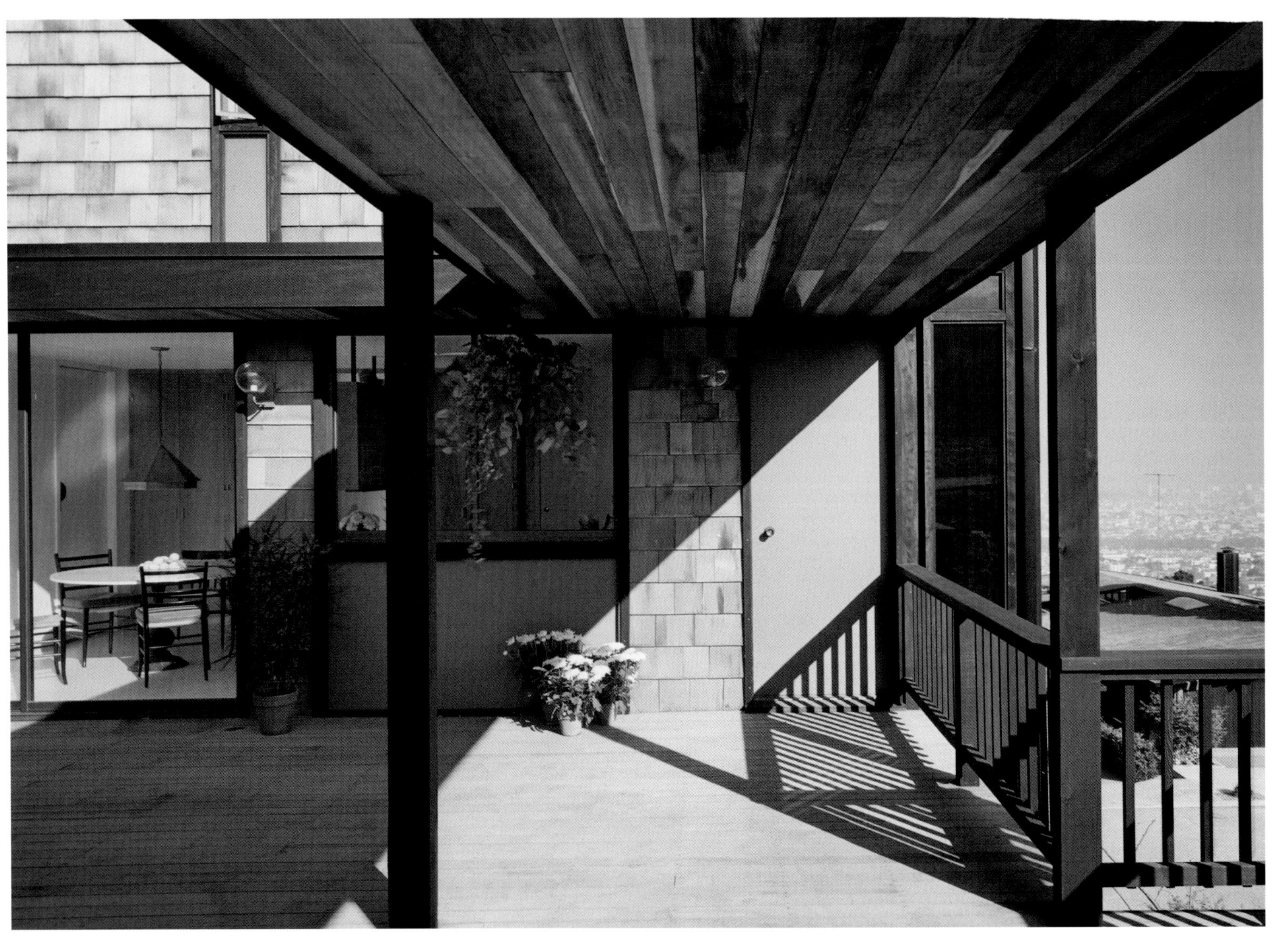

Heuman House, San Francisco.
Marquis & Stoller, 1966.

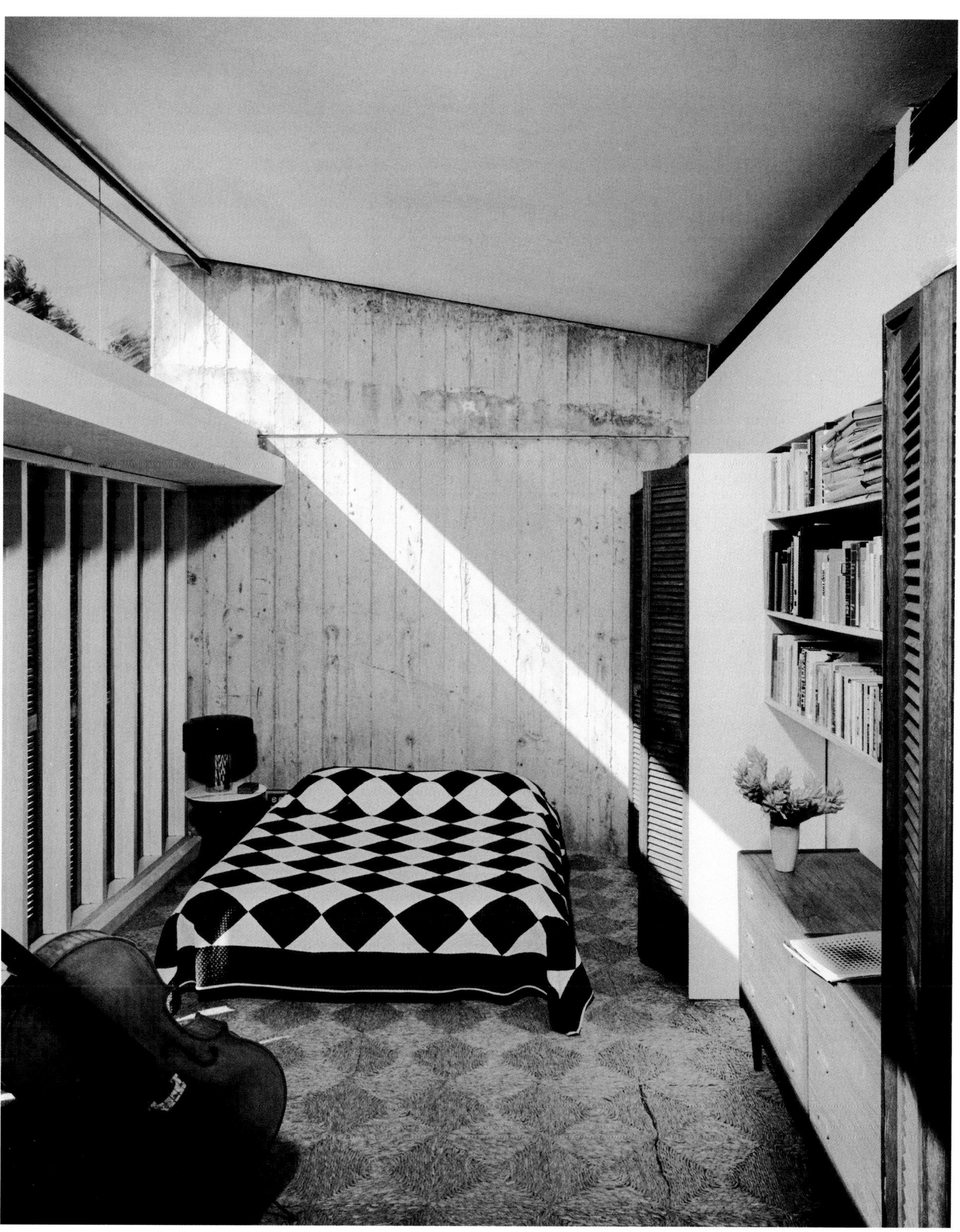

Marvel House for *House Beautiful*, 1970.

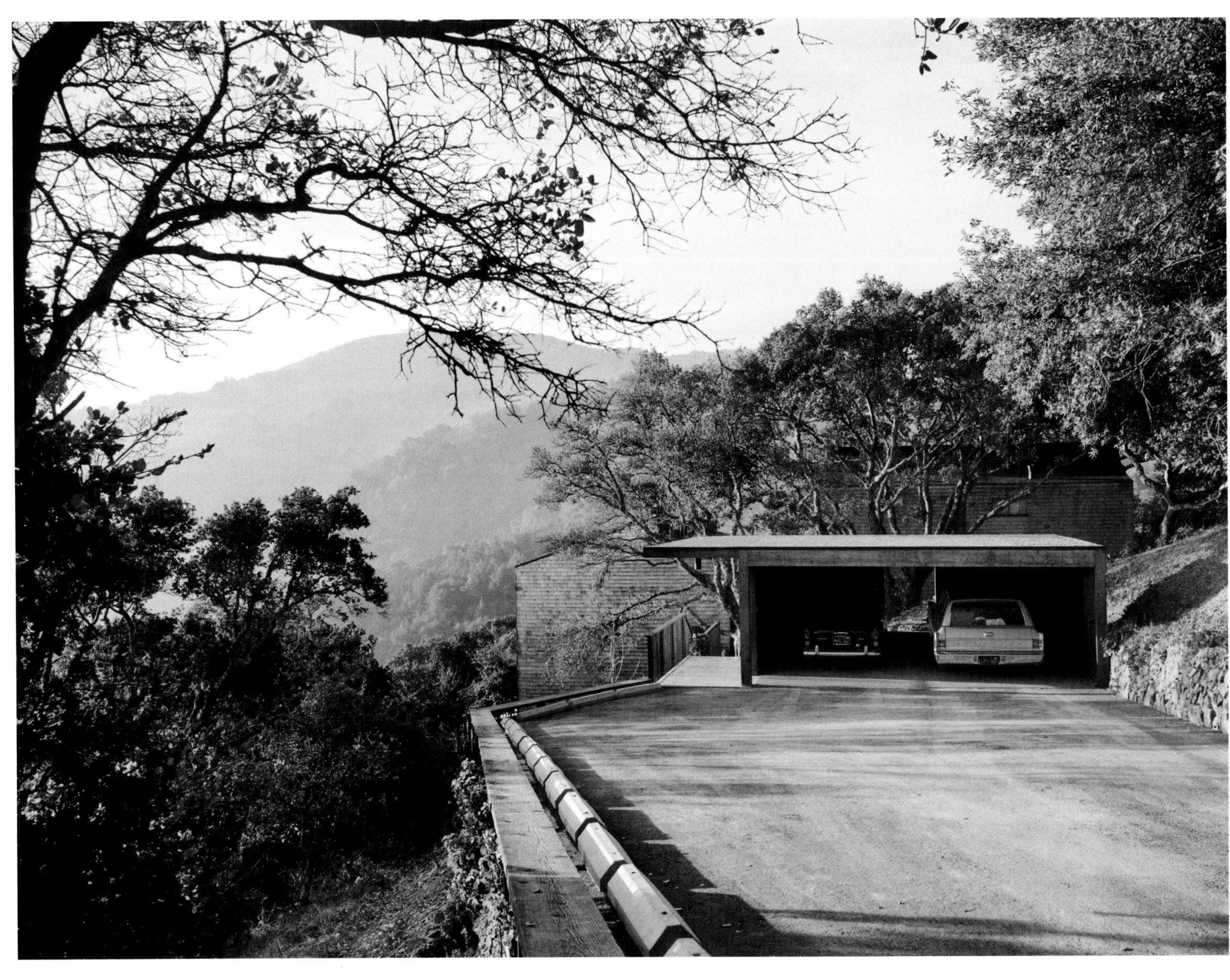

Blair House, Mill Valley, California.
Marquis & Stoller, 1952.

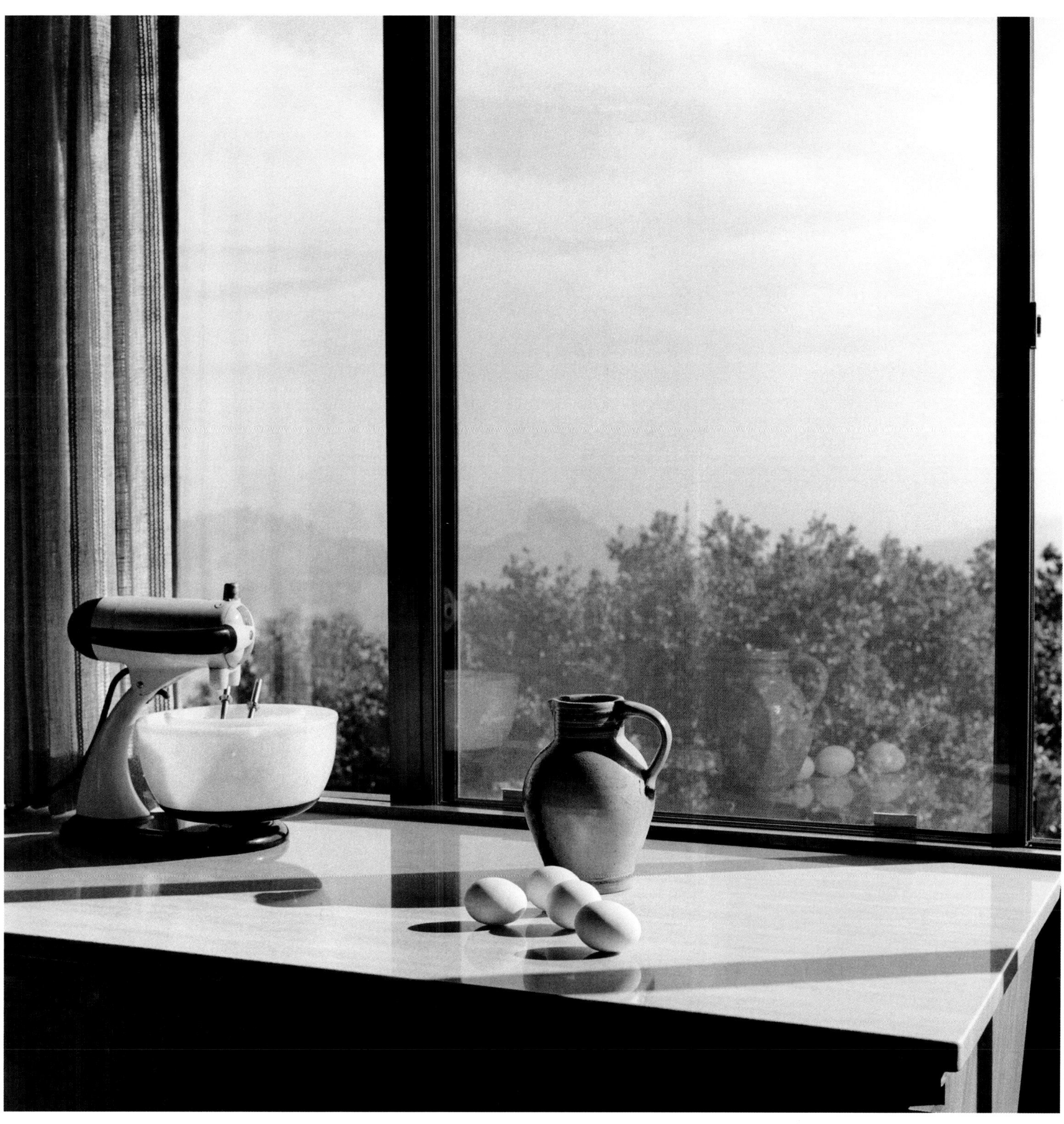

Blair House, Mill Valley, California.
Marquis & Stoller, 1952.

Equipment Timeline

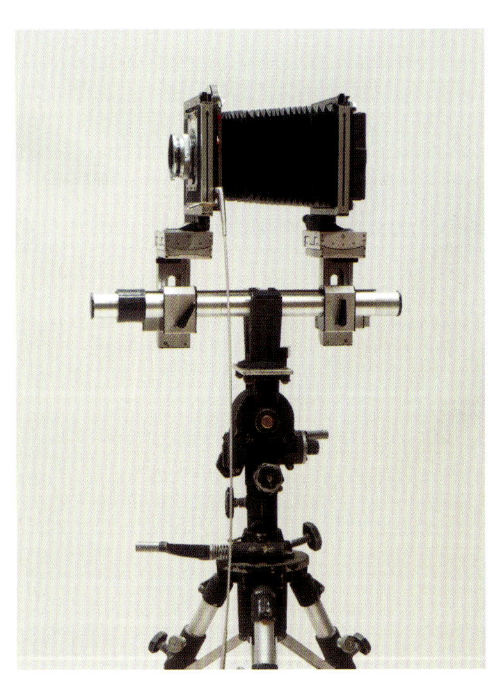

Ezra Stoller used a variety of cameras with 35mm, 120mm, 4 × 5, and 8 × 10 film. This timeline describes the camera kits, lenses, and equipment that he used throughout his life.

LARGE FORMAT CAMERAS

Purchased circa 1934–38, used until the late 1950s

1. Deardorff 8 × 10″ (V8 OS) field camera, masking slides, and recessed lens boards. Manufactured by L. F. Deardorff & Sons (1923–49).

2. Deardorff 8 × 10″ (V8) field camera lent by Stoller, who was in the Army, to Paul Strand, who was in the Signal Corps. Strand used it as a copy camera and painted the front standards black to reduce reflections. Manufactured by L. F. Deardorff & Sons (1923–49).

3. Linhof Technika II 4 × 5″ field camera. Manufactured by Linhof (1937–43).

Purchased circa 1957, used until the late 1960s

4. Sinar Norma 8 × 10″ monorail camera with 4 × 5″ and 8 × 10″ rear standards. Manufactured by Sinar AG (1948–70).

Purchased circa 1970, used until the late 1970s

5. Sinar P 4 × 5″ monorail camera with built-in leaf shutter. (Stoller liked how this camera had a leaf shutter independent of the lens shutters, allowing him to have consistent exposure from lens to lens.) Manufactured by Sinar AG (1970–83).

Purchased circa 1980, used until the late 1980s

6. Super Cambo 6 × 9 cm monorail camera. (Stoller purchased new, modern lenses for this camera but opted to use older Graflex 6 × 9 backs, which had uneven sharpness across the film plane.) Manufactured by Cambo BV (1970s).

LARGE FORMAT LENSES

Large-format lenses were forward compatible and stayed in his custom-machined tin box throughout the decades. The lenses, listed here by acquisition date, were all mounted to new lens boards as he changed camera brands and formats, moving down from 8 × 10″ to 4 × 5″ and then briefly to a 6 × 9 cm roll film camera at the end of his career.

Purchased in 1930s, used until the late 1940s

1. Voightlander Braunchweig Heliar 15 cm, f/4.5 lens (serial #2766986).

2. Dagor 6.5″, f/8 lens in Linhof board and Graflex Shutter (serial #756672). Manufactured by C. P. Goerz American Optical.

Purchased late 1940s–50s (for 8 × 10″ format)
3. Dagor 9.5″, f/6.8 lens with an ILEX No. 3 Acme Synchro Shutter (serial #768562). Manufactured by C. P. Goerz American Optical.
4. Dagor 12″, f/6.8 lens with an Alphax Synchromatic Shutter (serial #793060). Manufactured by C. P. Goerz American Optical.
5. Ektar 14″, f/6.3 lens with a No. 5 Universal Synchro Shutter (serial #OM295). Manufactured by Ilex Optical Company for Eastman Kodak.

Purchased in the 1960s (for 4 × 5″ format)
6. Angulon 6.8/210mm lens (serial #6359808). Manufactured by Schneider-Kreuznach (1960).
7. Technika Super-Angulon 8/121mm lens (serial #7354110). Manufactured by Schneider-Kreuznach (1961).
8. Sinar Symmar 5.6/135mm lens (serial #8412985). Manufactured by Schneider-Kreuznach (1963).
9. Angulon 6.8/165mm lens (serial #10985846). Manufactured by Schneider-Kreuznach (1967).
10. Super-Angulon 5.6/90mm lens (serial #10790847). Manufactured by Schneider-Kreuznach (1967).
11. Sinar Super-Angulon 5.6/75mm lens (serial #10478636). Manufactured by Schneider-Kreuznach (1967).

Purchased in the 1970s (for 6 × 9 cm format)
12. Super-Angulon 5.6/47mm lens (serial #11443820). Manufactured by Schneider-Kreuznach (1970).
13. Super-Angulon 5.6/65mm lens (serial #12967695). Manufactured by Schneider-Kreuznach (1974).

MEDIUM AND 35MM FORMAT CAMERAS AND LENSES

Hasselblad System, purchased in the early 1960s
1. Hasselblad SWC (Super-Wide Camera) with Biogon 38mm f/4.5 lens (serial #1990377). Manufactured by Carl Zeiss/Hasselblad.
2. Hasselblad 500C camera. Manufactured by Hasselblad.
3. Distagon 60mm f/5.6 lens (serial #2678755). Manufactured by Carl Zeiss/Hasselblad.
4. Planar 80mm f/2.8 lens (serial #2575592). Manufactured by Carl Zeiss/Hasselblad.
5. Sonnar 150mm f/4 lens (serial #1849389). Manufactured by Carl Zeiss/Hasselblad.
6. Planar 250mm f/5.6 lens (serial# 2860158). Manufactured by Carl Zeiss/Hasselblad.
Stoller also used an unknown Rolleicord prior to obtaining the Hasselblad System.

Leica M System, purchased in the 1950s and used until 1990s
1. Leica M2 rangefinder cameras (serial #940298 and #935092). Manufactured by Leitz Camera (1958).
2. Summilix 75mm f/1.5 lens (serial #732429). Manufactured by Leitz Camera.
3. W-Nikkor-C 3.5 cm f/1.8 lens with Leica M adapter (serial #181875). Manufactured by Nippon Kogaku Japan (Nikon).
4. Summaron 35mm f/3.5 lens (serial # 1567483). Manufactured by Leitz Camera
5. Summicron 50mm f/2 lens with "eyes" (serial #1571681). Manufactured by Leitz Camera.
6. 35mm f/2.5 type R1 lens (serial #239329). Manufactured by P. Angenieux, Paris.
7. Leicameter M (hot shoe mounted meter). Manufactured by Leitz Camera.

Nikon SLR Systems, purchased in the 1960s and 1970s, used until 1990s
1. Nikon F SLR (single-lens reflex) camera (1960s).
2. Nikon F2 SLR camera (1970s).
3. Nikon F3 SLR camera (1980s).
4. Nikkormat EL SLR camera (late 1970s).
5. PC-Nikkor 28mm f/4 lens (serial #174580). Manufactured by Nikon.
6. PC-Nikkor 35mm f/2.8 lens (serial #867602). Manufactured by Nikon.
7. Micro-Nikkor 55mm f/2.8 lens. Manufactured by Nikon.
8. Zoom-Nikkor Auto 43–86mm f/3.5 lens (serial #508955). Manufactured by Nikon.

LIGHTING

1. Until 1975, Stoller was using a combination of screw-in "hot lights" and then 200- or 500-watt flashbulbs in standard hardware reflectors to light his interiors. The blue-tinted lights were controlled with various flags and gobos; he tripped the lights with a portable battery or by plugging the system into a household socket. Sometimes multiple "pops" of the flashes were required to light a scene at the desired luminance for large-format capture; this involved assistants wearing welding gloves to swap out the hot lights, without disturbing the scene or moving the camera. (Stoller became a licensed dealer for the bulbs because he used such a large quantity.)
2. Around 1975, Stoller reluctantly purchased and experimented with Dynalite portable stroboscopic flash units.
3. Stoller used reflective spot meters for determining light levels outdoors, but with the flashbulbs, exposure was determined by the number of bulbs used and their distance from the walls or objects in the room. ("When we were outside, the exposure always seemed to be the same.")
a. Luna-Pro sbc Incident/Reflective-Light Meter. Manufactured by Gossen.
b. Auto-Spot 1º Reflective Spot Meter. Manufactured by Minolta.

FILM

1. Film formats: Stoller first used 8 × 10″ and 4 × 5″ film on his Deardorff and Linhof cameras, respectively, while a student at New York University in the 1930s. His first architectural projects were photographed with both cameras, but in the 1950s he switched to mostly 8 × 10″ black-and-white negatives and positive transparency film, shifting down from 8 × 10″ to 4 × 5″ rear-standard on his Sinar Norma for the economy of an assignment or when a scene needed a wider lens (which were initially available only in 4 × 5″ format). Stoller photographed personal work in 35mm and 120mm roll film format, using a mix of slide, negative, and black-and-white film.
2. Black-and-white film: Stoller used a wide variety of black-and-white sheet and roll films. Some of the earliest suffer from cellulose triacetate degradation, or "vinegar syndrome." The roll films are almost impossible to identify since they all read "Kodak Safety Film" and use a complex code that indicates only which plant manufactured the film.
3. Color reversal film (transparency/slide film): Stoller used Kodachrome 4 × 5″ transparency as early as the 1940s, later switching to a mixture of Ansco transparency and Kodak Ektachrome film (surprisingly, the more "economical" Ansco has held better color) throughout the late 1950s to the end of his commercial career in the early 1980s. Stoller often saw color as a necessity of commercial work but insisted that black-and-white film was his preferred medium.
4. Color negative film: Stoller started experimenting with color negative film as early as 1965 and used it intermittently thereafter. Initially, it was supposed to resolve the necessity of photographing both in color and black and white for each scene through its ability to produce a color darkroom print, a positive slide through internegative printing or contact process, and a black-and-white print on Kodak Panalure paper. Stoller used color negative film intermittently throughout the rest of his career.

Catalogue of Projects

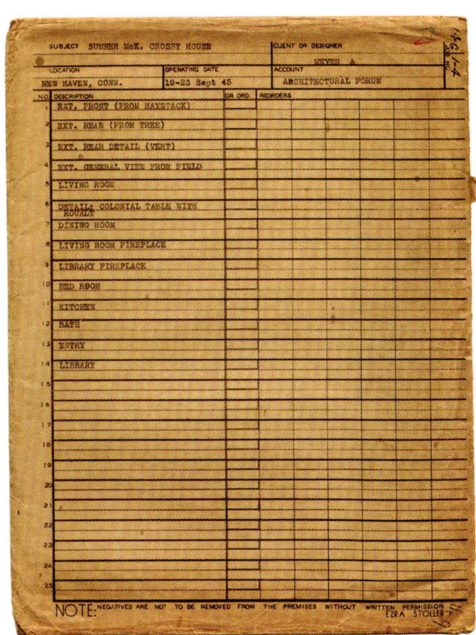

SUBJECT SUMNER McK. CROSBY HOUSE

CLIENT OR DESIGNER MEYER A.

LOCATION NEW HAVEN, CONN.

OPERATING DATE 19-23 Sept 45

ACCOUNT ARCHITECTURAL FORUM

NO.	DESCRIPTION
1	EXT. FRONT (FROM HAYSTACK)
2	EXT. REAR (FROM TREE)
3	EXT. REAR DETAIL (VERT)
4	EXT. GENERAL VIEW FROM FIELD
5	LIVING ROOM
6	DETAIL: COLONIAL TABLE WITH ROUALT
7	DINING ROOM
8	LIVING ROOM FIREPLACE
9	LIBRARY FIREPLACE
10	BED ROOM
11	KITCHEN
12	BATH
13	ENTRY
14	LIBRARY

NOTE: NEGATIVES ARE NOT TO BE REMOVED FROM THE PREMISES WITHOUT WRITTEN PERMISSION EZRA STOLLER

This project list is compiled from the handwritten and typed notes in the Ezra Stoller card catalogue that documented assignments from 1939 through his last professional project in 1993. It reveals the range of Stoller's projects, the intensity of his travel schedule, and his constant engagement with his work.

1939

Coney Island · Surrey Motors · Stuyvesant Housing Project · Federal Advertising · Pierce Nichols House · Jay Lord Haberdashery · Duplex Fabrics · Janney House · Bullock's · Kimball House · Korchein Housing Model · McKinsey and Company · Henry Hebbeln House · Flah Department Store · Hotel Pierre · Lord Jeff Showroom · Tafel Parents' House · Store Model · Lincoln Mercury · Weinstein Fur Salon · Evangelist Church · Rockwood School · American Commercial Model · Kimball House in Winter · World's Fair, Finnish Pavilion · World's Fair, Irish Pavilion · World's Fair Views · Bookcase · Lederer Store · Breuer House · MIT Field House · Littaur Center, Harvard · Massachusetts General Hospital · Shepley House · Shepley Beach · Ayres House · List House · Memorial Hospital · Ansco Exhibition · Sheffield Farms Building Seal Test · World's Fair, Wastebasket at Court of States · World's Fair, House of Jewels · World's Fair, Aviation Building

1940

Brandeis, Wein Faculty Center · Belmont Hill · Appelman Art Glass Company · Weiss House · Adrian Dress Salon · Spingold Residence · Eunice Shops · Sloan-Kettering Building · Craig Stanton Office · Gotham Lighting Fixtures · Noguchi Table for Herman Miller · Synagogue Model · Container Corporation of America · Ruffin and Payne Lumber Yard Building · Chapin House · Cooper Graham House · Producer's Distributing Company · Benjamin Rosenthal House · Fultis Self-Serve Restaurant · Martha West Shop · Fortune Layout · Paris Theater · Schwann House · Emerson House · MIT Gas Turbine Laboratory · WMCA Radio Station Construction · Korchien Harmon Housing Model · Marcel Rochas · Millman House · Katz Model · Lightolier · Church Model · Hospital Model · WMCA Inter-City Broadcasting Company · Jack Dempsey's Restaurant · Longchamps Restaurant · Louis Levy Boat: "We Three" · Longchamps Kitchen · Tanglewood Music Shed · Croton Falls Church · Longchamps Restaurant · Northwestern University · Glendale Housing Development · Lindley House · Kassler House · Mary Lyons School · A. S. Beck Shoe Store · Shaw Walker Showroom · World's Fair, Hall of Pharmacy · Statue of Doctor Sims · Harbor Sideshow Room · Welfare Hospital · Le Bas Lillian · Steckler Shop · W. T. Grant Department Store · A. S. Beck Shoes · Goodman Apartment · Pedac Model, Collier's House of Ideas · Dr. Mehlman's office

1941

Black Mountain Development Model · Barton's Bonbonniere · Stoller Apartment · Time Offices · L. .K Thorne Apartment · Frederick Field Interiors · Greenbriar Gardens Restaurant · Otis Underwear Counter Display · Wallachs · Shelter Fold System · Le Bas Lillian Park Avenue · Trade Winds · Sixty-Eight Restaurant · Goodall Decorative Fabrics · Portrait of Hamas Children · Converted Luncheonette Cars · Toffenetti Restaurant · Opera at Julliard · Central Knitwear Mills · Helen Stoller Post Office Mural · Mack Sepler Store · Barton's Bonbonniere · Sherman Clinic Model · Hoffman Pressing Machine Model · Mission of St. Peter Claver · North Country School · Robsjohn-Gibbings Chair · Juilliard Opera · Metropolitan Museum Exhibit · Loewi Apartment · Metropolitan Museum exhibit · Newman Apartment · Office Life Cartoons at Shaw-Walker · Noguchi Sculpture · George Katrina Sculpture · Mrs. Armand Deutsch Apartment · Longfellow Building · Metropolitan Museum Exhibit · Federal Loan Agency Building · Desk Pad · S&H Parking Center · Redex Display · George P. Marshall Residence · Mrs. Joseph B. Platt · Tiffany Glassware · Uline Ice Arena · Shaw Walker Office Models · Douglas House · Race Track Renderings · Reid House · Tichy House · Rich House · Quincy Shaw McKean House/Margaret Sargent House · Small Cottage · Federal Works Agency Exhibit, World's Fair · Smith Apartment · Air Hill Homes · Leonard Baskin Sculpture · Albert E. Hoffman, Portrait · Kleinman Bros. Fur Showroom · Mary Ginsberg House · Bogner House · William T. Grant Residence · Wheaton College Alumnae Building · Pabst Sales Company Building · Gunderson Glass Works · Sixth Avenue Association Exhibit · Mavitran Exhibit · Curtis House · Collier House of Ideas · Franklin-Bush Office · Van Raalte Sales and Showroom · Ziff Davis Publishing Company Office · Pickerill House · Krakauer Piano Empress Model · Pane Apartment · American Machinery

& Foundry Products · Bartos Thompson Office · Upjohn Booklet · Rockefeller Center Home Center Lobby · WMCA Brochure · Ilka Chase Sloan House of the Year · Wanamaker's Decorators' Apartments · Terrace House · Regency Room Rock Center Home Center · Pepsi-Cola Accessories · Chamberlain Cottage · Edna Ferber House · Terzaghi House · Monk's House · Christmas Packages · Camp Tamiment Golf Club · Summit Chapel · Unity House · Hunter College · Green Mansions · Simon and Schuster Offices · Buttenweiser House · Cherry Lawn School · Cabot Farm · Frank House · Nemeny and Geller Spec House · Imogene Wolcott House · Neiman Marcus · Altschul House · Kingsborough Housing Project · Conger Goodyear House · Astor Hotel, Columbia Room · Kawalsky House · Sidney R. Shurcliff House · Abbott Kimball · Sculpture · Berkwit House · Westboro Homes · P. S. F. Garage · Hunt & Winterbottom Showroom · Philadelphia Evening Bulletin · Rumford Chemical Works · Carl Koch House · Bedford Shirt Company Showroom · Cushman House · Economy Apartment · Snake Hill House · Pittsburgh War Housing Model · Lord and Taylor Couch/Bed · Gropius House, View from · Salvation Army Building · Saint Barnabas Home · Joseph Rose House · Canada Dry · Tafel Apartment · Hunter Shop · Gerber House · Nelson House · British Railways · Saint Barnabas Home for Women · Hunter's Department Store Model · Knopf Apartment Cabinet

1942
Apartment · Cedar Chests · Silverware & China · Wildcliff Junior College · Recording Session for Night Shift · Artek of New York Shop · Priest's Vestments · OEM, Night Shift · Orloff Products · Scope Magazine 3 for Upjohn · Remodeled Furniture · OEM, O. Levant Conducting · Mangel's Office · Sonorama · Recording Session with Paul Muni · Magnavox Radios · Corsetorium · Colony Restaurant · Beaunit Mille · House Interior · George Wallace House · A. J. Harriman House · South Portland Shipyard · Abele House · Duplan Silk Mills · Bedspread Ideas · Morris Ketchum & Jed Reisner, Portrait · Service Men's Center, Times Square · Kalisher & Barry · Farmington Farm House · Woodhouse Garden · House in Lewiston · Whitney House · Life and Fortune Xmas Cards · St. Patrick's High Altar · Model · Wheaton College, Science Building and Library Addition · Scope Magazine · 4 for Upjohn · Brooklyn Project Model · Wallachs · Thru-View Blinds · Catheron House · Lawrence House · Neil House · Six Moon Hill Miscellaneous · Paul Grotz House · 30 Broad Street · House on Long Island · Idella La Vista · Plaza Hotel, Persian Room · Morris Park House

1943
Darcy Advertising Agency Offices · London Shoe Store · Dana London · Apartment · Morris Ketchum · 9 Ash Street House · Tremont Avenue Overpass Model · Standard Oil Bayway Refinery · Van Wesep House · Scovill Manufacuring Company · Brainard Field Dining Room · Grey Advertising · Pepsi Cola Plant · Cherry Point Housing Project · Scope · 5 for Upjohn · Duplan Silk Mills · Orangeburg Camp Model · Robert Silberstein House · Pomerance House · Wood House · Sarah Lawrence College · Idlewild Airport Model · Housing Models · Patients in doctor's waiting room · Propaganda film, stills

1944
Standard Oil Bayway Refinery · South Portland Housing Project · Bath Housing Project · Colonial House · Bath Iron Works · John E. L. Huse Memorial School · Hyde Windlass Company · St. Mark's Church · Houses in Colonial Style · Fairfax School · Barre Auditorium · American Locomotive Company · Scope · 5 for Upjohn · Furniture Models 1945 Noguchi table and chessboard · Grover Cronin Department Store · Time Reception Room · Daily News Building · Fortune Experimental Project · Shelter Fold System · Sversky House · Airport Model · Air Stadium · Gaines House · Fried Garage · Nelson Office · Sumner McK. Crosby House · Sonneborn Offices · Joan Geiger Apartment

1945–46
Puerto Rico Hotel Model · Camp Shanks/Camp Kilmer · Dow House · G. Stone House · Stubbins House · Yost House Model · Wills House · Harris House · G. Keck House · Camp House · Fortune Offices · Charles of the Ritz · Little Kitchen · Kitchen · Large Kitchen · Kitchen · Frank House Model · White Lab's Preparation of Ointment Pads for Upjohn · Storage Wall · Arts of the Pacific, Museum of Modern Art · Good Housekeeping, Model Home of Bianchini-Férier Silk Showroom · Loeb House Model · Model of Clark House · Model Bedrooms · Model House · Weldwood · Rosengren House · Model of Johnson & Johnson Plant · House Model · Model Bedroom · Geller House · Coney Island · George Jessel Vaudeville Performance

1946
Goodall Showrooms · Jackson House · Zerbe House · Kreble House · Snake Hill · Cole House · Winter House Model · General Panel · Frost House · CBS Studio · Collins House Prefab · SA Housing Project Models · Sculpture by José de Rivera · Krene Showroom · Fisher House · Neiman-Marcus Children's Shop · Kawneer Exhibition · Paraffin Company of America Showroom · Herman Miller Furniture, Noguchi and Nelson · Michigan State Capitol, Model Offices · Shoe Store · Taliesin East · Taliesin West · Snake Hill · House Model

1947
Red House Model · Hahn Shoe Store · Herman Miller Furniture · House Model · Devon Dennett Workshop · Silicone Plastics for Fortune · Army Post Office Fixtures · Herman Miller Furniture · Gilbert Tompkins House · Nichols House · du Pont, Homsey Offices · MIT Radiation Lab · MIT School of Architecture · RCA Exhibit · Closets · Johnson & Johnson Baby Products Plant · H. K. Porter Factory · Koch Kitchen · Kurt Versen Lamps · Lighting Story · Clark House · North Country School, Little House · Green Mansions New Lounge · H. J. Heinz Model · Astrophysics & Astronomy for Fortune · Power in the West for Fortune · Model Churches · Jefferson Memorial Model · Akston Apartment · Idea House II · Better Philadelphia Exhibition · Freedom Train · Tamiment Golf Club · Unity House · Stubbins House · Bitter House · Rantoul House · Philadelphia Human Interest Story · Pope Leighey House · Ketchum Gina Sharp Offices · Allied Artists Guild · Young Years Shop · Holly Store

1948
Union Fern Store · Foley Bros. Department Store · Houston Back Yards · Chicago Tribune Addition · Hospital Model · Socony Vacuum Model · Fiberglas Building · South American Church Model · Stubbins Model · Arts & Ends · Hathaway Bedroom · USDA Kitchen · New Designs · SA Community Center Model · Highlander Folk School Model · Al & Dick Restaurant · Apartment House, East 91st Street · Burdines Department Store · Miller Residence · University of Miami · Barney Stock Store · Lustron House · Esso Lounge · Allis House · Bantam Cock Restaurant · Chittern House · Clarke House · Coleman House · Eisele Guest House · General Panel Home Prefab Project · Halsey House · Heil House · Knowell House · Maston House · Mauer House · McDonald House · Moore House · Saxton Pope House · Radditz House · Whitney Smith House · Southern California Home · J. A. Stein House · J. Van Cleef House · Watzek House · Yeon and Jorgenson Houses · Mills House · Equitable Building · Oregonian Building · Esso Building at Rockefeller Center · Menefee House · Gardner Gamwell House · House on Madison at 87 Street · Marshall House · Yerbe House · Nantucket Homes · Terrace Plaza Hotel · Monticello · Upjohn Project · South American Theatre · Burtin Booklets · NYU Bellevue Medical Center Model · Christmas Decorations · Helena Rubenstein Apartment · Ain House Model · Standard Vacuum Oil Model · Knoll Showroom · Federal Telecomm, ITT Tower · Philadelphia Back Yards · Upjohn Display for Fortune · Antonin Raymond House · Farney House · Besser Manufacturing Company Exhibit · Sharp House · City of LA Stadium Model · Stein House · Adams House · Parton House · Dean House · Dean Kitchen with Mrs. Dean · Michaels House · Holmes House · Stoller House Wiring · Sherry Wine and Spirits · Surrey Motors Company · Acorn House · Hermitage · Belle Mead House · SS Exeter interiors · Will Burtin Exhibit · SS Exeter exteriors · Adrenalin Cartex Building · Saint Barnabas Home · Carl Koch Kitchen · Bayer Cadillac showroom · Bigelow-Sanford Carpet Company · RCA Information Booth · Al and Dick Restaurant · Farmers Consumers Dairies

1949
Ladies Home Journal Offices · Rudolph House (not Paul Rudolph) · Upjohn Products · New York Life Insurance Model · Arthur J. Olsen House · Moore House · Doctor's hands for Upjohn · Clark House · Windswept Apartments · University of Miami Housing · Stein House · University of Miami Students Club · Bloomingdales · Howard Johnson's Restaurant · Arthur Murray's Dance Studio · MoMA House and Breuer Portrait · Comstock House · Kimmel House and Rayburn House · Keyes Office · Keyes Apartment · Baxter House · Wohl Studio Apartments · Rutgers University, publicity show · Printing Story for Fortune · Devon Dennett Tables · Binder House · Penicillin · Bottles on a Shelf · Drug Store · Sanchez House · Piano, Newhouse · McKesson and Robbins Warehouse · Lillian Russell House · Miami Parking Garage · A-D Exhibition Booklet · Siegrist House · Finney House, Revere House · Florida Southern College · Brewster House · Wohl House · Richard Berlin Kitchen · Russell House · Breuer House in MoMA Garden · Yeakley House · Regional Design Studies · George Nakashima House · Altman's room set up · Tea Gardens · Estes House · Bryant House · MIT Baker House · Fred Raske Apartment · Smith House · Stoller House · Glass House · August Trip Ads Kalamazoo · Fortune cover · Appleman House · Upjohn Ads · Television Studios · Garden · Dewey House · Andrews House (Shaker) · Murtagh House · Eldridge House · Underwood House · Howlett House · Robert McMillan House · Fletcher House · Harkness House · Sherwood House · Curry House · Sills House · Clack House · Howell House · Louis McMillen House · Martin House · Dretzin House · Alfred E. Smith Housing Project · John Morris House · Great Neck Gardens · 7 AM Strip Project · Recruiting Manual · Sculpture · Philadelphia Subway · Furrier's Dental Clinic · Circular Apartment Model · Bank Building and Equipment Company · Gotham Carpet · Parsons House · Finsven Showroom · Lever House Model · Fuldner Furniture · Stech House · United Nations Construction · Lamps · Davis Delaney Printing Press · Concrete House Model

1950
Development Project · Freight Car · Caribe Hilton · Arnold Newman, Portrait · Vocational Training School · Fort Hamilton Veterans Hospital · Deeds House · Breuer House at MoMA Garden · Heller House · Upjohn Fibre Neg · Miller Cottage · Wedding House · Florida Southern College · Denman House · Savannah Regional Architecture · Burdine's Department Store · Upjohn Health Stores · Jackson House Model · Butterflies · Upjohn Gelfoam · Ain House at MoMA Garden · 6 St. Luke's Place Apartment · Geranium Garden · Cameron Clark House · Florida Southern College · University of Michigan Model · Edward Wormley Apartment · Nathaniel Newhouse Apt, Piano · Organ Story · Obzansky House · House of Design · East Hampton Regional Architecture · Model House · Self-Service Market · Blythe Park Elementary School · Covington Fabrics · Basket Chair · Royal Barry Wills House · Dupont Story · Hudson Valley Regional Architecture · Wormley Portfolio · Upjohn Hematoma Tape Measure · Line of Pills for Upjohn · Upjohn trip to Kalamazoo · Chicago Tribune Tower Model · United Nations · Upjohn Blood Corpuscles · Pan American Building Model, New Orleans · Ford Model · Bathroom · DeVilbiss Showroom · Caribe Hilton · Kootz Gallery/House Model · Fitchburg Youth Library · Eastgate Apartments · Fitchburg Youth Library Fireplace · Schaefer House · John Notman House · Hunter/Cook House · Leuthardt Nurseries · Holiday House · Sage House · Upjohn Anti-Biotic Display Model · Nathan Hale House · Lewis House · Schwarzenbach House · Esmund Shaw House · Lawrence and Lundsgaard Houses · Hotpoint House · Friedman House · Stonington Houses · Vernon Sears Game Room · Johnson Wax Tower · Adelman House · Jacobs II House · Pew House · Cedar Rock · Taliesin East · Pace Setter House · Abraham & Strauss Drawing · Madison Unitarian Church · Frank Lloyd Wright, Portraits · Harvard Graduate Center · Providence Houses · Calder Show at MIT · Meyers Climate Control House

1951
First National Bank · Sandifer House · El Panama Hotel · Syntex Story · University of Panama · Taliesin West · Pittsburgh Plate Glass Company · Knife Fork and Spoon Exhibit · Kahn Apartment · Palazzo Giustiniani · Dwight Deere Wiman Estate · Spool Package · A. C. Koch House · Seabrook Plantation · Earle House · Cocoon House Healey House · Reid House · Hotel Statler · Upjohn Ampules · Zelda Kaplan House · University of Florida · Cabana Colony Hotel · Rowell House · Burnette House · Leavengood House · Farmington Stonington Providence · Upjohn Hands · Upjohn Unicaps · Royal Barry Wills Parish House · Riley House · Fitch House · Corning Glass Center · Skyline · Houston Shopping Center Model · Lionni House · Upjohn Glassware · Great Neck · Radio Shack · Maurice Segal House · Wellesley Housing Project · McCammond House · Christopher House · Fitch House · Lou Baker House · Schindler Residence · Rosen House · General Motors Technical Center · Offices of Linewebber, Yamasaki and Hellmuth · US Gypsum · Yamasaki House · Winograd · Applebaum House · Pearson House · Gilbert Burke House · Yale Physics Lab

Model · Philadelphia Zoo · 600 Fifth Avenue · Sorrento House · Rosenberg House · Hand Holding Graduate for Upjohn · United Nations and Skyline from Boat · Hilton Hotel Turkey Model · Diamond House · Thigh for Upjohn · Medicine Chest for Upjohn · Mack House · Duveen Building · New York Skyline · Heating Coils · Urban Furniture Company · Rich's Department Store · Baker Residence · Furniture Groups · Neiman Marcus Preston Center · Miami Research · Burdines Department Store · Alfred Politz House

1952
House of History · William Zeckendorf Properties · Capitol Hill Model · CBS Television City studio · Eames Office · Coney Island Hospital Model · Dumbarton Morris House · Amsterdam Hospital · Museum of Modern Art Lounge · Office with Contemporary Art Collection · United Nations General Assembly · Webb House · Melton House · Sterling House · Rice House · Haskins House · Coward House · Parker Pacesetter House · Adler House · Riley Streate House · Zeckendorf Office · Mounted Flies for Upjohn · Holmes Elementary School · Fisherman Setup for Upjohn · Shell with pill for Upjohn · Washington Heights Bank · Museum of Modern Art offices · Hechinger House · Keyes House · England House · Lever House · Tulip Hill · Carrier air conditioner UN · Manhattan House · Kitchen Laundry Setup for Upjohn · Pan American Ticket Office · Chaffee House · Little House · Lever House · Five Fields · Attleboro School · Isaacson House · Keith Lombard Sample Houses · Five Fields · Sam Glazer House · Scherman Studio · Taunton Housing Project · Harvard, Burr Lecture Hall · Mass Gen Hosp Research Lab · Conantum · McKay Lab for Applied Science · Bayer Cadillac · Oneto House/J. E. Miller House · Clark House · Stowe Hof · Hodgson House · Osborne House · Wolosoff House · Chinese Book for Upjohn · Bronxville Skylight · Magazine and Buffet Table · Kenneth Welsh House · Warren Platner House · Eero Saarinen Office · Anthony House · Eric Brown House · Dr. Ina Harper House · Upjohn trip September · Container Corporation for Scope Magazine · Mossberg House · Stendler House · Brenner House · Sheffield Building · Upjohn Cortisone Plant Frontispiece · TV Setups for Upjohn · House on Long Island · O'Brien House · Chermayeff House · York National Bank · Smithsonian Exhibition · Donald Dodge/Spite House · May House · Lady Pepperell House · Tate House · Zimmerman House · Alexander Girard House · Scope Shots for Upjohn · Wright Bathroom · Olivetti Exhibit MoMA · Edward Durell Stone Office · Tafel Apartment · CBS Television City Studio · Hoeffer Porch/Skylight · Wormley Apartment · Florida House · Johansen House · Jones and Laughlan Steel Works · Widdicomb Furniture · Trade Signs for Upjohn

1953
Guide to the Bride · Nakashima Furniture · CBS/Columbia Records · Titelman House · State Department Education Center Europe · United Nations General Assembly · Segal Apartment · Wolosoff Bathroom · Textured paper designed by Will Burtin for Upjohn · Plumer Kitchen · Raymor Barbecue · George Washington Carver School · Fraternity House Model · Waldin House · Howard Johnson's Motor Inn · Walker Guest House · Sanderling Beach Club · Super House and Hook House · Connecticut Mutual Life Insurance Company Office · Barry Apartment · Dr. Sacks House · Fehr House · Segal Apartment/Lustig Office · McCalls Office · Henry Holt Office · Price House · Garden City Offices · Federal Reserve Bank · Herman Miller · Jones Steel and Iron Company · Greenville Office Building Model · Metlon Corp · Heinz Offices and Factory · Yamasaki House and Robinson House · Taylor House · General Motors office · Parker House · Baldwin Building · Biscayne Annex Post Office · Stockstrum House · Hutzler Bros. Company · Pottsgrove · Gould House · Aspendale Downes House · Germantown · Atkinson House · Rock Hall · Gore House · Stony Brook,2 LI Lovelies · Pereira and Luckman Offices · Stevenson Apartment · Garden · Pahlman · Ford Model · Tesoro House · 600 Fifth Ave Factory · Manufacturers Trust Company Model · Unicorn Tapestry at Cloisters · Yale Medical School Housing · Bayview Houses Model · McLeod House · Hamilton House · Kronenberg House · Harvard Kresge Hall · Harvard Chapel Memorial Panel · Loomis School · Parzinger Booth · Homsey House · Weiting House · Gordon Gibbs House · Aldrich Hall · Dunbar Chairs · Floating Islands Model · Mosler Safe Door · Hunter House · Cabot House · Lee Mansion · Ruggles House · Johansen House · Rufus Stillman House · Burdines Beauty shop · Ryder House · Parker Kitchen · Koch II House · Usonian House at Guggenheim · House of Cards · Hamilton Metal Products Grill · Usonian House at Guggenheim · New York Savings Bank · Nieman Marcus · Upjohn Proof Negatives · Crawford Homes · Upjohn · Mayan Restaurant · Geodesic Dome, wood construction

1954
Mayan Restaurant · L and T Table Setups · Project X, Chicago · Dr. Walter's Office · CBS Columbia Records · Dreher Bonnett Hill Farm · Frank Lloyd Wright House Bathroom · 60 Sutton Place · 1 Wall Street · Nakashima Chair · Millard House · Gamble House · James House · Walker House · Olivetti, San Francisco · Norman Kopmeier House · Mervin LeRoy House · Ludekins House · Millard House La Miniatura · Meteor Crater Museum · Charles Greene House · Hollyhock House · Ennis House · Coliseum Model · Dr. Green House · School · Yacht Club · Parker House Firescreen · Crozant House · Hunt Henderson House · Jordan House · Scope Magazine · 5 · Coke House · McDowell House · O'Rear House · Museum of Modern Art Restaurant · Guggenheim Museum Model · Dutton House at Shelburne Museum · School Model · Scope Cover Shell Fish for Upjohn · Olivetti, Chicago · Connecticut General Model · Wiley House · Guest House at Glass House · Schlumberger Building · Tremaine Barn · Orbach Apartment · Olivetti, New York · Northwest Airlines · Haselton House · Ridgeway School · St. Phillips Church · Japanese House at MoMA Garden · Thomas and Betts Offices · Peter Schweitzer Paper Company · Ball House · IBM Booklet · Rauwolfia Roots for Upjohn · United Nations · Wheaton College Infirmary · Wheaton College Dining Room · Wheaton College Housing · Lakeside School · Lynnfield High School · West Parish School · Andover High School · Saks Fifth Avenue · Japanese House at MoMA Garden · Home Furnishings Show · Experimental Liquor Shots for Upjohn · Pier Development Model · Manufacturers Trust · Aviation Trade School Model · Hollow Tree School · Franzen House · Time Life Models · Add-on House · Macy's Roosevelt Field Model · Whitney Museum · McNiff House · Nakashima Showroom · Model House Project · Farney House · Virgin Island Model · Portfolio House Model · Fortune Story: 25 Years · Levittown · Jensen House · Josephson House · Burt Friedman House · IBM Building Shots · Esso Products

1955
Sears Roebuck · Dania Fronton · Burdine's · Rice House · Zollner House · Fleet Sonar School · Price House · Herbert Johnson House · Gimbel House · University of Miami Ring Theatre · Florida Southern College, Industrial Arts Building · Summer Furniture, Puerto Rico · Land Pictures · IBM 702 Machine · Kitchen of Tomorrow · IBM Cardatype · Family of Man at MoMA · High Voltage Corporation · City and Suburban Homes · Inland Steel Model · Pan American Insurance Company Building · Tourneau Semisphere · House Model · Fleischmann Liquor Labels · Stencil Letters for Upjohn · Wallach's, Yonkers · Norcross House · New Delhi Embassy Model · Garden Shed · Permascreen House · Columbus Hotel Lobby · Plastic Pools · Bruil House · Kornbloom House · London Terrace · IBM Cores and Transistors · SS Stockholm · John Hill Apartment · City and Suburban Laundry · Leopold Kitchen · Kneses Tifereth Israel Synagogue · Wallach's, Fifth Avenue · Philadelphia Inquirer Gravure Plant · Hutzler Lunch Bar · Chestnut Lodge · Catalano House · Hollywood Beach Hotel · Wyatt Building · Neill D. Coates House · Van House · Mass House · Air Force Academy Model · Lake Shore Drive Apartments · Chicago Municipal Garage · Princeton Houses · Emerson Foote House · Hoffman Motors BMW Showroom · Ziegler Apartment · LHJ Project House · Liberty Life Insurance Company · Oak Ridge High School · TVA Johnsonville Plant · General Electric Appliance Park · Reynolds Metals, Arkadelphia · St. Louis Airport · Army Records Center · Bristol Primary School · Grosse Point University School · Ford Headquarters · Ford Rotunda · Dearborn School · Budd Company, Chase Plant · Carnegie Tech Donner Hall · Kermit Schaeffer House · Johnson Builder's House · Boswell Tea House · IBM 705 · Frank Lloyd Wright Plaza Apartment · IBM New 702 Center · Arvida Bridge · MIT Kresge Auditorium · Lombardy Hotel · Art Nouveau Furniture story · Tempestini House · Refrigeration Le Prieure · Notre Dame du Haut, Ronchamp · Istanbul Hilton · Unite d'Habitation · New Canaan Country Club · Vets Park School · Church · Mile High Center · Bruce Payne Office, Rockefeller Center · General Motors Technical Center · Pills and Indian Headdress for Upjohn · Dr. Goodyear House · Child's note with pills for Upjohn · Brandeis Chapels · MIT Chapel/Kresge Auditorium · North East Elementary School · Kaufman House · Cleveland Houses · Lombardy Hotel · Chase Manhattan Bank Model · Molecular Gene Model · Woodlawn Plantation · Gunston Hall · Thalhimers Department Store · Portfolio House · 3 · Albree E. Miller Residence · Florida Furniture · Shapiro Screened Porch · Mass Tile Shots · Lucerne Hotel · Cohen House · Davidson House · Stoller Fireplace

1956
Bronx Municipal, now Jacobi, Hospital · Barrie's Restaurant · IBM EDPM Center · Plastics in America Exhibit for United States Information Agency · Measuring Boy for Upjohn · Medicine Cabinet for Upjohn · Shoreham Hotel · 35th Street Apartments · Suitcase for Upjohn · Esso Building · St. Louis Airport · Burden Model · Marschalk and Pratt · Transylvania College for Upjohn · Pahlman Apartment · IBM · Ivar Bryce House · Olson Apartment · Richardson House · Grove Theatre · Newkirk Houses · Claude Hutchinson House · Jordan Marsh · Biscayne Federal Bank · Miami Library · Biggs House · Philip Hiss Offices · Hiss Development House · Choate (now Severs) House · Chastain House · Rodieck House · Burke House · Bedroom, Seaview Hotel · Seagram Building construction · Garden House · Nivola Sculpture · LHJ Portfolio House · 4 · Loewy Apartment · Hotpoint Exhibit · Berlin Conference Hall Model · Noyes House · City and Suburban Offices · IBM Endicott · Elizabeth Halloran House · George Eastman House · Campbell Whittlesey House · Hollis Baker Jr House · Old Farm Hill Homes · Richard Litsey House · Carmona House · Gayer House · Marko House · Washington House of Ideas · Federal Reserve Bank · Dunbar Tables · Eden Roc Hotel · Sears Root Chemicals · IBM 702 Building · IBM Kingston · Flemington Garden · Library Model · Rhode Island Hospital · Felix DeWeldon House · George Whitney House · Harvard Botany Building · Ames Gate House · Holy Name School and Convent · Colonial Park School · Dean House · Donald David House · Robert Buck House · BoatJen · Design Research · IBM Endicott, September '56 · Socony-Mobil Building · Plattsburgh State Teachers College · University Club of New York · Morgan Library · Ralph Ackeman House · Wyeth Labs · Boissonas House · Starkey House · Shrodes House · Ladd House · Cliff May House · Station WCKT · Geyer Terrace · Stylon of Miami Showroom · Eden Roc Murals · Apartments · Cohen Bath · Tile Tables · Service Employees Building · Rosen Apartment · Reynolds Metals Plant · Curtiss-Wright Facility

1957
Americana Hotel · Gimbel House Decorations · Biscayne Kennel Club · Storefront and Offices of Plumers · Root Chemical Products · Walden House · Ryder House · First Federal · Atlas Sewing Center · Elliot McKiever Insurance · Sea Crest Hotel Lounge · Grosvenor House Lobby · American National Bank · Coates and Dorsey Insurance · NYC Backyard · Erwin Wasey Offices · Fletcher House · White Plains Jewish Community Center · Baxter Reese House · Air Force Academy Model II · World House Galleries · Montefiore Hospital · Mayan Ruins · Hotel Mayaland · Ford Motor Company · Hotpoint Kitchen · Goldberg House · Miami Crippled Childrens Center · Neuvohnes House · Bickford House · Kenilworth House · Grand Bahama Freeport · Don White House · Kasdin House · First Federal Savings and Loan · Palm Beach Towers · Mass Kitchen and Rug · Cohen Bathroom · Sears · Grand Bahama Freeport · Plumer House · Mass Rugs · Law Office · Kenneth McClave House · Hollis Caswell Residence · Sheraton Hotel · Roosevelt Field · Connecticut General Life Insurance · Borgatta House · Garden Houses · Sheraton Escalator · Portfolio House · Willis Mills House · Riess House · Schmidlin House · Macht House · Small Traditional House · Ewing House · Pepsi Cola Building Model · Alcoa House · Old Farm Hill G. House · Theme House Model · Jewell House · Bank Office · Jewell House Tile · City Garden · Kalamazoo Exhibit · Brook Lodge · Leonhardt House · Coney Island Hospital · MIT Compton Labs · Curtiss-Wright Labs · Otto Spaeth House · Curtiss-Wright Facility · Chetwynd Apartments · YW-YMHA · Morrow House · Coolidge House · Osborn School · Schwartzman House · Cell Model · Astor Plaza Model · Milwaukee War Memorial · Geigy · Tiffany Glass · 717 Fifth Avenue Model · Portfolio House · Gould Guest House · Bliss House, Captain's House · Grady Vocational School · Peter Mehlich Promotion · IBM Vanguard Project · IBM Business Machine Show · Ed Winter Apartment · Connecticut General Plate Glass · IBM Card Plant · IBM SBC · IBM Endicott · IBM Poughkeepsie · Tile Work · IBM Service Bureau Corporation · CCNY Technology Building Model · CIT Building · Time and Slave Typewriter · Beattie House · Cell Model, 24' cell · IBM Cryatron · Connecticut Aerial

1958

Libby Owens Illinois Model · Sherry Wine and Spirits Cellar · Washington DC Housing Project · 44 Wall Street · Outdoor Furniture · Kitchens House · Litzy Bathroom · Lockhart House · Rosarian Academy · Curran House · Stamford Presbyterian Church · Decorations at Stoller House · Coral Harbour Club · Forum Restaurant accessories · Chase Manhattan Bank construction · Corning Glass · Washington Housing Model · Baldwin High School · Cell Model, progress shots · SOM Offices · Hoffman House Stone Work · Baker Bath · LHJ Gardens · Kips Bay Model · Irwin Miller House · Inland Steel · Warren Petroleum Company · Douglas Aircraft · Franklin National Bank · Dollar Savings Bank · Lincoln Square Center Model · Bruno Graf House · Upjohn Model · Graham Miller House · Alliance Machine Company · Taber House · DeFlores Residence · Seagram Building · B and J Meininger House · Smith College · Northampton Hotel · Dracut High School · Lowell Elementary School · Grafton Elementary School · Brandeis, Slosberg and Mailman Buildings · Brandeis, Ullman Amphitheater · Brandeis, Rabb Graduate Center · Brandeis, Stoneman Infirmary · Wolbach House · Maynard C. Ford House · Reynolds Metal Building · Memorial Fountain Model · B. and A. Miller Gardens · Shade Story · General Mills · Girl Scouts of America · Bunshaft Apartment · Skidmore, Owings & Merrill Offices · Indoor Outdoor Furniture · Sterling House · Classic Furniture · Heinz Factory · National Homes Model Homes · Beth Abraham Hospital · Hill Apartment II · Karl Middeleer Gardens · Peter Mehlich Organization · Worcester Medical Building · IBM Owego · IBM Lexington · IBM Rochester · Davis House · Graham Miller House · Hogarth House · Cloverleaf Bowling Lanes · Dorado Beach Club · Barkin Levin Plant · Brenaman House · CBS Labs · IBM Sleepy Hollow · Preston Moore House · Luft Playhouse · IBM 305 RAMAC · Lincoln Square Center Model · SS Jerusalem · Summer Furniture at Krisiloff House · Canada House · IBM Education Building and 7070 · IBM Reader Sorter · Standard Vacuum · Mutual Benefit Life · IBM SBC · Equitable Model · Banque Lambert Model · Mass Model · Summer Furniture · A. L. Cohen House · J. and F. May House and orchids · Deering House · Burkhardt House · Harkavy House · Hiss House/Umbrella House · Riverview High School · Roosevelt and Freidin Offices · Presbyterian Church Model

1959

Brain Model for Upjohn · Miller Furniture · 1107 Broadway · Upjohn Packaging · Yale, Ingalls Rink · Idlewild JFK Airport · CIT Marble · Hans Wegner Furniture · Dr. Edward LaSalle Apartment · Allstate · First National City Bank Model · Cell Model · National Homes, Price House · Aerials Tract Housing Miami Havana · McAllister Hotel · Roney Plaza Hotel · Gulf Stream Hotel · George Ketchum House · IBM Ad · Avco Research and Development Center · Good Samaritan Home · Warson Woods School · Guggenheim Museum · IBM World Headquarters · Marble Yard · Corning Glass/Steuben Glass Building · Vogeler House and Moravian Graveyard · Hanes House · Eyre House/Eastern Shore · Upshur House · Wharton Place · Mackay House · Nam Sang Boat · S. F. B. Morse House · Virginia Stanton Refrigerator · IBM Tokyo · Izukin Sushi · Tokyo Metropolitan Government Building (former), Tocho · Ehime Convention Center · Kagawa Prefecture Building · Hiroshima Peace Memorial · Hiroshima Children's Library · Imbari Municipal Office · Shizuoka · Tange Residence · JAL Stewardesses · Tokyo Olympic Facilities · Angkor Wat, Bantei Srei · Rees House · Imperial Hotel · Old Tea House · Jim Thompson House · Prince and Princess Chumbot residence · Katsura · Storage Story/ Flower Arranging School · Japanese Gardens · Sliding Panel Story · Kurashiki · Mr. Ito and Bonsai · Sen Tea Ceremony · Nara · Pagoda/Contemporary housing · Ryokans · Cell Model 2, 6' cell · McComas Research Center · Handicrafts · Food at Four Seasons Restaurant · Hartman House · Park West Village · Decorated Box · Painted Furniture · Corbett House · Institute of Muscle Disease · Stewart Maxwell Swimming Pool · Summer Furniture · Hoover floor washer · Colgate Medical Center · Queensbury Hotel · Guggenheim Museum · Capital Park Apartments · Atlanta House · Aqueduct Racetrack · LHJ Portfolio House · Chase Manhattan Bank · NYU Loeb Student Center · Union Carbide Display · Guggenheim Auditorium · Guggenheim Museum: Portraits · Chase Bank Signage · Union Carbide · Ambassador Hotel · Marco Wolff House · Calvin Goodrich House · Ketti Frings House · Frank House · Robert Marquis House · Harry Camp House · Steiner Kitchen · Four Seasons Restaurant · Fern Story · Bennington College Library · George McCandlish House · MIT Campus Model · First City National Houston Model · Ganz Apartment · Stone Lantern

1960

Barnard College · Sriberg Baths · Evergreen Plantation · San Francisco Plantation · Pepsi Cola Building · Pavelle House · 9201 Bay Shore Drive Apartment Building · Saphier House · Summer Furniture at Pavelle House · Yale Beinecke Library Model · Upjohn products · NUMEC · Upjohn ads · Japan still lifes · Lincoln Center Model · Sarasota High School · Institute for Human Relations · Ski Lodge · Brain Exhibit · Shibui Color · Studio Exteriors Winter · Nat Owings House · Dry Flowers at James House · Virginia Stanton Tables · Thomas Church Gardens · Shopping Center in California · Patterson House · Swimming Pools California · IBM San Jose · Wright Ludington House · Hakon Gardens · Lloyd Flood House · Stuart Pharmacy · Japanese Still Lifes · Brandeis Goldfarb Library · Knox House · Shaw House · Deering Milliken · Dirksen Senate Office Building · Church Tower Model · Japanese Screen · Wellesley Library · First National City Bank, Idlewild JFK Airport · LHJ Portfolio House · Salmenhaara Pottery · Villa Mairea, Gullichsen House · New School for Social Research · Paul Crocker House · LHJ Portfolio House · Gunther House · H. F. Johnson House · Hill Bedroom · Amster Table Setting · G. Wally House · The Eyrie · Fletcher Ashley House · Robinson Pool · Rockefeller Gallery · Oriental Carpets · Kimberly Clark · Robert Bosch · Manufacturers Trust Mural · Union Carbide · Wyatt Garden · Bronxville Garden · IBM Exhibit Building Model · Munson Williams Proctor Institute · Libby Owens Ford · IBM Research cover · Philip Morris Offices · Royal Orleans · Heinz England Model · Stuffed Shirt Restaurant · First City Bank of Pasadena · Ryan House · Lawenda House · McGuire House · IBM Yorktown Construction · Deems Apartment · Home for the Aged · Colonnade Apartments · Yuasa Apartment

1961

Amon Carter Museum of Western Art · Magnavox Research Labs · El Dorado Golf Club · Palm Springs Pools · George Nelson Apartment · Union Carbide Exhibition · First City National Bank · Wetherill House · Frank Kaufman House · World Trade Center Model · Gurrentz House · Scandinavian Craft Objects · Idlewild Airport, Arrivals Building · Idlewild Airport United Airlines · Emhart Model · Dexter Cummings House · Seton Lindsey House · J. Seward Johnson House · Rasbach House · David Frame House · Winterbotham House · John Carter House · Dallas Gardens · Hanna House · Duncan House · Thomas J. Stanton, Jr., House · La Strada Restaurant · Von Strom Garden · McGuire Furniture · Rasbach House Kitchen · Willis Polk Building · Richard Rosenthal House · Nelson Rockefeller Retreat · Mary Bass Garden · Matthews House · LHJ Portfolio House 14 · Brandeis Buildings · New Haven Housing · Schulman House · IBM Typewriter Detail · IBM Phrenology Head · Nelson Rockefeller House · First National City Bank · Peterkin House · Hartford Life Insurance · Johnson Furniture · Peterkin House · Prefab House · Fort Worth Bank · Michael Keeler House · Frisselle House · Doan House · Charles Breed House · Pepinsky House · Sessions Village · IBM Yorktown · Eastman Kodak Exhibit Model · Sherry-Lehmann Liquor Shots · Upjohn Headquarters · Castle House · S. Perlov House · Tom Owen House · Monmouth Shopping Center · Edward Kuzon House · Union Carbide · Alcoa Model apartment · Faile House · Edward Thrower House · Rhodes Perdue House · Eve Johnson House · Woodstock School Library · Brandeis, Rose Art Museum · Macht House · Alside Prefab · First Unitarian Church · Lincoln Center Repertory Theater Model · Hotel Governor Clinton, Rooms · Yardley International Offices and Plant · Balcony House · Yale Model · Schlumberger Offices · Moss Rouse Company · University of Illinois Assembly Hall · Richard Bennett House · Roderer Champagne · Pittsburgh Center No 4 · Ketchum MacLeod and Grove office · Lincoln Center Dance Theatre Model · Lincoln Center Opera House Model · Humberto Arellano House

1962

Albright Knox Art Gallery · Seymour Knox Foundation · United Nations Hammarskjold Library · JAL Exhibit at Dallas Museum of Art · IBM Executary Portable Dictation Unit · Erieview · Dallas Square Plaza · John Hancock Insurance · Houseboats · Bruce Alspach House · Swenson House · General Capital Building · Flagler Federal Building · International Design Center · Pan American Insurance Building · Peter Mehlich Offices · Mayer House · Gade House · Monarch Bay · McIntyre House · Georgia Pacific · Hope Foote House · Dean Carter House · Doane House · Pfund House · Swigert House · Green Johnson House · Methodist Church · Robert Silverstein House · TWA Terminal at Idlewild Airport · Yale University, Stiles and Morse Colleges · New Trends

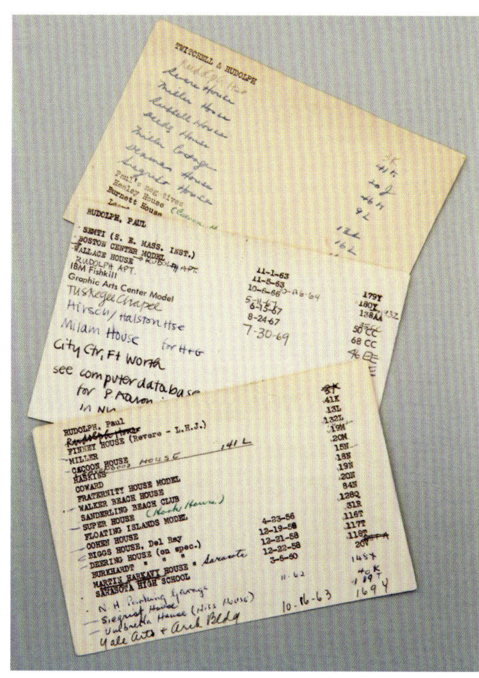

in Design/Architect Portraits · Lincoln Center, Avery Fisher Hall · Pittsburgh Art Center Model · Ulrich Franzen Portrait · IBM Executary Backyard · New York Story · Stable Gallery · Bundschuh House · Wells House · Cullman House · Chase Bank · Epstein House · Directional Furniture · CBS Building Excavation · Hobbs House · Dr. and Mrs. Carlson House · Cummins Engine Company · Cummins Engine Facility Model · Oakbrook Shopping Center · Central Motor Bank · Broadwater Beach Hotel · Isbell House · Noxema Building Warehouse · Dushin House · Johnson Jr House · Berkeley Science Center Model · J. P. Stevens Carter Plant · J. P. Stevens Plant, Clemson · J P Stevens Plant, Milledgeville · J. P. StevensPlant, Slater · Eldon Industries Showroom · Guy Henle House · Hotel Geneva · Helen Whiting Dress Factory · J. P. Stevens Office Building · Nakashima House/Studio · IBM Executary Living Room Scene · AGA Kitchen · IBM Machines and Models · E. N. Clark House · Temple Israel · New Haven Parking Garage · Phillips Academy · Phillips Academy, Rabbit Pond Dormitories · Huglin House · FOB 5 Office Model · Land and Sea Model · Alside Homes · Hubbard House Remodel · Asmat Exhibition at MoMA · J. M. Clark House · Mrs. Harold Snow House · Sam House · Kitt Peak Solar Observatory · Tavern on the Green · Charles Addams Apartment · Summer Furniture at Caulkins · Cowle House · Capital Park Apartment interiors · Harbor Square Model · Upjohn Metabolism Model · Burton Tremaine Apartment · Ben Shahn House · Smithsonian Exhibit

1963

Philharmonic Hall Restrooms · Wing House · Piney Point Elementary School · Houston Museum of Fine Arts, Cullinan Hall · Pittsburgh YWCA · Slater Kitchen · Palm Beach Design Showroom · Ralph Anderson House · Guiberson House · Doyle Cotton Bath · Hertz House · Achille Colpere House · Emhart (demolished 2003) · American Republic Model · New Haven Church Street Model · Fleeger House · Roddy Burdine House · Savage House · Galveston · Mental Hospital Model · Bronx State Hospital · Renewal and Redevelopment Office · Gordon Carroll House · Polaroid Advertisement · AT&T Exhibit · FOB 5 Model · AT&T Murray Hill · House of Ideas · Albany Empire State Plaza Model · Stewart/Lapham House · United Carbon · Petroleum Club of Houston · Gilbert Hahn Jr Residence · Tatum House · John Hancock Building · Tom Owen Kitchen · Tonkens House · Tonkens Body Shop · Neiman-Marcus · Phoenix Mutual Life Insurance · Famous Photographers School · Mount Sinai · Assembly Pavilion Model · Ernest Office and Portrait · Alcoa Plaza Model · University Hospital interiors · Jules Gregory House · Tabler House · Andover Domes · Lillian Lee House · Clint Thompson House · Wilmarth House · Wilmarth House 2 · Rodef Sholom Synagogue · Marin County Civic Center · Chermayeff House · Houghwout House · Ment House · Smallen House · Philip Johnson Pavilion · Tennessee Gas Building · Hammarstrom House · Chapel of St. John the Fisherman · Dumbarton Oaks Museum · Community

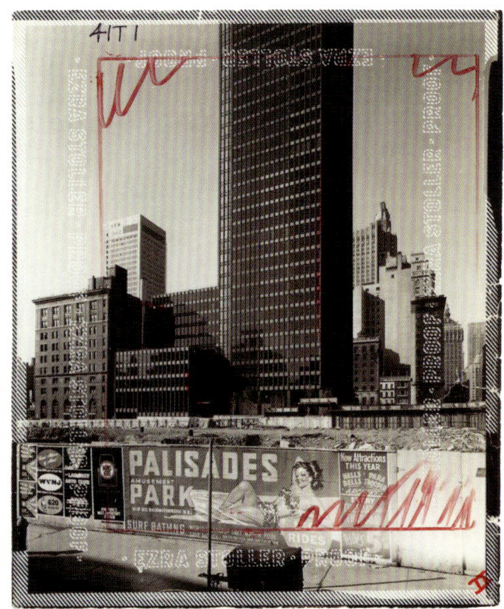

Hospital of the Monterey Peninsula · Green House · Lee House · Paulsen House · Montgomery House · Sheldon Museum of Art · Blitman House · N.C. State Legislature Building · Yale, Beinecke Library · Wooster Square Conte School · Yale Geology Buildling · Cummins Airplane · Roofless Church · Fleschner House · Cummins Metropower · Cummins Advertisement · Fallingwater · Yale Art + Architecture Building · Yale University, Old Art Gallery · Pine Knoll House · SEMTI Model · Boston Center Model · Dr. Katzin Apartment · Kennedy Center Model · Business Men's Assurance Company Building · Hansel Nowling House · Perpetual Savings and Loan Main Office · Perpetual Savings and Loan Branch · Loyola University, Foley Communications Center · Psychiatric Institute · UC Sanitation Lab · Kleiner House · Sandors Kitchen · Joe Lowe Corp Building · Brunswick Exhibit Model · Phoenix Mutual Insurance Building · International Trade Mart Model · Burndy Library

1964

Polynesian Village Model · Einstein Research Building · Pine Bluff Civic Center Model · AT&T Bell Laboratories · B. Altman's Radnor Model · Nutone and Orbit Kitchen · Metropolitan Opera Model · 777 Third Avenue · Katzin Kitchen · IBM Type and Ribbons · Allen Saalburg at Work · AT&T Long Lines Building · American Airlines Admiral Club · Crescent Park Apartments · Bert Stern Studio, Photographer Portraits · New York Civic Center Model · Xerox Showrooms · Levitt Office Building Model · Matthews Apartment · Hamilton College Bristol Center Model · Lincoln Center · Cadman Plaza Hotel · IBM Typewriters · Gerald Tonkens's Cars and Horse · Xerox Offices · Philip Morris Operations Center · Collins House · Lake House · 400 S. Ocean Blvd. Apartment House · Lost Tree Village House · Saul Eig House · Jorge Arango House · Miami Lakes Builders House · Gallery of Contemporary Art, 2 Columbus Circle · Dallas Square Model · Carnegie Hall · Worlds Fair, New York State Pavilion · House of Ideas · Marco Wolff House · Cal Tech Beckman Auditorium · John Deere Company · Lehigh Furniture Showroom · Rockefeller Japanese Garden · Bell Labs · Air Force Museum Model · Julimar Farm Gardens · Dulles Airport · Dumbarton House · Cowles House · New York University Hospital · P.S. 199 · Ford Foundation Model · White Plains Parking Garage · Henredon Heritage Furniture in Florida · Hope Lutheran Church · Van Cortlandt House · Ford Styling Offices · City Federal Savings and Loan · Levitt Strathmore at Stonybrook · National Geographic Society · M. Gordon Residence · George Hickey House · Container Corporation · Chicago Civic Center construction · Brunswick Building · Equitable Building · Chestnut-Dewitt Building · New York State Theater Lighting · Bunshaft House · Lehigh Furniture Bank Table · TWA at LaGuardia · Metropolitan Museum Blumenthal Patio · North House · Pools by Rafferty and Goodman · Silver House · Kassnar House · Worlds FairSpanish Pavilion · Clark University · Bowdoin College, Coles Tower · Columbia, Md., Model · Morris Lapidus Office · Chrysler Sales & Service Training Center · Brookline Model, The Farm · High Fidelity Story · Pace Setter House · Bates Mills

1965

Rautbord House · Mizner Ruins · Lehigh Furniture · Grove Bay Village · Upjohn Annual Report · Beber Porch · Snyder Garden House · Stanley Garden House · Henry Harris House · Teleford House · Winter Haven Bank · Dewers House · Gerstenberg House · P. Jefferson Garden · James David Gallery · Simpson House · Lincocin for Upjohn · Coe House · IBM Type · Case House · Grossett and Dunlap · William Beck House · Fontana Apartments · McGuire Apartment · Maura House · Blum Apartment · High Fidelity Magazine · Equitable Savings and Loan · Helen Stern Apt, Marina City · Great Southern Life Insurance · Royal National Bank · Bethlehem Steel · Dammann House · Kummer House · Lincoln Center Metropolitan Opera · Chase Manhattan Bank exteriors · Borge House · American Republic Insurance Company · Federal Reserve Bank · Neiman Marcus · Knights of Columbus Model · Chromosome Model · Del Corso Apartment · Gaea Pallavicini Residence · Banque Lambert · Clark Gum and Personna Razors · Heinz England Offices · Heinz England Research · English Decorating · Roger Vivier Apartment · Boissonas House · Edmund Bory Apartment · Louis Carre House · Mary Quant Dining Room · Boots Chemical Nottingham Model · Moulin de l'Auro · Shrine of the Book · Lionni House · Museum of Modern Art Garden · Collodi House · Henry Moore portraits · Bloomingdales · TWA Ad · Lincoln Center · Lincocin Vials · Gould House · Jack Lenor Larsen House · Moses Research Tower · Wallace House · Fleeger House · Benton House · Rohm and Haas Building · Ewald Garden · David Kend House · Dansk offices · Levitt Office Building · E. H. Stern Greenhouse · John Jay House · Cleveland Jewish Community Federation Headquarters · Paducah City Hall · Brunswick Lobby Exhibit · Storey House Addition · Henry Lambert Landscape Addition · Steves Residence · Tulsa Civic Center · Albert Herbert House · Derujinisky Bath · Carlton Centre Model · SUNY Albany · Thomas Adams House · IBM Building · Security Mutual Insurance Company

1966

John Hancock Chicago Model · Brunswick Executive Offices · NorthPark Shopping Center · Greenhouse Spa · Neiman Marcus Main Store · Lombard House · ABC Building · Lincocin Human Figure for Upjohn · Ponce Museum · Macy's · Uniondale Public Library · Heritage Furniture · Wicker Furniture · Joe Lambert Apartment · Eaton Center Model · Anderson Clayton · Massapequa Telephone Building · Roma Prov. 2836 · Oster House · Lincocin Dental and Pediatric for Upjohn · Lagerwall House · Metcalf House · Simpson House · Kemp Caler House · P. Pulitzer House · Dodge Campaign · Mad River House and Scouting · NY Stock Exchange Model · NYU Bobst Library Model · Wiltwyck School for Boys · Debos House · Angel House · Martinez Apartment · Felipe Ozma de Porras House · Bermudez House · Amoral Apartment · Gomez Hacienda · Doors in South America · Obregon House · Farina Pool · Mariano Soyer Apartment · Larsen Fabrics · Machu Picchu · Pisac · Urabamba · Modern Houses and Churches, Ecuador · Cruchaga Apartment · Roberto Burle Marx and work · Bernades House · Rio de Janeiro General Views · Triana House · Lincocin with Syringe Capsule for Upjohn · One Wall Street · Asgrow Advertising Building · Yale Lab of Clinical Investigation · LBJ Library Model · Chromosome Model · Esherick House · Ford Foundation Mock Up · Dr. Serrell House · Light House · Surge Lab · David Adler Houses · Richard Rogers House · Whitney Museum · Lincocin Head for Upjohn · Huntington National Bank · Greenwich Hospital · Gallery at The Glass House · Echavarria House · Shaio House · Cartagena General Views · Apt House · South America Miscellaneous · Bogota Library and Museum · Saeng House · Garden and Door Details · Lima and vicinity, General Views · Agua Caliente · Gunston Hall · Herman Miller Showroom · Lincoln Center Reperoty Theatre/Library · Williams College Greylock Center · Kostelanetz Apartment · American Bible Society Building · Brown University Barus & Holley Building · Marx House · American Bible Society Building · Princeton Institute for Advanced Study · National Life Insurance Building Model · Henri Jova Residence · Plakatoris House · Brandeis, Spingold Theatre · Burroughs Corporation · Bethesda Fountain · Jones Beach restaurant · Lincocin for Upjohn · Sealectoboard · Stubbins House · World Bank Model · Hunting Lodge (Birthday House) · 131 St. Nicholas Ave Apartments · Colombian Information Center · Hammond Museum Gardens · North/Ment House for Bellows Club · Patterson Hospital · Bedford Middle School · Richard Rodgers House (Rock Meadow) · Colburn House · Mallory House · Queens Hall of Science · John Moony House · Shell Building Model · Ox Ridge Elementary School · Anawalt House · Heuman House · Simon Fraser University and Vancouver spec · New Trier High School · AT&T Ad Stubbins House · John F. Kennedy Federal Office Building · Davis House · Williamsburg Paint Story · Allied Chemical · Burns and Roe Company · Ethel Walker School

1967

Richard C. Lee High School · Marcel Breuer portrait at Whitney · Heritage Village · Heineman House · Mostly Architecture Exhibition: Ezra Stoller · Port Chester Instrument Company · Dr. Richard Lyons House · Campbell House · The Meadows · Smith House · McGuire Furniture · Pittsburgh Art Center Model · Sunbeam Electronics · Miamarina Model · Umbrella Story · Kimball House · George Reed House · Florida Apartments · Dr. Charles Beber House · IBM Paris Exhibition Model · Glenn Fardig House · Osman House · Goldman Goldstein Office · Marine Acoustical · Webb House · Maximo Presbyterian Church · Eaton Center Model · Morris House · WAC Miller III House · Korach Apartment · Heliotron at Kansas State University · National Center for Atmospheric Research · Paul Rudolph Apartment · Ford Foundation Theatre Model · Andrew Rockefeller House · Zurcher House · IBM Boulder · Main Place Dallas · David Graham House · Bennett House · New Trier High School · Gordon Smith House · Orchard House · IBM Los Gatos · Kilkenny Design Workshop · Durrow Abbey · IBM Fishkill · Rogers House · Noxzema Offices · TAC Offices Brattle Street · Radcliffe Library, now the Radcliffe Institute for Advanced Study at Harvard · Hirschhorn Museum Model · Temple Beth Zion · C. V. Starr Building Model · Roanoke Hospital · John Deere Company · Worcester Foundation · Taylor House · Upjohn Orinare Cardiac · Duncan House · Rockland Housing · Kennedy Grave, Arlington Cemetery · Rousso House · Graphic Arts Center Model · George Nakashima Workshop · Rousso House Bath · Chicago Civic Center Plaza and Picasso Sculpture · Connecticut Mutual · Lehigh Furniture by Warren Platner · William Gregory House · Dart House · Edward W. Bennett House · John Hancock Chicago construction · Gateway Center · DeWitt and Chestnut Apartments · Dorchester Apts on Midway · United Airlines Offices · Inland Steel Research · Hitz House · Beyer House · Indianapolis Housing Authority · Glenn Taylor House · Colby College Dorms · Mount Anthony High School · North Bennington Fire House · Feeley Fire House · Smith House · PIC Instruments · McGraw-Hill Building Model · East Greenwich High School · Fitchburg Library II · Robie House snapshots · IBM Hemisfair Exhibition Model · John Rockefeller House · Hollins College Science Building · Horizon Towers · Cambridge Homes · Ford Foundation Building · Whitney Museum interiors · Robert Sarnoff Offices · American Can Company Model · SUNY Buffalo Model

1968

Capillary Exhibit Model for Upjohn · Muscle Exhibit Model for Upjohn · Lincocin with Spaeth family for Upjohn · Spinnaker House · Wheary House · Ski Houses · KRON TV Station · Alcoa Building · Blair House · Oakland Coliseum · Oakland Museum · Beneficial Life Insurance Plaza · Music Center · Union Bank Building · Moonhole · 140 Broadway · Woolworth Donahue House · First National Bank and PGA Clubhouse · Cousins House · Palm Beach Pool · Holbrook House · Semon House · Les Combs House · John N. Simpson House · Frick Collection · Time Life Building · League School · Virginia National Bank · Max Hoffman House · Sherwood House · Potlatch Club · Hoshour House · IIT Gym, Keating Hall · Skokie National Bank · Georg Jensen International Showroom and Platner portraits · Shopping Center · Boots Company Headquarters · Brumwell House · Brumwell Hut · Bannenberg II House · Lockwood House · History Library Cambridge · University of East Anglia · Hicks and Zarak Showroom · Henderson Weekend Cottage · Marine Midland Buffalo Model · Kostanecki House · Hartford Center Model · Lake County National Bank · Evangelical Theological Seminary · Naperville Church · River Oaks Shopping Center · CIBC Model · Metropolitan Museum Facade Model · Norwegian Prefab · L'Enfant Plaza Partitions · Kreeger House · County Federal Bank · Furniture by Hugh Smallen · Tower East · The White House · L'Enfant Plaza · Amherst Music Building · Hartford Group Building · Des Moines Art Center · Bethlehem Steel, H and J · Thomas Apartment Rug · Capillary or Inflammation Model · W. Hawkins Ferry House · Rotterdam Model · New York Buildings, various · Richard Foster House · John Johnston House · Kennedy High School · Mt Sinai Hospital Model · Manitowoc Savings Bank · COS Building/Huff Medical Center · 500 Michigan · Hartford Plaza

Bank · Wentworth, Hamilton Ontario, Model · Clark University, Dana Center · Metropolitan Life Insurance Company Tower · Colby College Field House · IBM Dictating Machine · Hoffman House · DeVido House · Cornell Social Science Model · Alley Theatre · Hendrix College Library · L'Enfant Plaza Theatre · Boston City Hall · Tapestry at Robinson House

1969
Hines Model II · Baker Furniture · Binoculars and comb for Upjohn · Neiman Marcus and Galleria · CI Design Showroom · CI Design file tray · Dictating Machine · Pan American Annual Report · Hecht House · CI Furniture Brochure · Solow Building Model · Bomser House · Hunt House · Merrill Hall Model · Everson Museum · Gray Taylor House · YMCA Park · Stamford Town Hall · Coats and Clark Building · Stamford Marina · Town Hall Plaza · Stamford Landing Marina · Wilton Church · Pet Incorporated · Bond Square Model · Skidmore, Owings & Merrill portraits · University of Massachusetts · Amherst Science Building · Schenectady Public Library · Reformed Church · Inflammation Model for Upjohn · Fitzpatrick House · Summer Street · Princeton Lab · Ney House · Stamford Marina Model · Dental Offices of Dr. Nathan Shore · Hirsch (now Halston) House · Mountain House · Trinity College, Jacobs Life Sciences Center · Oliver Vanderbilt Offices · Tuskegee Institute Chapel · One Main Place · Narcotics Rehab Center · Wagner College · Community Services Building · Saltzman House · Sea Train Terminals · Manufacturers Hanover Trust · Greenwich Library · Bendick House · Ford Motor Credit Building · Mt Sinai Hospital Labs · Briarcliff Junior College · Iranian Embassy · General Motors Building · Yeshiva University Library · SUNY Stony Brook · Colonial Williamsburg interiors · Chicago Transit CTA Dan Ryan · United Nations Development Model · Juilliard School · CDC Model · Rockefeller Mennen Portrait · 45 E. 89 Street · IBM Building 57 and Madison · Hudson River Museum · Michael Pollen House · Geller House · Novo Model · New England Center for Continuing Education · Administration Building · Mt. Holyoke Theatre · Lord & Taylor · William Bell House · Pierre S. DuPont IV House · Krannert Center · Princeton Faculty Club · Main Place · CIBC Model II · Macmillan Bloedel Building · Pan Am Boeing 747 · Yale Math Building Competition · IBM Building Model · Olivetti Underwood Factory · Yale Math Competition II · Ft Lauderdale Yacht Basin blueprints · Portraits II Shell Oil

1970
Pan Am Boeing 747 at JFK and Seattle · Guarneri House · John Hancock Center · Steelcase Showroom · Westbeth Artists Housing · Design Research · Robert Heath · Kennedy Memorial Model · Table by Skidmore, Owings & Merrill · Enzymes for Upjohn · Enzymes and Hand for Upjohn · Cornell Book Store · Enzymes and Flask for Upjohn · Northwestern University Library · Marvel House · John Kane House · Ponce Housing · Ruth Merrill House · Princeton Physics Lab · Coast Guard Barracks · Oakland Post Office · San Clemente College · Sleepy Hollow High School · Bank of America · Palo Alto Civic Center · Stanford Child Hospital · Stanford University Medical Center · Atherton House · Airequipt Projector · Watsonville Hospital · The Sequoias · Bank of Stockton · Kennedy Memorial · Tandy House · Gerald Hines offices · Beekman Downtown Hospital · Omaha National Bank · National Life and Accident Insurance Company · Laurel Printing · Bassett Hospital · Harvard Law School · Spectrum Arena · Meier Models, various · Lounge Chair X · Gardens Digest · Limbic System Media Graphics for Upjohn · Lufkin House · American Can Company · The Mill at Burlington House · Worcester Museum School · Buffalo Model · Bath House · City Federal Savings Bank · World Bank · Sandy Cove Condominiums · Cecil House · St. Mark's Episcopal Church · New Canaan Presbyterian Church · Quaker Oats Offices · Faye Dunaway Apartment · UPenn Hockey Rink · Fredonia and Bronx School Models · Paul, Weiss, Rifkind, Wharton & Garrison Offices · Tour Fiat Model · Tony Smith Sculpture · US Gypsum Company · Treadwell Corp Offices · US Steel

1971
Koizim House · John Carl Warnecke office · Seatrain · Models of Modular Homes · Synagogue Model · Interiors of Two Homes · Phillips Exeter Academy, George H. Love Gymnasium · First Wisconsin Center Model · Neiman Marcus, Bal Harbor · Bal Harbour Shops · J. Seward Johnson House · Knoll Furniture · Presbyterian Church · Fallingwater · IBM Copier · Mark Firestone House · Miamarina · Flagler Federal · Alfred Browning Parker offices · Florida House · David Rockefeller House · Bronx Developmental Center Model · University of Chicago, Regenstein Library · Northwestern Biology Labs · Lyndon Baines Johnson Library · City National Bank · IBM Austin · Robie House · Anderson House · Schools in Providence · Harvard Currier House · Benjamin Thompson House · Marine Midland Bank · Allied Chemical · O'Hare Plaza · Westinghouse Building · Pepsico · Hoffman La Roche Headquarters · Genesee Crossroads Plaza · Harvard Business School, Burden Hall · Worcester Center Mall · United Nations Ecology Model · IBM Brochure and Tetrahedron · House in Old Westbury · Weyerhaeuser · Laney College · Kaiser Ordway Building · Columbus Republic · Pollen House · Cleo Rogers Memorial Library · First National Bank of Boston · Schering-Plough · Tupperware International Headquarters · Bedford Stuyvesant Pool · Sam Weiner House · Karastan Carpet · Parker House · One Shell Plaza · Brooklyn Redevelopment Model · Welfare Island Model · Douglas House Model

1972
Paul Strand Exhibit · Frick Collection Interiors · Ehrlich Apartment · Olympic Tower Model · Olivetti Model I · Valerian Rybar Apartment · Latter Meltzer Building · Northeast Utilities · Xerox Offices · Harvard School of Education, Gutman Library · SUNY Purchase Neuberger Museum Purchase construction · Waldorf Astoria Hotel · First Wisconsin Madison Model · Wells Tobacco Model · Platner House · First of Illinois Bank Model · Norwalk High School · Pennzoil Place Model · First City National Bank · SUNY Oswego · Water Tower Place Model · Bacardi International Headquarters · Kent Memorial Library · Combustion Engineering · Eastman Kodak · One Liberty Plaza · Twin Parks, UDC Bronx · Kimbell Art Museum · Art Museum of South Texas · Levolor Blinds at Kodak Building · John Deere Company · 919 Third Ave · Third Ave Post Office · Manufacturers Hanover · Harvard Divinity School, Rockefeller Dorms · Harvard GSD, Gund Hall · Cogan House · CI Styrofoam furniture · Yale Club Lobby · Olivetti Model II · Tottenville High School · Olney School · Engel House · Connecticut General Life Insurance · Warren Platner office shots · Geier House · Philip Morris Research Center Tower · Boston Public Library Addition · Boston Five Cents Savings Bank · Kimbell Art Museum

1973
Alexandra Adler portrait · Philip Johnson Various · Olivetti Model III · Lobster Chair by Warren Platner · Tile · Executive Chair by Warren Platner · AIA Headquarters · Pennzoil Place Model · Ernest S. Bird Library · Square House · Bulgari Jewelry Store · Mira Amagasu House · Boston Model · George Nakashima work and family · House on the Sound · MGIC Headquarters · Plaza Towers · Stillman Room · Bross House · John Garraty House · Citicorp Model · 45 E. 89 Street · One Battery Park Plaza · SUNY Purchase, Neuberger Museum · Worcester Housing · Engle House · Keystone Building · CIBC · City Federal Savings · Kykuit · Amherst Fields · Philip Morris, Richmond · City Federal Savings Bank · MIT Housing · UMass Medical Power Plant · Westchester County Courthouse

1974
Carlton Centre · Westinghouse Research · Warren Platner furniture · Teknor Apex offices · Hoffman BMW Headquarters · McGraw Hill Building · Sears Tower · First Wisconsin Milwaukee · First Wisconsin Madison · Exxon Building · Douglas House · General Electric · St. Joseph Valley Bank · Celanese Building · Kirkland College · Dartmouth Science Center · Boston City Hall · White Plains Library · Hirshhorn Museum · General Reinsurance · Shamberg House

1975
Penick Company Offices · Hampshire College, Prescott House · Marine Midland Branch Bank · Fourth Financial Center · Kagen Banks · Baxter Travenol Labs · Crate & Barrel · Allen Lambe House snapshots · Harris Trust · Models, various, Meier · Monroe Rehabilitation Center · Illinois National Bank · Sinai Temple · Vassar · Albany Mall Construction · New Harmony Atheneum Model

1976
Robert Lawther House · Bank of Tokyo · Bronx Developmental Center · San Francisco Housing Authority, Turk Street · UC Santa Barbara · Robin Hood Dell · Shawmut Bank · Knoll Research · Windows on the World · Providence Journal-Bulletin · University of Rochester · Tour Fiat · Wills Tobacco · Equibank · Maidman House · Cooper Union gallery

1977
Continental Grain · Central Park Project · Salk Institute of Biological Research · Rockefeller Center buildings, Sixth Avenue · Barell House · BancOhio · United Nations Complex · Summer Furniture by CI Designs · United Nations Plaza Hotel · Albany Mall · Dartmouth College, Hopkins Center · Wesleyan Models · IBM Armonk interiors · Apartment, Office, Portrait, Model · Reception House · Greenwich House Model · Union Church

1978
East Wing, National Gallery of Art · Wong House · Maine House · Texaco · Rockefeller Japanese House · Rockefeller Collection, Apartment Interior · McCullough House and Standard Brands Models · National Commercial Bank of Jeddah Model · Kripacz House · Asian Objects from Rockefeller Collection · Colombier

1979
London Model · Woodlake · Taubman House · New Harmony Atheneum · Standard Brands · United Nations, General Assembly · New Rochelle Library · Richard Stockton College · CUNY, Aaron Davis Hall · Keiler House · International Year of the Child · Providence Atheneum

1980
UNC, Colvard Building · Mecklenburg County Courthouse · Equitable Life Insurance · WAYS Radio Station · Tower Model · Residence Model · Kogod Office · Robson Square and Provincial Law Courts · Wesleyan University · Red Oak · Simon Frazer College · Corning Glass Building

1981
Ezra Stoller Exhibition · Chase Manhattan Offices · Instituto Cultural Dominicano · Urasenke Chanoyu Tea Center · AT&T Long Lines · Wesleyan, Fayerweather Beckham Hall · Hartford Seminary · Katonah Gallery · High Museum Model · Renault Model I · Libbey-Owens Illinois Model

1982
Asia Society and Angkor Wat Show · Klein House

1983
Stoller Greenhouse · Chapel by Bruce Goff · Johnson & Johnson · Montpelier · Biggs House · High Museum · Clifty Creek School · Monticello · University of Virginia · Tryon Palace and New Bern · Ocracoke · Currie House · Renovated Schoolhouse

1984
Giovannitti House · Pittsburgh House · City Center

1985
Museum fur Kunsthandwerk · Centre Pompidou · Neue Staatsgalerie · Des Moines Art Center · Monet Gardens · Springfield (Kuzon) House

1986
Harvard, Sackler Center · Harvard, Carpenter Center

1987
Madison Square Garden Model · Housing for the Elderly

1988
Hague City Hall Model · Canal Plus Model

1989
People's Bank · Cornell AAC Model · Alvar Aalto Glassware

1991
National Museum of Western Art · Carl Milles Sculpture · Seagram Building

1993
House in Greenwich

Acknowledgments

From a collection of photographs, envelopes on shelves, to a book. How far back do we go to determine the steps required and to thank those involved? We begin our thanks with Mr. Photographer, of course, for his eye, energy, and commitment, and for setting up the systems that preserved the material and made it accessible, useful, and important. We also recognize the architects, designers, and editors who worked with Ezra Stoller over many years and who made these images possible.

After Ezra died in 2004, David La Spina, a young photographer working with the Esto archive, suggested digitizing the images in order to show, for the first time, the scope of the collection. He initiated the project and worked on it with Justin Stewart over the next few years. During that time ARTstor became interested in the Stoller work, and with that organization's valuable help many of the important projects were scanned to high-resolution, pre-press standards making the images more accessible. Ezra Stoller's images are moments in time, documents of an era, and important works of art in themselves.

In 2006, a phone call from Joshua Heller initiated a project that included a broad overview of Stoller's photography as a two-part exhibition displayed first in 2009 and continuing through 2012 at 1050 K Street in Washington, D.C. Following that exhibition, we began to work on this project together. Our book grew out of the Washington, D.C. exhibition, with additional contributions by Akiko Busch, John Morris Dixon, and Andy Grundberg.

The Esto staff has worked tirelessly on the collection as it moved from film to digital and to final files selected and prepared for this publication. We are grateful to Christine Cordazzo, Susan Herpel, Amanda Jinks, David La Spina, Morunda Moore, and Ryan Rothman. Jamie Chan and Maggie Hartnick helped with text and image editing. In addition, Yossi Milo and Alissa Schoenfeld of the Yossi Milo Gallery have presented the photographs in a new light, and we thank them for their enthusiasm. We are also pleased to acknowledge the support of Ronald Abramson and the Graham Foundation for Advanced Studies in the Fine Arts. Thanks also go to Michelle Komie, Sarah Henry, and Heidi Downey of Yale University Press, and to Yve Ludwig of Pentagram.

Nina Rappaport
Erica Stoller

Contributors

Erica Stoller
Erica Stoller is the daughter of Ezra Stoller. She directs Esto, the agency that handles the archive of her father's work, represents a group of working architectural photographers, and maintains a library specializing in images of the built environment. Stoller, a graduate of Bennington College, is also a sculptor.

Nina Rappaport
Nina Rappaport is an architecture critic, a curator, a historian, and an educator. She is publications director at Yale School of Architecture; director of the project Vertical Urban Factory; and professor in the Syracuse in New York City program. She is author of *Support and Resist: Structural Engineers and Design Innovation* (Monacelli Press, 2007), co-author of *Long Island City Connecting the Arts* (The Design Trust and Episode Books, 2006) and of numerous essays. She curated exhibitions of the work of Ezra Stoller at the 1050 K Street Galleries in Washington, D.C., in 2009 and 2011.

Andy Grundberg
Andy Grundberg is a critic, curator, teacher, and consultant of the arts. He is chair of the photography department of the Corcoran College of Art and Design. He was a photography critic for the *New York Times* from 1981 to 1991.

John Morris Dixon
John Morris Dixon is an architecture journalist, serving for many years at *Progressive Architecture* and *Architectural Forum*. His work also appears in *Architect, Architecture, Architectural Record,* and *Competitions*. He has edited five volumes of the series *Urban Spaces* (Visual Reference Publications), as well as *The Atlas of American Architecture* (Rizzoli).

Akiko Busch
Akiko Busch writes about design, culture, and the natural world. Her books include *Geography of Home: Writings on Where We Live, The Uncommon Life of Common Objects: Essays on Design and the Everyday,* and *Patience: Taking Time in an Age of Acceleration* (Sterling). She was a contributing editor at *Metropolis* magazine for twenty years and is a current contributor to *American Craft*.

Index

Page numbers in *italic* type indicate illustrations.